A PRINCETON COMPANION

Sponsored by the Class of 1919,
Princeton University

A Princeton Companion

Alexander Leitch

PRINCETON UNIVERSITY PRESS

Princeton, New Jersey

Published by Princeton University Press, Princeton, New Jersey
In the United Kingdom: Princeton University Press,
Guildford, Surrey

Library of Congress Cataloging in Publication Data will
be found on the last printed page of this book

This book has been composed in VIP Caledonia

Printed in the United States of America
by Princeton University Press,
Princeton, New Jersey

ALEXANDER LEITCH '24 was an editor of the *Princetonian*
and a member of the Press Club as an undergraduate.
Thereafter he served the University for forty-two years
under Presidents Hibben, Dodds, and
Goheen as director of student employment,
director of public information,
secretary of the Graduate Council,
assistant to the president, and, from 1936 until his retirement
in 1966, as Secretary of the University.

TO THE MEMORY OF
MARY LANCASTER LEITCH
1912-1972
ALEXANDER LEITCH, JR.
1943-1970
MATRI FILIOQUE
IN AMORE DEDICATUS

PREFACE

This book is the work of many hands. Besides my own, there were, to begin with, those of W. Beaumont Whitney, II, who persuaded the Class of 1919, of which he was then president, to commit funds that might otherwise have been used for a fiftieth reunion class book to the support of a badly needed Princeton history. Then there were those of my successor as Secretary of the University, Jeremiah S. Finch, who suggested to the Class of 1919 that I might make creditable use of their funds in my retirement years. Next were added, indispensably, those of Herbert S. Bailey, Jr., Publisher to the University, who endorsed the kind of book I proposed for publication by the University Press. The foregoing triumvirate has for over a decade conspired to devise every conceivable means to help get the job done, never publicly admitting the possibility that the author might be finished before the manuscript. Beau Whitney has on a moment's notice come up to Princeton from Philadelphia whenever he was asked, urging the project on with soft-spoken persistence. Jerry Finch, a master of clear and concise statement and widely knowledgeable about all aspects of Princeton, proved a valued consultant on style and content from beginning to end. Herb Bailey cheered the project on its way, kept matters within manageable limits, and toward the end was instrumental in finding other hands to help speed it to completion.

The kind of book projected was the work of another triumvirate: my wife, my son Sandy, and me. Sandy, a member of the Princeton Class of 1965, then a graduate student at Harvard, advised against my undertaking a conventional history for which I lacked proper credentials. Accordingly, we three, in frequent meetings in our living room, worked out the idea for a book of articles in alphabetical order about every facet of Princeton life and history from 1746 to the present that would be a useful work of reference and also one to browse in; and we called it *A Princeton Companion*. Until their deaths, they both contributed immeasurably to the preparation of articles that set the mode for what was to follow. I have dedicated this book to their memory. The Latin inscription I have used is taken from the Rothschild Arch (q.v.), which links the University Chapel and Dickinson Hall.

Still another pair of strong hands took up work on the *Companion* when my old friend, Nelson P. Rose '31, in town for the graduation of his second Princeton son, asked whether I didn't need research and editorial assistance and then gave his own affirmative answer with a spontaneous and very generous gift for that purpose, an example later followed by other eminent Princetonians. He helped in other ways, too. Carefully reading all the many articles I sent him for criticism, he helped clean up grammar and tighten syntax, quoted passages from Lincoln's second inaugural as examples of alternatives to over-long sentences, supplied pithy anecdotes from a richly stored memory of his own undergraduate days, and always found something to commend.

Presidents Goheen and Bowen helped with funds at their disposal and gave their enthusiastic encouragement, as did Emeritus President Dodds.

Midway in the writing, financial support of the *Companion*, received a much needed stimulus at the hands of another old friend of Princeton's and of mine, Grant ("Bill") Oliver '25. His cheerful persuasion brought substantial gifts from himself, Brooks Emeny '24, Dorothy Hubbell ['24], Lewis Mack '25, S. Barksdale Penick '25, T. Edmund Beck '26, Robert M. Walker '32, and Rawleigh Warner, Jr. '44. A few years later, when a further transfusion appeared necessary, Bill teamed with Beau Whitney to secure generous gifts from themselves, William A. Kirkland '19, Ernest C. Savage '19, Benjamin Strong '19, Harold H. Helm '20, James F. Oates, Jr. '21, Brooks Emeny '24, Henry B. Guthrie '24, Rudolph J. Schaefer '24, Frank H. Connor '25, and Horace H. Wilson '25. All of these Princetonians, along with the Class of 1919, merit the applause of all who find the *Companion* to their liking.

At about the same time, at the suggestion of Herb Bailey and Jerry Finch, an effort was begun to obtain the help of faculty and alumni in writing certain articles. Ultimately some seventy persons responded; their names will be found at the end of the articles they contributed. These contributions, which represent about a fifth of the contents, helped bring the book to earlier completion; in not a few cases they gave it added scholarly authority and literary quality.

Various faculty and alumni helped to enlist authors or to read and make suggestions about completed articles, among them—in addition to Bailey, Finch, Whitney, and Oliver—Carlos Baker, Morroe Berger, David P. Billington, Joseph L. Bolster, Jr., John Tyler Bonner, Julian P. Boyd, J. Douglas Brown, W. Frank Craven, Frederic E. Fox, Donald W. Griffin, Robert C. Gunning, David W. Hirst, Ernest F.

Johnson, Frances F. Jones, Sheldon Judson, Richard A. Lester, Arthur S. Link, Dorothy Lupichuk, Henry D. Smyth, Lyman Spitzer, Jr., Joseph R. Strayer, Willard Thorp, Leslie L. Vivian, Jr., and Thomas H. Wright, Jr., and my two old Princeton friends, Alan W. Carrick '23 and Frederick S. Osborne '24.

As a member of the sponsoring Class of 1919, Doug Brown took a particular interest in the project. Besides writing four articles himself, the Emeritus Provost and Dean of the Faculty drew on his long experience with the faculty to suggest those I might ask to write articles and enlisted some recruits himself over lunch at Prospect.

Emeritus Davis Professor of American History, Frank Craven, another productive writer and good recruiting agent, was an especially generous adviser and consultant. His door was always open and I went through it frequently to have my history checked and to be cheered by his good-humored counsel.

Carlos Baker showed me how to sharpen the focus of a story along with other tricks he had learned in his long writing career. On receiving a limp answer to his question about the *Companion*'s progress when he encountered me dragging my way up Nassau Street one blustery March day, the Woodrow Wilson Professor of Literature volunteered to take on another long piece—he had already done two—and arranged for two more excellent ones by a younger colleague.

Grateful acknowledgment is also due various other kinds of assistance. Useful suggestions about athletic articles were made by Asa S. Bushnell '21, Charles R. Erdman, Jr. '19, R. Kenneth Fairman '34, Samuel C. Howell '50, Gordon G. Sikes '16, Donald C.

Stuart, Jr. '35, Daniel F. Sullivan, and Sanford G. Thatcher '65. Indispensable archival aid was provided successively by M. Halsey Thomas, F. James Dallett, Constance K. Escher, Edith James, and Earle E. Coleman. An old New Hampshire hill-walking companion and former *Washington Post* editor, Kenneth Dole (Harvard '24) gave a helpful perspective on a variety of articles.

I thank my daughter Margie and my son Colin for many helpful suggestions and for their enduring warm support.

With the help of the gifts previously mentioned, the *Companion* benefited by a succession of talented research and editorial assistants: Margaret Rindfuss, Elizabeth Reilly '73, Phyllis Benjamin '76, Elizabeth Billington '76, Leslie Mitchner, and Stuart Mitchner. Because their tenures were longest and fullest, three of them merit special mention. A member of the first coeducational class, Liz Reilly was able to supplement her conscientious and effective work with helpful contemporary insights gained during her pioneering four-year passage through Princeton. A faculty daughter who served the *Companion* longest, Elizabeth Billington's clear-headed and disciplined approach to any problem presented to her and her fine sense of what is appropriate made her an indispensable ally in every phase of our work. Stuart Mitchner, an author with strong academic qualifications, brought to our project an experience in research and a skill with words that made his contribution invaluable.

In the closing stages we were fortunate to be under the capable guidance of Gail Filion, staff editor at the University Press. Her experience, imperturbability, and good nature did much to ease the way in bringing our endeavor to a successful conclusion.

* * *

Those who have contributed their means, their talents, and their time can take satisfaction from knowing that they have helped produce a volume that provides in readily usable form detailed information about the diverse elements of Princeton's heritage and its ongoing life. Included among some 400 articles are the following:

Biographical sketches of 125 eminent Princetonians—all its presidents, some deans, half a hundred other professors, and a number of trustees and other alumni. (Except in the case of the presidents, the *Companion* follows the practice of other publications—e.g., the *Dictionary of American Biography* and the *Dictionary of Scientific Biography*—and does not include a sketch of any person living at the time the manuscript was prepared.)

Historical articles about Princeton's trustees, its charter, its seal, and its endowment.

A description of the organization and development of the Faculty, and histories of all the University's departments of instruction and research, and many of its special programs.

Similar accounts, fully exploring origins, of student social life, extracurricular activities, and various branches of athletics.

Accounts of the origin and development of the preceptorial method of instruction, the four-course plan, and the honor system in examinations.

Articles about the annual commencement and baccalaureate exercises, honorary degrees, the salutatory, the valedictory, and Princeton's centennial, sesquicentennial and bicentennial celebrations.

Articles on such varied features of Princeton—old and new—as its founding, its colors, its cheers, Nassau Hall, the origin of "Old Nassau"; and the Computer Center, the Third World Center, and women at Princeton.

Full accounts of alumni activities, especially the alumni college, the alumni parade, annual giving, and reunions.

An historical account of the development of the campus and of its different architectural styles, and individual histories and descriptions of various of its buildings.

Lists of Princetonians who have been awarded Nobel and Pulitzer prizes and of faculty members who have been elected to the different honorary scholarly societies.

An extended coverage of Princeton's tradition of national service, including a summary of Woodrow Wilson's Sesquicentennial address, "Princeton in the Nation's Service," a list of Princeton alumni who were members of the Continental Congress, an account of the part played by the Princeton members of the Constitutional Convention of 1787, and lists of those alumni who, since the nation's founding, have been presidents, vice-presidents, cabinet officers, senators, representatives, supreme court justices, ambassadors, governors of states, and college and university founders and presidents.

In a book of this kind, errors of both commission and omission are bound to occur, and I will appreciate being informed, through Princeton University Press, of any the reader may find.

Alexander Leitch

A PRINCETON COMPANION

Admission to Princeton in the early years was based entirely on a knowledge of Latin and Greek, but by 1760 entering freshmen were required also to understand the principal rules of "vulgar arithmetic." The president of the College personally examined each applicant and determined whether or not he should be admitted. Early one morning in the 1790s, Titus Hutchinson, who had come down from Vermont, called at Tusculum to apply for admission, and after morning prayers and breakfast with President Witherspoon, was grilled by him in Latin and Greek and admitted, with the understanding that he was to occupy the coming vacation with the studies in which he was behind. (Hutchinson graduated with honors in 1794 and later became chief justice of Vermont.)

Population was thinner then, and so was the proportion seeking a college education. Writing to a trustee in 1803, Chemistry Professor John Maclean, Sr., ended his letter: "We got another student today." Thirty years later his son, Vice-president John Maclean, Jr., received a visit from James Moffat, a twenty-two-year-old immigrant printer from Scotland sent to see him by a mutual friend, and after an hour's conversation about Latin and Greek, informed the young man, who had been unaware of what was transpiring, that he had been admitted to the junior class. (Moffat gave the valedictory at graduation in 1835 and was later professor of classics in the College and the father of five Princeton-educated sons.)

Oral entrance examinations continued until well past the middle of the nineteenth century, when they began to be superseded by written examinations, first given only in Princeton, and after 1888 also at strategic points across the country. With the founding of the College Entrance Examination Board in 1900, Princeton honored the board's examinations as well as its own, and after 1915 required them of all applicants.

The great increase in the number of applicants for admission to American colleges following the First World War led the trustees in 1922 to adopt a policy of limited enrollment and selective admission in order to preserve the essential features of Princeton's residential life and to maintain its standards of individual instruction. At the same time they created the office of director of admission, subsequently occupied by Radcliffe Heermance, 1922-1950; C. William Edwards '36, 1950-1962; E. Alden Dunham III '53, 1962-1966; John T. Osander '57, 1966-1971; Timothy C. Callard '63, 1971-1978; and James W. Wickenden, Jr. '61, 1978-   .

During his twenty-eight years as first admission director, Radcliffe Heermance pioneered in the development of selective admission procedures, established close relationships with secondary schools in all parts of the country, and helped guide and develop the College Entrance Examination Board, of which he was chairman from 1933 to 1936. Another pioneer during the formative years of selective admission was Psychology Professor Carl C. Brigham, who did innovative work in aptitude testing and was later chiefly responsible for the development of the College Board's Scholastic Aptitude Test, first given in 1926.

In the 1930s Princeton adopted a special plan of admission without examination for students of exceptional achievement and promise in the Far West and South, where school programs did not fit them specifically for College Board examinations. Thanks to this program and the missionary efforts of nation-wide Alumni Schools Committees, the geographical distribution of members of freshman classes was substantially broadened.

This temporary Princeton solution anticipated a more general and permanent one which came in 1940 when the College Board replaced examinations based on a set curriculum with objective tests that endeavored to cover the common elements of what was taught in schools throughout the country. This change brought marked increases both in the number of applicants for admission to Princeton and the number of schools from which they came.

A significant development, more recently, concerned blacks and other minority groups. Although a few blacks studied privately with President Witherspoon as early as 1774, and although, beginning in the last quarter of the nineteenth century, black students occasionally earned University degrees, the first appreciable influx did not begin until the 1960s when the University adopted an active recruitment policy for minority students. By 1976, the freshman class of 1980 included ninety-two black students and eighty-nine members of other minority groups —Puerto Ricans, Mexican Americans, native Americans, and Asian Americans.

The admission process was further broadened in 1969 when Princeton began undergraduate coeducation, with separate admission quotas for men and women. That year, 171 women matriculated, 69 as transferring sophomores, juniors, or seniors, 102 as members, along with 819 men, of the freshman class of 1973. The trustees adopted a policy of equal access for men and women in 1974 and at the same time determined that the undergraduate body should remain at approx-imately its existing size for the forseeable future. In 1976, the freshman class of 1980 numbered 736 men and 380 women, drawn from a record number of applicants—10,305.

In meeting the responsibilities involved in a necessarily comprehensive and painstaking process of selection, the admission director and his staff rely on help from alumni and undergraduates. More than 130 Alumni Schools Committees across the country act as liaison between the University and secondary school students in their communities, helping the applicants get a clearer picture of what Princeton can offer them and making certain that the Admission Office has a full knowledge of each candidate's capabilities. On campus, an Undergraduate Schools Committee helps prospective students obtain a first-hand acquaintance with Princeton by arranging meals, overnight accommodations in dormitories, attendance at classes and lectures, and meetings with faculty.

In 1976 the University's admission objectives were summed up by Admission Director Callard in these words:

Princeton seeks to enroll a student body that will be characterized by both excellence and diversity. While the University is interested in many kinds of excellence, superior past academic performance and significant promise for future academic growth must clearly be the fundamental considerations in evaluating candidates.

But Princeton is no less interested in the personal credentials of its applicants and is particularly concerned to find evidence of such qualities of personal character as honesty and trustworthiness, which are so crucial to the health of a residential university community like Princeton's. Beyond personal integrity, the University is continually looking for evidence of such important qualities as curiosity, initiative, energy, imagination, sensitivity, concern for others, commitment, persistence, creativity, leadership, and a sense of responsibility—qualities which clearly relate to academic as well as nonacademic aspects of an applicant's potential performance at Princeton, yet which are sometimes more easily perceived in the record of an applicant's nonacademic pursuits.

The director of admission and his staff are responsible only for undergraduate admissions. Graduate admissions are made by the dean of the Graduate School after reviewing the recommendations of the departments concerned.

Advisory Councils for the academic departments were established in 1941. Each council consists of from three to fifteen members appointed by the trustees for three-year terms; nominations are made by the departments in consultation with the Alumni Council. Membership is not restricted to alumni, but at least one member of each council must be an alumnus. Meetings for consultation and conference are held at such times as are mutually agreed upon by the advisory council and the department concerned. Close to 500 persons serve on some forty advisory councils.

Aerospace and Mechanical Sciences, The Department of, which was formed in 1963 by a merger of the departments of Mechanical and Aeronautical Engineering, traces its roots back to the early 1920s when Arthur M. Greene,

Jr. (q.v.), came to Princeton to establish a Department of Mechanical Engineering and to serve as dean of the newly created School of Engineering (q.v.).

Classes were held in the old School of Science, with a makeshift laboratory in a boiler house across Washington Road, until the John C. Green Engineering Building was constructed in 1928. Starting with only two young assistants in mechanical engineering, Dean Greene taught over half the courses in the department in addition to performing his administrative duties. Louis F. Rahm and Alfred E. Sorenson joined the slowly expanding department in 1926; Lewis F. Moody as professor of fluid mechanics and machine design arrived in 1930.

During the Depression, graduating seniors, unable to obtain employment, returned for graduate study, spurring the development of both the engine and hydraulics laboratories. By 1941, when Dean Greene retired and was succeeded as dean and chairman by Kenneth H. Condit, the Department of Mechanical Engineering was both well staffed and equipped, permitting it to acquit itself well during the hectic war years when year-round teaching of military and civilian students was the order of the day.

In the summer of 1941, when the United States was developing the technological and industrial base that would give it world leadership in the design and manufacture of aircraft, Dean Condit invited Daniel C. Sayre (q.v.) to conduct a three-month study of the "possibility and desirability" of introducing courses relating to aeronautical engineering into the curriculum of the Mechanical Engineering Department.

Although recognizing the limited nature of this original intent, the energetic and irrepressible Sayre made such a strong case for the creation of a separate Department of Aeronautical Engineering that his suggestions were adopted, and in early 1942 he found himself both Princeton's first professor of aeronautical engineering and the new department's entire faculty.

With keen competition for available talent in the rapidly expanding aeronautical field, building a departmental staff was not easy, but Sayre succeeded in enlisting Alexander A. Nikolsky, who had helped Sikorsky develop the helicopter, and Harry Ashworth, a skilled machinist and instrument expert. These three, aided by a few graduate assistants, and equipped with a small wind tunnel on a balcony of what is now Aaron Burr Hall, were the entire department until the end of the war. Then began a steady increase in faculty and a meteoric rise in achievement that culminated in the department's recognition as a leader in the field by the mid-1950s.

The first of the new faculty to arrive was Courtland D. Perkins, fresh from Wright Field. Later, between various leaves of absence to serve as chief scientist to the Air Force and as assistant secretary of the air force for research and development, Perkins pioneered in-flight test analysis of aircraft stability and control. His research interests led to the creation of the Flight Dynamics Laboratory, a unique facility for an academic institution, in which theory is tested in actual flight.

Rapidly outgrowing its balcony, the department moved to a series of buildings near Lake Carnegie and to installations behind Palmer Stadium that had housed wartime research in physics. The plan of development aimed at maintaining a strong undergraduate program, but concentrated on graduate

training and research. A Master's program was begun with the inception of the department in 1942, a doctoral program in 1949.

Experimental as well as analytical research supported these graduate programs. The strange constructions with which Nikolsky's students probed the idiosyncrasies of helicopters caused interested comment. The racket of supersonic wind tunnels and rocket firings brought outraged protests. It was clear that new quarters were needed.

Already contending with the cancer that would take his life five years later, Sayre spearheaded the effort that led to the acquisition in 1951 of the property formerly occupied by the Rockefeller Institute for Medical Research and to its development as the James Forrestal Campus (q.v.). The University at last had a place to house research that, in Sayre's words, "makes loud noises or bad smells," and the department moved to these new quarters with alacrity. It was here that Charles Conrad, third man to walk the moon, completed his undergraduate studies in 1953.

Recognition of the stature the department had achieved came with Harry F. Guggenheim's selection of Princeton as the site for one of two jet propulsion research centers. (The other was at the California Institute of Technology.) In 1954 Luigi Crocco of the University of Rome was appointed first Goddard Professor of Jet Propulsion. His work in combustion theory along with Martin Summerfield's studies of solid propellants had a profound effect upon rocket engine development during the next decade.

In 1951 Sayre relinquished the chairmanship to Perkins in order to give full time to the direction of the Forrestal Campus. Under Perkins, research activities expanded until there were active programs in the entire aerospace field, ranging from low speed flight to hypersonic reentry.

In 1963, in recognition of overlapping interests, coupled with declining enrollments in mechanical engineering, the two departments merged to form the Department of Aerospace and Mechanical Sciences under Perkins's leadership. Activities of the new department reached an all-time high in 1967 with a research budget of almost $3.25 million and with an enrollment of 140 graduate and 125 undergraduate students.

The late 1960s and early 1970s were difficult years. With increasing national anguish over war in Vietnam came campus unrest and a wave of revulsion at the ills produced by the misuse of technology. Since the department was deeply involved in a technology closely linked in the public mind with weaponry, it inevitably suffered decreasing enrollments and had to face critical investigations to determine the appropriateness of its research on a campus greatly concerned with the needs of humanity.

That the research was demonstrated to be of high calibre and in no way unsuited to the University was not sufficient for the departmental faculty. With characteristic vigor they turned their talents toward solutions of societal problems. Research narrowly aimed at aircraft systems broadened its focus to include all modes of transportation. Combustion investigations moved from studies of rocket motors to problems of noise, of air pollution, and even of the dangers of smoking. Gas dynamicists turned to problems of energy conversion and control, while the aerodynamicists, not to be outdone, started work on high efficiency windmills for power generation.

By 1974, as Perkins retired as chairman, the changes had had effect. Enrollments were recovering, research budgets were expanding, and the department, under the new leadership of Seymour M. Bogdonoff, was facing the future with confidence.

David C. Hazen

Afro-American Studies Program, The, was organized in 1969 to concern itself, the faculty committee said, "with the history, the culture and the current situation of twenty-five million Americans of African origins." Earlier in the 1960s, interdepartmental interest in this field had been focused in two research conferences on scholarly approaches to Afro-American Studies held under the auspices of the Straus Council on Human Relations. In the program's first year, twenty-six undergraduates—half of them white—concentrated in Afro-American Studies, and more than 500 took one or more of its elective courses.

In the belief that "the black experience is a special case of American experience," the program was designed to provide an opportunity for interdisciplinary and comparative study "of the position and experience of people of African ancestry in the United States, seen in relation to the experience of black people in other parts of the world."

The program is supervised by an interdepartmental committee and involves twelve cooperating departments and schools: Anthropology, The School of Architecture and Urban Planning, Art and Archaeology, Economics, English, History, Philosophy, Politics, Psychology, Religion, Sociology, and the Woodrow Wilson School. Students enter the program through one of the cooperating departments or schools.

In the program's early years, the University received an $88,300 grant from the Ford Foundation for the development of undergraduate Afro-American studies and a $215,000 grant from the Rockefeller Foundation for the support of graduate studies and faculty research.

F. Sheldon Hackney, a specialist in the history of the American South, was chairman of the committee that designed the program. Chairmen of the program have included C. Sylvester Whitaker, Jr. (Politics), John R. Willis (Near Eastern Studies), and since 1973, Howard F. Taylor (Sociology).

Alexander, Stephen (1806-1883), under whose influence astronomy first developed as a separate discipline at Princeton, graduated with honors from Union College at eighteen. A cousin and also a brother-in-law of Joseph Henry (q.v.), he collaborated with Henry in his scientific investigations at Albany Academy and accompanied him to Princeton in 1832, when Henry became professor of natural philosophy. Appointed tutor in mathematics in 1833 and professor of astronomy in 1840, Alexander's association with the College continued for fifty years.

Alexander gave Princeton's first discrete course in astronomy; he was well liked by his students, who called him "Stephy." The College's first astronomy building, the Halsted Observatory, which stood on University Place from 1869 to 1932, was built through his influence and from his plans; however, a telescope was not installed until after his retirement. Working with only his own small telescope, he carried on a steady program of research, published many papers, and studied comets, including the great comet of 1843, whose sudden appearance excited American interest in astronomy. He also studied the atmospheres of Venus, Mercury,

and Jupiter, led expeditions for the Coast and Geodetic Survey and the National Academy of Sciences to observe solar eclipses, and in collaboration with Henry, conducted experiments on the relative heat of sunspots. He was president of the American Association for the Advancement of Science in 1859 and was chosen as one of the original fifty members of the National Academy of Sciences in 1862.

The winter before he died, Alexander concluded his astronomical observations of more than half a century by observing the 1882 transit of Venus across the disk of the sun. This phenomenon, not due to occur again until 2004, was well covered from a Princeton point of view, as it was also observed in Princeton by Alexander's immediate successor, Charles A. Young (q.v.), and in Oyster Bay, New York, by a five-year-old boy named Henry Norris Russell (q.v.).

Alexander Hall, one of the University's most useful buildings, was erected in 1892 as a convocation hall for commencement exercises and other large gatherings. It was given by Harriet Crocker Alexander in honor of her husband, Charles B. Alexander 1870, his father, Henry M. Alexander 1840, and his grandfather, Archibald Alexander hon. D.D. 1810, all of whom served as Princeton trustees.

During its early years the building was used for the sesquicentennial celebration, for Woodrow Wilson's inauguration as president, and for the Stafford Little Lectures given by ex-President Grover Cleveland. For thirty years freshmen were welcomed and seniors graduated in Alexander, but by 1922 commencement exercises had outgrown the building and thereafter were held in front of Nassau Hall. After Marquand Chapel burned in 1920, Alexander was used for Sunday services until the University Chapel was completed in 1929.

Designed by William A. Potter in a Romanesque style, Alexander is rich in ornate detail. Although it cannot be considered a complete success aesthetically, the big, round, granite and brownstone building has always seemed able to meet the changing needs of succeeding generations and to accommodate many different activities —student mass meetings, political gatherings, football rallies, concerts, lectures, and speeches. Among those who have spoken from its rostrum have been Andrew Carnegie, William Jennings Bryan, Albert Einstein, Will Rogers, Eleanor Roosevelt, Norman Thomas, Adlai Stevenson, William Douglas, C. P. Snow, Madame Nu, Eugene McCarthy, George Wallace, David E. Lilienthal, and Art Buchwald.

Alumni College was founded in 1970 to provide, as the Alumni Council announced, "an intensive period of study and dialogue for those whose curiosity and intellectual interest reach beyond their normal daily pursuits." It was an outgrowth of the faculty-alumni forums, an earlier Princeton venture in continuing education initiated in 1951 by the Class of 1926 at its twenty-fifth reunion and an increasingly popular part of the June reunion weekend ever since.

The first Alumni College met at the Princeton Inn College during the postreunion week of 1970, and this on-campus meeting became an annual feature of the Alumni Council's program. Other Alumni Colleges, lasting from two to fourteen days, were gradually organized outside of Princeton, in response to alumni demand.

Unlike the Faculty-Alumni Forums, which are open to all alumni in attendance at reunions, Alumni Colleges are residential, and enrollment is limited in order to give participants more opportunity for interaction with their teachers and each other. The Princeton faculty usually comes from an assortment of disciplines and is sometimes supplemented by authorities in other fields outside the University. A typical program includes lectures, precepts, seminar discussions, films, field trips, and social and recreational activities. "An open admission policy" is followed, spouses, children, and friends being welcome as well as alumni.

By the mid-seventies five or six Alumni Colleges were meeting each year in the Far West, the Middle West, and at various places along the eastern seaboard from Massachusetts to Florida, exploring topics that ranged in time from the Middle Ages to the last thirty years in American history, and often matching the subject with the setting: "The Yankee Spirit" at Martha's Vineyard; "New York: Profile of a City" at the Princeton Club of New York; "At the Edge of Wilderness" at the Blairstown Education Center near the Appalachian Trail in northwestern New Jersey.

At the first Alumni College abroad, conducted at Rouen in the summer of 1976, a student body of thirty-five, representing classes from 1925 to 1965, engaged in an eleven-day study of modern France under the guidance of a faculty that included two Princeton professors of romance languages, an architect and a lawyer (both alumni, practicing in France), and the United States ambassador to France.

"Alumni who attend Alumni Colleges," the Alumni Council concluded after six years experience with the program, "come to study and learn, and they are not often disappointed."

Alumni Council, The, traces its antecedents to the Committee of Fifty, organized in 1904 to raise funds for "the immediate necessities and future development of the University." Chief among the immediate necessities was Woodrow Wilson's newly announced preceptorial system. Aspiring to a broader function, the Committee of Fifty transformed itself in 1909 into the Graduate Council, which after almost fifty years changed its name to Alumni Council. The council has provided leadership for alumni activity through the medium of standing committees on alumni associations, athletics, class affairs and reunions, communications, schools, and undergraduate activities. Among its most significant contributions have been the institution of advisory councils for the academic divisions of the University, the launching of Annual Giving, and the development of the Alumni College.

In 1920 the council brought all of the Princeton alumni organizations into a centralized Alumni Association, replacing the Alumni Association of Nassau Hall, which had been founded in 1826 "to promote the interests of the College and the friendly intercourse of its graduates." The Alumni Association, of which every alumnus is *ipso facto* a member, meets twice a year, as does the Alumni Council, which is, in effect, the association's executive body.

The Alumni Council is composed of presidents of alumni classes and regional alumni associations, and also includes all former chairmen who are life members, and a group of appointed members. The total membership is about 280.

Chairmen of the Committee of Fifty,

the Graduate Council, and the Alumni Council have been: Cleveland H. Dodge 1879, Parker D. Handy 1879, Charles Scribner 1875, Francis Speir 1877, Walter E. Hope '01, Francis G. Landon 1881, Ambrose G. Todd 1884, Walter L. Johnson 1897, Lawrence G. Payson '16, Chauncey Belknap '12, Robert M. Green '13, Harold H. Helm '20, Lewis N. Lukens '17, Richard K. Stevens '22, John C. Williams '25, George E. Clark '29, Chandler Cudlipp '19, Dorrance Sexton '33, Walker W. Stevenson '35, George C. Denniston '27, William P. Wright, Jr. '33 Grant Sanger '31, T. Henry Dixon '40, D. Bruce Merrifield '42, Mortimer H. Chute, Jr. '56, Frederick L. Redpath '39, George Faunce III '47, and Donald P. Dickson '49.

Secretaries have been: George W. Burleigh 1892, Harold G. Murray 1893, V. Lansing Collins 1892, Alexander Leitch '24, Thurston J. Davies '16, Donald W. Griffin '23, Joseph G. Bradshaw '40, Charles L. Taggart '51, David G. Rahr '60, Daniel N. White '65.

In 1961, after a quarter of a century as secretary of the council, Donald Griffin was appointed general secretary, serving until his retirement in 1964. William D. Lippincott '41, previously dean of students, was executive director from 1968 to 1972. David Rahr has been director since 1972.

Alumni Day was first observed on Lincoln's birthday in 1915. It was organized to give alumni a glimpse of campus daily life when the University was in session. About a hundred alumni joined in what the *Alumni Weekly* called "an intellectual pilgrimage to their Alma Mater," highlighted by a meeting of the Alumni Association in the Faculty Room of Nassau Hall.

The following year, Alumni Day took

place on Washington's birthday, the traditional date until 1955, when it began to be observed on the Saturday nearest February 22nd. Gradually, attendance outgrew the Faculty Room, and since the late 1930s, Alumni Association meetings have taken place at formal luncheons (held successively in the old University Gymnasium, Baker Rink, Dillon and Jadwin Gymnasiums), preceded by faculty panel discussions and lectures, and followed, since 1970, by the annual Service of Remembrance.

The luncheon program, which includes brief remarks by the president, is the occasion of the annual presentation of the Woodrow Wilson Award, the James Madison Medal, the Pyne Honor Prize, and the Freshman First Honor Prize. Announcement is also made of nominations for alumni trustees, with reports on the progress of Annual Giving and of other benefactions to the University. The day's program is rounded out by an undergraduate debate, athletic events, and a reception at the John Maclean House.

Alumni Directory, The, first appeared in 1888 with the names and most of the addresses of some four thousand living graduates and former students. It was compiled by two graduates of the Class of 1877, Professor William Libbey, Jr., and Trustee M. Taylor Pyne, who spent several years gathering addresses with the help of class secretaries. Libbey and Pyne also edited the second edition in 1892 and the third in 1896. Thereafter new editions were issued at three- or four-year intervals, by the Office of the Secretary from 1902 to 1917, by the Alumni Council Office from 1921 to 1948, by the Bureau of Alumni Records beginning in 1952. The twenty-fifth edition, published in 1974, by the Alumni Records Section of Printing, Mailing and Alumni Records, listed the names (and the addresses of all but 1,964) of some 44,000 alumni of the College and the Graduate School and of about 4,900 undergraduate and graduate students then in residence.

Alumni Parade, The, held annually on the Saturday before Commencement as the climax of class reunions, originated in the 1890s but, as now conducted, is related to an earlier alumni event: beginning soon after the Civil War, alumni classes had been taking part, on Commencement Day, in an ordered procession to the place of their dinner meeting where "an excellent and abundant meal" was followed by five or six alumni speeches, "both grave and witty, serious and mirthful."

The more lighthearted Saturday parade grew out of the baseball rivalry between Yale and Princeton. Their teams first met in 1868, and twenty years later began playing one of their several games at Princeton on the Saturday before Commencement. Alumni attendance grew, and now and then a class back for a reunion would march to the game behind a band. In 1897, stimulated by a torchlight procession of alumni at the Sesquicentennial celebration the previous fall, all the "reuning" classes joined in a parade to the game. Thus began the most colorful event of the annual Commencement program.

For many years, the P-rade (as it came to be known) formed in front of Nassau Hall, moved across the Campus to '79 Arch, down Prospect Avenue, through the Thompson Gateway, and around University Field, passing in review before the president's box behind first base.

At first the sole decoration worn by

returning alumni was a badge with class numerals on it. Gradually classes began to distinguish themselves by using class hats, balloons, parasols, large palm leaf fans, and before long younger classes were wearing colorful costumes, carrying humorous signs, and sometimes performing comic stunts.

In 1907, the Class of 1897, dressed as Dutch boys, made an arresting sight—and sound—as they clattered along in their wooden shoes.

A year later, the Class of 1898 marched as a Roman Legion, with tunics, buskins, shields, and swords, wheeling at their head a reproduction of the Arch of Trajan, on which was emblazoned:

A·I·N·T·T·H·I·S
A·T·R·I·U·M·P·H

In 1909, not long after Princeton had been given its lake by the Scottish-American Andrew Carnegie, the Class of 1904 appeared in an orange and black tartan highland dress, led by a bagpipe band of highlanders in bonnet, kilt, and sporran. As the stalwart drum major whirled his baton, the double-jointed drummer pummeled his drum, and the pipers piped their martial airs, the long line of '04 Highlanders presented the appearance of a Scottish regiment on parade, winning the crowd's thunderous applause.

In 1910 the Class of 1900 paraded in long gowns as suffragettes, with the former football player "Big Bill" Edwards, leading on horseback, as an improbable Joan of Arc.

In 1916, when interest in the preparedness movement was mounting, the Class of 1906 wore the top hat, chin whiskers, white-starred blue tailcoat, and the red and white striped trousers of Uncle Sam.

At the "Victory Commencement" of 1919 a throng of alumni, happy to be back from the war, formed the longest and most colorful P-rade up to that time. That year Alumni Day coincided with Flag Day, and at the conclusion of the parade, a band struck up "The Battle Hymn of the Republic," and five thousand alumni marched across University Field, waving their flags from right to left with each step—"a moving sight," the *Alumni Weekly* reported, "which brought the 10,000 spectators to their feet."

An even longer P-rade took place in 1946 when 7,300 alumni returned to Princeton for a "Victory Reunion." The procession reached a climax on University Field with the massing of service flags showing the number in each class who had served in the war and the number who had given their lives.

In general, classes have tended to wear costumes through their fifteenth or twentieth reunions, class blazers and occasionally gay umbrellas with class numerals through their fiftieth, and thereafter, blazers or simply hatbands with class numerals.

Over the years, alumni have appeared as Mexican bullfighters, Roman gladiators, convicts, Spanish toreadors, pirates, zouaves, French artists, Apache dancers, Roman emperors, pierrots, cowboys, Anzacs, French sailors, Confederate soldiers, Indians, the French Foreign Legion, African hunters, chefs, firemen, baseball players, spacemen, and even as tigers.

Live animals have added excitement from time to time: in 1906 a troupe of trained lions, in 1923 two tigers, in 1949 three elephants who led the clowns of '44 around the field and then knelt in front of the president's box.

Bands have always been an indispensable element. Every class celebrating a major reunion (i.e. those occurring at five-year intervals) has usually had one, and occasionally one or two classes celebrating "off-year" reunions have had them, too. At times there have been as many as thirty bands punctuating the long procession—brass bands, bagpipers, fife and drum corps, all-girl bands—and at the head of the column, the University Band.

Rain put an occasional damper on the P-rade, but only once—in 1953—did it force a cancellation of the parade (and of the game). Some classes insisted on marching anyway, staging an impromptu parade in the R.O.T.C. armory. After the storm abated, the twenty-fifth-year Class of 1928 marched to "Prospect," called out President Dodds, and, with him at their head, marched to University Field and back to the Cannon, accompanied by the University Band.

From 1961 to 1967 the Alumni P-rade proceeded to Clarke Field, rather than to University Field, where the Engineering Quadrangle was built; and in 1966 a further change was required when Yale found that it could no longer keep its team together for the post-season Princeton Commencement game. A game between the Varsity and a team of alumni provided a temporary focus for the P-rade in 1967. Since 1968 the P-rade has terminated in an Alumni Association meeting, the alumni once more marching to their Commencement gathering as their predecessors did in 1865—now without the abundant meal and extensive oratory to follow, but with the color, music, and fun that have, since the Golden Nineties, been essential ingredients of this unique event.

Alumni Weekly, The Princeton (PAW), was founded on April 7, 1900, as ". . . a long distance telephone . . . to keep a live connection between the University and its alumni . . . for their mutual enlightenment, benefit and satisfaction." It replaced the *Alumni Princetonian*, a weekly edition of the *Daily Princetonian* that the undergraduate editors had been putting out for six years but that had sold subscriptions to only 500 of the then 6,000 alumni.

Jesse Lynch Williams 1892, a former *Nassau Lit* editor and later a Pulitzer Prize winner, was editor of the *Weekly* during its first four years; he gave it (as a later editor said) "a flying start and a bright tone." Edwin Mark Norris 1895, the second editor, devoted twenty-one years to the magazine. Subsequent editors and their years of service have been: W. Irving Harris '20 (1925), Asa S. Bushnell '21 (1925-1930), John T. Rodgers '22 (1930), Edmund S. De-Long '22 (1930-1931), Datus C. Smith '29 (1931-1940), Douglas E. Stuart '35 (1940-1942), Frederick S. Osborne '24 (1942-1946), Ernest T. Stewart '41 (1946-1951), Philip W. Quigg '43 (1951-1955), John D. Davies '41 (1955-1969), Landon Y. Jones, Jr. '66 (1969-1974) and since 1975, Charles L. Creesy '65.

These editors have all doubtless shared the hope expressed by the fourth editor, Asa Bushnell, that, "in the thousands of widely scattered Princeton homes, the query 'Has the *Weekly* come yet?' might be heard more regularly than 'What, is the *Weekly* here again?' "

They would probably assent, also, to the valedictory statement of the eleventh editor, Philip Quigg: "With few exceptions, alumni magazines with the greatest editorial freedom are the most readable and in the long run serve best the institutions for which they exist. . . . If perchance the present editor has upon occasion been critical, we hope it may have added further cre-

dence to the burden of his message—
that Princeton is the best old place of
all."

Published and printed by Princeton
University Press, with an editorial
board of five members (three of whom
are appointed by the Alumni Council,
two by the Press), the magazine is distributed to virtually every alumnus
through group subscriptions paid for by
the classes and until 1977 was the only
college alumni publication in the
United States appearing weekly. That
fall, it changed to biweekly publication
during the academic year in order to
offset rising costs and also to give the
staff time to cover campus news more
thoroughly in larger issues. The change
only involved a reduction from
twenty-eight to twenty-one issues a
year, and PAW, as it was now formally
known, still led all other American
alumni magazines in the number of issues published annually.

The 1977 change also affected the
Weekly's association with the quarterly
magazine *University*, founded in 1959
as a means of communication with
alumni of the Graduate School, parents
of undergraduates, and other non-
alumni friends. Under the new arrangement, *University* was to be made
up of articles previously printed in
PAW, with *University*'s retiring editor,
William McCleery, serving as consulting editor during the transitional year.

University had a turn-of-the-century
counterpart in another quarterly which
began in 1889 as the *Princeton College
Bulletin* (after 1896 the *Princeton University Bulletin*) and continued until
1904. The *Bulletin* contained in rudimentary form some of the features
of both the *Alumni Weekly* and *University*, as well as of the *Weekly Bulletin*
and the *Bibliography of Princeton Publications*.

Ambassadors and ministers who have
attended Princeton number more than
a hundred and have served throughout
the world in approximately seventy
countries and missions, including the
following:

ALBANIA
Post Wheeler 1891 (1933-1934)

ARGENTINA
John W. Garrett 1895 (1911-1914)
Norman Armour '09 (1939-1944)

AUSTRIA
Gilchrist B. Stockton '14 (1930-1933)
H. Freeman Matthews '21
    (1957-1962)
John P. Humes '43 (1969-1972)

BAHAMAS
Ronald I. Spiers MPA '50
    (1973-1974)

BELGIUM
Leonard K. Firestone '31 (1974-1976)

BOLIVIA
William Austin Seay 1850
    (1885-1887)
Robert G. Caldwell Ph.D. '12
    (1937-1939)

BURUNDI
George W. Renchard '30 (1968-1970)

CAMBODIA
William C. Trimble '30 (1959-1962)

CANADA
R. Douglas Stuart '08 (1953-1956)
Livingston T. Merchant '26
    (1956-1958; 1961-1962)
W. Walton Butterworth, Jr., '25
    (1962-1968)
Adolph W. Schmidt '26 (1969-1974)

CEYLON
Bernard A. Gufler '25 (1959-1961)

CHILE
Norman Armour '09 (1938-1939)
Ralph A. Dungan, Jr., MPA '52
    (1964-1967)

CHINA
John V. MacMurray '02 (1925-1929)

CHINA (Taiwan)
Karl L. Rankin '22 (1953-1957)

CONGO
Edmund A. Gullion '35 (1961)
Robert H. McBride '40 (1967-1969)

COSTA RICA
Nathaniel P. Davis '16 (1949-1951)
Whiting Willauer '28 (1958-1960)

CUBA
Joshua B. Wright 1899 (1937-1939)

CZECHOSLOVAKIA
Joshua B. Wright 1899 (1934-1937)
Edward T. Wailes '25 (1961-1962)
Jacob D. Beam '29 (1966-1969)

ECUADOR
Findley Burns, Jr. '39 (1970-1971)

FINLAND
Bernard A. Gufler '25 (1961-1963)
Tyler Thompson '30 (1964-1969)

FRANCE
John Armstrong 1775 (1804-1810)
Edward Livingston 1781 (1833-1835)
Richard Rush 1797 (1847-1851)
William Lewis Dayton 1825
  (1861-1864)
David K. E. Bruce '19 (1949-1952)
John N. Irwin II '37 (1973-1974)

GABON
Richard Funkhouser '39 (1969-1970)

GERMANY
David K. E. Bruce '19 (1957-1959)

GREAT BRITAIN
Richard Rush 1797 (1817-1825)
Joseph Reed Ingersoll 1804
  (1852-1853)
George Mifflin Dallas 1810
  (1856-1861)
John Gilbert Winant '13 (1941-1947)
David K. E. Bruce '19 (1961-1969)

GREECE
Henry R. Labouisse '26 (1962-1965)

GUINEA
William H. Attwood '41 (1961-1963)

HONDURAS
Whiting Willauer '28 (1954-1958)

HUNGARY
Joshua B. Wright 1899 (1927-1930)
Nathaniel P. Davis '16 (1949-1951)

ICELAND
Tyler Thompson '30 (1960-1961)

INDIA
Robert F. Goheen '40 (1977-   )

IRAN
Richmond Pearson 1872 (1902-1907)
Edward T. Wailes '25 (1958-1961)

IRAQ
Edward S. Crocker '18 (1948-1952)

ITALY
John P. Stockton 1843 (1857-1861)
John W. Garrett 1895 (1929-1933)
Breckenridge Long '03 (1933-1936)

IVORY COAST
John F. Root '40 (1969-1974)

JAPAN
Roland S. Morris 1896 (1917-1921)

KENYA
William H. Attwood '41 (1964-1966)

KUWAIT
William Stoltzfus '46 (1974-1976)

LAOS
Charles W. Yost '28 (1954-1956)
Christian G. Chapman '43
  (1974-   )

LIBYA
John L. Tappin '28 (1954-1958)

MALAWI
William C. Burdett '41 (1970-1975)

MALTA
John C. Pritzlaff, Jr. '47 (1969-1972)

MAURITANIA
Holsey G. Handyside MPA '53
  (1975-   )

MEXICO
John Forsyth, Jr. 1832 (1856-1858)
Robert H. McBride '40 (1969-1972)

MOROCCO
Samuel R. Gummere 1870
 (1905-1909)
Charles W. Yost '28 (1958-1961)

NETHERLANDS
William Lewis Dayton 1858
 (1882-1885)
Henry van Dyke 1873 (1913-1917)
John W. Garrett 1895 (1917-1919)
H. Freeman Matthews '21
 (1953-1957)

NICARAGUA
Aaron S. Brown '35 (1961-1967)

NIGERIA
Donald B. Easum Ph.D. '53
 (1975-   )

PARAGUAY
Post Wheeler 1891 (1929-1933)

PERU
William P. Cooper '17 (1946-1948)

PHILIPPINES
William E. Stevenson '22
 (1961-1964)
G. Mennen Williams '33 (1968-1969)

POLAND
Jacob D. Beam '29 (1957-1961)

PORTUGAL
Robert G. Caldwell Ph.D. '12
 (1933-1937)
Frank C. Carlucci '52 (1975-1977)

RUMANIA
Richard H. Davis '35 (1965-1969)

RUSSIA
George Washington Campbell 1794
 (1818-1821)
George Mifflin Dallas 1810
 (1837-1839)
George Henry Boker 1842
 (1875-1878)
(See U.S.S.R. for later appointments)

SAUDI ARABIA
William A. Eddy '17 (1944-1946)
Nicholas G. Thacher '37 (1970-1973)

SOMALIA
Roger Kirk '52 (1973-1975)

SOUTH AFRICA
Edward T. Wailes '25 (1954-1956)

SPAIN
John Forsyth 1799 (1819-1823)
Norman Armour '09 (1944-1945)
Peter M. Flanigan '45 (1975-1976)

SWEDEN
H. Freeman Matthews '21
 (1947-1950)
W. Walton Butterworth, Jr. '25
 (1950-1953)

SWITZERLAND
Shelby Cullom Davis '30 (1969-1972)

SYRIA
Charles W. Yost '28 (1958)

TANGANYIKA
William K. Leonhart Ph.D. '43
 (1962-1965)

TRINIDAD AND TOBAGO
John F. Symington, Jr. '33
 (1969-1973)

TURKEY
George Henry Boker 1842
 (1871-1875)
John V. MacMurray '02 (1936-1942)
Ronald I. Spiers MPA '50
 (1977-   )

URUGUAY
Joshua B. Wright 1899 (1930-1934)

UPPER VOLTA
Donald B. Easum Ph.D. '53 (1971-
1975)

U.S.S.R.
George F. Kennan '25 (1952-1953)
Jacob D. Beam '29 (1969-1973)
(See Russia for earlier appointments)

VENEZUELA
Allen Thomas 1850 (1888-1892)
John W. Garrett 1895 (1910-1911)
Norman Armour '09 (1950-1951)

YUGOSLAVIA
Karl L. Rankin '22 (1958-1961)
George F. Kennan '25 (1961-1963)
William K. Leonhart Ph.D. '43
 (1969-1971)

*Representatives to Special Missions
with rank of Ambassador*

UNITED NATIONS, NEW YORK
Adlai E. Stevenson '22 (1961-1965)
Charles W. Yost '28 (1969-1971)

INTERNATIONAL ATOMIC ENERGY
COMMISSION, VIENNA
Henry DeWolf Smyth '18
(1961-1970)

NORTH ATLANTIC TREATY
ORGANIZATION AND EUROPEAN
REGIONAL ORGANIZATION,
PARIS
John C. Hughes '14 (1953-1955)
James Harlan Cleveland '38
(1965-1969)
Donald Rumsfeld '54 (1973-1974)
David K. E. Bruce '19 (1975-1976)

EUROPEAN ECONOMIC COMMUNITY
W. Walton Butterworth '25
(1958-1962)

American Academy of Arts and Sciences, The, chartered at Boston in 1780, is the second oldest learned society in the United States, exceeded in age only by the American Philosophical Society. The "end and design" of the Academy, according to its charter, is "to cultivate every art and science which may tend to advance the interest, honor, dignity, and happiness of a free, independent, and virtuous people."

Princeton professors who have been members of the Academy, and the years of their election, follow:*

1840	Joseph Henry
1841	John Torrey
1849	Arnold Guyot
1850	Stephen Alexander
1871	Charles A. Young
1874	James McCosh
1901	Henry Fairfield Osborn
1912	William Berryman Scott
	Woodrow Wilson

1914	Edwin Grant Conklin
1917	Allan Marquand
1918	Edward Capps
1921	Henry Norris Russell
1923	Oswald Veblen
1931	Edward C. Armstrong
	Frank J. Mather
	Robert K. Root
1932	Morris W. Croll
1933	Carroll C. Pratt
1934	Edwin W. Kemmerer
	Theodore Leslie Shear
	Jacob Viner
	Howard C. Warren
1936	Frank A. Fetter
1940	Hermann Weyl
1943	Hugh Stott Taylor
1944	C. Rufus Morey
	John von Neumann
1948	Arthur F. Buddington
	E. Newton Harvey
1949	Julian P. Boyd
	Gilbert Chinard
1950	Eugene P. Wigner
1951	Edward C. Kendall
	Walter T. Stace
1952	Donald F. Hornig
1953	Lyman Spitzer, Jr.
1954	Martin Schwarzschild
	Joseph R. Strayer
	John A. Wheeler
1956	Henry D. Smyth
1957	Emil Artin
	Carl G. Hempel
1958	Henry Eyring
	Colin S. Pittendrigh
1959	P. J. Conkwright
	Harold W. Dodds
1960	J. Douglas Brown
	Alonzo Church
1961	Fritz Machlup
	John W. Milnor
	Roger H. Sessions
1962	Gordon A. Craig
	Robert F. Goheen
	Roman Smoluchowski
	Oliver Strunk

1963　Walker Bleakney
　　　　Robert H. Dicke
　　　　Charles C. Gillispie
　　　　E. H. Harbison
　　　　Walter J. Kauzmann
　　　　Thomas S. Kuhn
　　　　Alpheus T. Mason
　　　　Frank W. Notestein
　　　　Arthur B. Pardee
　　　　Erik Sjöqvist
　　　　Ernest G. Wever
　　　　Samuel S. Wilks
1964　Richard P. Blackmur
　　　　Rensselaer W. Lee
　　　　John W. Tukey
　　　　Richard H. Wilhelm
1965　Georges Florovsky
　　　　Marvin L. Goldberger
　　　　Wallace D. Hayes
1966　Val L. Fitch
　　　　Joseph J. Kohn
　　　　Marshall N. Rosenbluth
　　　　Carl E. Schorske
　　　　Arthur S. Wightman
　　　　Sheldon S. Wolin
1967　James W. Cronin
　　　　Donald C. Spencer
　　　　Gregory Vlastos
1968　Valentine Bargmann
　　　　Stuart N. Hampshire
　　　　Harry H. Hess
　　　　Lawrence Stone
1969　John T. Bonner
　　　　Joseph Frank
　　　　Noboru Sueoka
1970　Marver H. Bernstein
　　　　Ansley J. Coale
　　　　Harry H. Eckstein
1971　William J. Baumol
1972　Charles Fefferman
　　　　Arthur S. Link
　　　　Dana S. Scott
　　　　Irene B. Taeuber
1973　William G. Bowen
　　　　Evelyn B. Harrison
　　　　Marius B. Jansen
　　　　Arthur S. Mendel

　　　　Sam B. Treiman
1974　Stephen L. Adler
　　　　Milton B. Babbitt
　　　　Victor H. Brombert
　　　　Kurt M. Mislow
　　　　William G. Moulton
　　　　Richard H. Ullman
1975　Gerald E. Bentley
　　　　Cyril E. Black
　　　　Edward T. Cone
　　　　John J. Hopfield
　　　　Edward Nelson
　　　　Jeremiah P. Ostriker
　　　　Robert C. Tucker
1976　John N. Bahcall
　　　　Jerome Blum
　　　　Fred I. Greenstein
　　　　Oskar Morgenstern
　　　　Albert Rees
1977　Robert May
　　　　Walter F. Murphy
　　　　P. James E. Peebles
　　　　Norman B. Ryder
　　　　Donald E. Stokes

* More than 150 non-faculty alumni have also been members, among them Benjamin Rush, William Paterson, Oliver Ellsworth, James Madison, Harlow Shapley (President, 1939-1944), Harold Medina, Frederick Osborn, Douglas Horton, George P. Berry, Alfred Barr, Adlai E. Stevenson, Philip Bard, Lewis Thomas, George P. Shultz, John G. Kemeny.

American Philosophical Society, The, the oldest learned society in the United States, was formed by Benjamin Franklin in 1743 and reorganized in its present form in 1769. It resulted from "A Proposal for Promoting Useful Knowledge Among the British Plantations in America," which Franklin circulated among a carefully selected number of "ingenious Men residing in the several colonies."

The society's *Transactions* (the oldest continued periodical in North America) and *Proceedings* include scholarly books, monographs, papers, and research reports that are distributed throughout the world. Erected in 1789, its headquarters, Philosophical Hall, is, after Independence Hall, the oldest building now standing on Independence Square in Philadelphia. The society's library contains collections particularly strong in Frankliniana, the history of science and culture in America, and North American Indian linguistics and archaeology. The society makes research grants, awards prizes, and, at its twice yearly meetings, provides for its members the companionship, in Benjamin Franklin's words, "of sensible, virtuous and elegant minds."

The fields for selection of new members are: 1) mathematical and physical sciences; 2) geological and biological sciences; 3) social sciences; 4) humanities; 5) administration, the fine arts, and public affairs. Membership is limited to 500 residents of the United States and 100 residents of foreign countries.

Princeton professors who have been members of the society, and the years of their election, follow:*

1769	John Witherspoon
1780	William C. Houston
1785	S. Stanhope Smith
1789	Ashbel Green
	Walter Minto
1805	John Maclean, Sr.
1831	Henry Vethake
1835	Joseph Henry
	John Torrey
1839	Stephen Alexander
1844	John S. Hart
1856	George A. Matile
1867	Arnold Guyot
1871	James McCosh
1874	Charles A. Young
1877	Cyrus Fogg Brackett
	Charles W. Shields
1886	William Berryman Scott

1887	Henry Fairfield Osborn
1896	William F. Magie
1897	Edwin G. Conklin
	Henry Burchard Fine
	John B. Hatcher
	William Libbey
	Leroy W. McCay
	Charles F. W. McClure
	Arnold E. Ortmann
	Francis Landey Patton
	Woodrow Wilson
1901	Dana C. Munro
1908	Charles H. Smyth, Jr.
1911	Augustus Trowbridge
1912	John Grier Hibben
	Oswald Veblen
1913	Luther P. Eisenhart
	George A. Hulett
	Henry Norris Russell
1915	Edwin P. Adams
1918	George H. Shull
1919	Ulric Dahlgren
1920	Edward Capps
1923	Karl T. Compton
	William J. Sinclair
1928	James W. Alexander
	Hugh Stott Taylor
1929	E. Newton Harvey
	Solomon Lefschetz
1931	Arthur F. Buddington
	Raymond S. Dugan
	Howard McClenahan
1932	Gilbert Chinard
	Edwin W. Kemmerer
	Charles P. Smyth
1935	Harold W. Dodds
	Frank A. Fetter
	Hermann Weyl
1936	Edward S. Corwin
1938	C. Rufus Morey
	John von Neumann
1939	Theodore Leslie Shear
1940	Frank J. Mather
	Howard P. Robertson
1941	Henry Eyring
	Thomas J. Wertenbaker
1942	Jacob Viner

1943 Julian P. Boyd
     Charles G. Osgood
1944 Eugene P. Wigner
1945 Frank W. Notestein
1947 Henry D. Smyth
1948 Elmer G. Butler
     Samuel S. Wilks
1949 Glenn L. Jepsen
1951 Edward C. Kendall
     John A. Wheeler
1952 Albert M. Friend, Jr.
1958 Wilbert E. Moore
1959 Robert R. Palmer
     Lyman Spitzer, Jr.
     Joseph R. Strayer
1960 Harry H. Hess
1962 John W. Tukey
1963 Ansley J. Coale
     Gordon A. Craig
     Fritz Machlup
1964 Kurt Weitzmann
1965 John W. Milnor
1966 William Feller
     Carl G. Hempel
     William Arthur Lewis
     Arthur S. Link
1967 Donald F. Hornig
1969 Frederick H. Harbison
1970 Gerald E. Bentley
     Lawrence Stone
1972 John T. Bonner
     Charles C. Gillispie
1973 Bernard Lewis
1974 Thomas S. Kuhn
1976 W. Frank Craven
1977 William J. Baumol

* In addition over a hundred non-faculty alumni have been elected, among them Richard Stockton, Benjamin Rush, William Paterson, David Ramsay, James Madison, Samuel L. Southard, George M. Dallas, Basil L. Gildersleeve, Livingston Farrand, Raymond B. Fosdick, Clinton J. Davisson, Hamilton Fish Armstrong, Wilder G. Penfield, George F. Kennan, Charles W. Yost.

Five Princetonians—four professors and one trustee—have been president of the society: William Berryman Scott from 1918 to 1925; Henry Norris Russell in 1931 and 1932; Roland S. Morris (a trustee of the University), from 1932 to 1942; Edwin Grant Conklin from 1942 to 1945 and from 1948 to 1952; and Julian P. Boyd, from 1973 to 1976.

Professor Conklin was executive officer of the society from 1936 to 1942, Dean Eisenhart from 1942 to 1959.

American Studies, The Program in (formerly American Civilization), was created by the Faculty on January 12, 1942, just five weeks after the United States entered the Second World War. Its aim was to give undergraduates an understanding of their own civilization and an appreciation of its significance among other world civilizations. The program began at an opportune time, but, as President Dodds said in announcing it, "it was not rushed to the printer to meet the demands of the hour," but was rather the product of a year's deliberation.

Interdepartmental in character, the program draws its faculty and students from thirteen cooperating departments: Anthropology, Architecture and Urban Planning, Art and Archaeology, Economics, English, History, Music, Philosophy, Politics, Psychology, Religion, Sociology, and the Woodrow Wilson School.

Each student in the program majors in one of the cooperating departments, with as much emphasis on the American field as the regulations of his department permit, and devotes his senior thesis to a topic related to American civilization. He also takes the program's one-term introductory course in the sophomore year, and its two one-term conferences in the junior year. The work of the conferences involves a cooperative study by students and faculty of a significant feature of American civilization, the reading of a paper by each student in the conference, and lectures by faculty specialists, visiting scholars, and public figures. Guest speakers have included Lewis Mumford, Margaret Mead, Reinhold Niebuhr, Frances Perkins, Perry Miller, Helen Lynd, Oscar Handlin—and Fidel Castro, whose visit to Princeton the night of April 20, 1959, to address the Conference on "The United States and the Revolutionary Spirit" soon after he became the premier of the Republic of Cuba, caused a campus-wide sensation.

For the faculty, the conference has been a means of cooperative scholarship and publication. Books that have grown out of the conference have included: *Foreign Influences in American Life* (1944), *Evolutionary Thought in America* (1950), *Socialism and American Life* (2 vols., 1952), *Religion in American Life* (4 vols., 1961), and *Blacks in America: Bibliographical Essays* (1972).

Professor Willard Thorp (English), the prime mover in the formulation of the program, was its chairman from 1942 to 1955. Other chairmen have been Stow S. Persons (History), James Ward Smith (Philosophy), John William Ward (History), Laurence B. Holland (English), Richard M. Ludwig (English), James M. Banner, Jr. (History), James M. McPherson (History), Emory B. Elliott, Jr. (English).

During World War II, the program conducted week-end courses in American studies for members of the British armed services stationed in this country. In gratitude the British government later sent the University a stone from the bombed-out House of Commons, which is embedded in the wall at the right of the main entrance to Firestone Library.

Annual Giving, the University's most important source of unrestricted operating income, began in 1940-1941. That first year, the organization and the "know-how" of later years were lacking, and the results were modest: 18 percent of the alumni and a few friends contributed $80,000. But the underlying spirit of this enterprise was evident from the start: one alumnus gave the proceeds of a short story he had just published, another let his class agent cash in two Yale football tickets he couldn't use, and all 150 members of the Class of 1898 contributed, making them the first class to achieve 100 percent participation. President Dodds told the class agents, "You men have started something which may well grow to be the most effective force for progress at Princeton."

In the second year, contributions picked up after the attack on Pearl Harbor, and when the campaign ended, 25 percent of the alumni, and friends, had given $102,000. During the war, foreign currency came in from alumni stationed in military theatres throughout the world; a Class of 1923 lieutenant colonel in Italy sent a thousand-lira note in Allied Military currency, its modest value enhanced by Marlene Dietrich's autograph.

Contributions grew steadily in the postwar period, and the tenth year, 1949-1950, the half-million dollar mark was passed. Non-alumni parents, in their second year of participation, contributed $60,000. This pioneering program, which eventually brought upward of $100,000 annually from approximately 2,000 non-alumni parents, was adopted by many other colleges.

Six years later, in 1955-1956, the

million-dollar mark was passed. Meantime, alumni participation was also growing steadily, and in 1958-1959 it reached 72.2 percent, the best attained by any college in the United States up to then. Contributing to this record were 2,000 alumni workers in some three hundred cities here and abroad, who followed up the appeals of sixty-odd class agents with telephone calls and visits, in a program that had been started in 1947-1948. Their work was especially valuable in combating procrastination, which is not only a thief of time but, Annual Giving holds, a cause, if not cured, of Lybunts. A Lybunt is one who gave *Last Year But Not This.* Regional workers also helped in recruiting Tybnols. A Tybnol (another Princeton-originated term) is one who gave *This Year But Not Last.*

The Class of 1898, which had 100 percent participation the first year of Annual Giving, continued blissfully ignorant of both Lybunts and Tybnols, maintaining their perfect record for twenty-five years.

In the 1960s, total contributions increased dramatically in response to expanding University needs. "More is expected of us," President Goheen told his fellow alumni, "because more is expected of Princeton. There is more to be learned today; more to be done." In the silver anniversary year, 1964-1965, Annual Giving celebrated "twenty-five years of thoughtful dependable support" by exceeding $2 million for the first time. Three years later, it reached the $3 million plateau.

In 1962 and again in 1968, Princeton received the American Alumni Council's Grand Award for Sustained Performance in Annual Giving; no other university had received this award more than once.

One factor in the rapid rise in total contributions in the 1960s was the growing participation of Graduate School alumni, first begun in 1957-1958. The seventy-eight contributors the first year had grown to 1,000 ten years later. Another factor was the support of corporations, who matched gifts of Princeton employees in a plan initiated in 1954-1955 by General Electric and who, in some cases, made additional corporate contributions. This support grew steadily until Annual Giving was receiving between $300,000 and $400,000 annually from 450 corporations. But the most important factor was the rivalry among alumni classes vying for the honor of contributing the most to Princeton. The Class of 1922 was the first to top $100,000, just before its forty-second reunion in 1964. Thereafter, classes preparing for major reunions led the way. In 1966, the Classes of 1926 and 1941 passed the $200,000 mark, and a year later, the Class of 1942 topped $300,000. In 1971 the fiftieth reunion Class of 1921 broke the $400,000 barrier, and three years later the twenty-fifth reunion Class of 1949 became Annual Giving's first half-million dollar class. The 1949 class agent, Ralph Glendinning, had started a few years earlier to prepare his classmates for their achievement with this counsel: "Make your contribution proportionate to Princeton's place in higher education—and to what having gone to Princeton has meant to you, your career, and your family."

In 1971-1972 a special Annual Giving effort in honor of President Goheen, on the eve of his retirement, brought in a record-breaking total of $3,805,872. The following year, another special effort in honor of newly elected President Bowen produced another record: $3,955,842. These results, President Bowen told the alumni, demonstrated once again their pride and confidence in Princeton. "We thank you for your trust," he said. "We shall strive to live up to it."

Following eight consecutive years in the $3 million range, contributions to Annual Giving in 1975-1976 exceeded $4 million for the first time in the program's thirty-six-year history. In the same year two other major records were set when the Class of 1951 became the first twenty-fifth reunion class to contribute as much as $700,000, and the fiftieth reunion Class of 1926 became the first class to pass the $2 million mark in accumulated contributions. The total achievement in the year of the nation's bicentennial—$4.4 million—represented a 26 percent increase over the previous year, the greatest one-year jump in Annual Giving history. This record sum was the equivalent of income from the endowment of more than $100 million.

Credit for Annual Giving's perennial success belongs, in part, to its small professional staff, which has been headed by Edgar M. Gemmell '34, Edward A. Myers '38, George J. Cooke, Jr. '22, Arthur J. Horton '42, and Joseph L. Bolster, Jr. '52. Credit also belongs to the legions of dedicated volunteers who have worked so effectively under the leadership of the Annual Giving chairmen, and who have each year, in the words of one chairman, "sacrificed their evenings, their weekends, and perhaps, temporarily, even the affection of their long-suffering families" to earn Princeton's "abiding thanks for a job well done." Annual Giving chairmen, since the beginning, have been: Harold H. Helm '20, Richard L. Kennedy '28, Ernest C. Savage '19, Richard K. Stevens '22, S. Barksdale Penick '25, Baldwin Maull '22, Franklin T. McClintock '25, Sidney Lanier '24, Geoffrey Stengel '37, Harry H. Neuberger '17, Arthur Gardner '23, Macpherson Raymond '40, Amos Eno '32, Gilbert Lea '36, Duncan Van Norden '35, Edward C. Eisenhart '42, F. Stark Newberry '27, Douglas H. Hahn '34, Robert P. Hazlehurst, Jr. '40, John F. Maloney, '35, Winthrop A. Short '41, Sharon Clay Risk '43, Roby Harrington III '51, and Charles T. Bellingrath '56.

Anthropology, The Department of, was established at Princeton in 1971; the main emphasis was placed on the study of cultural and social anthropology including linguistics, and because it was a small department, neither archaeology nor physical anthropology was stressed. Within a few years, the department developed a reputation as a place for specialized work in the theoretical problems of symbolism and cultural change—areas of research within cultural anthropology that were undergoing a good deal of ferment and development during the late 1960s and early 1970s. Faculty and graduate research focused on such topics, among others, as religious systems; ritual performances; political ideologies; language and its relation to culture; myth and folktales; cultural conceptions of kinship; and psychological aspects of culture, drama, art, and folklore.

Princeton's first course in cultural anthropology was given in 1946 by Sociology Professor Kingsley Davis; this introductory course was subsequently taught for ten years by Sociology Professor Melvin Tumin, and then at various times until 1965 by anthropologists Lloyd A. Fallers, Paul J. Bohannan, Peter Kunstadter, and David W. Crabb—all frontiersmen of Princeton anthropology, who were responsible for developing additional undergraduate and graduate courses in the field.

Originally, anthropology was a part of the curriculum of the Department of Economics and Social Institutions. This department divided in 1960, when the Department of Sociology and Anthropology was established. In 1965 a separate Program in Anthropology was launched; it was directed by a faculty committee under the chairmanship of Cyril E. Black (1965-1966), David W. Crabb (1966-1970), and Martin G. Silverman (1970-1971).

In 1971 an independent Department of Anthropology was established, with Martin Silverman as first chairman. He was succeeded by Hildred Geertz in 1973, and by James W. Fernandez in 1978.

Hildred Geertz

Architecture and Urban Planning, The School of, was founded in 1919 (as the School of Architecture) under the leadership of Howard Crosby Butler 1892, but architectural study had begun at Princeton almost a century earlier with physicist Joseph Henry's (q.v.) arrival in 1832. Among Henry's hobbies was the study of construction, design, and landscaping. His drawings formed the basis for the first long-range building plans of the College, and the quadrangle in back of Nassau Hall remains approximately as he laid it out. He gave lectures on the history and appreciation of architecture, later continued by Albert B. Dod 1822, a mathematician. Interest was sufficient in the 1860s to generate plans for a four-year professional course in architecture, but nothing came of these plans.

Two names are important in the record of architectural teaching at Princeton, Allan Marquand 1874 and Howard Crosby Butler 1892. Professor Marquand, an art historian and head of the Department of Art and Archaeology, began the first regular instruction in architecture in 1882; he inspired many architects as well as artists and art history teachers. It was largely due to his influence that Butler, an archaeologist, returned to the Princeton faculty in 1902. Thereafter, architectural courses were offered regularly by Butler in the Department of Art and Archaeology.

A renewed effort to create a professional course in architecture was begun in 1916 by a group of former Princeton students who had gone on to architectural schools and who had found their work at Princeton an admirable foundation for professional training. After the war, in 1919, Butler announced that Princeton would offer professional training in architecture. The principles on which that training would be based are similar to those of today. It was Princeton's belief that an architect should have a well-rounded education in liberal studies and should approach his profession primarily as an art, that he should understand and appreciate other arts in relation to architecture, and that he should be taught the science of building construction as a part of his training in design, rather than as an end in itself. Princeton inaugurated the plan for an architectural course that would begin in freshman year and continue without break through two years of graduate work, leaving room for the inclusion of liberal electives. Within the last decade most architectural schools have abandoned their five-year programs in favor of a similar six-year plan of study. The first student to receive a professional degree in architecture from Princeton was Robert B. O'Connor M.F.A. 1920, a graduate of

Trinity College, who later followed Stephen F. Voorhees '00 as the University's supervising architect.

Raymond Bossange was made director of the school upon the death of Howard C. Butler; he in turn was followed by Sherley W. Morgan '13. Morgan was first appointed to an instructorship in architectural drawing in 1916, and after World War I he and E. Baldwin Smith Ph.D. 1915 returned as assistant professors. These two teachers were responsible for the school's development over the next thirty years, and succeeded in making Princeton's School of Architecture one of the foremost in the country.

Sherley Morgan appointed Jean Labatut as resident design critic in 1928 following Frederic D'Amato's untimely death. This appointment was made upon the recommendation of two alumni of the school, Alexander P. Morgan '22 and Gordon McCormick '17, who had worked with Labatut in Paris. Jean Labatut's ability to bring out the best in his students, his sound judgment, and his artistic integrity contributed greatly to the success of the school during his thirty-nine-year teaching career at Princeton. The school was awarded many medals in national competitions, and individual students won five Paris prizes and four Rome prizes in architecture as well as other awards during Labatut's tenure. He himself was the first recipient of the award for distinction in education jointly sponsored by the American Institute of Architects and the Association of Collegiate Schools of Architecture. Many of Labatut's students are currently teaching architecture all over the world and many are deans or directors of their schools.

In 1930 Frank Lloyd Wright gave his first lectures in the United States at Princeton. These lectures, sponsored by the Kahn Foundation, were later published as a monograph, *Modern Architecture*—Wright's first American book on his philosophy and his work.

Princeton entered the urban planning field with the creation of the Bureau of Urban Research in 1941, founded by Jean Labatut and managed by an interdepartmental committee, to establish source material for urban studies. Melville C. Branch '34, its first director, was ably assisted by Dorothy Whiteman. As part of the Bicentennial Celebration, 1946-1947, the school was able to conduct a three-day conference on Planning Man's Physical Environment, which was directed by Arthur C. Holden '12 and Henry A. Jandl M.F.A. 1937. It brought together leading architects, teachers, planners and writers from all over the world, including Alvar Aalto, Frederick J. Adams, Sigfried Giedion, Walter Gropius, Richard Neutra, Carlos Contreras, Mies Van der Rohe, William Wurster and others. The final session juxtaposed the contrasting views of its principal speakers Robert Moses and Frank Lloyd Wright.

Another important innovation, in 1949, was the Princeton Architectural Laboratory, a center for experimentation in architectural expression and technology. Here Princeton's contributions to architectural research were begun, and later, a pioneer study on metal curtain walls for buildings was conducted. The results of this study were published from 1953 to 1957, after Robert W. McLaughlin '21 had assumed the directorship of the school following Sherley W. Morgan's retirement in 1952. Also during this period the brothers Victor and Aladar Olgyay conducted a systematic study of the effects of climate and environment upon man and his shelter. Their book, *Solar*

Control and Shading Devices remains the primary source for architects and planners in the field of architecture and its relation to the physical environment.

Under McLaughlin's directorship the school became an entity separate from the Department of Art and Archaeology in 1952. As the school expanded, the faculty included many visiting architects, notably Enrico Peressutti from Milan and Sven Silow from Stockholm. Another frequent visitor to the school, R. Buckminster Fuller, inspired students with the investigations he conducted in architectural structural theory. During one of his visits, the students designed, fabricated, and built a 40-foot tension-integrity sphere at the laboratory.

In 1963 the school moved from its cramped quarters in McCormick Hall to its new home, a building designed by a Baltimore architectural firm of which two principals were Princeton alumni, Charles Nes '28 and L. McLane Fisher '23. In 1963, also, the school lost by retirement one of its most active teachers, Francis A. Comstock '19, a member of its faculty for almost forty years.

In 1965 Robert W. McLaughlin retired as director of the school. In recognition of the increasing role which the school had assumed within the University during his administration, the title of director was changed to dean. Robert L. Geddes was appointed the first dean, and Henry A. Jandl became executive officer in charge of departmental administration. Under Geddes's leadership new faculty were added and changes were instituted in the curriculum, emphasizing values, concepts and methods, to provide the beginning architectural student with the broadest possible liberal education

and, at the same time, to provide introductory courses for students in other disciplines in the area of urban studies, and man-made environment, and historical studies.

The Research Center for Urban and Environmental Planning was established in 1966. One of its first contract projects in 1967 was a Planning and Design Workbook for Community Participation. At this time, the name of the School of Architecture was changed to include Urban Planning, and concurrently the school established a master's degree program in urban planning in cooperation with the Woodrow Wilson School of Public and International Affairs. These innovations, soon followed by a Ph.D. program in urban planning, represented a major step by the school in meeting the challenge of the changing needs and goals of society.

Henry A. Jandl

Armstrong, Hamilton Fish '16 (1893-1973), was a founder and for fifty years editor of the American quarterly review *Foreign Affairs*.

He was born and lived all his life on West Tenth Street in New York; his book *Those Days* recounts the experience of growing up in Greenwich Village. In his undergraduate years he showed his editorial bent by earning places on the *Nassau Lit* and the *Daily Princetonian*. As editorial chairman of the *Prince* his senior year, when women's suffrage was being debated in New Jersey, he spoke out in favor of giving the vote to "the other half" of the human race. But his interest in international matters was a later development. At graduation he reported to the *Nassau Herald* that he was still undecided about his future occupation, and it was not until he became a military attaché in Belgrade at the end of the First World War that his life-long interest in foreign affairs was kindled.

During his half-century with *Foreign Affairs*, he traveled widely, studied closely the problems of many countries, and came to know the leading statesmen of the world. His knowledge and judgment in assessing international problems gave the quarterly a worldwide reputation and influence. Everyone who knew him was impressed by the rare personal qualities of "the Gentleman from Tenth Street," as James Reston called him. Arthur Schlesinger, Jr., said he treated everyone, "old or young, famous or unknown, with the same generous courtesy and concern. It was more than manner . . .; it was a genuine youthfulness of mind and openness of heart."

In his eightieth year Armstrong summed up his thoughts about America's place in the world with these words:

> The direction is not backward in nostalgia, to the virtues of our forefathers. . . . The direction is forward, to recognize and accept the present ills of our society and to set about curing them—by rehumanizing ourselves, by readopting civility as part of good behavior, by recognizing that history can inform the future . . . by welcoming diversity of opinion as an essential element of strength in a democracy.

Art and Archaeology, The Department of, has had a long and illustrious history. Its rudimentary beginnings go back to a course of lectures on architecture given first in 1832 by physicist Joseph Henry (q.v.), Professor of Natural Philosophy. The year before, the study of Roman antiquities had been mentioned in the catalogue—an indication that Princeton was the first college to offer the subject of archaeology. Fifty years later, in 1882, Allan Marquand (q.v.), the first great name in the department's history, was appointed to the faculty. Marquand, with Charles Eliot Norton of Harvard, shares the distinction of having been the first to see the immense cultural benefit of the history of art to the American student and to introduce its serious study into American university life. Before the end of the nineteenth century Marquand taught ancient art and archaeology, Arthur L. Frothingham taught "monastic art," and Howard Crosby Butler (q.v.), who later became first Master of the Graduate College, gave graduate courses in early Christian and mediaeval architecture. Thus Princeton was the first college to offer consistent undergraduate and graduate work in classical and mediaeval art—subjects that have never ceased to play a dominant part in the department's history.

During the first quarter of the twentieth century, Marquand was not only writing his famous books on the della Robbia family of sculptors, but, as the department's first chairman, was building a staff of scholars in the history of art whose teaching and writing during the second quarter of the century were to bring Princeton national and international renown. Among them were Charles Rufus Morey (q.v.), who became the most formidable historian of mediaeval art in America; Frank Jewett Mather, Jr., a gifted writer on many aspects of art who gave courses on Italian and northern European painting; George Elderkin, historian of Greek art; Albert M. Friend, masterly preceptor and brilliant medievalist; and W. Frederick Stohlman, another fine mediaevalist, who also gave enlightening lectures on Renaissance sculpture.

The two decades after Morey became chairman in 1924 were the department's period of greatest power and influence. Morey rounded out the department by appointing five new members, all of whom added to Princeton's fame: two mediaevalists—Ernest De-Wald, who also gave a popular course in Italian painting, and Kurt Weitzmann, the celebrated Byzantinist; George Rowley, the father of Princeton's studies in Far Eastern art; Richard Stillwell, the distinguished classical archaeologist; and Donald Egbert, whose courses in American art and architecture widely influenced the study of these subjects in this country. Morey raised large sums of money for departmental endowment and for the Marquand Library, founded by Marquand and now one of the great art libraries of the world. He also established the world-famous Index of Christian Art (q.v.), a photographic record with bibliography of works of Christian art produced before 1400—an invaluable aid to scholarship. And under Morey the department's great period of colonization began. While Harvard by and large staffed the country's museums, Princeton in good measure provided teachers and departmental chairman for a relatively new discipline that was beginning to expand across the country. This spreading of Princeton's heritage has continued ever since. Finally Morey started the department's handsome publication fund. With the Princeton Monographs in Art and Archaeology (numbering 41 volumes) and with the series in the History of Manuscript Illumination, Princeton is, in programmatic publication in the history of art, ahead of every American university.

Morey's successor, in 1945, was Baldwin Smith, a great teacher and an eminent historian of ancient and early Christian architecture. He added to the staff three young men who became distinguished teachers and scholars in their fields: David Coffin in Renaissance architecture; John Rupert Martin in the Baroque art of Italy and northern Europe; and Robert Koch in the Northern Renaissance, a field in which Bert Friend had earlier given a memorable course. During Smith's chairmanship, Princeton's tradition of field archaeology, initiated by Butler's early expedition to Sardis, and carried forward in the great collaborative dig at Antioch in the 1930s, entered a new phase with the model and productive excavation of the ancient Greek city of Morgantina in Sicily under Richard Stillwell and another eminent classicist who had joined the department in 1951, Eric Sjöqvist, formerly archaeological secretary to King Gustav of Sweden.

Under Rensselaer Lee, who succeeded Smith as chairman in 1956, funds were secured for a new expedition, directed by Kurt Weitzmann and by George H. Forsyth, Jr. '23 of the University of Michigan (the University of Alexandria in Egypt was a co-sponsor), to the ancient monastery of Mt. Sinai. This led to the publication by Forsyth of the monastery's architecture and by Weitzmann of its great apse mosaic and its unique collection of early Byzantine paintings. Also plans were completed for the new McCormick Hall and for the Art Museum (qq.v.), then ably directed by Patrick J. Kelleher. Graduate work and museum collections in oriental art developed imposingly under Wen Fong who persuaded the eminent Japanese scholar, Shujiro Shimada, to join the faculty; and the department acquired among others Felton Gibbons, a rising star in the field of Italian Renaissance art. Several preeminent scholars at the Institute for Advanced Study have greatly strengthened the graduate curriculum. Under Lee's chairmanship Erwin Panofsky was persuaded to teach courses regularly; Millard Meiss also contributed to instruction and with his wife endowed a fund for the purchase of photographs.

During the chairmanship of Lee's successors, Coffin (1964-1970) and Fong (1970-1973), the department maintained and increased its offerings in the traditional fields. It also kept up with the times in establishing new courses in twentieth-century art, Spanish art, and graphic arts, the art of Latin America, and the art of photography, the last taught by Peter Bunnell, director of the Art Museum, and first incumbent of the new chair in photography endowed by David H. McAlpin '20 in 1972.

Under Coffin the department's new buildings were completed, and strong appointments in classical art were made to replace Stillwell and Sjöqvist, who had retired: Theodore Leslie Shear, Jr., field director of the excavations in the Athenian Agora, and Evelyn Harrison, the first woman to be appointed a full professor in the department (lost, unfortunately, in 1974 to the graduate Institute of Fine Arts at New York University).

Under Fong, one of the country's most distinguished young scholars in the field of Chinese painting, important acquisitions continued to enrich the oriental collections in the Art Museum; also three women were added to the faculty, and after coeducation the department's enrollment increased notably as women showed strong interest in its courses.

As this is written, John R. Martin is serving his fourth year as chairman. His international repute as a teacher-scholar, his energy, and his sense of the department's great history and tradition augur well for its future.

Rensselaer W. Lee

Art Museum, The, almost equidistant from Nassau Hall and the main portal of the Chapel, can be located from afar by Picasso's imposing "Head of a Woman" (one of the Putnam Memorial sculptures, q.v.), which stands in front of the glass facade. The museum's dominant characteristic is a refreshing openness. It shares an entrance with McCormick Hall, which houses the Department of Art and Archaeology and the Marquand Art Library, and occupies the site of the original Romanesque-style structure, built in the 1880s when the new department was organized by Allan Marquand 1874 (q.v.). He felt strongly that students should be given access to original works of art and insisted that a museum be part of the program. The department, library, and museum soon outgrew this building, but it was not until the end of the First World War that relief could be obtained. Then McCormick Hall was built to accommodate the department and library, thus allowing the museum more space in the old quarters.

When Marquand retired in 1922 after four decades of developing the University's resources in art and archaeology, administrative responsibilities were divided; C. Rufus Morey became chairman of the department and Frank Jewett Mather, Jr., became director of the museum, a position he held long past the conventional retirement age until men began to return from military service in World War II. Under Mather the museum continued to grow until its walls fairly bulged, but conditions during the war and urgent priority for the University Library made it necessary to defer expansion. Ernest T. DeWald, like his predecessors a specialist in Italian art, became director in 1946 and, not long before retiring in 1960, was involved with plans for the new building, designed by Steinmann and Cain and made possible by the University's $53 million drive. Completion of the plans and then two years of functioning only as an office in Green Hall Annex marked the beginning of Patrick J. Kelleher's directorship. The excitement of installing the University's works of art in the new museum, many of them not seen for years because of inadequate space, culminated in the dedication of the building in June 1966 and in the rewarding response of enthusiastic visitors to the round of activities that were possible in the new structure. Peter C. Bunnell, who succeeded Kelleher as director in 1973 and returned to full-time teaching in the Department of Art and Archaeology five years later, developed and guided a dynamic program that reached beyond campus and community. In 1978 his successor, Fred S. Licht, came back to Princeton, where he once taught, to carry on the continuous challenge of putting the Museum to stimulating use for all concerned with achievement in the visual arts.

Many alumni and friends contributed to the new building; the entire quota was met by designated gifts. The most generous individual donor was Carl Otto von Kienbusch '06, a steady benefactor since his student days. The concerted effort of the Class of 1929, which adopted the museum as its special project, assured final success.

Through the decades the museum has received generous help in developing the collections. During the first years Marquand established an endowment for the purchase of works of art. Other endowments followed: The Caroline G. Mather Fund, given by Professor Mather, his brother and sisters, in memory of their mother; The Laura P. Hall Memorial Fund, left by Clifton R. Hall of the Department of History, to provide for additions to the collections of prints and drawings he bequeathed; The John Maclean Magie and Gertrude Magie Fund and the Fowler McCormick '21 Fund for acquisitions; the Mildred Clarke Pressinger von Kienbusch Memorial Fund for publishing the museum's semi-annual bulletin which Mr. Kienbusch sponsored from its beginning in 1942. Several other funds, not endowed, but replenished periodically, give generous assistance in various areas of the museum's operation. The Friends of the Museum, formed in 1950, have provided for purchases of works of art, in addition to generating support for the exhibition program.

Every museum works within defined borders to be effective. Since Princeton's is a teaching museum, the scope of the collections is approximately that of the art department's curriculum. It ranges in time from ancient cultures (the Mediterranean world, the Far East, and Meso-America) to the present. Geographically, the emphasis is upon western Europe, China and Japan, Central America, and the United States. Particular areas of strength are in classical antiquities; Italian paintings; prints, photographs and drawings of European and American schools; Chinese paintings and ceremonial bronzes. The museum's possessions are exhibited on a rotating basis, which is determined largely by the requirement of certain courses. Loan exhibitions are arranged to supplement the permanent collections, as well as to bring in material the museum does not attempt to collect. Certain collections (e.g., prints and drawings), by their nature cannot be shown frequently, but are available by appointment to serious students and scholars.

Allan Marquand made many gifts, including one of the Museum's treasures—Hieronymous Bosch's painting, "Christ before Pilate." Frank Jewett Mather's collection of Italian drawings includes many gems, among them a study by Carpaccio for one of his wall-paintings in Venice. The 1938 bequest of Dan Fellows Platt 1895 provided an unusually rich concentration in drawings by Italian seventeenth-century artists; his Italian paintings include important early works that dovetail well with the generally later Italian paintings given in 1935 by Henry White Cannon '10. A collection of about five hundred Chinese snuff-bottles bequeathed by James A. Blair '03 is admired by specialists and amateurs alike. In 1947, in honor of the University's Bicentennial, DuBois S. Morris 1893 presented his collection of Chinese paintings, which contains an outstanding Sung Dynasty landscape. Through the years Carl Otto von Kienbusch '06 underwrote the acquisition of many objects. The ideal donor, he imposed no preferences and, as a result, the collection named in memory of his elder son and namesake represents many periods and places. A striking object in this collection, and one of the museum's masterpieces, is a polychrome wooden statue of Kwan Yin of the Sung Dynasty. The 1933 bequest of Junius S. Morgan 1888 brought to the museum an important group of Greek vases and an extraordinary assemblage of prints, including a nearly complete

series of the engravings and etchings of Jacques Callot. A new area of collection was initiated in 1971 when David H. McAlpin '20 gave about five hundred photographs and a fund for the purchase of additional examples of photography as an artistic medium.

The present museum and its collections are a fitting fulfillment of the pioneering efforts of the first two directors, Professors Marquand and Mather, who together served for more than half a century. A bronze plaque in the entrance court records their great contribution to Princeton:

> BY SCHOLARSHIP, VISION, AND
> GENEROSITY, THEY MADE
> POSSIBLE A COMMUNITY OF
> STUDENTS AND WORKS OF ART.

Frances F. Jones

Astrophysical Sciences, The Department of, came into being in 1962 when the trustees and faculty approved a recommendation of the Department of Astronomy that its name be so changed and its scope enlarged to include graduate programs in plasma physics and in atomic and molecular physics as well as in astronomy and astrophysics.

Astronomy at Princeton was originally taught as a part of "natural philosophy," usually by professors who were primarily mathematicians. Walter Minto, called from Scotland by President Witherspoon in 1787 as professor of mathematics and natural philosophy, was the author of a treatise on the newly discovered planet Uranus. Andrew Hunter, Jr., Class of 1772, held the title Professor of Mathematics and Astronomy, 1804-1808.

The College was proud of its Rittenhouse Orrery—a clock-like planetarium—acquired in 1771, but it had difficulty raising funds for an observatory.

After the Nassau Hall fire of 1802, the trustees asked John Maclean Sr., who then held the professorship of mathematics and natural philosophy, "to select from the materials remaining after the rebuilding of the college such parts as may be necessary for the building of an Observatory," but nothing came of this proposal.

Astronomy began its development as a separate discipline under Stephen Alexander who, beginning as a tutor in mathematics in 1833, was appointed professor of astronomy in 1840. He gave the first separate course in astronomy, made observations on a small telescope in his home, published some twenty scientific papers, and by his patience and enthusiasm for his subject secured benefactions for the Halsted Observatory, completed from his plans in 1872. This observatory was one of the inducements that lured Charles A. Young from Dartmouth as Alexander's successor in 1877; others were the promise of an observatory office and residence built on Prospect Avenue in 1878, and of a 23-inch telescope installed in the Halsted Observatory in 1882.

Young was the founder of a distinguished dynasty of observatory directors, who with the exception of a few years, have represented a direct line of teachers and students. Seven years following Young's retirement in 1905, Henry Norris Russell, who graduated from Princeton in 1897 and took his Ph.D. under Young in 1900, became director. On Russell's retirement thirty-five years later, he was succeeded by Lyman Spitzer, Jr., who graduated from Yale in 1935 and earned his doctorate at Princeton under Russell in 1938.

Young pioneered in solar spectroscopy, using a spectroscope of his own devising to study the colors given off by light from the sun in order to determine the elements present in the sun's atmosphere. He was the author of an authoritative work on *The Sun* and four textbooks, said by Harlow Shapley to be "models of clearness and balanced presentation," on which most of the next generation of American astronomers were nurtured.

While Young was primarily an observer, his successor, Henry Norris Russell, was chiefly a theorist who used mathematics and physics to explain the observations of others. With Eddington and Milne in England and Karl Schwarzchild in Germany, Russell laid much of the foundation of modern astrophysics.

Carrying on Young's study of the chemical composition of the sun, Russell brought to the investigation exact physical theory that made it possible for the first time to specify the relative amounts of the different elements present in the sun's atmosphere. "His detailed recipe for the solar atmosphere" (in Professor Spitzer's words) is known to astronomers as the "Russell mixture" and has been widely used in theoretical work on the sun and the stars. The surprisingly overwhelming abundance of hydrogen which he found (92 percent by volume) was later confirmed by others for stars in general and exerted a profound influence on all of astronomy.

Russell also became a leading authority on stellar evolution—the birth, growth, decay, and death of a star. He and the Danish astronomer, Einar Hertzsprung, independently discovered a certain regularity in the relationship between the brightness of stars, their colors, and their spectral class; the diagram illustrating this relationship is usually called the Hertzsprung-Russell diagram.

Under Russell, Princeton became the foremost center for the analysis of eclipsing variables: double stars—so close together they appear as a single star—whose orbital motion around one another, accompanied by periodic eclipses, results in a systematic change in brightness, which when measured can be used to learn the relative sizes of the two stars. Russell worked out the theory and method of analysis in 1912, and for many years the most precise measurements of light variations were made by his colleague, Raymond S. Dugan, in thousands of painstaking observations. Another colleague, Newton L. Pierce, who studied under Dugan, carried on his teacher's work, using electronic techniques.

Professors Russell, Dugan, and John Q. Stewart collaborated on a two-volume textbook (1927) that "essentially revolutionized astronomical teaching and astronomical textbook writing in America."

On Russell's retirement in 1947 Lyman Spitzer, Jr., succeeded him as director of the Observatory and, several years later, as Charles A. Young Professor of Astronomy. At the same time Martin Schwarzschild, then thirty-five, was called from Columbia as professor of astronomy; he was later appointed Eugene Higgins Professor of Astronomy. The appointment of Spitzer, one of Russell's students, and of Schwarzschild, son of Russell's famous contemporary, Karl Schwarzschild, led to a dramatic expansion in Princeton's role as a center of astronomical research, mostly in the two fields of theoretical astrophysics and of observational space astronomy. This expansion has been financed in part by University funds, in part by substantial grants from the federal government through the Office of Naval Research, the National Science Foundation, the National Aeronautics and Space Administration, and the Air Force.

Spitzer has continued Russell's work in theoretical astrophysics, making pioneering calculations of the temperature of the very rare gases in interstellar space and investigating many aspects of the problem of star formation. Schwarzschild has also carried on the study of stellar evolution begun by Russell, with his investigations on the interior of stars, confirming, for the interior of the sun, Russell's discovery of the great abundance of hydrogen and helium in the solar atmosphere. By careful calculation of the changes in the interior of a star due to the burning of its nuclear fuel, Schwarzschild has been able to find its age corresponding to a given present position on the Hertzsprung-Russell diagram.

In 1951 Spitzer instituted on the Forrestal Research Campus a program (originally called Project Matterhorn but later named the Plasma Physics Laboratory) for studies of basic plasma physics and the possibilities of controlled thermonuclear power. This program brought an influx of specialists in plasma physics who have given Princeton great strength in a basic subject that may hold the key for solving the future energy problems of mankind: John M. Dawson, Edward A. Frieman, Harold P. Furth, Melvin B. Gottlieb, Martin D. Kruskal, Russell Kulsrud, Carl R. Oberman, Thomas H. Stix, and Shoichi Yoshikawa.

Schwarzschild has pioneered in the use of giant balloons to hoist telescopes 80,000 feet into the stratosphere, to get clearer pictures of the sun and other stars and planets. In a series of flights in 1957 and 1959 a 12-inch balloon telescope (Stratoscope I) enabled Schwarzschild and his associates to obtain the sharpest and most detailed photographs of the sun ever taken. A 36-inch balloon telescope (Stratoscope II) was developed in 1963 and was used to obtain unprecedentedly sharp photographs of planets and stellar systems. Before his death in 1976, Professor Robert E. Danielson was closely associated with Schwarzschild in this work.

Spitzer has also been responsible for conceiving and developing, as part of NASA's Orbiting Astronomical Observatory program, a special satellite project to study the composition and physical structure of inter-stellar gases and dust clouds in space. This equipment, which was launched in August 1972 on a satellite named *Copernicus*, contains a 32-inch telescope, an ultraviolet spectrometer, and auxiliary electronic equipment to measure the ultraviolet light absorption characteristics of cosmic clouds and the gaseous atmospheres of the brighter stars. *Copernicus* is in earth orbit at a height of about 500 miles, well beyond the 30 or 40 mile ozone layer, where the strong absorption of ultraviolet light by the ozone precludes such measurements. Astronomers from all over the world have come to Princeton to use this instrument in their researches. John B. Rogerson has been associated with Spitzer on this project; other members of the group have been Kurt Dressler, Donald C. Morton, Donald G. York, and Edward B. Jenkins.

Morton has headed up another innovative program in space astronomy. By means of equipment carried 80 miles high in a rocket, he and his associates were able to make observations of stars from above the earth's atmosphere. In 1965 they launched a rocket carrying a telescope with photographic equipment, which obtained for the first time detailed spectra of two stars in ultraviolet wavelengths which do not reach Earth's surface. Since that time other Princeton rocket-carried telescopes have obtained additional such information previously denied to astronomers. In particular, this program has unexpectedly shown that hot stars are blowing their atmospheres out into space at speeds of thousands of miles per second.

The department's facilities were greatly enhanced in 1966 by the installation of a 36-inch reflecting telescope in the FitzRandolph Observatory, which had been built in 1934 to replace the Halsted Observatory, and by the completion of the department's modern home, Peyton Hall, which replaced its former headquarters in the old Observatory of Instruction on Prospect Avenue.

The appointment in 1971 of John N. Bahcall as professor of astronomy in the Institute for Advanced Study, succeeding Bengt Strömgren, who first held this position, further intensified the light given off by Princeton as a center for the astrophysical sciences, as has the presence from time to time, as visiting professors at the Princeton Observatory, of luminaries such as Walter Baade (Mt. Wilson Observatory), Subrahmanyan Chandrasekhar (Yerkes Observatory), Fred Hoyle (England), Jan H. Oort (The Netherlands).

Athletics. Until 1800 outdoor exercise for Princeton students usually took the form of walking, horseback riding, canoeing down the Millstone River, and hunting small game in the hills and fields nearby. The first quarter of the nineteenth century saw an increase in more violent forms of physical activity, including occasional duels and frequent struggles with "townies" when the cry of "Nassau! Nassau!" would bring half-clad students rushing from their beds to rescue their comrades and defend the college honor.

Although there were no intercollegiate football contests until 1869, as early as 1844 the quadrangle between East and West College was the scene of many spirited football games. Frequently the entire student body would turn out, divide themselves into teams, and endeavor to kick the ball until it touched the wall of either East or West College. The fall of 1857 brought a more organized form of athletics with the formation of a cricket club and two baseball clubs. The following year saw the emergence of the Nassau Baseball Club, which played its first game away from Princeton two years later.

During the early days the teams had little system or organization; the best player was usually the leader. The first step toward a more formal mode of operation occurred when the players elected one of their members as captain, with sole charge and management of the games and players. The next step was the development of the Football and Baseball, and later the Track, Associations, whose student boards of directors ran into criticism after gradually usurping the authority of the captains and were reduced in 1876 to two-man undergraduate committees.

The alumni were admitted to a share of management in 1885 when a graduate advisory committee of three was established by the Baseball Association. This scheme was so well received that, before the year closed, the various student associations had agreed to give the graduate advisory committee general supervision over all athletics of the college—the first step toward consolidation of athletic interests. In 1886 an executive committee composed of un-dergraduate representatives from all the associations was organized to take charge of the grounds and general athletic interests of the college.

The final steps toward consolidation came with the adoption of an alumni proposal that each association turn over all surplus monies at the year's end to a University Fund managed by a regularly elected officer eventually known as the general athletic treasurer. In 1890 the graduate and under-graduate committees joined in the formation of the Princeton University Athletic Association, a year later incorporated under the laws of New Jersey. The general athletic treasurer became the first full-time officer to have administrative responsibility for all athletic programs.

At the same time, the faculty appointed a committee on outdoor sports to investigate and approve the academic standing of the individual players and to see that games and hours of training did not interfere with study.

The amalgamation of the faculty and alumni committees into a Board of Athletic Control came in 1900. Under the chairmanship of Dean Howard McClenahan '94, with G. R. Murray '93 as general athletic treasurer/secretary, this board gave general supervision to the organization of sports in Princeton.

In 1923 Dr. Charles W. Kennedy '03 took over the chairmanship. Asa S. Bushnell '21 was appointed secretary of the board in 1928 and three years later became graduate manager of athletics. In 1932 Dr. Joseph E. Raycroft succeeded Dr. Kennedy as chairman; the same year brought the retirement of G. R. Murray after thirty-two years of service to Princeton's athletic interests.

The Board of Athletic Control was replaced by the University Council on Athletics in 1934, with Burnham N.

Dell as chairman and Asa S. Bushnell secretary.

In 1937 the Athletic Association was formally dissolved and reconstituted as an integral part of the University. In 1939, Bushnell left Princeton to become the head of the Central Office for Eastern Intercollegiate Athletics and R. Kenneth Fairman '34 was appointed graduate manager of athletics, a designation changed to director of athletics in 1941. Howard Stepp was acting director during Fairman's military service in World War II.

The last major change in the administrative structure of athletics occurred in 1947 when a single Department of Physical Education and Athletics was established, bringing the physical education and intramural programs under one departmental purview with intercollegiate athletics. Major increases in Princeton's athletic plant took place during Fairman's leadership with the construction of the Caldwell Field House and the Jadwin Gymnasium as well as adjacent baseball, football, and lacrosse fields. Fairman also laid the groundwork for the successful entry of women into the Princeton athletic picture before he retired in 1972 after 35 years in charge of Princeton athletics.

Royce N. Flippin, Jr.'56 took over the directorship of physical education and athletics in 1973. Shortly after his arrival, the department added "Recreation" to its masthead in recognition of the growing interest in lifetime sports, recreational activities, and health fitness on the part of large numbers of the student body, faculty and staff.

Samuel C. Howell

Baccalaureate Address, The (originally called a sermon), is one of Princeton's oldest traditions. The earliest recorded address was delivered by President Samuel Davies in 1760 to the eleven members of the graduating class. Entitled "Religion and Public Spirit," it treated a topic that has been a frequently recurring theme. "Serve your Generation," he told his students.

Live not for yourself but the Publick. Be the Servants of the Church; the Servants of your Country; the Servants of all. . . . Esteem yourselves by so much the more happy, honourable and important, by how much the more useful you are. Let your own Ease, your own Pleasure, your own private Interests, yield to the common Good.

Davies's address was delivered in the prayer hall of Nassau Hall. In modern times, the baccalaureate has been given in the University Chapel, and as in Davies's day, it takes place on the Sunday preceding commencement. The service begins with an academic procession and includes scripture readings and prayers, anthems by the choir, and hymns by the congregation. Since 1972 the address, originally delivered by the president, has been given each year by a different speaker chosen by the president from the alumni or the faculty.

Speaking from the text "We are unprofitable servants: we have done [only] that which was our duty to do" (Luke 17:10), President Woodrow Wilson in 1909 told the graduating seniors that the education they had received had made them

in some special sense citizens of a spiritual world in which men are expected to do more than make a living; in which they are expected to enrich the day they live in with . . . something given freely, from their special store of knowledge and of instructed principle, for the service of their neighbors and their communities and for the enlightenment of mankind.

(A half-century later, the Class of 1909 reprinted this sermon for their fiftieth reunion, and Judge Harold R. Medina read it at their memorial service.)

Although a common thread has run through many baccalaureates, sometimes they have reflected specifically the times in which they were given. Among President Harold W. Dodds's twenty addresses, for example, one, given in 1937, during the Depression, treated the concept "preoccupation with security breeds insecurity"; another, delivered in 1941, the year the United States entered the Second World War, discussed "The Anatomy of Courage"; and a third, given in 1949, in the early days of the cold war, considered the question, "Which comes first, the integrity of the individual or the authority of the state?"

President Robert F. Goheen, in his last baccalaureate, in 1972, told the graduating seniors that their generation, more than most of his, had an awareness of, "indeed a passionate concern for," contemporary problems. He reminded them that the solution to these problems "requires, more often than not, the combining of humanitarian empathy with much tough-mindedness, much sophisticated knowledge, and a long view." He emphasized the contributions universities can make to this effort; they are, he said, "continually trying to extend the range and precision of human understanding, and . . . to help us make contact with the deepest resources of human wisdom as a basis for action."

In 1975, Gregory Vlastos, Stuart Pro-

fessor of Philosophy, applied to Princeton the text "Unto whomsoever much is given, of him shall be much required" (Luke 12:48), and cited two principal obligations of the University: the pursuit of excellence in the advancement and dissemination of knowledge, and the practice of brotherhood. Regarding the second requirement, he pointed out that in recent years Princeton had moved closer than ever before to the "ideal of a humane community which opens its doors to all and treats all within its doors with that equal respect which is the moral right of every human being and the constitutional right of every American."

Professor Vlastos told the seniors that the "sacred thing we call 'a human life' " existed in each one of them, and that for him "the final sanction of morality" was "reverence for that sacred thing in every human being," which was why he believed that "at the deepest level" the University's intellectual and moral obligations converged.

Baker Memorial Rink is dedicated to the legendary Hobart Amory Hare Baker '14, one of Princeton's finest athletes. He was an All-American halfback noted for his headlong habit of catching punts on the run (and without a helmet), yet he found his true greatness in hockey. In his day he was regarded as the greatest amateur hockey player ever developed in North America. No other player had his uncanny ability to weave in and out of the opposing defense, constantly changing his pace and direction. As he would take the puck behind the Princeton goal and set fly on one of his rink-long rushes, the crowd would yell, "Here he comes!" When he continued his amateur career with the St. Nick's Club in New York, the sign "Hobey Baker

Plays Tonight" would go up, and the line of limousines would stretch for blocks.

A fighter squadron commander in the First World War, he met an ironic death testing a repaired plane with his orders home in his pocket. A memorial service was held at the University, in which President Hibben declared, "The spirit of the place was incarnate in him, the spirit of manly vigor, of honor, of fair play, and the clean game." Later a $250,000 campaign for an artificial-ice rink was announced as his memorial, the first collegiate rink in this country. It was an intercollegiate effort; 1,537 men from thirty-nine colleges contributed, including 90 from Yale and 172 from Harvard. The building is in the familiar Gothic mode, made of random ashlar Princeton stone with pointed arches and mullioned windows. An illuminated case standing in the lobby contains Hobey's picture, his skates, his pucks, and his biography.

John D. Davies

Band, The University, made a modest debut on October 9, 1920 when twenty undergraduates dressed in black sweaters and white flannel trousers appeared in Palmer Stadium and played Princeton songs during, and between halves of, the Princeton-Maryland football game.

Thirty-five years later, the October 17, 1955, issue of *Sports Illustrated* pictured on its cover that year's Princeton band—attired in orange-and-black plaid blazers, gray flannel trousers, white shoes, and straw hats—to illustrate a typical Princeton football Saturday "filled with the color of autumn and the noise of Princeton's highly polished [seventy-six piece] brass band" making "the welkin ring for Old Nassau."

Around the same time, the band, whose numbers eventually topped a hundred, introduced satirical half-time shows and began performing, in small but lively groups, at home basketball and hockey games.

In 1951, some of the marching band's more accomplished members formed a concert band, whose winter concerts in McCarter Theatre and spring concerts on the steps of Nassau Hall became Princeton traditions. Three years later, Princeton joined Yale in a New York concert (described as not "half bad" by a *New York Times* music critic, who admitted to being an ex-Harvard bandsman), and in May 1971 celebrated the University Band's fiftieth season in a joint performance with Harvard at Lincoln Center. During the Spring Recess of 1975, the concert band toured California, bringing its music to West Coast alumni and friends, from San Diego to San Francisco.

In 1969, the marching and concert bands were among the first Princeton organizations to benefit from the talents of the newly arrived women students. In recent years, the marching band has led the annual Alumni Parade, and the concert band has played the music for the Commencement procession.

Conductors of the University Band have included Richard F. Goldman, 1951 to 1955; Robert L. Leist, from 1955 to 1971; and since 1971, David Uber.

Baseball, Princeton's oldest sport and once one of its most popular, first came into prominence in 1858 when some freshmen from Brooklyn organized the Baseball Club of the Class of 1862 of Nassau Hall, which played intraclub matches every day except Sunday.

Later, members of other classes

joined in, and on October 22, 1860, Princeton met its first outside opponent, playing an Orange, New Jersey, team to a 42-42 tie (balls were livelier then and the pitching less sophisticated) in a long nine-inning game that was called on account of darkness. Four years later, on November 22, 1864, Princeton played its first intercollegiate game, defeating Williams 27 to 16. Four years after that, while on a tour of New England, the Princeton team helped initiate Big Three athletic competition (the visitors were defeated both times, by Harvard 17 to 16, by Yale 30 to 23).

Three Princetonians made notable contributions to the game in the early years. William S. Gummere 1870 was the first baseball player to use the hook-slide, stealing second successfully by throwing himself feet first under the second baseman's tag, in an exhibition game with the Philadelphia Athletics in the spring of 1870.

Joseph McElroy Mann 1876 was the first college pitcher to control the curve ball and use it successfully in a game. He saw Candy Cummings, a professional pitcher with the Hartford, Connecticut, Club, give an exhibition of curve-throwing in the fall of 1874, and that winter he developed his own curve ball by constant practice in the corridors of Nassau Hall. His highly effective use of this novel delivery, on May 29, 1875, in New Haven, Connecticut, enabled him to pitch the first no-hit game in the history of baseball, amateur or professional. Only two Yale batters got as far as first base, on errors, and Princeton won 3 to 0. There have been half a dozen Princeton no-hitters since then, but Mann's is still the closest to a perfect game on record: he faced only 28 batters.

William S. Schenck 1880 was the first

catcher to use a primitive kind of chest protector: copies of the *Princetonian* stuffed beneath his shirt. After the 1880 Harvard game, a Boston sporting goods manufacturer learned of this contrivance from Schenck, and within a year had developed a rudimentary form of the present pad.

Another phenomenal pitching performance came in Princeton's 13 to 0 victory over Yale in its Big Three championship season of 1896. In that game, pitcher Ros Easton 1898 struck out sixteen Yale batters, a record all the more remarkable because at that time no foul ball was counted as a strike. (Years later, Easton set another record when as class agent he made 1898 the first class to achieve 100 percent participation in Annual Giving.)

THE CLARKE YEARS

In 1897, Bill Clarke, then catcher for the Baltimore Orioles, came to Princeton to help correct some of the Varsity team's flaws. He returned again for short periods in 1899, 1900, and 1901, and then in 1909, on his retirement from professional baseball, became Princeton's first full-time baseball coach.

The 1897 team won the Big Three championship, and so did the Clarke-helped teams of 1899, 1900, and 1901. A notable player of this era was catcher Frederick Kafer 1900, whose classmates later gave a cup in his honor, awarded annually to the outstanding varsity player.

Princeton continued to win the Big Three championship with near regularity, failing to take it in only two years from 1903 through 1912. From 1907 through 1909, pitcher "Biggie" Heyniger '09 won every Big Three game in which he started: four against Yale and five against Harvard, four of the latter shutouts. Against Yale in 1912, Sanford White '12, shortstop and cleanup batter, scored five runs and took part in two double plays. King Lear '14 (his proper name was Charles Bernard Lear) pitched every inning of the four Big Three games in 1912, beating Yale twice and Harvard once; he later pitched for Cincinnati.

Among Clarke's best teams were the 1923 team, which won 21 out of 25 games (nineteen of them in a row), and the 1924 team, which won 19 out of 23. Leading players of this period were shortstop Moe Berg '23, pitchers Charlie Townsend '24 and Charlie Caldwell '25, and third-baseman Jimmie Boohecker '25. Boohecker was an ideal lead-off man; "he would do anything to get on base," Clarke once said, "even to the extent of declining to respond to the instinct of self-preservation when the pitcher threw one in his direction." In 1924 Caldwell and Townsend shut out Yale, Caldwell 1-0 in New Haven, Townsend 7-0 in the Commencement game at Princeton. Throughout the Commencement game—the last of his career—Townsend coolly preserved a slowly developing no-hitter as well as a shutout, four times striking out the last Yale batter of the inning with one or two men on base.

Berg later played professional baseball for fifteen years, mostly as catcher. He was considered the most scholarly player in the big leagues, and his story-telling made him a great favorite in the bull-pen. A good student who never forgot what he had learned in Professor Bender's course in linguistic science, his talent for picking up new languages greatly impressed his teammates on a barn-storming trip to Japan in the 1930s. During the crossing, Berg spent a good deal of time in the ship's engine-room practicing Japanese with a Japanese fireman, and when the team arrived in Tokyo, Babe Ruth and the others were grateful for Berg's ability to read signs and to talk with cab drivers and hotel clerks. In World War II, he served as a spy for the Office of Strategic Services and obtained valuable information about Germany's progress in the race with the United States to develop an atomic bomb.

When Clarke gave up coaching in 1927 for six years, Byrd Douglas '16, Harry B. Hooper, and then John H. Jeffries, Jr. '23 took his place. During this period, Herman A. Heydt '29 pitched sixteen innings without giving up a single walk in a 4-3 victory over Cornell his senior year.

In 1934 Clarke resumed coaching for another decade. Throughout his long career, his teams generally had stronger pitching than hitting. "Hitting's a gift," Clarke once told a *Princetonian* reporter investigating this phenomenon, "just like God Almighty hanging a good arm on you." Providence, which continued to provide Clarke with good pitchers—one of them, George Lauritzen '37, pitched a 9-0 no-hitter against Lehigh in 1935—also favored him with four league batting champions in his last years: Rolf Paine '37 (.452), Brooks Jones '40 (.467), Bill MacCoy '42 (.452), and Roy Talcott '43 (.385). Talcott's batting record was a notable achievement for his position—pitcher. In Clarke's last decade, two teams won Eastern Intercollegiate League championships—1941 and 1942. Talcott and MacCoy stood out among some very fine players these years. Talcott had a 12-0 pitching record the first year, 9-0 the second. MacCoy, who was captain in 1942, scored the winning run in two decisive extra-inning games, against Yale in the tenth inning, against Harvard in the fourteenth. MacCoy was killed in a plane crash while serving in the United States Air Force in World War II; he is memorialized by a bronze plaque on Clarke Field given by his family.

After Clarke's retirement in 1944, there was a seven-year interregnum before the beginning of Eddie Donovan's era in 1952. Charlie Caldwell '25 coached in 1945 and 1946, Matt Davidson in 1947 and 1948, and Emerson Dickman in 1949, 1950, and 1951. Caldwell's team won the Eastern Intercollegiate League championship in 1945; Dickman's teams won it in 1949, shared it with Army in 1950, and won it again in 1951. The 1951 team, which had the best record overall (20-6) since the 1923-1924 period, also won the NCAA District 2 championship.

These years were highlighted by a number of outstanding pitching performances. In 1945 Henry Rohner '48 won both halves of a double-header against Dartmouth, pitching all eighteen innings and allowing only three hits in each game. Bob Wolcott '48 pitched four shut-outs against Big Three teams during his three Varsity years. In 1950 sophomore Ray Chirurgi '52 was the pitcher of record in all of Princeton's league victories, and in 1951 Dave Sisler '53 had a phenomenal earned run average of 0.99; he later pitched in the major leagues for six years.

DONOVAN'S QUARTER-CENTURY

Eddie Donovan was coach from 1952 through 1975. His 1953 team was Eastern Intercollegiate as well as Big Three champion. Outstanding in later years were the 1960 and 1965 teams, both Big Three champions, and the 1971 team, which finished with a 22-7-1 record. In 1971 Donovan was voted District 2 Coach of the year.

Good pitching continued to be Princeton's chief asset. Four pitchers threw no-hitters: Harry Brightman '52 against Fordham in 1952, Dave Douglas '60 against Manhattan in 1960, Anton Schoolwerth '63 against C.C.N.Y. in 1961, and Graham Marcott '67 against Villanova in 1966.

The 1953 pitching staff scored nine shutouts; Dick Emery '55, who produced five of them, was pitcher of the year in District 2 of the NCAA. Jack Hittson '71, who had a 9-0 won-lost record, was an All-American pitcher his senior year.

Donovan was blessed with several outstanding hitters: Joe Golden '53 batted .361 and Arnold Holtberg '70 (an All-American catcher) .356 their senior years. Bob Schiffner '71 had a three-year batting average of .332, the best in Princeton history. Ray Huard '71 set another Princeton record his senior year by hitting five home runs in a single season.

Len Rivers, a member of the football coaching staff since 1973, succeeded Donovan as baseball coach at the end of the 1975 season. His 1976 team finished second in the Eastern League with a 10-4 record and reached the semi-finals of the ECAC Mid-Atlantic Regionals where it was eliminated by St. John's, the eventual champion. During the season, Mike French '76 pitched five shut-outs, equaling the Princeton record set by Dick Emery '55 in 1953.

Basketball was invented in 1891 by James Naismith, a physical education instructor at Springfield College in Massachusetts, who had been asked to develop a new game that would provide an interlude between the football and baseball seasons more exciting than the gymnastic exercises the students were then grumbling about. Naismith thought that, indoors, it would be safer to throw a ball than kick it, and that it would be a more interesting game if, to score, the ball had to be thrown into a small receptacle. Peach baskets were used for this purpose when Naismith's ideas were first tried out, and soon the new game was called "basketball."

Princeton's first team, formed in 1901, played twelve games and, by virtue of a decisive goal by Bill Roper '02 in the last minute of the final game, ended with a 7-5 record for the season. At a postseason dinner in the old Princeton Inn the manager announced that the team had cleared expenses and had a dollar and twenty-five cents in hand for the next season.

In the winter of 1901-1902, Columbia, Cornell, Harvard, Yale and Princeton formed the original Eastern Intercollegiate Basketball League, joined in later years by Penn, Dartmouth, and Brown. Columbia, Penn, and Yale dominated this league in the first two decades. In 1916 Princeton tied for the championship but lost the play-off game to Penn.

At first the Princeton coach, usually a member of a professional team in Trenton, showed undergraduates how to play the game by scrimmaging against them in practice sessions, leaving substituting and strategy during actual games to the captain. The first resident coach was Fred W. Luehring, who joined the newly founded Department of Hygiene and Physical Education in 1911, and coached for eight years through 1920.

In the twenties, Princeton was second only to four-time champion Penn, winning championships in 1922 and 1925, losing two others by a single goal in the play-offs in 1927 and 1928, and finishing second, as well, in 1923 and 1924. The 1925 team compiled a 21-2 won-lost record, which half a century later had still not been equalled. Three Princeton seniors, James H. Lemon, Robert C. Hynson, and Stephen C. Cleaves, led the league in points scored that season. Arthur Loeb Hemmersley '24 was named All-American in 1922 and 1923, Carl M. Loeb, Jr. '26 in 1926.

Columbia and Penn shared honors in the thirties, and Dartmouth was undisputed leader in the forties. In 1932 Princeton tied for first place with Columbia and won the play-off for the championship, and the next year R. Kenneth Fairman '34, later director of athletics, was named All-American. The 1942 Princeton team tied for first place but lost the play-off to Dartmouth. Its defensive leader was Dewey Bartlett '42, later governor of Oklahoma; its leader in rebounding, Bud Palmer '44, who became captain of the New York Knickerbockers in their early years and later New York's Public Events Commissioner and a radio and television announcer.

THE FIFTIES

In the fifties Princeton had the edge in a continuing struggle with Dartmouth: each won the championship three times, but Princeton was more often second. Princeton took the title outright in 1950 and 1952 and won it in 1955 in the play-off of a triple tie with Columbia and Penn. That year's captain, Harold F. Haabestad, Jr. '55, who was selected for the all-Ivy team in his senior year, became the first Princetonian to score more than 1,000 points in his career, with a three-year total of 1292. Princeton tied for first place two other times but lost the play-offs, in 1954 to Cornell and in 1959 to Dartmouth, both times as a result of baskets scored by the opponents as the final buzzer sounded. In 1959 the same five players—the Belz brothers, Carl and Herm, Jim Brangan, Joe Burns, and Artie Klein—started every game for Princeton, setting an Ivy League record for durability. Carl Belz, who was captain, was twice all-Ivy.

The winning teams of the fifties were produced by Franklin C. Cappon, University of Michigan 1924 and an honorary member of the Princeton Class of 1924. He had become coach in 1939 and, except for the war years, carried on until he died of a heart attack in the Dillon gym locker room after a practice session with his team in November 1961.

Frank Deford '61 gave this graphic and affecting word-picture of Cappon in the *Alumni Weekly*:

In a profession in which men are renowned for their behaviour during a basketball game, Cappy Cappon stood quite by himself among coaches. Until the game was over, the man never did anything but frown. There were degrees of frowning, of course, but his gamut of expression seldom ventured too far from that of a basic frown. A mournful frown, a disinterested frown, and if it was possible—and it was—a frown of satisfaction. . . . And when something happened that there wasn't a frown to express completely, Cappy would cup his hands or rise to his feet and bellow the words: "What-'rya doin' out there?" When the game was over, the frown would stay quite in place if Princeton lost. But if they won, he would finally smile just a bit, a smile that looked both modest and embarrassed. . . .

As a teacher, he was recognized not only for his record, but for his

perfection of the weave offense, and for substituting but rarely. "If you start five men, they should be your best men, and if they're in shape, and play the way they should, there should be no need to substitute," he said once. He paused and added, "but more important than all that, I haven't got anybody worth a damn on the bench."

THE SIXTIES

In the sixties Princeton won seven titles (1960, 1961, 1963, 1964, 1965, 1967, and 1969), lost the play-off for an eighth one (1968), and finished in the first division the other two seasons (1962 and 1966). Four coaches took part in this achievement. Cappon got things off to a good start and Jake L. McCandless '51 carried on in 1961 and 1962. Willem van Breda Kolff '45, one of Cappon's players and one of Palmer's teammates on the Knicks, served from 1963 through 1967; he was named coach-of-the-year in 1965. Peter J. Carril took over in 1968.

Jim Brangan, the 1960 captain who was twice all-Ivy, delighted the Princeton fans with his good shooting, his aggressive defense and his smart play generally. When Cappy took him out two minutes before the end of his last game, the crowd gave him a five-minute standing ovation.

High scorer in the early sixties was Pete Campbell '62, who broke Haabestad's 1955 record with a career total of 1451 points. Campbell was all-Ivy three times; his classmate Al Kaemmerlen, an outstanding rebounder and captain in 1962, was all-Ivy twice.

In 1963, 1964 and 1965, Princeton attained the highest level of excellence it had ever known, winning three successive league championships for the first time in its history. This achievement was due primarily to the performance of Bill Bradley '65, a complete and dedicated player, who not only provided a classic example of team play but led the league in scoring all three varsity years.

As a freshman Bradley sank 57 successive free throws, a record unmatched by any other player, college or professional. As a sophomore he led the league in rebounds, field goals, free throws, and total points, and, when he fouled out after scoring a record-breaking 40 points in an NCAA tournament game with St. Joseph's in Philadelphia, was given an unprecedented ovation.

In his junior year he made 51 points against Harvard, more than the entire opposing team had scored before he was taken out, and his 33.1 points-per-game average that season set an Ivy League record.

In the summer of 1964 Bradley was the youngest member, and the captain, of the gold-medal winning United States basketball team at the Olympics in Tokyo.

In his senior year, when he was captain, he led Princeton to the highest national ranking it had ever had in basketball. It placed third behind UCLA and Michigan in the NCAA tournament as a result of an 118-82 victory over the University of Wichita in the consolation game of the semi-finals.* In the Wichita game Bradley scored 58 points, an NCAA tournament record.

Bradley's career total of 2503 points ranked third after the collegiate record of 2973 Oscar Robertson set at the University of Cincinnati in the late fifties and the 2538 Frank Selvy scored at Furman in the middle fifties. He was a unanimous all-Ivy selection in 1963, 1964, and 1965; Art Hyland, captain in 1963, was the only other Princetonian named all-Ivy during this era. Bradley

was named All-American all three years and shared with Gail Goodrich of UCLA the player-of-the-year honors in 1965. That year he was selected as the winner of the Sullivan Award as the amateur athlete "who did the most to advance the cause of good sportsmanship during the year." He was the first basketball player ever to win this award, and the second Princetonian (Bill Bonthron '34, the miler, won it in 1934). Best known of the extensive writing about Bradley while he was at Princeton was John McPhee '53's *New Yorker* profile, later published in expanded form as a book, *A Sense of Where You Are*.

After graduating from Princeton, Bradley was a Rhodes Scholar at Oxford for two years. He then joined the New York Knickerbockers and contributed to their winning of the N.B.A. championship in 1970 and 1973.

The 1967 team compiled a 25-3 won-lost record—Princeton's best since 1925. This team set a league record for the largest number of points (116) made in one game—against Dartmouth (42) at Hanover. It set another record when it provided three-fifths of the annual all-Ivy team (Gary Walters '67, Joe Heiser '68, Chris Thomforde '69), as did the 1968 team (Heiser, Thomforde, and Geoff Petrie '70), occurrences unprecedented since these selections by Ivy League coaches were begun in 1954. In 1968, Heiser, then captain, sank 91.8 percent of his free throws, which made him the best college foul shooter in the country that year.

The 1969 team, in Coach Carril's words, "was born of adversity and indignities." Early in the season it was frustrated by Villanova, embarrassed by Duke, and humiliated by UCLA and North Carolina. It then went on to do what a Princeton team had never done before: it won all fourteen league games, the first time any Ivy team had gone undefeated in league competition since 1951. The three front-court men, Captain Chris Thomforde '69, center, and Geoff Petrie '70 and John Hummer '70, forwards, all twice all-Ivy selections, were outstanding. Petrie and Hummer, co-captains in 1970, followed Bradley into professional basketball. Petrie who was N.B.A. co-rookie-of-the-year in 1971, became a top scorer for Portland. Hummer played for Buffalo, Chicago, and Seattle.

THE SEVENTIES

Penn resumed its domination of the Ivy League in the early seventies, winning six championships through 1975. Princeton became stronger as the decade advanced, placing third in 1970 and 1971, second in the next four successive years, and first in 1976 and 1977.

Brian Taylor was a principal factor in the success of the 1972 team, which missed tying Penn for the championship only by losing a two-point upset to Dartmouth. All-Ivy in 1971 and 1972, All-American in 1972, and the only Princeton player after Bradley to score 1,000 points in two years of Varsity play, Taylor left college at the end of his junior year to accept a contract with the New York Nets. He was A.B.A. rookie-of-the-year in 1973 and later played with the Kansas City Kings and the Denver Nuggets.

The Princeton team of 1973, led by Captain Ted Manakas, ranked third in defense nationally. Manakas was a unanimous choice for the All-Ivy team and later played for Kansas City-Omaha in the National Basketball Association.

In 1974, Princeton ranked among the top five college teams nationally both in defense and free-throw shooting. The captain and center, Andy Rimol, was drafted on graduation, by the Buffalo Braves.

Although the 1975 team finished second to Penn in the Ivy League with a 12-2 record, it swept its final thirteen games for the longest major college winning streak that year, and the last four victories in Madison Square Garden (over Holy Cross, South Carolina, Oregon, and Providence) gave Princeton a stunning championship in the National Invitation Tournament and twelfth place in the final Associated Press national rankings. The championship was the first ever won by an Ivy team in any postseason basketball tournament. Reporters called the Princeton team "patient," "smart," and "poised," observing that it "combined a probing offense with an aggressive man-to-man defense." Starting guards Armond Hill and Mickey Steurer won special recognition, Hill as all-Ivy, Steurer as a member of a twelve-man squad selected by the Eastern College Athletic Conference.

The 1976 team, co-captained, like its predecessor, by Armond Hill and Mickey Steurer, won the Ivy title 14-0 and finished the season impressively 22-5 overall. Two of its members were drafted by professional teams, Armond Hill, a unanimous all-Ivy selection, by the Atlanta Hawks, and Barnes Hauptfuhrer by the Houston Rockets.

In 1977, Princeton retained the Ivy League title 13-1, while posting a 21-4 record over-all. Frank Sowinski '78, who led the league with a .767 field goal shooting percentage, was a unanimous All-Ivy selection and had the added distinction of being named Ivy League basketball player of the year.

Both the 1976 and the 1977 teams led the nation in defense and were also noted for the way they moved the ball around, patiently waiting for the open man and the good shot—hallmarks of Pete Carril's coaching. Other coaches frequently said his teams gave clinical demonstrations of how basketball should be played. Playing Princeton, one of them declared, was like going to the dentist—"It's painful, but it does you a lot of good."

The 1978 season brought Princeton a tie for second place in the Ivy League, All-Ivy selection for both co-captains, Frank Sowinski and Bill Omeltchenko, Pete Carril's eleventh winning season in as many years at Princeton, and a book by Dan White '65 called *Play To Win: A Profile of Princeton Basketball Coach Pete Carril*.

WOMEN'S BASKETBALL

Coached by Penelope Hinckley and later by Pat Walsh, the women's basketball team, first organized in 1971, has been increasingly successful in intercollegiate competition, gaining four straight Ivy championships in 1975, 1976, 1977, and 1978. In 1976 Princeton won the AIAW Eastern Small College Tournament, and in 1978, it placed two women on the Ivy all-tournament team—Margaret Meier '78 and C. B. Tomasewicz '79, who was also voted the tournament's most valuable player. The development of a tight one-on-one defensive style contributed to the women's continuing success, which brought growing University community interest and support.

* Princeton was eliminated in the first round of the NCAA tournament in 1952, 1960, 1963, 1969, 1976, and 1977; in the second round in 1955, 1961, 1964, and 1967.

Bayard, Samuel (1767-1840), a Philadelphian of Huguenot ancestry, was valedictorian of the Class of 1784 at the age of seventeen. He became well known in the law and in public service—as clerk of the United States Supreme Court, prosecutor of United States claims before the British admiralty courts, presiding judge of Westchester County—and when he was forty returned to live in Princeton. He became the first mayor of the borough, and was for a time presiding judge of the court of common pleas of Somerset County and a member of the state assembly. At different times he served the College as librarian, trustee, and treasurer; he was a founder and a trustee of the Seminary. The street on which he lived was named Bayard Lane in his honor.

Bedford, Paul (1875-1967) came to Princeton to see his first commencement when he was a boy of sixteen still undecided about where to go to college. He accompanied the pastor of his church in Wilkes-Barre, Pennsylvania, Francis B. Hodge 1859, who was a Princeton trustee. Bedford liked to recall that, soon after their arrival, he met "a spinster lady of Victorian virtues," who cautioned him about the behavior of alumni at their reunions. Thus alerted, he watched very carefully, and the more he saw of "alumni jubilation," he said, the more he envied the alumni. "Their companionship and their loyalty to class and college" so impressed him that he thereupon determined to go to Princeton instead of Yale.

Two years later, in 1893, he entered Princeton and here, in the middle of the Golden Nineties, discovered interests and developed tastes that he cultivated all his life: good food and drink, friendships, athletics, music, history and politics—the last enlivened by Woodrow Wilson's brilliant lectures.

After graduating from Princeton in 1897 and from the University of Pennsylvania Law School in 1900, Bedford returned to Wilkes-Barre and joined his father in the practice of law. He became a leader in his profession and in civic affairs, president of the trustees of Dr. Hodge's old church, an active Wilsonian Democrat, and—in the opinion of many—the first citizen of the community.

Bedford was elected an alumni trustee in 1930, a charter trustee in 1934, and, after his retirement in 1946, served as trustee emeritus until his death in 1967, at the age of ninety-two. He was chairman of the trustee committee that raised funds for the building of Firestone Library and founder of the Friends of Music at Princeton, its honorary chairman and one of its most faithful and generous supporters. A devoted follower of football and baseball, he was for many years one of the two trustee representatives on the University Council on Athletics; in 1934 he donated the funds for Bedford Field, which is used for intramural athletics.

Bedford was chairman of the commencement committee from 1941 through 1967. Every spring he entertained the committee at a dinner at the Princeton Inn which he took delight in planning and which, in its sumptuous detail, was reminiscent of the Golden Nineties: cocktails and caviar; fresh fruit; terrapin soup laced with sherry; shad with roe, and new asparagus with Hollandaise sauce, accompanied by Bedford's favorite wine, a choice Moselle called Bernkasteler Doktor und-graben; salad; ices and cakes with champagne; coffee; liqueur, and cigars.

During the twenty-seven years that Bedford was chairman, his was the most sought-after committee in the University; its membership increased from five to twenty and no one ever resigned.

His annual report on commencement was a highlight of the October meeting of the Board of Trustees. He expatiated eloquently on such topics as the "degustation of food and beverages," the skill of the faculty marshals in getting the procession to move "with celerity uncontempered by cunctation," and the vagaries of the weather. After the 1959 commencement he was able to report an unbroken record of twenty-five successive outdoor commencements, an achievement he thought only fitting for a university with the motto *Dei sub numine viget*, though he always credited any favorable weather to the committee's efforts.

In his reports, Bedford always had a kind word for alumni reunions—those times of jubilation that "the spinster lady of Victorian virtue" had first called to his attention years before. He considered them "the core and kernel of Princeton's widespread loyalty," from which stems "active alumni support for every Princeton cause." Bedford himself was able to celebrate his seventieth reunion with one other classmate.

At the Commencement exercises in 1965, nine days before Bedford's ninetieth birthday, President Goheen read this tribute:

As gay at heart, as young in spirit today as he was at his own Commencement in 1897, he has graced the meetings of the Board of Trustees for thirty-five years, delighting them with his humor, impressing them with his wisdom. Like Falstaff, he is not only witty in himself, but the cause of wit in other men. To the city of his birth, Wilkes-Barre, he has devoted his professional life and his noble instincts for charity and social work; to his alma mater he has given decades of cheerful service and leadership, and each loyalty has served to enrich the other. . . . The past six presidents of Princeton have been entertained at his hospitable family home in Wilkes-Barre, and the last three have been richer for his sympathetic friendship extended over his own gourmet board. He is a man who, as Dr. Johnson said, keeps his friendships in repair. As chairman of the committee for raising the funds for Firestone Library, and as perennial godfather of the Department of Music, he has unwittingly reared his own best tributes from this University. Today we honor in affection and gratitude the Chairman of the Commencement Committee for the past twenty-five years, that Prince of Princetonians, Paul Bedford of the Class of 1897.

Beer jackets of white denim, with a distinctive design imprinted on the back, have been worn by undergraduates in the spring of their senior year during the greater part of this century. The practice was started by a small group in the Class of 1912 who, while quaffing beer and carving their initials on the tables of the old Nassau Inn, noticed that the foam from their steins sometimes spotted their clothes. In order to avoid dry-cleaning bills, they adopted the blue denim overalls and jackets of workmen. The next year, with the first signs of spring, the whole Class of 1913 donned overalls and jackets, this time white, and, although they were more a means of class identification than drinking uniforms, called them beer suits. Beer suits disappeared during World War I but were revived in 1919, partly in protest against high clothing prices.

The Class of 1920 were the first to use a design; they wore black arm bands to mourn the passing of John Barleycorn. Other classes also recorded the effects of Prohibition on the backs of their beer jackets, 1922 by a beer mug with wings, 1923 with a tiger pursued by a camel. The Class of 1925 depicted a tiger crushed by four heavy tomes, in token of the burden imposed on them by the new Four Course Plan.

The Class of 1930's design, "a perfect bust," was prompted by several seniors' purloining a copy of Venus de Milo from McCormick Hall, but it was also interpreted by some as commemorating the 1929 stock market crash. The Class of 1934 celebrated the contribution it had made to Princeton's undefeated football season of 1933 in the context of the National Recovery Act of that same year by portraying the NRA initials and legend "We did our part."

The Class of 1941, graduating during World War II, pictured a helmeted tiger sitting on a bomb-shaped world with a burning fuse. After the war, overalls were dispensed with, and since then only jackets have been worn.

In the fifties and sixties less attention was paid to symbolizing events of senior year and more to rearranging what came to be regarded as basic elements of beer jacket design: tigers, beer, girls. The Class of 1962's "the lady and the tiger" made effective use of the numerals 62 for the essential curves of the lady, while the Class of 1963's "astrotiger" rode in a space capsule, a foaming mug in one paw. A once-in-a-century opportunity was exploited by the Class of 1964—a tiger behind a ball marked with $\sqrt{64}$.

Beggs, George Erle (1883-1939), Professor of Civil Engineering, was internationally known for his invention of a means of predetermining the stress resistance of bridges, dams, and similar structures. This method, which involved making celluloid scale models, placing test weights on them, and measuring the strains with instruments he devised, was used by him when a consultant for the Arlington Memorial Bridge, the Stevenson Creek Dam, the San Francisco-Oakland Bridge, and the towers of the Golden Gate Bridge. The Beggs deformeter gauges have been used by engineers throughout the world for the solution of problems relating to indeterminate structures.

Beggs was born in Ashland, Illinois; he earned his A.B. from Northwestern University in 1905, and a civil engineering degree, with highest honors, from Columbia University in 1910. He joined the Princeton faculty as instructor in 1914, became a full professor in 1930, and chairman of the Department of Civil Engineering in 1937. He was also chairman of the Engineering Foundation, a cooperative arm of the several national engineering societies organized for the furtherance of research.

His students admired him for the thoroughness and clarity of his teaching, and his colleagues for the active part he took in the life of the University and in the engineering profession. Beggs Hall, one of the six units of the Engineering Quadrangle, built in 1962, is named for him.

Belcher, Jonathan (1681/2-1757), governor of the Province of New Jersey from 1747 to 1757, granted Princeton its second charter and helped its advancement in many other ways; the College, his fellow trustees declared in 1755, viewed him as "its founder, patron, and benefactor."

A native of Cambridge, Massachusetts, he graduated from Harvard in 1699, second in a class of twelve, accumulated a fortune at an early age as a merchant in Boston, and then occupied himself with a succession of public offices: tithingman and town accountant of Boston, member of the Massachusetts Council, governor of Massachusetts and New Hampshire, and finally, during the last decade of his life—to quote from his commission, which is preserved in the University Library—"Captain General and Governor-in-Chief of the Province of New Jersey and territories thereupon depending in America, and Vice-Admiral of the same."

Belcher had a quick temper and a sharp tongue, which aggravated the troubles that every royal governor faced in reconciling colonial interests with those of the Crown, and earned for him many enemies in Massachusetts and New Hampshire whose intrigues brought about his dismissal in 1741. He was, however, able to convince the English court that he had been maligned by his political enemies, and after living in England for several years he was appointed to the New Jersey governorship.

Soon after his arrival in New Jersey in 1747, Belcher, a Congregationalist, adopted the infant college of the dissenting Presbyterians as his own and busied himself in its promotion for "better enlightening the minds and polishing the manners of this and neighboring colonies." Finding the legality of the College's original charter under attack—it had been granted by Acting Governor John Hamilton, whose authority was questioned—Belcher granted a second one on September 14, 1748. The charter provided for twenty-three, rather than twelve, trustees, thus permitting the governing board to broaden and strengthen its representation politically and religiously (see article on *Charter*). Eight weeks later at the College's first commencement, the trustees conferred on

Belcher Princeton's first honorary degree.

Belcher encouraged the trustees to raise funds for a college building and a house for the president and, in the dispute as to where the College was to be settled, threw his influence in favor of Princeton—"as near the center of the Province as any and a fine situation."

Just before the College moved from Newark to Princeton Belcher gave the trustees his library of 474 volumes, his full-length portrait, his carved and gilded coat-of-arms, a pair of terrestrial globes, and ten framed portraits of kings and queens of England. In their address of thanks the trustees asked his permission to name the first building, then being erected in Princeton, Belcher Hall. Modestly—and providentially—the governor declined this honor and persuaded them to name it Nassau Hall for "the glorious King William the Third . . . of the illustrious House of Nassau," who was held in high regard by dissenters as a champion of religious freedom and political liberty.

Although only six of Belcher's books have survived, he is still held in honor as the library's oldest benefactor: when Firestone Library was built in 1948, the governor's arms were carved in stone over the main entrance along with those of the University. His portrait and those of the ten English monarchs were destroyed during the Revolution. The portrait of Belcher that now hangs in Nassau Hall was obtained from an English descendant of the governor and presented to the University in 1953 by Carl Otto von Kienbusch '06.

Bender, Harold H. (1882-1951), M. Taylor Pyne Professor of Indo-Germanic Philology and first chairman of the Department of Oriental Languages and Literatures, spent all forty-one years of his versatile and productive career at Princeton.

After receiving his Ph.D. at Johns Hopkins and pursuing further study at the University of Berlin, he joined the faculty in 1909. He began teaching German to freshmen and sophomores, and soon was teaching Gothic, Old Norse, Sanskrit, Lithuanian, and his famous course in linguistic science to graduate students.

A specialist in Lithuanian philology, he demonstrated in one of his major publications the relationship between Lithuanian and other Indo-European languages. In another important book he located the original home of the Indo-Europeans in eastern central Europe. As chief etymologist for Webster's New International Dictionary, with the assistance of seventy other scholars he revised the etymologies of over half a million words. This monumental achievement brought him worldwide recognition as an authority on the etymology of the English language.

Bender was a founder of the Linguistic Society of America and president of the American Oriental Society. He was an honorary doctor of philology of the University of Lithuania, and was decorated by Lithuania for his assistance during her struggle for independence.

An amateur criminologist, he gave the state police expert help in their investigation of the Lindbergh kidnapping and other cases. His colleagues thought that, for him, tracking down criminals was as interesting as "tracing the origin of obscure words to some remote corner of the world or dim period of antiquity."

He conducted most of his classes and did most of his research at home, and when it was necessary for him to come to the campus he usually came by taxi. He was a tireless worker with an amazing capacity for concentrated work. It was not unusual for passers-by to observe the light in his study at 120 Fitz-Randolph Road burning long after midnight.

His colleagues praised him for his critical insight and his acumen and what, they said, was an even rarer quality, his creative imagination. "His own joy in what he was doing, and his conviction of its importance, were contagious. To numberless students, he was an unsurpassed example of the teacher-scholar."

Bicentennial, The, of Princeton's founding on October 22, 1746, was celebrated in a year-long series of events in 1946-1947. The "concatenation," as Professor Charles G. Osgood called it in his book on the celebration, began in September with a sermon in the Chapel by the Archbishop of Canterbury and ended with an address by President Truman in front of Nassau Hall at the concluding convocation in June. Intervening were three other convocations, and in between these "gaudy days" were sixteen conferences of scholars and men of affairs, brought together to help recover some of the momentum that had been lost during the war years and to try to chart what lay ahead.

President Dodds made three major addresses at the convocations in October, February, and June. During the course of the year, he also conferred honorary degrees on some hundred eminent persons, including Niels Bohr, John von Neumann, Arnold J. Toynbee, Alvar Aalto, Erwin Panofsky, Reinhold Niebuhr, Salvador de Madariaga, Jacques Maritain, Trygvie Lie, General Dwight Eisenhower, Sec-

retary of State George Marshall, and President Truman.

The chief designer of the Bicentennial Conferences was Dean J. Douglas Brown, who directed a series of conferences in the fall; Professor Whitney J. Oates directed a series in the winter and spring. Most of the conferences were led by Princeton professors and were concerned with broad topics in their several fields of scholarship, e.g., "The Future of Nuclear Science," Eugene P. Wigner; "The Humanistic Tradition in the Century Ahead," Donald A. Stauffer; "The University and Its World Responsibilities," Gordon A. Craig and Cyril E. Black. The conferences were attended by scholars and men and women of affairs from all parts of the world.

The October convocation, commemorating Charter Day, began with an academic procession from Nassau Hall to the Chapel; the undergraduate band, grouped about the Cannon, played as an accompaniment a hitherto unperformed march by Beethoven. At the exercises the choir and the glee club sang an anthem, "Let Us Now Praise Famous Men," composed especially for the occasion by Professor Edward T. Cone.

The February convocation was held in the Chapel on Washington's Birthday, even more snowbound than usual in the late Princeton winter. At the luncheon that followed, alumni and guests heard Secretary of State George C. Marshall make his first address since taking office.

The Bicentennial Year reached its climax with a brilliant series of events during the days from June 14 to 17. These included: on Saturday, the dedication of the new Dillon Gymnasium and a musical review of Princeton history, narrated by José Ferrer '33; on

52 BICENTENNIAL PRECEPTORSHIPS

Sunday, a service of remembrance in the Chapel and a festival concert by the Boston Symphony Orchestra, led by Serge Koussevitsky; on Monday, a service of dedication, the laying of the cornerstone of Firestone Library, a formal reception of visiting delegates, a garden party at the Graduate College, and a dinner for 1,700 guests; and on Tuesday, the final convocation of the celebration.

At the convocation, an audience of five thousand persons seated in front of Nassau Hall watched an academic procession that included such celebrities as President Truman, former President Hoover, General Eisenhower, Field Marshall Viscount Alexander of Tunis (the Governor-General of Canada), Admiral Nimitz, Chief Justice Vinson, Judge Learned Hand, Governor Driscoll, Albert Einstein, Eugene Cardinal Tisserant, T. S. Eliot, and Serge Koussevitsky. The procession was swollen to a thousand persons by delegates from universities and colleges in all parts of the United States and in forty-three foreign countries. They walked in the order of the founding of their universities beginning with twelfth-century Salamanca and thirteenth-century Paris, Oxford, Cambridge and Toulouse, and ending with several American colleges established in the 1940s. Their presence, President Dodds told them at the reception of delegates on the preceding day, was "more than a gracious gesture of friendship"; it was an indication "of the comity of purpose that makes scholars everywhere citizens of one world-wide commonwealth."

President Truman said the need for educated people in public life, which Grover Cleveland had stressed at Princeton's Sesquicentennial fifty years before, was now greater than ever, and

in this connection praised the program of the Woodrow Wilson School.

The guiding spirit in the development of the Bicentennial Year was Walter E. Hope '01, chairman of the executive committee of the trustees and of the executive committee for the Bicentennial. Serving as chief marshal at the various convocations was Chauncey Belknap '12, clerk of the Board of Trustees. The chief organizer and coordinator was Arthur E. Fox '13, assistant to the president, secretary of the Bicentennial executive committee. Colonel Fox left a file of Bicentennial procedures and methods, "complete to the most minute detail," in the University archives. There it awaits his successor in 1996.

Bicentennial Preceptorships, which were conceived soon after the University's two hundredth anniversary in 1946-1947, were first awarded in 1950. Their purpose is to recognize young faculty members of high promise and to encourage the development of their teaching capacity and scholarship. Each award is made for a period of three years and provides a year's leave of absence at full salary for scholarly work, along with an allowance for research expenses.

Ten preceptorships were endowed with gifts from the Classes of 1931 and 1936 and bequests from Philip Rollins 1889 and Beulah Rollins, Arthur H. Scribner 1881, Mrs. Helen Annan Scribner, and Ferris Thompson 1888; others are supported through Annual Giving.

Bicycle Racing on Princeton University grounds began in 1879. A year later, during the first running of the Intercollegiate Games, Princeton won the two-mile event, and won again in 1900 when the competition was held under the auspices of an independent Intercollegiate Bicycle Association. Princeton's best known rider in the early days was Bert Ripley '01, famous for his "scaled cat sprint" (back arched, shoulders low) and the winner of hundreds of races, including the five-mile competition at the 1898 Intercollegiate Games.

Although the 1890s may have been the period of most intense cycling activity, the 1960s saw a dramatic renaissance, with Princeton winning five consecutive National Intercollegiate Championships between 1961 and 1966. Among the leading riders on these championship teams were Leif Thorne Thompson '65, Mikk Hinnov '66, and three-time Olympian John Allis '65.

In 1976 Princeton cyclists departed from one long-held tradition when they admitted women to the team.

Frank J. Quinn
Dick Swann

Big Three was the name given Harvard, Yale, and Princeton in the days when they settled "between them," as the *New York Times* once put it, "the question of primacy in football," and overwhelmed their other opponents in the process. At a time when games were ninety minutes long, as against today's sixty minutes, and schedules were also somewhat longer, Princeton rolled up a season's score of 637 to 25 in 1885; Harvard dominated by a record margin of 765 to 41 in 1886; and Yale shut out everybody, 698 to 0, in 1888. Huge totals like these reflected single-game landslides over smaller colleges (e.g., Yale 142, Wesleyan 0; Princeton 140, Lafayette 0; Harvard 102, Amherst 0), but they included substantial victories over colleges of approximately equal size (e.g., Princeton 82, Rutgers 0; Harvard 77, Cornell 0; Yale 64, Michigan 0).

These scores were made before football had spread to the West and the South, with the help of Big Three football stars who went out in the 1890s and early 1900s to coach at such colleges as Chicago, Wisconsin, Iowa, Minnesota, Purdue, California, Stanford, North Carolina, Virgina, and Vanderbilt. There were many from Princeton and even more from Yale—eight members of Yale's famous 1888 team became coaches.

The Big Three dominated football for half a century, until 1919. Princeton football historian Donald Grant Herring '07 said that November 1 of that year marked "the beginning of the end" of their reign. That was the Saturday that previously unheralded West Virginia beat a very good Princeton team 25 to 0. The decline was further evidenced in 1921 when Centre College of Kentucky, whose student body numbered 264, upset Harvard 6 to 0, and again in 1922 when the University of Iowa, playing its first intersectional game, defeated Yale 6 to 0.

Although originally drawn together by their mutual interests, the Big Three have had their differences among themselves. The only unbroken football relationship among them is the one between Princeton and Yale which dates from 1873. Harvard and Yale, who first played each other in 1875, sustained a two-year break in the 1890s when Harvard dropped Yale from its schedule. The Harvard-Princeton series, which began in 1877, was interrupted on Harvard's initiative for almost all of the two decades from 1890 through 1910, and on Princeton's from 1926 through 1933; both interruptions began during periods of especially intense rivalry when feelings ran high, and there were

54   BIOCHEMICAL SCIENCES

charges and countercharges of excessive zeal on and off the field. But these football breaks did not preclude friendly gestures in other areas. Soon after the 1926 break, Arthur Sachs (Harvard 1901) made a handsome gift to Princeton and Harvard to support the publication of *Art Studies* (which was jointly edited by their art departments), wishing thus, he said, to stress Harvard and Princeton's friendly relations in terms of cooperative scholarship at a time when their "desirable" relations in athletics had become "overemphasized."

As early as 1916, the Big Three had attempted to counteract this "overemphasis." That year, in an effort to keep "the spirit and the associations of professionalism out of college sports," the presidents of the three universities adopted a statement of principles setting common standards for athletic eligibility both as to scholastic standing and financial aid. A supplementary agreement, adopted in 1922, reduced the length of football schedules and outlawed spring practice and postseason games. Except for the years of the last Harvard-Princeton break, when there were dual agreements between Yale and Harvard and Yale and Princeton, the Harvard-Yale-Princeton agreement continued in effect until 1945, when the three universities entered into a similar arrangement with the other members of what became the Ivy League (q.v.).

Over the years the Big Three concept spread to other sports, from baseball to wrestling, and even after the organization of the Ivy League, retained some of its original influence. In 150-pound rowing, Harvard, Yale, and Princeton crews have since 1922 annually competed for the Goldthwait Cup, and there have been special Big Three

meets in cross-country. With coeducation, the Big Three idea has taken hold in a number of women's sports, including field hockey, whose Princeton adherents proudly celebrated their third successive Big Three championship in 1975.

Biochemical Sciences at Princeton had their official beginning in 1961 when a Program in Biochemical Sciences was initiated. Courses in this field had previously been given by the Biology Department for many years. In fact, in the 1920s E. Newton Harvey gave one of the earliest undergraduate biochemistry courses in this country. Other biochemically oriented courses were presented during the intervening forty years, particularly by Aurin M. Chase.

The need for a more chemically oriented sort of biology became apparent to the University during the 1950s, as the spectacular successes of biochemistry and molecular biology in explaining life's mysteries achieved general acknowledgment. A committee of biology and chemistry faculty members formulated a plan for bringing biochemists to Princeton, to be members of either department and to be housed in the new Moffett Laboratory and in Frick Chemical Laboratory. The first appointees were Jacques R. Fresco in 1960 (chemistry) and Arthur B. Pardee in 1961 (biology), a member of the Princeton faculty until 1975, when he accepted appointment as professor in the Sidney Farber Cancer Institute of the Harvard Medical School.

The program has grown in numbers of both faculty and students; in 1974 there were about 12 faculty, and a student-faculty ratio considerably above the University average. Teaching has also been stressed at the graduate level; research and work with postdoctoral fellows has been extensive, with grants for sponsored research amounting to $1.4 million. Noteworthy events in the growth of the program were the construction in 1964 of a new wing of Frick Laboratory—half for biochemical sciences—and the achievement of departmental status in 1970. Chairmen have been Arthur B. Pardee (1961-1967), Charles Gilvarg (1967-1973), Bruce M. Alberts (1973-1974), and Jacques R. Fresco (1974-   ).

In 1977, work was started on the construction of a new building (on William Street, adjacent to Frick) designed not only to provide much needed additional space and modern biochemical laboratories but also to permit the consolidation of all of the department's activities.

Arthur B. Pardee

Biology at Princeton goes back to 1830 when the great American botanist John Torrey (q.v.) accepted a part-time faculty appointment and began giving courses in botany to the undergraduates. Following Torrey, various professors from other disciplines (for instance, a professor of German and Italian) gave lectures in botany and zoology. However, it was not until the formation of the School of Science in the 1870s that Princeton had a full-time biologist on the faculty. President McCosh first attempted to obtain Theodore Gill, a leading zoologist, from the Smithsonian Institution, but much to the president's embarrassment the trustees turned the appointment down because Dr. Gill was a Darwinian. After some further searching, the trustees enthusiastically approved the president's calling the Reverend George Macloskie from Ireland to become the Professor of Natural History at Princeton. Professor Macloskie was an ama-

teur naturalist with degrees in divinity and law. Many years later, he told his distinguished successor, Edwin Grant Conklin (q.v.), in what Dr. Conklin termed a "humorous confession," that he accepted because he "wanted to see America for a few years and thought he might learn enough natural history on the way over to keep ahead of the boys." In fact he was a splendid teacher and wrote a textbook of elementary botany in 1883. Furthermore, he contributed some important parts on plants to the highly respected *Reports of the Princeton Expedition to Patagonia*. He was, of course, not a Darwinian and believed in what was called theistic evolution. He is perhaps best known for his spirited attempt to interpret the Bible in terms of modern science, in which he suggested, among other things, that Jonah could not have resided in the whale's stomach; he must have been in the laryngeal chamber.

The first stirrings at Princeton of biology as we know it today came from geology and paleontology. The famous geologist Arnold Guyot had a number of brilliant students, three of whom in particular straddled biology, paleontology, and geology. They were Henry Fairfield Osborn, William Berryman Scott, and William Libbey Jr. All three graduated from the college in 1877. The first two studied abroad in a number of laboratories, including that of Thomas Henry Huxley in London. Huxley was a most vigorous proponent of a unified science of life, i.e., biology, rather than the more traditional fragmentation into the separate study of plants and of animals. Undoubtedly Osborn's and Scott's exposure to this modern view had the favorable effect of ultimately producing a biology department at Princeton at a time when most universities had separate botany and zoology departments. All three of these remarkable men became assistant professors at Princeton in 1881. Professor Libbey remained in physical geography, while Professor Osborn left for the Museum of Natural History after ten years. But Professor Scott (q.v.) became intimately involved in the formation of the first Department of Biology. Although Blair Professor of Geology, he taught courses in biology also, and after President Woodrow Wilson first formed the Departments of Geology and Biology in 1904, Scott was chairman of both for four years, a staggering thought in modern times.

The year 1908 was an important one for biology at Princeton. It not only marked the beginning of the construction of Guyot Hall; it was also the year when Edwin Grant Conklin was persuaded by President Wilson to become the first full-time chairman. The president said that he wanted to build a "great school of biology" at Princeton, and some years later Professor Conklin reported that he was carried away by Wilson's splendid vision of the perfect place of learning, and he told the president he would "like to have a part in its development." As one looks back over the changes since 1908 it is clear that in the case of biology the "development" has been enormous, and it did not stop with Conklin's retirement in 1933.

Before Guyot Hall was built, biology was housed in various scattered locations over the campus, including the top floor of Nassau Hall. When the building was finished in 1910, the department had a faculty of five, and the new quarters, which they shared with the Department of Geology, were positively commodious. Today the faculty has quadrupled and has long since burst the seams of its end of Guyot Hall. Several steps were taken to meet the department's burgeoning needs. First, part of the natural history museum was converted into two floors of laboratory space. This was possible because the museum has an extremely high ceiling, said to have been built especially to accommodate the skeletons of large animals; in fact until recently a giraffe stood with head unbowed in the center of the main hall. Then, in 1960, the Moffett Laboratory was added to the south end of Guyot Hall, almost doubling the department's space. The second floor of Guyot Hall has recently been converted into a splendid, modern library, and the department has overflowed into Eno Hall, formerly occupied by the Psychology Department. There is also, northwest of Princeton, the Stony Ford Field Station, whose ninety acres of beautiful wood and meadow (and the restored barn it uses for its headquarters) are employed for experimental work in ecology and animal behavior.

Between 1908 and 1977 there have been only four chairman of the department, rather an unusual record. Edwin Grant Conklin served twenty-five years, Elmer Butler for fifteen years, Arthur Parpart for seventeen years, and John Bonner for twelve years. Edward Cox became chairman in 1977. Similarly, the elementary biology course has passed through relatively few hands, although as student enrollment has increased more faculty have been invloved. This was, for years, Conklin's famous course, which inspired so many undergraduates. He was followed by Wilbur Swingle and, in more recent years by Colin Pittendrigh, who was later dean of the Graduate School.

There have been some important milestones in the teaching program of the department. In 1920, E. Newton

Harvey (q.v.) started what must have been the first undergraduate course in biochemistry in the country. In the early 1960s, a program in biochemistry was started up by Arthur Pardee. This program, made up of professors in biology and chemistry, became a separate department in 1970. Another new development has been the introduction of two new areas of teaching and research: neurophysiology and behavior, and ecology and evolution (population biology). The former was organized by Vincent Dethier in 1967, and the latter by Robert MacArthur in 1965. Besides these new subjects, the department has strengthened its faculty in developmental and cell biology (so vigorously initiated by Professor Conklin), and in genetics. The latter began in 1915 when Conklin persuaded George Harrison Shull to come to Princeton. Professor Shull had already achieved renown for his work on hybrid vigor; he was one of the co-discoverers of hybrid corn.

At the moment, the world is in a golden age for the biological sciences. The interest and importance of the subject grows steadily. Princeton is fortunate in being one of the most desirable places to do graduate study; and the undergraduate enrollment, with the strong increase in interest in medicine and the life sciences in general, has more than doubled in the last few years. The department no longer lies obscurely in the laryngeal cavity of the whale.

John Tyler Bonner

Bishop, John Peale '17 (1892-1944) who is remembered mainly as a friend of Scott Fitzgerald '17 and Edmund Wilson '16 deserves to be better known for his own contribution to American letters.

Having postponed entering college for three years because of illness, he was twenty-one when he came to Princeton from Charles Town, West Virginia. Dean Gauss, who came to know him from his classes in French and Italian literature as well as from Bishop's work on the *Nassau Lit*, said that he came with "a more carefully thought out and more accomplished mastery of the technique of English verse" than any other undergraduate in the talented group then writing for the *Lit*.

Scott Fitzgerald was drawn to the *Lit* group by his great admiration for Bishop, who became the model for Tom D'Invilliers, the patrician poet in *This Side of Paradise*. "John looked the poet he was," Dean Gauss wrote. "There was an air of distinction about all that he did. . . . Even as a freshman, he had a self-possession and a self-mastery which gave him the poise and bearing of a young English lord. Scott's unruly Irish temperament, his irresistible love of glamour made these aristocratic qualities something he would forever envy but never acquire and I feel confident they suggested that Burke's Peerage type of name, D'Invilliers, which he gave John in the novel."

Edmund Wilson also greatly admired Bishop; he was later to call him the most distinguished poet ever graduated from Princeton. Bishop succeeded Wilson as managing editor of the *Lit*, and later, on their return from the war in France, brought out with him a collection of their verse and prose, *The Undertaker's Garland*.

In later life Bishop wrote poems for his two Princeton contemporaries, "No More the Senator," an exhortation to a friend (Edmund Wilson) to give up serious political activity and to withdraw into private virtue, and "The

Hours," an elegy on Scott Fitzgerald.

Over a period of twenty-four years he published four books of poetry, a volume of short stories, a novel, and many critical essays, besides serving on the staff of Paramount Pictures, as managing editor of *Vanity Fair*, and as poetry reviewer for the *Nation*.

Professor Joseph N. Frank, who wrote two essays on Bishop's work, said that he was "that rare thing in American literature, a . . . writer who, though incapable of supreme creative achievement, keeps alive a sense for the highest values."

> It is this type of writer [Professor Frank declared] whom the French delight to honor, recognizing their importance for the continuance of a vital cultural tradition. . . . Bishop, it would appear, was quite conscious of the rôle his type of writer could play in American life. Asking what the example of France could mean for America, he answered, "It means that we must find a way to reconcile our own past with the vast past of Western civilization." Perhaps the greatest praise we can give John Peale Bishop is to say that in his own devotion to the values of art, he helped American literature take a step forward in achieving that reconciliation.

In 1948 Wilson edited Bishop's collected essays, and in the same year, Allen Tate, another close friend, edited, with a preface and personal memoir, his collected poems.

Blackmur, Richard P. (1904-1965), became one of America's foremost literary critics—and one of Princeton's most distinguished professors—without the benefit of an academic degree. During the years after his graduation from the

Cambridge, Massachusetts, High and Latin School, he worked in a Cambridge bookstore and sat in on lectures at Harvard, but he did not become a candidate for a degree, choosing to attend, in fellow critic Leon Edel's words, "the school of his own bold intelligence." He began his literary career as a regular contributor to *The Hound and Horn*, one of the earliest and most influential of America's "little magazines." In 1935 the publication of his first volume of essays, *The Double Agent*, marked the beginning of what was to become known as the New Criticism, a school of criticism that revolutionized the teaching of literature in American universities by directing the student's attention to a close analysis of the language of literary works.

The independence that permitted Blackmur to develop his talents outside the framework of a formal college education was also at the center of his writing, with its "avoidance of academic stereotypes"—one of the virtues singled out for mention by his colleague Allen Tate, whose recommendation brought Blackmur to Princeton in 1940 to help conduct Dean Christian Gauss's Creative Arts Program. The same independence characterized his twenty-five year teaching career at Princeton. A faculty tribute prepared by Professors Edward T. Cone, Alan S. Downer, and Edmund L. Keeley described Blackmur as a man who provided "a constant challenge to both intellect and imagination," a challenge available to any colleague, student, or friend; those who chose to accept the challenge "became participants in a continuing conversation." According to these associates, Blackmur's "informal talk produced a comprehensive body of criticism," and displayed an immense range of knowledge "coupled with a profound but simple wisdom, a 'natural piety' that rooted his critical constructions, no matter how elaborate or abstruse, in his native New England soil."

Blackmur himself may have best defined the power that made him a memorable teacher. "Only those have force," he once wrote in reference to Dean Gauss, "who know it is not theirs unless it is given to others." Students who took his courses in poetry, literary criticism, and creative writing have testified to his success in conveying his own gift of force, perhaps most appropriately in the words of one who wrote, ". . . if I were to tell the truth, next time I'm asked 'Where do you come from?' I'd say, 'I come from R. P. Blackmur.'"

His literary reputation was based on his poetry as well as his criticism. The first of his three books of poetry, *From Jordan's Delight*, was praised by Allen Tate as "one of the most distinguished volumes of verse in the first half of the century," and his six collections of criticism, in the estimate of the *Kenyon Review*, made him one of the two or three contemporary critics "likely to endure." His critical range took him from the studies of modern poetry in his first book to the discussions of politics and the cold war in later works like *The Lion and the Honeycomb*. He lectured frequently here and abroad, and enjoyed the distinction of being the first man of letters to hold the Pitt Professorship of American History and Institutions at Cambridge University. He was Princeton's first Hodder Fellow, a member of the American Academy of Arts and Sciences, vice-president of the National Institute of Arts and Letters, and a Fellow in American Letters at the Library of Congress.

Blackmur conceived and found the necessary financial support for the Christian Gauss Seminars in Criticism (q.v.) in 1949, and directed them from 1957 to 1965. According to one participant, English critic-novelist Alfred Alvarez, "they turned out to be the brightest intellectual happenings in Princeton." At impromptu parties after each seminar, Alvarez wrote, "Blackmur . . . would argue in fierce, sidelong bursts and with obvious enjoyment far into the night." Professors Cone, Downer, and Keeley concluded their tribute to Blackmur with this commentary on the seminars, which they called "one of his enduring legacies to the University":

> Once a colleague was asked, "What is the real purpose of the Gauss Seminars?" He replied, "They make it possible for Blackmur to talk with his friends." Many would have considered this justification enough.

Blair Hall, the University's first collegiate Gothic dormitory, was a Sesquicentennial gift of John Insley Blair (1802-1899), a trustee of Princeton from 1866 to 1899.

As a boy in Warren County, New Jersey, Blair left school at age eleven to work in a country store. At eighteen he owned his own store, at twenty-seven he was operating a chain of five general stores and four large flour mills. He next acquired an interest in the iron mines at Oxford Furnace and helped found the Lackawanna Coal & Iron Company. He then helped organize the Delaware, Lackawanna & Western Railroad and later, the Union Pacific Railroad. At one time he was president of sixteen railroads and was reputed to own more miles of railroad right-of-way than any other man in the world.

In 1864 he endowed the professorship of geology then held by Arnold

Guyot; it is Princeton's second oldest endowed chair. Asked for a few remarks after his installation as a trustee in 1866, he reminded the Board that his own formal education was limited; he had spent most of his life learning addition and now, he said, "I have come to Princeton to learn subtraction." He gave the funds for Blair Hall in 1896; it was built in 1897. He did other exercises in subtraction in favor of Blair Academy in Blairstown, N.J., and of the Presbyterian Church, making gifts of land and money toward the building of more than a hundred churches in towns he had helped lay out along the route of the Union Pacific and other western railroads.

Blair Hall was designed by Cope and Stewardson, who were among the first to apply the Tudor Gothic style to American college dormitories. Blair Hall is considered their masterpiece.

In 1907 Blair's son, DeWitt Clinton Blair 1856, who was also a trustee 1900-1909, gave the extension of Blair Hall that terminates in a gateway tower on University Place.

When first built, Blair, Little and the Gymnasium marked the western boundary of the Campus. Originally the Pennsylvania Railroad tracks came to the foot of the broad steps leading up to Blair Arch, which served as the entrance to the Campus for visitors arriving by train. This was a convenience for most people but a mixed blessing for students living in Blair; the puffing engine parked below often kept them awake and the soot from its smokestack blew into their rooms. In 1918 the railroad station near the foot of the steps was moved a quarter of a mile to the south and the intervening tracks taken up, making way for the post-World War I dormitory development that Blair Tower now overlooks.

Boker, George Henry 1842 (1823-1890), a founder and the first editor of the *Nassau Monthly* (as the *Lit* was called in its early years), was tall, handsome, and patrician, with, a friend thought, "the form of Apollo and a head the counterpart of the bust of Byron." He was the College's best poet since Philip Freneau 1771, and an equally ardent patriot: "If there is one offence in a nation, which we should willingly forgive," he said in one of his contributions to the *Nassau Monthly*, "it is the undue pride and admiration of its great men."

In later life he published two volumes of poetry, wrote a number of plays, six of which were produced, and served as United States Minister to Turkey and to Russia. His most successful play was the verse tragedy, *Francesca da Rimini*, based on the story of Paolo and Francesca; it was first produced in 1855 and revived, with great acclaim, in 1882 and 1901. Most widely known of the patriotic verse he wrote during the Civil War was his "Black Regiment" (celebrating the charge of the Negro troops at Port Hudson in 1863), which moved Oliver Wendell Holmes to write him an enthusiastic note of praise.

Boker's poem, "Our Heroic Themes," which he read before the Phi Beta Kappa Society of Harvard on July 20, 1865, contained one of the earliest tributes to Abraham Lincoln. It concluded:

No king this man, by grace of God's intent:
No, something better, freemen,—President!
A nature modelled on a higher plan,
Lord of himself, an inborn gentleman!

Bowen, William Gordon was installed as seventeenth president of Princeton on June 30, 1972, and began his presidency on the following day. In a simple ceremony in Nassau Hall's historic Faculty Room, witnessed by members of the Board of Trustees and representatives of the faculty, administration, students, and alumni, he took the oath of office on the Bible that originally belonged to President John Witherspoon.

Born on October 6, 1933, in Cincinnati, Ohio, he was valedictorian and class president at Wyoming High School and top-ranking scholar, student body co-chairman, and Ohio Conference tennis champion at nearby Denison University. He came to Princeton in 1955 as a Woodrow Wilson Fellow in the Graduate School and the following year married Mary Ellen Maxwell of Cincinnati. In 1958, when he was not quite twenty-five, he took his Ph.D. and joined the faculty as an Assistant Professor of Economics and a research associate in the Industrial Relations Section, winning appointment a year later as Jonathan Dickinson Preceptor. He became director of graduate studies in the Woodrow Wilson School at thirty, Professor of Economics and Public Affairs at thirty-one, and provost at thirty-three, and was elected president when he had just turned thirty-eight.

Bowen was regarded as an outstanding teacher by both his department and his students and for a number of years gave the introductory course, Economics 101. (As president, he has continued to teach sections of the course.) A tireless scholar, he wrote numerous books and articles. After publishing two early studies on the wage-price issue and on wage behavior in the postwar period, he brought out a report on the effects of Princeton's involvement with the government in the operations of the

University, *The Federal Government and Princeton University*. Following a research trip to the United Kingdom in 1962, he published *Economic Aspects of Education*, which included a skillful analysis of university financing in the United States and Great Britain. A year later, he and William J. Baumol were named research directors of a Twentieth Century Fund study of the economic foundations of theatre, opera, orchestra, and dance in the United States. Their *Performing Arts: The Economic Dilemma*, published by the Fund in 1966, was described by one critic as a landmark study of the economics of culture. On leave of absence in 1966-1967 as a McCosh Faculty Fellow, he worked with T. A. Finegan of Vanderbilt University to complete *The Economics of Labor Force Participation*, which reviewers called the most authoritative work of its kind.

During his years as provost, Bowen was deeply involved in the University's conversion to coeducation, its program to increase the enrollment of minority group students, and its efforts to bring the budget more closely in line with income. Under his guidance, a priorities committee formed to advise on budget cutting outlined various ways to reduce Princeton's financial deficit, producing a report so impressive that the American Council for Education sent copies of it to 4,000 educational institutions as a model. Thanks to the committee's recommendations, and record support from Annual Giving, a balanced budget was achieved for the fiscal year 1971-1972 after two years of successive deficits.

Although Bowen's expertise in the economics of education was a significant factor in his election as president, the choice was further influenced by a general recognition of his enormous energy and broad intelligence, and, in the words of a faculty colleague, "his easy manner, his delightful sense of humor, his ability to get along with people and to listen and to understand their point of view, and his ability to take quick and decisive action once his mind was made up."

In his brief remarks at the installation ceremony in Nassau Hall in 1972, President Bowen said he found his induction "a very humbling experience," having had an opportunity to observe at first hand "the variety and intensity of the pressures that beat upon the office and the person holding it." But he was encouraged, he said, by the sources of strength the president could draw upon, and particularly by the power of the very idea of Princeton as a place of learning given life for over two hundred years by trustees, faculty, administrative staff, alumni, and students under the leadership of his predecessors—all sixteen of whom were looking down upon the assembly from their portraits on the walls with, he noted, "an occasional hint of skepticism in the eye."

I know [he continued] that Princeton future, no less than Princeton past, will draw strength from the great array of people who care about her and from the spirit that binds all of us together. This strength is represented here today in this historic room. Those of us gathered here, coming from different generations, different backgrounds, different regions, different vocations, possessing an extraordinary variety of viewpoints and perspectives, nevertheless share an abiding commitment to this University.

This is not to say that we shall always agree; nor should we. Contention is the life blood of any good university, for there has never been a single path to the truth and it is by testing ideas that we sharpen them and make them serviceable. But the spirit of our advocacy is as important as its quality. May all of us, and the many more whom we represent, continue to study and to think independently, to exercise our freedom, but always with mutual respect, with compassion as well as precision, with courage and good humor, and with the best interests of this University ever in mind. It is in this spirit that I now look forward to doing what I can, with you, for Princeton.

Boyd, James (1888-1944) was born in Pennsylvania and brought up in North Carolina. At Princeton he wrote verse and fiction for the *Tiger* and was its managing editor in his senior year. After graduation in 1910, he studied at Trinity College, Cambridge, and served overseas with the Army Ambulance Service in World War I. He then returned to North Carolina, where he wrote five historical novels. His two best known are laid in North Carolina, *Drums* (1925), during the American Revolution, and *Marching On* (1927), during the Civil War. *Roll River* (1935) is about his native Harrisburg, *Long Hunt* (1930) and *Bitter Creek* (1939) about the frontier West.

The Manuscripts Room of Firestone Library is dedicated to Boyd's memory. Inscribed on a silver tablet are these words of his:

The belief that leads to a democracy is this: that every man has something sacred about him. This sacredness is held to be inherent and perpetual: no ruler, no religion, no group of men, no government is justified in violating it. It is the first principle of man's life and nothing takes precedence over it.

Brackenridge, Hugh Henry (1748-1816), a powerfully built, twenty-year-old Scotsman with a booming voice and fierce countenance, must have captured the attention of his younger classmates when he entered the class of 1771. Instead of courting the Muses, he appeared better suited for clearing the barrens of York County, Pennsylvania, to which his parents had emigrated from Scotland when he was a child. But as his quick and lasting friends James Madison and Philip Freneau soon recognized, this farmer's son possessed impressive classical learning, oratorical skills, and a wit as ready as his fists. With his passion for knowledge and for moral and public good, Brackenridge had before him a career in public service and letters that would lead him to the bench of the Pennsylvania Supreme Court and to the first rank of early American writers.

An avid Whig at Princeton and later a Jeffersonian democrat, Brackenridge joined Freneau, Madison, and others in forming the American Whig Society to counter the conservative Cliosophic Society. These activities led Freneau and Brackenridge to collaborate on *Father Bombo's Pilgrimage to Mecca in Arabia*, a satire on American manners that may be the first work of prose fiction written in America. They also combined their talents in composing a patriotic poem of epic design, "The Rising Glory of America," which Brackenridge read at the commencement exercises of 1771 at Nassau Hall.

After his graduation Brackenridge sought a calling through which he could best attain his lifetime goal of educating Americans for liberty. He completed his training for the ministry, taught for

some time, and served successfully as headmaster of a Maryland academy. The Revolutionary War found him as an army chaplain preaching fiery patriotic sermons to the soldiers. Hoping for a wider sphere of influence, he started the *United States Magazine* in Philadelphia in 1778, but its lagging subscriptions convinced him to change his profession and location. He took a law degree and moved to the tiny village of Pittsburgh, where he later reflected that his aim in "offering myself to the place" was "to advance the country and thereby myself."

Soon a distinguished citizen of Pittsburgh and founder of the first western newspaper, *The Pittsburgh Gazette*, he was elected to the state assembly, where he fought for the adoption of the Federal Constitution and obtained state endowments for the establishment of the Pittsburgh Academy (University of Pittsburgh). Outspoken and uncompromising, he lost a bid for re-election because he followed his conscience and opposed popular sentiment in supporting federal controls; and he also nearly lost his life when he attempted to mediate the Whiskey Rebellion.

During his years as a judge (1799-1814), Brackenridge continued his untiring efforts to instruct the people. In addition to a steady flow of satires, narratives, and published sermons, he devoted himself to his masterwork, *Modern Chivalry*, a long comic narrative in the tradition of *Don Quixote* and *Tom Jones*. Written, he said, as an entertaining lecture on morals and society for "Tom, Dick, and Harry of the woods," the novel exposes the folly of a people whose ignorance and greed causes them to elect corrupt and hypocritical leaders. Through this work, published in several volumes between 1792 and

1815, Brackenridge finally achieved his goal of reaching a large portion of the people with his moral precepts. His novel was called "a textbook for all classes of society," and his son reported that his name "became a household word for half a century."

In recent years modern reprintings of his writings and critical re-evaluations have greatly enhanced his literary reputation, placing Bracken-ridge squarely at the beginning of a democratic tradition in American litera-ture that includes Whitman and Twain. Like them, Brackenridge was often dis-couraged by the folly of Americans, but he never lost faith in the ultimate pos-sibilities of an educated democratic people.

Emory B. Elliott, Jr.

Brackett, Cyrus Fogg (1833-1915), first Joseph Henry Professor of Physics and founder of the Electrical Engineering Department, was born on a farm in Parsonfield, Maine. He put himself through Bowdoin College by teaching in country schools, graduating in 1859 when he was twenty-six. While con-tinuing to teach, he studied medicine at Bowdoin and at Harvard, and received his M.D. degree from the Medical School of Maine in 1863. For ten years thereafter he held professorships of natural science, chemistry, zoology, geology, and physics at Bowdoin.

In 1873 Brackett was called to Princeton to occupy a new chair in physics founded in honor of Joseph Henry [q.v.]. He soon became an ad-viser to the trustees in their efforts to improve instruction in scientific sub-jects and was also influential with the faculty in the development of the scien-tific curriculum. One of his first tasks was to build up the College's equip-ment, which, after Henry's departure in 1848, had been allowed to fall behind

new developments in physics. He was mechanically skillful, and constructed much of the apparatus needed for his ingenious lecture demonstrations him-self.

Brackett believed that physics should be an essential part of every student's education; and he drew upon literature and philosophy as well as other sciences to arouse interest in his subject. He was generally regarded as one of the most brilliant lecturers of his day and one of the most stimulating influences in the intellectual growth of his students.

Brackett's own interests were stimu-lated by the developments in electricity of the seventies and eighties. He was closely associated with Thomas Alva Edison, who frequently sought his ad-vice and counsel, and developed a dynamometer to measure the power delivered by Edison's early generators. He was also acquainted with Alexander Graham Bell and testified in the litiga-tion that established Bell's claims to the basic patents for the telephone.

Brackett's lecture room, according to tradition, was the first electrically lighted classroom in America. He con-structed a dynamo and battery system for this purpose soon after Edison in-vented the incandescent lamp. He also rigged up Princeton's first telephone line, which extended from his labora-tory in the School of Science to Profes-sor Young's office in the observatory on Prospect Avenue.

He was thus led, in 1889, to under-take the development of a school of electrical engineering, leaving respon-sibility for undergraduate courses in physics to his associate, Professor Wil-liam F. Magie [q.v.]. The program of the new school was designed for college graduates with a strong background in mathematics, physics, and chemistry, and it emphasized advanced study of general electrical science.

With Professor William A. Anthony of Cornell (who initiated the electrical engineering course there), Brackett wrote a *Textbook of Physics* (1884), which was widely used in the closing years of the last century. He was elected to the American Philosophical Society in 1877 and became a charter member of the American Physical Society when it was organized in 1899. He drew upon his early medical training both as chairman of the University's Sanitary Committee, originally in charge of the college infirmary, and as president of the Board of Health of New Jersey from 1888 to 1908.

Brackett's engaging personality won the warm regard of colleagues and students. It also inspired the gift of Palmer Physical Laboratory by Stephen S. Palmer, father of Edgar Palmer '03, one of Brackett's students in electrical engineering, and its endowment by David B. Jones 1876 and Thomas D. Jones 1876, two of his early students in physics. Palmer Laboratory was completed in 1908, the year Brackett, then seventy-five, retired. Commenting on Brackett's retirement in his annual report, President Wilson wrote:

Few college careers have been more notable than his. He worked in the quiet field of mind whose achievements are not talked about outside the circle of those who are intent upon science or letters, and gave his brilliant gifts to the work of teaching and organization rather than to the work of investigation for which he was so admirably fitted; but the application of his fine force to the work he had to do produced remarkable results in developing the study of physics at Princeton.

Princetonians gave Brackett an ovation at Commencement in 1910 when President Wilson awarded him the honorary degree of Doctor of Laws.

Brackett is memorialized by a lectureship, founded by the Princeton Engineering Association in 1921, and by an endowed professorship in physics, donated in 1927 by Thomas D. Jones 1876 to give expression to "a debt of gratitude" he said he owed Brackett "as a teacher and friend."

Brackett Hall, one of the six units of the Engineering Quadrangle built in 1962, is also named for him.

Bric-a-Brac, The, undergraduate yearbook, first appeared in 1876. The founding editors hoped their "compact and comprehensive summary of every feature of the college" would help fill the gap left by the college catalogue, which, they felt, did not sufficiently represent the interests of undergraduates. The editors of the second issue voiced sentiments frequently shared by their successors: "Though meeting with delay and discouragement, we have persevered and now offer [this year's] *Bric-a-Brac*, hoping it will meet with favor." In 1966 the editors were still struggling with an age-old problem: "If your picture is fuzzy and your name spelled backwards, we apologize, but we did our best."

The *Bric*, which began as a 96-page 5½ by 9 inch paperback, had, within a decade, doubled its pages and acquired a hard cover. It continued to grow and assumed a 9 x 12 inch format in 1937.

One *Bric* editor, Mahlon Pitney 1879, became a supreme court justice. Several became college presidents: John Grier Hibben 1882 (Princeton), Robert C. Clothier '08 (Rutgers), Henry P. Van Dusen '19 (Union Theological Seminary), Paul Havens '25 (Wilson). A few became writers, editors, or publishers: Booth Tarkington 1893, Ernest Poole '02, Maxwell Struthers Burt '04, Peter Schwed '32, Donald Clive Stuart, Jr. '35, Andrew Turnbull '42.

Brown Hall (1892) was the gift of mathematics professor Albert B. Dod's sister, Mrs. David B. Brown, in memory of her husband; she was also the donor of Dod Hall (q.v.). This dormitory was designed by John Lyman Faxon, who, like other architects of his era, was a votary of the Italian Renaissance style. He modeled Brown after a Florentine palace, but, as Professor Thomas J. Wertenbaker later observed, "the completed building, with its heavy lines . . . had little of the charm of Italian architecture."

Bunn, B[enjamin] Franklin '07 (1875-1971) probably knew, and was known by, more members of the University than any other Princetonian in this century. His popularity on the campus carried over into the community at large: in his time no citizen was better known than he.

As manager of the University Store 1908-1947, he was universally appreciated as the dispenser of the store's annual rebate checks, which he personally handed out to waiting queues several weeks before Christmas. For many years he served as a timer at football, basketball, track, and swimming contests. For half a century he was graduate treasurer of the Triangle Club and accompanied the club on its annual Christmas trip. For almost as long he was graduate treasurer of the *Daily Princetonian*, the *Princeton Tiger*, and a number of other student enterprises. For a score of years he was manager of the McCarter Theatre. The seniors summed it up in their Faculty Song:

Oh, Bacon Bunn, you crafty guy,
Your finger is in every pie;
But once a year you do relent,
And give us back our ten per cent.

The nickname "Bacon Bunn'" came from a popular student snack—crisp bacon in a roll—sold by the Jigger Man. Once during the depression of the 1930s Bunn reduced the store's rebate to eight percent but managed to follow his customary practice of trading in his Buick every other year, as the seniors noted in another version of his verse in the Faculty Song:

Oh, Bacon Bunn, you went too far,
In buying that new Buick car.
Oh, Bacon, you're a clever gent,
But where's our other two percent?

A farmer's son from Chester County, Pennsylvania, whose schooling had been interrupted by responsibilities at home, Bunn entered Phillips Exeter Academy when he was 25 and Princeton three years later at 28. He worked his way through Exeter by taking care of the headmaster's furnace, at Princeton by working in a student-managed bookstore. On graduation in 1907 he became a clerk in the recently founded University Store and in 1908 became its manager.

He had a finger in every pie in the Princeton community, too. He was a founder and officer of the University Laundry and the Princeton Savings and Loan Association, and a director of the Princeton Water Company. He was mayor of Princeton Borough and later of Princeton Township, the only person ever to occupy both offices. For thirty years he was president of the trustees of the First Presbyterian Church and helped select five of its pastors. He was a director of the United Fund, the Princeton Hospital, the Chamber of Commerce, and a trustee of the Westminster Choir College.

Bunn was chairman of a citizens' committee that raised funds for the purchase of a ceremonial mace presented to the University at the 200th anniversary of the opening of Nassau Hall—a symbol of the long and close relationship of the University to the Princeton community. In 1963 the Princeton Chamber of Commerce gave him a "man of the years" award and in 1965 the Princeton Y.M.C.A. established an award in his name, given annually for outstanding community service. Bunn's name is perpetuated in the University by a basketball award established in 1931 and by a prize for sophomores on the business staff of the *Daily Princetonian* set up by the senior business board in 1964.

At the University's Bicentennial in 1947, when Bunn received an honorary degree of Master of Arts, he was cited as follows:

Faithful steward for forty years of the many trusts committed to him by the Princeton community, untiring ally of the University administration and faculty under three presidents; counsellor and friend of generations of undergraduates, his sturdy loyalty is an inspiration to all Princeton men.

Burr, Aaron, Sr. (1715/6-1757) was Princeton's second president, but because his predecessor, Jonathan Dickinson, died the year he took office, it was Burr who did most of the work of organizing the College and making it a reality. Burr's work was also cut short by death, but during the ten years he served, the curriculum was devised, the student body enlarged tenfold, new friends made for the College, substantial gifts obtained, and a permanent home found in Princeton.

Burr was born in Fairfield, Connecticut, and graduated from Yale at the head of his class in 1735. After studying divinity at New Haven, he was called to the Presbyterian Church in Newark, New Jersey, where he conducted a classical school similar to Dickinson's at Elizabethtown. He was associated with Dickinson in the founding of the College and was the youngest clergyman among its original trustees. On Dickinson's death in October 1747, he was induced to take the embryonic college under his care in Newark and a year later was formally elected president.

Ezra Stiles, then tutor and afterwards president of Yale and an intimate acquaintance of Burr's, noted in his diary that Burr was a "small man as to body, but of great and well improved mind. . . . a hard student. A good classical scholar in the 3 learned Tongues [Hebrew, Greek, Latin] . . . well studied in Logic, Rhetoric, Natural and Moral Philosophy, the belles Lettres, History, Divinity, and Politics. He was an excellent Divine and Preacher, pious and agreeable, facetious and sociable; the eminent Christian and every way the worthy man."

These talents Burr applied to the College with diligence and devotion, beginning with his inauguration at the first Commencement on November 9, 1748, when he delivered, from memory, a forty-five minute oration in Latin, and conferred an honorary degree on the College's leading patron and benefactor, Governor Jonathan Belcher (q.v.). He carried on the instruction of the students with the assistance of one tutor and later, as enrollment grew, of two. The students boarded out in town and attended classes in the parsonage and later in the county courtrooms above the county jail, which was not far from the Presbyterian Church.

Burr was a bachelor when he assumed the presidency. Some four years later, on June 29, 1752, he married Esther Edwards, third daughter of the celebrated divine, Jonathan Edwards (q.v.) of Stockbridge, Massachusetts. The wedding took place in Newark and the senior class gave a piece of silver as a wedding present. Joseph Shippen, Jr., a member of the junior class, wrote his father that President Burr had "made a visit of but three days . . . at Stockbridge, in which short time, though he had not . . . seen the lady these six years, I suppose he accomplished the whole design." The bride was fifteen years younger than her husband, who was then thirty-six. Young Shippen admired her beauty and thought her "rather too young for the president." As he came to know her better he discovered that she possessed qualities not unsuitable for a president's wife: "I think her a woman of very good sense," he wrote, "of a genteel and virtuous education, amiable in her person, of great affability and agreeableness in conversation and a very excellent economist."

Burr served for three years without salary, and filled both the offices of pastor and president until 1755 when, at the request of the trustees, he was relieved of his pastoral duties to devote full time to the College. He drew up the first entrance requirements, the first course of study, the first set of rules and regulations, and supervised the erection of the first building, Nassau Hall, to which he, his two tutors, and seventy students moved in November 1756.

President Burr did not have long to enjoy the fruits of his endeavors. Soon after the removal to Princeton, the illness of one of the tutors obliged Burr to perform his duties as well as his own.

The growing needs of the College also required him to make frequent trips through the colonies in search of funds. It was on returning from one such arduous trip that he learned the news of the death of his close friend and ally, Governor Belcher. He sat down at once in spite of exhaustion and a high fever to write the funeral sermon. Two days later he rode his horse to Elizabethtown, where he delivered the sermon, although "it was seen that he was fitter for his bed than the pulpit." He returned to Princeton grievously ill and died several weeks later at the age of forty-one. He was buried in the Princeton Cemetery—the first in the President's Lot—after a service conducted, as he had requested in his will, "in the plainest manner consistent with decency," and the money thus saved applied to charitable uses.

In Benjamin Franklin's *Pennsylvania Gazette* Burr's death was reported as follows:

> September 29, 1757. Last Saturday died the Rev. Aaron Burr, President of the New Jersey College, a gentleman and a Christian, as universally beloved as known; an agreeable companion, a faithful friend, a tender and affectionate husband, and a good father; remarkable for his industry, integrity, strict honesty, and pure, undissembled piety; his benevolence as disinterested as unconfined, an excellent preacher, a great scholar, and a very great man.

Esther Burr survived her husband by less than a year; she died of smallpox at the age of twenty-six, leaving their two children, four-year-old Sarah and two-year-old Aaron, Jr. Sarah married Tapping Reeve 1763 (q.v.), who was to be Chief Justice of Connecticut. Aaron, Jr., who graduated from Princeton in

1772, became the third vice-president of the United States.

Burr, Aaron, Jr. (1756-1836), third vice-president of the United States (1801-1805), was thought to be one of the most brilliant students graduated from Princeton in the eighteenth century. Woodrow Wilson said he had "genius enough to have made him immortal, and unschooled passion enough to have made him infamous." His father was Princeton's second president; his maternal grandfather, Jonathan Edwards, was Princeton's third president. The younger Aaron Burr was left an orphan when he was two years old, his father and mother (and both maternal grandparents) having died within a year. He did not respond well to the discipline of his austere uncle, Timothy Edwards, several times running away from home and attempting to go to sea. He entered the sophomore class at Princeton at the age of thirteen and graduated with distinction at sixteen in 1772, a year after James Madison and Philip Freneau. He was a member of the Cliosophic Society and for his Commencement Oration chose the prophetic topic "On Castle Building."

Burr studied theology for a while and then law. After the Revolutionary War, in which he served with distinction as a field officer, he took up the practice of law in New York City and entered politics, serving as a member of the New York state assembly, attorney general of New York, and United States senator. In the presidential election of 1800, he received the same number of electoral votes as Thomas Jefferson, but the tie was broken in the House of Representatives in Jefferson's favor, and Burr became vice-president.

Four years later, on July 11, 1804, in the historic duel at Weehawken, New Jersey, Burr mortally wounded his professional rival and political enemy, Alexander Hamilton. Thereafter came his errant political adventures in the West, his trial for treason, and his acquittal.

Burr's chief counsel at the trial was Luther Martin 1766, a fellow member and one of the founders of the Cliosophic Society. A few years before his death, the society invited Burr to preside at its commencement meeting, and its members took part in the procession at Burr's funeral in Princeton in 1836. President Carnahan preached the funeral sermon in Nassau Hall (in which he decried the evils of dueling). Escorted to the Princeton Cemetery by members of the faculty, students, alumni, a military band, and the Mercer Guards, Burr was buried with full military honors at the foot of his father's and grandfather's graves in the President's Lot.

Burr, Aaron, Hall, named in 1977 for Princeton's second president, occupies the southeast corner of Washington Road and Nassau Street. Built in 1891 as a chemical laboratory, it later housed the Department of Chemical Engineering and is now the home of the Department of Anthropology.

Butler, Howard Crosby 1892 (1872-1922), archaeologist and Professor of the History of Architecture, was first Master in Residence of the Graduate College and first director of the School of Architecture. In his early student days he played leading roles in the first productions of the newly founded Triangle Club and helped organize the college's third eating club, Tiger Inn, whose clubhouse he later designed. In his senior year, under the influence of Professor Allan Marquand, he acquired a serious interest in the history of art, which he further developed in graduate study at Princeton, the Columbia School of Architecture, the American Academy in Rome, and the American School of Classical Study at Athens. He organized and led three archaeological expeditions into the Syrian Desert and two expeditions for the excavation of ancient Sardis, discovering there long-hidden treasures that enriched modern knowledge of Lydian, Greek, Syrian, and Roman civilizations. The diplomatic skill and the personal courage Butler demonstrated on these expeditions were legendary. Professor Marquand told of Butler's braving the Bedouins of the Syrian desert, unsupported by the guards usually considered necessary, and of how, on another occasion, when all the others had run to their quarters for firearms, Butler, unassisted and armed only with a bamboo cane, quelled an insurrection among the natives at Sardis. "His tact and personal bravery . . . invested his expeditions with the charm of romance" which was carried over into his teaching, where he also demonstrated "a subtle instinct for divining and evoking the latent powers of those he taught."

As Master in Residence, first at the experimental graduate hall "Merwick" and then at the Graduate College itself, his serenity, self-discipline, and intellectual integrity exerted an influence attested to by many of the graduate students of that era.

As Professor of Architecture, "he stood almost alone," in Professor Marquand's words, "in transcending his subject and in revealing it against its broad and deep historic background both as complete in itself and as an organic part of human achievement." His teaching inspired a group of alumni architects to initiate a movement that resulted in the establishment of the School of Architecture in 1920, with Butler as first director.

"If we were to ask for a motto for his life," said Dean West, "I think the saying of an old Italian scholar would be most fitting: 'I go to wake the dead.' Professor Butler did wake the dead,—dead impulses in students to newness of life, dead cities of the Orient rising again under his magical touch."

A portrait of Butler hangs in Procter Hall in the Graduate College and the following inscription, discovered on a Christian tomb in northern Syria by his first expedition, appears in his memory on a stone in the vestibule: "I sojourned well; I journeyed well; and well I lie at rest. Pray for me." His name is perpetuated by a professorship in the history of architecture created in 1931 by gifts from his former students.

Cabinet officers who attended Princeton and the presidents under whom they served are as follows:

SECRETARY OF STATE

JEFFERSON
James Madison 1771 (Va.) 1801-1809

MADISON
Robert Smith 1781 (Md.) 1809-1811

JACKSON AND VAN BUREN
Edward Livingston 1781 (La.) 1831-1833
John Forsyth 1799 (Ga.) 1834-1841

TYLER
Abel P. Upshur 1807 (Va.) 1843-1844

EISENHOWER
John Foster Dulles '08 (N.Y.) 1953-1959

SECRETARY OF THE TREASURY

MADISON
George W. Campbell 1794 (Tenn.) 1814

J. Q. ADAMS
Richard Rush 1797 (Pa.) 1825-1828

TYLER
George M. Bibb 1792 (Ky.)
1844-1845

NIXON
George P. Shultz '42 (Ill.) 1972-1974

CARTER
W. Michael Blumenthal M.P.A. '53
Ph.D. '56 (Mich.) 1977-

SECRETARY OF WAR*

MADISON
John Armstrong 1776 (N.Y.)
1813-1814

TAYLOR
George W. Crawford 1820 (Ga.)
1849-1850

GRANT
William W. Belknap 1848 (Iowa)
1869-1876
James D. Cameron 1852 (Pa.)
1876-1877

SECRETARY OF THE NAVY*

JEFFERSON
Robert Smith 1781 (Md.) 1801-1805

MONROE
Smith Thompson 1788 (N.Y.)
1818-1823

MONROE AND J. Q. ADAMS
Samuel L. Southard 1804 (N.J.)
1823-1829

JACKSON AND VAN BUREN
Mahlon Dickerson 1789 (N.J.)
1834-1838

TYLER
Abel P. Upshur 1807 (Va.) 1841-1843

GRANT
George M. Robeson 1847 (N.J.)
1869-1877

F. D. ROOSEVELT AND TRUMAN
James V. Forrestal '15 (N.Y.)
1944-1947

SECRETARY OF DEFENSE*

TRUMAN
James V. Forrestal '15 (N.Y.)
1947-1949

FORD
Donald Rumsfeld '54 (Ill.) 1975-1976

ATTORNEY GENERAL

WASHINGTON
William Bradford, Jr. 1772 (Pa.)
1794-1795

WASHINGTON AND JOHN ADAMS
Charles Lee 1775 (Va.) 1795-1801

JEFFERSON
Robert Smith 1781 (Md.) 1805

MADISON
Richard Rush 1797 (Pa.) 1814-1817

JACKSON
John M. Berrien 1796 (Ga.)
1829-1831

ARTHUR
Benjamin H. Brewster 1834 (Pa.)
1881-1885

JOHNSON
Nicholas deB. Katzenbach '43 (Pa.)
1965-1966

SECRETARY OF COMMERCE

JOHNSON
Alexander B. Trowbridge '51 (N.J.)
1967-1968

SECRETARY OF LABOR

NIXON
George P. Shultz '42 (Ill.) 1969-1970

SECRETARY OF HOUSING
AND URBAN DEVELOPMENT

JOHNSON
Robert C. Wood '44 (Mass.) 1969

* When the national military establishment was reorganized under the head of a Secretary of Defense in 1947, the office of Secretary of War was discontinued and the Secretary of Navy was no longer given cabinet rank; nor were the newly instituted Secretaries of the Army and of the Air

Force. Princeton incumbents of the latter posts have been: Secretary of the Army—Frank Pace, Jr. '33 (Ark.) 1950-1953 (Truman); Stephen Ailes '33 (W.Va.) 1964-1965 (Johnson); Martin R. Hoffman '54 (Va.) 1975-1976 (Ford). Secretary of the Air Force—James H. Douglas '20 (Ill.) 1957-1959 (Eisenhower); Dudley C. Sharp '27 (Tex.) 1959-1961 (Eisenhower).

Caldwell Field House, The, is a memorial to Charles W. Caldwell, Jr. '25, head coach of football from 1945 through 1956. It was built in 1963 with donations from his family and from some 3,500 alumni and friends.

As an undergraduate, Caldwell played center and fullback on Roper's 1922 "Team of Destiny" and was a star pitcher on the baseball team (he later had a tryout with the New York Yankees and played briefly in several games). He was assistant football coach at Princeton for three years, and head coach at Williams for seventeen, before his appointment as Princeton's head coach in 1945. A keen student of the game, he developed a new kind of single wing football, adding to the traditional power plays of that formation elements of deception, which he borrowed from the modern T.

One of Caldwell's favorite words for an effective team or player was "solid." Another, which he used to describe a quality he thought indispensable to success was "desire." He himself possessed abundant desire, and the results he obtained in the dozen years he was coach were eminently solid. His teams won six successive Big Three championships in the years 1947 through 1952, two more than the previous record, which Harvard teams set under Percy Haughton in the years 1912 through 1915. Caldwell's teams of 1950 and 1951, both Lambert Trophy winners as the best in the East, won every game—the first time Princeton had two

perfect seasons in succession since full-length schedules were introduced in 1878 (the teams of 1874 and 1875 won all their games—two each). Caldwell was voted Coach of the Year in 1950 and given the annual award of the Touchdown Club of New York in 1952. He was stricken with cancer of the pancreas early in the season of 1957 and died November 1 in his fifty-sixth year. President Goheen summed up his career succinctly: "Charlie was an inspiring teacher who devoted his life to the education of young men."

The Caldwell Field House contains dressing and training facilities for teams that use the neighboring athletic facilities—Palmer Stadium, the Jadwin Gymnasium, and a half-dozen playing fields. The Field House is larger than it looks—only one of its two-and-a-half stories shows above ground level—and, because of its flexible design, more serviceable even than its true size would suggest. Dressing rooms are convertible to dormitories for visiting teams, and coaches' offices to dressing rooms for officials at game time. The Class of 1925 Room, a pine-paneled, carpeted lounge, is used by coaches for conferences with their staffs and their teams, and by families of players waiting to meet them at the end of a game. A medical treatment center is equipped for treating sprained muscles, wrenched joints, and other aches and pains suffered in contact sports.

Caldwell is also remembered by a trophy, established by the undergraduate body in 1957, awarded annually to that senior on the varsity football squad who has shown the greatest improvement.

Campbell Field, one of the playing fields east of Palmer Stadium, was created in 1962 by his family and friends as a memorial to Tyler Campbell '43, who gave his life in the Second World War. All-American lacrosse defenseman, class president-elect and varsity club president-elect, Campbell left college at the end of his junior year to enlist in the army as a private in the mountain troops. Graduated from Officers' Candidate School as a 2nd lieutenant, he led his men on the invasion beachheads of Sicily, Salerno, Anzio, and southern France, was wounded twice and twice promoted in the field, reaching the grade of captain. He was killed in action in France while commanding an infantry company of the 7th Army, two years after leaving college. Edwin G. Baetjer II '43 and John Gregg Thomas, Jr. '43, Campbell's close friends and clubmates, also died in service.

Campbell Hall was the gift of the Class of 1877, a strong competitor with 1879 for first place among the outstanding classes graduated during the McCosh presidency or, for that matter, during the entire nineteenth century. The building was named for John A. Campbell (1856-1938), a banker and a leading citizen of Trenton, who was president of the class all four years in college and for fifty years thereafter.

It took the class less than an hour to raise most of the funds for the dormitory—a unique instance in the long history of alumni generosity. The necessary pledges poured forth in a spontaneous outburst during a high-spirited dinner at their thirtieth reunion in 1907. Woodrow Wilson's friend and classmate, Cleveland H. Dodge 1879, who was present as a guest, said it was the greatest show he had ever attended—a judgment supported by the verbatim report of the proceedings preserved in 1877's class history, put out at its fiftieth reunion.

The leading actors in the performance were John Campbell, M. Taylor Pyne, George Allison Armour, J. Howard Ford, and Frank S. Layng. The last three were known as "the three shortstops"—not because they had played baseball but because they had stopped short of graduation.

Pyne, a trustee of the University, precipitated the outburst when, speaking of the University's need for more dormitories, he reminded his classmates that 1879 had given Seventy-Nine Hall and ten other classes had each given an entry in Patton, and asked whether 1877 couldn't be counted on for an entry in one of the other new dormitories.

"No, no!" Armour called out, "Let's give the whole dormitory." Someone else shouted, "Three cheers for Princeton," and Layng said, "We've got to give more than three cheers, we've got to give our money, our good money."

As Pyne continued speaking, Armour passed his calling card up to President Campbell, who followed Pyne's speech, by reading this cryptic message: "3 shortstops $15,000." Armour got up and explained that he and Ford and Layng wanted to start the ball rolling because they were so grateful for having spent one year at Princeton. After Armour observed that "those who have been here four years will probably want to do a good bit more than that," Pyne said, "Put me down for $10,000," Henry Fairfield Osborn followed with, "I'll bring it up to $30,000, John," and Layng added "this short-stop makes it $35,000." Someone called for three cheers for Frank Layng, and they were given.

"If he had graduated," President Campbell reflected, "I believe he would have given us an entire dormitory, completely furnished."

Someone asked how much the dormitory would cost; Campbell said he assumed at least $100,000. A half-dozen men called out pledges from $500 to $5,000. Campbell held up another of Armour's cards. This one pledged $5,000 in memory of a classmate who had recently died. Men from other classes who were guests at the dinner got caught up in the excitement and soon there were pledges from '74, '75, '76, '78, and '79.

There was a flurry of $500 pledges —most of them $100 a year for five years. One was from a man who was attending his first reunion. We're mighty glad to see him here," Campbell said, "He's a fine-looking fellow and we're proud of him." Campbell then announced that Henry B. Thompson, another trustee, had doubled the contribution he had previously made.

> VOICE: Good for Harry.
> SECOND VOICE: Give him another bottle of wine.
> PRESIDENT: We now have $56,000, we ought to work up to $77,000 tonight.

More contributions followed, small and moderate. President Campbell hoped no one would be too modest about speaking out. Layng advised, "Send out for three more bottles and we'll get the rest." A minute later Campbell announced an additional $10,000 from Pyne and another calling card from Armour with $5,000 in memory of still another recently deceased classmate. Then, according to the verbatim report:

> FORD [the third shortstop]: I understand that I'm down for $1,000; I'd like to increase that to $5,000.

Campbell announced that contributions were now well over $77,000 and that he was appointing a committee of seven to carry the project to completion. This unplanned part of the Class's dinner program then ended as follows:

> PYNE: When I spoke earlier, I thought that, with great effort, the Class might raise $17,000 for an entry in a dormitory. The Class of '79 had to work a year before they got as much as we've raised tonight. I never felt so proud of our class, as I do at this moment.
> LAYNG: Take another drink from that cup, Armour.
> ARMOUR: Not on your life. I would give forty then.
> PRESIDENT CAMPBELL: I think we ought to stand up and sing Whoop 'Er Up for '77.
> SONG: Oh, we'll whoop 'er up for '77.

The Class soon raised the balance needed, Cram, Goodhue, and Ferguson drew up the plans, and Campbell Hall was ready for occupancy in the fall of 1909.

Campus. The use of the word *campus* (Latin for "field") to mean the grounds of a college originated at Princeton. Its earliest recorded use is found in a letter Charles C. Beatty 1775 wrote to his brother-in-law Enoch Green 1760 on January 31, 1774: "Last week to show our patriotism, we gathered all the steward's winter store of tea, and having made a fire in the Campus, we there burnt near a dozen pounds, tolled the bell and made many spirited resolves."

Previously *yard* was the word used at Princeton, as it was at Harvard (where it was first used in 1639) and other colleges. An example of this usage occurs in a letter James Madison 1771 wrote to his father on July 23, 1770. Referring to the interception by Princeton students of a letter a group of New York merchants had addressed to the merchants of Philadelphia, asking them to break the agreement not to import British goods, he said: "Their letter . . . was . . . burnt by the Students of this place in the college Yard, all of them appearing in their black Gowns and the bell Tolling."

In a monograph on the use of the word *campus* in the *Publications of the Colonial Society of Massachusetts* (Volume III, 1897), an etymologist, Albert Matthews (Harvard 1882), suggests that the word may have been introduced by President John Witherspoon who came to Princeton from Scotland in 1768. Matthews reasons that Witherspoon, accustomed to the city universities of Scotland, must have been struck by the different aspect at Princeton where the college grounds consisted of a perfectly flat field with no enclosures, and was therefore moved to apply to the grounds "a classical term which fitly described their character."

The word *yard* remained in use at Princeton after the introduction of *campus* and for some time the two terms were used interchangeably. Thus, while the faculty in 1787 spoke of "the back campus of the College," the trustees referred in 1802 to "the west side of the College yard," and then in 1807 to "the front Campus."

Gradually *campus* won out over *yard*. In 1833 it appeared in print for the first time in a book by an Englishman, James Finch, *Travels in the United States and Canada*, in which he writes of Princeton: "In front of the College is a fine campus ornamented with trees." In 1851, Benjamin H. Hall (Harvard 1851) in his *College Words*

and Customs, noted that at Princeton "the college yard is denominated the *Campus*." After the Civil War the word spread to other colleges and was finally given lexicographical recognition by inclusion in the *Century Dictionary* of 1889. Samuel Eliot Morison in *Three Centuries of Harvard* (1936), referring to Princeton's adoption of *campus* in 1774, wrote, "One by one every other American college has followed suit, until Harvard alone has kept her Yard."

BEGINNINGS OF THE CAMPUS

The College possessed no grounds for the first six years after its founding in 1746. Classes were held at Elizabethtown in the parsonage of President Dickinson and later at Newark in the parsonage of President Burr and, when numbers grew, in the county courthouse, in a room above the jail. The trustees sought another location, "more sequestred from the various temptations attending a promiscuous converse with the world, that theatre of folly and dissipation"—and one nearer to the center of the Province. Then, in the winter of 1752-1753, the village of Princeton won from the town of New Brunswick the right to become the permanent home of the College by securing for it, as stipulated by the trustees, £1,000 proclamation money, ten acres of cleared land, and 200 acres of woodland to provide fuel.

The citizens of Princeton primarily responsible for this achievement were John Stockton (father of Richard Stockton 1748), Thomas Leonard (a trustee of the College), John Hornor, and Nathaniel FitzRandolph, all large landowners. All four contributed to the £1,000 fund and secured subscriptions from others. In December 1752 Stockton and Leonard gave 200 acres of woodland a mile or so north of the village (about where Witherspoon Street now meets Route 206), and Hornor gave seven acres of cleared land in the same vicinity.

At their winter meeting on January 24, 1753, the trustees voted to accept Princeton as the place of the College "when Mr. [Fitz] Randolph has given a Deed for a certain tract of land four hundred feet Front and thirty poles [495 feet] depth, in lines at right angles with the broad street where it is proposed that the College shall be built." The day after this meeting Nathaniel FitzRandolph and his wife Rebeckah gave the trustees a deed for "a certain plot of land bounded Northward by the King's Highway, and containing about four acres and a half." In his private journal FitzRandolph noted that although the deed mentioned a consideration of 150 pounds, he "never did receive one penny of it," since "that was only to confirm the title."

After the Revolution, when the College was in financial straits, the trustees sold the 200 acres given by Stockton and Leonard and the seven acres given by Hornor.

GROWTH OF THE CAMPUS

FitzRandolph's four and one-half acres provided the site of Nassau Hall (and what came to be called the Front Campus), to which President Burr and his pupils moved in 1756. At a sheriff's sale four years later the trustees bought land surrounding three sides of the College. These five or six acres widened the Front Campus and added what came to be known as the Back Campus, ending at a line just behind what was to be the site of Whig and Clio Halls.

For eighty-five years the Campus remained unchanged. Then, through small accretions by purchase and gift over a period of thirty years, it gradually increased in size to about twenty acres.

In 1878 Robert L. and Alexander Stuart of New York bought a house and thirty-five-acre estate called "Prospect," adjacent to the Campus, and gave it to the College for use as the residence of President McCosh. Their gift more than doubled the acreage of the Campus, providing precious space for the growth of the College and later of the University.

In 1889 the grounds were quadrupled when the residuary legatees of the estate of John C. Green (who was a generous supporter of the College during President McCosh's administration) purchased and presented the Potter Farm, consisting of 155 acres of meadow and woodland extending from the Campus to the canal between Washington Road and the railroad. "This magnificant gift," M. Taylor Pyne, chairman of the committee on grounds and buildings, told the trustees, "preserves forever our beautiful view, and leaves ample room for the growth of the University for many years to come." It made it possible to say, Pyne added, that Princeton now possessed "the finest Campus of any College in America."

About this time alumni took great interest in securing land for the University. Among their leaders were the South East Club, a group who had lived in the south entry of East College in the 1870s: Howard Russell Butler, William Allen Butler, and Bayard Henry of the Class of 1876; M. Taylor Pyne and Henry B. Thompson, 1877; Percy R. Pyne Jr., 1878; C. C. Cuyler, Cleveland Dodge and William Earl Dodge, 1879. For many years they met annually at a dinner at which M. Taylor Pyne, the first of their number to be elected a trustee, spoke of the College's needs.

Their efforts began to bring results in 1905. At the commencement meeting of the trustees that year, Pyne, as president of the Springfield Association whose twenty members had contributed to the cause, presented a deed for a 230-acre tract lying between the Theological Seminary and Stony Brook, on which a golf course had recently been laid, and where the Graduate College was later to be built. That same day, James Laughlin, Jr. 1868, as president of the Olden Association, presented a deed for the ninety-three-acre Olden Farm, extending from the ridge of Prospect Avenue to Stony Brook on the east side of Washington Road. This farm became the site of athletic facilities and playing fields, faculty housing, and a center for mathematics, physics, and astrophysics.

A year later, the creation of a lake, which Howard Russell Butler prevailed upon Andrew Carnegie to finance, resulted in the University's acquisition of some 400 acres—the lake itself and land fronting it for over a mile and a half (see *Lake Carnegie*).

Howard Butler, acting as Carnegie's attorney in acquiring thirty-three parcels of land needed for the lake, struck a snag in his negotiations for a small strip of about three acres just east of Harrison Street. This the Gray family refused to sell unless their entire farm of 107 acres was purchased; and Carnegie, for his part, was unwilling to buy upland. Howard Butler's brother, William Allen Butler, organized a syndicate of South East Club members and others to purchase the farm, which they were able to do through a down payment, a bank loan, and a mortgage. After the loan was paid off, Butler induced his mother to satisfy the mortgage, enabling the syndicate in 1912 to present the deed for the property to the trustees. The major part of this gift, named the Butler Tract, was used for graduate student housing, a smaller part, retaining the name Gray Farm, for faculty housing.

In 1917 Bayard Henry obtained gifts from alumni and friends that permitted the University to negotiate, under his guidance, with the Pennsylvania Railroad to move the Princeton station from the foot of Blair Tower to its present location, thus releasing about seven acres of land, which the University used for six dormitories south of Blair Hall along University Place.

At the spring meeting of the trustees in 1922, Henry informed the board that he and several other alumni would donate the Mather farm, extending south from Lake Carnegie along Washington Road, if the University would purchase the Schenck farm, adjoining it on the west, which had just come on the market. The board accepted the donation and made the additional purchase, thereby adding 216 acres to its holdings and giving the University ownership of all the land that lies between Washington Road and the line of University Place from Nassau Street to U.S. Route 1. That same year M. Taylor Pyne bequeathed twenty-five houses and lots and twenty-seven and a half undeveloped acres in the Broadmead section, east of the Olden Farm.

In 1951 the University acquired 825 acres—the largest land acquisition in its history—by its purchase of the grounds and buildings of the Rockefeller Institute for Medical Research a few miles northeast of the central Campus. This area, used for advanced research in science and engineering, was named the James Forrestal Campus (q.v.).

The Major farm of one hundred

acres, adjoining the Forrestal Campus to the east, was acquired in 1967.

By 1970 the University's grounds comprised 2,325 acres.

ARCHITECTURE AND LANDSCAPING

In the College's early years the Georgian style of Nassau Hall prevailed, with two minor but conspicuous exceptions. The style was followed in twin buildings, a library and a refectory (later Stanhope Hall and Philosophical Hall) erected in the early 1800s on either side of Nassau Hall, and in twin dormitories, East College and West College, constructed in the 1830s on either side of the Back Campus. The two exceptions came a few years later when Whig and Clio were built in the style of classical Greek temples.

A more permanent break with the Georgian tradition came after the Civil War, in the administration of President McCosh, with the erection of Ruskinian Gothic buildings such as the Chancellor Green Library (now the Student Center). Chancellor Green's replacement of Philosophical Hall altered the formal symmetry of the Campus, by foreshadowing the more extensive alteration that was to come with the razing of East College to make way for Chancellor Green's companion, Pyne Library.

The McCosh administration brought an advance in landscaping, which had had modest beginnings with the planting of sycamore trees in front of the president's house in 1765 and of elm trees on the Front Campus in the 1830s.

President McCosh, who brought a Britisher's love of gardens with him when he arrived in 1868, took pleasure in laying out the grounds and locating the buildings, and under his care and planning the Campus began to take on a park-like appearance.

The Ruskinian Gothic of the McCosh era was followed, after a few divergences such as Alexander Hall (Romanesque) and Brown and Dod dormitories (Italian Renaissance) by the Tudor Gothic of Oxford and Cambridge, adopted at the time of the Sesquicentennial through the influence of Professor Andrew Fleming West, the organizing genius of that celebration, and M. Taylor Pyne, chairman of the trustees' committee on grounds and buildings. From the completion of Pyne Library and Blair Hall in 1897 to the building of Firestone Library fifty years later, collegiate Gothic was the prevailing architectural style at Princeton, achieving its highest expression in McCosh Hall, Holder Hall, the Graduate College, and the University Chapel.

The long-range development of the Campus was facilitated by the creation of the office of supervising architect and the appointment of Ralph Adams Cram as first incumbent in 1907. Henry B. Thompson, who succeeded his classmate, Pyne, as chairman of the committee on grounds and buildings, was influential in this appointment as he was in that of Beatrix Farrand as first consulting landscape gardener in 1915.

Cram made the first master plan for the Campus. He visualized two main axes, one extending south from the rear of Nassau Hall, the other east and west from the tiger gateway between Blair and Little along McCosh Walk to Washington Road. The north-south axis he conceived was later accented by the construction in 1969 of the plaza and steps, guarded by tigers, between Whig and Clio Halls.

Stephen F. Voorhees '00 was supervising architect from 1930 to 1949, Robert B. O'Connor from 1949 to 1954. When he died in 1965, Voorhees left a fund for the beautification of the Campus. Douglas Orr was consulting architect (a title adopted in 1954) from 1954 to 1966. Pietro Belluschi was appointed to this office in 1966 and was succeeded by Charles H. Warner, Jr. in 1975.

Orr devised a new master plan that added another east-west axis farther south, extending from the tennis courts to Palmer Stadium. After 1948 collegiate Gothic gave way to a variety of modern architectural styles in buildings such as the Engineering Quadrangle, the Woodrow Wilson School, the Art Museum, Fine and Jadwin Halls, and the newer dormitories.

Most of the beautiful planting on the Campus was the work of Mrs. Farrand. She began with the Graduate College and by the time she retired she had overseen the planting of trees and shrubs around some seventy-five buildings. Her successors as consulting landscape architect (the slightly altered title was adopted in 1946) have been Alfred Geiffert, Jr. from 1943 to 1958, Markley Stevenson from 1958 to 1961, Michael Rapuano from 1961 to 1974, and since 1974, Robert L. Zion.

Successors of Henry B. Thompson as chairman of the trustees' committee on grounds and buildings have been Franklin D'Olier 1898 from 1928 to 1942, Dean Mathey '12 from 1942 to 1949, Sanford G. Etherington '06 from 1949 to 1951, Henderson Supplee, Jr. '26 from 1951 to 1974, and since 1974, Richard R. Hough '39.

Cannons, Princeton. The Big Cannon in the center of the quadrangle back of Nassau Hall and the Little Cannon between Whig and Clio Halls were both left in Princeton after the Revolution, and both loomed large in student life in the nineteenth century.

After lying on the Campus for years, the Big Cannon was taken to New Brunswick during the War of 1812 to defend that city from possible enemy attack. It remained on the common there until one dark night in 1835 when the Princeton Blues, a military company of citizens of the town, loaded it on a wagon and headed back to Princeton. Their wagon broke down at the outskirts of the town, and they abandoned the cannon at the side of the road. There it lay until another dark night a few years later, when about a hundred students, led by Leonard Jerome 1839 (maternal grandfather of Winston Churchill), hoisted it onto a heavy wagon they had engaged, along with a team of horses and driver, brought it to the campus, and—before Vice-president Maclean could intervene—dumped it in front of Nassau Hall. In 1840 it was moved and planted muzzle down in its present location.

Since the 1890s, the Big Cannon has been the focus of championship football bonfires and the seniors' class day exercises in June. It inspired Joseph F. Hewitt '07 and Arthur H. Osborne '07 to compose "The Princeton Cannon Song" ("With cheers and songs we'll rally round The Cannon as of yore/And Nassau's walls will echo with the Princeton Tiger's roar").

The Little Cannon was the cause of the celebrated "Cannon War" with Rutgers in 1875, when it was taken to New Brunswick by Rutgers students under the mistaken impression that it was a lost cannon belonging to that city. After a retaliatory raid by Princeton students and some sharp correspondence between the presidents of the two colleges, a joint committee was appointed by the respective faculties and the dispute settled amicably, Princeton students agreeing to return some muskets they had taken from New Brunswick, Rutgers students the cannon they had taken from Princeton.

The day the New Brunswick chief of police brought the Little Cannon back to Princeton, President McCosh and the whole college assembled between the two Halls to greet him. The Nassau Hall bell rang and the President made a speech. He said he was reminded of the contest over Helen in the Trojan War and suggested that the Cannon War should be immortalized in a new *Iliad*, written in Greek and in hexameter verse. The students cheered wildly, but there is no evidence that McCosh's effort to give the Cannon War a cultural turn bore any fruit. The "War," however, was well covered by the press.

Capps, Edward (1866-1950), noted champion of Greek-American friendship who was Professor of Classics at Princeton from 1907 to 1935, became interested in the classics at Illinois College in his native Jacksonville. He received his A.B. there in 1887, took his Ph.D. at Yale in 1891, and later studied in Greece and Germany. He taught at Illinois College, at Yale, and at the University of Chicago (where he was the founder and editor of *Classical Philology*), before being called to Princeton by Woodrow Wilson in 1907.

Capps's Princeton colleagues were soon impressed by his abundant energy and his loyalty to his beliefs and friends. As a member of the faculty committee on the graduate school, he sided with Wilson in the Wilson-West controversy over the location of the graduate college, taking a vigorous part in debate at faculty meetings and supporting Wilson to the end. One of the founders of the American Associa-

tion of University Professors, he was a leader during its first fight for academic freedom and served for a term as its president. He was also president of the American Philological Association.

He was the first American editor of the Loeb Classical Library, the series of texts of classical authors with English translations, regarded in the profession as a notable achievement of American scholarship.

Most of his adult life Capps was closely identified with Greece. "With Lord Byron removed from the field," the *Alumni Weekly* once said, "Professor Capps would win any contest for 'best-known foreigner in Greece.'" He first went there in the fall of 1893 as a member of the American School of Classical Studies at Athens, and the following spring took part in the School's excavation of the theater at ancient Eretria. He returned to Athens for further study in 1903, this time deciphering and collating a series of tablets about the theater, which also contained important data on that city's military and political history.

At the end of the First World War, Capps spent two years in Greece as American Red Cross Commissioner and another year as United States Minister to Greece, on appointment of President Wilson. During this period, he played a leading role in the founding of Athens College, which later named a building in his honor, citing him as an "inspiring teacher of Greek life and letters . . . and for nearly half a century a champion of friendship between Greece and America."

Capps was chairman of the managing committee of the American School of Classical Studies at Athens for twenty years. In this capacity he organized the most spectacular of all American archaeological ventures, the excavation of the Agora of ancient Athens, securing the Greek government's necessary cooperation, John D. Rockefeller, Jr.'s financial support, and Professor T. Leslie Shear's expert services as director. He was influential in obtaining the gift of the Gennadius Library, which made the School an international center of Byzantine and Neo-Hellenic studies.

Following his retirement from the University in 1935, he served as acting director of the American School in Athens for a year, and was then visiting professor at the Institute for Advanced Study for five years. Thereafter he continued to work on the Loeb Classical Library and to read his favorite Greek authors with students who met with him at his home on Mercer Street. Shortly before his eightieth birthday he went to Oxford to accept a Doctor of Letters degree *honoris causa*; he had previously been honored by Illinois College, Oberlin, Harvard, Michigan, and Athens, and had been twice decorated by the Greek government.

At the centennial of his first alma mater, Illinois College, his family and friends founded there the Edward Capps chair of Greek and Latin.

Carnahan, James (1775-1859), was a man of simple, solid virtues whose thirty-one-year tenure as ninth president of the College (1823-1854), was the longest in its history. He was born and reared in Pennsylvania, where his father farmed, first near Harrisburg, then near Pittsburgh. In 1798 James and his friend Jacob Lindly (later president of Ohio University) entered the junior class at Princeton after an arduous trip over the Allegheny Mountains. Having only one horse (Lindly's), they used a system, called "ride and tie," by which each rode a number of miles

every day and then, tying up the horse to await his companion, walked as many more.

After his graduation in 1800, Carnahan served as tutor at Princeton, studied theology with President S. Stanhope Smith, and preached for six years, before resigning because of a throat aliment that troubled him all his life. He then founded and conducted a classical seminary in Georgetown, D.C., and had been there eleven years when he was notified of his election to the presidency of the College.

Not having kept in touch with developments at the College, Carnahan was unprepared for what he found when he assumed the presidency: the divided counsels of the trustees and the conflicting views and interests left by Ashbel Green's administration. He thought of resigning at once, but young Professor John Maclean, Jr. persuaded him to carry on. The period of decline continued, reaching its lowest ebb five years later, when enrollment dropped to eighty students. Carnahan thought of recommending the closing of the institution, but John Maclean proposed a plan for strengthening the faculty that resulted in his being elected vice president of the College.

From that time on, as a trustee later observed, the College had an administration "in which two colleagues labored as one man." Reviewing the achievements of this partnership on his retirement in 1854, Carnahan was able to report a restoration of harmony between the trustees and faculty, the doubling of student enrollment and the tripling of the Faculty, the erection of East and West Colleges and Whig and Clio Halls. Carnahan paid tribute to Maclean's energy, zeal, and devotion. Maclean for his part praised Carnahan's freedom from personal ambition and said that his faithfulness and success in conducting the affairs of the College entitled him to the lasting gratitude of its alumni and friends.

Carnahan was genuinely modest about his own achievements. What he hoped people would remember about him, he sometimes told his family during his last years, was that it was he who planted the trees in the front Campus.

Carnegie Lake was created in 1906 by the construction of a dam at Kingston that impounded the confluence of Stony Brook and the Millstone River, producing a sheet of water three and a half miles long and 800 feet across at its widest point.

It was the gift of the Scottish-American steel maker, Andrew Carnegie. He had built a number of lochs in Scotland and was easily persuaded to finance one for Princeton by Howard Russell Butler and his brother, William Allen Butler, both of the Class of 1876, They and some of their college friends were determined that undergraduates should have a better place for rowing than the old canal that had been tried in the 1870s and found wanting.

The Butlers succeeded where James McCosh and Woodrow Wilson failed. President McCosh had made repeated efforts to interest his fellow Scot in his plans for the College but without success. Meeting Carnegie at the railroad station on one visit, McCosh told him how honored he was to welcome him to Princeton. Carnegie replied that he had always had a warm spot in his heart for Princeton, to which Mrs. McCosh replied with spirit, "Indeed, Mr. Carnegie, we have seen no evidence of it as yet."

While the negotiations for the lake were in progress President Wilson tried unsuccessfully to interest Car-

negie in making a substantial contribution to the endowment of either the graduate school or the preceptorial system. Later when Wilson again asked for help and Carnegie answered, "I have already given you a lake" (Ray Stannard Baker relates), Wilson replied, "We needed bread and you gave us cake."

But the general response to Carnegie's formal presentation of the lake on December 5, 1906, was enthusiastic. Carnegie came down from New York in a special train with five dozen friends. President Wilson, Dean Fine, and M. Taylor Pyne met them at the station, which was then at the foot of the Blair Arch steps. Climbing the steps, Carnegie smiled at a banner that hung from an undergraduate's room in Blair Tower with the words "Welkum to the Laird of Skeebo [the name Carnegie had given his estate in Scotland]." Later when the academic procession, led by Wilson and Carnegie, arrived in Alexander Hall for the ceremonies, his smile broadened as students in the balcony suddenly began to sing, to the tune of the then popular song "Tammany,"

> *Carnegie, Carnegie*
> *He is giving us a lake—*
> *You can hear the breakers break;*
> *Carnegie, Carnegie*
> *Andy, Andy, you're a dandy*
> *Carnegie.*

The creation of Lake Carnegie did more than provide a place for undergraduate rowing, and for canoeing, sailing, fishing, and skating by members of the Princeton community. Aside from the aesthetic and healthful advantages that resulted from flooding a large marshy area, Carnegie's gift involved the purchase of hundreds of acres adjacent to the lake, giving the University invaluable room for development it might not otherwise have been able to secure.

In the 1960s it became apparent that Lake Carnegie was being threatened by some of the problems that beset larger bodies of water. One problem, reflecting poor land use over three decades, was the accumulation of sediment washed in by Stony Brook from the communities it drains. The other problem was the more recent, rapid deposit of sewage carried by the Millstone River from nearby towns, where expansion of sewage treatment facilities had not kept pace with rapid growth of population. Extensive dredging was undertaken to solve these problems in the early 1970s.

Castro, Americo (1885-1972), Emory L. Ford Professor of Spanish, divided a half-century of scholarly· work almost equally between Spain and the United States and, in the words of the citation for the honorary Doctor of Letters the University conferred on him in 1963, "gracefully exemplified the union of [these] two great cultures."

He was born of Spanish parents in Brazil and educated in Spain and France. He took his doctorate at the University of Madrid in 1911, and four years later won appointment through competitive examinations to its chair in the history of the Spanish language. In 1925 he published *The Thought of Cervantes*, a fundamental work that opened a new epoch in studies of the author of *Don Quixote*.

Castro was a strong supporter of the Spanish Republic when it was established in 1931, serving as its ambassador to Germany and also in its Council of Public Instruction and its Division of Cultural Relations. He left Spain when Franco rose to power in 1937

and, after teaching at the Universities of Wisconsin and Texas, accepted a call to Princeton in 1940.

Castro was regarded as one of the world's most distinguished Hispanists. His magnum opus, *Spain in Her History* (1948), was considered a notable innovation in modern Spanish historiography. Written in Spanish, this work was later translated into English, Italian, German, French, and Japanese. He also earned international recognition as a teacher, serving as visiting professor at universities in Argentina, Chile, Mexico, Cuba, Puerto Rico, Germany, and throughout the United States.

According to his colleagues, Castro was unusually successful in solving the problem of teaching the literature of one land to students of another: "Don Americo succeeded not only in making what was obscure intelligible, and what was alien understandable, but in arousing . . . fervor and enthusiasm. . . . This he was able to do not so much because of his extraordinary scholarly competence as because of his commitment to teaching as a priestly and prophetic calling."

Catalogue, The, as we know it today, made a rudimentary appearance in 1819, the College having functioned happily and successfully without one for over seventy years.

An earlier "catalogue" appeared in 1770, but it was of another kind: a listing of all the officers and graduates since the College's founding. For more than a century it retained the use of Latin for it headings (*Praesides, Curatores, Facultas Artium*) and for most given names. This cumulative roll appeared triennially from 1786 through 1886, again in 1896, and in 1906 culminated in the *General Catalogue of*

Princeton University 1746-1906. Meantime, the Alumni Directory (q.v.), containing names and addresses of *living* alumni, made its first appearance in 1888.

The 1819 prototype of today's annual college catalogue was entirely in English; its twelve pages consisted of a list of the current "officers and students of Nassau Hall." Beginning in 1821, the catalogue added a list of studies for each class and a half-page "advertisement," giving the dates of Commencement and the fall and spring vacations. In 1829 the "advertisement" grew to three pages with a list of courses offered and brief references to admission procedures, expenses, the library, and scientific apparatus.

The Catalogue grew with the College and the University, increasing from eighteen pages in 1844 to 668 pages in 1941. Beginning in 1942, information about graduate work was published in a separate *Graduate School Announcement*, and beginning in 1958, descriptions of courses for undergraduates and other material of special interest to them was issued in a separate *Undergraduate Announcement*. In recent years, the different issues of the Catalogue have been undergoing changes in format and design reflecting changes in the University itself.

Centennial Anniversary, The, of the College was celebrated at the Commencement of 1847, "this being the occasion," Vice President John Maclean, Jr., explained, "on which the members of the one hundredth Senior Class were admitted to their first degree in the Arts." Present besides the graduating seniors and their families were a large number of alumni, delegates from other colleges, the vice president of the United States (George Mifflin Dallas

1810), the governor and several ex-governors of New Jersey, a justice of the United States Supreme Court, the chief justice and chancellor of New Jersey and of Delaware, and other dignitaries.

The celebration lasted only two days—Tuesday and Wednesday, June 29 and 30—but the committee on arrangements managed to pack into that brief period a remarkable volume of oratory. There were three sessions on Tuesday and two on Wednesday. All but the last were held in the First Presbyterian Church, filled, the committee in its enthusiasm reported, "with an audience which for beauty, intellect, and respectability could scarcely be surpassed."

At the first session on Tuesday, Chief Justice Henry W. Green 1820 (later the Chancellor Green for whon the present student center is named) gave an address formally opening the new law school, which proved short-lived, ceasing operations only a few years later.

At the second session James W. Alexander 1820, the Centennial historian, spoke over two hours, "with such eloquence," the committee unhesitatingly reported, "that the audience sat in rapt attention, missing not a single word."

On Tuesday evening eight representatives of the junior class delivered orations, a student from Ireland on "The Faded Shamrock," one from Mississippi on the question, "Why Has America No National Literature?"

At the graduation exercises Wednesday morning, twenty-three of the sixty-two seniors receiving bachelor degrees delivered orations.

In the afternoon a dinner was served to 700 persons in a large tent in back of Nassau Hall. The toastmaster, trustee James S. Green, son of ex-president Ashbel Green, offered thirteen formal toasts—without wine! "Our hearts are full to overflowing" he said, "we need no additional excitements." To six of his toasts there were responses, by Vice-President Dallas, ex-Governor William Pennington 1813, and others. The program concluded with nine impromptu toasts, some with responses, honoring President Carnahan, physicist Joseph Henry, the oldest living graduate Samuel Baldwin 1770, and others. At the end Robert McKnight 1839 of Pittsburgh, who was later a congressman, offered a toast to *"Nassau Hall and her Sons*—The *tie* which binds her absent sons increases as the *square* of the distance"—a sentiment, the committee noted in its official report, "received with a most agreeable sensation by all present."

Chancellor Green Student Center was originally the college library building, which was given in 1873 by John C. Green and named for his brother, Henry Woodhull Green 1820, Chancellor of New Jersey in the 1860s. Its architecture was inspired by the Ruskinian version of Venetian Gothic then popular in England.

After Pyne Library was built adjacent to Chancellor Green in 1897, they both served as the University library until the completion of Firestone in 1947. Chancellor Green's conversion into a student center seven years later was made possible largely through a twentieth reunion gift of the Class of 1934.

Chapel, The University, continues a tradition of public worship that goes back to Princeton's founding in 1746. For the first ten years of the College's existence, daily services were celebrated in the studies of the first two presidents—the Reverend Jonathan Dickinson, in Elizabethtown, and the Reverend Aaron Burr, in Newark. After the College moved to Princeton in 1756, a prayer-hall in Nassau Hall (for a time the meeting place of the Continental Congress on state occasions, and now the Faculty Room) was used for services until 1847, when the first chapel was built. This chapel, described in a novel of that period as "a beautiful smile on a plain face," was replaced in 1882 by the larger Marquand Chapel, gift of Henry G. Marquand, and thereafter was known as the "Old Chapel" until it was razed in 1896 to make way for Pyne Library. Marquand Chapel was destroyed by fire in the spring of 1920. Services were then conducted in Alexander Hall until 1928. The cornerstone of the University Chapel was laid in 1925, and it was dedicated on Sunday, May 31, 1928.

THE DEANS

Until 1928 the president of the University was directly responsible for supervision of the Chapel programs. That year the office of dean of the chapel was created by the trustees and the Reverend Robert Russell Wicks of Holyoke was appointed as the first incumbent. In the same year, the chair of Dean of the Chapel of the University was endowed by their families in memory of the Rev. Wilton Merle-Smith and Judge Walter Lloyd-Smith, twin brothers in the Princeton Class of 1877. The gift also provided for a deanery to house the dean and his family. Dean Wicks challenged the unexamined premises of many undergraduates and demonstrated the vitality of the Christian faith in the modern world. On his retirement in 1947, Wicks was succeeded by the Right Reverend Donald B. Aldrich, former Bishop Coadjutor of the Protestant Episcopal Diocese of Michigan and a charter trustee of the

University. An experienced pastor, Dean Aldrich counseled students compassionately in the confused times following World War II. Owing to ill health, he resigned in 1955. He was succeeded by the Reverend Ernest Gordon, an ordained minister of the Church of Scotland and a former minister of Paisley Abbey—situated in the same town where the Reverend John Witherspoon served as minister of the Laigh Kirk (low church) before his call to the Princeton presidency in 1768.

REQUIRED CHAPEL ATTENDANCE

The College of New Jersey was firmly rooted in the fertile soil of the Great Awakening. One of its emphases was that an individual was accountable before God for his life, his neighbors, his country, and his back yard. This resulted in a personal discipline of prayers, praise, and thanksgiving. For 136 years after the College began, students were required to attend morning prayers (originally at 5 a.m.) and evening prayers daily, and morning and afternoon services on Sunday. These requirements were a source of student complaint and frequent pranks. Stories that have come down from alumni of that period recall that once the seats of the "Old Chapel" were tarred, at another time the benches were literally buried in hay, and at still another a cow was discovered up near the pulpit just before the morning service began.

Irreverence of students was apparently most noticeable during long prayers. President Emeritus Maclean continued to take part in the services during James McCosh's presidency. He was accustomed to praying not only for the nation and for the College but also for everyone associated with their respective administrations. On one Sunday he concluded his lengthy litany with additional prayers for the Seniors, the Juniors, and Sophomores, and then, Henry Fairfield Osborn 1877 recalled, "as the Reverend Doctor reached the Freshmen, a roar of laughter proceeded from the seemingly reverently bowed heads of the entire student body. At this unexpected 'Amen' Doctor McCosh became very impatient. After the disturbance was duly quelled and the Doxology sung with unusual fervor, he was heard to remark: 'Surely Doctor Maclean is in his dotage; he ought to have more sense than to pray for the Freshmen.' "

This remark is not surprising from a divine who is alleged to have opened a prayer, soon after the publication of one of his most successful books, with these words: "O Thou who has also written a book."

By 1882, changing views of life's priorities brought the abolition of required attendance at daily vespers, and in 1902 the required Sunday afternoon service was also discontinued. By 1905 attendance at morning prayers (then held at 7 a.m.) was required only twice a week, and in 1915 this requirement was given up entirely. Protests continued about Sunday chapel. A "Chapel Strike at Princeton," as headlined by New York newspapers in 1914, turned out, in the *Daily Princetonian*'s version, to be "a lengthy attack of bronchitis . . . [during] a lengthier prayer. . . . At the conclusion of the prayer, the pitiable cough subsided, and the service continued uninterrupted." The *Prince* said the incident demonstrated the conviction of students that Sunday chapel should end promptly at noon; "this is their religion."

A few years ago, the writer received a visit from one of the ringleaders of this incident, who had been expelled for his contribution. He later went on to study at a theological seminary and became a professor of theology.

Required attendance at Sunday chapel ended eventually: for upperclassmen in 1935, for sophomores in 1960, and, finally, for freshmen in 1964. The trustees' decision to remove the last vestige of compulsion was made, in their official words, "in the best interests of a freer, more honest, creative expression of religion."

STUDENT RELIGIOUS ORGANIZATIONS

For more than a hundred years the student-organized Philadelphian Society (1825-1930) carried on an active program in religion and social service. This society early espoused the cause of foreign missions and in later years was responsible for the founding of Princeton-in-Asia and the Princeton Summer Camp. The various activities of this old Princeton institution, later carried on by the Student-Faculty Association (1930-1946) and the Student Christian Association (1946-1967), have been continued under the auspices of the Chapel Fellowship and its related social service organization, the Student Volunteers Council (1967-   ).

DENOMINATIONAL SOCIETIES AND CHAPLAINS

In 1925 President Hibben forbade the Reverend Frank Buchman, founder of the Oxford Group and later of Moral Rearmament, to appear on campus, in consequence of a conflict about his controversial techniques, particularly as practiced by recent converts. (It was the contention thus aroused that led to the dissolution of the Philadelphian Society.) In the 1926 report of the University commission on Buchmanism, the hope was expressed that the new chapel and its minister would be a means of achieving religious harmony on the campus.

The achievement of this harmony has been one of the Chapel's functions. The denominational societies, and their chaplains, cooperate with the work of the University Chapel and contribute to its activities. There are eleven of these societies. The oldest of them, the Episcopal Procter Foundation, was begun in 1876 as St. Paul's Society. The Presbyterian Westminster Foundation, the Catholic Club (later the Aquinas Institute), the Methodist Wesley Club, and the Evangelical Fellowship were organized in the 1920s. After World War II the Jewish Hillel Foundation, Lutheran Student Fellowship, Baptist Student Fellowship, Unitarian/Universalist Fellowship, Christian Science Organization, and the Orthodox Christian St. Photius Society were founded. The University makes its facilities available to the denominational societies for services and meetings and extends various courtesies and privileges to the chaplains.

In 1957 these courtesies and privileges were withdrawn from Father Hugh Halton because he had conducted his ministry in such a way that he had alienated from himself not only Protestant members of the University but devout Catholics as well. Thereafter the air cleared; since 1966 daily services for Catholics have been conducted in the University Chapel.

THE RECENT YEARS

The first noticeable consequence of the abolition of the last Chapel requirement in 1964 was a decline in attendance by freshmen and an increase in attendance by upperclassmen. When the Class of 1967 graduated, attendance took a rapid plunge due to the departure of 300 seniors who had been active members of the Chapel Fellowship. It was the growth of this fellowship in the years preceding the abolition of the requirement that insured the continuation of the Chapel's place on the campus. It was made up of diverse groups representing a wide range of interests, such as study, discussion, religious drama, social service, music, Chapel administration, and charitable enterprises.

Although the building was once called, by some, Princeton's two-million-dollar protest against materialism, and, by others, a great white whale (not elephant!), its architectural strength has contributed to its place as the center of spiritual life on the campus. It is seen to be the one building that exalts the whole of creation and humanity. Since 1957 it has been kept open daily from 8 a.m. to 12:30 a.m. to serve the needs of the University community; the closing service each day is an Organ Epilogue from 11 p.m. to 12:30 a.m. Sunday services are held during the twelve months of the year.

Rather than a decrease, there has been a marked increase in the number of services held in the Chapel, which has resulted in a problem of scheduling the number requested. Since 1970 attendance at services has noticeably increased, and the degree of student participation is greater than it has ever been. An undergraduate deaconate of twenty-five men and women represents the needs, concerns, and interests of the Chapel Fellowship and of the student body as a whole.

A significant portion of the Chapel's budget comes from annual gifts of the Friends of the Chapel. Religious, medical, educational, and charitable services engaged in by alumni are supported from Chapel offerings of from $12,000 to $15,000 a year.

It is in the Chapel that the University comes together as a community. This is true not only at Opening Exercises, Baccalaureate Services, annual memorial services for members of the University and again for alumni, funerals and weddings; it has also been true on occasions of national tragedy such as the assassinations of President John Kennedy, his brother Robert, and Martin Luther King, Jr. Because it provides a center for community, it attracts a large number of alumni and visitors to its services. It has also been a bridge between town and gown, and between the several academic communities of Princeton. The Thanksgiving and Christmas services are mostly for the benefit of townspeople.

Organ and choral music are an important part of the Chapel program. They have both come a long way since the days when Yale's President Ezra Stiles after a visit in 1770 declared the organ in Nassau Hall "an innovation of ill consequence," and when John Adams, later President of the United States, reported after *his* visit to Princeton in 1774, "The Schollars sing as badly as the Presbyterians at New York." The standard set by today's choir and musicians at the weekly services is one of excellence, and the Christmas Vespers and the Milbank Concerts are outstanding events in the University's musical calendar.

Since the retirement of the noted Bach organist Carl Weinrich in 1973, the organists have been students who have performed with a dedication and loyalty that has done much to achieve the ideal of a University community of worship. The same can be said of a chapter of student organists who sustain the Organ Epilogue seven nights a week in term. All the musical activities are supervised by Walter Nollner, Director of Music in the Chapel since 1973.

THE CHAPEL'S
CONTINUING PURPOSE

The University Chapel provides a place where people can come in reverence to face the ultimate mystery of creation and existence. This continuing purpose is well expressed in one of the prayers that were said in the Litany of Dedication when the Chapel's doors were first opened in 1928:

> That, for all who with troubled hearts and minds here seek comfort and healing, this house may be as a hiding place from the wind and a covert from the tempest, as rivers of water in a dry place, as the shadow of a great rock in a weary land.

Ernest Gordon

NOTE: For a description of the architecture, sculpture, and windows of the University Chapel, see: Richard Stillwell, *The Chapel of Princeton University*, Princeton University Press, 1971.

Charter, The, which created the corporation originally known as The Trustees of the College of New Jersey, was granted in the name of King George II and "passed the Great Seal" of the Province of New Jersey on October 22, 1746.

This charter authorized the erection of a college "for the Education of Youth in the Learned Languages and in the Liberal Arts and Sciences," designated seven men, with five others to be chosen by them, to be the trustees of the college, and ordained that "the said Trustees and their Successors shall forever hereafter be, in Deed, Fact & Name a Body corporate & politick. . . ."

The charter granted the trustees and their successors full power and author- ity to acquire real and personal property, to erect buildings, to elect a president, tutors, professors, and other officers, to grant degrees, and to establish ordinances and laws "not repugnant to the Laws and Statutes of . . . Great Britain, or . . . of New Jersey, and not excluding any Person of any religious Denomination whatsoever from . . . any of the Liberties, Privileges, or immunities of the . . . College, on account of his . . . being of a Religious profession Different from the . . . Trustees of the College."

The original charter was issued by John Hamilton, president of the Council of the Province of New Jersey, who was acting as governor at the time. Because Hamilton's authority was questioned, the legal status of the College came under attack, and a second charter was therefore issued in 1748 by Jonathan Belcher, newly appointed governor of the province.* It corresponded, for the most part, to the charter of 1746, but it increased the maximum number of trustees from twelve to twenty-three, made the governor of New Jersey a trustee ex-officio, and stipulated that twelve trustees were to be inhabitants of the State of New Jersey.†

In 1780, the Council (i.e., Senate) and General Assembly of the State of New Jersey, on petition of the trustees, confirmed the royal charter of 1748 with minor changes, one being that each trustee swear allegiance to the state in which he resided instead of to the king of Great Britain. A further legislative enactment, adopted in 1799, required him also to affirm his intention to support the Constitution of the United States. Still another, adopted in 1866, directed him to swear to perform the duties of his office faithfully and impartially, thus adding the third article of the oath each new trustee has taken ever since.

On February 13, 1896, the corporation adopted a resolution changing its name to The Trustees of Princeton University. President Patton publicly proclaimed this change on October 22, 1896, the 150th anniversary of the granting of the first charter.

The "yearly clear value" of real and personal property the trustees were allowed to acquire for the purpose of the corporation was limited at one time to the equivalent of 20,000 bushels of wheat. Since 1903 the corporation's capacity to receive real and personal property has been—legally—unlimited.

In 1963, the Board of Trustees adopted a complete revision of the charter, simplifying and modernizing its language to reflect the requirements and benefits of present law and corporate practice. This revision was filed with the Secretary of State as constituting the current Certificate of Incorporation of The Trustees of Princeton University.

* The text of the charters of 1746 and of 1748 is given in Thomas Jefferson Wertenbaker's *Princeton 1746-1896*, pp. 396-404.

† An amendment adopted in 1926 provided that thereafter there should be from twenty-three to forty trustees, the exact number to be fixed from time to time in the by-laws. The number who were to be residents of New Jersey was reduced to eight and, by another amendment in 1963, to one in addition to the governor and the president of the University.

Cheers became a part of the Princeton student's way of life sometime in the late 1850s or early 1860s. The first cheer, "Hooray, hooray, hooray! Tiger siss-boom-ah, Princeton!" was adapted from the "skyrocket" cheer of the Seventh Regiment of New York City. Princetonians of the early 1860s re-

membered fifty years later hearing the Seventh Regiment give this cheer from their railroad coaches at the Princeton depot on their way to Washington, a few days after the outbreak of the Civil War. But a member of the Class of 1860 was pretty sure that he had heard a classmate give the rocket cheer in Professor Schenck's chemistry class in the spring of their senior year. The "tiger" (the word itself or a roar) was a common element in early cheers, generally. Its use in the rocket cheer did not refer to the Princeton mascot; he came later (see *Tiger*).

The Princeton skyrocket cheer was quoted by Rudyard Kipling in his story *A Matter of Fact* (1892): An English newspaperman, encouraging his reluctant American colleague, a Princeton graduate, to cable a fantastic story about a sea serpent to the New York *World*, ends his exhortation with the words "Sizz! Boom-ah!"

Sometime in the 1890s, the skyrocket cheer developed into the "locomotive," Princeton's longest-used and most distinctive cheer, which starts slowly and picks up increasing speed, suggesting the sound of a locomotive:

'Ray 'ray 'ray
Tiger, tiger, tiger
Sis, sis, sis,
Boom, boom, boom, ah!
Princeton! Princeton! Princeton!

In another cheer, used in the first half of the century, first Nassau and then Tiger were spelled out three times, followed by "fight, team, fight." Still another, the "short" cheer, was used principally to honor individuals: "R-r-r-ay, Lourie."

Cheering played a more important part in football games in earlier years. With no band, time-outs were filled with locomotives and Nassau cheers, and with no public address system, the infrequent withdrawal of a player was greeted with a short cheer in his honor. And, as a *Philadelphia Press* reporter brought out in his account of Yale's 29 to 5 victory over Princeton in 1900, the cheering did not end with the game. When the Yale adherents danced about on the field to celebrate their victory, he reported, the Princeton stands responded with "the steady, deep pulsation of the locomotive." Even after everyone else had left the field and darkness was closing in, "still in obedience to the cry of a white-hatted figure up on the fence, a knot of Princetonians cheered—cheered the team, cheered the scrub, cheered the team man by man, cheered Princeton, and last of all . . . sang in husky voices each verse of *Old Nassau.*"

In recent years cheering has been less ritualistic, more responsive to the immediate situation, with rhythmic chants such as "go-Tiger-go," "take that ball away, heh, heh, take that ball away," and the one-word call first used for basketball, later applied also to football: "DE-fence," repeated time and again.

While cheering has become less important, the activities of the cheerleaders have become more spectacular, with tumbling on the sidelines, and push-ups under the goal posts to recount the points after each Princeton score. Cheerleaders were once chosen for their prominence on campus (sometimes as captains or managers in other sports); more recently they have been selected because of their special talents for the acrobatics of cheerleading.

Chemical Engineering was first offered at Princeton in 1922 as a special program administered jointly by the Department of Chemistry and the newly formed School of Engineering, which drew on existing courses in both fields. The senior professor of physical chemistry, Hugh Stott Taylor, watched over the fledgling program and groomed one of his graduate students, Joseph C. Elgin (whose undergraduate work at the University of Virginia was in chemical engineering) for its eventual leadership.

On receiving his Ph.D. in physical chemistry in 1929, Elgin was appointed Princeton's first instructor in chemical engineering, responsible for developing the new department's courses and facilities. He prepared himself by spending eight months as a guest of the M.I.T. chemical engineering department, then regarded as one of the best in the country. On his return he set up quarters in the old chemical laboratory, which housed the department until 1962, when it moved into its present home in Maclean Hall in the Engineering Quadrangle. One of Elgin's first students, John C. Whitwell (B.S.E. 1931, Ch.E. 1932), became his colleague in 1932. Two years later Elgin and Whitwell were joined by Richard H. Wilhelm (q.v.), who had just received his doctor's degree in chemical engineering at Columbia. This triumvirate laid the foundations of the Department of Chemical Engineering.

Their first task was to build from scratch an undergraduate curriculum in chemical engineering. In this they were later joined by Richard K. Toner, who came from New York University in 1942, and by Ernest F. Johnson, who came from the University of Pennsylvania in 1948. Undergraduate enrollment in the department grew steadily and at one time was larger than any other engineering department in the University. In 1946 a Ph.D. program was added to the original Ch.E. (later

M.S.E.) program of study, and in April 1948, a student in the department earned the first doctor's degree ever granted in the School of Engineering.

By 1954, when Elgin gave up the chairmanship to become dean of the School of Engineering, the department had grown to an enrollment of 100 undergraduates and twenty-five graduate students, and a faculty of seven.

Further growth, particularly in graduate instruction and research, came under the leadership of the second chairman, Richard H. Wilhelm, with the added assistance of new members of the department, including Professors Leon Lapidus, William R. Schowalter, Robert C. Axtmann, and Bryce Maxwell. In 1966 the department was cited by the Cartter report of the American Council on Education as having the second most attractive chemical engineering graduate program in the country. When Professor Wilhelm died suddenly in 1968, fourteen years after he assumed the chairmanship, the faculty was twice as large as when he took over, there were three times as many graduate students, the department had expanded into chemical reactor engineering, transport phenomena, and control and optimization theory, and had been one of the first to make extensive use of computer technology.

The third chairman, appointed in 1968, was Leon Lapidus, a member of the Princeton faculty since 1953, widely known for his work in the application of computer techniques in chemical engineering, for which he was given the Professional Progress (1966) and William H. Walker (1973) Awards of the American Institute of Chemical Engineers. Two departmental areas of instruction and research developed during his chairmanship were the Pol-

ymer Science and Materials Program, directed by Bryce Maxwell, recipient of the 1976 Society of Plastics Engineers' international award, and the Fusion Reactor Technology Program, closely integrated with the Plasma Physics Laboratory, and directed by Ernest Johnson, who has been associated since 1955 with the laboratory's program of research directed toward controlled fusion. Under Lapidus, the department reached out into new areas of research such as biochemical engineering, energy conversion, and pollution control. The interest in pollution control was underlined in 1971 when the name of the Professorship of Chemical Engineering for Nuclear Studies, then held by Robert Axtmann, was changed to Chemical Engineering for Environmental Studies, with the agreement of the Mobil Oil Corporation, which was then supporting it. Professor Axtmann was first chairman of the University's Council on Environmental Studies and of the School of Engineering's topical program on Energy Conversion and Resources, which offers undergraduate engineering students an opportunity to supplement their departmental major with intensive study not only of energy conversion and energy resources, but also of the environmental impact of energy technologies.

In May 1977, the department suffered its second major loss in less than a decade with the sudden death of Leon Lapidus. Arrangements were made for Ernest Johnson to serve as chairman through the academic year 1977-1978, and for William R. Schowalter, associate dean of the School of Engineering since 1972, to assume the chairmanship in 1978.

Chemistry at Princeton may be divided, like Ceasar's Gaul, into three parts: pre-World War I, between the wars, and post-World War II. But there was a continuity of spirit from the earliest years to the latest, suggested by Hugh Stott Taylor, chairman of the department from 1926 to 1951, with these words, at the dedication of the Frick Chemical Laboratory in 1929:

> May the vivifying influence of Maclean in the early days of Science at Princeton be an inspiration to those who follow him in tasks of teaching and seeking in Chemistry.

Dean Taylor was referring, of course, to John Maclean (q.v.), a medical doctor who in 1795 was appointed Professor of Chemistry, at that time a rare title in this country. Maclean carried the banner of Lavoisier's New Chemistry to the New World, and set up, in Nassau Hall, the first undergraduate chemistry laboratory in America. The following year a new chair was created, Professor of Chemistry and Natural History, and Dr. Maclean was its first incumbent, reflecting his competence in other sciences as well.

Because of its association with medicine, chemistry enjoyed a preeminence among the sciences throughout the nineteenth century, and was a required subject for all Princeton students. Toward the end of the century, when exploration of the nation's mineral resources became important, the faculty included mineralogists Henry B. Cornwall and Alexander H. Phillips, and the analyst LeRoy W. McCay, a student of Bunsen and discoverer of the thio-arsenates. McCay's colleagues included Lauder Jones in nitrogen chemistry, and George Hulett, who was an authority on standard cells, but whose greatest discovery, many thought, was Hugh Stott Taylor (q.v.), whom he brought to Princeton in 1914.

This young Englishman (later knighted by both Pope Pius XII and Queen Elizabeth II), an inspiring teacher, a bold leader, and the recipient of innumerable honors for his pioneering work in catalysis, set the pattern for research and teaching at Princeton for the next half-century.

These were exciting times for research. The atmosphere in the laboratory was so thickly permeated by catalysis that it prompted the observation that Princeton was the only major American university that did not need to offer a course in catalysis, since the students were absorbing it by osmosis. Dean Taylor ascribed catalytic action to "active spots" on vast inert areas of catalyst surfaces, spots so few that they could be rendered inactive by tiny amounts of poisons. This concept also paved the way for other discoveries. The chain reaction theory of inhibition catalysis was elucidated and illustrated with rows of falling dominoes in Princeton in 1928, decades before the domino theory became a political byword.

During this period, Frick Laboratory became world-famous for researches in photochemistry and the mechanisms of chemical reactions. When heavy water was discovered in 1931, and used as a tool in these areas, there was more heavy water (about a test-tube full!) in Frick than anywhere else in the world.

Notable scholars attracted to Princeton during Taylor's chairmanship included N. Howell Furman, president of the American Chemical Society in 1950 and first recipient of its Fisher Award in Analytical Chemistry; the physical chemists Charles P. Smyth and Robert N. Pease, authorities in dipole moments and combustion kinetics, respectively; and the organic chemists, Eugene Pacsu in carbohydrates, and

Everett S. Wallis, who made notable contributions in the areas of molecular rearrangements and especially in hormone research with his pupil Lew Sarett (cortisones) and Nobel Prizeman Edward Kendall (thyroxin and cortisone). For fifteen years, from 1931 to 1946, Henry Eyring was a bright star in the chemistry department firmament, developing the theory of absolute reaction rates and applying it to chemical and biological processes, viscosity, diffusion, and ion transport. A devout Mormon, Eyring left Princeton to become Dean of the University of Utah Graduate School. Arne Tiselius's work in electrophoresis and Willard Libby's in carbon dating were researches initiated in Frick Laboratory for which they were later to receive Nobel Prizes. Arthur Tobolsky's brilliant researches in the field of polymers were unfortunately cut short by his untimely death in 1972.

Lecture demonstrations have been a Princeton heritage since the days of Dr. Maclean. As early as 1795 the trustees allocated £2000 for additions to the library and for "philosophical apparatus" for Dr. Maclean's demonstrations. From Dr. Maclean's share of this generous allotment—eight times the president's annual salary—the sum of 75 cents had to be used to pay a fine that the College incurred for transporting Maclean's equipment from Philadelphia on a Sunday. Later, the trustees purchased extensive chemical apparatus from one of Maclean's successors, John Torrey (q.v.), another medical doctor, who lectured to the students on chemistry and natural history from 1830 to 1854. Princeton alumni will recall interesting lectures in organic chemistry by Fred Neher, Gregg Dougherty, and Everett Wallis, and also the lively lecture demonstra-

tions in freshman chemistry by William Foster, Alan Menzies, Charles Smyth, Hubert Alyea, and John Turkevich.

During World War II, Taylor and Furman journeyed daily to Columbia University, where Taylor was associate director of that branch of the Manhattan project. Charles Smyth was a member of the ALSOS mission sent to Europe by General Grove ("alsos" is Greek for "grove") to search for German secret weapons. Under the Government Engineering Science and Management Training Program, all members of the department conducted, in Newark, Elizabeth, and Bound Brook, graduate courses for over 3,000 chemists in industry.

The postwar years brought radical changes to the department, because the making and manipulation of molecules now required expensive machines, costly to operate. The annual chemistry budget for operating expenses, exclusive of maintenance, which was $30,000 from 1920 to 1950, rose to nearly $2,000,000 by 1968, much of this for project research.

By the late 1950s Dean Taylor's colleagues had passed on; a new staff was assembled by Donald Hornig, who was chairman from 1958 to 1964. A large new wing, generous gift of an anonymous donor, doubled the research space in Frick in 1964, and housed a biochemistry faculty that later formed a separate department (q.v.).

The chemistry department is not large; there are approximately twenty faculty, thirty seniors, and eighty graduate students. But it teaches nearly a thousand undergraduates each year, many of them premedical students and engineers. The postdoctoral research group grew from only a few in 1950 to over sixty in 1974.

The current faculty, composed of experienced young men and distinguished older chemists, has a variety of interests. Whereas the group associated with Dean Taylor were most active in physical chemistry, a major new area of strength is now in organic and organometallic chemistry. Of the senior faculty, Professors Kurt Mislow, Edward Taylor, and Maitland Jones, Jr., are synthesizing new organic molecules, some mirror images of one another, some containing foreign atoms of sulfur, silicone, phosphorus, or thallium; and still others with unusual ring arrangements or special configurations to reveal significant functional groups. The physical chemists, Professors John Turkevich, Walter Kauzmann, Leland Allen, Donald McClure, Victor Laurie, and Robert Naumann, are investigating the nature and strengths of chemical bonds, submicroscopic molecular arrangements, catalytic effects, electronic and photochemical processes, proteins, and nuclear transmutations.

Modern instruments in the Frick Laboratory include numerous spectrometers (infrared, ultraviolet, microwave, Raman, and laser-Raman beams); also Nuclear Magnetic Resonance, Electron Spin Resonance, and gas chromatographic, molecular beam, electron-microscope, mass spectrometer, and x-ray instruments. A variety of advanced computers are kept busy interpreting data, or suggesting novel methods for synthesizing new molecules.

From the researches of these chemists, their colleagues, and their students, there will doubtless issue, to return to the words of Dean Taylor,

. . . new findings, new discoveries, new ideas . . . to keep bright the tradition of progress in scientific

truth which Maclean initiated at Princeton.

Hubert N. Alyea

Chinard, Gilbert (1881-1972), first permanent Meredith Howland Pyne Professor of French Literature and a leading authority on Franco-American relations, was born in France and trained at the University of Bordeaux and the Sorbonne. He came to the United States in 1908 and taught at Brown, the University of California, and Johns Hopkins before joining the Princeton faculty in 1937. He occupied the Pyne chair until his retirement in 1950 and continued to live in Princeton until his death shortly after his ninetieth birthday.

His *Thomas Jefferson, The Apostle of Americanism* (1929) and his *Honest John Adams* (1933) were acclaimed by critics as the most readable one-volume biographies of their subjects. Another major work was his *L'Apotheosis de Benjamin Franklin*, published in Paris in 1955. He wrote and edited more than forty books and published almost two hundred articles and reviews, mostly on Chateaubriand, Thomas Jefferson, and Frenchmen in America. He sent a copy of the bibliography of his writings that appeared in the *Library Chronicle* in 1965 to a former student inscribed: "en souvenir d'un demisiecle de vagabondage litteraire." The "vagabondage," a colleague later observed, expressed well Chinard's characteristics as a scholar: "the extensiveness of his interests, the richness of his knowledge, the alertness of his imagination . . . the ease and grace with which he achieved new and lively insights. What he collected in his intellectual wanderings in the history of France and the United States will stand at the top of all research in Franco-American relations."

His associates found him "a man of great conviction, courage, and integrity, with a . . . keen wit and humor." They liked to recall his characteristically modest "I discovered it tout à fait par hasard," which, one of them said, "always announced a wondrously productive chance."

Chinard was accorded signal honors both in America and in France. He was president of the Modern Language Association of America, a member of the American Philosophical Society, a fellow of the American Academy of Arts and Sciences, a commander of the Legion of Honor, and a laureate of the French Academy. He was awarded Princeton's honorary degree of Doctor of Humane Letters in 1959.

Christian Art, The Index of, in McCormick Hall records all known works of Christian art produced before 1400. Originated by Professor Charles Rufus Morey (q.v.) in 1917 with a shoebox full of file cards, the Index has grown to a collection of 100,000 photographs of works of art and a file of over 500,000 cards, which catalogue and analyze iconographically these art works.

The Index has expedited and clarified scholarly investigations, earning a reputation as an incomparable humanistic research tool for medieval scholars as well as art historians. For example: A scholar cataloguing a European museum collection, anxious to date a cross holding the key to identification of other objects, wrote to the Christian Art Index as well as to the director of another museum, reputed to have a similar cross. The museum director confirmed the likeness of the crosses, supplied a date, and expressed surprise

at the inquiry—he had thought his the only existing one of its kind. The Princeton Index, however, sent the scholar photostatic reproductions of seven other crosses, similar in all essential details, and cited a publication that convincingly dated the execution two centuries earlier than the museum director had.

Alison Smith MacDonald did the first formal cataloguing from 1918 to 1920. Phila Calder Nye, director from 1920 to 1933, kept the project going, when funds were lacking, with voluntary assistance from nine women (known as the Nine Muses). In the twenties the Index acquired an endowment of $200,000; in the thirties its resources were further increased by expendable gifts of $156,000. Helen Woodruff, director from 1933 to 1942, worked out the form for recording descriptive and bibliographical information that has been the Index's hallmark ever since. William L. M. Burke was director from 1942 to 1951. Rosalie B. Green succeeded him in 1951.

So helpful has the Index been in saving scholars hours—even weeks or months—of research time, that four complete copies have been made available elsewhere: at Dumbarton Oaks in Washington, D.C. (1940), at the Vatican (1951), at the University of Utrecht in the Netherlands (1962), at the University of California, Los Angeles (1964).

Martha Lou Stohlman

Christian Student, The, was the name undergraduates gave a statue that stood on the lawn just south of Pyne Library, diagonally across from Murray-Dodge Hall, in the years immediately before and after World War I. The life-size bronze statue, depicting an undergraduate in football uniform, an academic gown slung over his shoulder, a pile of books in his left arm, was a memorial likeness of W. Earl Dodge 1879, leader of a group of students who formed the Intercollegiate Y.M.C.A. in 1876 in nearby East College (q.v.). Remembered by his classmates as "'79's great hero of college days," captain of the championship football team, president of the student religious organization, the Philadelphian Society, an honor student who graduated near the top of his class, Earl Dodge died suddenly at the age of twenty-five. The statue was given by his brother Cleveland H. Dodge 1879.

The "Christian Student" was the work of Daniel Chester French, who also did the figures of Joseph Henry and Benjamin Franklin flanking the entrance to Palmer Hall, and John Harvard in Cambridge, Alma Mater at Columbia, and Lincoln in the Lincoln Memorial at Washington, D.C. Erected in 1913, the statue was twice torn down: the first time in 1929 by some seniors during a spree the night of Commencement; the second time in 1930 as one of several episodes during a riot that grew out of a football rally (those found chiefly responsible were expelled for a year). The second time it was torn down, the statue was put in storage; it was later placed on permanent loan at Stockbridge, Massachusetts, in the Daniel Chester French Museum, which was subsequently turned over to the National Trust for Historic Preservation.

Civil Engineering, the oldest kind of non-military engineering—it was so named to differentiate it from the military variety—was first taught at Princeton in 1875 by Charles McMillan (q.v.), the first engineering professor in the newly established John C. Green School of Science, and the founder of the department that the *Princeton Engineer* many years later called "the granddad of the School of Engineering."

McMillan educated the earliest generation of Princeton civil engineers single-handedly, but as enrollment grew, additional appointments were needed, and within fifteen years he had been joined by three others who were to follow life-long careers in the department. Frederick Newton Willson, like McMillan a graduate of Rensselaer, organized the department's work in graphics in 1880 and taught that subject for forty-three years; much interested in the construction of bridges, he celebrated his eightieth birthday on the catwalk atop one of the towers of the Golden Gate bridge. One of McMillan's first four students, Herbert Stearns Squier Smith (known to generations of students as H2S Smith) taught applied mechanics, water supply, and hydraulics for forty years; he was secretary of the civil engineering faculty for most of his career (and secretary of the Princeton Class of 1878 for sixty-two years). Another McMillan student, Walter Butler Harris 1886 (who, while still an undergraduate, designed and built the first jetty on the Atlantic coast), taught railroad engineering and surveying for forty-five years and by the time of his retirement in 1934 had left his mark by laying out a large part of the newer University campus and designing twenty-five faculty houses in the Broadmead area.

Charles McMillan retired in 1914 and was succeeded as chairman by Frank H. Constant, who served until 1937. The year of McMillan's retirement also marked the arrival of George E. Beggs (q.v.) who became internationally known for his pioneering work in the model analysis of bridges and other structures. Beggs was the mainstay of the departmental program in structural engineering, which was further strengthened in the late thirties and early forties by the addition of Gregory P. Tschebotarioff in soil mechanics and Hans F. Winterkorn in soil physics.

Beggs followed Constant as chairman, serving for two years until his death in 1939. He was succeeded by Philip Kissam (1939 to 1946) and Elmer K. Timby, who resigned in 1949 to enter private practice. Like his old teacher Professor Harris, Kissam initiated hundreds of undergraduates into the techniques of surveying during his forty-four years in the department. The chairman from 1950 to 1961 was W. Mack Angas, who, as a vice-admiral in the United States Navy, had supervised the construction of sixteen bases by the "seabees" in the Southwest Pacific during World War II, and who, at Princeton, founded the department's River and Harbor Program, which flourished during the fifties and sixties.

A change in the departmental structure came in 1966, when the department merged with the geological engineering department, which had been founded in 1922 and had been particularly strong during the fourteen-year chairmanship (1940-1955) of Blair Professor of Geology W. Taylor Thom, Jr. The Department of Civil and Geological Engineering, which resulted from the merger, continued until 1974, when geological engineering became a program within the Department of Civil Engineering under the direction of William E. Bonini (a member of both the civil engineering and the geological and geophysical sciences departments).

Another interdepartmental plan of study brought under the aegis of the department at this time was the Basic Engineering Program, first instituted in 1938 by Kenneth Condit to meet the needs of students wishing to prepare for administrative and economic phases of an engineering career in industry or government. Most recently, basic engineering has been supervised by Howard Menand, Jr. (director from 1964 until his retirement in 1977), and since 1977 by P. Michael Lion, chairman of the interdepartmental committee in charge of the program.

Norman Sollenberger's ten-year chairmanship (1961-1971) was marked by substantial expansion of the department's Ph.D. program and the recruitment of new faculty, reinforcing Princeton's strong tradition in structural engineering while developing a new theoretical undergirding in mechanics.

Those added in structural engineering included Robert H. Scanlan (an authority on vibrations and structural dynamics), David P. Billington (thin shell concrete structures), and Robert Mark (experimental stress analysis). Billington and Mark, who also teach in the School of Architecture and Urban Planning, have been particularly concerned with developing fruitful relations between humanistic and engineering teaching and research, involving, for example, structures of historical and cultural interest such as bridges and Gothic cathedrals.

Increased strength was brought to the department's research and instruction in mechanics—the other part of its current graduate program in structures and mechanics—by the addition of Ahmet S. Cakmak (a specialist in the mechanics of materials), Peter C. Y. Lee (elasticity theory), and, later, A. Cemal Eringen (theory of mixtures).

Another addition to the department under Sollenberger's chairmanship was J. Stuart Hunter, a specialist in the use of statistical methods for problem solving and decision making in engineering, and also a leader in the Basic Engineering Program.

Under Professor Cakmak, who became chairman in 1971, the department gave special attention to strengthening the Program in Water Resources and to the development of a new Transportation Program. Jointly sponsored since the early sixties by the Departments of Civil Engineering and Geological and Geophysical Sciences to contribute to the solution of "the increasingly acute water resources problem attending world population growth," the Water Resources Program was revitalized in the seventies under William E. Bonini and later, George F. Pinder, who came to the department from the United States Geological Survey.

The Transportation Program was organized in 1972 under the aegis of the civil engineering department as a multidisciplinary project involving faculty and students from the School of Engineering and Applied Science, the School of Architecture and Urban Planning, and the Woodrow Wilson School of Public and International Affairs. Directed by Civil Engineering Professor P. Michael Lion, the program has generated a considerable amount of original research, with both student and faculty involvement in a number of outside projects, among them an assessment of transit alternatives for Trenton, commissioned by that city, and an analysis of the Conrail system and its potential as a profit-making venture, commissioned by Congress. More recently, under the direction of Alain L. Kornhauser, the program has ex-

plored ways of increasing the productivity of the railroads in cooperation with shippers, rail management and labor, and the federal government.

In the seventies the Department of Civil Engineering experienced a substantial rise in enrollment—an increase Professor Cakmak attributed to the department's efforts to make its programs relevant to contemporary life and attractive to students interested "in applying their technical knowledge to actual problems of social concern." By 1976-1977 Civil Engineering had risen to fifth place among the thirty-two departments of instruction in the number of undergraduate majors, surpassed only by the traditional leaders, History, English, Economics, and Politics.

As it passed its hundredth birthday, the "granddad" of Princeton engineering appeared quite spry, and not only able but eager to adjust to the times and to join with other disciplines— some younger, some older—in the search for solutions to contemporary problems.

Class of 1912 Pavilion was given by that class in 1965 "in memory of Sanford B. White [1888-1964] beloved class president for many years and one of Princeton's great athletes." Designed by Eldredge Snyder '22, the Pavilion stands between the Pardee and Gulick playing fields south of Guyot Hall, its orange, black, and white striped roof topped by two 1912 pennant weather vanes.

Sanford White was an All-American end who was chiefly responsible for Princeton's winning the Big Three football championship in his senior year. In the Harvard game he picked up a fumble and ran ninety yards for a touchdown and later tackled an opposing runner behind his goal line for a safety to give Princeton an 8 to 6 victory. A week later he recovered a fumble and ran seventy yards for a touchdown to achieve a 6 to 3 victory over Yale. White also played a big part in Princeton's Big Three baseball championships of 1910, 1911, and 1912 as shortstop and cleanup man in the batting order. Against Yale in 1912, he scored five runs, pulled down a line drive and took part in two double plays. In later life White was secretary of the International Harvester Company in Chicago.

Classics at Princeton is coeval with the College itself. The first of the rules drawn up by President Aaron Burr in 1748 went as follows:

> None may expect to be admitted into College but such as being examined by the President and Tutors shall be found able to render Virgil and Tully's Orations into English; and to turn English into true and grammatical Latin; and to be so well acquainted with the Greek as to render any part of the four Evangelists in that language into Latin or English; and to give the grammatical connexion of the words.

The emphasis on classics in eighteenth-century education at Princeton —and its diurnal rigor—is well set forth in a letter dated February 13, 1750, from freshman Joseph Shippen of Philadelphia to his father: "But I must give you an account of my studies at the present time. At seven in the morning we recite to the President lessons in the works of Xenophon in Greek, and in Watt's 'Ontology.' The rest of the morning, until dinner time, we study Cicero *de Oratore* and the Hebrew Grammar."

Throughout the nineteenth century, classical studies, like the College, flourished *Dei sub Numine*. Of the twenty or more professors, adjunct professors, and senior tutors who taught the subject, nine were Doctors of Divinity, and (a further sign of grace) thirteen were College of New Jersey Bachelors of Arts. In the first half of the century there was only one Ph.D. (from Göttingen); in the last half there were relatively many. Princeton was moving toward university status. As early as 1869 a fellowship had been established for advanced study in classics.

Prominent classicists in the 1880s were Samuel R. Winans, Andrew Fleming West, and John H. Westcott. The history of the modern department begins with these three. Winans, a future dean of the faculty, became Professor of Greek in 1883; West, Professor of Latin in 1883 and Professor of Pedagogics in 1885. Westcott became Professor of Latin in 1889. Later, as head of the department under Woodrow Wilson, Westcott guided it to prominence with excellent appointments of numerous young men of great promise, many of whom became distinguished scholars: William Kelly Prentice (1900) in Greek history, epigraphy, and archaeology; David Magie (1905) in Roman history; Duane R. Stuart (1905) in Latin literature and ancient biography. West, raconteur par excellence, persuader supreme of powerful alumni, was already head of the Graduate School when Wilson became president of the University. Their clash over the location of the Graduate College reverberated for many years. In 1907 Frank Frost Abbott and Edward Capps were called from the University of Chicago. Abbott gave strength in Roman historical studies and Capps brought renown in Greek drama, epigraphy, and archaeology. Capps was also a man of affairs: American Red Cross commissioner in Greece 1918-19; United States Minister to Greece 1920-22; organizer of the American excavation of the Athenian *Agora* begun in 1930 under Professor T. Leslie Shear.

In 1912, the year John Grier Hibben became president, Allen Chester Johnson joined the faculty. He was a Roman historian and an outstanding papyrologist, cataloguer of the Greek papyri in the Princeton collection, and editor of the Princeton studies in papyrology. In 1919, the department gained Paul Coleman-Norton in Roman studies and Shirley Weber in Greek studies; Weber left in 1940 to become librarian of the Gennadeion of the American School in Athens.

The first quarter of the twentieth century was a time of national prestige for the department and of its greatest power within the University. Even as late as 1929, all Liberal Arts freshmen (400 of them) had to offer four years of Latin for admission and take a fifth year in college—vestiges of a fading educational elitism, it has been said. In 1930 the requirement was abolished; Classics ceased being a vested interest and thus gained freedom to prosper on its own merits.

In 1927, Arthur L. Wheeler, specialist in Roman drama, was called from Bryn Mawr to take over the chairmanship of the department from Capps. He was succeeded in 1932 by Duane R. Stuart. The late twenties and the thirties brought judicious appointments such as those of Whitney J. Oates, Greek philosophy, founder of the Special Program in the Humanities and of the Council of the Humanities, originator of the idea of the Woodrow Wilson Fellowship Program; Francis R.B. Godolphin, literary criticism, Roman elegy,

English literature and the Classics; John V.A. Fine, Greek history, mentor of graduate students; George E. Duckworth, Roman drama and ancient epic. Under their guidance the department emphasized the development of "service" courses that made available, in translation, the values and ideas embodied in the classics. While the concentrators became fewer, those who made significant, meaningful contact with classical culture became far more numerous.

After World War II Godolphin became dean of the college and Oates became chairman of the department. In the following years there were added to the staff Anthony Raubitschek, Greek studies; Frank C. Bourne, Roman history and law; Robert D. Murray, Greek tragedy and lyric poetry; Robert F. Goheen (later president of Princeton) Greek drama; and James I. Armstrong (who not much later became president of Middlebury College) Homeric studies. In the fifties, and most of the sixties, departmental graduate studies flourished. Under the leadership of Erik Sjöqvist and Richard Stillwell of Art and Archaeology the Program in Classical Archaeology, enthusiastically supported by the department, grew strong. The department made new affiliations on the graduate level with linguistics, philosophy, and comparative literature. Close ties were maintained with Classics at the Institute for Advanced Study; many of its members, such as Harold Cherniss in Greek philosophy, Benjamin Meritt in Greek epigraphy, and Homer Thompson in archaeology, contributed seminars in various years. Princeton became, and still remains, a world center for classical studies.

In 1961 Samuel D. Atkins, whose field is Indo-European and classical lin-

guistics, succeeded to the chairmanship. A new generation moved to tenure in this decade. David Furley was
called from the University of London to
help run the Program in Classical Philosophy. Arthur Hanson, Latin literature, and W. Robert Connor, Greek
history, came from the University of
Michigan. T. James Luce was added in
Roman studies, John Keaney in Greek
studies, and Bernard Fenik in Homeric
studies. The department survived the
generation gap, student alienation,
and proliferating permissiveness.

A brave new world started in the
seventies. With the advent of coeducation, the University enrollment was
larger and so too was the department's.
Ann L. Bergren, Lois V. Hinckley,
Janet M. Martin, and Carroll Moulton
were added at the Junior level. Janet
Martin's subsequent promotion to Associate Professor made her the first
woman to attain tenure rank in the department. Edward J. Champlin and
James E. Zetzel later joined the junior
staff, and Froma I. Zeitlin came as Associate Professor. Interest flourished in
medieval studies and in comparative
literature, and the graduate program
remained healthy despite severe pressures on academic hiring. Under the
able leadership of W. Robert Connor,
chairman from 1972 to 1977, the department maintained its national profile. T. James Luce became chairman in
1977. Always keeping in mind the
Greek admonitions *meden agan* (nothing in excess!) and *euphemeite* (speak
with silence!), one may, with caution,
say that the future appears promising.

Samuel D. Atkins

Cleveland, Grover (1837-1908) and his
wife first visited Princeton in October
1896, when he made an address at the
Sesquicentennial Celebration. At that
time, too, began his friendship with
Andrew Fleming West, the chief organizer of the celebration, who was later to
be dean of the graduate school. The
Clevelands liked Princeton so much
they decided to live here at the close of
his second term as president. With Professor West's help, Cleveland arranged
for the purchase of a colonial mansion
surrounded by spacious grounds at 15
Hodge Road which he named "Westland."

The Clevelands moved into Westland in March 1897, and soon took a
central place of honor and affection in
the community. During their visit at
the Sesquicentennial they had re-
viewed a torchlight procession of
alumni and students from the steps of
Nassau Hall; one of the signs the undergraduates carried read "Grover,
send your boys to Princeton." This invitation was somewhat premature since
the three Cleveland children were all
girls. But the next fall, the Clevelands'
first son, Richard Folsom, was born,
and the undergraduates welcomed his
arrival with an oracular announcement,
on the campus bulletin board, that he
would enter Princeton with the Class of
1919 and play center on a championship football team all four years.*

Westland became the mecca for undergraduate processions after triumphs
in athletics or debating or other times
of student jubilation. Cleveland would
come out on the porch and respond
with a few pleasant words and sometimes even lead a locomotive cheer.
The students paraded to his house
every March 18th to cheer him on his
birthday and when he reached seventy
gave him a silver loving cup, which Professor John Grier Hibben presented on
their behalf. "I feel young at seventy,"
Cleveland told them, "because I have

here breathed the atmosphere of vigorous youth."

The ex-president made many acquaintances and some close friends in the faculty. West was the closest and was a frequent caller at Westland. Hibben also went there often. Paul van Dyke, the historian, was Cleveland's favorite hunting and fishing companion. Cleveland befriended John Finley when he came to Princeton as professor of politics, and built a house for his use in a corner of his spacious grounds. Years later Finley recalled that, as the house was nearing completion, he had discovered water in the cellar. When he felt obliged to mention it Cleveland replied, "Well, my dear fellow, what did you expect, champagne?" Cleveland once heard Woodrow Wilson read Wordsworth's "Character of the Happy Warrior," and it became his favorite poem.

Cleveland presided at Princeton-Yale debates and other campus meetings, and at Commencement each year walked at the head of the academic procession at the side of the president of the university. In 1899 Henry Stafford Little, of the Class of 1844, founded a public lectureship, stipulating that Cleveland should be its incumbent as long as he lived. Cleveland accepted and lectured once or twice each year before capacity audiences in Alexander Hall on such subjects as "The Independence of the Executive," "The Venezuelan Boundary Controversy," "Government in the Chicago Strike."

In the fall of 1901 Cleveland was elected a trustee and thereafter took an active part in University affairs until his death. He thought it "a serious thing to be a trustee of Princeton" and gave painstaking attention to all the details of the operation of the University that came before the board. He spoke for the trustees at Woodrow Wilson's inauguration in 1902 and at the dedication of the Faculty Room in Nassau Hall in 1906. In 1904 he was appointed chairman of the trustees' committee on the graduate school and became a staunch advocate of the plan for its development; he wrote a fellow trustee that it was "laying the foundation of Princeton's largest element of future greatness." He sided with Dean West in his dispute with Woodrow Wilson about the location of the graduate college. Cleveland also opposed Wilson's quad plan, in part because he feared it would delay realization of the graduate college. He sought to influence Andrew Carnegie to contribute to the university's endowment and it was during one of Carnegie's visits to Westland that the scheme of creating a lake for Princeton was first broached.

Cleveland died at Westland on June 24, 1908. The simple funeral services at the house, attended by the family, President Roosevelt, others eminent in the government, and Princeton friends, closed with Henry van Dyke's reading of "The Happy Warrior." ("Who comprehends his trust, and to the same / Keeps faithful with a singleness of aim.") He was buried in the Princeton cemetery.

Woodrow Wilson wrote in his President's Report that the trustees had felt the power of Cleveland's character in all their deliberations, that "there was an unmistakable tonic in mere association with him. . . . He did much more than give the prestige of his great name to the university: he served it with thoughtful intelligence and conscientious devotion."

Cleveland's association with Princeton is commemorated by the Cleveland Tower of the Graduate College, erected in 1913 by popular subscription—"a tower of strength and beauty," ex-President Taft said at its dedication, "and most expressive of his character."

* This prophecy was fulfilled in part. Richard Cleveland *did* enter, and did graduate, with the Class of 1919. But he played football only one year—he was fullback on his freshman team which beat the Yale freshmen—and thereafter concentrated on track. However, his son, Thomas Grover Cleveland '49, was a varsity guard for three years, in two of which the team beat Harvard and Yale.

Clio Hall, originally the home of the Cliosophic Society, was built in 1893 at the same time as its identical neighbor, Whig Hall (q.v.). After the Cliosophic Society merged with the American Whig Society in 1929 to form what is commonly known as Whig-Clio, Clio was used for a variety of purposes and became for a time the home of the Department of Music. In 1963, on the completion of the Woolworth Center for Musical Studies, the building's interior was renovated, and it has since been used by Personnel Services and later also by Career Services.

Coffin, Robert P. Tristram (1892-1955), poet, novelist, and essayist, earned an A.M. at Princeton after graduating from Bowdoin in 1915 and before going to Oxford as a Rhodes Scholar. Two of his poems appeared in a selection of Princeton verse published by Princeton University Press in 1916 and thirteen in another Princeton anthology published by the Press in 1919. While teaching at Wells College and Bowdoin College, Coffin wrote thirty-seven books—poems, novels, biographies, and essays. His *Strange Holiness* won the Pulitzer Prize for poetry in 1935.

College and University Founders. Princeton graduates have been founders or first presidents of the following institutions:

AUSTIN COLLEGE, Sherman, Texas

Daniel Baker 1815 was chiefly responsible for securing its charter in 1849 and was its president from 1853 to 1857. The trustees proposed naming the college for him, but he declined the honor.

BROWN UNIVERSITY, Providence, Rhode Island (1764)

James Manning 1762 was its first president, David Howell 1766 its first tutor, Nassau Hall the model for its first building, and Princeton the source of its original course of study and customs.

DICKINSON COLLEGE, Carlisle, Pennsylvania

Begun as a school in 1773, it was chartered as a college in 1783. Benjamin Rush 1760 was chiefly responsible for securing the charter, for naming the college after his fellow patriot, John Dickinson, and for bringing its first president from Scotland. A century and a half later, in 1933, the college honored him by naming a large addition to its grounds, the Benjamin Rush Campus.

HAMILTON COLLEGE, Clinton, New York

The Rev. Samuel Kirkland 1765, missionary to the Oneida Indians, in 1793, with the help of Alexander Hamilton, founded the Hamilton Oneida Academy which in 1812 was reorganized as Hamilton College.

HAMPDEN-SYDNEY COLLEGE, Hampden-Sydney, Va.

In 1776 the Rev. Samuel Stanhope Smith 1769 founded and became first rector of Hampden-Sydney Academy, which was chartered as a college in 1783. When he returned to Princeton as professor of moral philosophy in 1779, his brother John Blair Smith 1773 succeeded him as president. Five of the original trustees were Princeton graduates, among them James Madison 1771.

HOBART COLLEGE, Geneva, New York

John Henry Hobart 1793, Protestant Episcopal Bishop of New York, led a movement in 1822 to reorganize Geneva Academy, begun in 1796, as Geneva College. In 1852 the College was renamed in his honor.

UNIVERSITY OF NORTH CAROLINA, Chapel Hill, N.C.

William Richardson Davie 1776 is called "the Father of the University." In 1789 as a member of the state legislature he drafted and introduced the bill that established "the first state university in the United States to open its doors to students." Later he was chiefly responsible for locating the university and providing for its future development. Joseph Caldwell 1791 was the first president. Two academic buildings across the street from each other are named for Davie and Caldwell. Caldwell is also memorialized by a shaft of marble in the center of the North Quadrangle. An old poplar tree under which, according to legend, Davie and his associates rested after surveying many sites and there decided to locate the University in Chapel Hill, is called the Davie Poplar.

OHIO UNIVERSITY, Athens, Ohio

Chartered in 1804, opened in 1808. The Rev. Jacob Lindly 1800 was the first member of its faculty and administered its affairs until 1822. The College's first two buildings were erected under his direction; one of them, ac-cording to tradition, was patterned after Nassau Hall. A college hall of more recent construction is named for him.

TRANSYLVANIA COLLEGE, Lexington, Kentucky

The Rev. John Todd 1749 and the Rev. Caleb Wallace 1770 were influential in securing a charter and endowment for Transylvania Seminary in 1783, and David Rice 1761 was the first chairman of its trustees. It became Transylvania University in 1798; since 1915 it has been called a college.

TUSCULUM COLLEGE, Greenville, Tennessee

The Rev. Hezekiah Balch 1766 was the first president of Greenville College in 1794. The Rev. Samuel Doak 1775 founded Tusculum Academy, later chartered as Tusculum College, in 1819. After the Civil War, the two colleges united and came to be known as Tusculum College.

UNION COLLEGE, Schenectady, New York

The Rev. Dirck Romeyn 1765 provided the leadership for the founding of Schenectady Academy in 1785 and for its reorganization as Union College in 1795. John Blair Smith 1773 was the first president of the college.

UNITED NATIONS UNIVERSITY, Tokyo, Japan

James M. Hester '46, who served as president of New York University from 1962 to 1975, became rector of the United Nations University at its founding in September 1975.

WASHINGTON AND JEFFERSON COLLEGE, Washington, Pa.

The Rev. John MacMillan 1772 and the Rev. Thaddeus Dod 1773 founded Washington Academy, later chartered as Washington College, in 1787. The Rev. John Watson 1797 was first president of Jefferson College (1802). The two colleges united in 1865.

WASHINGTON AND LEE UNIVERSITY, Lexington, Va.

Begun in 1749 as Augusta Academy, it was called Liberty Hall in 1776, Liberty Hall Academy in 1782, Washington Academy (following a gift from George Washington) in 1798, Washington College in 1813, and Washington and Lee University (following Robert E. Lee's presidency) in 1871. The Rev. William Graham 1773, a Princeton classmate and friend of Light-Horse Harry Lee, was in charge of the institution from 1774 to 1796 and its first president after its incorporation. "To his exertions, more than to those of any other one man," Henry Howe wrote in *Historical Collections of Virginia* (1845), "the institution owes its establishment, and its continuance during . . . troublous times."

College and University Presidents. Colleges and universities that have been headed by presidents who attended Princeton number more than a hundred, in thirty-six states from Alabama to Washington, and in seven foreign countries: China, Egypt, Greece, India, Lebanon, Pakistan, and Turkey. Those with significant Princeton associations include:

ALLAHABAD CHRISTIAN COLLEGE, Allahabad, India
Sam Higginbottom '03 (1932-1950)

AMERICAN UNIVERSITY, Beirut, Lebanon
Bayard Dodge '09 (1923-1948)

BROWN UNIVERSITY, Providence, Rhode Island
James Manning 1762 (1765-1791)
Howard R. Swearer '54 (1977-   )

CENTRE COLLEGE, Danville, Kentucky
William C. Roberts 1855 (1898-1903)
Walter A. Groves A.M. '23 (1947-1957)

CHARLESTON, COLLEGE OF, Charleston, S.C.
Elijah D. Rattoone 1787 (1809-1810)
William P. Finley 1820 (1845-1857)

COLGATE UNIVERSITY, Hamilton, New York
Everett N. Case '22 (1942-1962)

COLORADO COLLEGE, Colorado Springs, Colorado
Charles C. Mierow '05 (1925-1934)
Thurston J. Davies '16 (1934-1948)

CONNECTICUT COLLEGE, New London, Connecticut
Charles E. Shain '36 Ph.D. '49 (1962-1974)

CORNELL UNIVERSITY, Ithaca, New York
Livingston Farrand 1888 (1921-1937)
James A. Perkins Ph.D. '37 (1963-1969)

DARTMOUTH COLLEGE, Hanover, New Hampshire
John G. Kemeny '46 Ph.D. '49 (1970-   )

DICKINSON COLLEGE, Carlisle, Pennsylvania
John McKnight 1773 (1815-1816)
William Neill 1803 (1824-1829)

DREXEL INSTITUTE OF TECHNOLOGY, Philadelphia, Pennsylvania
James Creese '18 (1945-1963)

FORMAN CHRISTIAN COLLEGE, Lahore, Pakistan
Rhea McC. Ewing '24 (1950-1968)

HOBART COLLEGE, Geneva, New York
Robert G. Hinsdale 1856 (1876-1883)
William A. Eddy '17 (1936-1941)

ILLINOIS COLLEGE, Jacksonville, Illinois
William K. Selden '34 (1953-1955)

KENYON COLLEGE, Gambier, Ohio
William B. Bodine 1860 (1877-1891)
Philip H. Jordan, Jr. '54 (1975-   )

LAFAYETTE COLLEGE, Easton,
Pennsylvania
William C. Cattell 1848 (1863-1883)
Ethelbert D. Warfield 1882
(1891-1914)

LAKE FOREST COLLEGE, Lake Forest,
Illinois
Daniel S. Gregory 1857 (1879-1886)
William C. Robert 1855 (1886-1893)
Richard D. Harlan 1881 (1901-1906)

LINCOLN UNIVERSITY, Lincoln
University, Pennsylvania
Isaac N. Rendall 1852 (1865-1906)
John B. Rendall 1870 (1906-1924)
William H. Johnson 1888 (1926-1936)
Walter L. Wright 1892 (1936-1945)

LINDENWOOD COLLEGE, St. Charles,
Missouri
Addison V. Schenck 1843 (1857-1862)
Jeremiah H. Nixon 1851 (1871-1876)
John A. Brown Jr. Ph.D. '52
(1966-   )

MASSACHUSETTS INSTITUTE OF
TECHNOLOGY, Cambridge. Mass.
Karl T. Compton Ph.D. '12
President 1930-1948; Chairman
of the Corporation 1948-1954)

MIDDLEBURY COLLEGE, Middlebury,
Vermont
James I. Armstrong '41 Ph.D. '49
(1963-1975)

NASHVILLE, UNIVERSITY OF, Nashville,
Tennessee
Thomas B. Craighead 1775
(1786-1806)
Philip Lindsly 1804 (1824-1850)

NEW YORK UNIVERSITY, New York
City
Jacob R.T. Frelinghuysen 1804
(1839-1850)
James M. Hester '46 (1962-1975)
John C. Sawhill '58 (1975-   )

OBERLIN COLLEGE, Oberlin, Ohio
William E. Stevenson '22
(1946-1959)
Robert W. Fuller Ph.D. '61
(1970-   )

OCCIDENTAL COLLEGE, Los Angeles,
California
Elbert N. Condit 1873 (1894-1896)
James W. Parkhill 1880 (1896-1897)
Silas Evans A.M. '00 (1917-1921)

OGLETHORPE COLLEGE, Atlanta,
Georgia
Samuel K. Talmage 1820 (1841-1865)
Thornwell Jacobs A.M. 1899
(1915-1943)

PENNSYLVANIA, UNIVERSITY OF,
Philadelphia, Pennsylvania
John Ewing 1754 (1779-1802)
Gaylord P. Harnwell Ph.D. '27
(1953-1970)

RICHMOND, UNIVERSITY OF,
Richmond, Virginia
George M. Modlin Ph.D. '32
(President, 1946-1971;
Chancellor 1971-   )

RIPON COLLEGE, Ripon, Wisconsin
Silas Evans A.M. '00 (1911-1917,
1921-1943)
Clark G. Kuebler g-33 (1943-1954)
Bernard S. Adams '50 (1966-   )

ROBERT COLLEGE, Istanbul, Turkey
Walter L. Wright Jr. '21 Ph.D. '28
(1935-1944)

ROCKEFELLER UNIVERSITY, New York,
N.Y.
Frederick Seitz Ph.D. '34
(1968-   )

RUTGERS UNIVERSITY, New
Brunswick, N.J.
William Linn 1772 (1791-1794)
Ira Condict 1784 (1794-1810)
Jacob R.T. Frelinghuysen 1804
(1850-1861)
Robert C. Clothier '08 (1932-1951)

TEMPLE UNIVERSITY, Philadelphia,
Pennsylvania
  Charles E. Beury '03 (1926-1941)
TUSCULUM COLLEGE, Greenville,
Tennessee
  Hezekiah Balch 1766 (1794-1810)
  George K. Davies '22 (1946-1950)
UNION COLLEGE, Schenectady, New
York
  John Blair Smith 1773 (1795-1799)
  Jonathan Edwards 1765 (1799-1801)
WASHINGTON AND JEFFERSON
COLLEGE, Washington, Pennsylvania
  John Watson 1797 (1802)
  James Dunlap 1773 (1803-1812)
  James H. Case Jr. '29 (1946-1950)
WELLS COLLEGE, Aurora, New York
  William E. Weld A.M. '09
    (1936-1946)
  Richard L. Greene Ph.D. '29
    (1946-1950)
WEST VIRGINIA, UNIVERSITY OF,
Morgantown, West Virginia
  Eli M. Turner 1868 (1885-1893)
  John R. Turner Ph.D. '13
    (1928-1935)
WESTMINSTER COLLEGE, Fulton,
Missouri
  William W. Hall Jr. '25 (1947-1955)
WILSON COLLEGE, Chambersburg,
Pennsylvania
  Ethelbert D. Warfield 1882
    (1915-1936)
  Paul S. Havens '25 (1936-1970)

College of New Jersey was Princeton's legal name during its first one hundred and fifty years. But the College was usually referred to as Nassau or Nassau Hall or Princeton College after it moved to Princeton in 1756. In the 1860s the College baseball team used the name "Nassau"; starting in 1870 all athletic teams were designated "Princeton." On October 22, 1896, the anni-

versary of the signing of the College's first charter, at the climax of the Sesquicentennial Celebration, President Patton announced that "from this moment what heretofore for one hundred and fifty years has been known as the College of New Jersey shall in all future time be known as Princeton University."

Collins, Varnum Lansing (1870-1936), who is gratefully remembered for his research and writing in Princeton history, was graduated from Princeton in 1892. In college he was the leader of the Glee Club, chairman of the Bric-a-Brac, and an editor of the Nassau Lit. He served his Alma Mater as reference librarian, preceptor, professor of French, clerk of the faculty, and, finally, as Secretary of the University from 1917 until his death in 1936.

Collins wrote an account of the Continental Congress at Princeton (1908), a history of the University (1914), a guide to the campus and the town (1919), and a two-volume biography of John Witherspoon (1925). "More than any other person," the *Alumni Weekly* said when he died, "he has given us a sense of Princeton's living continuity."

Colors. Princeton's orange and black came into use soon after the Civil War. On April 5, 1866, a freshman named George K. Ward 1869 observed at a class meeting that many other colleges had their distinctive colors but Princeton had none, and he suggested that orange would be appropriate since William III of the House of Nassau, in whose honor the first building had been named, was also Prince of Orange. His suggestion met with instant favor with his classmates but failed to win general approval in the other classes. Ward persisted, however, and a little over a year later, on June 26, 1867, when his teammates in the Class of 1869 Base Ball Club assembled at Princeton Junction for their trip to New Haven to play the Yale Class of 1869, he provided them all with badges of orange ribbon with " '69 B.B.C." printed on them in black ink. It proved an auspicious occasion for the first recorded use of Princeton's colors. Sporting their badges, the team had a pleasant trip by train to New York and overnight on the steamer "Elm City" up Long Island Sound to New Haven; heard a speech by President Andrew Johnson who was making a tour of New England and happened to be in New Haven; came from behind with two runs in the ninth inning to win, 19 to 18; and, still wearing their badges, had supper with their Yale opponents at a New Haven hotel where the Yale players magnanimously sang "Oh, here's to Nassau Hall / For she's bully at baseball!"

More general and formal use of Princeton's colors came a year later. In response to a petition from all four undergraduate classes, the Faculty on October 12, 1868 resolved to permit students "to adopt and wear as the College Badge an orange colored Ribbon bearing upon it the word 'Princeton.' " Two weeks later at the inauguration of James McCosh as eleventh president of the College, such badges, arranged for by the Class of 1869, were much in evidence and the use of orange (with black printing) became official.

The combination of orange and black was accidental and the two colors were not associated in the undergraduates' minds until the fall of 1873 when a freshman named William Libbey, Jr., 1877, on a dare from his classmate, Melancthon W. Jacobus, sported a necktie made of yellow and black silk which he had seen advertised in Cambridge, England, the preceding summer, as "The Duke of Nassau's colors." His wearing of the necktie was used as evidence to prove Princeton's prior right to the colors to a committee from Rutgers that had become interested in orange and black. The following spring, Libbey arranged through his father, a New York merchant, for the manufacture in a Paterson silk mill of a thousand yards of orange and black ribbon for use at an intercollegiate rowing regatta in Saratoga, N.Y., on July 15, 1874. He gave pieces of the ribbon to members of the freshman crew for hatbands and sent the remainder to a store in the Grand Union Hotel at Saratoga, three miles from the lake where the races were rowed, to be sold as "Princeton's colors." When the Princeton freshmen won the first race, the Class of 1877 commissioned one of its members, who happened to have with him a very fast trotting horse, to hurry to the hotel to buy up all the ribbon, but by the time he arrived every inch had been sold.

Thereafter orange and black appeared in the attire of athletic teams and in 1888 as the title of a song that soon won a place in Princeton lore. In 1896, the year of the Sesquicentennial, the trustees adopted orange and black as the official colors for academic gowns despite a plea by Professor Allan Marquand 1874 that Princeton's colors be changed to orange and *blue*, which he had discovered were the true colors of the House of Nassau (and of the Netherlands whence New York City gets *its* orange and blue). Professor Marquand made a strong case for his proposal, on aesthetic as well as historical grounds, but by now too much sentiment had been attached to the colors that had been in use for several decades to permit giving them up. "It matters not whether we got them by accident or design," the feeling was said to run, "We have them, and will never change them, so long as eye and voice can unite in praise of 'dear old Princeton and the Orange and the Black.' "

Commencement, the ceremony of conferring degrees, marks the end of the academic year, and the beginning of the careers of those graduating. As early as the fourteenth century, at Cambridge University, a student who had passed the requisite examinations was said to "commence Bachelor of Arts (or Master or Doctor)," and the occasion when he took his degree was called commencement.

At Princeton's first commencement, held in 1748 in the Newark "meeting-house" of which President Aaron Burr was pastor, seven persons took degrees: Jonathan Belcher (q.v.), royal governor of the Province of New Jersey, who was awarded an honorary master's degree, and six young men who had passed their examinations for the bachelor's degree. These few "commencers" were the objects of much oratory. At the morning exercises (one of the trustees reported in a New York newspaper), the clerk of the board read *in extenso* the 3700-word royal charter that Governor Belcher had granted the College. In the afternoon, President Burr delivered from memory an "elegant Oration in the Latin Tongue" that lasted three quarters of an hour, and, after public disputations in Latin by the six candidates and the conferring of degrees, the student salutatorian spoke in Latin for half an hour, after which the president prayed in English and dismissed the assembly. These proceedings gave "universal Satisfaction, even the Unlearned being pleased with [their] Solemnity and Decorum."

After the College moved to Prince-

ton in 1756, commencement was held in the prayer hall in Nassau Hall until 1764 when more adequate space became available in the First Presbyterian Church's new building. Latin continued to be the language of choice, but, according to contemporary newspaper accounts, the proceedings were enlivened by an occasional speech in English and by music. In 1760 Benjamin Rush (q.v.) "in a very sprightly and entertaining Manner delivered an ingenious English Harangue in Praise of Oratory," and the graduating seniors sang two compositions by President Samuel Davies.

Under President Witherspoon commencement took on a revolutionary flavor. In 1770 the entire graduating class wore American-made clothes, and in 1771 (when James Madison graduated) Hugh Henry Brackenridge read a prophetic poem on "The Rising Glory of America," which Philip Freneau and he had written. The commencement of 1783 was made memorable by the presence of George Washington and members of the Continental Congress, then meeting in Princeton.

For almost a century, commencement took place in the fall. Coming at the end of the harvest season, the occasion became a public holiday for the entire countryside, and speakers at the exercises in the church (President John Maclean recalled) had to compete with the crowds on the street outside, "drinking, fiddling and dancing, playing for pennies, and testing the speed of their horses." In 1844, on petition of the faculty, the trustees advanced commencement to June.

Exercises continued to be held in the First Church until 1892, when Alexander Hall was completed. Alexander, in turn, was outgrown, and beginning in 1922 commencement was held in front of Nassau Hall except when rain forced the ceremonies indoors.

The modern commencement season lasts almost a week. Alumni begin returning for class reunions on the preceding Wednesday, take part in faculty-alumni forums on Thursday, Friday, and Saturday morning, and the alumni parade (q.v.) on Saturday afternoon. Sunday is given over to the baccalaureate service (q.v.) in the morning, the president's garden party in the afternoon, and a band concert at night. Monday is devoted to class day exercises, departmental receptions for seniors and their families, and at night the senior promenade, held in recent years on the plaza between Jadwin and Fine Halls, with fireworks in nearby Palmer Stadium.

Commencement exercises on Tuesday include an invocation, the singing of "Faith of Our Fathers," the Latin salutatory (q.v.), the conferring of bachelor degrees, the recognition of honors graduates, the valedictory (q.v.), the conferring of master, doctor, and honorary degrees (q.v.), brief remarks by the president, and the singing of "Old Nassau."

These ceremonies, lasting about an hour, follow an academic procession of trustees, faculty, and degree candidates, wearing traditional cap, gown, and hood, brightened by the colors of Princeton and many other universities. They are directed by a dozen faculty marshals in orange silk gowns and black velvet da Vinci caps. Since 1896, when the college became a university, the chief marshal's baton has been wielded by William Libbey, Jr., V. Lansing Collins, Robert M. Scoon, E. Baldwin Smith, Robert W. McLaughlin, Jr., Richard Stillwell, Erling Dorf, E. Dudley H. Johnson, Carlos H. Baker, and David R. Coffin.

Comparative Literature, The Department of, has enjoyed a brief but substantial history at Princeton. The graduate program, which began under an interdepartmental committee in the Council of the Humanities in 1962, gathered a nucleus of four faculty members from 1966 to 1970 and emerged as an independent department in 1975. Its formation was requested by both graduate and undergraduate students, and strengthened by faculty members, who had taught comparative courses in other departments of literature for several years.

At present they form a faculty of fifteen members—thirteen full professors, and two assistant professors supported by funds from the Mellon Foundation. In addition to English, the linguistic coverage of the department consists of the major European languages—French, German, Italian, Russian, Spanish, Latin and Classical Greek; Near and Far Eastern languages will be more effectively represented in the future. The historical range of the faculty leads from antiquity to the modern period.

The department offers an enlarged graduate program and undergraduate concentration in Comparative Literature. The purpose of the graduate program is essentially to train new teachers in the field, that of the undergraduate program to provide a liberal, humanizing discipline for the study of language and literature as a whole. In relation to the Humanities at Princeton, Comparative Literature draws on the specialities of surrounding departments and lends them broad, generalizing kinds of strength. All students are asked to major, in effect, in one literature, and so benefit from the other departments, their faculties and courses; their students, in turn, are invited to enroll in courses in Comparative Literature, forums where central literary issues, regardless of national boundaries, may be discussed.

More specifically, the strengths of the department include the history, theory, and practice of literary criticism, the study of literary forms— particularly narrative forms, the epic and the novel—the classical tradition and the main chronological periods, all considered from an international, intercultural, perspective.

Robert Fagles

Compton Brothers, The, were among the most illustrious alumni of the Princeton Graduate School. All three graduated from the College of Wooster, where their father, a Presbyterian minister, was dean and professor of philosophy, and all three earned their Ph.D.'s at Princeton. Karl T. Compton (1887-1954), who received his Ph.D. in 1912, was professor of physics and chairman of the department at Princeton, and later president and chairman of the corporation of Massachusetts Institute of Technology. Wilson M. Compton (1890-1967), who received his Ph.D. in 1915, taught economics, served the lumber industry and then the federal government as a specialist in forest conservation and timber management, and became president of the State College of Washington, later Washington State University. Arthur H. Compton (1892-1962), who received his Ph.D. in 1916, was a distinguished service professor at the University of Chicago, a Nobel Prize winner in physics (1927), took a leading part in the development of the atomic bomb, and was for a time chancellor of Washington University in St. Louis. The

trustees named one of the two quadrangles which were added to the original Graduate College in 1963 the Compton Quadrangle in their honor.

Wilson M. Compton, then the lone survivor of the three, spoke on their behalf at the dedication of the Compton Quadrangle on May 9, 1964. "I classify all the teachers I have had in three categories," he said, "those I have forgotten, those I have forgiven, and those I will never forget. In the last category I would include Frank Albert Fetter and Edward S. Corwin. My brother Karl, if he were here, would name, I am sure, William F. Magie and O. W. Richardson; my brother, Arthur, William F. Magie and Luther P. Eisenhart."

Computer Center, The, was established in 1962 under Electrical Engineering Professor Edward J. McCluskey, Jr. Located in the Engineering Quadrangle, the first computer was an IBM 7090. Serving primarily the scientific and engineering communities, the computer was enlarged, replaced, and enlarged again to accommodate the rapidly growing demand for service. McCluskey was succeeded as director by Roald Buhler in 1966. Under Buhler's direction, the University, with generous support from the National Science Foundation, built the current Computer Center building at 87 Prospect Avenue, behind Stevenson Hall. Installed in the new building in 1969 was an IBM 360/91, one of the largest and fastest scientific computers available at the time. Buhler stepped down in 1970 yielding the reins to the current director, Dr. James F. Poage '55.

Although designed for research use, the IBM 360/91 also proved adequate to the task of providing service to students and administrators. Convenient remote job entry stations located in various buildings around the campus allow the users to submit work and receive results without traveling to the Computer Center. Princeton joined the modern world of time-sharing in 1975 when it acquired an IBM 370/158. Now users can employ the computer to obtain answers to extremely complex problems almost instantaneously. Graphics terminals are available that plot results immediately on video screens. At the push of a button a printed copy of the plot can be obtained. No longer is it necessary to tediously plot results in a laboratory notebook.

For the individual user, the computers are fun and exciting; for the University, they are indispensable tools in today's research, instruction, and administration.

James F. Poage

Conklin, Edwin Grant (1863-1952), eminent biologist and teacher, came to Princeton from the University of Pennsylvania in 1908, at the invitation of President Woodrow Wilson, to become the first full-time head of the Department of Biology. Chairman for twenty-five years, he organized and guided the early development of the department; as lecturer in the introductory biology course, he inspired thousands of undergraduates; as investigator, he carried out fundmental research both in Guyot Hall and, in the summer, at the Marine Biological Laboratory in Woods Hole, Massachusetts, on the embryonic development of eggs of marine animals. His strong interest in the philosophical implications of biology and particularly of evolution

put him in great demand as a public speaker. At the end of his long life he estimated that he had given at least a thousand lectures before a wide variety of audiences, crusading for the acceptance of the concept of evolution.

He was born in Waldo, Ohio, the son of a busy "horse and buggy doctor." Following his early education in rural schools he entered Ohio Wesleyan University. In great need of money, especially for the purchase of books, he dropped out for half of his third year to teach at a one-room school. In college he was active in debates and oratorical contests. His professor of natural history aroused his interest in collecting and identifying fossils and the shells of mussels and snails; he later asked Conklin to serve as assistant in the museum.

Conklin considered entering the ministry and was ordained as a lay preacher; but, needing money to pay off his debts after graduation, he took a position at Rust University in Mississippi, a missionary college for Negroes, where for three years he taught Latin, Greek, English, history, and all the sciences. He later said he was "glad to have this opportunity for which I longed, to take part in a most necessary and humane work." However, his interest in biology became strong enough for him to choose it for his life work, and he left to enter graduate school at Johns Hopkins.

During the summer of 1890 Conklin was at Woods Hole searching for suitable material for a doctoral thesis in embryology. He chose the easily available eggs of a marine snail and discovered that following fertilization these eggs divide according to a fixed and striking pattern, which enabled him to follow individual cells and their descendants to their final location in the various organs of the larva. Through this "cell lineage" the origin of the larval structures could be traced back to different regions of the egg. In later years he successfully extended these studies to eggs of other marine animals and demonstrated that an undivided egg, far from being a homogeneous mass of protoplasm, possesses a remarkable degree of organization in its cytoplasm. He further refined his investigations through various experimental techniques, such as the isolation of cells, application of centrifugal force and use of salt solutions. At a time when biologists tended to be overawed by the importance of the genes located in the nucleus, he elucidated the role of the cytoplasm of the egg in the early differentiation of the embryo, an essential but much neglected aspect of development.

Conklin's scholarly achievements were recognized by his election to the American Philosophical Society when he was only thirty-four; he was later its executive officer (1936-1942) and president (1942-1945 and 1948-1952), the only member ever elected twice to this high office—the second time at the age of eighty-five. He was also a member of the National Academy of Sciences, president of several scientific societies, and a member of several foreign learned societies and academies.

A deeply religious man, Conklin was much concerned with the relations between science, ethics, and religion, a subject on which he wrote several books, published numerous magazine articles, and gave many speeches. Conklin believed that scientific evidence of man's animal ancestry need not undermine religious faith or belief in human dignity. "The real dignity of man," he once wrote, "consists not in his origin but in what he is and in what he may become." Perhaps the most conclusive statement of his point of view is found among the last words of his brief, posthumously published "spiritual autobiography": "No one can furnish scientific proof of the existence or nature of a divine plan in the fulfillment of which men may cooperate, but it is evident that such an ideal lends strength and courage to mortal men."

However great Conklin's scientific achievements were, his most enduring legacy may have been the personal influence he exerted on those who were fortunate enough to come into close contact with him. His contagious enthusiasm, his deep concern for others, his readiness to encourage and support young people have been decisive factors in many lives.

Gerhard Fankhauser

Constitutional Convention of 1787, The, was attended by more alumni of Princeton than any other American or British institution. Representing their states were nine men who had studied under Presidents Burr, Finley, and Witherspoon:

Alexander Martin 1756 (North Carolina)
William Paterson 1763 (New Jersey)
Oliver Ellsworth 1766 (Connecticut)
Luther Martin 1766 (Maryland)
William C. Houston 1768 (New Jersey)
Gunning Bedford, Jr. 1771 (Delaware)
James Madison 1771 (Virginia)
William R. Davie 1776 (North Carolina)
Jonathan Dayton 1776 (New Jersey)

Five of the college alumni at the convention had attended William and Mary, five Yale,* three Harvard, three Columbia, two the University of Pennsylvania, one Oxford, one Glasgow, and one had studied at three universities in Scotland. (Twenty-five of the fifty-five members of the convention, including George Washington and Benjamin Franklin, had not attended college.) The large number of graduates of Nassau Hall at the convention reflected the wide geographic distribution of its graduates generally. Princeton's alumni were delegates from six states, while Yale (which stood next in this respect) were from four, and all of Harvard's were from Massachusetts. Three of the Princetonians represented New Jersey, two North Carolina, and one each Connecticut, Delaware, Maryland, and Virginia.

Outstanding in the New Jersey delegation was William Paterson (q.v.), described by William Pierce (a Georgia delegate whose notes include interesting character sketches of convention members) as a man of great modesty who always picked the right time and the right way to enter a debate and never spoke "but when he [understood] his subject well."†

William Churchill Houston, previously professor of mathematics and natural philosophy at Princeton, was, at the time of the convention, clerk of the Supreme Court of New Jersey.

Jonathan Dayton, son of a storekeeper in Elizabethtown, had served with distinction in the Revolution, and, at twenty-six, was the convention's youngest delegate. Pierce, an army comrade, said that Dayton had "an impetuosity in his temper" that was injurious to him, but that he also had an "honest rectitude."

Alexander Martin, who headed the North Carolina delegation, had been a colonel in the Revolution, but after having been cleared of court-martial charges of cowardice in the battle of Germantown, had resigned his commission. He was later governor of his state—"a Man of sense," Pierce said, but "no Speaker."

The other Princetonian from North Carolina, William Richardson Davie, a tall and elegant figure, was only thirty. A daring officer in the Revolution he had since become an accomplished lawyer.

Oliver Ellsworth (q.v.), tall, dignified, and commanding, was an able member of the Connecticut delegation. A supreme court judge in that state, he showed himself "a Gentleman of a clear, deep, and copious understanding; eloquent . . . in public debate; and always attentive to his duty."

Gunning Bedford, Jr., who had been class valedictorian in 1771, was attorney general of Delaware. Slender and handsome as a student, he was by 1787, according to Pierce, "very corpulent." He was an impressive speaker, but a nervous one, apt to be hasty and impetuous.

Luther Martin, attorney general of Maryland, was an acknowledged leader of the bar with a prodigious memory that enabled him to win his cases more by weight of precedent and knowledge of law than by his powers of expression. Pierce found him "so extremely prolix, that he never speaks without tiring the patience of all who hear him."

James Madison (q.v.) was an influential member of the distinguished Virginia delegation. "Every Person," Pierce wrote, "seems to acknowledge his greatness. He blends together the profound politician with the Scholar

. . . and tho' he cannot be called an Orator, he is a most agreeable, eloquent, and convincing Speaker. . . . [He is] a Gentleman of great modesty, with a remarkable sweet temper."

PRINCETON'S ROLE
IN THE CONVENTION

Three major proposals were considered by the convention. The Virginia Plan was generally favored by the large states and those laying claim to western land. It sought a strong national government with two legislative houses elected on the basis of population. The New Jersey Plan, favored principally by the small states, called for equal representation of the states in a single legislative body. The Connecticut Compromise, which broke the deadlock, proposed a lower house, elected in proportion to population, and an upper house, in which each state, regardless of size, would have equal representation.

A Princetonian was influential in the formation of each of these proposals. The Virginia Plan was outlined in resolutions presented by Governor Edmund Randolph, but "internal evidence," Yale professor Max Farrand (Princeton 1892) found, "shows much of Madison's handiwork in forming these resolutions."‡ The New Jersey Plan was presented and vigorously defended by William Paterson. Although each of the three delegates from Connecticut has been credited by one writer or another with bringing about the compromise, it was Oliver Ellsworth who made the motion that "in the second branch . . . each State shall have an equal vote," and during the debate he seems to have borne the brunt of the attack on the compromise by the large-state men.

Paterson was supported in his advo-

cacy of the New Jersey Plan by Jonathan Dayton, the junior member of his delegation, Gunning Bedford of Delaware, and Luther Martin of Maryland, all of whom spoke ardently—and sometimes immoderately—on behalf of the small states. At one point Dayton called the Virginia Plan "an amphibious monster." At another, Bedford said that if the large states persisted in the Virginia Plan, the small ones would "find some foreign ally of more honor and good faith," who would "take them by the hand and do them justice." Luther Martin, during a spell of extremely hot weather, delivered a two-day harangue in defense of state sovereignty "with much diffuseness & considerable vehemence," Madison observed in his record of the debates. Martin refused to sign the Constitution and later campaigned unsuccessfully in Maryland against its ratification.

At the conclusion of the convention, Madison sent a copy of the Constitution to Thomas Jefferson in Paris. It was impossible, he wrote Jefferson, "to consider the degree of concord which ultimately prevailed as less than a miracle." Madison's own contributions to this successful outcome were considerable. An important participant in the debates, respected by both allies and opponents as the leader of those favoring a strong national government, he was, in Professor Farrand's words, the "leading spirit" of the convention and the "master builder" of the Constitution.

All of the Princeton delegates except William Churchill Houston (who died of tuberculosis a year after the convention) went on to eventful careers, either in the federal government they had helped to create or in their own states. Most conspicuous, of course, was James Madison, who served the federal government twenty-four years as a member of the House of Representatives, secretary of state, and president. Although he had once said that his labors at the convention had "almost killed" him, he outlived all the other delegates and spent his last years, in his eighties, at Montpelier, receiving visitors and answering letters, still explaining and expounding the Constitution.

* Including Oliver Ellsworth who studied there, 1762-64, before coming to Princeton.

† "Notes of Major William Pierce on the Federal Convention of 1787," in *American Historical Review*, January 1898.

‡ *The Framing of the Constitution of the United States* (Yale University Press, 1913).

Continental Congress, The (1774-1789) numbered among its members Princeton alumni representing all of the colony-states except Massachusetts. The Congress also benefited from the services of two officers of the College: President John Witherspoon, a member for six years, and Trustee Elias Boudinot, president of the Congress in 1782-1783. In the summer and early fall of the latter year, the Congress met in Princeton.

Following is a list of delegates who attended Princeton, compiled from biographical sketches of members of the Continental Congress in the 1972 edition of the *Biographical Directory of the American Congress*, and further supplemented by material in *Princetonians 1748-1768: A Biographical Dictionary*.

CONNECTICUT
Oliver Ellsworth 1766 (1777-1784)
Jesse Root 1756 (1778-1783)
Pierpont Edwards 1768 (1787-1788)

DELAWARE
Gunning Bedford, Jr. 1771
(1783-1785)

GEORGIA
*Joseph Habersham (1783-1784)
*John Habersham (1785)

MARYLAND
*Benjamin Rumsey (1776-1778)
John Henry 1769 (1778-1781,
1784-1787)
Nathaniel Ramsay 1767 (1785-1787)

NEW HAMPSHIRE
Samuel Livermore 1752
(1780-1782, 1785)

NEW JERSEY
Richard Stockton 1748 (1776)
Jonathan D. Sergeant 1762 (1776,
1777)
Nathaniel Scudder 1751
(1777-1779, 1778-1781)
Frederick Frelinghuysen 1770
(1778, 1779, 1782, 1783)
William C. Houston 1768
(1779-1781, 1784, 1785)
William Burnet 1749 (1780-1781)
John Beatty 1769 (1783-1785)
Jonathan Dayton 1776 (1787-1789)

NEW YORK
Walter Livingston 1759 (1784, 1785)

NORTH CAROLINA
*Joseph Hewes (1774-1777, 1779)
Benjamin Hawkins 1777
(1781-1784, 1786, 1787)
Alexander Martin 1756 (1786-1787)

PENNSYLVANIA
Benjamin Rush 1760 (1776, 1777)
Joseph Reed 1757 (1777, 1778)
Jonathan B. Smith 1760 (1777-1778)
Joseph Montgomery 1755
(1780-1782)
James R. Reid 1775 (1787-1789)
Henry Wynkoop 1760 (1779-1783)

RHODE ISLAND
David Howell 1766 (1782-1785)
James Manning 1762 (1785, 1786)

* Although attendance at Princeton was indicated in the *Biographical Directory of the American Congress*, precise confirmation of the fact was not possible when this list was compiled.

Controller, the office of, was established in 1920 with George C. Wintringer as first incumbent. A graduate of the Class of 1894, he returned to Princeton in 1912 to occupy the new office of secretary of business administration, and eight years later took on added duties and assumed the title of controller. The controller and his staff keep the books and collect all monies due the University; they disburse salaries and wages to the faculty and staff and amounts due others for goods and services. When the office was established in 1920, the funds so handled totaled about $1.25 million annually. Fifty years later they were in excess of $70 million.

Controllers have been:

George C. Wintringer 1920-1941
Gail A. Mills 1941-1961
Wilbur M. Young 1961-1975
Raymond J. Clark 1975-

Corwin, Edward S. (1878-1963), third McCormick Professor of Jurisprudence and first chairman of the Department of Politics, was considered the leading expositor of the intent and meaning of the Constitution. Born on a farm near Plymouth, Michigan, he first developed his interest in constitutional law at the University of Michigan, where he was Phi Beta Kappa and president of

the Class of 1900, and at the University of Pennsylvania, where he completed his doctoral work in American history under the guidance of John Bach McMaster (q.v.) in 1905.

It was McMaster who turned Corwin toward Princeton. During a discussion of his "approaching jobless condition" at Sunday evening supper with the McMasters in June of 1905 (Corwin later recalled), his mentor suggested that he "run over to Princeton and apply to Woodrow Wilson for one of those preceptorships they're handing out over there." This he did the next day, armed with an "extraordinarily flowery" letter of introduction from McMaster. Everything proceeded "easily and delightfully" during his interviews with President Wilson and with Professor Winthrop More Daniels, chairman of the Department of History, Politics, and Economics, and several days later he received word that he had been appointed a Princeton preceptor at the salary he had suggested would be necessary "if I was ever to induce my creditors to lose interest in me." That fall Corwin joined Wilson's original group of preceptors and began an association with Princeton that was to last almost sixty years.

Though he considered Wilson "the most impressive human being" he had ever met, he didn't always agree with him, once vigorously challenging some of the president's more conservative views at a departmental meeting, much to the consternation of apparently everyone but Wilson, whose high regard for his outspoken young colleague prompted him to select Corwin to update his book *Division and Reunion* in 1908. Ten years later, in 1918, Corwin was appointed to the chair first occupied by Wilson, the McCormick Professorship of Jurisprudence, which he held until his retirement in 1946. When a separate Department of Politics was formed in 1924, Corwin became its first chairman, serving in that post until 1935.

Corwin's performance as a teacher led seniors repeatedly to vote his undergraduate course, Constitutional Interpretation, "most difficult" and "most valuable." Because of his erect posture and military bearing, he was affectionately known to generations of graduate students as "The General." According to his former student, Alpheus T. Mason, who succeeded him as McCormick Professor, he had the special gift "of reaching within each person, of discovering something firm and worthwhile, of encouraging him to stand on it," and the ability, "rare among teachers, . . . to judge young men, not by what they are, but by what they may yet become."

Corwin's influence eventually extended beyond the campus to the federal government, which he served in 1935 as an adviser to the Public Works Administration, and in 1936 and 1937 as a special assistant and consultant to the attorney general on constitutional issues. The independence of mind that had impressed Wilson also characterized Corwin's response to Roosevelt, whom he publicly supported on the plan to enlarge the Supreme Court and publicly opposed three years later when Roosevelt broke tradition and ran for a third term.

Of the more than twenty books Corwin wrote, the best known and most influential are his studies of the Constitution and the presidency. His most successful book was written at the suggestion of his companions in the Snuff Club—a small cross-departmental group that included Corwin, E. G. Conklin, Luther P. Eisenhart, Chris-

tian Gauss, Duane Reed Stuart, among others—who, after hearing several papers he read to the club, urged him to write an exposition of the Constitution for the general reader. *The Constitution and What It Means Today*, first published by Princeton University Press in 1920, continues in print after thirteen revised editions and numerous translations. His later book, *The President, Office and Powers* (1940), was still considered the "Bible" in its field when a newly revised fourth edition appeared in 1958.

A distinctive characteristic of Corwin's literary style, as observed by Alpheus Mason, was his "penchant for arresting comment and devastating wit" which "reflected the man and his mind—sharp, penetrating, and sometimes astringent." The flavor of his style is evident in his comments on judicial review ("American democracy's way of covering its bet") and the cabinet ("an administrative anachronism" that should be replaced by a legislative council "whose daily salt does not come from the Presidential table.") The same quality marked his conversation. When a colleague asked about a newly appointed Supreme Court Justice, "He's not a very big man, is he?" Corwin replied, "No, but then, it wasn't a very big vacancy." Not above enjoying an occasional pun, he was heard to observe—upon Frank Murphy's appointment to the Court in 1940—"Now we'll have justice tempered with Murphy."

Corwin's retirement ended neither his service to the government nor his willingness to take issue with it. As editor of the Library of Congress's legislative reference division, he directed a research project that resulted in a massive volume, *The Constitution Annotated: Analysis and Interpreta-*

tion. In 1954 he became chairman of a national committee opposed to the Bricker amendment to restrict the president's treaty-making powers, and during President Eisenhower's illness the following year, he scored the administration for granting too much power to the president's assistant, Sherman Adams.

A president of the American Political Science Association, winner of the American Philosophical Society's Franklin Medal and Phillips Prize, and the recipient of honorary degrees from Michigan and Princeton, he was among the scholars singled out for citation at the Harvard Tercentenary. Other honors came in 1952 when the original Woodrow Wilson Hall was redesignated Edward S. Corwin Hall, and on Constitution Day 1961 when Corwin was cited for his "brilliant service to both institutions—the Constitution and Princeton University." On that occasion one of his former students, Adlai E. Stevenson, recalled how much his undergraduate days at Princeton had been enriched by Corwin's "warmth, his wisdom, and his wit."

Although Corwin never wrote the "single, monumental" book he planned, the corpus of his work according to Professor Mason, "advances the frontiers of every significant aspect of his subject":

> Generally recognized as the most learned and discriminating of all our modern constitutional authorities, Corwin was a scholar's scholar. Historians, political scientists, and legal practitioners join in proclaiming his preeminence. The law itself reflects his own pointed dictum: "If judges make law, so do commentators." Corwin is in the great tradition of Cooley and Kent. His contributions are sources of learning and understanding—hallmarks to emulate and revere.

Corwin Hall at one time stood on Washington Road near Prospect Avenue, where it was erected in 1951 to house the Woodrow Wilson School of Public and International Affairs. The architect, Stephen F. Voorhees '00, used red brick with limestone trim to blend with Seventy-Nine Hall across the street. To preserve a handsome old copper beech tree he started the building farther from the corner than he otherwise would have done and to keep out traffic noises he restricted windows to the north and east sides. On the west, the long unbroken expanse of brick wall to the right of the main entrance which confronted one approaching from McCosh Walk troubled many people. Soon after its completion there appeared on it in foot-high white letters, so well executed it was suspected they were done by a student of architecture, these words from Shelley's *Ozymandias*: "Look on my work, ye mighty, and despair!"

The building was moved almost a hundred yards northeast to its present site on May 20, 1963. This engineering feat was accomplished by the New York firm of Spencer, White, and Prentiss, using hydraulic jacks to push the building along twelve steel tracks. The actual moving took only twelve hours but two months were needed to prepare for it and another three months to secure the building to its new foundation.

When the new Woodrow Wilson building was completed in 1965, the old one was assigned to one of the School's chief allies, the Department of Politics, and to the Center of International Studies, and its name changed from Wilson Hall to Corwin Hall in honor of Edward S. Corwin, Wilson's successor as McCormick Professor of Jurisprudence and the first chairman of the Department of Politics.

Council of the Princeton University Community (CPUC, U-Council) is primarily a deliberative and consultative body, with authority to "consider and investigate any question of University policy, any aspect of the governing of the University, and any general issue related to the welfare of the University; and to make recommendations regarding any such matters to the appropriate decision-making bodies . . . or to the appropriate officers of the University."

The Council also has authority to "make rules regarding the conduct of resident members of the University community," to oversee rule-making by other bodies within the University community, and to oversee all applications of rules.

The Council normally would not consider matters primarily academic in nature.

A Special Committee on the Structure of the University chaired by Professor Stanley Kelley, Jr., proposed the creation of the Council in May 1969. Sometimes referred to as "Kelley's Republic," the Council was designed as "a permanent conference of the representatives of all major groups of the University" where "they could each raise problems that concern them and . . . be exposed to each other's views."

The Council first met on October 27, 1969. Typically it meets once a month, October through May, with special meetings as needed.

Following a series of Charter amendments in the fall of 1975, membership of the Council was set at 50, including 6 senior officers of the administration, 15 faculty members, 12 under-

graduates, 7 graduate students, 6 staff members, and 4 alumni. The president of the University is the presiding officer of the Council and chairman of its Executive Committee.

Much of the work of the Council is conducted through its standing committees, including the Executive Committee, Committees on Rights and Rules, Governance, Priorities, and Resources, and the Judicial Committee. Special committees also have been established from time to time.

Robert K. Durkee

Cowell, David (1704-1760), a Presbyterian minister of Trenton, N.J., was a hard-working trustee of the college in its early years and served briefly as acting president in 1757-1758. "Few invested with the same trust," said President Davies "discharged it with so much zeal, diligence and alacrity." Cowell graduated from Harvard in 1732 and three years later was voted his M.A. in absentia, "he being far distant preaching the Gospel at New Jersey."

Unable to support himself by the contributions of his parishioners, "he gave some part of his time," Davies said "to the study and practice of physic [medicine], in which he made no inconsiderable figure."

Cowell was named a trustee of the College in the charter of 1748, and it was he who was commissioned by the Board of Trustees to carry its thanks to Governor Belcher for "granting so ample and well-contrived a charter." He promoted a lottery for the College and, since New Jersey refused to sanction it, persuaded a Harvard classmate who lived in Stamford to manage the drawing in Connecticut, where lotteries were permitted. He conducted the negotiations that led to Samuel Davies's acceptance of the Board's invitation to become fourth president of the College. *Sibley's Harvard Graduates* quotes from one of Cowell's letters to Davies, observing that Cowell "was describing the college at Princeton in terms unlike those since employed by other Harvard men":

> The College ought to be esteemed of as much importance to the interests of religion and liberty as any other institution of the kind in America. God, at first, in a most remarkable manner owned and blessed it. It was the Lord's doing. He erected it; for our beginning was nothing. He carried it on till it was marvellous in our eyes.

Creative Arts Program, The, precursor of three later programs in Creative Writing, Theatre and Dance, and Visual Arts, was first organized in 1939 by a faculty committee under the leadership of Dean Christian Gauss.

The original program was supported by a five-year grant from the Carnegie Corporation that made possible the enrichment of opportunities for undergraduates with particular aptitude and interest in music, painting, sculpture, and writing. For student composers of music, regular courses in harmony and composition were supplemented by weekly meetings with Professor Roger Sessions. Students interested in drawing and painting worked with James E. Davis '23 and Alden Wicks '37. Classes in sculpture were conducted by Joseph Brown, the boxing coach, in the cellar of Dean Gauss's residence, the Joseph Henry House. Students with talent in writing worked with Allen Tate, poet and critic, who came to Princeton as first resident Fellow in Creative Writing.

Under Dean Gauss's watchful eye, the program survived the Second World War in modified form and began to blossom again soon afterward. Other committee chairmen who guided the development of the program during the next two decades were English Professors Donald A. Stauffer, Carlos Baker, R. P. Blackmur, and Edmund Keeley; Architecture Professor Francis A. Comstock; Music Professor Edward T. Cone; French Professor E.B.O. Borgerhoff; and Philosophy Professor Arthur Szathmary.

Allen Tate's successors as Visiting Lecturers in Creative Writing have been well-known poets, critics, and novelists, among them R. P. Blackmur, John Berryman, Joseph N. Frank, Delmore Schwartz, Richard Eberhart, Leslie A. Fiedler, Sean O'Faolin, Philip Roth, Elizabeth Bowen, and Theodore R. Weiss. A number of Visiting Lecturers became permanent members of the faculty. Tate's immediate successor, Richard P. Blackmur, stayed on as professor of English. Joseph N. Frank, who served in the fifties, later returned as Professor of Comparative Literature, and in the sixties Theodore R. Weiss was given continuing appointment as Professor of English and Creative Arts. Several Visiting Lecturers were alumni of the program: William M. Meredith '40, Louis O. Coxe '40, Bink Noll '47, George P. Garrett '52, José Donoso '51, and Galway Kinnell '48. Another Princeton graduate who taught creative writing in later years was John McPhee '53, who led a workshop in the literature of fact.

Successors to James E. Davis and Alden M. Wicks as Resident Critic in Painting included Hereward L. Cooke, Jr., William C. Seitz, Stephen Greene, Hyde Solomon, Joseph J. Stefanelli, Esteban Vicente, George Ortman, and Thomas B. Cornell.

In 1966 the program was given a home in the Nassau Street School, now called 185 Nassau, which had just been acquired by the University. Joseph Brown fell heir to the school's old gymnasium for his sculpture classes, and there was space enough for additional sculpture studios and five painting studios. In its new home the program grew rapidly. Enrollment in courses in creative writing, musical composition, and painting doubled. A playwriting workshop, conducted by William McCleery, playwright and editor of the quarterly *University*, was added to the offerings in creative writing, and extracurricular woodcarving under Economics Professor William Baumol supplemented the regular courses in sculpture.

In the early seventies, the rapid growth of student interest in the creative arts led to further expansion of the original program, and by 1975 there were three separate programs—Creative Writing, Theatre and Dance, and Visual Arts.

CREATIVE WRITING

Throughout this period of change, the mainstays in Creative Writing have been Edmund Keeley '48, who became director of this program in 1971 after guiding the original Creative Arts Program through its previous five years, and Theodore Weiss, who had been associated with the original program since 1967. Keeley, a novelist and translator, has received the Rome Prize of the American Academy of Arts and Letters and has been nominated for the National Book Award in translation. Weiss, a poet and critic, received the Brandeis Award in Poetry and is editor, with his wife, of the *Quarterly Review of Literature*.

THEATRE AND DANCE

A number of the workshops in acting, directing, and playwriting are taught by members of the professional repertory company of McCarter Theatre, while courses in modern dance have the benefit of the experience and skill of a professional dancer and choreographer, Ze'eva Cohen. The director of the program since it assumed separate status in 1975 has been Daniel Seltzer '54, who came to Princeton in 1970 from his position as director of Harvard's Loeb Drama Center. An example of the program's balance of the academic with the professional was provided by the director himself in 1976 when he received a *Theatre World* award and a Tony nomination for his performance in a Broadway play—an accomplishment he managed while on leave from his regular duties as a professor in the Department of English.

VISUAL ARTS

The Visual Arts Program has developed a broad range of offerings in many fields—drawing, painting, sculpture, film history and criticism, photography, printmaking, typography, graphic design, and ceramics. One of the program's best known Visiting Lecturers was film director Marcel Ophuls, whose widely acclaimed documentary *The Memory of Justice* was made, in part, during his stay at the University. Sculpture was still the province of Joe Brown (until his retirement in 1977), along with James Seawright, a maker of modern kinetic sculptures and director of the program since 1975. Previous directors were architect Michael Graves, 1971-1973, and art historian Rosalind Krauss, 1974-1975.

The primary aims of the three programs have remained essentially the same as those stated by the faculty committee for the original Creative Arts Program—"to allow the talented undergraduate to work in the creative arts under professional supervision while pursuing a regular liberal arts course of study, as well as to offer all interested undergraduates an opportunity to develop their creative faculties in connection with the general program of humanistic education."

Cricket made its first appearance at Princeton in 1857 and, despite the *Nassau Lit*'s prediction that "the college authorities would stop it, as there was something wicket in it," it has been played here sporadically ever since. The Nassau Cricket Club played several outside matches in the 1860s and 70s. In this century, cricket has been played at the Graduate College chiefly by graduate students from the British Commonwealth in intramural matches, although teams played occasional games with other colleges in the 1950s and early 1960s. In the mid-seventies, both undergraduate and graduate members of a revived cricket club competed in the newly-formed Eastern Seaboard Cricket Conference.

Cross-country running, a popular intramural diversion at Princeton as early as 1880 when the Hare and Hounds Club was founded, began auspiciously as a varsity sport in 1899 with John Cregan 1899 winning the first intercollegiate championship meet ever held.

Fitting sequels to Cregan's notable achievement came in 1914, when Donald Morrison '15 finished second in the IC4A Championships, and again after the First World War, when Princeton teams placed second in the Intercollegiates in 1919, 1920, and 1921, and

won the first triangular meet with Harvard and Yale in 1922.

In the thirties, Bill Bonthron '34 excelled, going undefeated his freshman, sophomore, and junior years. He and his classmate Charles M. Reed finished arm-in-arm in a first place tie in every dual meet their sophomore year. The 1937 team was undefeated and won the Big Three meet, in which its captain Frederic Rosengarten '38 placed first.

After the interruption of World War II, Princeton cross-country reached a high point when the 1949 team went undefeated in dual meet competition, took the Big Three championship, and placed second in the Heptagonal cross-country championship meet.* That year's captain, Stan Johnson '50, won the triangular meet with Harvard and Yale for the third time in his varsity career. In the 1950s six Princeton harriers came in first in Big Three meets: Dick Snedecker '51 (1950), Al Pittis '52 (1951), Toby Maxwell '53 (1952), Jack Vodrey '57 (1954), Rod Zwirner '59 (1956), and Mike Kingston '62 (1959). Maxwell (who placed first in every dual meet his senior year) and Vodrey were second in the Heptagonals. Most successful of all was Zwirner, who as a sophomore won every dual meet and was also individual champion in the Heptagonals.

The University's thinclads, as the *Prince* has sometimes called them, were strong contenders in dual competition and in the various championship meets throughout the 1960s and the early 1970s. Seven years after Princeton's second-place finish in the 1968 Heptagonals, the 1975 team captured Princeton's first championship, an example followed by the 1976 and 1977 teams, who produced Princeton's second and third Heptagonal championships. The 1975 championship team, one of the best in Princeton's history, also placed first in the Big Three meet, second in the Intercollegiates, and fifteenth in the National Championships. Captain Larry Tractenberg '76 tied for first place with his teammate Craig Masback '77 in the Big Three meet, and finished third in both the Heptagonals and the Intercollegiates.

In the early years, cross-country was under the supervision of special coaches, but since the 1930s it has been the responsibility of track coaches Mattie Geis, 1932-1956; Peter Morgan, 1956-1970; and Larry Ellis, since 1970.

A woman's cross-country team organized in 1976 placed fourth in the first Ivy League women's championship meet in November of the same year.

* The seven teams constituting the heptagon in 1939 when the meet was first organized eventually grew to ten (the eight Ivy League teams plus Army and Navy).

Cuyler Hall was built in memory of Cornelius C. Cuyler, a New York banker who was a trustee of the University from 1898 until his death in 1909. His had always been "a magical name for any 1879 man," his classmate, Woodrow Wilson, then governor of New Jersey, said at the dedication of the building in 1912, and it was "singularly appropriate" that a dormitory "symbolic of the democratic life and the comradeships of the University" should bear his name. "He always meant to me a singular stimulation," Governor Wilson concluded, "he imparted his own energy to everything he did. Let us hope that his spirit will in some degree touch the life of this dormitory."

Dallas, George Mifflin (1792-1864), eleventh vice president of the United States (1845-1849), was a graduate of Princeton in the Class of 1810. His father was a prosperous lawyer and man of affairs in Philadelphia who served as Madison's Secretary of the Treasury 1814-1816. The younger Dallas entered public life three years after he left Princeton as secretary to the chairman of the commission that negotiated the treaty ending the War of 1812. He was mayor of Philadelphia, United States senator, and Minister to Russia prior to his election as vice president; later he was Minister to Great Britain. His biographer called him "conservative and cosmopolitan, precise and dignified . . . the gentleman in politics." Princeton conferred an honorary LL.D. on him in 1857, about the same time the citizens of a thriving community in northeast Texas named their newly incorporated town for him.

Davies, Samuel (1723-1761), fourth president of Princeton, was born in New Castle County, Delaware. His parents could not afford to send him to college but were determined that he should be trained for the ministry. He studied in Samuel Blair's famous school at Fagg's Manor, Chester County, Pennsylvania, was licensed to preach by the Presbytery of New Castle when he was twenty-two, and was ordained as an evangelist to Virginia a year later.

In Anglican Virginia, where dissenters were subjected to constant vexations, he built up a strong Presbyterian membership and became the advocate and defender of their civil rights and religious liberties. He conducted services in seven houses of worship dispersed through five counties, riding horseback through fields and forests to minister to his scattered congregations. A sufferer from tuberculosis, "he preached in the day and had his hectic fever by night," but was nevertheless "resolved that while life and sufficient strength remained, he would devote himself earnestly to the work of preaching the gospel." As a principal founder and first moderator of the Presbytery of Hanover, which comprised all the Presbyterian ministers in Virginia and North Carolina, he was considered "the animating soul of the whole dissenting interests in these two colonies."

In 1753 Davies and Gilbert Tennant, another well-known Presbyterian minister, were chosen by Princeton trustees to go to Great Britain and Ireland in search of donations for the College. Davies kept a diary of the mission, which was later published. Their five-week ocean voyage from Philadelphia to London was rough. The ship smelled; they were both seasick, and Davies suffered from the toothache, but they prayed alternately in their cabin for the success of their mission. Their prayers were answered. During their eleven-month stay in the British Isles, they secured donations—some individual gifts including three guineas from Oliver Cromwell's great-grandson, but chiefly church collections—sufficient to build Nassau Hall and the president's house and to found a charitable fund "for the education of pious and indigent youth for the gospel ministry." Davies, then only thirty, preached some sixty sermons. Near the end of his stay he had an apoplectic fit but recovered sufficiently to undertake the voyage home. The return trip lasted thirteen weeks and was tempestuous. Storms threatened to engulf the vessel, and Davies was saddened by the curses of the sailors and perplexed as to what to do about them, they were "so habituated to blasphemy."

In 1758 Davies was elected to succeed Jonathan Edwards as president of the College, but declined election, partly because of a reluctance to quit his pastoral work in Virginia, partly because he knew that while a majority of the trustees had voted for his election, a minority shared his own belief that Samuel Finley, a member of the Board, was better qualified for the office. The trustees subsequently reelected Davies and persuaded him to accept. He took up his duties on July 26, 1759. Eighteen months later, on February 4, 1761, he died of pneumonia, in his thirty-eighth year, a few weeks after having been bled for "a bad cold."

During his brief tenure Davies raised the standards for admission and for the bachelor's degree, instituted monthly orations by members of the senior class (an important part of undergraduate education at Princeton for more than a century), composed odes to peace and to science which were sung at Commencement, and drew up a catalogue of the 1,281 volumes in the college library "to give Information to such who are watching for Opportunities of doing good; and to afford particular Benefactors the Pleasure of seeing how many others have concurred with them in their favourite Charity."

Davies left his mark as scholar and patriot on his students, particularly the eleven members of the Class of 1760 whom he taught as seniors. "Whatever be your Place," he told them in his baccalaureate address, "imbibe and cherish a public spirit. Serve your generation." This they did. Among the eleven were a member of the Continental Congress, chaplains in the Continental Army, judges in Maine and Pennsylvania, the founder of a college in North Carolina, a member of the United States House of Representatives, and a signer of the Declaration of Independence.

Davies was long remembered as one of the great pulpit orators of his generation. Patrick Henry, who as a boy had frequently heard him preach, acknowledged Davies's influence on his own oratory. Davies's sermons went through four editions in the United States and nine editions in England, and for more than fifty years after his death were among the most widely read of any in the English language.

At Princeton, Davies was loved and respected; as one trustee wrote another, "There never was a college happier in a president."

Davis Center for Historical Studies, The, established in 1968, is named for Shelby Cullom Davis '30, who in 1964 gave the University more than $5 million for support of the Department of History. Davis, who graduated from the department with highest honors and has served as chairman of its advisory council since 1941, made this gift to assure the continuance of excellence in scholarship and the teaching of history at Princeton University.

The income from the Davis Fund is used in a variety of ways. Two chairs have been established: the George Henry Davis '86 Professorship of American History, which honors the donor's father, and the Shelby Cullom Davis '30 Professorship of European History. (Davis won a doctoral degree at the University of Geneva, and he later served as United States Ambassador to Switzerland.) In addition, funds are provided for the purchase of books for the University Library, for exploratory ventures in undergraduate teaching, for graduate student fellowships, for special costs of research by members of the department, and for the Davis Center, the most innovative part of the expanded program.

The Center's chief function is to conduct the Davis seminar in which members of the faculty, visitors from other institutions, graduate students, and selected undergraduates participate. For periods of time from one to four years, the members of the seminar direct their attention to a single theme or aspect of history in which they have a common interest. Topics represent relatively new approaches to the study of history, involving the investigation of neglected subjects or the application of new methods to older subjects. Emphasis is placed on interdisciplinary approaches and on topics that do not restrict participation to specialists in a single geographical area or period of time. Each year a number of scholars from other institutions are brought to Princeton as Visiting Davis Fellows, with no obligations other than to take part in the seminar and to pursue researches related to its current theme. The end product is intended to be a published work embodying the more significant papers developed through the seminar.

Among the themes chosen for study have been "The History of Higher Education," "The History of Popular Religion," and "The History of Popular Culture." The first publication was a two-volume work, *The University in Society*, published by Princeton University Press in 1974, and edited by Lawrence Stone, who has served as director of the Davis Center since its establishment. The Davis Center was the original sponsor of *Princetonians, 1748-1768: A Biographical Dictionary*, edited by James McLachlan and published by Princeton University Press in 1976.

W. Frank Craven

Dean, the office of, came into being in 1883. Since then deans have proliferated—all told there have been ten kinds (eight of which have persisted):

Dean of the Faculty 1883
Dean of the Graduate School 1901
Dean of the Departments of Science
  1909-1928
Dean of the College 1909
Dean of the School of Engineering
  1922
Dean of Freshmen 1925-1943
Dean of the Chapel 1928
Dean of Students (later Dean of
  Student Affairs) 1954
Dean of the Woodrow Wilson School
  1964
Dean of the School of Architecture
  1965

The Chairman of the University Research Board (1959), while not called a dean, is accorded rank equivalent to a dean by the trustee bylaws.

The work of deans is arduous and sometimes invidious (President McCosh's word for it), but some forty persons who have been deans have generally shown staying power and devotion. Given their stature, it is remarkable that so few of them have gone on to college or university presidencies—Luther P. Eisenhart received seven presidential calls during his several deanships, and it is probable that every dean has received at least one call.

Deans are generally held in high regard, and their title considered an honorable one, though Dean McClenahan once announced that he preferred to be called "mister"—having just read in the *Times* that the police had picked up the dean of New York pickpockets.

To fill its deanships the University has raided the English and physics departments more frequently than any others. Longest terms have been completed by Andrew West (Graduate School), 27 years; Henry B. Fine (Faculty, Departments of Science), 25 years; Christian Gauss (College), 21 years; J. Douglas Brown (Faculty), 21 years; Luther P. Eisenhart (Faculty, Graduate School), 20 years; Arthur M. Greene, Jr. (School of Engineering), 19 years; Robert R. Wicks (Chapel), 19 years.

Dean of the Chapel has charge of the services and the preaching in the University Chapel and general supervision of religious activities of the University. Incumbents have been:

Robert R. Wicks 1928-1947
Donald B. Aldrich 1947-1955
Ernest Gordon 1955-

Dean of the College is an office which came into being in the spring of 1909 when President Wilson recommended to the trustees that the superintendence of discipline previously vested in the dean of the faculty be vested in a new dean to be called the dean of discipline. By the time the name of the first incumbent appeared in the catalogue that fall, his title had become dean of the college. In 1946 the dean of the college was made responsible for the enforcement of rules relating to undergraduate scholastic standing, and for oversight of the services and agencies designed to promote the academic development of undergraduates; in 1954, responsibility for undergraduate discipline and extracurricular activities (and in 1957 athletic activities) was assigned to a new officer, the dean of students. Occupants of the office of dean of the college have been:

Edward G. Elliott (politics)
  1909-1912
Howard McClenahan (physics)
  1912-1925

Christian Gauss (modern languages)
1925-1946
Francis R. B. Godolphin (classics)
1946-1955
Jeremiah S. Finch (English)
1955-1961
J. Merrill Knapp (music) 1961-1966
Edward D. Sullivan (French)
1966-1972
Neil L. Rudenstine (English)
1972-1977
Joan S. Girgus (psychology) 1977-

Dean of the Departments of Science
was a title borne by only one man,
Henry B. Fine. He was appointed to
the post in 1909 and held it until his
death in 1928. This deanship was
created by the trustees at President
Wilson's request to provide general
administrative oversight of the Departments of Mathematics, Physics, Astronomy, Chemistry, Biology, and
Geology, and of the development of instruction in various fields of engineering. After Dean Fine's death, these
duties were assigned to the dean of the
faculty.

Dean of the Faculty, oldest and high-
est-ranking deanship, was established
by the trustees in 1883 as a means of releasing the incumbent president, James
McCosh, then seventy-two years old,
from certain onerous duties, and of thus
persuading him to remain as president
as well as professor of philosophy. A
by-law adopted by the trustees charged
the dean of the faculty "with oversight
of whatever does not pertain directly to
the work of instruction, such in particular as the discipline of the College, the
assignment of rooms and the sanitary
condition of the Institution." As thus
defined, this continued to be the dean

of the faculty's function until 1909
when, with the creation of the office of
the dean of the college, his original
duties were assigned to the new dean,
and the dean of the faculty took over
from the president the administrative
oversight of the application and enforcement of rules and standards of
scholarship in the University, the
chairmanship ex-officio of the faculty
committee on examinations and standing, and the responsibility of discharging the general duties of the president
in his absence or disability.

During the post-World War II years,
as the dean of the college assumed increasing responsibility for the academic
life of undergraduates, the dean of the
faculty shared with the president increasing responsibility for oversight of
departments of instruction and concern
for the well-being of the faculty. In
1967, the incumbent of the newly
created office of provost took over from
the dean of the faculty the responsibility of acting for the president, in his absence or disability, in the general
supervision of the University. Deans of
the faculty have been:

James O. Murray (English)
1883-1899
Samuel R. Winans (Greek)
1899-1903
Henry B. Fine (mathematics)
1903-1912
William F. Magie (physics)
1912-1925
Luther P. Eisenhart (mathematics)
1925-1933
Robert K. Root (English) 1933-1946
J. Douglas Brown (economics)
1946-1967
Robert R. Palmer (history) 1967-1968
Richard A. Lester (economics)
1968-1973
Aaron Lemonick (physics) 1973-

Dean of Freshmen, 1925-1942, was Radcliffe Heermance who was also director of admission. As dean of freshmen he was charged with administrative oversight of the academic work of the freshman class and direction of the board of advisors. Burnham N. Dell was dean of freshmen for one year 1942-1943. Thereafter, the duties of this office were absorbed by the staff of the dean of the college.

Dean of the Graduate School, second oldest deanship, was established in 1901. Its incumbent is responsible, under the president, for graduate studies, for the curriculum of the Graduate School and for the residential Graduate College. Deans of the Graduate School have been:

Andrew F. West (Latin) 1901-1928
Augustus Trowbridge (physics) 1928-1933
Luther P. Eisenhart (mathematics) 1933-1945
Hugh S. Taylor (chemistry) 1945-1958
Donald R. Hamilton (physics) 1958-1965
Colin S. Pittendrigh (biology) 1965-1969
Aaron Lemonick (physics) 1969-1973
Alvin B. Kernan (English) 1973-1977
Nina G. Garsoian (Near Eastern Studies) 1977-

Dean of the School of Architecture and Urban Planning, previously the director of the School of Architecture, has administrative oversight, under the president, of the University division founded in 1919 as the School of Architecture and renamed in 1969 the School of Architecture and Urban Planning. Incumbents have been:

DIRECTOR
Howard C. Butler 1919-1922
Raymond Bossange 1923-1926
Sherley W. Morgan 1928-1952
Robert W. McLaughlin, Jr. 1952-1965
DEAN
Robert L. Geddes 1965-

Dean of the School of Engineering and Applied Science, is the title of the administrative head of the University division founded as the School of Engineering and renamed in 1962 the School of Engineering and Applied Science. Incumbents have been:

Arthur M. Greene, Jr. (mechanical engineering) 1922-1940
Kenneth H. Condit (mechanical engineering) 1940-1954
Joseph C. Elgin (chemical engineering) 1954-1971
Robert G. Jahn (aerospace and mechanical sciences) 1971-

Dean of Student Affairs (formerly Dean of Students) oversees undergraduate social, extracurricular, and athletic activities, is responsible for matters relating to the conduct and discipline of undergraduates, and has supervision of the proctors. This deanship was established in 1954. Its incumbents have been:

William D. Lippincott 1954-1968
Neil L. Rudenstine 1968-1972
Adele S. Simmons 1972-1977
J. Anderson Brown, Jr. 1977-

Dean of the Woodrow Wilson School of Public and International Affairs, previously the director and before that the chairman of the Administrative Committee, has administrative oversight, under the president, of the School of Public and International Affairs, founded in 1930 and named in 1948 for the University's thirteenth president. Incumbents of this office have been:

CHAIRMAN OF THE ADMINISTRATIVE
  COMMITTEE
Harold W. Dodds 1930-1933

DIRECTOR
DeWitt C. Poole 1933-1939
Dana G. Munro 1939-1958
Gardner Patterson 1958-1963
Lester V. Chandler 1963-1964

DEAN
Marver H. Bernstein 1964-1969
John P. Lewis 1969-1974
Donald E. Stokes 1974-

Degrees awarded by American colleges in the colonial period were adopted from those then in use at Oxford and Cambridge. The original charter that King George II granted Princeton in 1746 empowered the trustees "for the encouragement of learning and animating the students . . . to diligence, industry and a laudable progress in literature," to "grant any such . . . degrees . . . as are usually granted in either of our universities or in any other college in our realm of Great Britain."

The chief degree so adopted was the Bachelor of Arts. In the medieval universities it had been a preliminary degree, enabling the holder to proceed to the master's degree, which alone enabled him to teach. The word *bachelor* was derived from the medieval Latin *baccalarius*, which had been applied in the eighth century to rustics, male and female, who were of low rank in the feudal hierarchy. The word was later extended to persons of subordinate positions in other systems: knighthood, the church, trade guilds, the universities, and finally, by its last extension, to unmarried men who presumably were still novices in the ways of the world generally.

On the continent the bachelor's degree continued to be an obscure way station on the road to the master's degree and later to the doctor's degree. But in England the bachelor's degree became the important one, and at Oxford and Cambridge the master's degree could be obtained several years after graduation merely by the payment of a few pounds. Similarly, a Princeton bachelor of arts could obtain a master's degree three years after his graduation simply by certifying that he had engaged in such professional studies as "divinity, law, or physick" and submitting "testimonials of good moral conduct signed by two or more gentlemen of Note and Veracity." This practice continued until the end of the nineteenth century when a more rigorous administration of higher degrees was instituted.

OTHER BACHELOR DEGREES

In addition to the time-honored Bachelor of Arts, other bachelor degrees have been offered at Princeton as follows: Bachelor of Laws from 1847 to 1852; Bachelor of Science from 1873 to 1930; Bachelor of Letters from 1904 to 1918; Bachelor of Science in Engineering since 1921.

The law degree was conferred on seven persons who completed a short-lived law course begun at the time of the College's centennial celebration.

The Bachelor of Science degree was introduced in the 1870s with the expansion of the science curriculum. Candidates for this degree were required at entrance to offer Latin but not Greek, although both languages were still required for the degree of Bachelor of Arts. It was later found that some students became candidates for the Bachelor of Science degree to flee Greek rather than to pursue science. In 1904, the Bachelor of Letters degree was accordingly introduced to distinguish students who wished to take a humanistic program without Greek from those who were really pursuing scientific programs. The Litt. B. Degree was discontinued in 1918 when Greek was dropped as an admission requirement for the Bachelor of Arts degree. At the same time, Latin was dropped as an entrance requirement for the Bachelor of Science degree but was retained for the Bachelor of Arts. This difference led to another anomaly, which came to light after the introduction of the four-course plan in 1923. It was found not uncommon for a B.S. candidate to major in art and archaeology or English, or for an A.B. candidate to concentrate in chemistry or biology, so that the difference in the degree related more to what the student had studied in secondary school than to what he had done in college. It was decided in 1930 that, in view of the nontechnical nature of undergraduate study in all the liberal arts and sciences, the same degree would be appropriate for work in every department. Beginning then, the degree of Bachelor of Arts was awarded in all departments except engineering, and the Latin entrance requirement was eliminated.

ENGINEERING DEGREES

From the time of their founding, the Departments of Civil Engineering (1875) and Electrical Engineering (1889) offered separate degrees (C.E. and E.E.). With the establishment of the School of Engineering in 1921, the first degree for all engineering departments was made Bachelor of Science in Engineering and the second degree, Master of Science in Engineering.

GRADUATE DEGREES

Modern graduate degrees were introduced in the 1870s with the inauguration of postgraduate study under President McCosh. At first there were two master's degrees—Master of Arts and Master of Science—and two doctor's degrees—Doctor of Philosophy and Doctor of Science (in the early 1890s the degree of Doctor of Letters was given twice); but by 1905 the other degrees were discontinued, leaving only two degrees, Master of Arts and Doctor of Philosophy, regularly offered for work in the liberal arts and sciences.

Other degrees at the Master's level have been offered as follows: Master of Fine Arts, in architecture from 1919 to 1970, in art and archaeology since 1919, in music since 1940; Master in Public Affairs since 1948; Master of Architecture since 1970; Master of Architecture and Urban Planning since 1970; Master in Public Affairs and Urban Planning since 1971.

In medieval universities the term *doctor* was introduced some time after *master*. *Master* and *doctor* were at first used synonymously, but in time *master* came to be restricted to the teachers of liberal arts and *doctor*, as a distinction, to the teachers of theology and law, and later of medicine. In Germany, *doctor* eventually came to be applied to advanced degrees in all faculties and it was the German system that was adopted generally in the United States. At Princeton the A.M. degree was often sought by those looking forward to secondary school teaching or writing or the diplomatic service, but in time it became, for the most part, a way station on the road to the doctorate. The Ph.D. became the degree for college and university teaching and for research in all the arts and sciences as well as in architecture, engineering, public affairs, and urban planning.

The following table shows the number of degrees conferred at Princeton's first Commencement in

1748, at fifty-year intervals thereafter until 1898, and at twenty-five year intervals since then:

	Bache- lors	Mas- ters	Doc- tors	Total
1748	6	—	—	6
1798	14	—	—	14
1848	74	—	—	74
1898	189	47	1	237
1923	383	68	18	469
1948	578	222	55	855
1973	920	301	225	1446

NOTE: These figures are exclusive of honorary degrees (q.v.).

Departments of instruction in the arts and sciences were first established at Princeton in 1904 as part of the reorganization of the curriculum that began soon after President Wilson's inauguration in 1902. Previously, the individual professor had presented his course proposals directly to the faculty after consultation with the president and other colleagues. With the increase in the faculty required for the introduction of Wilson's preceptorial system, and the greater complexity of the curriculum, organization of the faculty by departments became indispensable, and the University accordingly drew "the several chairs in related subjects of study" into the following eleven departments: Art and Archaeology; Biology; Chemistry; Classics; English; Geology; History, Politics, and Economics; Mathematics; Modern Languages; Philosophy; Physics. These were in addition to two existing departments of civil and electrical engineering. (Astronomy, one of Princeton's oldest disciplines, became a department a few years later.)

After 1904, through various evolutionary processes, the number of departments more than doubled. History,

Politics, and Economics became separate departments, and later Economics generated Sociology, which in turn produced Anthropology, Modern Languages and Literatures separated into Germanic, Romance, and Slavic Languages and Literatures, and a new department of Oriental Studies subsequently divided into East Asian and Near Eastern Studies. Psychology and Statistics, originally subfields of Philosophy and Mathematics, became separate departments. Other new departments were added after a period of incubation under the wing of another department (Music), of a faculty committee (Religion), or of the Council of the Humanities. (Comparative Literature). Biochemical Sciences was developed by the two departments from which it derived its name. By these different means the number of separate departments in the arts and sciences had grown to twenty-six by 1976.

In addition, two of the three professional schools—the School of Architecture and Urban Planning (1919) and the Woodrow Wilson School of Public and International Affairs (1930)—have functioned as departments; and the School of Engineering and Applied Science (1921), has embraced the four departments of Aerospace and Mechanical Sciences; Chemical Engineering; Civil Engineering; and Electrical Engineering and Computer Science. Thus, by 1977, the total number of academic departments came to thirty-two.

Articles about these departments and schools will be found under the appropriate headings.

Another related academic resource, which the University has been developing with increasing effectiveness since the late 1930s, brings together faculty members from different departments in interdisciplinary programs of instruc-

almost as many programs as departments. A few of them are described in separate articles: Afro-American Studies, American Studies, Creative Arts, History and Philosophy of Science, Linguistics, Teacher Preparation. Other programs range from Applied Mathematics, Classical Archaeology, and Demography to Neuroscience, Political Philosophy, and Transportation, and include, for example, international and regional study of Africa, East Asia, Latin America, Modern Europe, the Near East, and Russia.

Other interdepartmental committees have functioned without the formal structure of a program, as in the case of the Women's Studies Committee, which encourages interdisciplinary consideration of the role of women in various societies and of the changing nature of social and political relationships between men and women.

Further aids to interdisciplinary study have been provided by councils that coordinate the activities of programs in their areas. The oldest and the largest is the Council of the Humanities which is described in a separate article. Created more recently have been councils on Environmental, International and Regional, and Urban Studies, and the Council of Masters, which coordinates the educational objectives of the various undergraduate dining and residential units.

Another vital element in the academic structure of the University is the special research unit. Some of the older ones, described in separate articles, include Industrial Relations, International Finance, International Studies, and Population Research. Other fields in which special research programs have been created include Chinese Linguistics, Criminal Justice, Development Studies, Econometric Research, Financial Research, New Jersey

Affairs, and Urban and Environmental Planning.

Dickinson, Jonathan (1688-1747), Princeton's first president, died after only four and a half months in office and is chiefly remembered for having been the leader of the little group who, in his words, "first concocted the plan and foundation of the College." To him, "more than to any other man, the college . . . owes its origin," wrote Professor William A. Packard in *The Princeton Book* (1879).

Born in Hatfield, Massachusetts, Dickinson was a member of the fifth class to graduate, in 1706, from the Collegiate School of Connecticut, which later changed its name to Yale College. He studied theology and in 1709, when he was twenty-one, was ordained minister of the church in Elizabethtown (now Elizabeth), New Jersey.

Dickinson served this church all his life, ministering to his flock as pastor, lawyer, physician and, in later years, as an instructor of young men preparing for professional study. Besides Elizabethtown, his field of labor embraced the outlying towns of Rahway, Westfield, Connecticut Farms, Springfield, and a part of Chatham. At one time, when diphtheria became epidemic, he was called to visit a family that lost eight of its ten children in two weeks, and, finding one of the children "newly dead," had the advantage of postmortem examination and "thereby a better acquaintance with the Nature of the Disease." He published a paper, *Observations on That Terrible Disease, Vulgarly Called The Throat Distemper*, which according to a latter-day historian of medicine, "evidenced a mind skilled in the appreciation of morbid phenomena . . . and an enlarged knowledge, for his time, of the principles of cure."

The Elizabethtown church was originally Congregational, as was Dickinson, but because he felt a need for stronger ties with other churches in meeting the Church of England's opposition to New Jersey dissenters, he persuaded his congregation in 1717 to change its form of government and place itself under the care of the Presbytery of Philadelphia. Dickinson became a leader of this presbytery and also of the higher ecclesiastical body of which it was a member—the Synod of Philadelphia, which twice elected him moderator.

As a former Congregationalist he exerted a moderating influence on the deliberations of his Presbyterian colleagues. In 1721 he protested an action of the synod that he thought exceeded its legitimate powers. The following year, he presented a paper on "the true limits of church power" so persuasively that the synod adopted it unanimously and then closed the meeting with "joyful singing" from the 133rd Psalm: "Behold, how good and pleasant it is for brethren to dwell together in unity!"

In 1729 Dickinson opposed a proposal that every minister in the Synod of Philadelphia should be required "to give his hearty assent" to the Westminster Confession of Faith. While personally accepting the doctrine set forth in the Confessions and Catechisms of the Westminster Assembly, Dickinson held on principle that the imposition of any creed was an infringement of the individual clergyman's rights.

At the same time Dickinson defended Presbyterianism from external criticism, publishing frequent articles in this cause. These earned him a reputation second only to Jonathan Edward's as a champion of Calvinism in America and as a writer on divinity. A century later, President Maclean wrote that "for *profound* thinking, but *not always correct* [italics his], he would assign the palm to Edwards; but for sound judgment and practical wisdom, to Dickinson." Dickinson's best-known book, *Familiar Letters to a Gentleman, upon a Variety of Seasonable and Important Subjects in Religion*, was frequently reprinted both here and abroad.

Dickinson was one of the leaders of a movement to found a "seminary of learning" in the Synod of Philadelphia. He and Ebenezer Pemberton, pastor of the Presbyterian Church in New York, were members of a committee appointed in 1739 to plan a fund-raising expedition to Great Britain for this purpose, but their plans had to be tabled when war broke out between England and Spain.

Meanwhile, the influence of the Great Awakening (see *The Founding of Princeton*) brought a division between the "New Sides" and the "Old Sides" in the Presbyterian Church. Dickinson and his associates in the Presbytery of New York, which he had helped form in 1738, were moderate New Siders who, while encouraging revivals, opposed their more violent excesses. They nevertheless defended the rights of the more zealous graduates of the Log College (q.v.) in their disputes with the Old Sides. When the Log College-dominated Presbytery of New Brunswick was expelled from the Synod of Philadelphia in 1741, and Dickinson and his associates were unable to bring about a reconciliation, they withdrew in 1745 to form, in association with the Presbytery of New Brunswick, the Synod of New York, and Dickinson was elected the first moderator.

Dickinson now revived his earlier interest in a much-needed college for the Middle Colonies. He was disappointed by Harvard's and Yale's opposition to the revival meetings of George Whitefield and by Yale's harsh treatment of his young friend, David Brainerd, who was dismissed because of his outspoken opposition to the faculty's conservative religious views. He also felt that the course of instruction offered by the Log College was inadequate.

It was against this background that Dickinson and three other pastors—Pemberton, Aaron Burr Sr., and John Pierson—and the three laymen whose support they enlisted—William Smith, Peter Van Brugh Livingston, and William Peartree Smith—began to plan the founding of the College (q.v.). Led by Dickinson, this group applied in vain to Governor Lewis Morris for a charter and, following his death, renewed their application to Acting Governor John Hamilton, who granted a charter on October 22, 1746.

The first trustees, including five Log College adherents enlisted by Dickinson and Pemberton, announced Dickinson's appointment as president in April 1747. Classes began the fourth week in May in Elizabethtown, with a student body of eight or ten members. One of Dickinson's divinity students, Caleb Smith, served as tutor and the parsonage served as the College—the only library available was Dickinson's, the classroom was probably his parlor, and the refectory his dining room. But the first months of the College's life were the last of Dickinson's. His sudden death on October 7, 1747, was reported in *The New York Weekly Post Boy* by his long-time coworker for the College, Ebenezer Pemberton:

Elizabethtown in New Jersey,
October 10

On Wednesday morning last, about four o'clock, died here, of a pleuritic illness, that eminently learned and pious minister of the Gospel and President of the College of New Jersey, the Rev. Mr. Jonathan Dickinson, in the sixtieth year of his age, who had been Pastor of the First Presbyterian Church in this Town for nearly forty years, and was the Glory and Joy of it. In him conspicuously appeared those natural and acquired moral and spiritual Endowments which constitute a truly excellent and valuable man, a good Scholar, an eminent Divine, and a serious, devout Christian . . . By his death our Infant College is deprived of the Benefit and Advantage of his superior Accomplishments. . . . Never any Person in these Parts died more lamented.

The portrait of President Dickinson in the Faculty Room in Nassau Hall was copied from an engraving prefixed to the Glasgow edition of his *Familiar Letters* and was presented to the College by the artist, Edward Ludlow Mooney, in 1872.

Dickinson Hall, home of the Departments of Economics and of History, is named for the first president of the College, Jonathan Dickinson. Built in 1930 as an extension of the wing of McCosh Hall on Washington Road and connected with the University Chapel by the Rothschild Arch, it completed the great court of which the Chapel and McCosh form two sides.

Dickinson replaced an earlier recitation and lecture hall of the same name, which stood for fifty years at the southwest corner of the site now occupied by Firestone Library and was lost in 1920 in the fire that also destroyed Marquand Chapel.

Dillon Gymnasium, designed by Aymar Embury 1900, was built in 1947 on the site of the University Gymnasium (destroyed by fire in 1944), and named in honor of Herbert L. Dillon '07, onetime football captain and a principal donor to the building fund. Dillon contains all of the facilities of its predecessor plus a six-lane pool, which is used for intercollegiate competition as well as for intramural purposes. Since Jadwin Gymnasium (q.v.) was built, the main part of Dillon has been used chiefly for classes in physical education and as a supplement to Jadwin for intramural sports.

Dod Hall, named for Professor Albert Baldwin Dod (1805-1845), was given to Princeton by his sister, Mrs. David B. Brown, who also donated Brown Hall (q.v.). Both dormitory buildings were designed by John Lyman Faxon in an Italian Renaissance style.

A precocious student, Dod entered the College when he was fifteen, graduated two years later in 1822, and was appointed professor of mathematics when he was twenty-five. John Maclean said he was unsurpassed as a teacher of this subject. Dod also taught political economy and architecture and was regarded by his students as one of their most stimulating teachers in these subjects as well.

Professor Dod is also remembered by a professorship of mathematics, endowed in 1869 by his son, Samuel B. Dod 1857.

Dodds, Harold Willis (1889-   ) fifteenth president of Princeton, was born in Utica, Pennsylvania, on June 28, 1889. His father, a Presbyterian minister, was professor of Bible at Grove City College in Pennsylvania, and Harold Dodds spent most of his youth on or near the college campus. He graduated from Grove City in 1909 and, after teaching school for two years, did graduate work in politics at Princeton (M.A. 1914) and Pennsylvania (Ph.D. 1917). He celebrated his doctorate by marrying Margaret Murray of Halifax on Christmas Day, 1917. During the war he served in the Food Administration, and then (1919-1920) taught at Western Reserve. He had already gained a reputation as an expert on problems of local government, and in 1920 he became secretary of the National Municipal League, a post he held until 1928.

The president of the league was the secretary of state, Charles Evans Hughes. Hughes formed a high opinion of his young executive officer and got him involved in the electoral problems of Latin America. As adviser to the president of Nicaragua, Dodds drafted the Nicaraguan electoral law of 1923 and helped supervise the remarkably peaceful and honest elections of 1928. In between, he was advisor to the commission that vainly sought to arrange a plebiscite that would end the long dispute between Chile and Peru over the provinces of Tacna and Arica.

During this period, Dodds gave lecture courses at various eastern colleges. In 1925 he joined the Princeton Faculty. He was promoted to full professor in 1927, and in 1930 was appointed chairman of the newly established School of Public Affairs (now the Woodrow Wilson School). During his chairmanship, he and his colleagues made an intensive survey of the government of New Jersey. They found much room for improvement in the administration of the state, and some of their recommendations were actually put into effect—an unusual event in the history of such reports.

Thus when the trustees chose Harold Dodds as president of Princeton in 1933, they were selecting a scholar who had had wide experience in administration and in public and international affairs. They were also selecting the youngest president of Princeton in over a century, which was just as well, considering the problems that had to be met during the next two decades. The Great Depression, the Second World War, and the postwar period of readjustment put severe and continuing strains on the University and its president. Not until 1950 did Princeton have what might be called a normal year, with adequate income, a large enough faculty, and neither too few nor too many students.

Just to have kept the University going during these troubled times would have seemed a satisfactory achievement to many men. Dodds did far more. The intellectual level of the University and the breadth of its interests increased steadily during his presidency. He had a remarkable talent for recognizing excellence. Bright young men were quickly promoted; first-rate scholars were attracted from other institutions; new departments and programs were created. He depended heavily, of course, on the advice of deans and department chairmen, but they gave him good advice because they knew that he would back them to the limit when they had good candidates, and that he had a sure instinct for detecting mediocrity. He could help lure a Jacob Viner from Chicago to strengthen the Department of Economics, and he could also see why Classics needed to promote a young instructor named Robert Goheen.

The creation of new departments and programs and the growth of a professional staff made it especially important to pay careful attention to appointments and promotions. The development of the Music Department (1934), the Office of Population Research (1936), the Creative Arts Program (1939), the Departments of Religion (1940), Aeronautical Engineering (1941), and Near Eastern Studies (1947), the great postwar expansion of the Woodrow Wilson School and of sponsored research programs vastly increased the size of the faculty and professional staff. A few figures will show the rate of growth:

	1933	1941	1946	1956
Faculty	327	391	514	582
Professional staff				237
Total				819
Undergraduates	2309	2434	3428	2948
Graduate students	293	267	514	636
Total	2602	2701	3942	3584

It should also be noticed that the ratio of teachers to students increased steadily (except for the postwar bulge of 1946).

The war years were especially difficult. Princeton adopted an accelerated program to give its students an opportunity to graduate before they entered the armed services. At the same time the army and navy sent hundreds of young men to the campus for general or specialized training. The number of students fluctuated widely from month to month. A faculty depleted by enlistments or calls to government service had to teach unfamiliar subjects at break-neck speed. Yet the basic ideals of a Princeton education were maintained and a remarkably high percentage of undergraduates who had left the University for military service returned after the war.

During all this turmoil Dodds remained steadfast in his belief in the value of liberal studies, and his conviction helped to steady the University. He made an effort to keep in touch with students in the services and strengthened their desire to return to college. At the end of the war he set up the Princeton Program for Servicemen, which made it easy for men to resume their education almost as soon as they were discharged.

Just as the University was adjusting to the return of students and faculty from the war, came the two-hundredth anniversary of the founding of Princeton. The year 1946-1947 was celebrated by an almost continuous series of scholarly conferences and three major convocations. Over a thousand scholars and men of affairs from all parts of the world attended these meetings. They helped to renew bonds broken by the war and to indicate the tasks to be undertaken by the new generation of scholars. As a continuing memorial of the anniversary, Bicentennial Preceptorships were established to give the most promising young assistant professors a year of free time for research.

Increasing the size and quality of the faculty was expensive. Improving retirement benefits and building new housing for the faculty was also expensive. Even more costly were badly needed additions to the physical plant. The Dillon Gymnasium (1947) replaced the old gym, destroyed in a disastrous fire. The Firestone Library (1948) gave students in the humanities and the social sciences an almost ideal place to do their work. The acquisition of the Forrestal Campus (formerly part of the Rockefeller Center for Medical Research) in 1941, gave engineering and nuclear physics badly needed space. Woodrow Wilson Hall (now Corwin Hall) provided a home for the Woodrow Wilson School. New dormitories took care of the growing student population.

To meet these expenses a constant search for money was required. Annual Giving started modestly in 1941 but soon became a major source of income ($80,000 in 1941, $1,281,000 in 1957). Dodds's request in 1938 for an increase in the number of endowed professorships was remarkably successful. Thirty new endowed professorships were established during his administration, almost doubling the number and more than doubling the income from this source. The windfall of the Higgins Trust (shared with Yale, Harvard, and Columbia) took some of the strain off the budget for the science departments. But, as always, it was the loyal support of alumni and friends who believed in the aims and achievements of the University that carried Princeton through a period of inflation and growing expenditures.

As Princeton grew, both physically and in intellectual stature, the task of administering the University became more complicated. Harold Dodds grew with the job; he was never overwhelmed by new problems or new responsibilities. He saw opportunities, not threats, in changes in American life, as he made clear in his little book, *Out of This Nettle, Danger . . .* (Princeton 1943). His quiet confidence gave confidence to others, and his sense of humor kept him from becoming dogmatic and inflexible. He could say of the alumni that their tradition of pressing advice on the president began when Benjamin Rush (1760) told Witherspoon what to do, of the faculty that in their relations with him they had displayed a "tolerance that often rose to the level of true Christian charity," of the students "that when young people start to think for themselves they always cause pain to their elders." Few university presidents of his generation had his stamina and his experience. It was fitting that after his retirement the Carnegie Foundation asked him to undertake a study which produced the book *The Academic President—Educator or Caretaker?*

Harold Dodds stated his beliefs about the role of the University most clearly at the final Bicentennial Convocation on June 17, 1947:

Princeton enters her third century with certain convictions as to what she wants her future to be. We shall uphold the banner of the general as the only safe foundation for the particular. We shall strive for quality rather than quantity; we have no illusions of grandeur that bigness will satisfy. As a residential university, we shall emphasize the community of students and teachers, believing that the life of the campus is a potent supplement to formal study and instruction. We shall always see to it that our students represent a democratic cross-section of American youth, geographically and with respect to economic circumstance. We shall strive to develop mental proficiency, and to this end work to maintain the highest scholastic standards, but we shall not forget that moral proficiency must be cultivated as well. We shall seek to advance learning as well as disseminate it. We shall remember that we were founded by God-fearing men and we shall strive to communicate to our students the sense of duty that made our forebears strong.

As she crosses the threshold of a new and fateful age, Princeton will strive to meet any challenge, to dare any adventure to preserve her integrity and to further her enduring purpose. Proud as we are of our history and grateful for the strength our heritage brings to us, we know that to rest on it can lead only to decay and destruction. We intend to be the progenitors of a stronger Princeton, not merely the beneficiaries of generations that went before us.

To sum up, the Dodds years were the years in which Princeton became a real university, a major contributor to knowledge and understanding throughout the world. They were also years in which teaching, and especially the teaching of undergraduates, reached new levels of excellence. Departmental and interdepartmental programs became broader, deeper, and more flexible. Wilson had set the goal of combining high scholarship and first-rate teaching. When he retired in June 1957, Harold Dodds had come nearer to realizing this difficult combination than any of his predecessors. As the faculty said in an address to the president, read at the last faculty meeting over which he presided:

You have steadfastly adhered to the belief that the ideal member of the Faculty is one who can both communicate and add to the knowledge of his subject. In maintaining this principle you have helped us to create a community of teacher-scholars which is the envy of other institutions. Princeton has grown, during your Presidency, in all the things which make a university—in intellectual eminence and in influence on our society. It is a better place for scholars to do their work than it was when you became President, and we are grateful for all that you have done to make it so. The years of your administration will long be remembered as a great period in the history of Princeton.

Joseph R. Strayer

Dodge Gateway, standing between 1901 and Henry Dormitories, was given in 1933 by Mr. and Mrs. Marcellus Hartley Dodge in memory of their son, Marcellus Hartley Dodge, Jr., '30, who was killed in an automobile accident in France soon after his graduation from Princeton; inscribed on the Gateway are these words from Jeremiah:

His sun is gone down
While it was yet day

Dodge-Osborn Hall (1960), which is part of Woodrow Wilson College (q.v.) bears the names of two New York families with many Princeton associations. It was given in memory of Cleveland H. Dodge 1879 and William Church Osborn 1883 (hon. LL.D. 1942) by members of their families and by the Cleveland H. Dodge Foundation.

THE DODGES

Cleveland H. Dodge (1860-1926) was the son of William Earl Dodge, Jr., industrialist and philanthropist, whose father was one of the founders of Phelps, Dodge, and Company, dealers in copper and other metals, one of the organizers of the Young Men's Christian Association in America, and a liberal benefactor of a college, later the American University of Beirut, which was founded by another son, D. Stuart Dodge.

Cleveland H. Dodge succeeded his father as national president of the Y.M.C.A. and was for many years president of the trustees of Robert College in Istanbul. He and his father gave Dodge Hall in memory of his brother, W. Earl Dodge 1879, who died a few years after graduation (see *Murray-Dodge*). Cleveland H. Dodge was a trustee of Princeton and a liberal contributor to its funds during the presidency of his classmate Woodrow Wilson. He was also the largest contributor to Wilson's presidential campaign funds in 1912 and 1916. During the First World War he directed the United War Work Campaign, which raised $170,000,000 for the Y.M.C.A., the Knights of Columbus, the Salvation Army, and other relief organizations. He also headed campaigns for the Red Cross, the Y.M.C.A. and repeated appeals for relief of sufferers in the Near East. To all of these charities he was himself a liberal contributor. In 1918 he sent his check for $1,000,000 to the Red Cross, and that same year, outbidding all other competitors, paid the Red Cross $55,000 for the presidential proclamation of its appeal bearing the personal signature of his old classmate.

Cleveland H. Dodge's twin sons distinguished themselves in education and philanthropy. Bayard Dodge '09 (hon. D.D. 1928) was president of the University of Beirut in Lebanon and after his retirement, a lecturer in Princeton's Department of Near Eastern studies. Cleveland E. Dodge '09 (hon. Phil.D. 1959) was president of the Near East Foundation, chairman of the board of trustees of Teachers College of Columbia University, a leader and benefactor of the Y.M.C.A., and an alumni trustee of Princeton. In 1972, in recognition of Bayard and Cleveland E. Dodge's service to Princeton and the Near East, members of their families established twin chairs in the University's Department of Near Eastern Studies bearing their names.

THE OSBORNS

William Church Osborn 1883 (1862-1951) was the son of William Henry Osborn, railroad president and philanthropist and one of the exposers of the Tweed Ring in New York City. His older brother, Henry Fairfield Osborn 1877, D.Sc. 1880 (hon. LL.D. '02), donor of the Osborn Clubhouse (q.v.), was Princeton's first professor of comparative anatomy and later president of the American Museum of Natural History in New York; one of his two Princeton sons, Fairfield Osborn '09 (hon. D.Sc. 1957) was president of the New York Zoological Society and a leading conservationist, widely known for his book, *Our Plundered Planet*.

A lawyer, William Church Osborn was generally regarded as one of New York's first citizens. Although he never ran for office, he was active in the political life of his city and state, serving as organizer and president of the Society to Prevent Corrupt Practices at Elections, as chairman of the New York State Democratic Committee, as founder, president and chairman of the Citizens Budget Commission. He was for fifty years president or chairman of the board of the Children's Aid Society and was also president of the Metropolitan Museum of Art. A trustee of the University for almost forty years, he served as chairman of the Princeton Fund Committee for a decade, and was a principal organizer of the Woodrow Wilson School of Public and International Affairs. The trustees later created a professorship in the School in his memory. Mrs. William Church Osborn was a sister of Cleveland H. Dodge; she gave the Dodge Professorship of History.

The William Church Osborns had three Princeton sons, the eldest of whom, Frederick H. Osborn '10, was a major-general in charge of the army's educational program during the Second World War, deputy representative of the United States on the U.N. Atomic Energy Commission, president of the Population Council, and a trustee of the University during the administrations of Presidents Dodds and Goheen.

By 1975, twenty-four members of four generations of the Dodge and Osborn families had attended Princeton.

Douglass Service Award, The, was established in 1969 by the Association of Black Collegians and named for Frederick Douglass, the nineteenth-century black leader who "epitomized in his life the revolution in the status of his race." It is presented annually to the student who "exemplifies the courage, integrity, intellectual honesty, and moral behavior that gives dignity and sense of purpose to Negro youth across the nation, and in so doing acts in accordance with the academic tradition of preparation for service embodied in the Princeton education." Recipients of the award during its early years were: William Roderick Hamilton '69; Brent L. Henry '69; Howard W. Bell, Jr. '70; Leonard G. Brown '71; Jerome Davis '71; Roderick Plummer '72; Karl E. Hammonds '73; Michelle Elizabeth Willis '74; Della Elizabeth Britton '75; Jerry D. Blackmore '76; Valerie Denise Bell '77.

Duckworth, George Eckel (1903-1972), second Giger Professor of Latin, was associated with the University as student (A.B. 1924, Ph.D. 1931) and teacher for almost half a century.

An authority on Roman comedy, especially Plautus, and on Horace and Vergil, he was known among classical scholars the world over for his studies of Vergil's use of the Golden Mean ratio in the *Aeneid*. He was one of the most productive scholars in the history of the Department of Classics. On his retirement in 1971, the department published and distributed to classical scholars here and abroad his bibliography, listing seven books and more than a hundred journal articles and reviews, and calling attention to hundreds of articles he had written for four encyclopedias. In tribute to his achievement, his colleagues quoted from Pliny: ". . . *Ille thesaurus est* [He is a storehouse of knowledge]."

His erudition, his enthusiasm for his subject, and his warm interest in his students made him an effective and popular teacher. When his last illness prevented him from meeting with classes, his undergraduate students helped him celebrate Vergil's 2000th birthday by coming to his house with a huge birthday cake and a commemorative scroll.

Duckworth was a trustee of the American Academy in Rome, a Guggenheim Fellow, and president of the American Philological Association.

Dulles Library of Diplomatic History, a two-story hexagonal addition to the Firestone Library, was built at its southeast corner in 1962. It has a reading room on the ground floor and contains in stacks on the floor below, among other American historical manuscripts, the personal papers of John Foster Dulles '08 (1888-1959), United States secretary of state from 1953 to 1959.

The papers begin with the Hague Conference in 1907, which Dulles attended while an undergraduate, and extend over a period of more than fifty years, through the American Peace Commission after World War I, the founding of the United Nations after World War II, the Japanese Peace Treaty in 1951, and Dulles's years as President Eisenhower's secretary of state, to his death in 1959.

During his first term as secretary of state, Dulles was persuaded by President Dodds that Princeton would be the appropriate place for the preservation of his personal papers, and in 1958 he worked out an agreement to this end. A year later, when Dulles became critically ill, Clarence Dillon, then under-secretary of state, and other friends and associates of the Secretary initiated a plan to donate an addition to the library to house the Dulles papers and stand as a tribute to him. A single letter from the original sponsors brought additional contributions from three hundred other friends and admirers. "This wonderful record of spontaneous and generous benefaction," President Goheen reported at the dedication of the Dulles Library in 1962, "was paralleled by the speed and grace with which the hexagonal addition to the Firestone Library was developed by the architects [R. B. O'Connor & W. H. Kilham]. One week following our meeting with the original sponsors, floor plans and elevations were ready, so that immediately thereafter Mr. Dillon and his associates were able to show Mr. Dulles, days before his death, sketches of the building almost exactly as it stands today."

When the plans were shown to Dulles, they were accompanied by a tribute which is recorded in one of the display cases of the Dulles Library:

In a troubled time, your unfaltering leadership and indomitable courage have given strength to the free world and, in future, when men live in peace, with freedom and justice, you will be remembered as a leading architect of that world.

East Asian Studies at Princeton had their roots in the Department of Oriental Languages and Literatures, established in 1927 to coordinate graduate work in Semitic and Indo-European philology. An undergraduate program was not contemplated at that time. Undergraduates nevertheless had access to excellent courses in Chinese art taught by George Rowley, and in Far Eastern politics taught by Robert K. Reischauer, who was on the faculty of the Woodrow Wilson School at the time of his death in Shanghai in 1937, and by David Nelson Rowe, who later moved to Yale. After World War II social science of the Far East was further developed with the appointments of William W. Lockwood in political economy and Marion J. Levy, Jr., in sociology.

But although some hesitant steps toward language teaching were taken during and after World War II, it was not until the appointment in 1956 of Frederick W. Mote, a graduate of Nanking, that the Department of Oriental Studies, as it then was known, began regular work in Chinese. Working with Ta-Tuan Ch'en, who joined him in 1959, Mote built a language program that trained students to utilize the formidable resources of the Gest Library (q.v.) and also to master the modern colloquial language. Later, Yu-Kung Kao came in Chinese literature, permitting Mote to return to his own specialty of history, where he was joined in turn by James T. C. Liu.

Work in Japanese began with the appointment of Marius B. Jansen in history in 1959; Japanese language and literature were offered after 1960, and directed by John Nathan after 1973. Meanwhile, a number of other men and women came in Japanese studies to balance the strength the Chinese program had already shown.

In 1961 an interdepartmental undergraduate program in East Asian Studies was set up under the direction of Jansen, and in 1969 the East Asian wing of the Department of Oriental Studies received independent status as the Department of East Asian Studies, also under his chairmanship. Later, Mote and Levy succeeded Jansen as chairman. Generous financial support by John D. Rockefeller III (1961), the Ford Foundation (1961), the Carnegie Corporation (1963), the federal Office of Education (1965), and the government of Japan (1973) enabled the University to staff strong undergraduate and graduate programs that ranked with the best in the United States.

A graduate program in Chinese and Japanese art and archaeology was established in 1958; Wen Fong and Shujiro Shimada made it the center for acquisitions and activities that produced holdings such as the Carter bronzes (1965) and exhibits recorded in publications like *Traditions in Japanese Art* (with Fogg Art Museum, Harvard, 1970) and *Studies in Chinese Connoisseurship* (Princeton, 1973). The Department of Religion began offering courses in Buddhism in 1960, and additional courses in the modern history, sociology, and politics of East Asia were made available. An experiment with Korean language, history, and politics proved unsuccessful, but a project in Chinese linguistics, begun in 1960, enriched the department's program, bringing a series of specialists to Princeton for conferences, research, and teaching.

East Asian Studies has from the first focused upon undergraduate mastery of the modern colloquial languages as the primary requirement for competence and understanding. Mote and Jansen worked with their colleagues at other universities in establishing Inter-University Centers in Tokyo and Taipei in the early 1960s, and qualified undergraduates were encouraged (through support provided by the Class of 1944) to take an additional, undergraduate year of intensive language work in East Asia. Princeton-in-Asia (q.v.) added other opportunities. In 1963 the Critical Language Program brought undergraduates from other colleges to spend a "junior year abroad in Princeton" working on East Asian, Near Eastern, or Russian language. Young women in this program, promptly labeled "critters" by Princeton undergraduates, were the first undergraduate students to break the sex barrier on campus. In 1966 a summer school, initially in Chinese, after 1970 also in Japanese, was established at Middlebury College with Princeton direction and cooperation.

By the 1970s, East Asian Studies had acquired a home in the old mathematics building, Fine Hall, now renamed Jones Hall (q.v.), and a full range of language, literature, history, and cognate courses, undergraduate as well as graduate, had brought the department into the mainstream of campus—and national—attention.

Marius B. Jansen

East College, Princeton's first building used exclusively as a dormitory, was erected in 1833. It stood on the east side of Cannon Green, facing its identical twin, West College (1836). With Nassau Hall on the north and Whig and Clio Halls on the south, East and West Colleges helped to form a quadrangle of

pleasing symmetry. The razing of East College in 1896 to make way for Pyne Library was called by some alumni "the Crime of Ninety-Six."

In its day East College was the undergraduate home of a number of eminent Princetonians. A notable group lived on the fourth and fifth floors of the south entry in the 1870s: Charles Scribner in '75, the two Butlers—Howard Russell and William Allen—and Bayard Henry in '76, Henry B. Thompson in '77, the two Pynes—M. Taylor in '77 and Percy in '78—and the two Dodges—Cleveland and Earl in '79. These nine called themselves the South East Club and for many years after graduation met annually at dinner to talk about the University and its advancement. They were especially interested in enlarging the campus, and their combined lifetime efforts secured for the University nearly a square mile of additional property. As individuals they gave five buildings and made large gifts to endowment. At one of their dinners they chipped in to endow a fellowship in the Graduate School and thus ensured a continuing remembrance of their dormitory and their group: it is called the South East Club Fellowship in Social Science.

East Pyne Building, originally Pyne Library, was built in 1897, the Sesquicentennial gift of Mrs. Percy Rivington Pyne, mother of Moses Taylor Pyne 1877 (q.v.). Designed by William A. Potter (architect also of Chancellor Green Library and Alexander Hall) in collegiate Gothic, it was used with Chancellor Green as the University Library until the completion of Firestone Library in 1948. Thereafter, as Pyne Administration Building, it housed various administrative offices until 1965, when, with the completion of New South Building, it assumed its present name and was renovated to accommodate offices and classrooms of various language and literature departments and programs and also to form the southern part of the Chancellor Green Student Center.

In niches just above the western arch at the foot of the tower are statues, by the Scottish-American sculptor, John Massey Rhind, of John Witherspoon and James McCosh, and, higher up, flanking the southwest corner, of James Madison 1771 and Oliver Ellsworth 1766 (qq.v.).

On the south side of the tower is a sun dial and beneath it Martial's epigram about the hours it records: Pereunt et Imputantur. (They pass away and are charged to our account.)

The court in the center of East Pyne is dedicated to the memory of Henry B. Thompson 1877, for many years chairman of the Trustees Committee on Grounds and Buildings, who as an undergraduate lived in East College (q.v.), which was razed to make way for Pyne Library.

Eating clubs came into being in the nineteenth century as a consequence of the College's inability to provide adequate dining facilities for its growing student population. With the banning of Greek-letter fraternities (q.v.) in 1855, the field was left open for the eating clubs to become the dominant social influence among undergraduates. Although still a distinctive feature of Princeton's non-academic life, they are no longer the center of it, now that the University offers its larger and more diverse student body a wider variety of dining and social alternatives than ever before. (See *Residential, Dining, and Social Facilities.*)

Originally, all undergraduates were required to take their meals in the commons operated by the college steward; his offerings brought frequent complaints and occasional disorder. Beginning in 1843, students were sometimes permitted to board with families in town, where the rate was higher than that charged at commons. In certain cases, however, (the 1846 catalogue announced) "select associations" of students had been formed whose expenses were even less than those in commons, and the arrangements thus made were "perfectly satisfactory and by some preferred to every other."

When the college refectory was permanently closed in 1856, all students began taking their meals in village boardinghouses, many of them in "select associations." In 1864, the newly founded *Nassau Herald* listed twelve such groups, by then called eating clubs. These clubs grew in number—there were twenty-five in 1876—but they were temporary, lasting four years at most, usually sporting playful names like "Knights of the Round Table," "Old Bourbon," "At Mrs. Van Dyne's," and some others that the hungry students of earlier years would have appreciated— "Hollow Inn," "Nunquam Plenus [Never Full]," and "More."

In the autumn of 1879 a group of upperclassmen rented Ivy Hall on Mercer Street (originally the home of the College's short-lived law school), engaged their own steward, and began a more formal kind of eating club than any previously known. Four years later, this group obtained the College's permission to incorporate and to erect a simple frame house on Prospect Avenue and thus became the first self-perpetuating upperclass eating club.

Ivy was followed in 1886 by the University Cottage Club, which got its start in the "University cottage" on University Place, and in the early 1890s by Tiger Inn, Cap and Gown, Colonial, Cannon, and Elm, which adopted common campus terms for their names. About a quarter of the juniors and seniors belonged to these seven clubs; the others continued to take their meals in casual groups in boardinghouses. "We were barely conscious that there were such clubs," Andrew C. Imbrie, life-long secretary of 1895, later recalled, "We could thumb our noses at them with complete self-respect."

The early 1900s saw the formation of six more clubs—Campus, Quadrangle, Charter, Tower, Terrace, Key and Seal—and by 1906 two thirds of the upperclassmen were eating regularly on Prospect Avenue. The newer clubs were housed in modest frame buildings, but the older ones now enjoyed handsome brick or stone clubhouses, some of them designed by architects of campus buildings.

The influence the clubs were exerting on student social life was now markedly greater than it had been in the mid-nineties. President Wilson called the lot of the third left out of clubs "a little less than deplorable." His particular concern was that the clubs separated the social from the intellectual interests of students, with the result that the University was in danger of becoming for them "only an artistic setting and background for life on Prospect Avenue."

Wilson's alternative to the eating clubs was continued in the Quad Plan he proposed to the trustees in 1907 (see *Residential, Dining and Social Facilities*). Under its terms, the clubs would either have to be abolished, or, if their cooperation could be secured, developed into smaller residential quads as part of the University itself. Though

this plan was eventually rejected, the controversy it engendered helped stimulate some long-term changes in undergraduate social life. One change came immediately. In 1908, when commons for sophomores was established in University Hall, as it had been for freshmen in 1906, freshmen and sophomore eating clubs, sometimes called "waiting clubs," were abolished by edict of the student Senior Council.

Meanwhile, formation of new upper-class eating clubs continued but at a slower pace. Four more were begun in the years before the First World War: Dial Lodge, Arch Club, Cloister Inn, and Gateway. Arch Club was short-lived, disbanding with the onset of the war. Eight more new clubhouses replaced frame-house "incubators," Cannor Club with a cannon before its main entrance, Dial Lodge, a sun-dial on its facade.

Over the years, clubs tended to develop group personalities. In *This Side of Paradise*, Scott Fitzgerald '17 gave a description of some of them, which, though a caricature, offered a colorful impression of certain recognizable club traits:

> Ivy, detached and breathlessly aristocratic; Cottage, an impressive melange of brilliant adventurers and well-dressed philanderers; Tiger Inn, broad-shouldered and athletic, vitalized by an honest elaboration of prep-school standards; Cap and Gown, anti-alcoholic, faintly religious and politically powerful; flamboyant Colonial; literary Quadrangle; and the dozen others varying in age and position.

In January 1917—around the time Fitzgerald was referring to—five sophomores issued a manifesto in the *Princetonian*, which declared that the club system operated against the best interests of the University. Their reasons were much like those Wilson had advanced ten years earlier. The spokesman for the group was Richard F. Cleveland '19, whose father, ex-President Grover Cleveland, had, as a Princeton trustee, opposed the quad plan. Under the group's leadership, some ninety sophomores pledged themselves not to join the clubs but to continue to eat at commons in newly built Madison Hall (q.v.) during their upperclass years. The Cleveland Revolt, as it came to be known, reached its climax during Bicker Week in March, but the reform it initiated was cut short the following month when Congress declared war on Germany, and normal college activities ceased for the duration of World War I.

Two more clubs—Court Club and Arbor Inn—were formed following the war, bringing the proportion of upperclassmen who were club members to 75 percent.

During the Depression, Gateway and Arbor Inn became insolvent and were taken over by the University. Arbor Inn's building on Ivy Lane was used thereafter for a succession of academic projects. Until World War II, Gateway was operated by the University as a non-selective club with a faculty member as master-in-residence. At the end of the war, the Gateway clubhouse on Washington Road was taken over by the enterprising new Prospect Club, which reduced costs by having all work, except cooking, done by its members. Founded in 1941, Prospect was obliged to disband in 1959 when it failed to attract enough members, owing, the *Princetonian* suggested, to greater interest in the new Woodrow Wilson Lodge, forerunner of Wilson College (q.v.).

Criticism of the clubs and efforts at reform, which had continued at frequent intervals following the Cleveland revolt, became more decisive in the fifties and sixties. In 1950 a declaration by over 500 sophomores that none would join a club unless all who desired membership received invitations introduced an era of "100 percent club membership" that lasted well into the 1960s. In 1966 ten student leaders published a report declaring that the club election or "bicker" system imposed "a false hierarchy on Princeton social life" and erected "artifical barriers among its students." They also asserted that because of the lack of sufficient social alternatives, bicker was "virtually compulsory." A year later fourteen upperclassmen resigned from the Ivy Club in protest against the bicker system.

In the late 1960s a special trustees' committee, under the chairmanship of S. Barksdale Penick '25, studied the club problem and related social questions in company with representatives of the faculty, undergraduates, and alumni. It recommended the creation of a variety of dining and social alternatives in order to reduce the disproportionate emphasis on membership in clubs that had developed over the years and to provide a better climate of living for all undergraduates.

The ensuing years brought an increase in the number of alternative facilities and a decrease in the number of independent clubs. When Key and Seal disbanded in 1968, its clubhouse and the adjoining building, which Court Club had given up four years earlier, were converted to a non-selective dining, social and academic gathering place called Stevenson Hall (q.v.). In 1970, the Princeton Inn College (q.v.) was created with purposes similar to those of Wilson College.

Three more clubs discontinued operations in the early 1970s and their buildings were used for other purposes—Elm and Cannon as quarters for University research programs, Cloister Inn as a club open to all alumni—but Cloister Inn was revived as an undergraduate eating club in 1977, and Elm Club, in 1978.

In order to meet changing student interests and attitudes, many of the clubs adopted features somewhat similar to those of the University's alternative programs. A number developed additional opportunities for contact between their members and faculty. Most admitted women; a few retained their traditional exclusiveness. Many became non-selective, granting admission on a first-come-first-served basis, and for those that remained selective the bicker procedure became more relaxed, with sophomores calling on the clubs instead of waiting anxiously in their rooms for visits from club bicker committees.

In 1978, thirteen of the original twenty private eating clubs were operating as such. A little more than half the junior and senior classes were members.

The complete list of clubs from the beginning follows:

Ivy Club 1879
University Cottage Club 1886
Tiger Inn 1890
Cap and Gown Club 1890
Colonial Club 1891
Cannon Club 1895-1975
Elm Club 1895-1973, 1978-
Campus Club 1900
Charter Club 1901
Quadrangle Club 1901
Tower Club 1902
Terrace Club 1904
Key and Seal Club 1904-1968
Dial Lodge 1907
Arch Club 1911-1917
Cloister Inn 1912-1972, 1977-

Gateway Club 1913-1937
Court Club 1921-1964
Arbor Inn 1923-1939
Prospect Club 1941-1959

Economics, The Department of. The subject matter that came to be called "political economy" and still later "economics" developed only slowly as a distinct field of study at Princeton. This was partly because of the late development and differentiation of "the social sciences" generally, and partly because of Princeton's devotion to her classical curriculum. Although, almost from the beginning in 1746, topics in political economy, along with those in many other fields, received attention in courses entitled "moral philosophy," there was no specific course in political economy until 1819. In that year the College initiated a one-term course that all students were required to take along with seven other courses in various fields. This constituted Princeton's entire curriculum in economics until 1890, and it was taught by men whose primary responsibilities were in such diverse fields as belles lettres, natural philosophy, mathematics, and jurisprudence.

The situation began to change in 1890, when Woodrow Wilson came to Princeton as Professor of Jurisprudence and Political Economy. Wilson moved the required senior course in political economy to junior year and introduced an "advanced" course, the History of Political Economy, as a senior elective. But Wilson's primary interests were in jurisprudence, law, and politics, and he was probably happy, therefore, to relinquish his teaching in political economy in 1892 to a newcomer, Winthrop More Daniels, who had been valedictorian of the Class of 1888. Daniels was the first specialized economist on the faculty and for nearly twenty years was the leader in developing economics at Princeton, both quantitatively and qualitatively. Professor Wertenbaker has reported that Daniels "caused a panic" by announcing that "economics would no longer be a snap," and only his able teaching and the growing interest in the subject permitted him to survive "the consternation caused by this bold break with tradition." In 1904, when the faculty was divided into departments, Daniels became the first chairman of the new Department of History, Politics, and Economics. By the time he left Princeton in 1911 to accept Wilson's appointment as chairman of the New Jersey Public Utility Commission, economics had grown markedly; there were now six faculty members, five undergraduate courses most of them extending over two terms, and some graduate seminars. Daniels was succeeded by Frank Albert Fetter, a distinguished economist who came from Cornell and was elected president of the American Economic Association in 1912. When economics was split off from history and politics to form a separate Department of Economics and Social Institutions in 1913, Fetter became its first chairman, and he was a key person in the growth of the department until his retirement in 1933.

Economics at Princeton expanded rapidly in the years between the two world wars. By 1929, its faculty had grown to 22 members. Its undergraduate curriculum included 13 courses and a program for independent work, and in terms of undergraduate majors it was one of the largest departments in the University. Graduate study in economics also rose markedly, although, consistent with University policy at that time, the number of graduate students was kept relatively small. Prior to 1920,

the University had awarded only five doctoral degrees in economics; 37 were awarded in the next two decades. Two research sections were established during this period: the Industrial Relations Section, headed first by Robert F. Foerster and then by J. Douglas Brown, who was later to become dean of the faculty; and the International Finance Section, headed by Edwin Walter Kemmerer. Several economists in the department achieved widespread recognition. Perhaps the best known were Fetter, who was widely esteemed as an economic theorist; Kemmerer, who achieved international repute as "the money doctor" (missions that he headed played leading roles in monetary reform in many foreign countries) and was president of the American Economic Association in 1926; and Frank Dunstan Graham, a recognized leader in the field of international economics.

Since World War II the department has experienced numerous changes, some stemming from changes in the scope and content of economics, and some from developments within the University. Economics grew at an unprecedented rate during this period, reflecting the rapid accumulation of empirical materials, new analytical techniques, and new fields of study and research. Macroeconomics became a major field, reflecting theoretical developments by Keynes and others as well as new national interest in the behavior of national income, employment, and price levels. New courses in economic development resulted from the rise of international concern for the plight of the less developed countries. The genesis of urban economics was a response to the growing problems of our cities. Econometrics developed as a useful technique for testing and quantifying economic theories, old and new; and mathematical economics emerged as a powerful technique of analysis. Virtually all branches of economics became more "scientific" in that they employed more empirical materials and more precise methods of analysis.

Developments within the University have also had strong impact on the size and role of the department. Undergraduate enrollments were swollen by the increased size of the student body and the continuing popularity of economics as a field of study. Most undergraduates took at least one course in economics—many still remember such outstanding teachers as William G. Bowen and Burton G. Malkiel—and a large number of them majored in the department. The expansion of the graduate school was accompanied by a commensurate increase in the number of graduate students in economics and expansion of the graduate curriculum. A heightened interest in economic research was reflected in both the growth of individual investigation and publication, and the creation of four new organizations: the Office of Population Research, headed first by Frank Notestein and then by Ansley J. Coale; the Econometric Research Program, directed first by Oskar Morgenstern and later by Gregory Chow; the Research Program in Economic Development, conducted by W. Arthur Lewis and then by John P. Lewis; and the Center for Financial Research, led by Burton G. Malkiel.

The creation of the graduate program in the Woodrow Wilson School in 1947 and its marked expansion after 1961 have engaged the efforts of many economists. Among those involved were Donald H. Wallace, who created the graduate program; Gardner Patterson, who presided over its expansion; John P. Lewis, who served as dean of the school; and William G. Bowen and Richard A. Lester, who served as associate deans. Many more economists are teachers in the program.

By the end of World War II most of the faculty who had carried the work of the department in the prewar period had retired and had not been replaced. The department had not only to provide for these replacements but also to make large net additions to its staff to meet its mounting responsibilities. To do this and also improve quality proved to be no easy task in an academic market in which able economists were scarce and in great demand. But somehow it was done. By the early 1970s the department had more than 40 members and was generally conceded to be well within the top seven or eight economics departments in the country. Only a few of the many members who contributed to this reputation can be mentioned here: Jacob Viner, one of the most versatile and eminent economists in the English-speaking world; W. Arthur Lewis, a leader in development economics; William J. Baumol, an outstanding economic theorist; Ansley J. Coale, a distinguished demographer; Fritz Machlup, an expert in international economics and president of the American Economic Association in 1966; Oskar Morgenstern, best known for his work in game theory; and Richard A. Lester, Frederick H. Harbison, and Albert Rees in labor and social economics. In the long run, of course, the future of any department depends on the quality of its younger members. On this score the department has ample reasons for optimism.

Lester V. Chandler

Edwards, Jonathan (1703-1758), third president of Princeton for a brief period in 1758, was born in East Windsor, Connecticut, where his father was pastor. The only son in a family of eleven children, he entered Yale when he was not yet thirteen and graduated four years later at the head of his class. He studied theology, preached in a Presbyterian pulpit in New York, and in 1724 returned to Yale as tutor for two years, the second year as senior tutor and virtual head of the college, the rectorship then being vacant.

In 1728 he succeeded his maternal grandfather as pastor at Northampton, Massachusetts, where his preaching brought remarkable religious revivals. But he alienated many of his congregation in 1748 by his proposal to depart from his grandfather's policy of encouraging all baptized persons to partake of Communion and instead to admit to this sacrament only those who gave satisfactory evidence of being truly converted. He was dismissed in 1750.

He moved to Stockbridge, Massachusetts, then a frontier settlement, where he ministered to a tiny congregation and served as missionary to the Housatonic Indians. There, having more time for study and writing, he completed his celebrated work, *The Freedom of the Will*.

Edwards was elected president of Princeton September 29, 1757, five days after the death of his son-in-law, Aaron Burr, Sr., second president of the College. He was a popular choice, for he had been a friend of the College since its inception and was the most eminent American philosopher-theologian of his time. But Edwards shrank from taking on "such a new and great business in the decline of life," feeling himself deficient in health, in temperament, and in some branches of learning. He finally yielded when a group of ministers persuaded him that it was his duty to accept. Late in January 1758, he came to Princeton, where he preached in the College chapel and gave out questions in divinity to the senior class for each to study and write "what he thought proper" before coming together to discuss them—an eighteenth-century seminar. The seniors spoke enthusiastically of the "light and instruction which Mr. Edwards communicated."

On March 22, 1758, he died of fever following inoculation for smallpox, and was buried in the President's Lot in the Princeton cemetery beside his son-in-law, Aaron Burr.

Edwards had three sons and eight daughters. The three sons were graduated from Princeton; one of them, Jonathan Edwards, Jr. 1765, became president of Union College. Three daughters married Yale graduates; one was Burr; another was Timothy Dwight, forebear of three Yale presidents.

In 1860 Edwards' great-grandsons had a copy made of Yale's eighteenth-century portrait of him and presented it to Princeton; it hangs in the Faculty Room in Nassau Hall.

Edwards Hall commemorates the College's third president, Jonathan Edwards. It was built in 1880 at the behest of President McCosh to fill "the clamant want" of a "new and plain dormitory to provide cheap rooms for . . . struggling students," and to reduce the number of freshmen compelled "to live beyond our walls and under no tutorial inspection." McCosh was sensitive to reports "zealously propagated by the friends of rival institutions" that Princeton was becoming a rich man's college and was not "making provisions for a class of persons for whom the College was originally instituted." He was also persuaded that the student disturbances that had brought the College unfavorable attention in the newspapers in the late 1870s "were hatched in extra-collegiate rooms in town." In the 1880s and 1890s Edwards Hall had a reputation for "plain living and high thinking" and for a time was known as "Poler's Paradise."

Einstein, Albert (1879-1955) first visited Princeton in 1921—the year before he received the Nobel Prize—to deliver five Stafford Little lectures on the theory of relativity and to accept an honorary degree. He returned again in 1933 as a life member of the newly founded Institute for Advanced Study and lived here for the remaining twenty-two years of his life.

Although his two-month visit to America in 1921 was made primarily to advance the cause of the Zionist movement, Einstein accepted Princeton's invitation to deliver the tour's most extensive series of scientific lectures because he felt more had been done here in relation to this theory of relativity than anywhere else in the United States. At ceremonies in Alexander Hall, President Hibben welcomed Einstein in German and conferred on him Princeton's honorary Doctor of Science, following the reading of a citation by Dean Andrew Fleming West, who saluted him as "the new Columbus of science, 'voyaging through strange seas of thought alone.'"

Scientists from all over the country packed McCosh 50 for all five lectures. Each lecture, which Einstein delivered in German, was followed with a resumé in English by Princeton physicist Edwin P. Adams, who was, the *Daily Princetonian* noted, among the leading American expositors of the relativity theory, along with his Princeton colleagues mathematician Luther P. Eisenhart and astrophysicist Henry Norris Russell. After being submitted to Einstein for revision and final approval, a transcript of the lectures was translated into English by Professor Adams for publication by Princeton University Press, which gained the distinction of being the first United States publisher to bring out a book by the world's most acclaimed living scientist. *The Meaning of Relativity* has been republished in five editions and is still in print.

After Einstein's acceptance of appointment at the Institute for Advanced Study in 1933, the University enjoyed a renewal of its earlier association with him. All four of his colleagues in the Institute's School of Mathematics—its first branch—had previously been professors in the University, and until the Institute erected its first building in 1939, Einstein's office (Room 109) and theirs were located in the University's original Fine Hall, a building that contained several decorative tributes to Einstein's genius—his relativity equations among the motifs in the leaded windows and his famous remark, "God is subtle, but he is not malicious," carved in the original German over the fireplace in the Common Room.

When the Institute's Fuld Hall was completed in 1939, Einstein took an office there on the ground floor, customarily walking the mile-and-a half between his white frame house at 112 Mercer Street and the Institute. He found his quiet life at Princeton "indescribably enjoyable," and wrote his friend, the physicist Max Born, that he had "settled down splendidly"—"I hibernate like a bear in its cave, and really feel more at home than ever before in all my varied existence."

His chief recreations in Princeton were playing the violin at musical evenings with friends, sailing in a little second-hand sailboat on Lake Carnegie, and walking in the countryside near the Institute.

During the Princeton years, Einstein continued his studies in general relativity, his critical discussion of the interpretation of quantum theory, and his work on a unified field theory, which was included in appendices to *The Meaning of Relativity* in its third, fourth, and fifth University Press editions. At the same time, he played an increasingly prominent role on the world stage as an advocate of nuclear control and world peace.

On the occasion of Einstein's seventieth birthday, some three hundred scientists gathered in Frick Chemical Laboratory for a symposium on his contributions to modern science, held under the joint auspices of the University and the Institute, whose director, J. Robert Oppenheimer, expressed the universal esteem in which Einstein was held by scientists the world over by referring to him in his opening remarks as "the greatest member of our brotherhood."

When Einstein died six years later in 1955, the *Daily Princetonian* devoted an entire issue to him, with tributes from friends and colleagues. Physics Department chairman Allen G. Shenstone, who was Einstein's neighbor on Mercer Street, said his character was "the most beautiful" that he had ever known. Henry D. Smyth, chairman of the University's Research Board and a former member of the Atomic Energy Commission, spoke of "the informality and simplicity which characterized his relations with lesser scientists of all ages," and declared that Physics at Princeton had "immeasurably benefited by his presence at the In-

stitute for Advanced Study."

A statement from the Institute voiced the feeling colleagues there "shared with all the world" that "one of the great figures of mankind's struggle for intellectual insight and moral improvement" had passed "into the indelible record of history where his lofty place has long been assured."

In the years since his death, Einstein's association with Princeton has been commemorated in a number of ways. A new United States postage stamp bearing a Philippe Halsman photograph of him was issued in Princeton under the sponsorship of the University and the Institute in 1966, on the eighty-seventh anniversary of his birth. Nine years later, a University professorship was endowed in his name with a $1 million grant from the International Business Machines Corporation, and Robert H. Dicke, a former physics department chairman known for his studies in the field of gravity and for important experimental tests of Einstein's general theory of relativity, was named first Albert Einstein Professor of Science. In the mid-seventies, plans were going forward for publication of Einstein's papers by Princeton University Press in a series expected to run more than twenty volumes—a project the *New York Times* called "one of the more ambitious publishing ventures of the century."

Eisenhart, Luther Pfahler (1876-1965) contributed to Princeton's development in many ways: as mathematician, teacher, chairman of his department; as chairman of the Committee on Scientific Research, dean of the faculty, dean of the Graduate School; and as father of the four-course plan.

Born in York, Pennsylvania, Eisenhart was graduated in 1896 from Gettysburg College where he excelled in baseball and mathematics. He completed all of the mathematics courses the college gave by the end of his sophomore year and spent his last two years studying mathematical problems on his own under the general guidance of his professor. This experience, he said later, gave him the idea for the four-course plan. He went on to graduate study at the Johns Hopkins University, where he found the emphasis on study and research and the low priority given to rules and restrictions congenial and stimulating.

After receiving his Ph.D. in 1900, Eisenhart was called to Princeton by President Patton as instructor in mathematics. He soon earned a reputation as a stimulating teacher and in 1905 was selected by Woodrow Wilson to be one of the original preceptors. He also made his mark as one of the elite group of promising young mathematicians brought together and nurtured by Dean Fine, and rose to the rank of full professor in 1909 when he was only thirty-three.

In 1925, following Eisenhart's work on the early development of the four-course plan, President Hibben chose him as dean of the faculty. Four years later, after Dean Fine's death, Eisenhart was also appointed chairman of the Committee on Scientific Research, named Dod Professor of Mathematics, and made chairman of the department. Eisenhart's continuation of the work begun by Fine brought Princeton to a preeminent place among the world's centers for mathematical study and prepared the way for the outstanding scientific contribution the University was able to make to the national effort in World War II. In the interregnum between the Hibben and Dodds presidencies, Eisenhart bore a major share of administrative responsibility. In 1933 President Dodds named him dean of the Graduate School.

Eisenhart's world renown as a creative mathematician, as summed up by his former student and colleague, Professor Albert W. Tucker, "stemmed from his fundamental publications in differential geometry and tensor analysis—an area spotlighted in the 1920s by Einstein's general theory of relativity. His greatest work was probably his *Riemannian Geometry* (Princeton University Press, 1926). After retirement he continued to publish with undiminished zest. His bibliography spans a period of over sixty years, during which time vast changes occurred in the area of mathematics in which he worked. Some of these changes he initiated, some he accepted, and some he ignored—but always he pushed steadily forward, consistently loyal to this chosen area of research."

As a teacher, Eisenhart was a skilled practitioner of his own dictum that "teaching methods . . . must be designed to encourage independence and self-reliance, to evoke curiosity, and stimulate the imagination and creative inpulse." His students recall that sometimes he would have to ask many questions before the student at the blackboard finally got the point, but then Eisenhart's "That's it! That's the way to do it!" always made the student feel that he himself had made the discovery.

THE FOUR-COURSE PLAN

Eisenhart's opportunity to introduce the four-course plan came in the early 1920s when President Hibben appointed a subcommittee of the Course of Study Committee to consider the question of reinstating honors courses, which had been discontinued during World War I. These honors courses, begun soon after the adoption of the preceptorial method in 1905, had never attracted many students, and the enrollment had been steadily dropping in the years before the war. Eisenhart persuaded the committee and then President Hibben, who in turn persuaded the faculty, to adopt a radical and more ambitious plan that "sought to elevate the plane of endeavor and attainment of the whole undergraduate body rather than to provide honors courses for a comparatively few students."

Under the new plan, every upperclass candidate for the A.B. would take four courses, instead of five as formerly, two of which would be in his field of concentration or department. In the free time made available to him by the reduction of the course load, the student would engage in independent study and, in his senior year, write a thesis on a subject of his own choosing. At the end of the senior year, he would take a written comprehensive examination on selected topics in his field of concentration. Honors would be awarded on the basis of this examination and the thesis combined.

Eisenhart's four-course plan was remarkable both for the emphasis it placed on independent study and for its support of the principle that honors at graduation should be open to all students and not just to a restricted group. This later provision was the most controversial feature of the plan. It was also the one in which Eisenhart believed most strongly. He insisted that grades made in underclass years did not constitute a reliable test of a student's ability to qualify for honors, and that, on the contrary, the capacity for intellectual achievement frequently did not become evident until a student had been allowed to function freely on his own in his chosen area of concentra-

tion. Eisenhart would cite with relish the instances of students who, after receiving mediocre grades in underclass years, found their interest aroused by independent work in upperclass years and had gone on to graduate with honors. At the same time, he held that it was not essential to win honors in order to derive benefit from the four-course plan. "The real test of an educational process," he said, "is what is becoming of the student as he proceeds with his education—how he is being prepared to continue his education and become an educated man."

Eisenhart had to contend with apathy and some opposition in the early days of the four-course plan. Many faculty members lacked enthusiasm for the new plan; it required more time and effort on their part, and some thought Eisenhart too optimistic about the level of work that could be expected of undergraduates. President Hibben, however, backed the plan wholeheartedly and threw the full weight of his influence into persuading the faculty to give it a fair trial. A number of the undergraduates felt that the plan was too specialized and even more thought it too hard. The spring after the plan became effective with the Class of 1925 at the beginning of their junior year, the Class of 1924 signified their luck in escaping the "misfortune" by wearing horseshoes on their beer jackets; the next year the Class of 1925 jacket showed a tiger crushed under four massive tomes. And when, in 1927, the seniors sang about Eisenhart on the steps of Nassau Hall, it was mostly in fun but a trifle in earnest:

Luther Pfahler Eisenhart,
Efficient from the very start;
But he's condemned in the eyes of
  man
For originating the four-course plan.

Skeptical alumni questioned whether the plan was appropriate for undergraduates. A number of them reported that the impression had been circulated among schoolboys that the four-course plan was burdensome, that it left undergraduates insufficient time for the usual college activities, that while it might benefit those who wished to devote their lives to academic pursuits, it was not suitable for others. These reports, coming as they did during a low period in Princeton's football fortunes, were accompanied by the further suggestion that schoolboys who were good at games were tending to look to other colleges. These discussions came to a head in the fall of 1930 and resulted in the Alumni Council's appointment of a committee to study the matter.

Eisenhart proposed that alumni who had had experience with the plan be asked their opinion of its value. A letter sent to graduates from 1925 through 1930 brought back a favorable response and concrete evidence from men in many different occupations that the plan was accomplishing what Eisenhart had promised it would. In support of his cherished belief in the stimulating effect of independent study, Eisenhart marshalled impressive figures: of the 1016 men in the Classes of 1925 through 1930 who had won honors at graduation, 17 had been fifth groupers as sophomores, 167 fourth groupers, 407 third groupers. His answer to the charge that the four-course plan was making study at Princeton too difficult, was that the percentage of undergraduates dropped for scholastic reasons in 1929-1930 was the lowest it had been in twenty-five years.

The Alumni Council eventually turned in a favorable report on the four-course plan. In the natural course of events Princeton's football fortunes

improved, and reports of schoolboy fears were no longer heard. In his later years Eisenhart had the satisfaction of knowing not only that the four-course plan had won general acceptance but that most Princetonians had come to regard the senior thesis, the capstone of independent study, as the most valuable element in their undergraduate education.*

In accomplishing all that he did, Eisenhart made effective use of his time—even the briefest moments. More important, he appeared never to waste energy giving vent to anger or frustration. He viewed human foibles with dry humor but without sarcasm, never indulging in arguments *ad hominem*; ideas were what concerned him. He was always receptive to questions and criticisms; and whether they came from faculty colleague or trustee, freshman or alumnus, Eisenhart would hear his critic out and then try to bring him around to his point of view, usually ending the demonstration of his proposition with a wrinkled smile and a persuasively urgent "Isn't that it? Isn't that it?"

Eisenhart served as president of the American Mathematical Society and of the American Association of Colleges, and as vice president of the National Academy of Sciences and of the American Association for the Advancement of Science. He became the executive officer of the American Philosophical Society in 1942 and continued to supervise its affairs long after his retirement from Princeton in 1945, commuting to Philadelphia once or twice a week through his eighty-fourth year.

At his death, his faculty colleagues said that "in two centuries of Princeton's history few scholars had done more to shape the future of the University," and the trustees declared that he had "earned an enduring place in the front rank" of those who had "made Princeton great."

A portrait of Dean Eisenhart hangs in Procter Hall of the Graduate College. The Eisenhart Arch, given in his honor by an anonymous donor in 1951, marks the western approach to the Graduate College from Springdale Road.

* The Eisenhart ideal of independent study received additional emphasis beginning in 1967; thereafter, each undergraduate working for the A.B. was required to take only four courses a term during freshman and sophomore as well as junior year and three during senior year.

Electrical Engineering, Department of. Originally, engineering was associated primarily with the construction of military fortifications and devices. Early in the nineteenth century the application of this rapidly developing body of knowledge for nonmilitary purposes was designated civil engineering. Thereafter, civil engineering encompassed all engineering practice until the late nineteenth century, when increasing knowledge and technological innovation led to specialization and division into various subfields. Electrical engineering was often the first specialty so identified in universities because of the great activity in electrical research, development, and invention of the 1870s.

The stage was set at Princeton when Cyrus Fogg Brackett (q.v.) arrived in 1873 as Professor of Physics. This remarkable, energetic man was most interested in electrical phenomena and their applications. He was a friend of Thomas Edison and often supplied the theoretical basis for the inventor's amazing practical intuition and insight. Brackett's interest led naturally to the establishment of a two-year graduate program, leading to the degree of Electrical Engineer, first announced in the 1889 Catalogue of the College of New Jersey. Although the engineering subjects have changed substantially since that time, the prerequisite education has remained much the same. In particular, the statement in the 1889 catalogue that "Mathematics will be treated as a working instrument of which the student has already acquired control . . ." is consistent with the continuing emphasis on applied mathematics in Electrical Engineering. Brackett's role in the establishment of Electrical Engineering at Princeton was recognized when the wing housing this department in the Engineering Quadrangle was named Brackett Hall.

Brackett's successor was Malcolm MacLaren, a practicing electrical engineer from Westinghouse who served as chairman throughout a period of educational change. The technological demands of World War I accentuated the need for engineering education, and special intensive programs were established in the University. This activity further increased the growing interest in undergraduate curricula, and when the School of Engineering was established in 1921, Electrical Engineering was one of five departments offering the Bachelor of Science in Engineering degree for undergraduate specialization in their fields.

MacLaren retired in 1937 and was succeeded by Clodius H. Willis (q.v.), an expert in power conversion who, during World War II, also faced the pressure of demands for increased engineering education. This time, the development of sophisticated electronic devices placed a relatively greater burden on electrical engineering educators, who were called on to produce graduates capable of dealing with such devices as sonar and radar. In addition to managing army- and navy-supported undergraduate programs, Willis directed a graduate radar training program. During this era, the department became expert at making necessary adaptations; the graduate radar program, for example, used a garage opposite the University Press as its principal laboratory.

In 1950, Willis resigned the chairmanship because of failing health, and Walter C. Johnson replaced him. This was again a period when educational adaptation was needed to accommodate the new directions and changing emphasis that had arisen from the technological developments of the war. In recognition of the growing importance of research requiring advanced mathematics and physics in addition to a high degree of engineering specialization, the Ph.D. program had been introduced in 1946. During Johnson's chairmanship, doctoral education and the accompanying faculty and student research became an increasingly important departmental activity.

In 1966 Mac Elwyn Van Valkenburg, a nationally know circuit theorist, came from the University of Illinois to assume the chairmanship. Under his direction, research and graduate education were further strengthened, and the undergraduate curriculum was revised to reflect the changing directions in the field.

Van Valkenburg returned to the University of Illinois in 1973, and Bruce W. Arden was called from the University of Michigan to become chairman. Arden's principal interests are in the area of computer science and engineering. The development of the electronic digital computer has had a marked impact on society in many ways; at the same time, it has profoundly changed many of the classical engineering problem-solving techniques. Consequently, undergraduate and graduate students are deeply interested in computing, and they are being educated to understand and use this powerful tool in engineering work. In the tradition of engineering at Princeton the Department of Electrical Engineering continues to provide a strong scientific education adapted to current methods and problems.

Bruce W. Arden

Ellsworth, Oliver (1745-1807), one of the nation's founding fathers and third Chief Justice of the United States, received half of his undergraduate education at Yale, and half at Princeton, where he graduated in 1766. In his junior year he and others founded the Well Meaning Club, which later became the Cliosophic Society.

Returning to his home in Windsor, Connecticut, he studied theology and then law, and was admitted to the bar in 1771. At first his law practice was so unremunerative that he had to support himself by farming and occasional woodchopping, and on days when the court was sitting he was obliged to walk from his farm in Hartford and back, a round trip of twenty miles, since he was too poor to keep a horse.

In 1775 he moved to Hartford. There his rise at the bar was rapid, and before long there were few important cases in Connecticut in which Ellsworth did not represent one side or the other.

He was a delegate to the General Assembly of the state that met soon after the Battle of Lexington, and throughout the Revolutionary War was a member of the Continental Congress. He was one of the delegates from Connecticut in the Federal Constitutional Convention, one of the first two senators from Connecticut, and, on appointment of President Washington, served as Chief Justice of the United States from 1796 to 1800.

At the Federal Constitutional Convention, William Pierce, a delegate from Georgia who kept careful notes about all his colleagues, said Ellsworth was "a gentleman of a clear, deep, and copious understanding, eloquent in . . . public debate . . . very happy in reply, and choice in selecting such parts of his adversary's arguments as he finds makes the strongest impressions, in order to take off the force of them so as to admit the power of his own." Ellsworth employed these talents to support the Connecticut Compromise, which broke the deadlock between the large states, represented by James Madison 1771 of Virginia, and the small states, represented by Ellsworth's fellow Well Meaner and Cliosophian, William Paterson 1763 of New Jersey.

Ellsworth made his greatest contribution while serving in the United States Senate by drafting the Judiciary Act of 1789; the court system it established has continued to the present with little change.

Yale conferred an honorary LL.D. on him in 1790; Princeton, in 1797.

Endowed Professorships first came into being at Princeton in the middle of the last century. In 1827 the newly formed Alumni Association of Nassau Hall stressed the importance of collecting funds for the endowment of professorships, but it was not until 1857 that Silas Holmes of New York City gave Princeton's first endowed chair—in "belles-lettres"—which was named for him. Others soon followed: in 1864 John I. Blair gave a professorship in geology that bears his name; in 1869 Samuel Bayard Dod 1857 gave one in

mathematics in memory of his father, Professor Albert Baldwin Dod; in 1870 John N. Woodhull 1828, a local physician, founded a chair in modern languages; and in 1872 John C. Green gave a physics professorship in honor of Professor Joseph Henry.

With the growing prosperity of the country, gifts for new chairs increased steadily and by 1900 there were sixteen. Thereafter, the number increased more rapidly: by the end of President Hibben's administration in 1932 there were thirty-five; by the end of President Dodds' in 1957, sixty-five; when President Goheen left office in 1972 there were eighty-seven. By 1976, there were ninety-eight professorships supported by special funds—ninety endowed by gifts or bequests, five supported by the Higgins Trust (established in 1950), and three by current grants. Named for professors, trustees, alumni classes, individual alumni, and other friends of the University, they were fairly evenly distributed among the several areas of learning. About a third of the University's full professors occupy these specially designated chairs.

Endowment. On March 25, 1745, ten men executed pledges totaling 185 pounds "for the purpose of Erecting a Collegiate School in the province of New Jersey for the instructing of youth in the Learned Languages, Liberal Arts, and Sciences." The pledges were made a year and a half before the first charter establishing the College of New Jersey was granted. The document provided that only the interest earned on the principal sum could be expended for current purposes: namely, the payment of the president's salary and the salaries of tutors, and that the principal was to be continuously reinvested to generate income for the future. These modest pledges—whose value proved to be less than the president's annual salary—marked the beginning of Princeton's endowment, funds that in the mid-seventies totaled over $450 million.

The classic definition of "endowment" is a gift made on the stipulation that the principal be maintained in perpetuity and that only income from investment of the gift be expended. In addition to gifts of this nature, the University's current endowment fund also includes gifts received without any such stipulation, and allocated by the trustees to function as endowment, as well as appreciation earned from the investment of endowment funds.

In absolute terms the Princeton endowment is one of the largest of any University in the country. Measured in terms of the size of the fund relative to the size of the University—for instance, by an approximate measure such as endowment dollar per student—Princeton's endowment ranks as probably greater than that of any university but Harvard. The income generated annually from the endowment now constitutes about 16 percent of the University's annual operating budget.

The endowment thus represents the legacy to the present of the past generosity of the University's supporters. The growth of the endowment also reflects the skill and insight of the trustees in managing Princeton's funds. In the late 1940s and early 1950s, when conventional wisdom indicated that an endowment fund should be invested largely in fixed-income securities, Princeton increasingly allocated its endowment to equities, with a strong emphasis on growth-type stocks. Such investments have tended to produce higher rates of return than so-called income stocks or bonds. In 1940 only 27 percent of the market value of our endowment was invested in common stocks; today about 75 percent of the fund is in equities.

This investment strategy has yielded superior results. For instance, from 1958 through 1975, Princeton's endowment earned more in capital appreciation and income than the stock market on average, a performance achieved by few institutional funds, college, corporate, or financial. A study by the National Association of College and University Business Officers shows that over a ten-year period ending June 30, 1975, Princeton's endowment performance ranked fourth out of eighty endowment funds examined.

Policy for management of the University's endowment is set by an Investment Committee of three trustees who constitute a subcommittee of the Finance Committee of the Board of Trustees. The University's chief financial officer sits with the Investment Committee. For many years, the Investment Committee approved in advance the purchase and sale of all securities, aided by John W. Bristol & Co. Inc., which served as investment adviser to the Committee—a role that firm (and a predecessor organization) played since the mid-1930s. In the fall of 1977, the Investment Committee adopted a new procedure by which the committee concentrated on policy, delegating responsibility for the day-to-day selection of securities for the University's portfolio to four investment advisers: John W. Bristol and Herbert E. Gernert of New York, Robert E. Pruyne of Boston, and Mitchell Milias of Los Angeles.

Paul B. Firstenberg

Engineering and Applied Science, The School of, owes its origin to the benefactions of John C. Green (q.v.), founder in 1872 of the School of Science, and to the pioneering efforts of two early professors in that school, Cyrus Fogg Brackett and Charles McMillan (qq.v.). McMillian, who was called in 1875 to fill a civil engineering chair endowed that year by Green, gave the College's first engineering course and organized its first engineering department. Brackett, who came in 1873 to fill a physics chair endowed that year by Green, gave new life to the teaching of physics and conducted the College's first graduate course in engineering—in the School of Electrical Engineering, which he began in 1889.

The civil engineers turned out by McMillan and the electrical engineers by Brackett were at first few in number, but by 1912 there were enough of them to organize the Princeton Engineering Association "to bring together the men of Princeton interested in engineering . . . to the single end that the interests, influence, and efficiency of Princeton University be advanced through its Department of Engineering." Enthusiastic about the professional training Princeton had given them, they were eager to have the University broaden its curriculum to include other branches of engineering.

Spurred on by this association, the University announced the formation of a School of Engineering in 1921, and in 1922 Arthur M. Greene, Jr. (q.v.) came from Rensselaer Polytechnic Institute as its first dean. Greene proved to be, in the words of his successor, Kenneth H. Condit, "a born teacher, an able administrator, and a dynamo of energy."

Under Greene's guidance, four-year undergraduate programs were offered in civil, chemical, electrical, mechanical, and mining (later geological) engineering, and one-year graduate courses leading to the corresponding engineering degree (later to the Master of Science in Engineering for all fields).

In 1928 the school was given a home of its own, named the John C. Green Engineering Building (now Green Hall), the old Green School of Science having been destroyed by fire shortly before.

With the help of the Princeton Engineering Association, advisory committees of practicing engineers were formed for all engineering departments in 1935. These groups set the pattern for the system of Advisory Councils for all departments of the University established in 1941. Out of their discussions evolved the Basic Engineering Program, which the faculty formulated in 1938.

Greene's devotion and energy gave the school a sure foundation. When he came to Princeton in 1922 there were 84 engineering students. By 1940, when he retired, the number had grown to 379. But perhaps his most important contribution was the staunch support he gave to the Princeton concept of engineering education, the combining of instruction in science and fundamental engineering subjects with courses in the liberal arts, to provide what President Hibben and he liked to call "Engineering Plus."

1940-1954

Kenneth H. Condit, who succeeded Dean Greene, was a graduate of Stevens Institute in mechanical engineering and of Princeton in civil engineering. He had been an editor of McGraw-Hill engineering journals and, for a time, executive assistant to the president of the National Industrial Conference Board. He had also been president of the Princeton Engineering Association.

Condit's deanship covered the difficult days of World War II and the immediate postwar period. A rapid development of government research plus a greatly expanded program of instruction for civilian and military engineers during the war was followed, in President Dodds' words, "by a broadening of all areas of teaching and research far beyond dimensions previously envisaged."

A new Department of Aeronautical Engineering, initiated by Daniel C. Sayre (q.v.) early in the war, became, in a very few years, a leader in its field. A pioneering interdisciplinary program in plastics was also begun; it later evolved into the Polymer Sciences and Materials Program. The undergraduate curriculum was enriched by the introduction of special programs which permitted students with special abilities to do work in two fields of engineering or to combine their study of one engineering field with additional concentration in a related field of science and mathematics. Two undergraduates founded *The Princeton Engineer* (q.v.), which faithfully mirrored the growth of the school in succeeding years. Graduate training, previously limited to the one year required for the M.S.E. degree, was gradually extended to include work for the doctorate: Ph.D. programs were introduced in chemical engineering and electrical engineering in 1946, in aeronautical engineering in 1949, in civil engineering in 1951, in mechanical engineering in 1952.

The growth of the school put a heavy burden on the Green Engineering Building, which had been designed to accommodate 400 undergraduates.

Chemical Engineering fell heir to the old chemical laboratory building next door; Aeronautical Engineering, to several buildings near the lake which had been built for the Physics Department during the war; and, with the help of the ever-loyal Princeton Engineering Association, funds were raised to build the Hayes wing on Green for mechanical engineering.

The acquisition, in 1951, of the property of the Rockefeller Institute for Medical Research and its development as the James Forrestal Campus (q.v.), under Professor Sayre's guidance as director and Dean Condit's as chairman of the administrative committee, provided excellent working space for the burgeoning Department of Aeronautical Engineering.

When Dean Condit retired in 1954, the engineering faculty was three times as large as when he took office; the number of undergraduates had increased from 379 to 528, the number of graduate students from 11 to 87.

1954-1971

Joseph Clifton Elgin, third dean of the school, brought to the office in 1954 twenty-five years' experience as the University's first teacher of chemical engineering, including eighteen as the first chairman of that department.

Outstanding among the school's achievements during his administration was the development of a new concept of engineering education, which left much of the traditional engineering art—the technology and the skills—to a period of apprenticeship in industry, and placed increasing emphasis on engineering science, which, in Elgin's words, is concerned with "the principles upon which all technologies and engineering skills are ultimately based."

The Departments of Chemical and Electrical Engineering had for some years emphasized the engineering science approach and this was now extended to the other departments. Undergraduate curricula were completely revised and graduate programs strengthened in response to Elgin's urging:

> With strong departments of mathematics and the natural sciences [he wrote], Princeton has an exceptional opportunity to bring its School of Engineering to the forefront in its contributions to graduate engineering education and the advancement of knowledge in the engineering sciences.

The faculty's efforts to this end were rewarded in 1962 when Princeton was one of five universities to receive grants of one million dollars each from the Alfred P. Sloan Foundation in recognition of the emphasis they had given the scientific approach to engineering education, which the Foundation sought to encourage nationally.

With these developments, the space shortage which the school had suffered increasingly since World War II made new quarters one of the most urgent needs to be met by the $53 Million Campaign. Canvassers sought $8 million for a new quadrangle for engineering science, and when that amount had been raised, Dean Elgin and his faculty were ready with plans for a center that would provide facilities for new patterns of instruction and for expanded programs of postgraduate education and engineering research.

In the fall of 1962, the school moved into the new Engineering Quadrangle, whose five connecting halls gave it four times the space it had had in the Green Engineering Building and its satellites, and whose library's book capacity was seven times that of its former library.

At the same time, the increasing emphasis the faculty had given to engineering science was recognized by changing the school's name to the School of Engineering and Applied Science. Changing orientations also brought a merger of Aeronautical Engineering and Mechanical Engineering to form the Department of Aerospace and Mechanical Sciences, and a change in the organization of Geological Engineering, which merged with Civil Engineering in 1966 and subsequently became a program in that department, offered in cooperation with the Department of Geological and Geophysical Sciences.

Having acquired more adequate space and equipment the school prospered through the 1960s. Interdisciplinary research and instruction were fostered by the initiation of programs jointly offered by several engineering departments, sometimes in cooperation with non-engineering departments, in such fields as solid state and materials sciences, water resources, geophysical fluid dynamics, environmental studies. In 1969 Elgin's leadership was recognized by the American Society for Engineering Education when it conferred on him its highest honor, the Lamme Award.

Elgin retired as dean in 1971. During the seventeen years of his administration the faculty almost doubled to ninety-seven, the annual volume of sponsored research more than tripled to $3.8 million, the number of graduate students almost tripled to 241, with the number of undergraduate students remaining about the same. But the most dramatic index of the school's growth was the increase in the number of engineering Ph.D.'s awarded in one academic year: from seven in 1953-1954 to fifty in 1970-1971.

THE 1970s

Robert G. Jahn, Elgin's successor as fourth dean of the school, did both his undergraduate and graduate work at Princeton. He won highest honors in mechanical engineering at graduation in 1951 and was joint winner of the annual Kusaka prize as the most promising student of physics when he took his Ph.D. in that subject in 1955. After teaching for seven years at Lehigh and California Institute of Technology, he returned to Princeton in 1962 as assistant professor of aeronautical engineering in the Guggenheim Laboratories for the Aerospace Propulsion Sciences, and in 1967 he became professor of aerospace sciences. In 1968 he published *Physics of Electric Propulsion*, the definitive text in its field; the following year he received the Curtis W. McGraw ['19] Award of the American Society of Engineering Education for his research in plasma propulsion.

In an interview reported in *University* soon after he took office in 1971, Dean Jahn outlined the distinctive role of the Princeton School of Engineering in this way:

Princeton is a very special place in terms of excellence of the overall academic program, size, heritage. We cannot pretend that we are a major technological institute like M.I.T. or Cal. Tech. Nor can we replicate a large university complex, like Michigan or Minnesota. We have a small engineering school which must flourish in the framework of a small, liberal, excellent university. That I regard as an advantage, especially in an era which favors individually tailored, liberal engineering education for its students. We must respond to the anti-technological criticism being heard today; more important, we must respond to the needs of society for solutions to some very pressing problems. What better place to do it than at a university which has well-developed programs in the humanities, social sciences, and natural sciences; and which has a heritage of engineering education that has always emphasized the development of the mind of the student more than the simple transfer of technical facts and techniques?

"Solutions to . . . pressing problems" were sought in a series of four interdisciplinary topical programs introduced in 1972 as added study opportunities for undergraduates: Bioengineering, Energy Conversion and Resources, Environmental Studies, and Transportation. The purpose of these topical programs was to demonstrate the relevance of fundamental engineering scholarship to urgent contemporary social problems. This new curricular dimension proved attractive to the students, and helped to reverse the anti-technology mood that prevailed in the early seventies. Enrollment in the freshman class, which had dropped to 135 in the fall of 1971, increased sharply to 185 in 1972, and reached an all-time high of 250 in 1976. The same period also saw the first significant enrollment of women in the school; in 1973 they constituted 11 percent of the entering class, and by 1977 nearly 18 percent of the University's undergraduate engineering students were women—almost three times the national average. The engineering faculty found equally encouraging a substantial increase in transfers of A.B. students into the school and the enrollment of many more A.B. students in engineering courses. In the words of Dean Jahn, the School of Engineering had achieved "full integration into the academic fabric of the University."

Engineering Quadrangle, The, was dedicated on October 13, 1962. Built at a cost of approximately $8 million with funds derived largely from the $53 million campaign, the Quadrangle consists of six interconnecting halls surrounding a central court, located on Olden Avenue between Nassau Street and Prospect Avenue on land formerly a part of the old University Field. The Quadrangle, whose floor area is the equivalent of that of seven Nassau Halls, contains 120 laboratories for research and instruction, over 125 faculty offices and graduate study spaces, 25 classrooms, a research library, a general purpose machine shop, and a lounge and convocation room. It was designed by the architectural firm of Voorhees, Walker, Smith, Smith and Haines.

Five of the halls, devoted to teaching and research, are named for faculty and alumni: John Maclean, Sr., Princeton's first professor of chemistry; John Thomas Duffield, Professor of Mechanics and Mathematics; Cyrus Fogg Brackett, founder of the department of electrical engineering; George Erle Beggs, Professor of Civil Engineering; and James E. Hayes, C.E. 1895 and E.E. 1897. The sixth unit, the library, is named for the class of 1900, which made the principal gift for its construction. The court at the center of the quadrangle is named for architect Stephen F. Voorhees '00, a university trustee.

English, Department of. Until well through the nineteenth century, English studies at Princeton, as elsewhere, were regarded as incidental to preparation for the ministry, law, or public life, and as a result instruction concentrated on grammar and composition, rhetoric, and elocution. President Witherspoon's lectures on eloquence in the early days of the College were the forerunners of such studies, and indeed of criticism of contemporary writers, for he had some uncomplimentary things to say about the style of "one Samuel Johnson."

Although the Rev. James W. Alexander, Professor of Belles-Lettres, delivered in 1838 what should probably be regarded as the first course of lectures in English literature, official recognition of this subject in the College catalogue had to wait until 1864 when John S. Hart was listed as "Lecturer on English Literature." Further evidence of increasing attention to English studies came in 1868, when the title of Joshua H. McIlvaine, second incumbent of the University's oldest endowed chair, the Holmes Professorship, was changed from "Belles-Lettres and Elocution" to "Belles-Lettres and English Language and Literature." In 1870 the first description of courses in English appeared in the Catalogue, almost certainly as a result of the introduction of a modified form of the elective system by President James McCosh, who had come to Princeton from Belfast two years earlier. But the main burden of instruction remained on composition, rhetoric, and language.

The mid-1870s brought two key appointments: Theodore W. Hunt as Adjunct Professor of Rhetoric and English, and James O. Murray as Holmes Professor. "Granny" Hunt, as he became affectionally known, was the first chairman of the English Department. Murray became the first dean of the faculty; a professorship was named after him.

The growing importance of English within an expanding curriculum during the last decade of the nineteenth century is apparent from the names of the eminent scholars and teachers who joined Hunt and Murray. These included: Bliss Perry, Professor of Oratory and Aesthetic Criticism; Henry van Dyke, first Murray Professor; and George McLean Harper, who relinquished the Woodhull Professorship of Modern Languages to succeed Perry as Holmes Professor. In 1902 Thomas Marc Parrott was appointed Professor of English.

The stage was now set for the establishment of a Department of English in 1904 and its rapid expansion a year later, when President Wilson added to the current nucleus of professors seven preceptors, among whom were: Gordon H. Gerould, Francis C. MacDonald, Charles G. Osgood, Robert K. Root, and J. Duncan Spaeth. With the addition, in the years immediately following, of such preceptors as Morris W. Croll and Charles W. Kennedy, the department attained a position of national prominence that it has continued to enjoy.

The founding members of the department embodied to a remarkable extent the qualities that came to be associated with Princeton's ideal of the teacher-scholar. English shared with Greek Literature, Roman Literature, and Philosophy the distinction of being the first of the humanistic departments to be able to offer, after the new Graduate School was founded in 1901, a full roster of graduate as well as undergraduate courses. The authoritative learning of the members of the English faculty enabled them to preside over a program of graduate studies that had only three or four rivals, while their devotion to humane values made them among the most popular and influential undergraduate teachers. Despite the scholarly reputations they built up through their publications, none was confined in intellectual range to his field of specialization. Harper combined pioneer research on Wordsworth with the teaching of courses covering the entire Renaissance; Parrott was equally at home with Shakespeare, Renaissance drama, and the broad field of Victorian literature; Osgood, celebrated for his *variorum* edition of Spenser, was also an authority on Milton and Johnson; Gerould, who introduced the first course entirely devoted to prose fiction, was known for his mastery of early narrative poetry, especially the ballad. Root, whose teaching embraced Chaucer, the eighteenth century, and a famous course in the history of the language, in addition held successively the positions of the departmental chairman and dean of the faculty. His brilliance as a teacher is commemorated in "Root's Alumni Preceptorial," a group of alumni who met with Root periodically for dinner and discussion of assigned reading from the 1920s until his death in 1950, and since then have continued to meet similarly with other members of the English faculty.

During the late 1920s and 1930s a new generation of teacher-scholars came forward. Hoyt H. Hudson, later departmental chairman, reaffirmed the University's ancient allegiance to rhetoric and public speaking. His successors were Wilbur S. Howell, who established an international reputation for his studies in the history of rhetoric, and Jeremiah S. Finch, who was later also dean of the College and secretary of the University. Spaeth had offered a course in American literature as early as 1919. Joining the faculty in 1926, Willard Thorp, with his studies in Melville and others, gave the department a leadership in American studies that eventuated in 1942 with the establishment of a Program in American Civilization. In 1939 he was joined by Lawrance R. Thompson, who that year was appointed official biographer of Robert Frost. They were joined subsequently by Richard Ludwig, who is chief bibliographer for the *Literary History of the United States*, of which Thorp was one of the founders; and still later by William Howarth, chief editor of an edition of Thoreau's complete works issued by Princeton University Press with the aid of the National Endowment for the Humanities.

Bliss Perry in the 1890s originated a tradition of brilliant literary criticism, carried on by an unbroken line, which included Morris W. Croll, Asher E. Hinds, who gave his name to the departmental library, Donald A. Stauffer, Richard P. Blackmur, and A. Walton Litz. Stauffer was chairman from 1946 until his early death in 1952. He and his successors as chairman, Carlos Baker and Willard Thorp, were primarily responsible for revising the curriculum to include a large number of courses in modern literature, although students were still required to be firmly grounded in earlier periods.

A course in advanced composition, first offered in 1915 , was taken over in 1922 by Herbert S. Murch, who made it a breeding ground for writers. In 1939 this instruction was formalized within the Creative Arts Program, with Allen Tate as first Resident Fellow in Writing. His distinguished successor, Blackmur, became Professor of English as well. In 1971 the Program in Creative Writing became a separate entity under the chairmanship of Edmund L. Keeley, novelist and translator of modern Greek poetry, assisted by Theodore R. Weiss, poet and editor of *Quarterly Review of Literature*, and a staff of visiting writers who came for one or two years. The establishment of the Ferris Professorship of Journalism and Public Relations in 1964, with Irving Dilliard as first incumbent, provided further opportunity for students to perfect their writing skill.

The decade preceding the Second World War had brought to the department two additional scholars of note, both Princeton Ph.D.'s: Maurice W. Kelley, who maintained the department's eminence in Miltonic studies; and Carlos Baker, whose published works extend from Shelley to the standard biography of Ernest Hemingway.

The postwar years were ones of rebuilding in many fields. Gerald E. Bentley, author of the seven-volume *Jacobean and Caroline Stage*, and Alan S. Downer, who was later chairman, expanded the teaching of dramatic literature. Other major appointments included Louis A. Landa in the eighteenth century with particular emphasis on Swift and Defoe, and Durant W. Robertson, Jr., author, notably, of *A Preface to Chaucer*, in medieval studies. Robert B. Martin, an accomplished writer in many fields, joined E.D.H. Johnson in guiding the expansion of Victorian studies. The appointments of Hans Aarsleff and of Albert H. Marckwardt guaranteed that the department would continue to encourage the attention to Old English and linguistics first nurtured by Theodore W. Hunt and Charles W. Kennedy.

The Departments of English and History have for many years shared, in friendly rivalry, the distinction of having the largest number of upperclass concentrators. With the advent of coeducation the number of outstanding students electing English studies increased notably. At the same time the department welcomed women to its teaching staff; their number had reached seven in 1974. In the preceptorial and lecture rooms of McCosh Hall, the department's teacher-scholar tradition continued to flourish.

E.D.H. Johnson

Eno Hall at the time of its completion in 1924 was, in Professor Howard Crosby Warren's words, "the first laboratory in this country, if not in the world, dedicated solely to the teaching and investigation of scientific psychology." It was named in honor of the principal donor, Henry Lane Eno, Research Associate in Psychology. Another donor, then anonymous, was Professor Warren, chairman of the department, for whom, as President Hibben pointed out, the laboratory was the realization of a dream he had long cherished.

The Department of Psychology occupied Eno Hall until 1963 when it was given larger quarters, along with the Department of Sociology, in John C. Green Hall. Eno was subsequently used by the Department of Biology to supplement its facilities in Guyot Hall.

Eno Hall was designed by Day & Klauder. Above its front door is the motto originally carved over the portal of the Oracle of Delphi in ancient Greece: *Gnothi Sauton* [Know Thyself].

Enrollment in the College of New Jersey when President Jonathan Dickinson began instruction in his Elizabethtown parsonage in 1747 probably numbered not more than ten students. During the College's first twenty-one years, the 338 students in attendance came from all but two of the thirteen colonies. Although the majority lived in New Jersey, New York, and Pennsylvania, more than a quarter were from New England, and a fair number from the South, thus putting the College "on the way to becoming a national institution well before there was a nation."*

After 1768, President Witherspoon was particularly successful in attracting students from the South, where earlier graduates had formed strong Princeton influences as ministers and teachers. Under Witherspoon, the College enjoyed a cosmopolitan flavor, with students "not only from almost every province," Philip Fithian 1771 wrote in his senior year, "but . . . also many from the West Indies & some few from Europe."

Enrollment reached 314 by 1860 and then fell off during and after the Civil War. It resumed its upward trend under President McCosh, with the number of undergraduates doubling in his administration and again in President Patton's and rising steadily under Presidents Wilson (1,289), Hibben (2,279), Dodds (2,948), and Goheen (3,903). In later years this rise was a controlled one, based on a policy of limited enrollment and selective admission adopted in 1922.

The Civil War reduced the flow of students from the South, and although they never regained their numerical prominence—at times half the student body had been southern—the general enrollment rise later in the century brought with it a proportionate increase in the number of southern students. Appreciable enrollments from the Middle West began in the 1880s and from the Far West in the 1920s. Although the largest number of undergraduates, as of 1976, continued to come from New York (917), New Jersey

(767), and Pennsylvania (442), there were substantial enrollments from states in New England, the South, the Middle West, the Southwest, and the Far West. In those regions the states with the largest enrollments were Massachusetts (302), Virginia (129), Illinois (94), Texas (124), and California (156), respectively.

Until the 1870s Princeton's enrollment was entirely undergraduate except for occasional non-degree postgraduate students. The number of candidates for higher degrees steadily increased under President McCosh, and by the time the Graduate School was formally established in 1901 there were 117. After the First World War, enrollment in the Graduate School was limited to 200, and then 250, but following the Second World War, a policy of controlled expansion was adopted, allowing a marked rise in the number enrolled.

A considerable influx of students from other countries after the Second World War added to the cosmopolitan character of the student body. In 1976 approximately 4 percent of the undergraduates and 22 percent of the graduate students came from outside the United States.

Two University decisions in the 1960s further increased the diversity of student enrollment: the adoption of an active recruitment policy for blacks and other minority groups, and the decision to admit women to the Graduate School and later to the undergraduate college.

By 1976, total student enrollment had grown to 5,775, with representatives from every state in the Union and from seventy countries on six continents. It consisted of 4,360 undergraduates, including 1,395 women, 346 blacks, and 351 members of other minority groups; and 1,415 graduate students, including 367 women, 38 blacks, and 185 representing other minority groups.

Earle E. Coleman

* James McLachlan, *Princetonians 1748-1768; A Biographical Dictionary* (Princeton University Press, 1976).

Evelyn College for Women created a pleasant stir in the borough of Princeton for ten years toward the end of the last century. Founded in 1887 by a 72-year-old clergyman and former Princeton professor, Joshua Hall McIlvaine 1837, who named it after Sir John Evelyn, seventeenth-century man of letters, the college was housed in two buildings about a mile east of the center of town, one on what is now called Evelyn Place, the other on the southwest corner of Nassau and Harrison Streets.

Although Evelyn had no legal connection with Princeton, it enjoyed most of the benefits of a coordinate college. President Patton, Dean Murray, and Professors Marquand and Young were on its board of trustees, and most of Princeton's senior professors lectured there. Enrollment was small, probably never more than fifty in one year, made up largely of daughters of professors in the College and the Seminary and sisters of Princeton undergraduates.

When the newly formed Colonial Club rented the house next door to Evelyn College for its first clubhouse, it found its competitive position strengthened vis-à-vis the three slightly older eating clubs, and although President McIlvaine complained to President Patton that Colonial's proximity meant the ruination of Evelyn, the club was allowed to enjoy its advantage until the expiration of its year's lease.

During the four-year depression that followed the Panic of 1893, hard times kept down enrollment and also diminished the chances of obtaining any sizable gifts for endowment and buildings. After President McIlvaine died in 1897, Evelyn College closed its doors forever, and Princeton had to wait almost three quarters of a century before education for women within its precincts became a reality. (See *Women*.)

Faculty. A persistent influence in the evolution of Princeton University has been the concept of a single, integrated faculty. As other universities have expanded, their faculties have usually divided into semiautonomous schools, held together more by financial controls and physical services than by common policies and objectives.

At Princeton, a single faculty, with the President presiding, oversees a wide range of educational functions including admissions, curriculum, instruction, research, discipline, examinations, standing, and extracurricular life. Through its standing committees, it advises the President on faculty appointments and advancements and on general university policy. It also provides a channel of communication and appeal to the Board of Trustees.

The integrated structure of the Princeton faculty as a policy-making body has survived because of the University's deep-set urge to limit size in order to sustain the quality of both its faculty and its students, to emphasize the fundamental branches of learning, to encourage their mutual reinforcement, and to preserve a common, man-centered approach to education in the liberal tradition. With but gradual expansion of the fields of study, and the close coordination of new fields to old, the need for atomization into sharply differentiated schools has been avoided.

Much of the work of the "Faculty of Princeton University" is done by elected standing committees. These include: (a) policy committees, such as those on the Course of Study, the Graduate School, Undergraduate Admission and Financial Aid, as well as the University Research Board; (b) advisory committees, such as those on Appointments and Advancements, Policy, and Conference; and (c) administrative committees, such as on Athletic Eligibility, Examinations and Standing, Library, Public Lectures, and the Schedule. Policy and administrative committees report to the faculty at its regular monthly meetings. The educational policies of the University have long been the product of thorough study and lively debate by a faculty which through these orderly procedures assumes an unusual degree of concern and responsibility. The president and deans exercise their influence upon these policies far more through their leadership in the faculty and its committees than through any assumption of *ex officio* authority.

The operating unit which implements the educational policies of the University is the department whose functions include the administration of instruction, the planning of curriculum, oversight of research activities and facilities, and the recruitment and development of effective teacher-scholars. The chairman of a department is appointed by the president, after consultation, from among its senior members. His term is limited, and rotation in office is normal. As with the faculty, the responsibility for departmental activities is shared by its members, through the assignment of functions to committees or representatives, whose work is closely coordinated by oversight and decision by the department as a whole.

The integration of the operating and planning functions of the teaching department with the policy and review functions of the University Faculty may be illustrated by two long-established procedures among many. In revising or expanding its curriculum, the department must recommend any change to the University-wide Committee on the Course of Study at the undergraduate level or to the Committee on the Graduate School in the case of graduate programs. If the change is approved by the appropriate committee, it is recommended to the University faculty for action. With Princeton's long tradition of a tightly controlled curriculum, the process of planning and review is thorough at all stages of the procedure.

The second procedure concerns the area of faculty appointments and advancements. The present quality, effectiveness, and morale, of the Princeton faculty is owing in large measure to the responsible participation of its senior members. To be appointed or promoted to or within the professorial ranks, a candidate must be judged by all the senior members of a department. If the candidate is approved by the department, a full and formal recommendation is sent to the dean of the faculty, who lays it before the Advisory Committee on Appointments and Advancements for careful study.

This committee, traditionally called the "Committee of Three," now includes four *voting* members elected annually by the faculty from among the chairmen of departments, one from each of the four major divisions of the University. The committee, with the president, the provost, the dean of the faculty, the dean of the Graduate School, and the dean of the College "in attendance," advises the president on all proposals for the appointment or advancement in salary or rank of faculty personnel beyond first appointment as an assistant professor. In addition to reviewing the extensive materials forwarded by departments, it may seek outside evaluations of candidates or ask chairmen to appear before it. After full discussion by all present, it is the vote of the *four elected members* of the committee which the president takes under advisement in exercising his sole responsibility of recommending action by the Board of Trustees.

Another consolidating influence upon the Princeton faculty, which exercises as great a degree of responsibility as in any American university, is the concept of continuing tenure, Attained only after the thorough-going review outlined above, whether through step-by-step advancement to the rank of associate professor, reappointment at that rank, or first appointment as a full professor, the award of tenure encourages the member to feel that he is a "managing partner" in an ongoing institution. His responsibilities are clear and rewarding at both the University and the departmental level. He comes to have a long-run stake in the overall quality of the institution and in the strength and progress of his own discipline within it. If there were no other argument for academic tenure in higher education, at Princeton it could be strongly defended as a force for enhancing faculty responsibility and morale, as well as for thoroughness and concern in the selection of those to whom it is awarded.

In American higher education generally, the usual justification of academic tenure is either, at the philosophical level, the assurance of academic freedom, or at the practical, personal level, the assurance of security against loss of job. In an older institution, with a tight-knit faculty, the major protection against arbitrary dismissal because of unpopular opinions is the tradition of the institution, supported by well-established procedures for faculty, presidential, and trustee review. At the same time, a strong feeling of mutual responsibility reduces the likelihood of the abuse of freedom. At the practical, personal level, it is unlikely at a strong, older institution that arbitrary terminations of senior personnel will become necessary for reasons of institutional finance. At Princeton, the policy of awarding continuing tenure has been far more a means of assuring a strong and responsible faculty than a needed safeguard of a long-cherished tradition of academic freedom.

J. Douglas Brown

Faculty Song, a ballad about their professors, has been sung by Princeton seniors on the steps of Nassau Hall on Spring evenings since 1895. The verses are generally irreverent, sometimes barbed, but seldom ill-natured. Campus favorites other than faculty members have been sung about, too. The tune, a sample verse, and the chorus are shown below.

The idea of the song was borrowed from students at Trinity College, Hartford, Connecticut by Andrew C. Imbrie, 1895, who composed the first verses. He and his classmates did not inquire about the origin of the tune at the time; years later they were delighted to learn from a Scottish bagpipe band that played the Faculty Song at a class reunion that it was an old Scottish ballad, "The Muckin' o' Geordie's Byre" ("The Cleaning out of the Dung from George's Cowshed").

The life expectancy of the average faculty verse is only a few years, but some have gone on for a decade or more. A verse for Professor William Berryman Scott, composed in 1902, was still being sung in 1919. Another, celebrating the arrival of the original preceptors in 1905, was still being sung

Arranged by
Kenneth S. Clark, '05

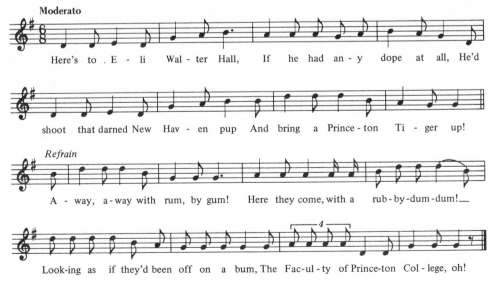

in 1930. Some of the best known personalities like Walter P. Hall, J. Duncan Spaeth, Dean Eisenhart, and Dean
Gauss, had a different verse sung about
them almost every other year. Countless verses have been sung over the
years.

Following are some of the favorites,
with identifying captions and the year
each was composed:

PROFESSOR WILLIAM BERRYMAN SCOTT
(1902)

Here's to Bill Geology Scott
He has a carboniferous knot,
He tells us how the earth was made,
And how the Lord his side-walks laid.

THE FIRST GROUP OF PRECEPTORS
(1906)

Here's to those preceptor guys,
Fifty stiffs to make us wise.
Easy jobs and lots of pay,
Work the students night and day.

PRINCETON'S 13TH PRESIDENT; THE
U.S.A.'S 28TH (1913)

Here's to Woodrow Wilson who
Cleaned up Taft and Teddy too;
So once a hundred years we'd nip
The presidential championship.

THE OSBORN PROFESSOR OF
BIOLOGY (1915)

Here's to Conklin, Edwin Grant,
Who knows the habits of the ant.
And why the present human shape
Is not exactly like the ape.

MARQUAND PROFESSOR FRANK JEWETT
MATHER (1920)

Here's to Mather, who teaches art,
What hair he has is mostly part.
He shows that he is not a prude
By inclination for the nude.

THE SECOND DEAN OF THE COLLEGE
(1923)

Here's to Dean McClenahan,

He cans as many as he can;
It seems to put his mind at ease
To reunite the families.

A TEACHER OF COMPOSITION,
EFFECTIVE BUT DOUR (1925)

Here's to Herbert Spenser Murch
Who seems as solemn as a church.
His looks would make you think indeed
His lunch and he had disagreed.

EISENHART AND GAUSS SUCCEED
MAGIE AND McCLENAHAN (1925)

Concerning deans, the old and new,
From history we get the clue:
The Irish refuse to make concessions,
And leave old Nassau to the Hessians.

FIRST DEAN OF THE GRADUATE
SCHOOL (1926)

Here's to Andrew Fleming West,
A Latin scholar self-confessed.
He lived to see a lifetime's hope
Constructed out of Ivory Soap.

GEORGE McLEAN HARPER, AUTHOR OF
WORDSWORTH'S FRENCH DAUGHTER
(1927)

Harper went to France to get
The red-hot dope on dear Annette;
And there performed a deed of note,
Revealing Wordsworth's one wild oat.

A VERSATILE DEAN THE OBJECT OF
ENVY DURING THE GREAT DEPRESSION
(1932)

Professor Gauss, he teaches French,
Dean Gauss, he judges on the bench,
Mr. Gauss don't write for fun;
He's got three jobs, and we've got none.

ERNEST GORDON, SCOTTISH DEAN OF
THE CHAPEL (1966)

All hail to Gordon, Earnest Dean,
Of Heaven and Hell, he paints the
*   scene;*
If you can take his brimstone brew,
You'll get your Scotch on Sunday too.

Fencing was introduced to Princeton in 1856, when Karl Langlotz, lately arrived from Germany, found temporary employment in teaching it to a class of fifty students; he subsequently taught German and composed the music to *Old Nassau*. Later in the century, sporadic fencing clubs fostered intramural competition. In 1905 a three-year spell of intercollegiate competition began when a devotee of the sport, Henry S. Breckinridge '07 (later president of the Amateur Fencers League of America) organized a team that beat Yale in 1906 and 1907.

A Fencing Association, organized in 1924, created such interest that fencing was recognized as a team sport and intercollegiate competition was begun in 1926. An outstanding performer in the early years was Tracy Jaeckel '28, who was intercollegiate champion in épée his senior year.

Captain F. G. McPherson, team coach in 1926, was succeeded a year later by Joseph De Vos, former fencing instructor at the court of Holland, who in turn was succeeded in 1933 by Hubert H. Pirotte, who was coach until the outbreak of World War II. During this period two Princeton fencers won individual titles at the Eastern Intercollegiates: William T. Pecora '33 (foil) in 1933, and Kirk Alexander, Jr. '37 (épée) in 1935; Princeton won the épée team title in 1940. The 1935 captain, Todd Harris, established annual fencing medals on his graduation and later organized alumni financial support.

Stanley S. Sieja became coach in 1946. His teams defeated both Harvard and Yale in 1949, 1952, 1956, 1959, and 1960, and again in ten successive years, from 1962 through 1971, winning its sixteenth Big Three championship in 1973. Princeton shared the Ivy crown in 1959, 1960, 1966, and 1969, and won it outright in 1975. At the Eastern Intercollegiates, Princeton won the épée team title in 1960, and both the foil team title and the three-weapon championship in 1969. At the annual NCAA tournament, Sieja's teams finished third in 1960 and 1965, took second place in 1961, and captured the national championship in 1964.

Eight of Sieja's fencers won individual championships. Five were Eastern intercollegiate champions: Chambless Johnston '51 (saber) in 1949; Paul Levy '58 (épée) in 1958; Frank Anger '61 (épée) in 1960; Richard Lawrence '72 (foil) in 1972; and James Neale '77 (épée) in 1977. Four were NCAA champions: Johnston (saber) in 1951; Henry Kolowrat '54 (épée) in 1954; Kinmot Hoitsma '56 (épée) in 1956; and William Hicks '64 (foil) in 1964. Three fencers were voted NCAA Fencer of the Year: Anger in 1961, Hicks in 1964, and John Nonna '70 in 1969. Sieja was elected Coach of the Year by the National Fencing Coaches Association in 1964, 1968, and 1976, and was inducted into the Helms Foundation Hall of Fame in 1967.

Fetter, Frank Albert (1863-1949), first chairman of the Department of Economics and Social Institutions, was a philosopher-theorist whose Indiana-Quaker upbringing drove him to use his great powers of theoretical analysis for the advancement of public policy and human welfare. The Economics Department still bears his imprint.

Born in Peru, Indiana, in 1863, Fetter was obliged to interrupt his course of study at Indiana University for eight years while he assumed the financial responsibilities of his disabled father. Finally graduating in 1891, he went on to Cornell, the Sorbonne, and to Halle, where he received a Ph.D. in 1894. He returned to Cornell as an instructor but soon left for a professorship at Indiana University. Stanford called him west in 1898, but he resigned three years later in protest against violation of academic freedom. He returned to Cornell, where his international reputation as an economic theorist grew rapidly during the next decade. In 1911, having refused earlier offers from Yale and Columbia, he accepted Princeton's invitation to become chairman of its combined Department of History, Politics, and Economics.

Two years later, Fetter became chairman of the new Department of Economics and Social Institutions. For eleven years, he guided the development of a rapidly expanding program. Although he officially retired as a professor in 1931, he continued as a special lecturer in economic theory for two more years, and as a productive scholar and a vigorous exponent of economic justice until his death in 1949 at the age of 86.

Some indication of the distinguished position that Professor Fetter attained among American economists was his election to the presidency of the American Economic Association when he was only 49. He was also a fellow of the American Academy of Arts and Sciences and an active member of the American Philosophical Society. In 1927, the Austrian Economic Society awarded him its Karl Menger Medal. He received his first honorary degree of LL.D. from Colgate at 46 and his last from Princeton at 82. He was much in demand by other universities as visiting professor or lecturer.

Professor Fetter's major scholarly contributions were in the field of fundamental economic theory, including the theories of value, the concepts of value and price, capitalization, time preference, interest, and rent. Influenced by repeated visits to Austria, he emphasized subjective and psychological factors. He was at heart a "welfare economist," often at odds with those he considered too concerned with "price economics." His incisive understanding of the factors in price determination, however, made him in later years a vigorous opponent of monopoly because of its effect upon the welfare of consumers. He was a prolific writer of scholarly articles. Most Princeton undergraduates of the 1920s studied, with mixed emotions, his famous texts, *Economic Principles* and *Modern Economic Problems*.

Professor Fetter was at his best in face-to-face interchange with colleagues and graduate students. Here his intellectual acumen, penetrating analysis, keen wit, and, above all, his intuitive integrity and warm personal charm came through. He was loved and admired not only for himself but also for his concern for people and their problems.

His insight, courage, and integrity were communicated with such friendly warmth and dry humor that his influence upon colleagues and students reached far beyond their hard-earned mastery of economic theory. He encouraged students to become involved in public service in solving the problems of education, poverty, mental illness, juvenile delinquency, and bad housing. His extracurricular activities in these fields became the basis of a pioneering Princeton course in sociology which, despite its campus label, "Travelling Gut," took many students for their first time into asylums, prisons, and slums, and deepened their understanding of human tragedy and social responsibility. By his example, he reinforced Woodrow Wilson's goal for Princeton—that its faculty and students should serve their fellow men by acts as well as by ideas.

J. Douglas Brown

Field Hockey began propitiously in November 1971 with the first contest between Princeton and Yale women on the day of the annual Yale-Princeton football game. Of all the Princeton-Yale athletic contests played that day, women's field hockey provided the only Princeton victory, with an historic 3-2 win over Yale.

For the first five years, the Princeton women never lost to the Yale women . . . nor to many other women either. The season records speak for themselves: 1971, 5-2; 1972, 7-3-1; 1973, 8-3; 1974, undefeated; 1975, undefeated. From 1972 through 1975 Princeton was the Big Three and Ivy League Champion.

During the same short five-year period, the women's athletic program was organizing and fielding fourteen intercollegiate teams and achieving an aggregate winning percentage of .800. The women's field hockey team has contributed greatly to that winning effort.

Merrily Dean Baker

Fine, Henry Burchard (1858-1928), the first and only dean of the departments of science, was one of the men who did most to help Princeton develop from a college into a university. He made Princeton a leading center for mathematics and fostered the growth of creative work in other branches of science as well. Nationally he was one of the group of men who, in Professor Oswald Veblen's words, "carried American mathematics forward from a state of approximate nullity to one verging on parity with the European nations."

Fine was the oldest of four children of a Presbyterian minister of Dutch ancestry in Chambersburg, Pennsylvania. His father died when the children were young, and they were brought up by their mother, an able woman of strong character. (Three of her children became educators: Dean Fine; John B. Fine 1882, founder of the Princeton Preparatory School; and May Margaret Fine, founder of Miss Fine's School.) The family came to live in Princeton in 1875, and Henry entered the College the following year, graduating in 1880.

Fine played the flute in the college orchestra, rowed on one of the crews, and served for three years as an editor of the *Princetonian*, where he began a life-long friendship with Woodrow Wilson 1879, whom he succeeded as managing editor. Fine was also one of the small group of undergraduates who took part in President McCosh's biweekly "library meetings" at Prospect.

He led his class all four years and was Latin salutatorian at Commencement. Although he specialized in Latin and Greek, he adopted mathematics as a career toward the end of his college course, largely through the influence of George B. Halstead 1875, a tutor of mathematics who communicated his enthusiasm for his subject to Fine.

After a postgraduate year as Class of 1860 Fellow in Experimental Science and three years as tutor in mathematics, Fine went to Leipzig to study with the eminent geometer Felix Klein. Although, according to his own account, he knew very little German and almost no mathematics, he developed so rapidly that he obtained his Ph.D. in a little more than a year.

After this brief contact with the main current of mathematics, Fine returned to Princeton in 1885 as an assistant professor. He was promoted to professor in 1889, appointed Dod Professor of Mathematics in 1898, and made chairman of the department when departments were first organized in 1904. Early in his career he published a few research papers but, as time went on, he devoted his energies more to teaching and to the logical exposition of elementary mathematics. According to Professor Veblen, his widely used textbooks, *A College Algebra* (1905) and *Calculus* (1927) were unexcelled in accuracy of statement and the adequacy with which they represented the subject. His *College Algebra* was not found easy by beginning students who, when first confronted with it, according to a Princetonian of that era, "decided that no one could understand it but Professor Fine and God." When the students of the following year were treated to a revised edition "they agreed that comprehension was probably now limited to Professor Fine alone."

FINE AND WILSON

After Woodrow Wilson returned to Princeton as professor of jurisprudence in 1890, he and Fine resumed the close friendship they had begun in college days, sharing both a serious devotion to the life of the scholar and a keen interest in college sports. They served together on a faculty committee on athletics and on another one that corrected abuses arising from the admission of "special students," who enjoyed the pleasures of college life without having to meet the academic standards required of candidates for a degree. Both also worked for the adoption of the honor system in examinations.

In 1903, shortly after he became president of the University, Wilson appointed Fine dean of the faculty, and

Fine's energies were thereafter devoted chiefly to university administration. He worked shoulder to shoulder with Wilson in improving the curriculum and strengthening the faculty, and bore the onus of the student dismissals made inevitable by the raising of academic standards. In the controversies over the quad plan and the graduate college, Fine supported Wilson completely. After Wilson resigned to run for governor of New Jersey in 1910, Fine, as dean of the faculty, carried the chief burden of the university administration during an interregnum of two years; and when the trustees elected John Grier Hibben as Wilson's successor, Fine, who many had thought would receive the election, magnanimously pledged Hibben his wholehearted support. "He was singularly free from petty prejudices and always had the courage of his convictions," Hibben later recalled. "Every word and act was absolutely in character, and he was completely dependable in every emergency."

After his election as president of the United States, Wilson urged Fine to accept appointment as Ambassador to Germany and later as a member of the Federal Reserve Board, but Fine declined both appointments, saying quite simply that he preferred to remain at Princeton as a professor of mathematics. Fine also declined a call to the presidency of Johns Hopkins University and several to the presidency of Massachusetts Institute of Technology.

DEAN OF THE DEPARTMENTS OF SCIENCE

The introduction of the preceptorial system in 1905 required a considerable expansion of the faculty in the humanities and social studies. Fine persuaded Wilson that a similar enlargement was desirable in the sciences, and, seizing the opportunity, began to build a department of mathematics of the first rank while at the same time helping his colleagues lay the foundations for strong departments in other sciences. In this endeavor he was greatly aided by the force of his personality, by his remarkable ability to discern talent in younger men before it had become widely recognized, and by an unselfish interest in furthering their careers.

For suggestions and advice, Fine turned first to his friend, Sir Joseph J. Thomson, the Cambridge physicist who had been his house guest at the University's Sesquicentennial Celebration in 1896 when Thomson received an honorary degree and had discussed with Fine the latter's hopes for making Princeton a scientific center. As a result, James Jeans came to Princeton in 1905 as professor of mathematical physics and O. W. Richardson the following year as professor of experimental physics. A survey of younger mathematicians in this country led to other promotions and appointments. Luther P. Eisenhart was promoted to a preceptorship and Oswald Veblen, Gilbert A. Bliss, and John W. Young were brought to Princeton at the same rank. When Bliss and Young were called elsewhere they were replaced by two equally brilliant mathematicians, George D. Birkhoff and the Scots J.H.M. Wedderburn. Professor Veblen recalled that Fine's department had the services of a considerable proportion of the best mathematicians of America in his time. "In every case," Veblen said, "these men were called in before they became well known, at the time when recognition meant the most to them. Though many of them stayed only a few years, their contact with Fine and his group was important both to them and in the

continuing growth of this group as an organism."

Fine recognized the genius of Henry Norris Russell 1897 when Russell was an undergraduate and saw to it that this future astrophysicist was given every opportunity to develop his talents at Princeton and that every means was taken to keep him there. It was Fine who later persuaded Russell's classmates to endow a research professorship for him. Fine was also instrumental in bringing Edwin Grant Conklin, the biologist, and George A. Hulett, the physical chemist, to Princeton.

In 1909 when the dean of the faculty's duties were lightened by the creation of the office of the dean of the college, Fine became in title what he had been in fact—dean of the departments of science. When Hibben became president in 1912, Fine resigned as dean of the faculty but continued as dean of the departments of science. In his last years he was able to seize another opportunity for the advancement of science at Princeton. Largely because of the confidence he inspired, the General Education Board offered Princeton a million dollars for research in pure science on condition that the University raise two million for the same purpose. The fund was completed in 1928, chiefly by the contributions of Thomas D. Jones 1876, a wealthy alumnus who was strikingly similar to Fine in qualities of intellect and character. Jones had become a close friend of Fine's during Wilson's presidency—a friendship commemorated by the Henry B. Fine Professorship of Mathematics, founded by Jones, and the Thomas D. Jones Professorship of Mathematical Physics, founded by Miss Gwethalyn Jones. As a further memorial, Jones and his niece gave a building for mathematics, named Fine Hall, which was built in 1930. When a larger building for mathematics was constructed in 1968, it was named Fine Hall (q.v.) and the former mathematics building, converted for use by other departments, was renamed Jones Hall (q.v.) in honor of the original donors.

Fine was one of the founders of the American Mathematical Society and its president in 1911 and 1912. In the summer of 1928, he went to Europe, where he revisited old scenes and old friends, and recovered to some extent, in the distractions of travel, from the sorrows he had suffered in the recent death of his wife and the earlier deaths of two of his three children. Professor Veblen who talked with him soon after his return, reported later that Fine "spoke with humorous appreciation of the change he had observed in the attitude of European mathematicians toward their American colleagues and with pride of the esteem in which he had found his own department to be held."

Tall and erect, Dean Fine was a familiar figure on his bicycle, which he rode to and from classes and used for long rides in the country. While riding his bicycle on the way to visit his brother at the Princeton Preparatory School late one December afternoon, he was struck from behind by an automobile whose driver had failed to see him in the uncertain light of dusk. He died the next morning without having recovered consciousness, three months after his seventieth birthday.

Shortly after Fine's death, Professor Veblen visited Europe and met some of the mathematicians Fine had seen on his last trip, many of them younger men who had met Fine for the first time.

They all spoke [Veblen wrote] of his charm of manner and of the impres-

sion they had gained of a man of serene strength and poise and wisdom. It was a striking testimony to the way in which a man's character can be written into his appearance and manner by a long and strenuous life.

Fine Hall, home of the Department of Mathematics and the Department of Statistics, was dedicated in 1970 as a memorial to Henry Burchard Fine (q.v.), the central figure in the early development of the mathematics faculty of the University. It replaced an older Fine Hall, built forty years earlier, which was renamed Jones Hall (q.v.).

Fine Hall, which with its neighbor Jadwin Hall forms a center for mathematics and physics, is just west of Palmer Stadium. Fine Hall comprises a long three-story building, topped by a tower of ten additional floors. It is separated from Jadwin Hall by a plaza covering the underground joint mathematics-physics library.

The long, three-story section contains classrooms and graduate student offices and studies. On the third floor is a common room with portraits of Dean Fine and two earlier Princeton mathematicians, Walter Minto and Albert B. Dod. On the second floor are two study rooms named for Luther P. Eisenhart, Fine's successor as chairman of the Department of Mathematics, and Samuel S. Wilks, founder of the Department of Statistics.

The vertical lines of the tower counterbalance the horizontal mass of Jadwin Hall and provide a focal point for this architectural unit. Each floor of the tower, except the topmost, contains seven faculty offices and one seminar room. The entire top story is devoted to a professors' lounge, whose large picture windows afford panoramic views of the campus and the surrounding countryside.

Fine Hall was designed by Warner, Burns, Toan and Lunde of New York City, and together with Jadwin Hall won in 1966 an Award of Merit in the Architectural Design Award Program.

Finley, Samuel (1715-1766), fifth president of Princeton, was a Scotch-Irishman who came to this country with his parents when he was nineteen. He is thought to have attended William Tennent's Log College (q.v.) at Neshaminy, Bucks County, Pennsylvania. His early career as an evangelical preacher was marked by an energetic, contentious, and sometimes acrimonious spirit that was not uncommon in the eighteenth-century religious revivals known as The Great Awakening. In Cape May he once carried on a two-day debate with a Baptist minister on infant baptism; he called a collection of sermons on the evils of another sect "Satan Stripp'd of His Angelic Robe. . . ." During a pastorate in Milford, Connecticut, he was arrested on his way to preach to the Second Society at New Haven, a "separatist" congregation then illegal under Connecticut law, and was expelled from the colony as a vagrant. For the next seventeen years he was pastor of the church at Nottingham, Maryland, where he also conducted an academy renowned for its standards of scholarship and for training such men as Benjamin Rush 1760, physician and signer of the Declaration of Independence, and Ebenezer Hazard 1762, United States postmaster general. With increasing maturity Finley became less contentious and more effective in his preaching. Ebenezer Hazard said his sermons "were calculated to inform the ignorant, to alarm the careless and secure,

and to edify and comfort the faithful." Finley was given an honorary degree by the University of Glasgow, the first Princeton president and the second American divine to receive an honorary degree abroad. Finley, who had been one of the original trustees of the college, succeeded Samuel Davies as president on May 31, 1761. At the time of his election he was regarded as "a very accurate scholar, and a very great and good man."

Finley's presidency was marked by steady growth in enrollment, by his planting of shade trees—two sycamores that he planted in front of the President's House (now the Maclean House) are still standing—and by his effective teaching. He was "a man of small stature, and of round and ruddy countenance," respected and beloved by the students. In his fifty-second year he died in Philadelphia, where he had gone for medical treatment; many students journeyed from Princeton to pay their last respects, and eight members of the senior class bore his body to the grave.

Midway in Finley's administration the trustees declared, "Our idea is to send into the World good Scholars and useful members of Society." Some of the 130 graduates Finley sent out during his five-year presidency more than fulfilled this modest purpose, notably the Rev. James Manning 1762, founder and first president of Brown University; William Paterson 1763, governor of New Jersey; the Rt. Rev. Thomas J. Clagget 1764, Bishop of the Protestant Episcopal Diocese of Maryland; the Rev. Samuel Kirkland 1765, founder and first president of Hamilton College (for whom Hamilton's sister college, opened in 1968, was named); David Ramsay 1765, physician and historian of the American Revolution; Oliver Ellsworth 1766, chief justice of the United States.

Samuel Finley Breese Morse, developer of the telegraph, was the great grandson of President Finley; in 1870 he gave the portrait of Finley which hangs in the Faculty Room in Nassau Hall.

Finney, John M. T. 1884 (1863-1942), was the only person ever to play football for both Princeton and Harvard. He was an end on the Princeton varsity his senior year and held the same position on the Harvard varsity during his first year at the Harvard Medical School. (The rule restricting eligibility to undergraduates had not yet been adopted.)

In Princeton's victory over Harvard his senior year, Finney scored Princeton's only touchdown. At the Harvard Medical School he abstained from playing against Princeton.

A scrappy player, Finney's hard tackle of a back in the Yale game his senior year led to an exchange of unpleasantries. The following week the *Police Gazette* asked Finney for his photograph to include with John L. Sullivan's in a gallery of "the leading exponents of the manly art of self-defense," but Finney did not avail himself of this honor. "I got credit," he later recalled, "for a lot of slugging that was going on around me, in which I had no other part than that of peacemaker."

Finney gave up football after his first season with Harvard in order to do justice to his medical studies. On receiving his M.D. and completing his internship at the Massachusetts General Hospital, he went to Baltimore, where as professor of surgery he was associated with men like William H. Welch, Sir William Osler, and William S. Halsted in developing the great medical school and hospital at Johns Hopkins. Finney specialized in surgery of the alimentary canal, for which he devised a number of important operative techniques.

As chief consultant in surgery for the American Expeditionary Forces in World War I, Finney organized new methods for administering surgical aid to the wounded at the front, and was decorated by the United States, France, and Belgium. He was elected a fellow of the Royal Colleges of Surgeons of England, of Ireland, and of Edinburgh, and in 1932 was awarded the Bigelow gold medal, one of the highest honors in surgery in this country. He was a founder and first president of the American College of Surgeons. He was also president of the American Surgical Association and of the Society of Clinical Surgery. He pioneered in the recruitment and training of black surgeons.

The son of a clergyman, he served as vice-moderator of the General Assembly of the Presbyterian Church, and was a trustee of Lincoln University and of the Princeton Theological Seminary. He was cited for his contributions to better understanding among Catholics, Protestants, and Jews.

Finney was elected a life trustee of Princeton in 1910 just before Woodrow Wilson resigned as president. He so impressed his colleagues by "his simple honesty of thought, speech and action" that less than two years later they invited him to be president. Finney knew the need was great (the Board, divided by the Wilson-West dispute, had previously had trouble agreeing on a candidate) and his loyalty to Princeton put him under great pressure to accept. "His mental anguish," said a colleague at Johns Hopkins, "was plain to see." But in the end, his innate love of medicine, and the obligation he felt to the young doctors under his guidance, prevailed. "After a most careful consideration from every point of view," he wrote, "I feel that I am better fitted for the work which I am now doing and that I should remain in Baltimore where my work is not yet done." Soon thereafter Finney and John W. Barr 1885, a newcomer to the board also not identified with either the Wilson or the West faction, used their balance of power to elect John Grier Hibben as president.

As chairman of the Trustees' Committee on Health and Athletics, Finney helped to plan the present McCosh Infirmary, to secure its staff, and to set its tone, consistent with his personal philosophy, as a place where the human as well as the scientific aspects of medicine were emphasized. He also helped in the development of the University's intramural and intercollegiate athletic programs.

The gentle Wordsworth scholar, George McLean Harper, Finney's closest friend in the Class of 1884, had a more rounded view of Finney's manly qualities than the *Police Gazette* had had. Finney's manliness, Professor Harper wrote in a memorial for the *Alumni Weekly*, "was compounded of many elements: physical strength and vitality, intellectual vigor and versatility, moral purity, social warmth, and loving-kindness." After reviewing Finney's professional and civic achievements and his many acts of self-sacrifice and charity, Harper concluded: "We, his classmates, bow our hearts in thankfulness for a life so noble."

Two of Finney's sons, John M.T. Finney, Jr. '15 and George G. Finney '21 became surgeons also. George Finney and his son, Redmond C.S. Finney '51 were trustees of Princeton, too.

Finney Field, used for football and lacrosse, was given in his memory by his family in 1957.

Fires have completely or partially destroyed campus buildings on six occasions: Nassau Hall in 1802 and 1855; Marquand Chapel and Dickinson Hall in 1920; John C. Green School of Science in 1928; University Gymnasium in 1944; and Whig Hall in 1969.

NASSAU HALL FIRES

The fire of 1802 started about one o'clock on the windy afternoon of Saturday, March 6, and in two hours only the blackened walls of Nassau Hall were left standing. President Smith declared the fire the result of vice and irreligion, and a trustee's investigating committee thought it was begun intentionally. George Strawbridge 1802 (later a supreme court judge in Louisiana) made an independent investigation and concluded that no student was in any way guilty; he thought sooty chimneys probably responsible.

The trustees made a public appeal for funds to rebuild Nassau Hall and in less than a year it was again ready for use.

The 1855 fire also occurred on a windy Saturday in March (the 10th). It started about eight o'clock in the evening and by midnight, once again, only the walls were left standing. This time there was no suspicion of incendiarism. Many students suffered large losses of clothing and furniture, but the Latin professor, George M. Giger, with the help of some tutors and students, rescued Peale's portrait of Washington and other valuable paintings from the portrait gallery. "Little Giger performed prodigies of valor," Alfred A. Woodhull 1856 wrote his mother, "and several times was so excited that he came near having a fight with the firemen." President John Maclean braved the smoke and flames to search for a student mistakenly reported trapped in an upper story room. "Johnny . . . got so nearly suffocated," Woodhull told his mother, "that a party of students scarcely saved him."

Nassau Hall was reopened for the lodging of students in August 1856, but the reconstruction was not completed until June 1860, when the trustees thanked God "for . . . raising up liberal friends, who by their generous contributions, have enabled us to rebuild our burnt Edifice, and to enlarge and improve it." One of the most "liberal friends" was President Maclean himself, who helped liquidate the unpaid balance of the rebuilding cost by giving up part of his salary.

FIRES IN THE TWENTIES

On Friday, May 14, 1920, a fire broke out in the original Dickinson Hall, which stood on the southwest corner of the present site of Firestone Library, and spread southward to Marquand Chapel, which stood just northeast of Murray-Dodge Hall. Dickinson and Marquand were completely destroyed, but the Joseph Henry House, which at that time stood between them, escaped with little damage. Volunteer firemen, helped by students in evening clothes—the eating clubs were holding their house parties and there was a freshman dance at the gymnasium— and by an engine company from Trenton, kept the fire from spreading to McCosh Hall, Prospect, and Palmer Laboratory. Marquand Chapel was replaced by the University Chapel in 1928 and the present Dickinson Hall was built in 1930.

The fire that demolished the John C. Green School of Science was discovered a little before midnight on Monday, November 16, 1928. The tower was already in flames when the firemen

arrived; by 4 a.m. the last of the roof had caved in and by daybreak the building was a smouldering mass. The Joseph Henry House, which had been moved to a new location just north of the School of Science (to make way for the University Chapel) again escaped unscathed. This fire created a shortage of laboratories and classrooms, which was not relieved until the completion of Frick Chemical Laboratory in 1929 and Dickinson Hall in 1930, but the loss of the School of Science, which the *Daily Princetonian* thought had been "conceived under an evil architectural star," was generally unmourned.

UNIVERSITY GYMNASIUM

The University Gymnasium, built in 1903, was destroyed by fire the morning of May 13, 1944. The fire was discovered and an alarm turned in at 2:47 a.m. by naval watches in Little and Patton Halls where members of the navy V-12 unit were quartered. The building was completely gutted and all its contents lost, since the dense smoke made it impossible for anyone to enter a door. Lost in the flames was Dr. Joseph E. Raycroft's library of some 2,500 volumes on health, sports, and physical education (partly restored later by gifts from friends), and scores of athletic trophies and relics, including a ball from the first Yale-Princeton football game of 1873. Heroic work by firemen and the University's grounds and buildings forces kept the fire from spreading to adjoining dormitories. The University Gymnasium was replaced by Dillon Gymnasium, completed soon after the end of the war.

WHIG HALL FIRE

The Whig Hall fire on Sunday, November 9, 1969, was discovered by a University proctor at 5:45 a.m. and was brought under control by firemen by

7:30 a.m. All but one of the exterior marble walls remained intact, but eighty percent of the wooden interior was destroyed, although most of the historic portraits of the American Whig-Cliosophic Society escaped damage. Renovations were completed in 1972.

No loss of life resulted from any of these fires; the only serious injury was a broken leg incurred by a spectator from Kingston in the Nassau Hall fire of 1855.

Firestone Plaza was given in memory of Roger S. Firestone '35, an inscription on one of its flagstones says, "For The Enjoyment Of All Who Pause Here Or Pass This Way." Designed by the University's consulting landscape architect, Robert L. Zion, the plaza's widened bluestone walkways, limestone benches and sitting steps, trees, shrubs, and ground cover draw together the much frequented campus area enclosed by Firestone Library, the University Chapel, Chancellor Green Student Center, and East Pyne Building. The plaza was constructed in 1976-1977 with funds contributed by Roger Firestone's widow, Anne Firestone, and his friend, charter trustee Laurance S. Rockefeller '32. Roger Firestone was the youngest of Harvey Firestone Sr.'s five Princeton sons, the principal donors of the library that bears his name.

Fitzgerald, Francis Scott Key (1896-1940) was a star-spangled Princetonian of the Class of 1917. The poet Robert Browning once wrote that the legend inside his heart was "Italy." With Fitzgerald it would probably have been "Princeton." He entered this earthly paradise in the fall of 1913 from the Catholic Newman School in Hackensack, squeaking past his entrance examinations that September by the narrowest margin, and hurling himself into extracurricular activities with so much enthusiasm that he barely survived his first two years.

After three months as a junior, he withdrew because of ill health and poor grades. Following nine months of rustication and recuperation at home in St. Paul, Minnesota, he re-entered as a beginning junior in the fall of 1916. He managed to complete that academic year and one month of his senior year before withdrawing again to enter Officers' Training in October 1917. The fact that he was never graduated failed to expunge and indeed probably enhanced his golden memories of Princeton, Cottage Club, Princeton football, the Triangle Club, *The Nassau Lit*, and the *Tiger*, to say nothing of the look and feel of Prospect Street in all seasons, and the mossy spires and gargoyles of the neo-Gothic campus.

Apart from Princeton, two great forces guided his tragically abbreviated life. One was writing, which enthralled him in childhood, took up many college hours, supported and harassed him in maturity, and continued to engage his devotion until his dying day. The other was his romance with Zelda Sayre, a southern belle from Montgomery, Alabama, whom he coveted, courted, and at last married, sharing with her a characteristically hectic life in America and Europe during their great heyday of the 1920s. It was a manner of life that his chief biographer, Arthur Mizener has called "at once representative and dramatic, at moments a charmed and beautiful success to which he and Zelda were brilliantly equal, and at moments disastrous beyond the invention of the most macabre imagination."

This Side of Paradise, which Scribner's published March 26, 1920, and advertised in the *Daily Princetonian* as a "Story about a Princeton Man," shows Fitzgerald making all he could of his years at Princeton. Dean Gauss once wrote of Fitzgerald that he had "a truly Apollonian profile like the head on some Greek medallion." The same might have been written of Amory Blaine, Fitzgerald's handsome and insouciant hero, who invents his way through various love affairs and much bad poetry and indulges his awakening brain with high intellectual bull sessions. However banal the novel may seem today, it set Fitzgerald off and running, and he became a regular contributor of short stories to *The Smart Set*, *The Saturday Evening Post*, and *Scribner's Magazine*. Selections from these appeared in *Flappers and Philosophers* and *Tales of the Jazz Age*, which helped to stamp Fitzgerald forever as a chief spokesman for the roaring twenties, while his second novel, *The Beautiful and the Damned*, accurately summarized in its title if not in its substance the present and future course of his life with Zelda. There was also a satirical play, *The Vegetable: or From President to Postman*, published in 1923. Two further short-story collections, *All the Sad Young Men* and *Taps at Reveille*, appeared in 1926 and 1935.

Fitzgerald's best work in fiction owed little or nothing to Princeton. *The Great Gatsby* (1925), generally regarded as his finest novel, eschewed the Princeton scene in favor of Long Island and New York City. *Tender is the Night* (1934) borrowed its title from Keats and its locale and characters from Fitzgerald's experiences on the French Riviera in the middle 1920s. Behind the stories of Gatsby's longing for Daisy Buchanan and Dick Driver's for the beautiful Nicole, one can discern some

of the tragic implications of Fitzgerald's love for Zelda, the gradual advance of whose mental illness darkened the last years of their marriage. From time to time he overcame his overdrinking and worked with some success as film-writer in Hollywood, where he gathered the material for his final though unfinished novel, *The Last Tycoon*. This was posthumously published in 1941 under the editorship of Edmund Wilson '16, with whom Fitzgerald had collaborated on "The Evil Eye" for the Triangle Club twenty-five years earlier, and whom he always revered as his "intellectual conscience." Besides Wilson, the best critics of Fitzgerald's work have nearly all been Princetonians, with biographies by Arthur Mizener '30, and Andrew Turnbull '42, and critical studies by Henry Dan Piper '39, and Robert Sklar '58. Turnbull also edited a volume of Fitzgerald's letters.

The eternal note of promise which everyone found in Fitzgerald's early work was well summarized by his classmate, John Peale Bishop '17, in a requiem called "The Hours."

No promise such as yours when like
  the spring
You came, colors of jonquils in your
  hair,
Inspired as the wind, when woods
  are bare
and every silence is about to sing.

The tragic circumstances of his life, and they were many, did not prevent his partial fulfillment of that promise because his heart was always in his best writing. Although he sometimes uttered harsh words about his Alma Mater, its image stayed undimmed until the end. When his heart ceased to beat, indeed at the very moment of his death far away in the city of Hollywood, he was scribbling notes in the margin of his copy of the *Alumni Weekly* beside an article about the Princeton football team.

The Manuscripts Division of the Library contains Fitzgerald's papers, which were given to the University by his daughter Mrs. C. Grove Smith in 1946.

Carlos Baker

FitzRandolph Gateway, The, main entrance to the Campus from Nassau Street, was erected in 1905, from the design of McKim, Mead and White, in fulfillment of a bequest from Augustus van Winkle, of Hazleton, Pennsylvania, in memory of his ancestor, Nathaniel FitzRandolph, who gave the land on which Nassau Hall was built.

FitzRandolph was the son of one of the original seventeenth-century Quaker settlers of Princeton. More than any other citizen of Princeton, he was responsible for raising for the College the money and land the trustees required of the citizens of the place where it was to be located—£1000 New Jersey money, ten acres of cleared land for the campus, and 200 acres of woodland for fuel—and thus enabled Princeton to win from its chief competitor, New Brunswick, the honor and benefits of providing the site of the college.

Besides riding among his neighbors to solicit donations, FitzRandolph himself gave twenty pounds and 4½ acres, described in the trustee minutes as "a certain tract of land four hundred feet front and thirty poles [rods] depth, in line at right angles with the broad street where it is proposed that the college shall be built."

FitzRandolph took great interest in the building of the college and recorded its progress in his journal: July 29, 1754, "Jos. Morrow set a man first to dig the college cellar." September 17, 1754, "the first cornerstone . . . was laid in the northwesterly corner of the cellar by . . . Mr. William Worth, the mason that built the stone and brick work, myself, and many others." November 1755, "the roof . . . was raised by Robert Smith, the carpenter that built the timber work." November 13, 1756, "Aaron Burr, President, preached the first sermon and began the school in Princeton College."

FitzRandolph was buried in the family burial ground, which was located where Holder Hall now stands. Workmen excavating for the foundations of that dormitory in 1909 discovered thirty-two old, unmarked graves there. At President Wilson's direction the contents of the graves were preserved in separate boxes and reinterred under the eastern arch of Holder Hall and a memorial tablet placed in the arch. President Wilson wrote the English and Dean West the Latin for the inscription:

NEAR THIS SPOT
LIE THE REMAINS OF
NATHANIEL FITZRANDOLPH
THE GENEROUS GIVER OF THE LAND
UPON WHICH THE ORIGINAL
BUILDINGS
OF THIS UNIVERSITY
WERE ERECTED

In Agro Jacet Nostro Immo Suo

(In our ground he sleeps,
nay, rather, in his own.)

FitzRandolph Observatory, The, on FitzRandolph Road, east of Palmer Stadium, replaced in 1934 the old Halsted Observatory, in use for sixty years on University Place where Joline Hall now stands. The Observatory contains a 36-inch reflecting telescope installed in 1966 to supersede a 23-inch refracting telescope used since 1882.

Football was first played at Princeton on crisp fall afternoons in the 1840s when students gathered behind Nassau Hall for impromptu games. Opposing teams were made up of residents of East and West Colleges or members of the Whig and Clio Halls; sometimes, all the A to L's were pitted against the M to Z's. After the Civil War, increasing interest led to interclass matches and eventually to an epochal event—the first American intercollegiate football game, between Princeton and Rutgers, in New Brunswick on November 6, 1869.

The twenty-five players from each college played in their street clothes, and the several hundred spectators stood around on the side or sat on a wooden fence. There were no coaches, no officials, no programs—the Rutgers *Targum*, on which we chiefly depend for the record of the game, tells us that Princeton's first goal was made "by a well directed kick, from a gentleman whose name we don't know, but who did the best kicking on the Princeton side." The *Targum* is equally silent about the identity of the first wrongway player in American football history, a Rutgers man "who, in his ardor, forgot which way he was kicking," and scored for Princeton instead of Rutgers. By agreement, the home team's style of play was used, and Rutgers won, 6 goals to 4; a week later, Princeton won the return match on its grounds, 8 goals to 0.

The game that Princeton and Rutgers played was a form of association football, forerunner of later-day soccer, as was the game that Princeton and Yale played in 1873 (Princeton 3, Yale 0) in a match that inaugurated the longest continuous rivalry in American intercollegiate football. Harvard, meantime, had been playing the "Boston game," which was more like rugby, and in 1875 Harvard beat Yale, 4 to 0, in a rugby-type match, inaugurating this series. At this game, two spectators from Princeton, Jotham Potter 1877 and Earl Dodge 1879, were so taken with rugby that they resolved to press for its adoption at Princeton. Despite strong sentiment for retaining association football—"rather less rowdyish and more scientific" than the Harvard game, said the *Nassau Lit*—Potter's and Dodge's views prevailed by a narrow margin at a spirited mass meeting. Subsequently, on Princeton's initiative, Columbia, Harvard, Princeton, and Yale representatives met on November 23, 1876, and formed the Intercollegiate Football Association, which adopted modified rugby rules.

Princeton's success, which had been marked in association football, declined temporarily with the change to rugby, but by 1878, when Woodrow Wilson and his classmate, Earl Dodge, were directors of the student-managed Princeton College Football Association, Princeton won all six of its games, defeating both Harvard and Yale in the same season for the first time.

American football, as it evolved from rugby, became so rough in its early years that after watching a Harvard-Yale match, bare-knuckle heavyweight boxing champion John L. Sullivan declared, "There's murder in that game." Princeton contributed its share of roughness with its invention of the "V-formation wedge," which compared favorably with other engines of attack such as Harvard's "flying wedge" and Yale's "tackles back" formation. There were repeated efforts at reform, but relief from the continuing hazards of football came only in 1906, when, in response to public outcry, the game was opened up with legalization of the forward pass and other rule changes designed to reduce injuries.

THE 1880s

Princeton excelled in kicking throughout the 1880s. In the 1882 Yale game, John T. Haxall 1883 place-kicked a 65-yard goal, setting an intercollegiate record that the outstanding college kickers of subsequent years found hard to equal. In the second half of the 1883 Harvard game, the home-grown Princeton captain Alec Moffat 1884 (son of a professor of Greek) kicked two field goals with his right foot and two with his left, thus accounting for 20 points in Princeton's 26-7 victory. Moffat is credited with inventing the spiral punt, further developed by "Snake" Ames 1890, another superb kicker and a slippery open field runner.

The teams of 1885 and 1889 won all their games. The 1885 team scored 637 points and allowed its nine opponents only 25—a Princeton record, which by now must be considered indestructible. After winning its other games by an average margin of 75 points, it came from behind in its last game to edge out Yale, 6 to 5, with the famous run of Tillie Lamar 1886. In the closing minutes a Yale punt bounced off the shoulder of another player into the outstretched hands of Lamar who, catching the ball on the run, streaked 90 yards for a touchdown.

A tower of strength on both the 1885 and 1889 teams was Hector Cowan, who played tackle for five years, the last two as a Seminary student. In the various "all-time" teams in vogue up to World War II, Cowan was mentioned more frequently than any other Princetonian.

THE 1890s

The 1893 team, which also had a perfect record, was remarkable for its strong defense—and for its spirit of thankfulness. Standing "naked and covered with mud and blood and perspiration" in the dressing room after their climactic 6 to 0 triumph over Yale (Richard Harding Davis reported in *Harper's Weekly*), the victorious Princeton players sang "Praise God From Whom All Blessings Flow. . . ."

The 1896 team marred an otherwise perfect record by incurring a scoreless tie with a strong Lafayette team, but was, nevertheless, considered Princeton's best team up to then, overwhelming teams like Penn State and Cornell and defeating Harvard, 12 to 0, and Yale, 24 to 6. This was the last year that Harvard and Princeton met until 1911.

In 1898, Princeton missed a perfect record by the same narrow margin as in 1896, suffering a 5 to 5 tie with Army, the only team it did not hold scoreless. Arthur Poe won a 7 to 0 victory over Yale by snatching the ball from an opponent's arms and dashing the length of the field for a touchdown. The next year he clinched an 11 to 10 victory over Yale by kicking a last-minute field goal, the only one he had ever attempted. His were the most memorable of many exploits of six brothers who played for Princeton from 1882 to 1902 (see *Poe Brothers*).

VERSATILE JOHN DE WITT

The 1903 team, undefeated and untied, scored 159 points against its eleven opponents, giving up only 6—all to Yale. Its captain, John DeWitt '04, a big fast guard, was probably Princeton's most complete player in the pre-forward-pass era. He could block, tackle, run with the ball, punt, drop-kick, and place-kick equally well. He used his talents most strikingly in the last game of his career, when Princeton gave Yale its first defeat in two years.

Yale scored its six points (five with a

touchdown and one with a kick) early in the game. Toward the end of the first half a Yale drop-kick was blocked, and DeWitt scooped up the ball and ran 75 yards for a touchdown; Roy Vetterlein '06, the Princeton quarterback, kicked the extra point, tying the score. With only a minute left to play in the game, DeWitt kicked a 43-yard field goal (then worth five points) from a difficult angle, for the winning score. That Monday morning, placards all over the campus jubilantly announced: John DeWitt 11, Yale 6.

In the formal picture of his team, broad-framed Captain John DeWitt is clad in a white sweater with a black P—the best that a Nassau Street store could produce in his size, at a moment's notice, to replace the soiled and torn jersey he had brought with him to the photographers studio. DeWitt's makeshift attire later became standard garb for captains of Princeton championship teams.

SAN WHITE'S RUNS

From 1903 until the outbreak of the First World War, Princeton was eclipsed by Yale, and then by Harvard, except for two seasons. In 1906 strong Princeton and Yale teams had perfect records until their last game, when they held each other to a scoreless tie. The Princeton captain that year was Herbert L. Dillon '07, later the principal donor to the gymnasium that bears his name.

In 1911 Sanford White, at end, scored all the points that brought Princeton its first Big Three title since 1896. Against Harvard he recovered a blocked drop-kick and ran 90 yards for a touchdown, "without a hand being laid on him," the *Alumni Weekly* reported. Later he tackled a Harvard back behind his own goal line for a safety, adding the two points needed to win, 8 to 6. Two

weeks later, on a field of mud, he picked up a Yale fumble at mid-field and raced goalward. The Yale safety caught him at the four-yard line, but White struggled across the goal line, with the Yale defender holding on, for the winning score of 6 to 3.

Less spectacular, but equally important, was the all-round play at tackle of Eddie Hart, captain in 1910 and 1911. One of the most powerful linemen who ever played for Princeton, he became a legend in the American Expeditionary Force during the First World War when, responding to an offer by a professional strong man in a Paris theatre to take on anyone in the audience, Hart, on orders from his colonel, went forward to the stage and threw the challenger into the wings.

In 1911, just before Hart's team was photographed, someone doing research on the rights and privileges of champions discovered John DeWitt in his white sweater. A similar sweater was made ready for Eddie Hart, thus transmuting the 1903 improvisation into tradition.

In 1912 Hobey Baker '14 scored 92 points, an individual Princeton season record for more than sixty years.

THE ROPER ERA

Bill Roper '02, who coached both the Dillon and the Hart teams, was head coach from 1919 through 1930. He was a great orator and a classic example of the inspirational coach. "Hell," one of his opposing coaches complained, "He's not a coach; he's an evangelist."

Roper's 1919 and 1920 teams tied Harvard and beat Yale; his 1922, 1925, and 1926 teams were Big Three champions. The 1920 team, captained by Mike Callahan, center, scored a decisive 20 to 0 victory over a Yale team led by Mike's older brother Tim, an all-American guard.

Stan Keck, a big, fast, all-American tackle—"the ubiquitous Mr. Keck," one reporter called him—was the leading blocker in 1920 and 1921, and Don Lourie, an all-American quarterback, was the star of the attack. Lourie was ably assisted by Hank Garrity, Ralph Gilroy, and Jack Cleaves. Their exploits moved Frank D. Halsey '12 and A.C.M. Azoy '14 to lyrical flights:

Lourie and Garrity, Gilroy and
    Cleaves,
Footballers flightsome as
    autumn-blown leaves,
Filling the Princetons with riotous
    joy,
Lourie and Garrity, Cleaves and
    Gilroy.

Gilroy and Cleaves and Lourie and
    Garrity,
No hope for Harvard or Yale to get
    charity;
Worthy a wager of all your wife's
    dowry—
Garrity, Cleaves, Gilroy and Lourie.

In 1922 Roper's "team of destiny," as it came to be known, completed Princeton's first perfect season since 1903. This team had little offense (some of its plays were made up on the field), but its defense was invincible. In most of its key games, the narrow margins of victory were provided chiefly by Ken Smith '24's field goals and extra points. Its most thrilling victory was over heavily favored Chicago. Trailing 18 to 7 (Chicago had missed all three of its extra points), with only twelve minutes left in the last quarter, Princeton rallied to score two touchdowns, and Ken Smith kicked the extra points, making the score 21 to 18. Five minutes later, with only seconds to play, Princeton held Chicago on fourth down, inches from the goal line.

During this game, a Princeton fan became so excited when Howdie Gray '23 grabbed a Chicago fumble and raced 43 yards for a touchdown that he whacked someone sitting in front of him with his rolled-up program. "Watch out there!" a man cried, "that's my wife you just hit." "Terribly sorry," the enthusiastic fan replied, "that's my son who just made that run!" "Oh," said the husband, "go ahead, hit her again."

The 1925 and 1926 teams were led by Ed McMillan '26 at center and John Davis '27 at guard, and expertly directed by Dan Caulkins '27 at quarterback. In the 1925 Yale game, Jake Slagle '27, a triple-threat halfback, took the ball from punt formation, stiff-armed and side-stepped several tacklers and, behind alert and effective interference, swept 92 yards for a touchdown that was reminiscent of the one Tillie Lamar had scored forty years before.

THE 1930s

Al Wittmer '22 was coach in 1931, Fritz Crisler (later coach and director of athletics at Michigan) from 1932 to 1937, Tad Weiman from 1938 to 1942, and Harry Mahnken in 1943 and 1944.

In 1932 the Class of 1936 freshman team won all of its games and held all of its opponents scoreless. In the three succeeding varsity years members of this class, together with some excellent players from neighboring classes, won 25 games and lost only one—an upset by Yale, 7 to 0, in 1934. Teams captained by Art Lane '34 and Pepper Constable '36 were undefeated and untied in 1933 and 1935. The 1933 team held seven of its opponents scoreless and gave up only 8 points to the other two. Donald G. Herring '07, who covered football for the *Alumni Weekly*, said the 1935 team was the best college team he had ever seen. It overpowered Harvard and Yale and then went on to overwhelm Dartmouth in the last game, played in a near blizzard and made further memorable by the presence of a twelfth man in Dartmouth's line-up during one of its goal-line stands—a spectator in mufti, unconnected with Dartmouth, but with a consuming passion for the underdog.

Princeton beat Yale in 1938, 1939, 1940, and 1941, at that time the longest string of Princeton victories in the history of the series. High scorers in these years were Dave Allerdice '41, one of Princeton's greatest passers (in three years he gained 2,492 yards by passing and set half a dozen other records), and Bob Peters '42, whose skill in running, passing, and kicking made him a powerful triple threat.

THE CALDWELL YEARS

Charlie Caldwell '25, a member of Roper's 1922 "team of destiny" and a coach at Williams for seventeen years, was head coach at Princeton from 1945 until his death in 1957. He developed a highly effective offense that added elements of deception, associated with the more modern T formation, to the power blocking of traditional single-wing football.

His teams won six successive Big Three championships, 1947 through 1952, bettering by two the previous record set by Percy Haughton's Harvard teams, 1912 through 1915. Six captains, accordingly, wore white sweaters and lit victory bonfires at the Cannon: Dick West '45 (a war veteran who graduated in 1948), Ed Mead '49, George Sella '50, George Chandler '51, Dave Hickok '52, and Frank McPhee '53.

Chandler's and Hickok's teams had 9-0 records in 1950 and 1951—Princeton's only consecutive pair of perfect seasons since the advent of full-length schedules in 1876. These teams contributed the major part of a winning streak of twenty-four games (1949-1952), a Princeton record. Both were awarded the Lambert Trophy as Eastern champions, both beat Yale by large margins, 47 to 12 and 27 to 0, and against Harvard, both set records for that series: in 1950, for the highest score, 63 to 26, and in 1951, for the widest margin of victory, 54 to 13. Their narrowest victory, 13 to 7, over Dartmouth in 1950, was ground out in the wake of a hurricane, in torrential rain, with an 80-mile gale blowing through the open end of the stadium; while the offensive team was in the huddle, an official had to hold the ball on the line of scrimmage to keep it from blowing away.

These years were replete with outstanding performances from players like Jack Davison, Homer Smith, George Chandler, Frank McPhee—and Dick Kazmaier. Davison scored four touchdowns against Harvard in 1949, a record for that series equalled in 1952 by Smith, who in that game set a Princeton single-game rushing record of 273 yards. That year Smith also added to the Lamar-Slagle tradition with his exciting 93-yard touchdown run against Yale. Chandler, a great blocker and a fine signal-caller, was the key man of the 1950 team, according to Caldwell. McPhee blocked seven punts in 1951.

Kazmaier ran, passed, and punted equally well. Only 5'11" and 170 pounds, his strong point was innate skill, perfected by concentration and practice, rather than power. His passes and punts were distinguished by their accuracy, his runs by his change of pace and of direction. He was the only offensive first-stringer from 1950 not lost through graduation, and Caldwell attributed the 1951 perfect season to Kazmaier's effort to improve his own 1950 performance, which set an example for his teammates.

His finest hour came in the fifth game of 1951 against strong, previously undefeated Cornell. He completed 15 of 17 passes for 236 yards, and carried for 124 yards, 49 in an explosive run from a double reverse. All told, he scored two touchdowns, passed for three more, and set up two others. The score was 53 to 15.

In his senior year, Kazmaier gained 1,827 yards, rushing and passing, the best in the nation. His career total offense, 4,354 yards, has long been a Princeton three-year record, as has his 35 scoring passes.

Kazmaier was a unanimous choice for all-American in both his junior and senior years, and he was voted the Heisman Trophy as the player of the year in 1951 by the biggest margin in the seventeen-year history of the award.

In 1950 Caldwell was voted coach of the year; in 1951 he stood fourth.

Princeton was unofficial Ivy champion in 1955. That year, Captain Royce Flippin '56 (later director of athletics) completed a four-year scoring campaign against Yale akin to John De-Witt's virtuoso performance half a century earlier. In Yale games his freshman and three varsity seasons Flippin ran for nine touchdowns and passed for two others, thus having a hand in eleven of the twelve touchdowns his teams scored against Yale.

THE COLMAN YEARS

Dick Colman, Caldwell's pupil at Williams, and for twenty years his assistant as line coach at Williams and Princeton, took over during Caldwell's last illness. From 1957 through 1968, he taught single-wing football with the same conviction as Caldwell and with similar results. His teams won 75 games and lost 33, matching the average (.694) that Caldwell's teams had compiled during his twelve-year stewardship. Princeton won the Ivy championship in 1957 (the League's second year) and in 1964, and shared it in 1963 and 1966, and won the Big Three title in 1958, 1964, 1965, and 1966. Six captains, consequently, wore white sweaters and presided at bonfires: John Sapoch '58, Fred Tiley '59, Bill Guedel '64, Cosmo Iacavazzi '65, Paul Savidge '66, and Walter Kozumbo '67.

The 1957 team rose from the ashes (i.e., their loss to Yale) to win the Ivy championship by overwhelming previously unbeaten but once tied Dartmouth, 34 to 14, in a game, marked by another end-of-the-season snowstorm, and John Sapoch's play-calling and blocking, Bob Casciola's defensive play at tackle, and Dan Sachs's running and passing. The 1958 team won Princeton's first Big Three title since 1952; against Yale it rolled up the largest score (50-14) that Princeton had ever made in this series.

The mid-sixties were golden years, brightened by Cosmo Iacavazzi's hurdling touchdown leaps, Stas Maliszewski's skillful line-backing, and Charlie Gogolak's renowned place-kicking. The 1963 team shared the Ivy title with Dartmouth, missing sole possession by a single point in its 21-22 loss to that team. The 1964 team achieved Princeton's first perfect season (9-0) since 1951, and set an Ivy League single-game record, beating Penn 55 to 0. In 1965 the opposing teams in Princeton's annual encounter with Rutgers were captained by twin brothers, Peter Savidge for Rutgers, Paul for Princeton. Poetic justice called for a tie game, but Charlie Gogolak's six field goals and two goals after touchdown led Princeton to a 32 to 6 victory. Gogolak ended his Princeton career that year, the possessor of six national collegiate kicking records; one was for 50 consecutive goals after touchdown, six more than the previous record, set by his older brother Pete at Cornell. The Gogolak brothers were soccer-style placement kickers who came to this country with their family from Hungary during the revolt of 1956. Both later kicked for professional teams.

The 1966 team tied Harvard and Dartmouth for the Ivy League championship and also won the Big Three title, as Larry Stupski '67 gave an approximate replay of Sam White's performance in 1911. Stupski made two key tackles which led to the upset of undefeated Harvard, 18 to 14. A week later, after Walter Kozumbo had blocked a punt with less than four minutes to play, Stupski grabbed the ball and ran 60 yards for the touchdown which beat Yale, 13 to 7—the sixth successive victory over the Elis, tying a record set in 1952.

In 1967 fullback Ellis Moore scored five touchdowns against Harvard, setting an Ivy single-game record, later equalled by Ed Marinaro of Cornell.

THE RECENT YEARS

Dick Colman resigned at the end of the 1968 season to become director of athletics at Middlebury College. He was succeeded by Jake McCandless '51, who had understudied Dick Kazmaier in 1949 and 1950, and had assisted Colman, chiefly as backfield coach, since 1958. McCandless transformed the Princeton offense from single-wing to T-formation. His 1969 team tied Yale and Dartmouth for the Ivy League championship. Two of his players later played professional football: running back Hank Bjorkland '72 (who set a Princeton career rushing record of 2,362 yards) and defensive tackle Carl Barisich '73 (an all-East as well as all-Ivy player). McCandless resigned at the end of the 1972 season, and was succeeded by Bob Casciola '58, who had played tackle under Caldwell and Colman, and had coached at Princeton, Dartmouth, and the University of Connecticut.

Although Princeton's football fortunes suffered a slump through the mid-seventies, autumn afternoons in Palmer Stadium were brightened periodically by fine individual performances that brought new records and awards. In 1973, Bill Skinner '74 set a Princeton career record with 75 pass receptions, while offensive guard and captain Bill Cronin '74 and running back Walt Snickenberger '75 were named all-Ivy. His senior year, Snickenberger also set a Princeton season scoring record of 16 touchdowns and received the Bushnell Award as Ivy League player of the year. The following year quarterback Ron Beible '76 led the Ivy League in yards gained by forward passing as well as in total offense, set Princeton season and career records for forward passes completed (123 and 293) and total yards gained by passing (1503 and 3662), and was one of thirty-three scholar-athletes awarded scholarships for graduate study by the N.C.A.A. That same year, wide receiver Neil Chamberlin '76 set Princeton season and career records for passes caught (44, 78), and open-field runner Mike Carter '77 led the Ivy League in both kickoff and punt returns. Defensive tackle Ted Schiller '77 was named All-Ivy in 1975 and All-East in 1976. In the latter year, offensive guard Kevin

Fox '77 was chosen as scholar-athlete by the National Football Foundation.

At the end of the 1977 season, Casciola was succeeded by Frank Navarro, previously head coach at Wabash College in Indiana.

LIGHTWEIGHT FOOTBALL

Princeton's 150-pound football teams generally gave a good account of themselves in the Eastern Intercollegiate League after its founding in 1931. Their longest period of excellence came in the late thirties and early forties when, coached by Harry A. Mahnken, their hard blocking and tackling earned them the title "The Fighting Fifties" and enabled them to win the championship five of the six years from 1937 through 1942. Some dozen years later, teams coached by Dick Vaughan enjoyed another spell of success, highlighted by the performance of the undefeated team of 1954, which won the league title by overwhelming Navy, champion the five preceding years. Under Coach Dan White '65, the mid-seventies saw another string of winning teams, most notably the 1975 eleven, which defeated perennial league leaders Army and Navy on the way to a tie with Cornell for the championship.

Football All-Americans, now a rare species at Princeton, were once quite numerous. Five were named to the initial All-America team of 1889 and five again in 1893. In only two of the years prior to World War I—1900 and 1909—did Princeton fail to place a single player on the first team. Thereafter, with the spread of football hegemony to the West and South, Princeton's representation declined. Five Princetonians were named to the first team in the twenties, one in the thirties, four in the fifties, two in the sixties.

The names on the following list are taken from the All-America selections made by Caspar Whitney for 1889-1896, Walter Camp for 1897-1924, Grantland Rice for 1925-1953, the Associated Press since 1925, and United Press International since 1926; in recent years, additional names have been taken from the NCAA Consensus All-America teams.*

All told, fifty Princetonians have been named first team All-American, three of them three times, ten twice:†

1889
K.L. Ames 1890 (fullback)
Roscoe H. Channing Jr. 1891 (halfback)
Hector W. Cowan 1888 (tackle)
William J. George 1889 (center)
Edgar Allan Poe 1891 (quarterback)

1890
Sheppard Homans, Jr. 1892 (fullback)
Jesse B. Riggs 1892 (guard)
Ralph H. Warren 1893 (end)

1891
Sheppard Homans Jr. 1892 (fullback)
Philip King 1893 (quarterback)
Jesse B. Riggs 1892 (guard)

1892
Philip King 1893 (halfback)
Arthur L. Wheeler 1896 (guard)

1893
Philip King 1893 (quarterback)
Langdon Lea 1896 (tackle)
Franklin Morse 1895 (halfback)
Thomas G. Trenchard 1895 (end)
Arthur L. Wheeler 1896 (guard)

1894
Langdon Lea 1896 (tackle)
Arthur L. Wheeler 1896 (guard)

1895
Langdon Lea 1896 (tackle)
Dudley Riggs 1897 (guard)

1896
John Baird 1899 (fullback)
William W. Church 1897 (tackle)
Robert R. Gailey P.G. (center)
Addison W. Kelly 1898 (halfback)

1897
Garrett Cochran 1898 (end)
Addison W. Kelly 1898 (halfback)

1898
Arthur R. T. Hillebrand 1900 (tackle)
Lew R. Palmer 1898 (end)

1899
Arthur R. T. Hillebrand 1900 (tackle)
Arthur Poe 1900 (end)

1901
Ralph T. Davis '04 (end)

1902
John R. DeWitt '04 (guard)

1903
John R. DeWitt '04 (guard)
Howard H. Henry '04 (end)
J. Dana Kafer '05 (halfback)

1904
James L. Cooney '07 (tackle)

1905
James B. McCormick '08 (fullback)

1906
James L. Cooney '07 (tackle)
L. Caspar Wister '08 (end)

1907
Edwin H. W. Harlan '08 (halfback)
James B. McCormick '08 (fullback)

1908
Frederick M. Tibbott '09 (halfback)

1910
Talbot T. Pendleton '13 (halfback)

1911
Joseph M. Duff, Jr. '12 (guard)
Edward J. Hart '12 (tackle)
Sanford B. White '12 (end)

1912
William John Logan '13 (guard)

1913
Harold R. Ballin '15 (tackle)

1914
Harold R. Ballin '15 (tackle)

1918
Frank L. Murrey '22 (quarterback)

1920
J. Stanton Keck '21 (tackle)
Donold B. Lourie '22 (quarterback)

1922
C. Herbert Treat '24 (tackle)

1925
Edward L. McMillan '26 (center)

1928
Charles H. Howe '29 (center)

1935
Jac Weller '36 (guard)

1950
Holland R. Donan '51 (defensive tackle)
Redmond C.S. Finney '51 (center)
Richard W. Kazmaier, Jr. '52 (halfback)

1951
Richard W. Kazmaier, Jr. '52 (halfback)
Frank M. McPhee '53 (defensive end)

1952
Frank M. McPhee '53 (defensive end)

1964
Cosmo J. Iacavazzi '65 (fullback)

1965
Charles P. Gogolak '66 (kicking special-
ist)
Stanislaw Maliszewski '66 (guard)

* Frank G. Menke, *The Encyclopedia of
Sports* (fourth revised edition), A. S. Barnes and
Company, 1969, pp. 374-396, and the NCAA *College Football Modern Record Book*, 1975, p. 56.
    † The following thirty-three Princetonians were
named second or third team All-American:
halfback Howard R. Reiter 1898, fullback Herbert Wheeler 1900, guard William H. Edwards
1900, halfback Horace B. Bannard, Jr. 1900,
tackle Williamson Pell '02, center Hubert F.
Fisher PG, halfback Walter L. Foulke '05,
fullback Sumner Rulon-Miller '05, guard Harold

H. Short '05, end Norman B. Tooker '06, guard Herbert L. Dillon '07, quarterback Edward A. Dillon '09, center Walter J. Phillips '09, tackle Rudolph C. Siegling '10, center Arthur Bluethenthal '13, halfback Hobart A. H. Baker '14, guard Wilbur J. Shenk '14, guard Frank T. Hogg '17, halfback David W. Tibbott '17, quarterback John K. Strubing, Jr. '20, halfback R. Maurice Trimble, Jr. '20, center Henry A. Callahan '21, end Armant LeGendre '21, halfback Martin H. Garrity, Jr. '22, guard Melville P. Dickenson '22, tackle Robert W. Beattie '25, end Edmund C. Stout, Jr. '25, halfback Jacob W. Slagle '27 ("the best all-round football player the game has known in years," according to Grantland Rice, who omitted Slagle from the first team only because injuries had forced him to spend much of his senior year on the bench), fullback Oliver E. Miles '29, tackle Charles B. Ceppi '34, end R. Kenneth Fairman '34, center Elwood McG. Kalbaugh '35, and halfback George J. Sella, Jr. '50.

Forrestal Campus, a major University facility for research and instruction, was established in 1951 on a 825-acre tract, three miles southeast of the main campus on U.S. Route 1. It was named for the first United States Secretary of Defense, James Forrestal '15, who, while secretary of the navy, had initiated government support of fundamental research in science and engineering.

The University purchased the land, with sixteen laboratory buildings, for $1,500,000 from the Rockefeller Institute for Medical Research, which relocated its Princeton activities in New York as part of what became Rockefeller University. It was at the Institute that Nobel laureates Wendell M. Stanley and John H. Northrup made their discoveries about the essential nature of viruses.

At first, Forrestal was devoted principally to research activities in aerospace and mechanical sciences. Added subsequently were three major research facilities: Project Matterhorn, later called the Plasma Physics Laboratory (q.v.); the federal government's Geophysical Fluid Dynamics Laboratory for theoretical research in meteorology and oceanography, moved to Princeton from Washington, D.C. in 1968; and the $40 million Princeton-Pennsylvania Accelerator, which provided unique research facilities for the study of elementary particles from 1957 until 1972 when, supporting funds being no longer available, it was closed and placed in stand-by condition.

In 1973 the University announced a long-range plan to influence the quality of development in the area surrounding the Forrestal Campus and at the same time to generate long-term income for its own educational objectives. Called the Princeton Forrestal Center, the project involved adding enough acreage to the original Forrestal Campus (both by purchase and the acquisition of developmental control) to bring the total area to 1,600 acres. Almost half of this land was to be retained for the Forrestal Campus and for open space, leaving the rest to be developed for office, research, and light industrial use, and for town houses, apartments, a hotel, and a shopping area.

Founding of Princeton, The, like that of Brown, Rutgers, and Dartmouth, was one of the consequences of The Great Awakening, the series of religious revivals that swept the English colonies in America in the eighteenth century. The Great Awakening had other important social and political consequences, too. It brought an upsurge in missionary activities among the Indians and the first important movement against slavery. Of special importance for Princeton, it increased opposition to the Anglican Church and the royal officials who supported it, and created a democratic spirit in religion that was allied to the insistence on political home rule that eventually brought independence from Britain.

The Great Awakening is said to have begun in New Jersey about 1720 with revival meetings in the Raritan Valley led by a Dutch Reformed pastor, Theodorus Jacobus Frelinghuysen, who emphasized the religion of the heart over doctrine and liturgy. It was carried on throughout the Middle Colonies under the leadership of zealous, evangelical graduates of the Log College (q.v.), founded in Pennsylvania about 1726 by Presbyterian William Tennent. In New England the movement was led by the stirring preaching of Congregationalist Jonathan Edwards at Northampton, Massachusetts. These and other revivalistic activities were stimulated in the years 1739 to 1741 by the tours of the English evangelist, George Whitefield. The activities spread with the preaching of Presbyterian Samuel Davies in Virginia and with later efforts of Baptists and Methodists in other parts of the South.*

In New England, where the movement was shorter-lived than elsewhere, the emotional, and sometimes fanatical, excesses of some of the followers of the revivalists left a bitter division in the churches between the "New Lights" and the "Old Lights." In the Middle Colonies a similar division between the "New Sides" and the "Old Sides" caused a split in the Presbyterian Church from 1741 to 1758 known as the Great Schism.

ORIGIN OF THE COLLEGE

The four originators of the College were members of the moderate wing of the New Sides. Three of them were graduates of Yale: Jonathan Dickinson, pastor at Elizabethtown; Aaron Burr, pastor at Newark; John Pierson, pastor at Woodbridge. The fourth, Ebenezer Pemberton, pastor of the Presbyterian Church in New York, was a graduate of Harvard. They believed in revivalism and welcomed George Whitefield to their pulpits, but they disapproved of the more contentious and intrusive methods of the New Sides graduates of William Tennent's Log College. Nevertheless, being ex-Congregationalists, they defended the rights of the Tennent men in their disputes with the Old Sides group that dominated the Synod of Philadelphia. After this synod expelled the Presbytery of New Brunswick in 1741 for defying a regulation that Log College graduates should not be ordained without an examination by a committee of the synod, Dickinson, Burr, and the others tried in vain to effect a conciliation. They then withdrew from the Synod of Philadelphia and joined with the Presbytery of New Brunswick to form the new Synod of New York in 1745.

Disappointed by Yale and Harvard's opposition to the Great Awakening and not satisfied with the limited course of instruction given at the Log College, they devised a plan for the establishment of a new college. The four ministers persuaded three leading lay Presbyterians in New York to join them. These three, also graduates of Yale were: William Smith, lawyer; Peter Van Brugh Livingston, merchant; and William Peartree Smith, a young man of independent means who was a generous supporter of the church and "an ardent patriot." Since there was at that time no college in existence between New Haven in Connecticut and Williamsburg in Virginia—a long distance to cover by horseback or stagecoach—the need for an institution of higher education in the Middle Colonies, they felt, was urgent.

Late in 1745 or early in 1746 these

seven men applied for a charter to Governor Lewis Morris, an Anglican, who refused their petition because, he said, his instructions inhibited him from granting such a charter to a group of dissenters. Following Morris's death, they applied anew to Acting Governor John Hamilton. Although also an Anglican, Hamilton was more liberal in his views than Morris and with the consent of his Council, on which there were a number of friends of the proposed College, he granted a charter on October 22, 1746. The Anglican clergy later complained that it was done "so suddenly and privately" that they "had no opportunity to enter a caveat against it."

A century and a half later the Anglican Acting Governor received this tribute from a latter-day Presbyterian, John DeWitt 1861, in a history of the College that he wrote for the Sesquicentennial Celebration:

The name of John Hamilton should be given a conspicuous place in any list of the founders of Princeton University. He granted the first charter; he granted it against the precedent made by the governor whom he succeeded in the executive chair; and he granted it with alacrity. . . . What is more remarkable, at a time when Episcopalian governors were ill-disposed to grant to Presbyterians ecclesiastical or educational franchises, he—an Episcopalian—gave this charter to a board of trust composed wholly of members of the Presbyterian Church. . . .

However, the college thus founded was not, as has sometimes been said, established under the auspices of the Synod of New York. The seven persons who, in the words of their leader Jonathan Dickinson (q.v.), "first concocted the plan and foundation of the College" were leading members of that body, but they acted independently as (the charter said) "well disposed & publick spirited Persons." The new institution, therefore, was not to be a synodical seminary of the kind that had been planned earlier by the Synod of Philadelphia, but a college of liberal arts and sciences. "Though our great Intention was to erect a seminary for educating Ministers of the Gospel," one of the founders† later wrote in a letter to another clergyman, "yet we hope it will be useful in other learned professions —Ornaments of the State as well as the Church. Therefore we propose to make the plan of Education as extensive as our Circumstances will admit." The College, furthermore, was not to be solely for Presbyterians: "The most effectual Care is taken in our Charter to secure the Rights of Conscience," the Trustee wrote in this same letter. "Persons of all persuasions are to have free access to the Honours & Privileges of the College, while they behave themselves with Sobriety and Virtue."

Five months or more after they obtained the charter, the seven original trustees chose for the remaining places they were empowered to fill five ardent New Siders: Samuel Blair, Samuel Finley, Gilbert Tennent, William Tennent, Jr., and Richard Treat, all graduates of the Log College except Treat, who was one of its close adherents. On April 27, 1747, the trustees announced the election of Jonathan Dickinson as president, and the College opened in his Elizabethtown parsonage during the last week of May. On President Dickinson's death the following October, the College moved to the Newark parsonage of Aaron Burr, who was elected the second president.

THE FOUNDING PERFECTED

When the first charter was attacked —the Anglicans contended that Hamilton was superannuated when he granted it and threatened to test its validity in court—the next governor, Jonathan Belcher (q.v.), a graduate of Harvard and a Congregationalist, issued a second one on September 14, 1748. It left intact the essential features of the first charter, but developed further the founders' concern for "State as well as Church" by making the governor of New Jersey ex-officio a trustee and including among those appointed to an enlarged board of twenty-three trustees, four members of the Provincial Council and other prominent laymen, two of whom were members of the Society of Friends, two of the Episcopal Church, and one of the Dutch Reformed Church.

Belcher's efforts on behalf of the College tended to eclipse the work of the earlier founders. Although he himself referred to the College as his "adopted daughter," the trustees, in proposing to name the first college building in Princeton for him, said they viewed him as the College's "founder, patron, and benefactor." *An Account of the College*, published by the trustees in 1764, even begins with the granting of the charter by Governor Belcher and the opening of the College in Newark under "Mr. President Burr, the first who officiated in that station."

Later historians—President Maclean, Professors Collins and Wertenbaker—have, with ample documentation, restored the earlier phases of Princeton's founding, President Maclean giving us this balanced view of Belcher's role:

The Governor was *not*, properly speaking, *the* founder of the College, in the sense of being its originator, for the College was in existence, and in active operation, before his arrival. He was not, therefore, to use a phrase of Lord Coke's, its *Fundator Incipiens*, although, in view of what he did towards the building up of the institution, he may be regarded as its *Fundator Perficiens*.

* Frelinghuysen received an honorary degree from Princeton in 1749, Davies in 1753, Whitefield in 1754. Two of William Tennent's sons became Trustees of the College; Edwards, its third president; Davies, its fourth.

† The letter, when given to the University in 1905, lacked the last page(s). Internal evidence suggests that it was written between 1748 and 1750, probably by Ebenezer Pemberton.

Freneau, Philip [Morin] (1752-1832) fulfilled the dream of his wine merchant father, Pierre Fresneau (old spelling) when he entered the Class of 1771 to prepare for the ministry. Well versed in the classics in Monmouth County under the tutelage of William Tennent, Philip entered Princeton as a sophomore in 1768, but the joy of the occasion was marred by his father's financial losses and death the year before. In spite of financial hardships, Philip's Scottish mother believed that her oldest of five children would graduate and join the clergy. Though he was a serious student of theology and a stern moralist all his life, Freneau found his true calling in literature. As his roommate and close friend James Madison (q.v.) recognized early, Freneau's wit and verbal skills would make him a powerful wielder of the pen and a formidable adversary on the battlefields of print. Freneau soon became the unrivaled "poet of the Revolution" and is still widely regarded as the "Father of American Literature."

Although Freneau had produced

several accomplished private poems before college, it was the intense experience of pre-Revolutionary-War Princeton that turned the poet's interest to
public writing. Political concerns led
Madison, Freneau, and their friends
Hugh Henry Brackenridge (q.v.) and
William Bradford, Jr., to revive the
defunct Plain Dealing Club as the
American Whig Society. Their verbal
skirmishes with the conservative
Cliosophic Society provided ample opportunities for sharpening Freneau's
skills in prose and poetic satire.
Charged with literary and political enthusiasm, Freneau and Brackenridge
collaborated on a rollicking, picaresque
narrative, *Father Bombo's Pilgrimage
to Mecca in Arabia*, which presents
comic glimpses of life in eighteenth-
century America. This piece, recently
acquired by Princeton and published
by the University Library (1975), may
well be the first work of prose fiction
written in America.

During their senior year Freneau
and Brackenridge labored long on
another joint project to which Freneau
contributed the greater share. Their
composition was a patriotic poem of
epic design, "The Rising Glory of
America," a prophecy of a time when a
united nation should rule the vast continent from the Atlantic to the Pacific.
At the commencement exercises of
September 1771, Brackenridge read
this poem to a "vast concourse of the
politest company," gathered at Nassau
Hall. The poem articulated the vision
and fervor of a young revolutionary
generation.

Freneau's life after Princeton was
one of change and conflict. He tried
teaching and hated it. He spent two
more years studying theology, but gave
it up. He felt a deep obligation to perform public service, and his satires

against the British in 1775 were written
out of fervent patriotism. At the same
time he distrusted politics and had a
personal yearning to escape social
turmoil and war. The romantic private
poet within him struggled against his
public role. Thus, paradoxically, in
1776 the "poet of the revolution" set
sail for the West Indies where he spent
two years writing of the beauties of nature and learning navigation. Suddenly
in 1778, he returned to New Jersey and
joined the militia and sailed the Atlantic as a ship captain. After suffering for
six weeks on a British prison ship, he
poured his bitterness into his political
writing and into much of his voluminous poetry of the early 1780s.

By 1790, at the age of thirty-eight,
with two collections of poetry in print
and a reputation as a fiery propagandist
and skillful sea captain, Freneau decided to settle down. He married
Eleanor Forman and tried to withdraw
to a quiet job as an assistant editor in
New York. But politics called again.
His friends Madison and Jefferson persuaded him to set up his own newspaper in Philadelphia to counter the powerful Hamiltonian paper of John Fenno.
Freneau's *National Gazette* upheld Jefferson's "Republican" principles and
even condemned Washington's foreign
policy. Jefferson later praised Freneau
for having "saved our Constitution
which was galloping fast into monar-
chy," while Washington grumbled of
"that rascal Freneau"—an epithet that
became the title of Lewis Leary's authoritative biography (1949).

After another decade of feverish public action, Freneau withdrew again in
1801, when Jefferson was elected president. He retired to his farm and returned occasionally to the sea. During
his last thirty years, he worked on his
poems, wrote essays attacking the

greed and selfishness of corrupt politicians, and sold pieces of his lands to produce a small income. He discovered that he had given his best years of literary productivity to his country, for it had been in the few stolen moments of the hectic 1780s that he found the inspiration for his best poems, such as "The Indian Burying Ground" and "The Wild Honey Suckle," a beautiful lyric which established him as an important American precursor of the Romantics.

Most students of Freneau's life and writing agree that he could have produced much more poetry of high literary merit had he not expended so much energy and talent for his country's political goals. In a way, though, he had fulfilled his father's hopes for him, for he had devoted his life to public service as a guardian of the morals of his society and as a spokesman for the needs of its people.

Emory B. Elliott, Jr.

Frick Chemical Laboratory was built in 1929 and named for Pittsburgh steelmaker Henry Clay Frick. His interest in the University had been cultivated originally by Dean West, who persuaded him to give the Graduate College the Procter Hall organ. In 1916 Frick expressed an interest in helping start a law school at Princeton, but agreed instead to give a chemical laboratory when President Hibben told him how urgently one was needed. Plans were drawn up, but Frick was appalled by the estimated cost of $1 million, which he thought due to inflated steel prices; the building was accordingly postponed.

Frick died in 1919, leaving almost $6 million to Princeton for its unrestricted use. All of his benefaction was used for endowment of faculty salaries, then badly needed, and it was not until late in the twenties that funds for the new laboratory became available through the Princeton University Fund. When the laboratory was completed in 1929, at a cost of $1,840,000, the trustees, mindful of Frick's earlier interest and his subsequent bequest, voted to name it for him.

Designed by Charles Z. Klauder, and constructed at the corner of Washington Road and William Street, the three-story building contains undergraduate laboratories, lecture rooms, faculty offices, and many research laboratories. A new wing at the rear, designed by O'Connor and Kilham, was completed in 1964 at a cost of $2 million, doubling the space available for research. It was made possible by an anonymous $1 million gift, supplemented by grants from the National Science Foundation and the National Institutes of Health, and other gifts. A $3 million renovation program, completed in 1975, brought substantial modernization. Funds for this purpose were contributed through the University's $125 million development program by the Kresge Foundation, the Haas Community Fund, and other donors.

On the second floor of the original building, above the entrance hall, is the chemistry library. Over a fireplace is inscribed a Latin version of a quotation from Ptolemy with which Dean Taylor (q.v.) ended his address at the dedication of Frick in 1929: NON EST MORTVVS QUI SCIENTIAM VIVIFICAVIT (He is not dead who has made knowledge live).

Fund Raising. Only two years after the College of New Jersey was founded in 1746, a trustee remarked that "the principal thing we now want is a proper fund to enable us to go on with this expensive undertaking." Naturally a committee was formed and Princeton's long history of fund-raising commenced.

In the beginning, subscriptions were sought from colonists in New Jersey, New York, and Pennsylvania. Lotteries were conducted in the College's behalf, and loyal sons returned to England for financial support and encouragement. The earliest fund-raisers, founding Trustee Gilbert Tennent and fourth president Samuel Davies, left the College in 1753 on a trip to Britain to appeal for support. A year-and-a-half later, with Davies nearly dead from seasickness, they returned home heartened by the generosity of their former countrymen who financed construction of the first college building. As stone upon stone was laid and the building began to take shape, the trustees asked "to dignify the edifice now erecting at Princeton" with the name of Jonathan Belcher, then the governor of New Jersey. But Mr. Belcher declined the honor (perhaps one of the nicest gifts anyone has given to the University!) and suggested the building be named Nassau Hall, as a memorial to King William III, House of Nassau.

Many subsequent forays to raise funds for specific purposes continued over the years. Left uneasy by these unrelated, ad hoc solicitations, President Maclean established a permanent endowment fund in 1853. But the endowment grew slowly, and Princeton depended largely on annual gifts to meet its operating expenses. Today both current gifts and endowment income make major contributions to the operating budget, accounting for about a quarter of the income.

From the very beginning, Princeton realized that her loyal, supportive alumni were her most important hope for continuing strength and sustenance. Systematic annual appeals to the entire alumni body began in 1940 with Annual Giving. That year $80,000 was realized, a modest beginning for the well-organized drives that attracted more than $5 million by 1977. Complementing these campaigns, which raise unrestricted support for the University, are more specific, formal solicitations conducted by the Development Office, established in 1956 to attract funds for endowment, construction, student aid, and other needs.

In 1959, the Office launched a $53 million campaign under President Goheen. Thanks mainly to alumni generosity, that goal was soon exceeded, and another development program, begun less than a decade later, raised $125 million for Princeton. Gifts from alumni (which by this time included women) were to remain the primary means of support; they were complemented by foundation, corporate, and government assistance. As President Bowen has suggested, it is because of these diverse sources of support that Princeton is able to retain its independence. Although ultimate responsibility for fund-raising still falls on the president and trustees, volunteer alumni advocates (headed by the Council for University Resources)— supported by a staff of 25 persons— coordinate the activities.

Over the years gifts to the University have ranged from a first folio Shakespeare to fellowships; from parcels of land—such as the original four-and-a-half acre plot presented in 1753 for the site of the College by Nathaniel Fitz-Randolph, or the three-and-a-half mile long Lake Carnegie given by Andrew Carnegie in 1906—to works of art. Memorials include some 100 endowed professorships and 700 scholarships.

Through Annual Giving Princeton is better able to support faculty salaries and purchase less glamorous yet essential items such as light bulbs and lawn mowers. The spirit and loyalty of alumni and other friends through the centuries continue to give renewed life to the thought of President Dodds: "We intend to be the progenitors of a stronger Princeton, not merely beneficiaries of generations that came before us."

Henry E. Bessire

Garrett, Robert 1897 (1875-1961), once told his classmates that he had, "in a manner of speaking," elected himself to the Princeton Board of Trustees. In the winter of 1905, he said, he was invited to become a trustee of Johns Hopkins, in his native city of Baltimore, where he had once been a graduate student. Because of his regard for Princeton and "his desire to serve her and her only," he asked the advice of President Wilson who unhesitatingly advised him to decline the Hopkins invitation. Garrett did so in February; in April he received an invitation from President Wilson to become a trustee of Princeton. Garrett took his seat on the board in June at the age of twenty-nine, and went on to serve the University for forty years as charter trustee and for sixteen more as trustee emeritus.

Garrett's father, Thomas Harrison Garrett, of the Class of 1868, died in 1888. While Robert Garrett and his two older brothers, Horatio W. Garrett 1895 and John W. Garrett 1895, were in college their mother lived at 1 Bayard Lane in the house later occupied by the family of Edgar Palmer '03, and now used by the University, to whom it was bequeathed by Mrs. Palmer, as a guest house. Mrs. Garrett's home was a center of hospitality for students in the 1890s; they later erected a tablet in her memory in Alexander Hall.

Robert Garrett excelled in track and field athletics as an undergraduate. He was captain of the team in both his junior and senior years. In 1896 he organized and personally financed an expedition of himself and three classmates to Athens for the first modern revival of the ancient Olympic Games. Garrett stood out among the competitors from all nations, winning two first places and two second. One of his firsts was in the discus throw, in which he had never competed before.

Another expedition, of greater ultimate consequence, which Garrett helped organize and finance was an archaeological expedition to Syria, led by Howard Crosby Butler 1892 (q.v.) in 1899-1900.

The interest engendered by this expedition stimulated Garrett to start his collection of Near Eastern manuscripts, which grew with the years and which, when he gave it to the University in 1942, consisted of 10,000 titles in Arabic, Persian, and Turkish, as well as several thousand Western manuscripts. The Garrett Collection is one of the principal scholarly resources of the Department of Near Eastern Studies and was one of the factors that enabled Professors Harold H. Bender and Philip K. Hitti to create a department of unique distinction in this country. The Garrett Collection of Near Eastern Manuscripts is still without a peer in the United States.

On his return from the archaeological expedition, Garrett entered the Baltimore investment banking firm of Robert Garrett & Sons, which had been founded by his great-grandfather and namesake, and in time he became chairman of the board. He also played a conspicuous part in the development of public recreational facilities, the Y.M.C.A., and arts museums in Baltimore.

Garrett's contributions to Princeton as trustee included the creation of the office of Consulting Architect (originally suggested to him by Professor Howard Crosby Butler); the metamorphosis of the Committee on Morals and Discipline, which he thought "dourly named," into the Committee on Morals and Physical Education, and its later division into two committees, one on Student Life, the other on Health and Athletics; the establishment of the Department of Health and Physical Education, bringing Dr. Joseph E. Raycroft here from Chicago as its first chairman; and, finally, the nomination of his fellow townsman, Dr. John M. T. Finney 1884 (q.v.), to membership on the Board.

Garrett was president of the Class of 1897 for sixty-four years. He had two Princeton sons: Harrison Garrett '33 (alumni trustee 1964-1968) and Johnson Garrett '35.

Gauss, Christian (1878-1951), one of Woodrow Wilson's original preceptors, first Class of 1900 professor of modern languages, and third dean of the college, had, in Edmund Wilson's phrase, "an imaginative gift of entering into other people's points of view." It was this quality that made him a great teacher of literature and an illuminating critic. It had much to do as well with his becoming, in his time, one of Princeton's most beloved figures and perhaps the best known college dean in America.

Gauss was born and brought up in a community of South German immigrants in Ann Arbor, Michigan, "the lovely little town," in his words "with the name like the title of a song." His father had come there from Württemberg in the late 1860s to escape Prussian domination, and when he had saved enough money to buy a house, had chosen one on Liberty Street instead of a more desirable one on Main Street, so that all their lives "his children would have the satisfaction of knowing that they had been born *in die Freiheitsstrasse*." Growing up in Ann Arbor, then a quiet village, Christian Gauss developed "a deep sense of belonging" to his community, which stayed with him all his life.

Gauss worked his way through the University of Michigan in three years. He had begun working after school early in life, and when he graduated from college at the age of twenty, he could already look back on a versatile career—as baker's boy, grocery clerk, farm hand, drug clerk, bill collector, bank clerk, tutor, and barkeeper at county fairs.

After college Gauss worked for a time as a newspaper correspondent in Paris (where he wrote about the Dreyfus case and talked in cafés with Oscar Wilde), taught at Michigan and at Lehigh, and was called to Princeton in 1905 as one of the youngest of the University's first preceptors. Two years later, at the age of twenty-nine, he was promoted to full professor. He became chairman of the Department of Modern Languages in 1912 and served until 1936. In 1925 he was appointed dean of the college and in 1929 was named first incumbent of a chair in modern languages endowed by his friends in the Class of 1900. He occupied both positions until his retirement in 1946.

Along the way he also served as literary editor of the *Alumni Weekly*, reorganizer and adviser of the Press Club, guide and friend of the *Nassau Literary Magazine*, trustee and vice president of Princeton University Press, chairman of the University Council on Athletics, and founder and first chairman of the Creative Arts Program (q.v.). He was made a Knight of the Legion of Honor by the French Republic and received honorary degrees from half a dozen universities.

TEACHER OF LITERATURE

Christian Gauss was a great teacher whose courses on Dante and on French writers of the Romantic Period profoundly influenced many Princeton students of literature in the first half of this century.

His memory was remarkable, and he brimmed over with literary allusions. Two of his favorite quotations were Ernest Renan's *La verité est dans la nuance*, which he translated: "The truth lies in fine distinctions," and Dostoevski's "We were all born on purpose to be together."

The eminent federal judge Harold R. Medina '09 said it was Gauss who first taught him to think. "He led and guided with so gentle a touch that one began to think almost despite oneself," Medina recalled. In a similar vein, Edmund Wilson '16, the literary critic, spoke of "how the lightly dropped seeds from his lectures could take root and unfold in another's mind."

Wilson also described the influence Gauss exerted on him, John Peale Bishop '17, F. Scott Fitzgerald '17, and other undergraduate writers for the *Nassau Literary Magazine* through the reading of Dante and Flaubert: "He made us all want to write something in which every word, every cadence, every detail, should perform a definite function in producing an intense effect."

Gauss brought to his teaching a breadth of learning that was matched by a wide interest in the affairs of the world, both historical and contemporary. This quality was celebrated in a verse of the Faculty Song sung by the seniors in 1915:

Here's to Gauss, called Chris-ti-an,
A most encyclopedic man.
He jokes and lectures, rhymes and
*   teaches,*
And raves about the Kaiser's
*   speeches.*

(This last line referred to Gauss's anti-Prussianism, inherited from his father, which led him to champion the Allied cause before the United States entered the First World War.)

Wilson, who dedicated one of his books of literary criticism (*Axel's Castle*, 1931) to his old Princeton teacher, thought Gauss himself a brilliant critic—"by far the best," so far as he knew, "in our academic world of that period." "Gauss's special understanding of the techniques of art," Wilson wrote, "was combined, as is not always the case, with a highly developed sense of history, as well as a sense of morality."

Donald A. Stauffer '23, who while an undergraduate was Gauss's secretary, and was later chairman of the Department of English, described Gauss's essential quality as a teacher in this way:

He had respect for mind wherever he found it. He supported alike the specialized research of scholars and the wildest outbursts of nineteen-year-old aesthetes. He was as good with grandchildren as with dignitaries. In the exchange of opinions, in the inquiry into values, he practiced liberty, equality, and fraternity.

DEAN OF THE COLLEGE

The announcement of Gauss's appointment as dean of the college in the spring of 1925 elicited a new verse in the Faculty Song:

Oh, here's to Gauss, who knows his
*   stuff,*
We liked him though his course was
*   tough.*
But when he's Dean we shall delight
In hating him with all our might.

Though written with tongue in cheek, these words did suggest the dire possibilities of any deanship, and especially one in an era plagued by Prohibition, the Depression, and the Second World War, but in Gauss's case the opposite came to pass. At the beginning, his determination that the eighteenth amendment (which he publicly opposed) should be strictly enforced because it was the law, brought some resentment, but most undergraduates learned to respect the integrity of his position.

There were riots, too, in the Prohibition era, to which Gauss reacted variously. One in the spring of 1926, which involved a good deal of noise and jostling and some jeering of volunteer firemen, but no violence to any person or property, he played down when called by the newspapers. "It was nothing but a Poler's Recess," he said, "complicated by a false alarm." But when, in the fall of 1930 after a football rally, excited students tore down the statue of the Christian Student (q.v.) and rushed out onto Nassau Street and rocked an interurban bus with women and children in it, he invoked the language of Swift's *Gulliver's Travels* and publicly castigated them for their "Yahooism." (The ringleaders were subsequently suspended for a year.)

It was particularly as dean that Gauss came to be appreciated for his sympathy and human understanding. "Through many trying meetings of the discipline committee," Nelson P. Rose '31, who was chairman of the *Princetonian* and of the Undergraduate Council, recalled, "you could not fail to sense his own pain at having to cause pain. . . . On campus issues you could not fail to realize that he was looking for a helpful middle ground."

Some of his most ardent admirers were those who had frequented the mourner's bench outside the dean's office. Archie Murray '34, later a sports writer for the *New York Evening Post*, who had "practically made a career of getting into trouble" when he was an undergraduate, said he nevertheless looked up to Dean Gauss as a father— "he was so eminently fair and his sense of humor never deserted him."

Dean Gauss, for his part, showed his regard for those he had had to discipline in the early years of his deanship by dedicating his book *Life in College* (1930) to them. "In nearly every case," he wrote, "the frankness, honesty, generosity and sportsmanship of these undergraduate 'malefactors' was such as to make me conceive a higher opinion of mankind."

Life in College was made up of a series of articles that had appeared in the *Saturday Evening Post*; articles by Gauss frequently appeared also in the *New York Times*, the *Saturday Review*, and the *New Republic*. During the Depression, when seniors were worried about getting jobs, they sang:

Professor Gauss he teaches French;
Dean Gauss he judges on the bench;
Mister Gauss don't write for fun;
He's got three jobs and we've got
*   none.*

As chairman of the University Council on Athletics, Gauss was impressed by the wholesome influence of football, "properly coached and conducted," and was a concerned follower of all the games. "We thrived on his love of victory," said Gilbert Lea '36, an end on the championship team of 1935, "but we were gratified most by his loyalty in defeat."

In the latter years of his deanship, Gauss commanded the same respect and admiration he had won at the beginning. "As a dean he was still in the best sense a teacher," John N. Brooks, Jr. '42, the writer, who in college was chairman of the *Princetonian* and a member of the Discipline Committee, recalled:

> An argument with him [at a meeting about extracurricular activities] was a profoundly educational thing. . . . Dean Gauss always took us and our point of view seriously, entering into every debate as vigorously as if the issues were all new to him. . . . For his disciplinary role . . . he might conveniently have become the gentle sentimentalist or the martinet, but Dean Gauss did not choose easy roles. He did not even exude an air of infallibility, which must be the easiest and safest of all airs for a dean to exude. . . . He somehow succeeded in making his office at 205 Nassau Hall, by its nature the most formidable precinct in all Princeton, into a place that even many of those who came there under duress remember with real affection.

Dean Gauss was a courageous champion of freedom, both within and without the University. "The first obligation of the undergraduate is to think without let or hindrance," he declared in reply to charges of radical tendencies at Princeton, Yale, and Harvard by Colonel McCormick in the *Chicago Tribune*, "and the first obligation of the professor is to make him do so." He was a member of the National Committee of the American Civil Liberties Union and an outspoken critic of the House Committee on Un-American Activities. After the Second World War he frequently spoke to black audiences in the South, and took quiet satisfaction in having been responsible for assembling for the first time a mixed black and white audience in a white church in Richmond.

In retirement Gauss worked on two projects for philanthropic foundations, one on religion in higher education, the other on promotion of the study of the humanities. He also served as president of Phi Beta Kappa. One autumn day in his seventy-fourth year he went to New York to deliver the manuscript of his introduction to a new edition of Machiavelli's *The Prince* and to attend a memorial service for the Austrian novelist, Herman Brock. That evening while he was waiting in the Pennsylvania station for the train to take him back to Princeton, his heart failed and he fell dead.

"One had always still expected something further from Christian, had hoped that his character and talents would arrive at some final solution," Edmund Wilson wrote in his memoir of Dean Gauss and then concluded:

> But . . . one sees now that the career was complete, the achievement is all there. He has left no solid body of writing; he did not remake Princeton . . . he was not really a public man. He was a spiritual and intellectual force. . . . His great work in his generation was unorganized and unobtrusive; and *Who's Who* will tell you

nothing about it; but his influence was vital for those who felt it.

> Chè in la mente me'è fitta,
> ed or m'accora,
> La cara e buona imagine
> paterna
> Di voi, quando nel mondo
> ad ora ad ora
> M'insegnavate come l'uom
> s'eterna. . . .*

* From lines 82-85 Canto XV of the *Inferno* in which Dante addresses his teacher, Brunetto Latini: "For in my mind is fixed, and now fills my heart, the dear, good, paternal image of you, when in the world hour by hour you taught me how man makes himself eternal." (Charles Eliot Norton's translation, Houghton, Mifflin Company, 1919)

Gauss Seminars in Criticism, The, named in honor of Dean Christian Gauss (q.v.), were instituted in 1949 to provide a focus for discussion, study, and the exchange of ideas in the humanities.

Normally five or six seminars are held annually. Each seminar is conducted by an invited guest, who presents material upon which he is working or which seems to him significant, at from two to six weekly meetings. Past seminar leaders have included W. H. Auden, Noam Chomsky, Leon Edel, Jacques Maritain, Sean O'Faolain, Sir Herbert Read, Paul Tillich, René Wellek, Edmund Wilson. Some twenty-five or thirty persons, invited from the University Faculty, the Institute for Advanced Study, and the community at large, participate in each seminar.

The Seminars are arranged by an interdepartmental committee, one of whose members serves as director. Serving in this capacity have been Professors Francis Fergusson (1949-52), E.B.O. Borgerhoff (1952-57, 1965-66),

Richard P. Blackmur (1957-65), and since 1966, Joseph N. Frank.

Geological and Geophysical Sciences, Department of. Instruction in geology was first offered from 1818 to 1822 by the Professor of Experimental Philosophy, Chemistry, and Natural History, Jacob Green, who gave courses in paleontology. Thereafter instruction in this area lapsed until 1855 when Arnold Guyot, a colleague of Louis Agassiz at Neuchatel, Switzerland, arrived in Princeton to begin what has become the present department. Continuous instruction has been given in geology or, more broadly, the earth sciences ever since.

Until 1873 Guyot was the sole faculty member in geology and physical geography. During the next ten years four men came to Princeton to offer instruction and carry on research in the general field of geology. Henry B. Cornwall, a chemist, taught mineralogy. William Libbey 1877, first to receive the doctoral degree at Princeton (1879), taught physical geography. William Berryman Scott 1877 arrived with Libbey in 1880 and began his long career in vertebrate paleontology. His classmate, Henry Fairfield Osborn, was in the section of biology. In those days the general subject of geology was handled in three separate divisions: applied chemistry and mineralogy, physical geography, and geology—and sometimes with the cooperation of the section of biology.

In 1904, when the Department of Geology was formally created, six men made up the faculty: in physical geography, Libbey; in mineralogy, Cornwall and Alexander H. Phillips (whose constant laugh is commemorated in the Faculty Song: "Ha Ha Phillips, he he he / Teaches mineralogy"); in vertebrate paleontology, Scott and Marcus

Farr; and in invertebrate paleontology, Gilbert Van Ingen. The following year Charles H. Smyth (father of two other Princeton professors, the chemist Charles P. Smyth and the physicist Henry De W. Smyth) arrived to teach petrology, and William J. Sinclair joined the vertebrate paleontologists.

Chairman of the new department was "Geology Bill" Scott, who gave an even fifty years of continuous service on the Princeton faculty from 1880 to 1930, equalling the record set by President John Maclean in 1868. During his fifth year as chairman, the department moved to Guyot Hall, which had been built with funds provided by the mother of Cleveland Dodge 1879.

Princeton's international reputation in the earth sciences during the early days of the department stemmed from the presence of Scott. But it was Smyth who attracted the graduate students, a fact Scott cheerfully recognized. Smyth taught courses in petrology and chemical geology, both relatively new subjects in this country. The popularity of these subjects and the related subject of mineralogy was probably due to the fact that most jobs were to be found in the fields of mining geology and mineral exploration. Not until the late 1920s and early 1930s did the expanding petroleum industry create large demands for people with paleontological and stratigraphic training.

From 1920 to 1930 a new generation of geologists arrived, all overlapping original members of the department. These men, who included Arthur Buddington, Arthur K. Snelgrove, Edward Sampson, W. Taylor Thom, Paul MacClintock, Glenn L. Jepsen, Erling Dorf, Richard M. Field, and Benjamin F. Howell, carried the department's distinction into the 1950s. On their retirement in the late 1950s, Thom, Bud-

dington, Howell, MacClintock, and Sampson had together served Princeton for 173 years.

During the immediate prewar years the department experienced a large increase in both undergraduate and graduate enrollments. During the war the faculty helped hundreds of armed forces trainees discover the techniques of map and terrain interpretation as part of their officer training.

Buddington served as chairman of the department for fourteen years and was succeeded in 1950 by Harry H. Hess, who served for sixteen years. Under Hess's leadership the department acquired its present form.

Hess, who was hired as a mineralogist in 1934, developed into a remarkable generalist. His interests extended from objects of microscopic size to ocean basins measured in thousands of kilometers, and ranged from the deep interior of the earth to the moon and beyond. His single most important achievement was the formulation, in 1960, of the concept of "sea-floor spreading." This idea, introduced as a bit of "geopoetry," literally shook the foundations of geology, giving the subject a framework as important to it as organic evolution, the periodic table, and the atom have been to biology, chemistry, and physics.

In the decade following World War II, new faculty members included John C. Maxwell (who succeeded Hess as chairman), Franklyn B. Van Houten, H. D. Holland, William Bonini, Sheldon Judson (who followed Maxwell as chairman), Alfred G. Fischer, Jorma O. Kalliokoski, and Hollis D. Hedberg.

Geophysics became an important part of the departmental program of instruction and research in the early 1960s; this significant addition was recognized in 1968 by changing the name

Department of Geology to Department of Geological and Geophysical Sciences. Walter Elsasser was followed by Robert Phinney, Fred Vine, Jason Morgan, and Anthony Dahlen. The work of this group soon attracted world-wide attention, particularly through the studies of Morgan and Vine. Building on the ideas of Hess, Vine demonstrated the reality of the timing of sea-floor spreading through magnetic studies of the sea floor, and Morgan defined and described the plates that make up the jigsaw puzzle of the earth's crust.

A well-known facility of the department is the Museum of Natural History in Guyot Hall. Originally called the E. M. Museum of Geology and Archaeology (after Elizabeth Marsh, the mother of William Libbey), it moved from what is now the Faculty Room in Nassau Hall when Guyot Hall opened in 1908. It has included among its directors Guyot (its founder), Libbey, Sinclair, and Jepsen. Its exhibits are drawn from excellent collections of minerals, rock types, vertebrate and invertebrate specimens. The department for many years has also served as a repository for some important ethnological collections from the American Northwest, the South Seas, Africa, and the southwestern United States.

As of the 1970s, the department maintained a cooperative program in Water Resources with Civil Engineering, another in Geophysical Fluid Dynamics with the National Oceanographic and Atmospheric Administration's Laboratory, and still another in Geological Engineering with the School of Engineering. The department had a full-time faculty of sixteen and, in addition, six visiting scientists. Its Ph.D. program enrolled between thirty and forty students, and under-graduate majors graduating each year numbered between fifteen and twenty-five.

Sheldon Judson

Germanic Languages and Literatures. For the first 84 years of Princeton's history, the College itself offered no instruction in modern languages—though it did authorize outsiders to serve as tutors, at the students' expense. The appointment of the first faculty member in German seems to have come as an afterthought. In 1832 Benedict Jaegar, A.M., an Austrian, was engaged as Curator of the Zoological Museum and Lecturer on Natural History. Perhaps because he was "a man of talent and learning, and an admirable teacher," he was also named Professor of German and Italian.

Jaeger discharged his diverse duties until 1843. Thereafter, German was taught by a succession of short-term instructors until the appointment in 1857 of the German-born Karl Langlotz (far better known as the composer of the music to "Old Nassau"), who served until 1869. At that time the study of modern languages was entirely voluntary, and as Langlotz later recalled, students would drop out until his class of forty members was reduced to "ten or so faithful ones."

The man who finally established modern languages as a regular part of the curriculum was President McCosh, in 1868, the first year of his administration. The man he appointed as the first John H. Woodhull Professor of Modern Languages was surely the most flamboyant holder of that distinguished chair: General Joseph Kargé. A native of Prussia, Kargé had studied at Breslau, Paris, and Berlin; had twice been imprisoned as a Polish freedom fighter; had fled to the United States and become a Civil War hero; and then, from 1869 to 1892, quietly taught German and French at Princeton. His arrival marked the beginning of a new era for the teaching of German. He was later joined by Herman C. O. Huss, and followed by Willard C. Humphreys, J. Preston Hoskins, George Madison Priest, and Max F. Blau.

Whereas 1869 marked the start of regular modern language instruction, 1904 marked its consolidation. In that year Woodrow Wilson established the Department of Modern Languages and Literatures. Among the "preceptor guys" whom he chose in 1905 were Priest and Harvey W. Hewett-Thayer. Alumni (including the writer, Class of 1935) remember the superb instruction that they received from the peppery Hoskins (who used to start off lectures by removing his false teeth), from their friend and mentor Priest (who translated Goethe's *Faust*), and from the gentle and humane Hewett-Thayer (who wrote *Hoffmann: Author of the Tales*).

From 1938 to 1940 the distinguished author Thomas Mann was Lecturer in German. Others who in these and later years joined the Department of Modern Languages and Literatures as teachers of German were Bernhard Ulmer in 1936 (retired 1976), Werner G. Hollmann in 1945 (retired 1976), Walter Silz in 1948 (in 1954 he went to Columbia), and Victor Lange in 1957 (retired 1977).

In 1958 German was made a separate department, with Lange as first chairman. Lange enlarged the size and scope of the new department through a number of appointments: in 1960 William G. Moulton, a linguist; in 1963 Michael J. H. Curschmann, a medievalist; in 1964 Theodore J. Ziolkowski (named chairman in 1973), with primary interest in modern German literature; and in 1966 Stanley A. Corngold, a teacher of German and comparative literature. During 1965-1970 Lange was president of the International Association of Germanists, and the 1970 congress of this organization was held at Princeton.

Princeton's German department, though relatively small, has come to be widely recognized as one of the most attractive in the country. Like many departments elsewhere, it provides instruction not only in literature but also in a practical command of German; and this aim is supported by a "summer work program," which annually enables many students to spend a summer actively using German in a German-speaking country. As in all other modern language departments at Princeton, the interests of faculty members extend beyond their own particular professional fields. Many teach courses in European literature, in general as well as Germanic linguistics, or hold joint appointments with Comparative Literature. Uniquely among modern language departments at Princeton, German offers three types of undergraduate majors: language and literature, language and linguistics, and culture and civilization.

William G. Moulton

Gest Oriental Library, The, which has been administered by the University since 1937, is one of the Western world's greatest Chinese collections. It includes among other treasures several thousand fine and rare editions that were printed before the Gutenberg Bible, and one of the world's three complete sets of the original 1728 edition of the famous 5,000-volume Chinese Encyclopedia. The Library's two thousand volumes on medicine constitute the largest collection of traditional Chinese medical books outside China and Japan.

This extraordinary library was founded by Guion M. Gest (1864-1948) and I. V. Gillis (1875-1948). Gest, a Quaker in religion and an engineer by profession, suffered from glaucoma. On a business trip to China, he met Gillis (then a naval attaché at the American embassy in Peking), who persuaded him to try an old Chinese eye remedy. Although this medicine did not cure the glaucoma, it gave Gest some temporary relief and led him to commission Gillis to buy Chinese books on medicine for him. Gest later extended his interest to other fields and for thirty years impoverished himself to provide Gillis with the funds required to indulge his love of books. In the end, his library numbered some 100,000 volumes.

In 1937, the Institute for Advanced Study, with help from the Rockefeller Foundation, acquired the Gest Library and housed it in a University-owned building at 20 Nassau Street. In 1948 the Institute transferred custodianship to the University and the collection was moved to Firestone Library. In 1972 the collection was moved to Palmer-Jones, the home of the Department of East Asian Studies. The University's East Asian Collections, which include the Gest Oriental Library, now total three hundred thousand volumes in the East Asian languages, in addition to the University's holdings in Western languages, making it one of the five largest East·Asian research collections in the Western world.

Gildersleeve, Basil Lanneau 1849 (1831-1924) was one of the most eminent men graduated from Princeton in the middle of the nineteenth century. Dean West called him "the most brilliant, richly furnished and powerful master in Greek studies" this country had produced. Professor Paul Shorey of the University of Chicago, himself a great Greek scholar, said that, during fifty years of American classical scholarship, "the figure of Gildersleeve had dominated throughout."

The son of a Presbyterian minister in Charleston, South Carolina, Gildersleeve read the Bible "from cover to cover" when he was five and before he was thirteen had learned enough Latin to get through Caesar, Sallust, Cicero, Virgil, and Horace, and enough Greek "to make out" the New Testament.

Such was his precocity that when he entered Princeton as a junior at the age of sixteen in 1847 he was able to devote most of his time to his own reading. "I gave a couple of hours to my classes each day," he recalled in a memoir about his student days which he wrote toward the end of this life, "and then ho! for the wide field of literature—English, French, German, Italian, Spanish." Through Carlyle, he was introduced to Goethe, "the most important of all the teachers I ever had." Besides his "multifarious, jubilant reading," he also indulged himself in "composition in prose and rhyme." He admired the physicist Joseph Henry, "our one great man," and respected John Torrey, who taught chemistry and natural history, and Stephen Alexander, who taught mathematics. "Stevie" so inspired him, he recalled, that although he had always hated mathematics, he passed the best examination in his class. But he found little to be learned from the "hit-or-miss" instruction offered in his own field of interest—the classics and letters generally. In the course in Greek he could not recall one syntactical question and there were only two lectures on Greek literature.

But my heart smites me [Gildersleeve wrote]. Remember that I am writing of Rev. John Maclean, Vice President of the College . . . and Professor of Greek, judged by a professor of Greek, not of good old Johnny, best beloved of all Princeton men, a man every inch of him, in his prime a swift-footed Achilles, who, according to tradition, gave the erring Hectors a start as far as the cannon and always caught them; Johnny who watched over me tenderly when I lay greviously hurt at the house where that angel, Miss Mary [Maclean's sister], prepared delicacies for me, and Bob Stockton dressed my wound, acquired in a frog hunt near Dr. Scudder's. Some day another professor of Greek will make mock of my old-fashioned fancies in the matter of syntax. Would that I had as fair a record otherwise as good old Johnny!

After graduating from Princeton in 1849, Gildersleeve spent three years in Europe, chiefly in study at German universities. To his teachers there and to Germany in general he acknowledged his indebtedness "for everything professionally in the way of apparatus and method, and for much, very much in the way of inspiration."

Shortly after his return from Europe, Princeton proposed that he join its faculty; but the position offered, he recalled years later, turned out to be so inferior to what he, "a conceited youngster," deemed his due as a Ph.D. with high honors from the University of Göttingen, that the negotiations were broken off with some acerbity on both sides.

For three years he pursued philological studies at home and nearly completed a novel. In 1856, just before his twenty-fifth birthday, he began a twenty-year career as professor of Greek at the University of Virginia. He also taught Latin for a time, but Greek remained his true love. A regular churchgoer, he kept himself awake during sermons by mentally translating them into Greek, sentence by sentence as uttered, a practice he recommended as "a peculiarly rewarding means of grace."

During the Civil War Gildersleeve became further disenchanted with Princeton "when the authorities thought it necessary to emphasize their loyalty to the Union in a way that exasperated all ardent Southerners like myself." Both of his Princeton roommates, who were Virginians, fell in the first major engagement of the war at Manassas. Gildersleeve himself was severely wounded while serving with the Confederate cavalry. In later years, his northern students shared with their southern compatriots admiration for his soldierly valor, of which they were continually reminded, as one of them wrote, "by the choliambic [limping] rhythm in his majestic gait."

When Johns Hopkins University was founded in 1876, Gildersleeve was the first of a small band of scholars invited to develop a school of graduate work and research. According to one of his first students, Francis G. Allison, later professor at Brown University, Gildersleeve liked to recount that "he was put by President Gilman into an empty room and told to 'radiate!' "

The bare room [Allinson wrote] was soon occupied by graduates of diverse colleges. . . . Whatever their previous training, the fortunate members of his Greek seminary, year after year, were confronted with a new vision, shining across wide vistas in literature and language. As in his more personal teaching, where a "mistake" was a "crime," so in the wider sweep of his seminary courses an ineluctable exactitude prevailed. No vagueness was acceptable. No unverified reference was legal. Paradoxically, however, he indulged himself in a rapid fire of allusions which sometimes shot over the heads of his bewildered, yet devoted, hearers. In spite of this, he stimulated more than he discouraged and, as net effect in after years, his former students, though far removed in space and time, were conscious of his actual presence, ready to challenge any inadequacy or inaccuracy in their written or spoken word.

In 1877, Princeton "held out an olive branch," as Gildersleeve put it, by inviting him to make the annual address before the Whig and Cliosophic Societies. But he "did not improve matters," he said, by the chief theme of his discourse, "an inquiry why Princeton, which had done so much for divinity, for medicine, for law, for legislation, for arms, had fallen so far short in letters." Gildersleeve meantime was making his own mark as a man of letters as well as a scholar. In 1880 he founded the *American Journal of Philology*, and for forty years his personality pervaded its pages. "His uncurbed satire," one of his associates said, "occasionally engendered resentment, but his fearless criticism had a tonic effect upon contemporary scholarship." He became famous also for his *Latin Grammar*, his *Syntax of Classical Greek*, his editions of Greek poets, notably Pindar, and several books of critical essays and scholarly studies.

In 1899, at the fiftieth anniversary of the graduation of his class, Princeton conferred on him an honorary L.H.D.—"the seal," he said, "of reconciliation." He took pride, also, in the fact that his son, Raleigh C. Gildersleeve, was the architect of McCosh Hall and Lower Pyne Building.

Gildersleeve had a tall, well-proportioned figure, an Olympian head with "dominating eyes, humorous or devastating as the occasion demanded," and in later life a full white beard. His students called him Zeus. He taught at Johns Hopkins until he was eighty-four and edited the *Journal of Philology* until he was eighty-nine. In his last years he spent most of his time in his book-lined study in his house in Baltimore, reading Greek and writing sonnets. One he wrote when he was ninety concluded:

I know this sonnet-writing is inanity.
It is not art. 'Tis nothing but a knack
With which I while away the dark-
*   some hours.*
I'll keep it up, though critics doubt
*   my sanity*
Till the pale postman comes whose
*   knocks attack*
Alike the poor men's cots and
*   princes' towers.*

When the "pale postman" knocked some two years later, Dean West delivered Princeton's tribute, concluding with a quotation from the Greek rhetorician and philosopher Longinus: "When the sun sets, its brightness departs and its greatness remains." And Professor Shorey noted that, at the memorial service for Gildersleeve at Johns Hopkins, all the speakers "dwelt not so much on the wit, the brilliancy, the scholarship, which they took for granted, as on the moral qualities of the man, the teacher, the companion, the helper, the friend."

Glee Club, The, was founded in 1874 in response to an editorial in the February *Nassau Lit*, in which Andrew Fleming West 1874 (later dean of the Graduate School) lamented Princeton's lack of such a society and urged the "University Quartet" to "take this matter in hand and push it energetically." That popular campus singing group acted quickly and vigorously; the Glee Club was formally organized at a student meeting in March and gave its first concert at Commencement time.

In its early years the Club had only thirteen members. Its modest repertoire consisted mostly of college songs, and included "Old Nassau," the opening number of the first concert.

In 1876 the newly formed Instrumental Club, a rudimentary orchestra, performed at the Glee Club's spring concert. This collaboration, which continued for almost a decade, was later taken up by the Banjo Club in 1884 and the Mandolin Club in 1890; they performed at Glee Club concerts until the early 1930s. Since then, as its capabilities have grown, the Club has sung with the University and other orchestras.

Very early the Club began scheduling concerts outside of Princeton, taking brief tours during the spring recess and then longer ones at Christmastime. In 1894 the Christmas tour extended as far west as Denver, Colorado.

By the opening years of this century the Club had become particularly active during the football season. At the games Club members sat together in order to take the lead in student singing between halves, a practice that continued until the founding of the University Band in 1920. There were also occasional concerts before important games, and in 1913 Princeton, Har-

vard, and Yale Glee Clubs began holding dual concerts on the eve of Big Three games, a custom followed with only a few lapses ever since.

The Glee Club had a succession of instructors but no steady professional guidance until 1907 when Charles E. Burnham was appointed director. He was succeeded in 1918 by Alexander Russell, who served until 1934, when, music having gained a place in the University's curriculum, the Glee Club became a responsibility of the music faculty. James Giddings became director in 1934, Timothy Cheney in 1940, J. Merrill Knapp in 1941, Russell Ames Cook in 1943, J. Merrill Knapp in 1946, Elliot Forbes in 1952, Carl Weinrich in 1953, and Walter L. Nollner in 1958.

The Club's musical development led to a number of notable achievements in the thirties. It joined with the Philadelphia orchestra under Leopold Stokowski in the American premiere of Stravinsky's "Oedipus Rex" in 1931 and in performances of Schönberg's "Gurrelieder" and Wagner's "Parsifal" in the next two years. It presented Bach's Mass in B Minor at the Metropolitan Opera House in 1935 and with the Vassar College Choir gave the first United States performance of Jean Philippe Rameau's "Castor et Pollux" in 1937.

The Club continued to sing with choral groups from Vassar, Bryn Mawr, Wellesley, Mount Holyoke, and Smith until a mixed Princeton chorus was formed after the advent of coeducation. In company with singers from Smith College, the Club toured Europe in 1965 and 1968, Mexico in 1969, and South America in 1971.

In the summer of 1965 the Smith-Princeton chorus gave concerts in Munich, Salzburg, Rome, and other cities, took part in the famous choral festival at Spoleto, made a radio and television appearance in Paris, and gave a final concert in the Chartres cathedral. In 1968 they sang a Josquin des Pres mass, a Bach cantata, and other works in West Berlin, Nuremberg, Prague, Vienna, and Venice, again concluding with a concert at Chartres, which was taped for radio and television. A French critic commended their "naturalness . . . dynamism . . . [and] truly contagious ardor of interpretation."

The visits to Latin America were also well received, In 1969 the Smith-Princeton singers appeared with the Mexican National Symphony in Mexico City's Palace of Fine Arts. They received standing ovations throughout South America in 1971. High points of their tour were appearances with the Argentine Air Force band at a Fourth of July celebration at the United States Embassy in Buenos Aires and with the National Symphony Orchestra of Brazil in a performance of Haydn's "Paukenmesse" in Rio de Janeiro.

The first foreign tour of an all-Princeton mixed chorus in the spring of 1972 was sponsored by the Yale-Harvard-Princeton Club of Jamaica. In Kingston the Glee Club sang to 16,000 schoolchildren on the front lawn of the prime minister's official residence, joining with them at the end in the Jamaican national anthem.

On the 1973 trip to Mexico the Glee Club was accompanied by a chamber orchestra. They preformed works of Brahms and Haydn and Latin American folk songs in five concerts, gave an informal concert at Ambassador Robert H. McBride '40's reception for them, and sang "Old Nassau" on top of the Pyramid of the Sun at Teotihuacán.

During the Latin-American tours the performers, who were guests in private homes in each country, took every opportunity to sing folk songs of the host countries as well as of the United States, and gave a number of free concerts in order to reach wide audiences. Everywhere they received a warm reception, caused in large part, Professor Nollner reported, "by the realization that we were coming to learn and to give of our art."

In 1974 the Club celebrated its hundredth birthday with a concert in Alexander Hall, repeated a few nights later in Carnegie Hall. An ensemble of men and women adding up to an appropriate total of 100 singers, accompanied by soloists and orchestra, presented works by Arnold Schönberg, who was born the same year as the Glee Club, as well as by Bach and Haydn. A *Times* critic complimented the singers on the "flexible, transparent, even airy, massed tone" they achieved in "a program chosen and presented with . . . taste and musical discrimination."

SMALL SINGING GROUPS

The quartet that originated the Glee Club in the 1870s has had its modern counterparts in small singing groups, the first of which spun off from the Glee Club before the Second World War. They called themselves the Nassoons and they became noted for their close harmony, exact blending of voices, and five- (rather than four-) part arrangements, some of which were handed down to them by their Glee Club director, a Yale Whiffenpoof.

The Nassoons were followed by two other men's groups, the Tigertones (1947) and the Footnotes (1959), and after the advent of coeducation by a women's group, the Tigerlilies, (1971), and a mixed ensemble, the Katzenjammers (1975).

For the initiated, each of these groups may have its own special style, but an average listener is apt to be most impressed by something they all share: the enjoyment they take in their singing and their ability to impart that enjoyment to those who listen. This they do at paid engagements at proms and club house parties, at alumni dinners and reunions, at southern resorts during the spring recess, and on more free-spirited occasions beneath Seventy-Nine Tower after football games and at the top of Blair steps with the first sign of spring or at Christmastime.

Goheen, Robert Francis, sixteenth president of Princeton, was born August 15, 1919, at Vengurla, Bombay Presidency, India, where his father, Dr. Robert H. H. Goheen, was a Presbyterian medical missionary. The son remained in India, except for furloughs that brought the family to temporary residences in Wooster, Ohio and Princeton, until he was fifteen, when he enrolled in the Lawrenceville School. After two years at Lawrenceville, he was graduated with honors.

For him Princeton was the logical choice of college. His grandfather, Joseph M. Goheen (also a Presbyterian missionary in India), had graduated with the Class of 1872. An uncle on his mother's side of the family, Rhea M. Ewing, was a member of the Class of 1924. An older brother, Richard R. P. Goheen, graduated in 1936. In the fall of that year, Bob, as he was commonly known to the very end of his presidency by a large part of the faculty and staff, began his own career at Princeton with the Class of 1940.

As a freshman Goheen won his numerals in both soccer and baseball. Thereafter he played on the varsity soccer team through three years in which two league championships were won.

After his graduation, while enrolled as a first-year graduate student, he coached a freshman soccer team that lost only to Pennsylvania and defeated a theretofore unbeaten Yale team. His eating club was Quadrangle, of which he served as president. He was a member of the Inter-Club Committee, the Intramural Athletic Association, Whig-Clio, the Undergraduate Council, and Phi Beta Kappa. He graduated with Highest Honors in the Humanities Program, and in 1940 shared with James H. Worth the M. Taylor Pyne Prize, the highest general distinction conferred upon an undergraduate.

In November 1941, after completing a year of graduate study with the Department of Classics, Goheen entered the army. During the preceding June, he had been married to Margaret M. Skelly of Wilmington, Delaware.

Upon graduating from Officer Training School, he was commissioned in May 1942 as a second lieutenant in the Infantry and assigned to the Military Intelligence Service in the War Department. In March 1943 he was reassigned to the First Cavalry Division, with which he served in the Pacific until the summer of 1945, receiving decorations that included the Legion of Merit and the Bronze Star with two clusters. During his last year of service, he was Assistant Chief of Staff, G-2 for the Division and held the rank of lieutenant-colonel.

After the war Goheen returned to Princeton to continue his graduate studies. In the fall of 1945 he became one of the three men to whom the first Woodrow Wilson Fellowships were awarded, under a program initiated at Princeton for the encouragement of young men to find a career in teaching and scholarship. He received the M.A. degree in 1947, and in 1948, after a year as a Procter Fellow, was awarded his Ph.D.

Goheen was immediately appointed as an Instructor in the Department of Classics, and in 1950 was promoted to an assistant professorship. His major scholarly work, *The Imagery of Sophocles' Antigone*, was published by Princeton University Press in 1951. He was the Arthur H. Scribner Bicentennial Preceptor from September 1951 to June 1954, and in 1952-1953, during his Bicentennial Preceptorial leave, a Senior Fellow in Classics at the American Academy in Rome.

After returning from his year of study abroad in 1953, Goheen became director of the National Woodrow Wilson Fellowship Program, a position to which he devoted half of his time through the following three years. The program had been greatly expanded since the initial appointment of three returning war veterans as fellows in 1945, having acquired the sponsorship of the American Association of Universities and won substantial funding by foundations. By the academic year 1954-1955 the men and women who had held, or then held, the fellowships numbered 478; twelve regional committees served, with the aid of special representatives on individual faculties, to select the fellows from the many who were nominated for the honor. Between meeting classes in Princeton, Goheen spent much of his time on the road and in the process became well known among educators across the country.

He was elected to the presidency of Princeton by unanimous vote of the trustees on December 7, 1956, and at the same time was promoted from the rank of assistant professor to full professor. When he assumed office at the age of thirty-seven on July 1, 1957, he be-

came the third youngest president in the history of the University (Aaron Burr, Sr., 1748-1757, had been thirty-two; Samuel Davies, 1759-1761, thirty-five).

In his annual report for 1967 to the trustees, President Goheen summarized the first ten years of his administration as a period of "growth and change . . . in almost every part of the university." The description is no less applicable to the entire span of fifteen years in which he served as president.

Although he repeatedly disclaimed any ambition to be known as a "building president," more was added to the physical plant during his administration than under any of his predecessors. Some twenty-five new buildings were constructed on the main campus, still others at the Graduate College and Forrestal. All told, if measured in terms of square footage under roof, the physical plant increased by 80 percent. In addition, many of the older buildings were renovated to provide more useful space for instructional departments.

Among the more important additions were the Art Museum, the Woolworth Center of Musical Studies, the Architecture Building, the Woodrow Wilson School, the Engineering Quadrangle, the Jadwin Gymnasium, the Computer Center, and the complex of Peyton, Fine, and Jadwin Halls constructed for the mathematical and physical sciences in the area immediately adjacent to Palmer Stadium. All of these buildings housed expanded educational programs.

This physical expansion was accompanied by a proportionate increase in the financial resources of the University. The annual budget grew from approximately $20 million to $80 million. Contributions by the general body of alumni through Annual Giving more than doubled, reaching a total of $3.8 million in the last year of Goheen's administration. More than twenty newly endowed chairs were established for members of the faculty.

The faculty grew in size from just under 500 to more than 700, thereby maintaining the enviable student-teacher ratio for which Princeton had become noted. The number of applicants for admission to the college in Goheen's last year was more than two and a half times the number who applied during his first year in office. Undergraduate enrollment increased from nearly 3,000 to almost 4,000. The number of graduate students more than doubled.

President Goheen was deeply committed to Princeton's traditional emphasis on teaching combined with scholarship. "Pursued together," he observed, "they generate an atmosphere of learning that invigorates and gives added point to both." In the growing strength of the Graduate School he saw a strengthening also of undergraduate teaching. A national survey of graduate programs of study sponsored by the American Council on Education in 1969 rated 26 departments of instruction at Princeton and ranked 20 of them among the top ten in the country.

The undergraduate program of study found a new flexibility and variety in its response to what the president described as "an exploding, booming, shifting world of knowledge and ideas." Provision was made for sophomore concentration, a reading period at the end of each term, a reduction in course requirements for underclassmen, a University Scholar Program, and student-initiated seminars. New interdepartmental programs were introduced, among them the History and Philos-

ophy of Science; Science in Human Affairs; Comparative Literature; and East Asian, Latin American, Russian, African, Afro-American, Urban, and Medieval Studies.

No less marked was President Goheen's active interest in the quality of student life. Without challenging the established eating clubs on Prospect Avenue, he assumed leadership in the creation of a number of alternative social facilities.

With new programs of study and alternative social facilities came also a new diversification of the student body. In 1969 for the first time women were enrolled as undergraduate candidates for a degree. As early as 1961, they had been admitted as candidates for degrees in the Graduate School, provided they could demonstrate some educational opportunity that was unique to Princeton, a condition abandoned in 1968. Simultaneously, the number of blacks and students representative of other disadvantaged minorities was greatly increased.

It was not by chance that a selection of President Goheen's addresses and other papers published by Princeton University Press in 1969 carried the title *The Human Nature of a University*. He had a sensitive regard for the individuals (and their individuality) who make up a university. He had too a gift for maintaining rapport with them, whether students or members of the faculty and staff. Perhaps it was this quality, as much as any other, that enabled Goheen, in the later years of his administration, to bring Princeton through the most troubled period in the history of American higher education free of enduring scars.

Having more than once expressed the opinion that in a time of rapid change fifteen years was as long as a president should serve, he announced his intention to retire more than a year before he actually retired on June 30, 1972. The *Princetonian*, in a special issue of May 1971 devoted to the "Goheen Years," hailed him as "a superlative example of what a university president should be." The graduating seniors at the following commencement gave him a spontaneous ovation.

A year later another ovation came from the faculty at its last meeting with Goheen in the chair. A tribute presented in behalf of the faculty by one of its senior members recalled chiefly the recent past, when "momentous decisions had to be made in an atmosphere charged with feelings of shock, outrage, and anger," and credited the president with "the leadership we needed in a period of anxiety and confusion." The tribute concluded: "It was not simply that we trusted your judgment, good as it has proved to be. We trusted you as a man. . . . We admired your dignity and calmness in times of stress, your open-mindedness and fairness in times of controversy, and your endless patience as we groped towards a solution of our problems. And it is because we trusted you and because you deserved our trust that Princeton still flourishes under the grace of God."

The citation for an honorary degree conferred upon Goheen at the commencement of 1972 came unusually close to capturing the essential qualities of the man: "In his eyes the function of the intellect is so lofty that it becomes a form of morality. Patient, always humane and trustworthy, he is personally humble at the very time that he is rockily steadfast (an unsympathetic witness might say stubborn), not because he fails to understand and respect the views of others but because he refuses to compromise his own enduring val-

ues. By never seeking popularity, by never worrying about his own image in the eyes of others, he has gained the affection and respect of the entire university and led it to new achievement, new unity."

On his retirement in 1972, Goheen became president of the Council on Foundations. In 1977 he was appointed United States Ambassador to India.

W. Frank Craven

Golf came to Princeton in 1895 when alumni, faculty, and undergraduates formed the Princeton Golf Club, later renamed the Springdale Golf Club, and laid out a nine-hole golf course, subsequently extended to eighteen holes. In the first tournament of the newly formed Intercollegiate Golf Association in 1897, Louis P. Bayard, Jr. '98 won the individual championship.

Although other Princetonians won individual championships—Percy R. Pyne 2nd '03 in 1899, Francis O. Rinehart '05 in 1903, and Albert Seckel '12 in 1909—it was not until 1914 and 1916 that Princeton won its first and second team championships.

In 1919 S. Davidson Herron '18, who had been a member of the championship team of 1916, beat Bobby Jones, then seventeen years old, for the national amateur championship. Herron was a member of the 1923 United States Walker Cup team.

Until the First World War, Yale led the Intercollegiate Golf Association, but after the war, Princeton came to the fore, winning the intercollegiate championship in 1919, 1920, 1922, and 1923. J. Simpson Dean '21 won the individual intercollegiate championship in 1921.

After an interval of three years, Princeton was on top again, taking the

1927, 1928, 1929, and 1930 intercollegiate championships. George T. Dunlap, Jr. '31 won the individual intercollegiate championship in 1930 and 1931 and the national amateur championship in 1933.

Another string of winning seasons came in the late 1930s. The 1937 team won the national intercollegiate championship, the 1938 and 1939 teams took the eastern intercollegiate championship, and the 1940 team tied with Louisiana State for the national intercollegiate championship.

Princeton enjoyed another period of supremacy immediately after the Second World War. The teams of 1946 and 1947 were undefeated in the regular season, and the 1947 team won the eastern intercollegiate championship in a day of exciting competition at the Atlantic City Country Club. In the morning semi-final round, Princeton nosed out Penn State when Harry E. Hall '48 won an extra-hole match by scoring an eagle 3 on the par 5 first hole, and in the afternoon final round against Navy, Dick Nash '45's hole-in-one on the par 3 eighteenth hole in the last match gave Princeton the championship.

William C. Campbell '45, captain of both the 1946 and 1947 teams, continued to excel in amateur golf after graduation. A member of seven Walker Cup teams and captain in 1955, he received the Bob Jones Award for Distinguished Sportsmanship from the United States Golf Association in 1956, and won the national amateur championship in 1964.

The sixties and early seventies brought consistently fine performances by Princeton golf teams, highlighted by the winning of eastern intercollegiate tournaments in 1961, 1968, and 1969, and Ivy League championships in 1972,

1973, and 1976. Winners of individual eastern intercollegiate championships were Mike Porter '69 in 1968 and Bud Zachary '70 in 1969.

Golf coaches since 1927 have included Walter R. Bourne, 1927-1945; Harry M. Kinnell, 1946-1966; Delos C. Schoch, 1966-1970; and Bill Quackenbush, since 1971.

Governors. Forty-two governors of nineteen states have been alumni of Princeton, ranging from eighteenth-century figures like "Light-horse Harry" Lee 1773 of Virginia and William Richardson Davie 1776 of North Carolina to twentieth-century notables such as Woodrow Wilson 1879 of New Jersey and Adlai E. Stevenson '22 of Illinois.

The complete list follows:

CONNECTICUT
Henry Waggaman Edwards 1797 (1835-37)

DELAWARE
Pierre S. duPont IV '56 (1976-   )

GEORGIA
Peter Early 1792 (1814-15)
George McIntosh Troup 1797 (1823-27)
John Forsyth 1799 (1827-29)
George Washington Crawford 1820 (1843-47)
Alfred Holt Colquitt 1844 (1876-82)

ILLINOIS
Adlai Ewing Stevenson '22 (1949-53)

MARYLAND
John Henry 1769 (1797-98)
Samuel Sprigg 1806 (1819-22)

MICHIGAN
G. Mennen Williams '33 (1949-60)

MISSOURI
Christopher S. Bond '60 (1972-1976)

NEW HAMPSHIRE
John Gilbert Winant '13 (1925-27, 1931-35)

NEW JERSEY
William Paterson 1763 (1790-92)
Aaron Ogden 1773 (1812-13)
Mahlon Dickerson 1789 (1815-17)
Samuel Lewis Southard 1804 (1832-33)
William Pennington 1813 (1837-43)
Daniel Haines 1820 (1843-44, 1848-51)
Joel Parker 1839 (1863-66, 1872-75)
Robert Stockton Green 1850 (1887-90)
Woodrow Wilson 1879 (1911-13)
Brendan T. Byrne '49 (1974-)

NEW YORK
Morgan Lewis 1773 (1804-07)

NORTH CAROLINA
Alexander Martin 1756 (1782-85)
Nathaniel Alexander 1776 (1805-07)
William Richardson Davie 1776 (1798-99)
David Stone 1788 (1808-10)
James Iredell 1806 (1827-28)
Daniel Gould Fowle 1851 (1888-91)

OHIO
George White 1895 (1931-35)

OKLAHOMA
Dewey Follett Bartlett '42 (1967-1971)

PENNSYLVANIA
James Pollock 1831 (1855-58)
James H. Duff '04 (1947-51)

RHODE ISLAND
William Henry Vanderbilt '25 (1939-41)

SOUTH CAROLINA
John Taylor 1790 (1826-28)
Patrick Noble 1806 (1838-40)

TENNESSEE
William Prentice Cooper, Jr. '17 (1939-45)

VERMONT
Isaac Tichenor 1775 (1797-1809)

VIRGINIA
Henry Lee, Jr., 1773 (1792-95)
William Branch Giles 1781 (1826-29)
John Rutherfoord 1810 (1841-42)

Graduate College, The, was dedicated on October 22, 1913. Designed by Ralph Adams Cram in close collaboration with the first dean of the Graduate School, Andrew Fleming West, this imposing group of connected Gothic buildings was the first residential college in America devoted solely to postgraduate liberal studies. (In Princeton usage, "Graduate College" refers to the residential and dining halls, "Graduate School" to the program of instruction.)

Situated on a hill half a mile from the main campus, the buildings of the College are unified by the random walls of brown and gray Princeton stone and slate roofs of green and blue. The ensemble consists of a lofty tower whose beauty of design has been compared with that of Oxford's Magdalen tower ("by *moonlight*, . . . a dream in silvery grays and whites," Dean West wrote to President Wilson); a great dining hall with hammerhead beams, an organ, and stained glass; a refectory, a library, a lounge, gardens with ivies from abroad and in its wall architectural fragments from Oxford and Cambridge; a handsome house for the dean, and a suite for the master in residence. The detailing is continuously interesting, with humorous depiction of student life in the form of exterior gargoyles and grotesques, and caricatures of trustees carved on the dining hall hammerheads.

The principal components of the Graduate College are memorials to founders, benefactors or their relatives, and distingished graduates.

Thomson College, the central quadrangle, is a memorial to United States Senator John R. Thomson 1817 provided by a bequest left by his widow, Mrs. J. R. Thomson Swann, the Graduate College's first benefactor.

Procter Hall, the College's formal

dining hall and chief public room, admired by experts in the field as a distinguished example of collegiate gothic, was given by William Cooper Procter 1883 in memory of his parents.

Pyne Tower, which contains the living quarters of the master in residence, was named for the donor, M. Taylor Pyne 1877, the chairman of the trustees' graduate school committee at the time the Graduate College was built. In the vaulted vestibule at the base of the tower there is a memorial to the Graduate College's first master in residence, archaeologist Howard Crosby Butler 1892, in the form of a translation of a Greek inscription he discovered on the Syrian desert, carved beside a fireplace; *I sojourned well, I journeyed well; and well I lie at rest. Pray for me.*

Wyman House, the residence of the dean of the Graduate School, was named for Isaac C. Wyman 1848, who left the bulk of his estate to the University Graduate College.

Between Procter Hall and Wyman House, a gateway opens into the Graduate College gardens, from which can be seen the heraldic sculptures and elaborate grotesques that decorate the west facade of Procter Hall. Their carving, according to E. Baldwin Smith, then Howard Crosby Butler Professor of the History of Architecture, "has more freedom, vigor, and originality than perhaps any other modern revival of the Gothic style."

The 173-foot Cleveland Tower, which flanks the main entrance, was erected by public subscription of "thousands of citizens of all parties in all walks and conditions of life from all parts of the United States" as a memorial to President Grover Cleveland, who, following his retirement from public life, was a trustee of the University and, as chairman of the trustees'

graduate school committee, was deeply interested in the planning of the Graduate College. The carillon in the belfry of the tower was given in 1927 by the Class of 1892.

A quadrangle known as the North Court was added, also in 1927, with a gift from William Cooper Procter and a grant from University funds. Two additional quadrangles built northwest of the original group in 1963 were named for Procter and for three illustrious alumni of the Graduate School, the Compton brothers (q.v.).

Designed by R. Tait McKenzie and given by William Cooper Procter, the bronze statue of Dean West on the upper terrace of the court of Thomson College was dedicated in the spring of 1928. Seated in the center of the original Graduate College buildings, the dean appears to be saying—as one of his contemporaries suggested it was given to him to say, in the words of his favorite Latin author, Horace—*"Exegi monumentum aere perennius"* (I have built a monument more enduring than bronze).

John D. Davies

Graduate School, The, was established in 1901, but its antecedents reach back almost to Princeton's beginnings. In colonial times some graduates returned to prepare for the ministry with the College's president. James Madison 1771, who remained at Princeton for six months after his graduation to read under President Witherspoon's guidance, was possibly the first Princetonian to pursue non-theological postgraduate study. He is sometimes called Princeton's first graduate student. Later the number of postgraduate students increased—there were twenty-three in residence in 1823—but their work was informal and they were not candidates for degrees.

President James McCosh began to lay the groundwork for the later development of the Graduate School shortly after his inauguration in 1868. Under his leadership in the 1870s, new professorships and graduate fellowships were created and systematized programs of study leading to master's and doctor's degrees on examination were adopted. When he retired in 1888, seventy-eight graduate students were enrolled in programs in art and archaeology, astronomy, biology, classics, geology, mathematics, philosophy, and physics.

Although McCosh began the transformation of the College into a university, the change was not formalized until the Sesquicentennial in 1896, when the trustees changed the name of the College of New Jersey to Princeton University. McCosh's successor, President Patton, did little to further a graduate program, and during his administration efforts toward this end were led chiefly by Andrew Fleming West 1874 (q.v.), Giger Professor of Latin. As early as the Sesquicentennial, West began to advocate not only higher priority for graduate studies but also a college to house graduate students. (In the 1890s "graduate college" and "graduate school" were often used interchangeably, but, as the terms evolved in the following decade, the Graduate College became a place to live, the Graduate School a division of the University's educational program.)

On December 13, 1900, the trustees voted to establish a Graduate School and appointed West as the first dean. After a term's leave of absence, he took up his duties in the fall of 1901, and the Graduate School of Princeton University became a reality.

West worked diligently to achieve two primary goals. He insisted upon a high quality of graduate work in which the student could relate his specialty to more general learning in "the household of knowledge" (to use West's phrase). He also sought the creation of the proper setting—a Graduate College—to help produce such rounded scholars.

When Woodrow Wilson became president in 1902, he shared some of West's general concerns but not his overwhelming enthusiasm for the Graduate College. Within a few years Wilson turned his efforts toward the preceptorial system and the quad plan, while West (who declined the presidency of M.I.T. in order to complete the Graduate College) devoted most of his considerable energy to seeing the College built.

The experimental "Graduate House" at Merwick seemed a hopeful sign of what the Graduate College could become. But financial support was not found until Mrs. Josephine Thomson Swann, who died in 1906, left the University $275,000 for the construction of a graduate college. In April 1908, after two years of debate about the site, the trustees voted to build the College near Prospect.

Wilson wanted the graduate students and undergraduates to live in close proximity, believing that strong mutual intellectual stimulation would result. West wanted the graduate students isolated from the distractions of undergraduate life, and he worked against the Prospect site. In May 1909, William Cooper Procter 1883, one of West's alumni friends, offered Princeton $500,000 for the Graduate College, provided an equal amount was raised from other sources and some site, other than Prospect, selected that would be satisfactory to him.

For a year there was bitter controversy involving the entire university, a controversy over the site and the character of the Graduate College, but one which had its origin in an ongoing rivalry between two strong-willed personalities, President Wilson and Dean West.

Procter favored locating the Graduate College near the golf links, and in October 1909 a majority of the trustees voted to accept his offer and his choice of site, much to Wilson's disappointment. Thereafter, new proposals and counterproposals developed—at one point Wilson proposed two graduate colleges, one on the main campus (to satisfy what he contended were Mrs. Swann's wishes), and one near the golf course. In February 1910, noting the unfavorable reception it was receiving from the president and his associates, Procter withdrew his offer.

In May 1910, when West was on the verge of resigning as dean, Isaac Chauncey Wyman 1848 died, leaving an estate estimated at over two million dollars (but, it later developed, worth only $794,000), for the Graduate College, to be built as West desired. Procter renewed his offer, and the trustees accepted it. Wilson, turning toward state and national politics, resigned the presidency of Princeton in October 1910. Construction of the Graduate College at the edge of the golf course began in May 1911, and it was formally dedicated on October 22, 1913.

During the twenty-seven years that Dean West administered its affairs, the Graduate School grew steadily. In addition to the fields covered in McCosh's day, graduate programs were now offered also in chemistry, economics, English, German, history, Oriental studies, politics, psychology, and Romance languages, leading to A.M. and

Ph.D. degrees and, after 1919, in architecture, leading to the M.F.A. (later to the degree of Master of Architecture or Master of Architecture and Urban Planning).

A further gift from William Cooper Procter in 1927 provided an addition to the Graduate College, called North Court.

West held that excellence could best be attained with a small number of well-qualified graduate students, and enrollment under him never exceeded 200—the limit set by the trustees in 1922. In his last report, in 1928, he spoke with pride of the achievements of the School's graduates. At that time, he pointed out, former members of his "society of scholars" made up one-fourth of the Princeton faculty and were eagerly sought for academic posts elsewhere; and many others had gained notable positions in the professions, diplomacy, research, and philanthropy.

In the next quarter-century, under West's successors, physicist Augustus Trowbridge (1928 to 1933) and mathematician Luther P. Eisenhart (1933 to 1945), applications for admission rose, particularly in the sciences, stimulated by the creation of the University's Foundation for Scientific Research, and by the outstanding record Princeton Ph.D.'s had made in winning National Research Council fellowships in mathematics, physics, and chemistry. In the Trowbridge years, the trustees raised the enrollment limit to 250, and as demand increased under Dean Eisenhart, almost all of the programs leading to terminal A.M. degrees were eliminated in order to make room for more Ph.D. candidates.

Since then, except in Near Eastern Studies, the A.M. degree has been offered only as an incidental degree, available after completion of a portion of the Ph.D. requirements. (The M.F.A. degree has continued to be offered in art and archaeology and in music, as have appropriate professional degrees at the master's level in architecture, engineering, public affairs, and urban planning.)

Dean Hugh Stott Taylor's administration, from 1945 to 1958, was one of great growth. With the return of veterans after World War II, the trustees removed the limitation on enrollment, which mounted steadily, eventually reaching 660. The large number of married veterans needing accommodations led to the opening of the Butler Tract Project, the Graduate School's first housing for married students. Existing student aid resources were increased by G.I. benefits; by corporate, government, and foundation gifts and grants; and by the Woodrow Wilson Fellowship Program (q.v.), which originated in Princeton. Fifth year programs in engineering, which had been in effect since 1922, but outside Dean West's fold, were incorporated into the Graduate School for the first time, and new doctoral programs were adopted in aeronautical, chemical, civil, electrical, and mechanical engineering as well as in architecture, music, religion, and sociology.

Expansion continued in the 1960s under physicist Donald Ross Hamilton, dean from 1958 to 1965, and under biologist Colin S. Pittendrigh, who took over when Hamilton resigned because of ill health. A maginificent gift of $35 million for the Woodrow Wilson School permitted the appointment of additional faculty and a marked increase in the number of graduate students preparing for careers in public and international affairs. In other areas, new Ph.D. programs were begun in anthropology, astrophysics, biochemical sciences,

comparative literature, East Asian studies, and statistics, as well as in such interdisciplinary programs as the history and philosophy of science.

Applications for admission increased sharply, and after the successful launching of Sputnik, federal funding for graduate fellowships increased substantially, particularly in science and engineering. Similar aid for students in the humanities and social sciences was provided in a number of ways, notably by the Ford Foundation's liberal financing of the Woodrow Wilson Fellowship Program and by federal fellowships provided by the National Defense Education Act. Under a policy of controlled expansion, enrollment under Dean Hamilton reached 1,150. It continued to grow under Dean Pittendrigh, reaching 1,440 before he resigned in 1969 to accept appointment as professor of biology at Stanford.

Increased housing needs were filled, for single students by the construction in 1963 of the Procter and Compton Quadrangles, just west of the original Graduate College, and for a growing number of married students, by the erection in 1966 of the Lawrence Apartments.

The rapid growth of the 1960s, which approached an enrollment of 1,500 by 1969, was followed by a period of consolidation in the early 1970s, made necessary by financial strains on the university and a decline in fellowship support for graduate students available from outside sources. Under physicist Aaron Lemonick, who served as dean of the Graduate School from 1969 until his appointment as dean of the faculty in 1973, and Alvin B. Kernan, Professor of English, who served from 1973 to 1977, enrollment leveled off at about 1,400.

As national demand for well qualified women and racial minority Ph.D.'s continued to rise, two University decisions in the late 1960s significantly increased their number at Princeton.

The first woman student had been admitted in 1961 under rules that limited admission to those women for whom the Princeton Graduate School offered a practically unique opportunity. This criterion was used until 1968, when admission without regard to sex became the University's policy. Thereafter, the number of women increased steadily, and by 1976 enrollment of women graduate students reached 367.

In the late 1960s a conscious effort was begun to increase the number of blacks and other minority groups enrolled in the graduate school. Less than a decade later, in 1976, there were thirty-eight blacks and 185 members of other minority groups.

In 1977 Nina G. Garsoian, formerly of Columbia University, accepted appointment as professor of Byzantine and Armenian Studies and ninth dean of the Graduate School, the first woman to occupy that position.

In national ratings of graduate programs Princeton has always done very well. Of the twenty-six Princeton departments mentioned in a 1969 American Council of Education study, twenty were ranked among the country's top ten departments in effectiveness of doctoral programs, twelve were among the top three, and two were first. These findings reflect the advantages of the close association of small groups of students with distinguished departmental faculties—from the beginning one of the great strengths of the Princeton Graduate School.

Minor Myers, Jr.

Greek-letter fraternities maintained a precarious existence in the College during the middle of the nineteenth cen-

tury. The first one made its appearance in 1843, and, at one time or another, twelve fraternities were represented by Princeton chapters—Beta Theta Pi, Chi Phi, Chi Psi, Delta Kappa Epsilon, Delta Phi, Delta Psi, Kappa Alpha, Phi Kappa Sigma, Sigma Chi, Sigma Phi, Theta Delta Chi, Zeta Psi.

Fearing that the fraternities would undermine college discipline and prove injurious to the old American Whig and Cliosophic literary and debating societies, the trustees and faculty, at the instance of President Maclean, adopted resolutions in 1855 requiring each entering student to sign a pledge that he would not join such an organization while in college. This pledge—which, according to the catalogue, was still being required as late as 1939-1940—was as follows:

. . . I pledge myself, without any mental reservation, that I will have no connection whatever with any secret society in this institution so long as I am a member of Princeton University; it being understood that this promise has no reference to the American Whig and Cliosophic Societies. I also declare that I regard myself bound to keep this promise and on no account whatever to violate it.

Nevertheless, some fraternities maintained an illicit existence, and it was not until 1875 that decisive action by President McCosh brought the dissolution of most of those still remaining, in spite of opposition from some New York alumni who sought unsuccessfully to persuade the trustees to remove the prohibition on fraternities. One or two seem to have lingered on surreptitiously until the early 1880s. Meanwhile, the formation, with College approval, of "select associations" of students in local boardinghouses marked the first stage in the development of what became a distinctive feature in undergraduate social life—the eating clubs (q.v.).

Green, Ashbel (1762-1848), eighth president of Princeton 1812-1822, and the second alumnus to serve in that post, was a native of Hanover, New Jersey. His father, Jacob Green, was a controversial and independent-minded Presbyterian minister and a trustee of Princeton. His mother, Elizabeth Pierson Green, was the daughter of John Pierson, one of Princeton's original trustees. Green was educated at home by his father and at the age of sixteen began a three-year stint as a local schoolmaster. He entered Princeton in the junior class and graduated as class valedictorian in 1783. His valedictory address was delivered before George Washington and other members of the Continental Congress, then meeting in Princeton.

Green must have impressed President Witherspoon favorably, for he spent the two years after his graduation as a tutor in the College, and another one and a half years as professor of mathematics and natural philosophy. During this period Green married the first of his three wives, Elizabeth Stockton, daughter of a prominent Princeton family. Undecided about the choice of a career, Green sought advice from Samuel Stanhope Smith 1769, later his predecessor as president. "Theology is not the road either to fame or wealth," Smith told Green. "The law, in this country, leads to those objects. But if you wish to do good, and prefer an approving conscience before all other considerations, I have no hesitation in saying you ought to preach the gospel." Green immediately decided to become a minister, studied with Witherspoon (whom he revered deeply and whose "Life" he later wrote), and in 1787 began an association with Philadelphia's Second Presbyterian Church that would last until 1812.

A medium-sized, stocky man of commanding presence, Green soon rose to a position of considerable prominence within his denomination. A long-term member of the Presbyterian General Assembly, he was its Stated Clerk from 1790 to 1803, and had the additional distinction of serving as chaplain to the United States Congress from 1792 to 1800. Green was noted for his energy and organizational powers; his interests and activities covered a wide area. But the two objects closest to his heart were missionary work and education. He was a member of the committee that drew up plans for the Princeton Theological Seminary, and he maintained a close association with that institution from its founding in 1812 until 1848. Green was equally concerned with the College, which he served as a trustee beginning in 1790. By the early 1800s it seemed to some that Princeton under President Smith was not producing enough Presbyterian ministers, was theologically suspect, and, worst of all, was the scene of constant student riot and dissipation. In 1812 Smith was eased out of this post, and Green assumed the presidency of the College.

Green was fifty years old when he took up his new position. Most of his mature years had been spent in the successful service of his congregation and his denomination. It was as the stern but kindly pastor, rather than the educator, that Green approached his presidency. Rigorous disciplinary rules were introduced and a heavily religious tone soon pervaded the College. "Dr.

Smith's works have all been expelled, and others substituted in their room . . . ," one student reported to his father. "There appears to subsist between these ministers of Christ but little harmony or love." Green's efforts bore some fruit in the form of religious revivals among the students, and, for a short period, in relative peace. It is almost impossible to evaluate Green's effect in raising academic standards at Princeton. "I fear it is an undeniable fact," he had reported to the trustees in 1813, "that the majority of those who have received degrees with us, for a number of years past, could not possibly have translated their own diplomas into English." Many must have thought that Green had wrought a change for the better in Princeton, for despite some serious student riots, enrollments increased during his administration.

Green's tenure as president ended in 1822. The immediate cause of his resignation appears to have been an effort by the trustees to ease Green's son Jacob out of the post of professor of natural philosophy. The larger cause may well have been Green's involvement with the affairs of the Theological Seminary to the detriment of those of the College. Whatever the case, Green went on to a long and extremely influential career as a prominent religious writer and journalist and a major force in the "Old School" wing of the Presbyterian Church.

Green's administration has sometimes been accounted a failure. In fact, the heavily authoritarian and evangelistic spirit that marked his regime would become characteristic of many American colleges in the mid-nineteenth century. Ashbel Green was simply a Victorian ahead of his time.

James McLachlan

Green, John Cleve (1800-1875) was the College's greatest benefactor during the presidency of James McCosh. By the time McCosh retired in 1888, Green and his residuary legatees had contributed "to the good of the College," President McCosh said in his farewell report, "upwards of a million and a half, perhaps two million dollars."

Green was born in Lawrenceville, New Jersey, and was a member of the first class to enter what became the Lawrenceville School. He did not go to college, but entered the employ of New York merchants with extensive foreign trade. He spent ten years as supercargo of ships visiting South America and China, and by the time he was forty had acquired an ample fortune in the China trade, derived from the tea and textile business and, after the end of the East India Company's monopoly, from the opium trade. This fortune he enhanced by investments in railroads, whose dividends often reached 15 percent. His three children having died young, he made substantial gifts to various philanthropies. He was a principal benefactor of the Deaf and Dumb Asylum and the Home for Ruptured and Crippled in New York City, and of the Lawrenceville School and the Princeton Theological Seminary, as well as of Princeton College.

Green secured for the College in 1866 the land that now forms the northeast corner of the main Campus. In 1870 he gave the College its first recitation building, named for his great-great-grandfather, John Dickinson, first president of the College. In 1873 he gave the College its first library building, named for his brother, Henry Woodhull Green 1820, Chancellor of New Jersey and a trustee, and the same year he also donated funds for a school of science, which was named for him.

He endowed the Joseph Henry professorship, and his legatees provided further funds for science and for civil engineering as well as for professorships in Latin and Greek. The benefactions from his estate continued into the 1890s and included the erection of the College's first chemical laboratory building at the corner of Nassau Street and Washington Road in 1891.

After the John C. Green School of Science burned down in 1928, the Engineering Building that had just been completed on Washington Road was named for Green; in 1962 when the School of Engineering moved into the new Engineering Quadrangle, its old building was assigned to other departments and called Green Hall.

A portrait of Green hangs in the Convocation Room of the Engineering Quadrangle.

Green Hall is named for the founder of the School of Science, John C. Green (q.v.). Built in 1927 from the design of Charles Z. Klauder, it was the home of the School of Engineering until 1963 when, with the completion of the Engineering Quadrangle, it was redesigned by Francis W. Roudebush '22 for the use of the Departments of Psychology and Sociology, previously located in Eno and 1879 Halls.

The new design entailed extensive remodeling and modernization, made possible by a National Science Foundation grant of $500,000 and matching University funds. A third story and a new wing were added and new floors were constructed within the old high-ceilinged laboratories, supplying considerably expanded library, classroom, office, and laboratory space. Also provided were a vivarium, a small anthropology museum, a computer room, and a faculty lounge, named for Herbert S. Langfeld, a former psychology department chairman.

Greene, Arthur Maurice, Jr. (1872-1953), was the principal organizer of the School of Engineering and served as its first dean. He had previously taught at the University of Pennsylvania (his alma mater), Drexel Institute of Technology, the University of Missouri, and Rensselaer Polytechnic Institute. He accepted the call to Princeton primarily because of its traditional emphasis on liberal arts courses as integral parts of an engineering curriculum. "The imagination of the engineer," he held, "should be equal to that of the novelist, the artist, the poet, or the preacher, for in many respects the work of all these creators is the same."

When Greene came in 1922 to organize the newly formed School of Engineering, he served not only as dean but as chairman of the new Department of Mechanical Engineering. As the only professor in that department, he carried a teaching load that would have been the despair of many younger colleagues. An undergraduate said in the *Alumni Weekly* that the only exercise Greene could find time for was that he got hurrying from one engagement to another, and that the best one could hope for was a fleeting glimpse of him leaving his class in hydraulics for an hour in his office before returning for another class in thermodynamics.

A born teacher and tireless worker, he wrote ten textbooks, served as president of the Society for the Promotion of Engineering Education, and designed the campus power plants at Missouri, Rensselaer, and Princeton.

Following his formal retirement in 1940, which climaxed a teaching career of almost half a century, Dean Greene continued to give a graduate course in engineering economics through 1952, thus achieving his ambition to teach until he was eighty.

Gummere, William Stryker 1870 (1852-1933), was captain of the Princeton team that met Rutgers in 1869 in the first intercollegiate football game played in America.

Gummere himself took greater pride in having been the first player to use the hook-slide in baseball—in an exhibition game between Princeton and the Philadelphia Athletics in the spring of 1870. Gummere, a great center fielder, got to first on a base hit and started to steal second. On the way down he saw that the catcher's throw would get to the bag ahead of him. Knowing that the catcher always threw the ball shoulder high and that the second baseman, Al Reach (later a manufacturer of sporting goods), invariably turned around to tag the runner standing up, Gummere threw himself feet first at the bag and buried his face in his right arm for protection. When the second baseman turned to tag him, he discovered Gummere stretched out under his feet, safely out of reach.

"What kind of a damned fool trick is that?" Reach demanded.

"That," said Gummere, smiling as he got up and dusted himself off, "is a device to evade being put out when running bases."

After graduating from Princeton in 1870 at the age of eighteen, Gummere studied law in his father's office in Trenton and was admitted to the bar in 1873. In the Class of 1870's twentieth reunion book, Gummere said he was a Republican. "Consequently," he added, "I have never held office. Republicans don't as a usual thing hold office in New Jersey." This pessimism proved premature. Five years later a Democratic governor appointed Gummere to the Supreme Court of New Jersey, and six years after that a Republican governor appointed him Chief Justice, a position he held until his death thirty-two years later. When he died at the age of 80, a Democratic governor, echoing the tributes of other judges, said that New Jersey had lost one of its greatest jurists and America one of its keenest legal minds, and that the "treasure store of legal opinion" that Gummere had left would be vital for generations "long after most of us are forgotten."

Guyot, Arnold [Henri] (1807-1884), who in 1855 began the first systematic instruction in geology at Princeton, was born at Boudevilliers near Neuchatel, Switzerland. He obtained his doctoral degree at Berlin with a dissertation on "Natural Classification of Lakes." Between 1839 and 1848 he taught physical geography and history at the Academy of Neuchatel. In 1848 the Academy was closed, and at the suggestion of his friend Louis Agassiz, he came to the United States. He gave a series of lectures at the Lowell Institute in Boston entitled "The Earth and Man," which became the basis for a highly successful text of the same name, recently reprinted (1971) by the Arno Press. In 1854 he was appointed Professor of Geology and Physical Geography at the College of New Jersey and the following year began what is now the Department of Geological and Geophysical Sciences. Guyot's interests were in glaciology, physical geography, meteorology, and cartography. His early studies on the flow of ice and the distribution of glacial erratics in Switzerland served to underpin the theory of glaciation that had been advanced and championed by his close associate Agassiz.

In this country his main activities focused on hypsometric measurements of the eastern mountains from New England to North Carolina, on meteorology, and on the reform of geographic teaching in colleges and secondary schools.

He was intimately involved in the formative years of weather forecasting in the United States and was responsible for selecting and equipping some fifty meteorological observation stations for the network developed through the efforts of Joseph Henry for the Smithsonian Institution. He spent many summers making barometric measurements to determine mountain elevations from Mt. Katahdin in Maine to Mt. Oglethorpe in Georgia along what is now the Appalachian Trail. He used these occasions as field exercises in which Princeton students could practice barometric techniques, an early example of the long tradition of Princeton geology to include students in faculty field research as part of their educational experience.

Guyot's many texts, geographic atlases, and wall charts continued to be pubished long after his death.

In 1856 he founded what is now the Princeton Museum of Natural History and continued to contribute specimens to it until his death at the age of 78. He was the first incumbent of the Blair Professorship of Geology, the second oldest endowed chair at Princeton. Three Mt. Guyots—in the White Mountains of New Hampshire, on the North Carolina-Tennessee line in the Great Smoky Mountains, and the Colorado Rockies—were named in his honor, as were the Guyot Glacier in southeastern Alaska and the Guyot Crater on the moon. The great flat-topped seamounts that characterize many parts of the ocean floor were named "guyots" in his

honor by Harry H. Hess. And of course there is Guyot Hall.

Few memorabilia remain of Guyot's life. At Princeton there are forty-six cloth wall hangings that he used for illustrative materials in his classroom. In Guyot Hall is the field toilet kit he carried on his mountain explorations. In Guyot Hall also are his handwritten labels of the glacial erratic stones he collected in the 1840s in Switzerland, the specimens themselves being long gone. In front of Nassau Hall stands the Guyot boulder, a glacial erratic given to Princeton by Arnold Guyot's former students at the Academy of Neuchatel.

Sheldon Judson

Guyot Hall, named for Princeton's first professor of geology and geography, Arnold Guyot (q.v.), was given to the University by the mother of Cleveland H. Dodge 1879. In planning what was to become the home of the biology and geology departments, Professor William Berryman Scott, then chairman of both, sent out a faculty committee to study other important American laboratory buildings. The floor plans, worked out by the departments concerned and drawn up by Professor Gilbert Van Ingen, were accepted by the architects Parrish and Schroeder with scarcely any change. "Being, thus, practically designed by the men who were to use it," Professor Scott said thirty years after the building's completion in 1909, "Guyot Hall has always been a very satisfactory place in which to work."

The building contained about two acres of floor space and some 100 rooms. The ground floor was assigned to the Natural History Museum so that it might attract the attention of people on their way to lecture-laboratory rooms and offices on other floors. On the second floor a large central reading room housed the two departmental libraries; they eventually outgrew this space and were separated.

In exterior design, Guyot followed the Tudor Gothic style inaugurated in Blair and Little Halls, but with the red brick and limestone trim first used in Seventy-nine Hall. Added as an extra Gothic feature, in keeping with Guyot's purpose, were many extinct and living animals and plants represented by stone carvings on the molding around the building—some 200 of them, students discovered in a survey they made in the 1950s. These gargoyle-like ornaments were created in the studio of Gutzon Borglum, sculptor of the Mount Rushmore presidential portraits, in South Dakota.

Several additions were made to Guyot in the 1960s to accommodate the growth of the two departments. The George M. Moffett Biological Laboratory was built in 1960 with funds provided by the Whitehall Foundation, established by George M. Moffett '04 and the National Institutes of Health. That same year a one-story addition was made for geology, and in 1964 a larger three-story addition for geochemistry and geophysics was built with help from the National Science Foundation. All three additions were designed by O'Connor and Kilham.

NATURAL HISTORY MUSEUM

The Natural History Museum, founded in 1856 by Arnold Guyot, had previously been housed in Nassau Hall in what is now the Faculty Room; it expanded rapidly after the completion of Guyot Hall. The museum possesses several hundred thousand geological, biological, and archaeological specimens. The mineralogical collections contain a sample of almost every available mineral and gem in the world. Fossil vertebrates brought back by Princeton scientific expeditions to the Far West, Patagonia, and elsewhere are internationally famous. There is also an excellent collection of fossil fishes, recovered in 1946 from rocks exposed by the excavation for Firestone Library. Museum specimens of special interest include skeletons of the sabre-toothed tiger, mastodon, three-toed horse, and giant pig, and the fossil of an Eocene perch preserved in the act of trying to swallow a herring.

Gymnastics, one of Princeton's oldest athletic activities, began as an informal exercise in the 1830s, and as an organized sport with the completion of Bonner-Marquand Gymnasium in 1870 and the appointment of George Goldie as its director. Goldie was a handsome Scot, with a full beard and great biceps; according to Professor Allan Marquand, one of his aptest pupils, "his skill in gymnastics, his cheerful temper, and his high character made him justly popular."

Under Goldie's influence, gymnastics became a prominent intramural activity which every year reached its climax in a Commencement exhibition. In the early 1890s Princeton gymnasts began to give outside exhibitions at Mount Holly, Philadelphia, Baltimore, and Washington, and a few years later took part in the first annual Yale-Princeton exhibition, which eventually became competitive. Additional meets were scheduled with other colleges and, with the establishment in 1900 of championship meets by the newly-formed Intercollegiate Gymnastics Association, the era of competitive intercollegiate gymnastics began.

Goldie retired in 1911, and Goldie Field was named in his honor. Other gymnastic teachers served for brief periods until 1925 when Richard Swinnerton began a term as coach which lasted until the outbreak of World War II.

In the forty-year period before the Second World War, Princeton gymnastic teams were frequently among the best in the East and in five years— 1908, 1916, 1927, 1931, and 1937— they were the best.

Three Princetonians won the eastern Intercollegiate all-round championship: Ernest W. Mecabe '08 in his sophomore and senior years, Jerome B. Wiss '17 in his sophomore and junior years, and Robley D. Snively, Jr. '28 in his sophomore year. Two others excelled in two individual events: Charles E. Claggett '31 was champion on the side horse in his junior and senior years and on the rings in his senior year. Thomas Gucker III '37 set a world's record by completing the twenty-foot rope climb in 3.8 seconds in his junior year, and he also won the side horse championship in his junior and senior years.

Other Princetonians who won individual eastern intercollegiate championships were: Louis E. Katzenbach '01, tumbling; Harrison G. Otis '02, flying rings; William A. Coulter '03, Charles W. Holzhauer '05, and Frank C. Roberts Jr. '16, horizontal bar; Wolfgang S. Schwabacher '18 and Philip B. Townley '20, club swinging; David S. Sheldon '23, side horse (in 1922 and 1923); Barent M. Ten Eyck '24, club swinging; Otto Crouse '24, tumbling; Richard R. Quay, Jr. '26, parallel bar; Christopher A. Beling '27, horizontal bar; Robley D. Snively, Jr. '28, flying rings (in 1927 and 1928); Richard D. Wallace '34 and George Harrison Houston, Jr. '37, rope climb; Carl Ferenbach II '37, flying rings.

Gymnastics at Princeton ceased during the Second World War and was not revived again until the founding of a Gymnastics Club in 1967 and the beginning of an annual Ivy League Gymnastics Meet in 1968. A women's gymnastic team began competition in 1974; it was coached by Meredith Dean Baker until 1976 when Ute Alt was appointed women's coach at the same time that her husband J. Douglas Alt was made men's coach. In 1977, Vickie Mayer '80 placed second in the competition for the women's Ivy League all-round championship.

Hall, Walter Phelps (1884-1962) was probably the most popular teacher of Princeton undergraduates in the first half of this century. He was a legend in his own lifetime, and, as Professor Joseph R. Strayer said, his death marked the end of an era on the Princeton Campus.

A graduate of Yale (1906) and Columbia (Ph.D. 1912), he came to Princeton as a history instructor in 1913, at the age of twenty-nine. Soon his name began to appear among the favorite teachers selected in the annual senior poll; when he retired thirty-nine years later as Dodge Professor of History, he had been first more often than any other member of the Faculty in his time.

For most of his career he lectured to sophomores on modern European history. His course was a prerequisite for history majors, and it was the stimulus of his teaching that attracted many students into that department and made it one of the largest in the University. He was, in Professor Strayer's words, "a powerful teacher," whose "strength lay . . . in a rare ability to dramatize human events, however remote, and to kindle the imaginations of youthful minds."

He was a favorite subject in the Seniors' Faculty Song; their changing verses about him provide a running account of his life and habits.

His bulldog, "Eli," was a frequent guest in the preceptorials he conducted during his bachelor days in 363 Cuyler Hall. Sometimes, to make a new group of preceptees feel at home, he would grab a sword from the wall and fling it into the air, and Eli would catch it in his mouth. The students were properly impressed, but they couldn't resist the temptation to suggest in the Faculty Song, that "if he had any dope at all",

He'd shoot that darned New Haven
* pup,*
And bring a Princeton Tiger up.

Hall was married to Margaret Nixon by President Hibben in 1923. After their marriage, the Halls lived in the country for a while, and he was frequently seen driving to the Campus with a horse and carriage. "Keeps his flivver in a stall," the seniors sang that year,

Buzzes in from Kingston way
In a "car" that runs on hay.

Another verse of the Faculty Song described Hall's annual lecture on his favorite historical character:

On Garibaldi's life and death
He yells himself quite out of breath.

A handsome, stockily built man, given to fancy vests, knickerbockers, and flowing ties, Hall usually carried a walking stick. Never without a pipe, he seemed to spend more time in preceptorials filling it than smoking it. Because he used a hearing aid, he was called "Buzzer."

Walter Hall was remarkable in that the influence he exerted on undergraduates when he was young continued undiminished as the gap in their ages widened, right up to his retirement. The basic reasons for this phenomenon have been well described by Professor Strayer, who was Buzzer's student, colleague, and, finally, his departmental chairman:

> . . . All human activity, every person he met, engaged him. In spite of personal affliction and of increasing deafness, he never burdened others with his own troubles. He had the great gift of making other people's interests his own. He gave himself freely, and he received in return the affection of his colleagues and of generation after generation of undergraduates.

His unorthodox methods of lecturing were legendary. He frequently sat on the desk and sometimes stood on it. Stories were handed down from class to class about celebrated examples of his uninhibited spontaneity. One recounted the time he lectured in his underwear. The explanation was simple enough. He had been drenched walking to McCosh in a driving rain; rather than call off the lecture or take the risk of catching cold, he peeled off all of his outer garments and held forth in his underwear. Another was about the dramatic way he roused a sleeping undergraduate in one of his 7:40 A.M. lectures. Suspecting that the student had been up all night in New York and had returned on the milk train, Hall quietly walked to the dozer's side, and with a broad grin shouted, as only Buzzer could shout, "Princeton Junction, change for Princeton!"

So many students and faculty wanted to attend his last lecture the year he retired, 1952, that it had to be shifted from McCosh to Alexander Hall. In his concluding words he told his students to rise above their fears and anxieties and to "keep a merry heart." A six-piece band led the audience in singing "For He's a Jolly Good Fellow," and he was given a seven-foot scroll with the signatures of undergraduate contributors to a fund in his honor, later enlarged by alumni gifts. This fund was to be used for a senior thesis prize in European history and for an annual lecture to be given by Buzzer "as long as he felt like it." He gave the lecture every year up to 1962 when he died, two days before his 78th birthday.

Recalling Buzzer's admonition to his students, Professor Strayer observed: "No man ever took his own advice better. To the very end, and for the lasting good of all those who knew him, Walter Hall did keep a 'merry heart.' "

Hamilton Hall, one of the smallest Gothic dormitories, and one of the most charming, was designed by Day and Klauder and built in 1911 with funds donated by the Classes of 1884 and 1885. It commemorates John Hamilton, president of the provincial council and acting governor of the Province of New Jersey who granted the first charter of the College of New Jersey on October 22, 1746, and thus, as reads the inscription on the limestone tablet in the low archway near University Place, "in the name of the King gave being to Princeton University."

Harbison, Elmore Harris (1907-1964), Henry Charles Lea Professor of History, was valedictorian and an outstanding member of the class of 1928. He not only won highest honors in history, but also was Triangle Club president, Phi Beta Kappa secretary, and a Philadelphian Society cabinet member. He did his graduate work at Harvard, where he took his Ph.D. in 1938 with a dissertation which, as *Rival Ambassadors in the*

Court of Queen Mary, later received the American Historical Association's Adams Prize. "Jinks," as he was affectionately known, returned to Princeton as instructor in 1933, and continued to serve the University until his death thirty-one years later.

He was, in the words of his friend and colleague, Professor Joseph R. Strayer, "a profoundly religious man, a learned and honest scholar" who "wrestled all his life with the problem of reconciling the apparent meaninglessness of history with the Providence of God." His struggle with this seeming paradox is clearly seen in his two most influential works, *The Christian Scholar in the Age of the Reformation* and a collection of his essays on *Christianity and History*. These books reveal his lucid expression, his subtle humor, his rejection of both dogmatism and skepticism, and, above all, "his profound conviction that, in spite of all appearances, there is no contradiction between Christian faith and historical reason."

In the introduction to a collection of essays published as a memorial to Harbison, he was described by two of his former students, Professors Theodore K. Rabb and Jerrold E. Seigel, as a rare example of the teacher "able to combine teaching, scholarship, and personal conviction so that each grows out of the other." His faith, and "the humanity of his attitude" toward that faith, they say, "ensured that his influence extended to colleagues and students who had spiritual commitments different from his own."

Harbison's convictions and his reasoned way of expressing them made him an effective committee member and trustee. Besides service on faculty committees, for which he was in frequent demand, he was chairman of the 1949 President's Committee on Student-Faculty Relations and for twelve years chairman of the Graduate Board of Trustees of the Student Christian Association. In addition, he was a fellow of the American Academy of Arts and Sciences and of the National Council on Religion in Higher Education, a trustee of Princeton Theological Seminary and of Lawrenceville School, and an elder of the Second Presbyterian Church of Princeton. He was also a trustee of the Danforth Foundation and helped establish its annual award for gifted college teaching in 1962. After his death the foundation named this award in his honor.

At their meeting following his death, the faculty paid him this tribute:

> Jinks raised important questions in his writing; his great gift as a teacher was to make his students raise important questions in their turn. He was a master of the Socratic method, and he could make it effective at all levels, from a freshman class to a graduate seminar. Like Socrates, he made his points with wit as well as with logic. His lectures were a joy to hear, and his dryly humorous criticisms were memorable. His precepts reached the level of dialogue of which Woodrow Wilson dreamed. As for graduate students, in case after case men who came to Princeton to specialize in other fields found themselves writing theses in Renaissance or Reformation history under Jinks. Knowing that they were to be teachers themselves, they were irresistibly attracted to a master of the art.

> In the long run, this will be Jinks's most important legacy. The next generation will revise his ideas about university organization, and rewrite his essays on Christianity and

history—for this is the nature of academic life. But the men of the next generation who do this will be, in great part, men who studied under Jinks. Through his students and his students' students, his ideas will live and his influence endure far beyond the end of our days.

Harlan, John Marshall '20 (1899-1971), was the eighth Princeton graduate to serve as Justice of the United States Supreme Court.

Public service was a hallmark of his family. His Quaker forebear, George Harlan, came to America from Durham, England, in 1687 and eight years later became governor of Delaware. His great-grandfather James Harlan was attorney general of Kentucky and a United States congressman from that state in the 1830s. His grandfather, for whom he was named, served from 1877 to 1911 as a Justice of the Supreme Court. He is best remembered as the sole dissenter from the Court's 1896 declaration of the so-called "separate but equal" doctrine in defense of racial segregation, which he denounced because, he said, "our Constitution is color-blind and neither knows nor tolerates classes among citizens." An uncle, Richard D. Harlan 1881, the first Princetonian in the family, was president of Lake Forest College, and another uncle, James S. Harlan 1883, was attorney general of Puerto Rico. His father, John Maynard Harlan 1884, practiced law and served as a city alderman in Chicago.

John Harlan '20 was outstanding in the student life of his generation, serving as chairman of *The Daily Princetonian*, chairman of the Senior Council, and president of his class in junior and senior years. After graduating with honors in 1920, he spent three years as a Rhodes Scholar at Oxford, taking an A.B. with a "first" in jurisprudence in 1923.

On his return from England, he began work with one of the nation's leading law firms while studying at the New York Law School. He earned his LL.B. in 1924, was admitted to the New York bar in 1925, and became a partner in his firm in 1931. In the late 1920s, as special assistant attorney general of New York state, he investigated the Queens County sewer scandals and helped convict a former Queens borough president of conspiracy. In 1940 he and a partner represented the New York Board of Higher Education in its unsuccessful attempt to retain Bertrand Russell on the faculty of the City College of New York.

During World War II he served as a colonel in the United States Army Air Force, in charge of the Operations Analysis Section of the Eighth Bomber Command in England. He was awarded the American Legion of Merit and the Belgian and French Croix de Guerre.

In the early 1950s, as chief counsel for the newly created New York State Crime Commission, Harlan helped investigate waterfront rackets in New York City and illegal gambling activities in several other communities. Later, he was one of four attorneys who successfully defended several members of the duPont family in a federal antitrust suit.

On nomination of President Eisenhower, he became a judge of the United States Court of Appeals for the Second Circuit in March 1954 and associate justice of the Supreme Court a year later.

Harlan was called a "lawyer's judge" as well as a "judge's judge." His opinions were so closely reasoned and so clearly written that lawyers often turned to him first for a succinct, fair statement of the issues. In reviewing his career, newspapers spoke of him as the court's "conservative conscience."

He was a strong believer in states' rights and an ardent defender of the rights of the individual. When the Court laid down its one-man, one-vote rule for state legislatures in 1964 he dissented, because he believed the vitality of the American political system was weakened by reliance on the judiciary for political reform; "the Constitution," he said, "is not a panacea for every blot upon the public welfare." But he frequently sided with the liberals and sometimes wrote the majority opinion for them. In 1955 he joined in the unanimous opinion directing the district courts to take such action as was necessary to bring about, "with all deliberate speed," the end of racial segregation in the public schools, which the Court had declared unconstitutional the previous year. In 1971 he wrote the majority opinion that found that wearing, in a courthouse corridor, a jacket bearing an obscene protest against the draft was constitutionally protected free speech.

Harlan was admired by his associates for his integrity, his modesty, his gentle humor and, in his last years (when he wrote some of his most notable opinions), for the courage with which he met the challenge of seriously failing eyesight. Among the many tributes paid him after his death, at the age of seventy-two, was one by one of his first law clerks, Harvard Law School Professor Paul M. Bator (Princeton class of 1951), who said in part:

> The private virtues—love of truth; kindness; respect for others; the kind of decency and straightforwardness which only a firm self-respect can produce; an utter honesty and

simplicity of spirit, combined with what the Psalmist cried out for, a heart of flesh rather than a heart of stone—these were the qualities that transfigured Justice Harlan's public acts. . . .

Nothing is more fashionable in our society than to serve the cause of democracy by keeping a jealous scrutiny lest others exceed their power. Nothing is less common than one who is equally scrupulous about his own. Justice Harlan was one of these rare public men. For him fidelity to law was fidelity to the whole law, every day and not every other day, fidelity not only to those rules which define other people's power but also those which limited his own. . . . Maybe his most enduring legacy will be this, that when the dark night of cynicism and hopelessness is on us, we can say, yes, fidelity to law is possible, is worthwhile, is real.

Harper, George McLean 1884 (1863-1947), a leading Wordsworth scholar and first Woodrow Wilson Professor of Literature, grew up in Shippensburg, Pennsylvania. His fellow-townsman, Robert Bridges 1879, encouraged him to come to Princeton, and later introduced him to Woodrow Wilson 1879, who became a life-long friend.

In college Harper was one of the most studious members of his class and, his classmates thought, one of the happiest and most exuberant. He won prizes for oratory in Whig Hall, and was co-managing editor of the *Nassau Literary Magazine*. In the fall of his senior year, he was instrumental in bringing Matthew Arnold to Princeton on his first lecture tour of the United States. "I got in correspondence with his lecture bureau," Harper later recalled, "secured the Second Presbyte-

rian Church as an auditorium, advertised the event, and persuaded some of my classmates to serve with me as ushers." Arnold was to be the guest of Dr. McCosh. But his acceptance of a railroad official's last-minute offer to have an express train make a special stop for him at Princeton Junction resulted in Arnold's arriving at Prospect from the Junction in a farmer's haywagon just as McCosh's coachman returned from the Princeton station with an empty coach. "Despite this inauspicious arrival," Harper reported, "the lecture was a great success."

After graduation Harper spent several years abroad in study and travel and in 1887 got a job through Robert Bridges, as assistant editor of *Scribner's Magazine*. Two years later he was called back to Princeton as instructor in French. He became Woodhull Professor of Romance Languages at age thirty in 1894, and in 1900, when Bliss Perry left to become editor of the *Atlantic Monthly*, was appointed to succeed him as Holmes Professor of Belles Lettres in the Department of English. Writing to his classmates about this time, Harper said he had helped, he believed, "to make French respected and hard to pass." His hope for Princeton was that it might be "the hardest University in the land to enter and remain in, and the pleasantest for real scholars." He also wished that "we had more poor men here, men prepared in the free public schools."

HARPER AND WILSON

Harper was one of Woodrow Wilson's closest friends, and also one of the first to greet the Wilson family when Wilson joined the faculty in 1890. Harper was then a bachelor and the Wilsons frequently entertained him at Sunday dinner, afterwards listening to his talk about poetry. Wilson, who once said he believed the best political thought was to be found in poetry, was particularly fond of Harper's hero, William Wordsworth.

In 1895 Harper married Belle Westcott, sister of the classicist, John Howell Westcott. The Harpers continued to enjoy a close relationship with the Wilson family after Wilson became president of the University. Once, however, in a faculty meeting, their friendship was badly strained. At the end of a long speech by Wilson, Harper rose and said, "We have had enough of this quibbling. Let us get on with the business." Wilson flared up and gave Harper a verbal scorching, which hurt his feelings. As he turned into his house, walking home after the meeting, Harper felt a hand on his shoulder and heard Wilson say, "Don't let this little spat spoil our friendship." The two friends made up and never referred to the quarrel again. "How many a friend Wilson would have kept whom he lost in the two great controversies of his career," Harper observed in recounting this incident, "if he had made such a brotherly gesture and spoken such reconciling words."

In the presidential campaign of 1912 the Harper family was invited to join the Wilsons in receiving the election returns. They attended the inauguration and were afterwards week-end guests at the White House. On Sunday afternoon, Harper later recounted, they all sat on a rug before an open wood fire, repeating some of their favorite passages of poetry.

Harper edited a volume of President Wilson's addresses in 1918. When the Woodrow Wilson Professorship of Literature was founded in 1926 by Edward W. Bok "to commemorate Wilson's mastery of spoken and written Eng-

lish," Harper was unanimously chosen to be its first occupant.

BIOGRAPHY OF WORDSWORTH

Harper's two-volume biography, *William Wordsworth, His Life, Works, and Influence* (1916), established him as a leading Wordsworth scholar. Previous biographies, in Harper's view, had scanted Wordsworth's romantic and insubordinate youth, when he was "burning with zeal for his fellow men and with the fire of a generous philosophy," and had given disproportionate prominence to his old age, "when his personal and literary adventures were at an end, and he had given up his gallant struggle on behalf of equality and simplicity."

Along with Professor Emile Legouis of the Sorbonne, Harper had discovered the facts concerning Wordsworth's natural French daughter, Caroline, by Annette Vallon, and in his biography had quoted extensively from a neglected collection of letters in the British Museum from Dorothy Wordsworth, the poet's sister, which contained frequent references to Caroline and to her approaching marriage.

In 1917, while serving as an orderly in the American Hospital at Neuilly, France, Harper continued his researches in the archives of Orleans and of the Prefecture of the Seine in Paris, where he found a record of the child's baptism and a certificate of her marriage which noted that she was the "daughter of William Wordsworth, landowner, residing at Grasmere, Kendal, in the county of Westmorland, England. . . ."

Having discovered the official records of Caroline's birth and marriage as well as other items about her mother's family, Harper decided "to give them as simply and correctly as possible" in a little book, *Wordsworth's French Daughter*, published by Princeton University Press in 1921. "I have made no attempt to deny that the origin of all this trouble was a wrong," Harper wrote, "but the unusual difficulties that stood in the way of a legal marriage between William Wordsworth [a Protestant and zealous Revolutionary] and Anne-Marie or 'Annette' Vallon [a Catholic and Royalist] should be and will be remembered."

Harper's discovery created a great stir in England and in America and inevitably found its way into the seniors' Faculty Song:

Harper went to France to get
The red-hot dope on dear Annette;
And there performed a deed of note,
Revealing Wordsworth's one wild
*   oat.*

One of his students, Thomas S. Matthews '22, said of Harper in the classroom:

. . . He was a quiet teacher, on the dry side, yet quite incapable of irony or sarcasm; an open and guileless expectancy was his natural frame of mind. Before you had been long in his class you became aware that he was not only giving you the benefit of the doubt but confidently trusting that you might, at any moment, tell *him* something not only original but true. And that he would be grateful for it, but not at all surprised.

Harper was a Socialist and once ran, unsuccessfully, for mayor of the Borough of Princeton on the Socialist ticket, the only man ever to do so. A friend of Norman Thomas '05, in 1940 he joined Thomas in expressing regret in letters to the *Alumni Weekly* that there were then no Negro students at Princeton.

He died of a heart attack on July 14, 1947, while sitting on the porch of his house on Mercer Street. He had just returned from taking his wife out to lunch to celebrate Bastille Day.

Professor Harper is memorialized by a graduate fellowship in English.

Harvey, Edmund Newton (1887-1959), who was generally recognized as the world's leading authority on bioluminescence, began his investigations in biology as a boy in Germantown, Pennsylvania, collecting "every conceivable natural object," as he later recalled, including "frogs in the family bathtub to lay eggs in the spring."

At the University of Pennsylvania, where he received a B.S. degree in 1909, he continued his enthusiastic pursuit of science. By the time he began graduate work in zoology at Columbia University, he had already participated in expeditions to Europe to collect alpine plants and to British Columbia to study ecology, won two scientific prizes, and worked for a summer at marine biological laboratories at Tortugas, Florida, and Woods Hole, Massachusetts, where his observations of sea urchin eggs led to his first publication. He had also become increasingly interested in the relatively new field of cellular physiology and had decided to make laboratory experimentation in this field his life work. He completed his doctorate in 1911, after only two years of study, with a thesis on the permeability of cells.

That spring, on invitation of the chairman of Princeton's biology department, Edwin Grant Conklin (q.v.), who had been one of his teachers at the University of Pennsylvania, Harvey gave a lecture in Guyot Hall on the subject of his Ph.D. thesis. After the lecture, he was promptly offered and accepted an instructorship, thus beginning at the age of twenty-three a career as Princeton teacher-scholar that was to last forty-five years. He became a full professor in 1919 and on Conklin's retirement in 1933 succeeded him as Henry Fairfield Osborn Professor.

His contributions to the department were many and varied. He initiated courses in general physiology and biochemistry, subjects only rarely offered in biology curricula of those years. A stimulating teacher, his lectures were noted for their clear and precise exposition, and his laboratory was always open to serious-minded students. In his research he was, in the words of an associate, Aurin M. Chase, "an explorer and pioneer" who "opened up new regions for others to develop," and all those who came in contact with him "absorbed some of his boundless enthusiasm and spirit."

Harvey's greatest scientific interest —bioluminescence—began during an expedition to the Great Barrier Reef of Australia in 1913. In later years he traveled extensively to observe luminescent organisms and to collect material for study at Princeton. He devoted four books and more than half of some 250 published papers to bioluminescence. "No one," his student and colleague Frank H. Johnson said, "ever has, and perhaps no one ever will, equal the untiring efforts . . . that Newton Harvey brought to bear on this subject. . . . Through his efforts, aided by the students he inspired, the Guyot Hall laboratory became the world's foremost center of research on bioluminescence. . . ."

He also continued to conduct research in other fields, such as cell permeability and the biological effects of supersonic waves, and, during the Second World War, decompression sickness and wound ballistics. He collaborated with Alfred L. Loomis in devising the centrifuge microscope and in pioneer studies in electroencephalography.

Harvey was a member of a score of learned societies, including the American Philosophical Society and the National Academy of Sciences. He served as president of the American Society of Zoologists, the American Society of Naturalists, and the International Society for Cell Biology, and was a founder and first editor of the *Journal of Cellular and Comparative Physiology*. Among the many honors accorded him were the Wetherill Medal of the Franklin Institute, the Rumford Medal of the American Academy of Arts and Sciences, and the grade of Officer of the *Ordem Nacional do Cruziero do Sul* of Brazil.

In 1916, Harvey had married Ethel Nicholson Browne, also a Columbia Ph.D., noted for her research on the sea urchin. Throughout their careers they shared laboratories at Princeton and, in the summer, at Woods Hole. When they retired in 1956, his departmental colleagues gave him and his wife gold keys (hers engraved with a sea urchin, his with figures of luminous organisms), making them, in his words, "members of an exclusive scientific fraternity of two." They had two sons, Edmund Newton Harvey, Jr. '38, and Richard Bennett Harvey '43, who earned doctorates in physical chemistry and medicine, respectively. Harvey was understandably proud that every member of his family had earned a doctor's degree.

Health Services, University. From the earliest days, health has been one of the essential concerns of the institution that began as the College of New Jersey.

When the College was relocated in 1756, among the advantages of the move from Newark cited by the trustees was their belief that "the little village of Princeton" was "not inferior in the salubrity of the air to any village on the continent."

Notwithstanding the benign atmosphere, the health records of the first five presidents were grievously poor; none of them reached the ripe age attained by most of their successors. Students, on the other hand, in spite of the poor fare in the refectory, the dampness and chill of some of Nassau Hall's chambers, and the backwardness of medical practice, managed to keep well. An epidemic of dysentery swept through the college in 1813, but there were no fatalities and President Green informed the trustees that a "chemical fumigation," prepared by Professor Elijah Slack from a formula in a foreign scientific magazine, had had "a most wonderful, speedy, and happy effect in purifying the atmosphere."

For the better part of the nineteenth century, health care was in the hands of two well-known Samaritans. John Maclean, Jr., whose father and both grandfathers were physicians, ministered to ill students during the forty years that he served as vice-president or president. Isabella McCosh, daughter of an eminent Scottish physician, nursed many students to health while her husband was president. Effective as they were, their individual ministrations did not obviate the growing need for a more substantial health service.

A search for better health facilities was intensified after the tragic typhoid epidemic of 1880, which resulted in ten deaths in a student body of 473. The epidemic brought about a thorough overhaul of the College's drainage system and the subsequent appointment of a standing faculty sanitary committee whose efforts led eventually to the construction in 1892 of the Isabella McCosh Infirmary (q.v.).

The next major developments in health service at Princeton came in 1910 and 1911 with the beginning of a mental health program and the founding of the Department of Health and Physical Education.

Princeton was the first American college or university to provide mental health care for its students—a distinction it owed to a graduate of the Class of 1886, Stewart Paton (M.D. Columbia). A man of independent means who had pioneered in the teaching of psychiatry at Johns Hopkins, Paton settled in Princeton in 1910, and for sixteen years gave the University his services as lecturer on neurobiology and as consultant on mental health for students. His counsel and treatment provided relief for disturbed and sometimes seriously maladjusted students who came to him for help, a service Princeton has carried on with continued effectiveness ever since. Later he assisted Yale, Dartmouth, Columbia, and other universities in setting up similar programs intended to give students some idea, as he put it, "of what Nature—and not the Faculty—intended them to do emotionally and mentally."

In 1911, Joseph E. Raycroft (M.D. Rush Medical College), who had been medical director at the University of Chicago for twelve years, was called to Princeton as founding chairman of the Department of Health and Physical Education. He held this position for twenty-five years, gaining wide recognition for the development of a comprehensive student health program and for broadening the base of athletics through intramural competition to include some ninety percent of the undergraduate body. He is remembered by the Raycroft Library in Dillon Gymnasium, which contains some 1,500 volumes on medicine and sport, brought together when he was eighty with the help of colleagues, alumni, and other friends, to replace his earlier collection, which had been lost when the old gymnasium was destroyed by fire in 1944.

The Raycroft administration saw the beginning in 1928 of a strong program in athletic medicine, ably directed for thirty-six years by Harry R. McPhee (M.D. Western Reserve University), a pioneer in the treatment and prevention of athletic injuries who also served as Head Team Physician for American athletes at four Olympic and two Pan-American Games.

Under the second chairman, Wilbur H. York (M.D. Johns Hopkins), who came from Cornell in 1936, the department's development was facilitated by the transfer of responsibility for physical education and intramural sport to the Department of Athletics in 1946. Under York's leadership the department utilized the many advances that were taking place in medical practice, instituting such measures as a tuberculosis case-finding program and an allergy clinic, and continuing to emphasize the use of preventive measures and the development of constructive health habits. At Cornell, Dr. York's close association with students and their problems had led to his founding of one of the early programs in mental health, and at Princeton he gave strong backing to the field pioneered by Dr. Paton and carried on by a full-time psychiatrist. As the trustees committee on health and athletics noted in 1962 at the time of his retirement, in the twenty-sixth year of his service, Dr. York is remembered by students and faculty for the kindliness and skill with which he treated "their varied discomforts of body and mind."

Under Willard Dalrymple (M.D. Harvard), who served as director for fifteen years from 1962 to 1977, the department's name was changed to University Health Services to emphasize the wider role it was called on to play. New responsibilities included an occupational health and safety unit, a program in sexual education, and a University Counseling Center, which brought together a number of previously scattered counseling activities. The staff of McCosh Infirmary had grown to include five full-time physicians, a physician's associate, and eleven nurses.

Louis A. Pyle, Jr. (M.D. Columbia), took office as the University's fourth medical director on July 1, 1977. A Princeton graduate of the Class of 1941, he had been a University physician since 1971, and associate director of the Health Services since 1972.

The University has been affected by three outbreaks of contagious diseases in this century: the 1916 infantile paralysis epidemic which led the University to postpone its opening for two weeks; the 1918 Spanish influenza pandemic which taxed McCosh Infirmary to the limit just as the University was opening for the new year; and the 1957 Asian influenza epidemic which overwhelmed the campus, requiring the conversion of the Student Center into an influenza ward with 100 beds. No student lives were lost in any of these outbreaks.

Henry, Bayard, 1876 (1857-1926), a life trustee for thirty years, represented the fifth generation of his family to serve in that office.

Descended also from Nathaniel Fitz-

Randolph, donor of the land on which Nassau Hall was built in 1756, Henry was one of a small group of alumni of the McCosh era who helped secure almost a square mile of land for the University early in this century. Henry himself procured the plot on Nassau Street where Holder Hall now stands and the tract on University Place occupied by the dormitories south of Blair Hall, one of which was named for his son Howard Henry '04, who died in service in France in World War I. He was also responsible for the University's acquisition of the land extending from Lake Carnegie to U.S. Route 1 between Washington Road and the Pennsylvania Railroad.

. Henry practiced law in Philadelphia, served in the select council of that city and in the state senate of Pennsylvania, was a leader in the Presbyterian Church and a director of many corporations. "His sense of responsibility was steady as a rock," Dean West said, "but his supreme trait was an utter unselfishness." These qualities were shown in 1906 when a trust company, in which Henry was a director, was threatened with ruin by the frauds of its president. On Henry's initiative the directors voluntarily contributed $2,500,000; every depositor was paid in full, and the bank's doors were reopened within sixty days of its failure. "A splendid comment," Dean West observed, "on Cicero's words: 'How much broader is the rule of duty than the rule of law!' "

Henry collaborated with M. Taylor Pyne 1877 in collecting thousands of manuscripts relating to Princeton's history. The fruits of their labors are found in the Pyne-Henry Collection, which has long been one of the University Library's treasures.

His concern for Princeton continued to the end of his life. In their memorial minute the Trustees made special mention of his loyalty and devotion and declared that the University "owes much to his great foresight in securing lands adequate for our future needs."

Henry, Joseph (1797-1878), the leading American scientist after Benjamin Franklin until Willard Gibbs, was a professor at Princeton from 1832 to 1846. His chief scientific contributions were in the field of electromagnetism, where he discovered the phenomenon of self-inductance. The unit of inductance, called "the henry," immortalizes his name. Henry is also remembered as the first Secretary of the Smithsonian Institution, where he made extraordinary contributions to the organization and development of American science.

Of Scottish descent, Henry was the son of a day-laborer in Albany, N.Y. As a small boy he was sent to live with his grandmother in a village about 40 miles from Albany. There he worked in a general store after school hours and at the age of thirteen was apprenticed to a watchmaker. As a young man he became interested in the theater and was offered employment as a professional actor, but in 1819 several well-positioned Albany friends persuaded him instead to attend the Albany Academy, where free tuition was provided. His interest in science had already been aroused by a chance encounter with a popular scientific book, and by 1823 his education was so far advanced that he was assisting in the teaching of science courses. By 1826, after a stint as a district schoolteacher and as a private tutor, he was appointed Professor of Mathematics and Natural Philosophy at the Academy. Here, in spite of a teaching schedule that occupied him seven hours a day, he did his most important scientific experiments.

Henry had become interested in terrestrial magnetism, which was then, as today, an important scientific topic. This led him to experiment with electromagnetism. His apprenticeship as a watchmaker stood him in good stead in the construction of batteries and other apparatus. Oersted and others had observed magnetic effects from electric currents, but Henry was the first to wind insulated wires around an iron core to obtain powerful electromagnets. Before he left Albany, he built one for Yale that would lift 2,300 pounds, the largest in the world at that time. In experimenting with such magnets, Henry observed the large spark that was generated when the circuit was broken, and he deduced the property known as self-inductance, the inertial characteristic of an electric circuit. The self-inductance of a circuit tends to prevent the current from changing; if a current is flowing, self-inductance tends to keep it flowing, or if an electromotive force is applied self-inductance tends to keep it from building up. Henry found that the self-inductance is greatly affected by the configuration of the circuit, especially the coiling of the wire. He also discovered how to make non-inductive windings by folding the wire back on itself.

While Henry was doing these experiments, Michael Faraday did similar work in England. Henry was always slow in publishing his results, and he was unaware of Faraday's work. Today Faraday is recognized as the discoverer of mutual inductance (the basis of transformers), while Henry is credited with the discovery of self-inductance.

In 1832, when Henry was 35, Yale's distinguished geologist Benjamin Silliman was consulted regarding the possible appointment of Henry to Princeton. Silliman replied, "As a physical philosopher he has no superior in our country; certainly not among the young men." Henry, always modest, had responded to tentative inquiries, "Are you aware of the fact that I am not a graduate of any college and that I am principally self-educated?"

Henry's initial salary at Princeton was $1,000 per annum plus a house. The Trustees also provided $100 "for the purchase of a new electrical machine &c." At that point the College was near bankruptcy and Maclean was trying to institute reforms and build up the faculty. Henry was a notable acquisition, and he found the lighter teaching schedule and the intellectual companionship at Princeton congenial, especially when his brother-in-law Stephen Alexander (q.v.) joined the faculty to teach astronomy. Henry worked with Alexander in the observation of sunspots and continued his own work on magnets, building for Princeton an even larger magnet than he had built for Yale, one that would lift 3,500 pounds. He also rigged two long wires, one in front of Nassau Hall and one behind, so that he was able to send a signal by induction through the building. Another wire from his laboratory in Philosophical Hall to his home on the campus (see Joseph Henry House) was used to send signals to his wife; this signal system used a remote electromagnet to close a switch for a stronger local circuit, and constituted in effect the invention of the magnetic relay. A similar arrangement was used by S.F.B. Morse in the invention of the telegraph; Morse had consulted Henry and had used one of his scientific papers. Later, Henry was called to testify in a patent suit involving the telegraph, *Morse* vs. *O'Reilly*. Although Henry had encouraged and helped Morse in his project, his testimony that the principle of the telegraph had been known to himself and to Professor Wheatstone in England undermined Morse's claim to originality. This led to much unpleasantness and controversy, but Henry's reputation emerged unscathed.

In addition to natural philosophy (physics), Henry taught chemistry, geology, mineralogy, astronomy, and architecture—in the words of Frederick Seitz, Ph.D. '34, former president of the National Academy of Sciences, he was "a very large economy package." A rather reserved and quiet man, he was nevertheless a popular teacher. The College gave Henry an opportunity, then unusual, to travel abroad on leave at full salary. In 1837 he met Faraday, Wheatstone, and other British scientists, to whom he explained his idea of "quantity" and "intensity" circuits (low and high impedance, in modern terms). He returned to Princeton with a variety of scientific equipment purchased abroad.

During his remaining years in Princeton Henry continued his electrical investigations, but also branched out into the study of phosphorescence, sound, capillary action, and ballistics. In 1844 he was a member of a committee to investigate the explosion of a gun during a demonstration on the new U.S.S. *Princeton*; the Secretaries of State and Navy and several congressmen were among the spectators killed. His experiments on gun castings on this committee led him into the subject of the molecular cohesion of matter.

In 1846, having received from an Englishman, James Smithson, a large bequest for the founding of an institution "for the increase and diffusion of knowledge among men," the U.S.

Congress established the Smithsonian Institution. A distinguished board was appointed, with instructions to find the best possible man to head the new Institution as secretary, and the invitation was soon extended to Henry. He was reluctant to leave Princeton and the opportunity to do his own scientific investigations. "If I go," he said to a friend, "I shall probably exchange permanent fame for transient reputation." But he finally accepted and threw his enormous energy and knowledge and experience into the development of the Smithsonian, which became the first great driving force in the organization and direction of American science.

Henry was one of the original members of the National Academy of Sciences and served as its second president. He was also a trustee of Princeton and president of the American Association for the Advancement of Science. When he died in 1878 his funeral was attended by the president of the United States with his cabinet, the chief justice and associate justices of the Supreme Court, by many members of both houses of Congress, and by many scientists and other illustrious personages.

In 1872, John C. Green, founder of the School of Science at Princeton, endowed a chair of physics in Henry's honor (held since then by C. F. Brackett, W. F. Magie, E. P. Adams, H. D. Smyth, and J. A. Wheeler). Almost a century later, when the main physics building, Jadwin Hall, was dedicated in 1970, the Physics Department manifested its continuing esteem for Henry by declaring that all of the laboratory facilities housed in Jadwin and Palmer Halls and the Elementary Particles Laboratory should be collectively known as the Joseph Henry Laboratories. Some of Henry's laboratory equipment is on display in the lobby of Jadwin Hall. His campus home, built to his design, is called the Joseph Henry House (q.v.). In Washington his statue stands before the old Smithsonian Building.

Herbert S. Bailey, Jr.

Henry, Joseph, House, The, was built in 1837 to the design of the eminent physicist of that name, and occupied by him until he left in 1848 to become the first secretary of the Smithsonian Institution in Washington. It was to this house that Professor Henry sent telegraphic messages (sometimes to order lunch) from his laboratory in Philosophical Hall, which stood where Chancellor Green Student Center now stands. The Joseph Henry House was made the official residence of the dean of the College soon after that office was created in 1909 and was so used through the incumbencies of Deans Elliott, McClenahan, Gauss, Godolphin, and Finch. In 1961 it became the home of William D'O. Lippincott, dean of students from 1954 to 1968, and executive director of the Alumni Council from 1968 to 1972. In 1973 it became the home of Aaron Lemonick, dean of the faculty and professor of physics.

In a community where well-traveled buildings are no rarity, the Joseph Henry House has made more journeys than any other. Three times since it came into being on the south side of Stanhope Hall it has had to move to make way for other buildings: in 1879 for Reunion Hall (which was razed in 1966), in 1925 for the University Chapel, in 1946 for Firestone Library. It now stands just north of Chancellor Green, across the Front Campus from the John Maclean House.

Hess, Harry Hammond (1906-1969), sixth Blair Professor of Geology, did his undergraduate work at Yale (B.S.

1931), where according to his own— possibly apocryphal—account, he failed his first course in mineralogy and was told there was no future for him in that field. Following two years as a mineral prospector in the bush country of Northern Rhodesia and three years of graduate study at Princeton under Arthur F. Buddington in petrology, Alexander H. Phillips in mineralogy, Richard M. Field in oceanic structure, and Edward Sampson in mineral deposits, he went on to become a mineralogist of world repute whose far-reaching contributions made him, in the words of a National Academy of Sciences memoir, "one of the truly remarkable earth scientists of this century."

Hess brought to his research a rare talent for precision work combined with a boldness in the formulation of sweeping hypotheses in which, as one colleague put it, "he took the whole globe as his province." His careful attention to detail was evident in his work on peridotite, the subject of his doctoral dissertation, and on other multramafic rocks—believed to be the principal components of the earth's mantle. The boldness and brilliant intuition for which he became even better known were manifested in his introduction of new concepts on the origin of ocean basins and island arcs (long, curved chains of islands), on mountain building, and on the cause of continental drift. Described by one of his scientific colleagues as "a fierce fighter for science," he was also known for his relaxed and quietly humorous guidance in committee work which, along with his good judgment in public affairs, made him a leader among the scientists who helped guide the development of the national space program.

After taking his Ph.D. degree at Princeton in 1932, Hess spent a year as an instructor at Rutgers and another as a research associate in the Geophysical Laboratory of the Carnegie Institution of Washington before joining the Princeton faculty as instructor in 1934. In 1950 he followed his principal teacher and close friend, Arthur Buddington, as chairman of the department and in 1964 succeeded him as Blair Professor.

During the thirties Hess participated in submarine gravity studies of the West Indies island arc, and, in order to facilitate operations on Navy submarines, he acquired a commission as lieutenant, junior grade, thus initiating a long association with the United States Naval Reserve, where he ultimately rose to the rank of rear admiral. Called to active duty in 1941, he discharged important wartime duties and, at the same time, kept alive his scientific curiosity. Early in the war, he developed a successful system for estimating the daily positions of German submarines in the North Atlantic, and in order to obtain a first-hand test of the effectiveness of his detection program, he served, at his own request, on a hazardous mission aboard the submarine decoy vessel *U.S.S. Big Horn*. Later he took part in four major landings in the Pacific as commander of the attack transport *U.S.S. Cape Johnson*. Utilizing the transport's sounding gear, he was able to take thousands of miles of depth soundings that led to his discovery of the flat-topped sea mounts—submerged ancient islands—that he later named "guyots" in honor of the Swiss geographer Arnold Guyot, founder of the Princeton geology department and first Blair Professor. One of the guyots found by others after Hess's initial discoveries was named "Hess Guyot" in his honor.

On his return to Princeton from war service, Hess organized, secured funding for, and directed the Princeton Caribbean Research Project. Supported by the University, the National Science Foundation, the Office of Naval Research, several oil companies, and the governments of Puerto Rico, Venezuela, and Colombia, this continuing program explored every aspect of Caribbean geology and provided a valuable training ground for graduate students from many parts of the world, producing thirty-four Ph.D. dissertations.

In 1960 Hess made his single most important contribution, which is regarded as "part of the major advance in geologic science of this century." In a widely circulated report to the Office of Naval Research, he advanced the theory, now generally accepted, that the earth's crust moved laterally from long, volcanically active oceanic ridges. "Sea-floor spreading," as the process was later named, helped establish the concept of continental drift as scientifically respectable and triggered a "revolution in the earth sciences." This report was formally published in his *History of Ocean Basins* (1962), which for a time was the single most referenced work in solid-earth geophysics.

Hess also made significant contributions to the affairs of his department, the University, and the national scientific community. During his sixteen years as chairman, the Department of Geology enjoyed substantial growth, later recognized by the change of its name to Department of Geological and Geophysical Sciences. During this same period Hess's faculty colleagues elected him to the Advisory Committee on Appointments and Advancements in eleven successive years and also the faculty advisory committee on the election of a new president in 1957, when Robert F. Goheen was chosen to succeed Harold W. Dodds. Following his election to the National Academy of Sciences in 1952, Hess was called on frequently to head national scientific committees, serving as chairman of the Academy's Committee for Disposal of Radioactive Wastes, the National Research Council's Earth Sciences Division, and the Academy's Space Science Board, which was established to advise the National Aeronautics and Space Administration on scientific aspects of the development of the national space program. At the time of his death, he was one of ten members of a scientific panel appointed to analyze rock samples brought back from the moon by the Apollo 11 crew.

Hess's achievements were widely recognized by fellow scientists. He was elected to the American Philosophical Society and the American Academy of Arts and Sciences, in addition to the National Academy of Sciences, and to foreign membership in the geological societies of London, South Africa, and Venezuela. He also served as president of the Mineralogical Society of America, as well as of the Geological Society of America, which gave him its highest award, the Penrose Medal, in 1966. That same year he was elected to foreign membership in the Academia Nazionale dei Lincei of Rome, the world's oldest academy of science, and became the first earth scientist from the Western hemisphere to receive its $32,000 Feltrinelli Prize. Three years later, just a few months before his death, Yale conferred on him an honorary degree of Doctor of Science.

His death, of a heart attack, occurred on August 25, 1969, in Woods Hole, Massachusetts, while he was presiding at a Space Science Board conference he had organized to reformulate the scientific objectives of lunar exploration. He was buried in the Arlington National Cemetery and was posthumously awarded the National Aeronautics and Space Administration's Distinguished Public Service Award.

In a Faculty memorial minute, his Princeton colleagues observed: "Harry Hess had a deep, almost a religious, reverence for the awesome order of the universe. He possessed that combination of a driving urge to discover truth and a profound humility before the vast truths yet unknown which is the mark of the truly creative scholar."

Hibben, John Grier (1861-1933), fourteenth president of Princeton, was born on April 19, 1861, in Peoria, Illinois. He entered Princeton with the Class of 1882 and at graduation was both class president and valedictorian. Following a year of study in Berlin, he attended Princeton Theological Seminary. On November 8, 1887, he married Jenny Davidson of Elizabeth, New Jersey. Ordained in the same year, he served Presbyterian churches in St. Louis and Chambersburg, Pennsylvania, until a throat ailment cut short his career in the church and turned him toward graduate studies in philosophy at Princeton where he became an instructor in logic in 1891 and received his Ph.D. in 1893. Four years later, he was named Stuart Professor of Logic, a subject he continued to teach, along with psychology and the Bible, until his election to the presidency on January 11, 1912.

The search for a successor to Woodrow Wilson had lasted for fifteen months. Hibben's nomination and election came at the hands of those trustees who had most resisted Wilson's reforms, and this posed a special problem for the new president, whose warm friendship with Wilson had rapidly cooled after Hibben had joined forces with Wilson's principal opponents in the Graduate School controversy, Moses Taylor Pyne and Dean Andrew F. West. The University had become sharply divided during the controversy, and Hibben felt that his most urgent task was to bring the factions together. At his first public appearance after the election, he set the tone for his entire administration. "If I am to prove myself worthy in some small way of the confidence reposed in me," he told the alumni of Orange, New Jersey, "my administration must make for peace. I wish to say to the alumni that which I said to the board of trustees on the day of election to this high office, and later to the faculty, that I represent no group or set of men, no party, no faction, no past allegiance or affiliation—but one united Princeton!"

Hibben's actions proved his words. One of his first acts as president was to seek out several faculty members of the Wilson faction and urge them to cooperate with him in continuing the work begun by Wilson. Many had feared, according to Professor William Berryman Scott, that the election of Hibben "signified the triumph of Wilson's enemies on the board as well as in the faculty." But, Scott acknowledged, "I was entirely mistaken," for Hibben's "genial and kindly nature" soon healed the breach, and even Wilson's strongest supporter, Professor Henry B. Fine, came in time to feel that Hibben was a "singularly happy choice."

Hibben's style in office was more that of the coordinator and mediator than of the dynamic, innovative leader. "Temperate yet effective," "tolerant, candid and fair," are the kind of comments that recur in the observations of col-

leagues, alumni and trustees. His popularity as a teacher and his reputation for fair-mindedness—celebrated by more than twenty-five successive classes in the faculty song: "Here's to Hibben, we call him Jack / The whitest man in all the Fac"—followed him into Prospect.

In the fall of 1913, Hibben presided over elaborate ceremonies attending the formal opening of the impressive new Graduate College. Former President Taft and Dean West gave the principal addresses. Set apart on a hill about a half mile from the heart of the campus, the College represented the triumph of the work and ideas of Dean West and trustee Pyne. As dean of the Graduate School under Presidents Patton and Wilson, West had exercised nearly autonomous powers. However, within a year, those powers were to be severely reduced by the trustees when they wrote new by-laws making the Graduate School in every aspect of its administration subject to President Hibben and the standing committees of the trustees and faculty. A possible future source of difficulty for Hibben's leadership was thus removed at the outset.

The outbreak of the European War in 1914 brought new problems for the University as for the nation. President Hibben was a strong advocate of preparedness and of intervention on the side of the Allies. When America entered in 1917, he lost no time in placing the University's resources at the disposal of the government. Army, navy and aviation training schools were soon busily functioning on campus, and many buildings, laboratories, and other facilities were made available to various research and operational programs. As the University donned khaki, Princeton men, too, flocked to the colors. By September 1918, there were only sixty undergraduates not in service. In all, more than six thousand Princetonians —faculty, alumni, graduate and undergraduate students—served in some branch of the armed forces. Of these, 151 made the supreme sacrifice. Hibben spoke out frequently in support of the war effort and was honored by President Lowell as a "leader in patriotic thought" upon the presentation of a Harvard LL.D.

As a cleric as well as an educator, Hibben was distressed by the extent to which secular forces seemed to hold sway over undergraduate minds and habits during the postwar period. These tendencies had been, he thought, "largely affected by the hypocrisy attending the Eighteenth Amendment, by false standards of living growing out of our period of fictitious prosperity and by a skepticism toward old concepts of morals and religion following the World War." All this had resulted in a greater emphasis on social activities, he reported, a more luxurious style of living, particularly in the eating clubs, and the development of "week-ending" as more undergraduates sought diversion away from Princeton—usually in the city. Among Hibben's remedies for these unhappy influences was the building of eight new dormitories—Pyne, Henry, Foulke, Laughlin, 1901, Lockhart, 1903, and Walker Halls—which permitted the housing of some 82 percent of the 2,200 undergraduates, a 28 percent increase over the situation immediately following the war. Also, the eating clubs, viewed as a "vexing problem" by Hibben no less than by his predecessor, were brought under new regulations regarding membership eligibility and self-government. Another restriction, which involved what Hibben considered one of the "most serious enemies"

of the residential life of Princeton, came in 1927 when, with the President's concerned approval, the trustees prohibited the operation of cars by undergraduates except in special cases. Hibben's plans for countering these centrifugal impulses of social life also included the establishment of a student center as a focal point for the meeting and interaction of all members of the community. These plans were well-advanced when the onset of the great depression forced their postponement. But, over the years, perhaps none of these physical structures has had as much effect in drawing together the various elements of student life as Hibben's appointment, in 1930, of the Council on Undergraduate Life, which has served to the present day as a most helpful sounding board and clearinghouse for undergraduate problems and concerns.

The special quality of Hibben's leadership emerged slowly over the years. It was his practice to look to the faculty for initiative in new programs, and he was invariably rewarded with the cooperation of leading members, many of whom had been recruited during the Wilson years. The preceptorial system was further developed and extended to sophomore courses, but the most significant curriculum reform under Hibben's stewardship came in 1923 with the inauguration of the "four course plan," or more formally, the "Upperclass Plan of Study." As Hibben reported to the trustees, this plan sought "to elevate the plane of endeavor and attainment of the whole undergraduate body" rather than that of a few students as provided by the old Honors Course program. The idea was to give the student more freedom during the upperclass years for independent reading in a particular subject in lieu of taking a fifth course. It all culminated in a senior thesis and a comprehensive examination period. Despite some initial doubts, the program quickly proved successful and was much emulated elsewhere. Professor Eisenhart as chairman of the Committee on the Course of Study had responsibility for organizing the new program and his efforts were the major ingredient in its continuing success. The plan endures in substance to this day in the Princeton program.

Hibben sought persistently to draw the faculty into closer relation with the president and trustees in the conduct of University affairs. His greatest success in this regard was the creation of a Committee on Appointments and Advancements consisting of three members of the faculty chosen by that body and charged with conferring with the president regarding his recommendations to the trustees. The "Committee of Three," later enlarged, became one of the most important liaison groups on campus. In the same direction, more members of the faculty were named to trustee committees to establish a better working relationship on university matters of joint interest. The faculty also benefited from the successful fund drive by the Graduate Council to raise salaries, and with an improved salary scale came a new system of retirement, pensions, and insurance.

The years after the war also brought a vast increase in the University's facilities for instruction and research. "Never in all her history," recalled one member of the faculty, "was Princeton the scene of such Aladdin magic as unfolded itself during the last twelve years of the Hibben administration." A Department of Oriental Languages and Literatures was established in 1922, and three new schools were created: in

1919, the School of Architecture; in 1921, the School of Engineering; and in 1930, the School of Public and International Affairs founded to carry forward the Princeton tradition for public service and later appropriately named for Woodrow Wilson. Significant support for faculty research also came with the establishment in 1922 of the Industrial Relations Section; in 1928, of the International Finance Section; and in 1929, of a three-million-dollar Foundation for Scientific Research made possible by a General Education Board grant, supplemented by gifts of alumni and other friends.

The endowment fund rose dramatically under Hibben and by the end of his administration topped more than $24 million, a 374 percent increase. The University benefited from the burgeoning national economy and grew in step through the loyal support of the alumni. The remarkable increase in the general endowment was paralleled by numerous generous gifts in the form of new buildings. Besides the eight dormitories already mentioned, the list included two other dormitories, Cuyler and Joline Halls; the North Court quadrangle at the Graduate College and five new undergraduate dining halls; six new buildings for instruction and research—McCormick, Eno, Green, Frick, Dickinson, and Fine Halls—Palmer Stadium, Baker Rink, McCosh Infirmary, McCarter Theater, faculty apartments on Prospect Avenue and College Road, and the magnificent new University Chapel, whose nave was named for Hibben by the trustees in recognition of his personal efforts to make the chapel a reality. In all, some thirty buildings were constructed during Hibben's administration while the total area of the campus doubled in size.

Growth of the faculty was also impressive—in quality as well as quantity—as the teaching force expanded some 73 percent under Hibben, who managed to retain most of the luminaries of the Wilson era and to add other accomplished or promising scholars. At the same time, the student body increased by nearly a thousand, even though a policy of limited enrollment and selective admission had been adopted in 1922.

In 1932, when Hibben retired, the University was by more than a full turn larger and, on every level, more advanced than it had been in 1912. Perhaps Professor Charles G. Osgood, a Wilson appointee, who went the distance under Hibben's temperate, wise, and corporate leadership, said it best when he characterized Hibben's administration as the "flowering and harvest of Wilson's plantings." Certainly few could match the service and devotion Hibben gave to the University and its constituents for more than forty years. "Princeton was Dr. Hibben's entire life," said one of his colleagues. "He was a man of warm and generous instincts," added Professor Osgood, "concerned with the individual case of every member of the Princeton household." The University was his "parish."

Hibben retired at the end of the school year in 1932, and a year later died in a tragic automobile accident that also fatally injured Mrs. Hibben. "He had a profound sense of fairness and justice," observed the trustees in their memorial minute, "and the wounds of time were healed by it."

David W. Hirst

History, The Department of. For a department that has been a favorite with undergraduates since the 1920s, History was a long time a-borning. Witherspoon lectured on history, and although he felt that it was "subservient to the interests of religion," he was also concerned with what would now be called social and intellectual history. History was used to fill a few small cracks in the curriculum in the nineteenth century, but it seems to have been largely chronology and made little impression on undergraduates. The first faculty member to have the title of Professor of History—Charles Woodruff Shields (1869-1882)—was also Professor of the Harmony of Science and Revealed Religion. He wrote a long (18 pages) and anguished letter to the trustees in 1872 begging to be relieved of his elective courses in history. His petition was refused, but finally, in 1883, William Milligan Sloane was made Professor of History and Political Science. He was a professional historian, author of a number of useful books, but he departed for Columbia in 1896.

Meanwhile, the two most famous writers of history at Princeton were not considered historians. John Bach McMaster (q.v.), whose *History of the American People* revolutionized the writing of American history was a teacher of engineering. A proposal that he be made a professor of history was turned down by scandalized trustees who thought that he should stick to his trade, and he took a chair at Pennsylvania in 1883. (Princeton made amends by giving him an honorary degree in 1925.) The other widely read Princeton historian was Woodrow Wilson (q.v.), who was actually a political scientist.

When Wilson set up the departmental system in 1904, history, politics and economics were lumped together. A young preceptor had to be a versatile man to jump from medieval history to international law to money and banking. A few survived these hardships and became distinguished scholars—notably Edward S. Corwin (q.v.) and Charles H. McIlwain (the latter, alas, lost to Harvard). Some relief came when economics split off in 1913, but it was only in 1924, under the pressure of the Four-Course Plan, that history was separated from politics.

Three key appointments determined the future of the history department. One of Wilson's last acts was to name Thomas Jefferson Wertenbaker (q.v.) to the faculty. Wertenbaker became an eminent writer on early American history, and a revered teacher of many graduate students. In 1912 the two Halls, "Beppo" and "Buzzer," joined the Department. They were entirely different in temperament and interest; one student wrote of the "aristocratic Mr. Hall who believes in democracy" [Beppo] and the "democratic Mr. Hall who believes in aristocracy" [Buzzer]. But they were both great undergraduate teachers, and they set such a high standard that no young instructor coming to Princeton could feel comfortable if he were a poor teacher.

This combination of solid scholarship and excellent teaching was reinforced when Dana Carleton Munro (q.v.) joined the department in 1916. For 20 years (1916-1936) first "old Dana" Munro (his son, Dana Gardner Munro, joined the Department in 1932), and then Wertenbaker held the chairmanship of the history department. They began the work of recruiting the remarkable group of young men who were to carry the department to a peak of professional excellence while making it one of the best teaching units in the University. These were the years of the famous freshman course called "Historical Introduction," taught first by

Joseph C. Green and then by John Pomfret. It was an exhausting course, both for those who took it and those who taught it. (Green took refuge in the State Department, Pomfret in the presidency of William and Mary, and later in the directorship of the Huntington Library.) But in spite of its rigorous nature the course gave students a taste for historical studies, and enrollments in the Department began to grow.

These were also the years in which Raymond Sontag, Robert Albion, Elmer Beller, Joseph Strayer, E. Harris ("Jinks") Harbison (q.v.), Robert Palmer, Gordon Craig, Cyril Black, and Eric Goldman began their Princeton careers. Sontag had played an important role in recruiting the younger members of the group, especially during his chairmanship (1939-1941), but he was lured to Berkeley in 1941. The others remained to form the nucleus of the postwar department.

The Second World War put the department in a difficult position. Many of the regular members left for service in the armed forces or in Washington. Meanwhile, the government flooded the campus with thousands of young soldiers, sailors, and marines, all of whom—it was considered—needed a course in American history to be saved. To teach these multitudes, the department recruited one of the most distinguished—if not the most professional —groups it ever had on its roster. Professors of art, philosophy, political science and music, who had few students in their own fields, became instant experts on the Revolution and the Civil War. The professor of music wrote a "Fanfare for History" in memory of his experience; it is said to be somewhat dissonant.

In 1945 the department came back to normal, as far as its personnel was con-

cerned, but found that the new generation of undergraduates had an insati-
able appetite for history of all sorts.
This posed three problems: to recruit
new members to handle the increased
enrollment, to add new fields to meet
the needs of a new age, and to keep
other universities from stealing its best
men. The first two problems were
solved more easily than the third.
Jerome Blum and Charles Gillispie
came immediately after the war; Frank
Craven (as a replacement for Wertenbaker) four years later. All three added
greatly to the strength of the department. "Young Dana" Munro had begun
teaching Latin American history before
the war; his work was continued by
Stanley Stein. Cyril Black built up a
strong program in Russian studies.
Then Charles Gillispie assembled a
remarkable group of men in History of
Science, while Marius Jansen started
Far Eastern Studies at a high level.
Joint appointments strengthened the
old ties between History and Near
Eastern Studies. A little later Robert
Tignor began giving courses in African
History. This was quite a change from
the old curriculum, restricted to Euro-
pean and American history and heavily
political in emphasis.

During the chairmanship of Joseph
Strayer (1941-1961) the department
reached the peak of excellence at which
Munro, Wertenbaker, and Sontag had
aimed. The teacher-scholar tradition
was stronger than ever. Harbison was
one of the best preceptors the University ever had and was an expert on the
Reformation. Craig's lectures rivaled
those of "Buzzer" Hall in popularity,
and his work on German history was
praised on both sides of the Atlantic.
Courses in Russian history (Black),
medieval history (Strayer), and American diplomatic history (Challener) drew

surprisingly large numbers of students.
Palmer's great book on the *Age of the
Democratic Revolution* was appearing;
Julian Boyd's remarkable edition of the
Jefferson Papers was well under way;
Arthur Link was getting out the first
volumes of the Wilson Papers. It was
generally recognized that Princeton
had one of the three or four best history
departments in the country. The
generous gift of $5,000,000 to the de-
partment by Shelby Cullom Davis '30
was a recognition of this eminence.

The premature death of Harbison
and the departure of Craig and Palmer
to other universities left serious gaps in
the department's program. Student
demands for new types of history and
more specialized courses complicated
the problem. The chairmen of the
1960s and early '70s (Blum, Stone,
Challener, and Gillispie) had much rebuilding to do. Lawrence Stone's willingness to come to Princeton from Oxford filled one of the biggest holes (sixteenth and seventeenth-century England), while Arno Mayer picked up the
work in modern Europe and Robert
Darnton took on eighteenth-century
Europe and the French Revolution.
Another group of promising young assistant professors (including, for the
first time, two women) was recruited.
As of 1976, Princeton was still considered one of the best places to study history, and undergraduate enrollment in
history was larger than that in any other
department.

Five Princeton historians have
served as president of the American
Historical Association: the elder Munro
in 1926, Wertenbaker in 1947, Boyd in
1964, Palmer in 1970, Strayer in 1971.

Joseph R. Strayer

**History and Philosophy of Science,
Program in.** The two disciplines united

in the program are as old as learning itself, although they have emerged as distinct enterprises only in this century. Philosophers since Aristotle have made the epistemological and metaphysical commitments of natural inquiry a major concern of philosophy, and many, ranging from Aristotle and Bacon to Whewell and Comte, have looked to the history of scientific thought for clues about its conceptual structure. From the outset, then, readers of philosophy at Princeton have had some exposure to history and philosophy of science, and the latter remains central to the philosophy curriculum.

Long of interest also to scientists, history of science began to form a special field of history in the 1930s and received its main impetus during the 1950s as the impact of science on modern society increasingly concerned scientists and educators (cf. Princeton's Committee on Science in Human Affairs established in 1962). Taught at Princeton on occasion by scientists before World War II, history of science became a regular offering in 1955-1956 with Charles C. Gillispie's survey course sponsored jointly by History and the Council of the Humanities.

The growing need for historians and philosophers of science led in 1960 to a special graduate program chaired by Gillispie under the auspices of the departments of history and philosophy, and the Council. Expansion planned in 1963 culminated in 1970 with a full staff of five historians and five philosophers. In 1968 the program, by then largely autonomous but still working closely with history and philosophy, increased its lecture offerings and established an undergraduate major.

Since its inception the program has shared the international reputation of its leading faculty. In particular, Gillispie, together with Charles Scribner, Jr. '43, conceived and directed the monumental *Dictionary of Scientific Biography* (14 vols., N.Y., Scribner's, 1970-76); Carl G. Hempel published fundamental studies on the nature of scientific explanation; and Thomas S. Kuhn, in pursuing and defending the thesis of his *Structure of Scientific Revolutions* (Chicago, 1962) set the tone for contemporary discussions of the scientific enterprise.

Michael S. Mahoney

Holder Hall forms the large quadrangle on Nassau Street, three sides containing dormitory rooms, the fourth cloisters, the whole dominated by Holder Tower. Noteworthy features are the heavy, slate roofs and the leaded casement windows of the dormitory, the vaulted passages of the cloisters, and the unique finials atop the pinnacles on Holder Tower—four bronze tigers-rampant—which also function as weathervanes.

Holder Hall was given in 1909 by Margaret Olivia Sage, widow of the financier, Russell Sage, and named at her request for her ancestor, Christopher Holder, "a member of the Society of Friends in America in the Seventeenth Century," a tablet in the arch beneath the tower tells us, "devout, loving, loyal to duty, patient in suffering."

Holder Hall was erected on the site of the unmarked graveyard of the family of Nathanial FitzRandolph, one of the College's early benefactors who is memorialized by a tablet in the east arch and also by the FitzRandolph Gateway (q.v.).

Holder and the adjoining dining halls were both designed by Day and Klauder, who, "in this great group,"

Ralph Adams Cram said, "reach the highest point in their authoritative interpretation of Gothic as a living style."

Honorary degrees have been awarded by Princeton since its earliest days. The degree of Master of Arts, *honoris causa*, was conferred on the governor of the Province of New Jersey, Jonathan Belcher, at the College's first commencement in 1748. For the first century and a half, however, most degrees were conferred by the trustees at their stated meetings and the recipients informed of the honor by letter from the clerk.

In 1895 the trustees amended their by-laws to provide that thereafter no honorary degree should be conferred except upon a recipient present in person. The Sesquicentennial Celebration the following year was the first occasion when honorary graduands assembled for the formal conferring of their degrees. There were fifty-six, the largest company ever honored at one time.*

In 1905 Dean West (q.v.) inaugurated the practice of reading a formal citation as he presented each graduand; he continued to do this through 1925. Others who followed him as University Orator were Deans William F. Magie, Augustus Trowbridge, Luther P. Eisenhart, and Donald B. Aldrich; and trustees Roland S. Morris, Walter E. Hope, Frederick H. Osborn, Fordyce B. St. John, James F. Oates, Jr., and John B. Coburn.

A few persons have received two honorary degrees. John Gilbert Winant '13 received an A.M. in 1925 while governor of New Hampshire and an LL.D. in 1943 as ambassador to Great Britain. The first woman to receive an honorary degree was Willa Cather (Litt.D. 1931). Ralph J. Bunche, Undersecretary of the United Nations, was the first black to receive a degree *honoris causa* (LL.D. 1951).

CITATIONS

Excerpts from a few citations follow:

GEORGE WASHINGTON GOETHALS, chief engineer of the Panama Canal: Cleaving the rugged isthmus to join the severed oceans, he has opened a safe and stately roadway for the ships of every sea. (1915)

ALBERT EINSTEIN: So today for his genius and integrity we, who inadequately measure his power, salute the new Columbus of science, "voyaging through strange seas of thought alone." (1921)

FERDINAND FOCH, Marshal of France: When shall his glory fade? Not till free men forget their measureless debt to France. Not till they forget that energy of soul in accord with truth and honor is the one superlative mark of manhood. (1921)

WILDER GRAVES PENFIELD '13, neurosurgeon: A strong and gentle man, with extraordinary dexterity he penetrates the recesses of the human brain and restores to lives of usefulness and happiness those who had been facing the future without a single ray of hope. (1939)

HAROLD R. MEDINA '09, presiding judge at the 1949 Communist conspiracy trial: In one of the most turbulent trials, in the face of vehement provocation, he maintained the rules of jurisprudence with patient resolve, dignity, and justice. (1951)

FRANCIS CLARK WOOD '22, heart specialist: For more than four decades he has fulfilled literally the divine exhortation to ease the hearts of men. (1964)

ANDREW WYETH, artist: . . . Probing past the facade of nature he has made the peculiarly American banks of the Brandywine and the bony skeleton of Maine serve as universal metaphors for the mystery of existence. (1965)

ROBERT OPPENHEIMER, director, Institute for Advanced Study: Physicist and sailor, philosopher and horseman, linguist and cook, lover of fine wine and better poetry, he has added distinction to an already great Institute and strengthened the Princeton community of learning. (1966)

MARIANNE MOORE: From baseball to basilisks to Brooklyn, the subjects of her poetry have the great breadth of life itself . . . [she contemplates] the world around her, with a glance at once keen and compassionate. (1968)

JOHN M. DOAR '44, civil rights advocate (later chief counsel for the House Judiciary Committee at the impeachment hearings in 1974): To [his] integrity, skill, and . . . courage . . . the slow but inexorable march of civil rights owes much of its progress. . . . Undramatically braving mobs, . . . this nonviolent man has never feared violence in the pursuit of noble goals. (1968)

RUSSELL W. BAKER, *New York Times* columnist: His persuasive blend of amusement and outrage puts him in danger of becoming the very thing he so often takes to task, a revered American institution. (1969)

BOB DYLAN: . . . one of the most creative popular musicians of the last decade. . . . Although he is now approaching the perilous age of 30, his music remains the authentic expression of the disturbed and concerned conscience of young America. (1970)

JOAN GANZ COONEY, creator of *Sesame Street*: It has been said that the devil ought not have all the good tunes, and she has shown that the admen need not have all the fun. (1973)

SERETSE KHAMA, President, Republic of Botswana: The evenhandedness of his policies and the example of his life make him an inspiration to all who look upon his troubled region of the world with the anxiety of hope. (1976)

* One hundred thirteen honorary degrees were conferred during the year-long celebration of the Bicentennial in 1946-1947; the largest number at any one convocation was thirty-six.

Honor System, The, has been a cherished tradition at Princeton since its establishment in 1893. While it has undergone some procedural changes, its central principle has been upheld—that students accept full responsibility for their conduct in written examinations. There is no proctoring; and an examination paper must bear the signed pledge, substantially as it was first drawn: "I pledge my honor that, during this examination, I have neither given nor received assistance."

The Honor System had its origin in student dissatisfaction with faculty proctoring of examinations. In 1893 the *Daily Princetonian* called for the establishment of a system whereby students would have "sole charge of examinations." Such a plan had been introduced at William and Mary and followed at the University of Virginia, where Woodrow Wilson had known it. Princeton student leaders gained the support of Dean James O. Murray, who presented a proposal at a faculty meeting, where Wilson's eloquent plea brought a favorable vote. An immediate success, the Honor System attracted wide attention in the press and on other campuses.

In 1895 the first Constitution of the Honor System, not greatly different from the present one, was adopted. It designated an Honor Committee of six, and provided that if a student were found guilty of a violation, the committee would recommend to the faculty his separation from the College. For conviction, two of six votes were required; this was subsequently changed to five of six. By unanimous vote of the student body at a mass meeting in 1921 the committee was enlarged to seven members and authorized to recommend leniency in exceptional cases.

During the 1920s an attempt was made to extend "the Spirit of the Honor System" to "cover the whole life of the students," but it was soon apparent that this would erode the Honor System itself, and the scheme was abandoned. Since then the Honor System has applied, as originally intended, only to written examinations. All other cases of misconduct go to the Committee on Discipline, composed of students and faculty members.

In 1975 the Constitution was further amended to provide the possibility of a one-year separation as well as permanent separation from the University, to enumerate the rights of the accused, and to place the power to amend the Constitution with the undergraduate governing body rather than a mass meeting.

Two long-standing practices, not in the Constitution, have contributed to the strength of the Honor System. Each entering student must state, by personal letter to the Honor Committee, his willingness to abide by the system and to report any violation observed. The latter requirement has often been questioned, but was implicit in the compact between faculty and students in 1893, whereby the students assumed responsibility for the conduct of examinations with the understanding that the individual's responsibility to the undergraduate body as a whole transcends any reluctance to report a fellow student. A second time-honored custom is a meeting of all entering students at the beginning of the academic year, at which members of the Honor Committee and an outstanding alumnus entrust the Honor System to the new students.

The Honor System is less a set of rules than a state of mind—that honesty in examinations is assumed—and is a common bond among Princetonians.

Jeremiah S. Finch

Hosack, David (1769-1835), a leading physician of his day and an eminent botanist and mineralogist, had strong ties with both Princeton and Columbia. The son of a New York wine merchant who came to America to serve under Lord Jeffery Amherst in the French and Indian War, he attended Columbia for two years and then transferred to Princeton, where he received a bachelor's degree in 1789. He made the change partly to escape from the distractions of the city, and partly to obtain the benefits of instruction by the distinguished faculty then teaching in Nassau Hall—"attractions," he said, which he "could not resist."

He studied medicine, first in New York, then in Philadelphia, where he lived with the family of his favorite teacher Benjamin Rush 1760. He later studied medicine and botany in Edinburgh and mineralogy in London, bringing back from Great Britain the beginnings of a mineralogical collection that he later gave to Princeton.

He was, successively, professor of botany and materia medica at Columbia College, professor of the theory and practice of physic at the College of Physicians and Surgeons, and president of the short-lived Rutgers Medical College, which he helped found.

Early in his career, he established "in the vicinity" of New York—actually where Rockefeller Center now stands—the famous Elgin Botanic Garden, named for his father's birthplace in northern Scotland. Here each year, at the end of the spring term, he held a strawberry festival, in order, he once told another teacher, to let his students see that he was practical as well as theoretical. "The *fragaria* is a most appropriate aliment," he reminded his skeptical colleague; "Linnaeus cured his gout and protracted his life by strawberries." Among those who partook of his strawberries and of his botanical knowledge was John Torrey (q.v.), who later taught botany and chemistry at Princeton and Columbia.

Hosack's circle of friends included Aaron Burr, Jr. 1772, and Alexander Hamilton. As the surgeon in attendance at their duel in 1804, he treated Hamilton after he was mortally wounded; and he was one of the pallbearers at Hamilton's funeral. Three years later, after Burr was tried for treason and acquitted, Hosack lent him passage-money to go abroad in order to escape the notoriety resulting from the trial.

Princeton awarded Hosack an honorary LL.D. in 1818, and commissioned his portrait by Rembrandt Peale in 1826; it hangs in Upper Eagle Dining Hall. When his friend Bishop John Henry Hobart 1793 died in 1830, Hosack was elected to succeed him as a

vice president of the Alumni Association of Nassau Hall, of which James Madison was then president.

In his time, Hosack was considered one of New York's first citizens. He was influential in social and civic affairs as well as in his profession. He was a founder of the New York Historical Society and the American Academy of Fine Arts in addition to Bellevue Hospital, and "his house was the resort of the learned and the enlightened from every part of the world." According to one of his medical colleagues, it was often observed by citizens of New York that DeWitt Clinton, Bishop Hobart, and Dr. Hosack were "the tripod on which our city stood."

House of Representatives of the United States has not been without a Princeton alumnus in its membership in any year since it first met in 1789. All told, more than 200 Princetonians have represented twenty-eight states and territories in the lower house of Congress.

Seven members of the Class of 1805 served in the lower house of Congress, three of them from Georgia. In more recent times, the Class of 1954 contributed three members: William H. Hudnut of Indiana, Donald Rumsfeld of Illinois, and Paul S. Sarbanes of Maryland.

Following is a list of Princeton Representatives, compiled from biographical sketches in the 1972 edition of *The Biographical Directory of the American Congress*, supplemented by additional information from annual Congressional directories since then. Where known, the Representative's party affiliation is given in parenthesis, viz.: American (A), Anti-Federalist (AF), Democratic (D), Federalist (F), Free Soiler (FS), Independent (I), Republican (R), Union War (UW), Whig (W).

ALABAMA

James T. Jones 1852 (D) 1877-1879, 1883-1889

Arthur Glenn Andrews '31 (R) 1965-1967

TERRITORY OF ARKANSAS

James W. Bates 1807 1819-1823

CALIFORNIA

John C.W. Hinshaw '16 (R) 1939-1956

COLORADO

Robert F. Rockwell '09 (R) 1941-1949

CONNECTICUT

Henry W. Edwards 1797 (D) 1819-1823

Stewart B. McKinney '53 (R) 1970-

DELAWARE

Gunning Bedford, Jr. 1771 1789

James A. Bayard 1784 (F) 1797-1803

James M. Broom 1794 (F) 1805-1807

Nicholas Van Dyke, Jr. 1788 (F) 1807-1811

Kensey Johns, Jr. 1810 (F) 1827-1830

Thomas Robinson, Jr. 1823 (D) 1839-1841

George B. Rodney 1820 (W) 1841-1845

William G. Whiteley 1838 (D) 1857-1861

Harry G. Haskell, Jr. '44 (R) 1957-1959

Pierre S. DuPont IV '56 (R) 1970-1976

GEORGIA

Peter Early 1792 1803-1807

George M. Troup 1797 (D) 1807-1815

John Forsyth 1799 (D) 1813-1818, 1823-1827

Thomas Telfair 1805 (D) 1813-1817

Alfred Cuthbert 1803 (D) 1813-1816, 1821-1827

John A. Cuthbert 1805 (D) 1819-1821

James M. Wayne 1808 (D) 1829-1835

Walter T. Colquitt 1820 1839-1840 (W), 1842-1843 (D)

Richard W. Habersham 1805 (D) 1839-1842

George W. Crawford 1820 (W) 1843

Alfred Iverson 1820 (D) 1847-1849

Alfred H. Colquitt 1844 (D) 1853-1855

ILLINOIS

Donald H. Rumsfeld '54 (R) 1963-1969

INDIANA

William H. Hudnut '54 (R) 1972-1974

KENTUCKY

*Addison White (W) 1851-1853

Thomas L. Jones 1840 (D) 1867-1871, 1875-1877

LOUISIANA

Edward Livingston 1781 (D) 1823-1829

MARYLAND

Samuel Smith 1795 (D) 1793-1803, 1816-1822

John Archer 1760 (D) 1804-1807

*Patrick Magruder 1805-1807

Stevenson Archer 1805 (D) 1811-1817

Thomas Bayley 1797 (D) 1817-1823

William H. Heyward, Jr. 1808 (D) 1823-1825

Ephraim K. Wilson 1789 (D) 1827-1831

Benjamin C. Howard 1809 (D) 1829-1833, 1835-1839

John T. Stoddert 1810 (D) 1833-1835

Richard B. Carmichael 1828 (D) 1833-1835

James A. Pearce 1822 (W) 1835-1839, 1841-1843

John T. Mason 1836 (D) 1841-1843

Joseph S. Cottman 1823 (W) 1851-1853

*Thomas F. Bowie (D) 1855-1859

Charles E. Phelps 1852 (U) 1865-1869

Stevenson Archer 1846 (D) 1867-1875

John V. Findlay 1858 (D) 1883-1887

Barnes Compton 1851 (D) 1885-1889, 1891-1894

John K. Cowen 1866 (D) 1895-1897

George A. Pearre 1880 (R) 1899-1911
Daniel B. Brewster '46 (D) 1959-1963
Clarence D. Long Ph.D. '38 (D) 1962-
Paul. S. Sarbanes '54 (D) 1970-1976

MASSACHUSETTS
John Bacon 1765 (D) 1801-1803
Jonathan Mason, Jr. 1774 (F)
    1817-1820
Abram P. Andrews, Jr. 1893 (R)
    1921-1936

TERRITORY OF MICHIGAN
*John Biddle (W) 1829-1831

MISSISSIPPI
*Henry G. Ellett (D) 1847

MISSOURI
Francis P. Blair, Jr. 1841 (FS)
    1857-1864
Roger C. Slaughter '28 (D) 1943-1947

NEW HAMPSHIRE
Samuel Livermore 1752 1789-1793

NEW JERSEY
Jonathan Dayton 1776 (F) 1791-1799
John Beatty 1769 1793-1795
Isaac Smith 1755 (F) 1795-1797
Thomas Henderson 1761 1795-1797
John H. Imlay 1786 (F) 1797-1801
James Linn 1769 (D) 1799-1801
John A. Scudder 1775 (D) 1810-1811
George C. Maxwell 1792 1811-1813
Richard Stockton 1779 (F) 1813-1815
Thomas Ward 1803 (D) 1813-1817
George Holcombe 1805 (D) 1821-1828
Isaac Pierson 1789 (W) 1827-1831
Silas Condit 1795 (D) 1831-1833
William Chetwood 1792 (D)
    1836-1837
William Halsted 1812 (W) 1837-1839,
    1841-1843
John P.B. Maxwell 1823 (W)
    1837-1839, 1841-1843
Littleton Kirkpatrick 1815 (D)
    1843-1845
James G. Hampton 1835 (W)
    1845-1849
George H. Brown 1828 (W) 1851-1853

Isaiah D. Clawson 1840 (W) 1855-1859
William Pennington 1813 (W)
    1859-1861
John L.N. Stratton 1836 (R) 1859-1863
John T. Nixon 1841 (R) 1859-1863
Charles Haight 1857 (D) 1867-1871
Frederick H. Teese 1843 (D)
    1875-1877
George M. Robeson 1847 (R)
    1879-1883
Henry S. Harris 1870 (D) 1881-1883
Robert S. Green 1850 (D) 1885-1887
Christopher A. Bergen 1863 (R)
    1889-1893
Samuel Fowler 1873 (D) 1889-1893
Mahlon Pitney 1879 (R) 1895-1899
Richard W. Parker 1867 (R)
    1895-1911, 1911-1919, 1921-1923
Ira W. Wood 1877 (R) 1904-1913
Walter I. McCoy 1881 (D) 1911-1914
Charles Browne 1896 (D) 1923-1925
Elmer H. Geran 1899 (D) 1923-1925
Franklin W. Fort '01 (R) 1925-1931
Charles R. Howell '27 (D) 1949-1955
Alfred D. Sieminski '34 (D) 1951-1959
Peter H.B. Frelinghuysen '38 (R)
    1953-1974

NEW YORK
Thomas Treadwell 1764 1791-1795
Edward Livingston 1781 1795-1801
L. Conrad Elmendorf 1782 (D)
    1797-1803
William Kirkpatrick 1788 (D)
    1807-1809
Robert L. Livingston 1784 (F)
    1809-1812
William S. Smith 1774 (F) 1813-1815
Nathaniel W. Howell 1788 1813-1815
James Wilkin 1785 (D) 1815-1819
Silas Wood 1789 (D) 1819-1829
Stephen Van Rensselaer 1783
    1822-1829
Samuel W. Eager 1809 (R) 1830-1831
Samuel J. Wilkin 1812 (D) 1831-1833
William Seymour 1821 (D) 1835-1837
Andrew D. Bruyn 1810 (D) 1837-1838

Obadiah Bowne 1841 (W) 1851-1853
Alexander H. Bailey 1837 (R)
  1867-1871
George B. McClellan 1886 (D)
  1895-1903
Charles A. Talcott 1879 (D) 1911-1915
Walter G. Andrews '13 (R) 1931-1941
Ralph A. Gamble '09 (R) 1937-1957
William F. Ryan '44 (D) 1961-1973
Otis G. Pike '43 (D) 1961-

NORTH CAROLINA
Nathaniel Macon 1777 (D) 1791-1815
David Stone 1788 (D) 1799-1801
*Willis Alston (D) 1799-1815,
  1825-1831
Nathaniel Alexander 1776 1801-1805
Evan Alexander 1787 1806-1809
William Gaston 1796 (F) 1813-1817
James W. Clark 1797 (D) 1815-1817
Jesse Bynum 1821 (D) 1833-1841
William Montgomery 1808 (D)
  1835-1841
Abraham W. Venable 1819 (D)
  1847-1853
Lawrence O. Branch 1838 (D)
  1855-1861
Richmond Pearson 1872 (R) 1895-1901
Lunsford R. Preyer '41 (D) 1961-
James G. Martin Ph.D. '60 (R) 1972-

OHIO
*Joseph H. Crane (W) 1829-1837
George White 1895 (D) 1911-1915,
  1917-1919
Michael A. Feighan '27 (D) 1943-1971

PENNSYLVANIA
John W. Kittera 1776 (F) 1791-1801
*James Armstrong (F) 1793-1795
David Bard 1773 1795-1799,
  1803-1815
John A. Hanna 1782 (AF) 1797-1805
William Crawford 1781 (D) 1809-1817
Amos Ellmaker 1805 1815-1816
John Sergeant 1795 (F) 1815-1823,
  1827-1829, 1837-1841
John Wurts 1813 (R) 1825-1827

Thomas H. Crawford 1804 (D)
  1829-1833
Alem Marr 1807 (D) 1829-1831
John G. Watmough 1811 1831-1835
George Chambers 1804 (W)
  1833-1837
Joseph R. Ingersoll 1804 (W)
  1835-1837, 1841-1849
Samuel W. Morris 1806 (D) 1837-1841
George W. Toland 1816 (W)
  1837-1843
*George M. Keim (D) 1838-1843
Henry Nes 1824 (I) 1843-1845,
  1847-1850
James Pollock 1831 (W) 1844-1849
Chester Butler 1817 (W) 1847-1850
Thomas Ross 1825 (D) 1849-1853
Henry M. Fuller 1839 (W) 1851-1853,
  1855-1857
William L. Dewart 1841 (D)
  1857-1859
Robert McKnight 1839 (R) 1859-1863
Charles J. Biddle 1837 (D) 1861-1863
William H. Armstrong 1847 (R)
  1869-1871
James D. Strawbridge 1844 (R)
  1873-1875
Hiester Clymer 1847 (D) 1873-1881
Edward Overton, Jr. 1856 (R)
  1877-1881
Harry White 1854 (R) 1877-1881
James B. Everhart 1842 (R) 1883-1887
John A. Swope 1847 (D) 1884-1887
Welty McCullogh 1870 (R) 1887-1889
Lawrence H. Watres '04 (R)
  1923-1931
William E. Richardson '10 (D)
  1933-1937

SOUTH CAROLINA
Robert G. Harper 1785 (F) 1795-1801
John Taylor 1790 (D) 1807-1810

TENNESSEE
George W. Campbell 1794 (D)
  1803-1809
John Rhea 1780 (D) 1803-1815,
  1817-1823

Nathaniel G. Taylor 1840 (W)
    1854-1855, 1866-1867
Hubert F. Fisher A.M. '01 (D)
    1917-1931

TEXAS
David S. Kaufman 1833 (D) 1846-1851
George W. Smyth 1831 (D) 1853-1855
Dudley G. Wooten 1875 (D)
    1901-1903
Joseph W. Bailey, Jr. '15 (D)
    1933-1935
Bruce R. Alger '40 (R) 1955-1965

VERMONT
Nathaniel Niles 1766 1791-1795

VIRGINIA
James Madison 1771 (D) 1789-1797
*John Brown 1789-1792
William B. Giles 1781 1790-1798 (AF),
    1801-1803 (D)
Abraham B. Venable 1780 1791-1799
Henry Lee, Jr. 1773 (F) 1799-1801
John Randolph 1791 (D) 1799-1813,
    1815-1817, 1819-1825, 1827-1829
Thomas M. Bayley 1794 (D)
    1813-1815
Charles F. Mercer 1797 (D) 1817-1839
Edward Colston 1806 (F) 1817-1819
*Robert S. Garnett (D) 1817-1827
Alfred H. Powell 1799 1825-1827
George W. Crump 1805 (D)
    1826-1827
John M. Patton 1816 (D) 1830-1838
*John J. Roane (D) 1831-1833
James H. Gholson 1820 (D) 1833-1835
James McDowell 1816 (D) 1846-1851
Alexander R. Boteler 1835 (A)
    1859-1861

WEST VIRGINIA
James M. Jackson 1845 (D) 1889-1890
Joseph H. Gaines 1886 (R) 1901-1911

* Although attendance at Princeton was indicated in the *Biographical Directory of the American Congress*, precise confirmation of the fact was
not possible when this list was completed. (None
of the unconfirmed cases was counted in determining Princeton's record of continued representation since 1789.)

Hudnut, William H. 1886 (1864-1963)
was the patriarch of a numerous and
distinguished Princeton family. He had
two Princeton sons—Herbert B. Hudnut '16 and William H. Hudnut, Jr.
'27—and seven Princeton grandsons—
Henry Hudnut Bischoff '49, Herbert B.
Hudnut, Jr. '53, William H. Hudnut
III '54, Robert K. Hudnut '56, David
B. Hudnut '57, Stewart S. Hudnut '61,
and Thomas C. Hudnut '69.

Both of his sons followed him into the
Presbyterian ministry as did two of his
grandsons, one of whom, William H.
Hudnut III '54, was congressman from
Indiana and later mayor of In-
dianapolis.

In a talk at an Alumni Day luncheon
in his senior year Stewart S. Hudnut
'61 spoke of the strong Presbyterian
and Princeton influences in his upbringing. His earliest childhood recol-
lection, he said, was of singing two
songs, "Jesus Loves Me" and "Going
Back to Nassau Hall."

The year Stewart graduated, the
University conferred an honorary degree on his grandfather who was celebrating the seventy-fifth anniversary of
his graduation.

Dr. Hudnut became the oldest living
graduate in 1962. Acknowledging word
of this distinction, he declared in the
Alumni Weekly: "My lot has been cast
with wonderful people and to those that
survive I give a cheer. I thank God that
my education was in Princeton and I
bless the University as it moves into the
light." He died in 1963 just short of his
ninety-ninth birthday.

Humanities, The Council of the, was
established in 1953 as a means of fostering significant teaching and research in
the humanities. Its program was devised by a faculty committee headed by
Professor Whitney J. Oates, and including Professors Carlos H. Baker, E.B.O.

Borgerhoff, Donald D. Egbert, George A. Graham, E. Harris Harbison, Harry H. Hess, Arthur K. Parpart, Allen G. Shenstone, E. Baldwin Smith, Joseph R. Strayer, and Ledger Wood.

On the premise that there is no study in the University that does not have humanistic aspects, the Council is governed by a committee consisting of a representative from each of the humanistic departments and also single representatives from the natural sciences, the social sciences, architecture, and engineering. This committee, in addition to its other duties, administers the Council's endowment, determines long-range policy in carrying out its purposes, supervises and coordinates interdepartmental programs in the humanities and nominates Fellows of the Council.

Six previously established programs came under the purview of the Council at its founding: the Special Program in the Humanities (superseded in 1964 by the Committee on Humanistic Studies), the Creative Arts Program (later divided into programs in Creative Writing, Theatre and Dance, and the Visual Arts), the Christian Gauss Seminars in Criticism, and programs in American, European, and Near Eastern studies. Subsequently, the Council helped develop programs in linguistics, classical philosophy, political philosophy, and comparative literature which became a department in 1975.

Regarded as the equivalent of "distinguished professors," Fellows of the Council devote up to half their time to teaching and the balance to research. Their work has led, in many instances, to the development of new teaching programs and to important publications. During their tenure as Fellows in 1957-1958, English professor Lawrance R. Thompson began his biography of Robert Frost, and politics professor Al-

pheus T. Mason brought to completion his work *In Quest of Freedom*. Two years earlier, historian Charles C. Gillispie had used his fellowship to work on an essay in the history of scientific ideas, later published as *The Edge of Objectivity*, and to prepare and conduct a course that eventually led to the University's program in the history and philosophy of science.

As Visiting Fellow in 1957-1958, Brown University classicist W. Freeman Twaddell, then president of the Linguistic Society of America, gave courses in linguistics and also acted as adviser to a Humanities Council subcommittee, which was planning a linguistics program, begun several years later. Another Visiting Fellow, I. I. Rabi, Columbia's Nobel laureate in physics, stimulated the development of a program in Science in Human Affairs and continued to act as its consultant for a number of years. Among other Visiting Fellows have been Martin Buber, Hannah Arendt, Rosamund Tuve, Richard Hofstadter, Reinhold Niebuhr, Erwin Panofsky, Isaiah Berlin, Denis Brogan, Elizabeth Bowen, Anthony Burgess, René Wellek, and Philip Roth.

A later development has brought the appointment of another group of Visiting Fellows for brief but intensive periods of one or two weeks. Each of these "Short-Term Fellows" undertakes a coordinated program of participation in graduate seminars, departmental colloquia, public lectures, and other activities involving them fully in the University community.

In the 1960s the Council sponsored a project to appraise American humanistic scholarship during the preceding several decades. This endeavor, undertaken on the invitation of the Ford Foundation, which made a $335,000 grant for the purpose, was planned by a subcommittee of the Council; its director, Rutgers historian Richard Schlatter, and many of the thirty-five scholars who participated were in residence in Princeton as Fellows of the Council while engaged on the project. Their work resulted in fifteen volumes of *The Princeton Studies: Humanistic Scholarship in America*, published by Prentice-Hall.

In its early years the work of the Council was underwritten by a grant from the Carnegie Corporation of New York. Other grants came later from the United States Steel Foundation, the George W. Perkins Foundation, and the Old Dominion Foundation. In 1962 the work of the Council was given added impetus by a $500,000 grant from the Avalon Foundation to endow a chair in the humanities.

Chairmen of the Council's interdepartmental committee have been Whitney J. Oates, professor of classics and first incumbent of the Avalon chair, 1953-1970; Samuel D. Atkins, professor of classics, 1970-1971; A. Walton Litz, Jr., professor of English, 1971-1974; and Edward D. Sullivan, professor of French and comparative literature and Oates's successor as Avalon professor, since 1974.

Ice hockey came into prominence at Princeton at the turn of the century. In those early days, the game consisted of two twenty-minute halves, and play was slower (there was a good deal of high lofting of the puck by the defense men), but according to Gresham Poe '02, one of the first Varsity players, much excitement was generated by bodychecking, "which was immensely enjoyed by the customers." The teams worked out on Stony Brook whenever it froze over but, because of the milder New Jersey winters, they had fewer chances for practice than their New England rivals.

Princeton was one of the founding members of an intercollegiate hockey league, which started in 1899. The first three championships of this league were won by Yale, the next three by Harvard. In 1907, when newly completed Lake Carnegie provided a better place for practice, Princeton gave Harvard its first defeat in four years, and won its first championship. Princeton won its second championship in 1910, when goaltender Clarence N. Peacock '10 allowed league opponents only two goals in five games, and rover Alfred G. Kay '12 scored half of Princeton's twelve goals.

Princeton took the championship again in 1912 and 1914, narrowly missing out in 1913, when it lost two out of three games to Harvard. This was Princeton's golden age of hockey, highlighted by the brilliant play of Hobey Baker '14, universally recognized at that time as the greatest amateur hockey player ever developed in the United States. Playing rover (a position eliminated in 1921, when hockey teams were reduced from seven to six players), he thrilled spectators with his ability to weave his way through the opposing team, change his pace and direction, and send the puck speeding into the net.

Baker, who served with distinction as a pilot and squadron commander with the A.E.F. in the First World War, was killed in an airplane crash soon after the armistice and just before his scheduled return to America. With funds contributed by his Princeton friends and admirers from many other colleges, Princeton built the Hobart Baker Memorial Rink (q.v.), which was dedicated on January 6, 1923.

Princeton had many fine teams in the

twenties and thirties, especially those in 1923 (12 victories, 5 defeats, and one tie), 1924 (11-6), 1929 (15-3-1), 1931 (14-5), 1932 (13-4-1) and 1933 (15-4); but it had to wait until 1941 for another championship. That year Princeton took first place in the Quadrangular League over Dartmouth, Harvard, and Yale, and the Hobey Baker Memorial Trophy came home for the first time since it was put up in 1934. Dan Stuckey '42 was the leading scorer on a team that was further remarkable for having in its line-up two sets of brothers: Captain George Young '41 and Don Young '43, and twins Bill and Jim Sloane '43.

Hockey suffered a four-year hiatus when Baker Rink was boarded over for use as a gym between the loss of the University Gymnasium by fire in 1944 and the completion of Dillon in 1947. Six years later Princeton had sufficiently recovered its momentum to win the Pentagonal League championship over Brown, Dartmouth, Harvard, and Yale.

The 1953 championship was due, in no small part, to the leadership of the captain, All-American center Hank Bothfeld, who set a three-year Princeton record of 103 points (i.e. the total of goals and assists), while drawing only three penalties. This team also included two brothers, Bill Gall '53, who set a one-season Princeton record of 40 points in 1951, and Peter Gall '54.

Bothfeld's career record was broken in 1960 by John McBride '60, who made 118 points in three years; he also bettered Gall's one-season record twice, raising it in 1959 to 44 points, and in 1960 to 54 points. McBride's three-year record was surpassed in 1963 by Johnny Cook '63, who during his varsity career made a total of 132 goals and assists.

In the sixties the 1968 team was outstanding; it had a 13-10-1 record and qualified for the E.C.A.C. post-season tournament, but lost there to Cornell, whose All-American goalie was the renowned Ken Dryden.

Keene Fitzpatrick, well-known track coach and football trainer, was Princeton's first hockey coach; he directed the three teams that Hobey Baker played on. Best known of his successors were three Ivy League products: Pudge Neidlinger, Dartmouth '23; Dick Vaughan, Yale '28; and Norm Wood, Harvard '54. Vaughan coached from 1935 through 1959, far longer than anyone else. A devoted student of the game, in 1939 he published a book on hockey that has been widely used by other coaches. In recent years two former professional players have been coaches: John Wilson of Detroit and the New York Rangers, from 1965 to 1967, and Bill Quackenbush of Detroit and Boston, from 1967 to 1973. Jack Semler, University of Vermont '68, was coach from 1973 to 1977 and was succeeded by Jim Higgins, Boston University '63, previously coach at Colgate.

A women's ice hockey team, first organized in 1972-1973, improved steadily and in 1977 finished second in the Ivy League.

Industrial Relations Section. At Princeton industrial relations connotes a broad range of interests and activities. Within its traditional orbit are the areas of personnel administration, unionism, collective bargaining, the economics of the labor market, and management organization and development, as well as company benefit plans and government social security programs. More recently, the Industrial Relations Section has broadened its scope to include analysis of manpower and educational systems in developing countries, the financing of education in the United States, race relations and discrimination in employment, and the new and expanding area of economics known as "investment-in-man" or human capital.

The Industrial Relations Section itself was inaugurated in 1922, at the suggestion of Clarence J. Hicks of the Standard Oil Company (New Jersey). Hicks, a pioneer in the progressive movement of personnel administration in large-scale industry, was instrumental in securing funds from John D. Rockefeller, Jr., to establish the section on a trial basis. Later Rockefeller provided a permanent endowment, and his son, John D. Rockefeller III, provided additional funds, which were subsequently augmented by contributions from over sixty companies and six national unions. By 1975, the section's annual income from endowment was well over $150,000, and additional funds were being provided by foundation and government grants for specific projects.

The section has had five directors. Robert F. Foerster was called from Harvard to start the enterprise. He was succeeded in 1926 by J. Douglas Brown, who, in a very real sense, was the section's philosopher, prime mover, and builder. He developed its program, inspired its researchers, raised money for its endowment, and was its guiding spirit for nearly thirty years. He was succeeded by Frederick H. (Fizz) Harbison, who served as director from 1955 to 1968; since then Albert Rees and Orley Ashenfelter have alternately served as director.

Throughout its history, the section has functioned as a clearinghouse of information for students, business executives, union leaders, and government officials. It has the oldest and one of the best industrial relations library services in the country, provides financial support for the research of graduate students and faculty members, and is the workshop for hundreds of undergraduates writing course papers and senior theses. It has always been housed in the university library, since 1948 in space provided by a gift from the Class of 1926.

Outside of Princeton, the section was probably best known for its annual fall Conference on Industrial Relations. For over twenty years, starting in 1931, these conferences, artfully led by J. Douglas Brown, were revered by the blue-chip corporations in America as a strategic instrument in development of personnel administration and the management of human resources in industry. Later, as other organizations expanded their activity in this area, the section turned to conferences on major issues in public policy and on research in the various branches of industrial relations.

The contributions of members of the section's core group have been numerous and significant. Brown was one of the principal architects of our nation's social security system. Richard A. Lester's research and government service in collective bargaining, social security, manpower economics, and employment of women are held in the highest esteem. Harbison was a pioneer in the formulation and testing of "the manpower approach" to educational planning in developing countries. Brown, Lester, and Harbison helped organize and were subsequently presidents of the Industrial Relations Research Association. William G. Bowen made significant contributions to the theory of wages. Ashenfelter has been a leading figure particularly in the measurement of racial and minority discrimination in industrial employment. And Albert Rees was called in 1974 by President Ford to head the nation's Council on Wages and Prices.

Last, mention needs to be made of the contributions of several of these men in the central administration of the University. J. Douglas Brown became dean of the faculty and later provost. Richard A. Lester was also dean of the faculty. William G. Bowen became provost and later president. Albert Rees was also provost. One might conclude with good reason that the association of these men with industrial relations at Princeton explains, at least in part, their excellent record of performance as university administrators.

Frederick H. Harbison

Institute for Advanced Study, The, although organically and administratively separate from Princeton University, has had, since its founding in 1930, close academic and intellectual relations with the University. Originally housed in Fine Hall, it soon developed its own institutional center in a square mile of beautifully wooded land at the southern edge of Princeton beyond the Graduate College and near the battlefield. The Institute's primary purpose has been "the pursuit of advanced learning and exploration in fields of pure science and high scholarship." It awards no degrees and usually admits to membership scholars who have already taken their highest degree.

The first director of the Institute was Abraham Flexner, who was succeeded in 1939 by Frank Aydelotte, in 1947 by Robert Oppenheimer, in 1966 by Carl Kaysen, and in 1976 by Harry Woolf. The Institute's endowment, provided by Louis Bamberger and his sister Mrs.

Felix Fuld, is administered by a board of trustees of fifteen members.

Since its earliest years, the Institute has held an eminent position in the fields of pure mathematics and mathematical physics. Albert Einstein and John von Neumann were among the creative leaders on its distinguished faculty. As years have passed, the Institute has expanded its areas of coverage. While the members of the School of Mathematics remain for the most part pure mathematicians, the members of the School of Natural Sciences are generally theoretical physicists, astrophysicists, and astronomers, with some who have worked in other sciences such as chemistry, biology, and psychology. The School of Historical Studies is broader in scope, including all learning for which the use of the historical method is a principal instrument. The major interests of the faculty have, however, been in Greek archaeology, philosophy and philology; Roman history; medieval history; and the history of philosophy and science. The School of Social Science is of more recent origin and has emphasized the use of the methods and perspectives of the various social sciences with the aim of elucidating the processes of social change.

The professors of the Institute carry on their scholarly work without having to offer formal courses or give examinations. Rather, the emphasis is upon the informal interaction of scholars in a community of scholars.

The Institute provides facilities for residence and study for approximately one hundred and fifty visiting members who are admitted each year for short periods to pursue scholarly projects away from their normal duties at their home institutions. These visiting members come from all parts of America, with approximately a third from Europe and Asia.

While the Institute maintains residential and other facilities necessary for academic life and provides the opportunities for continuing intellectual interaction within its own community of scholars, it also gains from a symbiotic relationship with the University, with its wider range of disciplines and larger faculty. A small, working library at the Institute is buttressed by the libraries of the University, to which Institute members have full access.

There is much opportunity for interchange and cooperation on an informal basis between the faculties of the University and the Institute, and the Princeton academic community has been enriched not only by the presence of distinguished members of the Institute's permanent faculty, but also by a flow of internationally recognized visiting scholars.

J. Douglas Brown

International Finance Section, The, which is associated with the Department of Economics, was established in 1929 to provide research as well as research training in a field of increasing importance in world affairs. Its first director, Edwin W. Kemmerer, had been chairman of commissions to stabilize the finances of ten countries on five continents. He had noticed a scarcity of qualified specialists and found that Princeton was singularly well equipped to train the needed experts.

The section was funded chiefly by a gift of $490,000 from Gerard B. Lambert '08 and his family in memory of James Theodore Walker '27, who died in an airplane accident two days after his graduation. Additional gifts, including $20,000 from Kemmerer himself,

together with funds transferred from general endowment, gave the Walker Foundation of International Finance a value of $690,000 in 1930. Its income has financed the section and the Walker Professorship of Economics and International Finance.

During the early years Frank Dunstan Graham, Frank Whitson Fetter, and Charles Ray Whittlesey were associated with Kemmerer, who was both Walker Professor and director of the section. After Kemmerer's death in 1945, Graham became Walker Professor. In 1949, Gardner Patterson was brought in to direct the section; associated with him in its research were Friedrich A. Lutz, and Jacob Viner, who on Graham's death in 1949, became Walker Professor.

Patterson relinquished the directorship in 1958, and Viner retired as Walker Professor in 1960. Thereupon, the two positions were reunited: Fritz Machlup was called from Johns Hopkins to serve in both capacities. On Machlup's retirement in 1971, Peter B. Kenen, called from Columbia, assumed both positions.

The major achievements of the section are threefold: (1) research and research training, (2) publications of singular importance and timeliness, and (3) organization of conferences with great influence on governmental and intergovernmental policies. The research findings of the directors and associates of the section have been published in five different series of essays, papers, and studies, as well as in scores of books and articles. Probably no other single source of knowledge on international financial affairs has been more extensively used and cited by scholars and writers in this field than the publications of the section.

The usefulness of the conferences is

demonstrated by the number of top officials of national governments and international organizations who participate. The "Joint Conference of Officials and Academics on International Monetary Reform," first convened in Bellagio, Italy, and widely known as the Bellagio Group, met eighteen times between 1964 and 1977, in Bellagio, Washington, and Princeton, as well as in eight other European centers. Another series of conferences, held in Bürgenstock, Switzerland, which became known as the Bürgenstock Group, included also practitioners from the private sector—executives of commercial banks and multinational corporations. Both types of conferences have been credited with having had a wholesome influence on international negotiations in monetary affairs.

Fritz Machlup

International Studies, The Center of, traces its antecedents to the Yale Institute of International Studies (1935-1951), whose director, Frederick S. Dunn '14, came to Princeton with seven associates in 1951. First incumbent of the Milbank Professorship of International Law and Practice, Dunn was director of the Center until he retired in 1961 when he was succeeded as director by Klaus Knorr (public affairs), who had come with him from Yale. Cyril E. Black (history) became third director in 1968.

The Center, which draws its membership from Princeton faculty and pre-doctoral students and visiting scholars from other institutions, encourages research in two interrelated fields—international relations (e.g., studies of world order, foreign policy, military affairs) and national development (studies of comparative politics and of modernization in countries at various levels of development). The Center's members include economists, historians, and sociologists as well as political scientists, and many of its group research projects involve multidisciplinary, comparative, and cross-cultural approaches.

The Center's Program in World Order Studies, which focuses on problems associated with developing a just and peaceful world order, was established in 1970 with a grant from Randolph P. Compton '15 and Mrs. Compton. Younger scholars are awarded predoctoral and postdoctoral fellowships named for the Comptons' son John Parker Compton '47, who was killed in World War II.

One of this program's first projects, "The Future of the International Legal Order," was directed by Cyril Black and Richard A. Falk (Dunn's successor as Milbank Professor), with the participaton of some forty scholars from twenty-eight institutions in this country and abroad. In 1973, the first four volumes that had resulted from this project received the Annual Award of the American Society of International Law, which cited the editors for having "persuaded some of the world's ablest minds to apply their highest talents to our most important problems."

Additional research and publication at the Center has involved a broad range of topics, including the modernization of Japan and Russia, the modernization of China, thermonuclear war, the politics of developing areas, revolution, guerilla warfare, problems of ecology.

Besides issuing research monographs and policy memoranda from time to time, the Center sponsors *World Politics,* an academic quarterly in international relations and national develop-

ment which political scientists rated
highest in quality among sixty-three
professional journals in its field in a
1975 survey. Ninety books were written under the Center's auspices during
its first quarter century, half of them by
scholars from other institutions in this
country and abroad.

Support of the Center has been provided by income from an endowment,
by appropriations from the Woodrow
Wilson School, and by University general funds. The Center has also received support from the Rockefeller,
Ford, and Compton Foundations, from
the Carnegie Corporation, from numerous individual gifts, and from various research agencies of the federal
government.

Ivy League is the name generally
applied to eight universities (Brown,
Columbia, Cornell, Dartmouth, Harvard, Pennsylvania, Princeton, and
Yale) that over the years have had
common interests in scholarship as well
as in athletics. Stanley Woodward, *New
York Herald Tribune* sports writer,
coined the phrase in the early thirties.

In 1936 the undergraduate newspapers of these universities simultaneously ran an editorial advocating the
formation of an "Ivy League," but the
first move toward this end was not
taken until 1945. In that year, the eight
presidents entered into an agreement
"for the purpose of reaffirming their intention of continuing intercollegiate
football in such a way as to maintain the
values of the game, while keeping it in
fitting proportion to the main purposes
of academic life." To achieve this objective two inter-university committees
were appointed: one, made up primarily of the college deans, was to administer rules of eligibility; the other,
composed of the athletic directors, was

to establish policies on the length of the
playing season and of preseason practice, operating budgets, and related
matters. Two other inter-university
committees on admission and financial
aid were added later.

As President Dodds pointed out at
the time, the general principles agreed
on by the eight universities were essentially the same as those set forth in the
Harvard-Yale-Princeton   Presidents'
Agreement of 1916 (see *Big Three*).

The first step toward organizing full
league competition came in 1952 with
the announcement that, beginning with
the fall of 1953, each college would play
every other college in the group at least
once every five years. This plan was
superseded in 1954 when the presidents announced the adoption of a
yearly round-robin schedule in football,
starting in 1956, and approved the
principle of similar schedules in "as
many sports as practicable."

Thereafter, the Ivy Group (as the
league was called in the Presidents'
Agreement of 1954) established
schedules in other sports, including
some in existing leagues with non-Ivy
members. As of 1977, the Ivy League
colleges competed, round-robin, in
football, soccer, basketball, and, with
certain variations as noted, in baseball
(also Army and Navy), fencing (except
Brown and Dartmouth), ice hockey
(except Columbia), squash (except
Brown, Columbia, and Cornell), swimming (except Columbia, but also Army
and Navy), tennis (also Army and
Navy), and wrestling (except Brown
and Dartmouth). Ivy championships in
cross-country and track were determined at the annual Heptagonal Meets,
in golf at an Ivy championship tournament, and in rowing at the Eastern Association of Rowing Colleges Regatta.

The mid-seventies brought the inclusion of women's teams in the Ivy League program with the institution of championship tournaments in basketball and ice hockey, and a move toward round-robin competition in field hockey, lacrosse, and other sports.

Other instances of increasing formalization of the Ivy League occurred in the seventies—two of them involving Princetonians.

Since 1971, the Bushnell Cup has been awarded to the Ivy football player of the year, who is selected by vote of the eight coaches. This trophy, presented to the Ivy League by the Eastern Association of Intercollegiate Football Officials, was named in honor of Asa S. Bushnell '21, the first commissioner of the Eastern College Athletic Conference, in appreciation of "his great contribution to the advancement of college athletics."

In 1973, to provide greater coordination of the athletic interests of the eight universities, the post of executive director of the Council of Ivy League Presidents was created, and Ricardo A. Mestres '31, financial vice-president and treasurer of the University, emeritus, was elected first incumbent. Mestres served in this post until 1976, when he was succeeded by James M. Litvack, visiting lecturer in economics and public affairs in the University.

Jadwin Gymnasium is a memorial to Leander Stockwell Jadwin '28, who was captain of the track team his senior year and who died of injuries suffered in an automobile accident in New York eight months after his graduation. He was, his teammate John McG. Dalenz '28 said at the gymnasium's dedication forty years later, "a young man who was dedicated but light-hearted, accomplished but with great modesty, competitive but magnanimous." One Sat-

urday in his senior year, Dalenz related, Jadwin went to New York to run in an A.A.U. indoor track meet. The next morning when his roommates asked him how he had done, he replied, "Oh, I didn't do so badly." It wasn't until they saw the headline in the *New York Times* that they realized the extent of his understatement: "Princeton's Jadwin Ties High Hurdle World Record."

When Jadwin's mother died in 1965, she left the University an unrestricted bequest of $27 million, and because the Jadwin family had some years earlier expressed an interest in a fieldhouse for indoor track and had made a substantial contribution for this purpose, the trustees decided to use part of the Jadwin legacy to complete the funds needed for a $6.5 million multipurpose athletic building and to name it for Stockwell Jadwin.

Ground was broken for the Jadwin Gymnasium in 1964, and construction was completed in 1969. At its dedication President Goheen called it a tribute to the director of athletics, R. Kenneth Fairman '34, who had "had a vision of what Princeton needed in the way of a multipurpose gymnasium and had put himself into the building of it."

Situated just below the open end of Palmer Stadium on a hillside overlooking Lake Carnegie, Jadwin Gymnasium is one of the University's largest structures, with more than enough total floor space to enclose eight football fields; it is also one of its most versatile buildings, providing year-round facilities for competition and practice in ten sports and for convocations, concerts, and lectures.

Designed by Walker O. Cain & Associates, Jadwin has two primary levels beneath a roof formed by three interlocking shells. On the upper level the first shell covers the entrance lobby. The area beneath the middle shell contains the main basketball court and four practice courts. Using temporary bleachers to supplement the fixed seats in the balcony, 7,500 spectators can be accommodated at a basketball game. At other non-athletic events, as many as 10,000 can be seated. The area beneath the third shell to the south contains an eight-laps-to-the-mile Tartan track, with a 310-foot straightaway and pole vault, high jump, and long jump locations, which can be converted into four indoor tennis courts.

The lower level has a large dirt floor for shot-put and weight-throw events in winter track meets, for indoor baseball practice in the early spring, and for indoor football, lacrosse, or soccer practice, when needed. Adjacent are six bituminous-surfaced tennis courts.

Intermediate levels beneath the entrance lobby contain a fencing room, a wrestling room, and thirteen squash racquets courts with spectator galleries.

Jadwin is Princeton's fifth gymnasium. Efforts to provide a suitable place "for the bracing of the bodily frame" (President McCosh's phrase) began in 1837 when a group of students in the Class of 1839 fitted up a gymnasium of sorts in an old building just off campus, but it was discontinued after they graduated.

The first gymnasium for the whole college—a stoveless, wooden, barn-like structure—was put up in 1859 near where Witherspoon now stands. Half the $984.31 cost was paid by students, half by the faculty. It was equipped with second-hand parallel and horizontal bars, pulleys with weights, a few swings with hand rings, and a mattress or two, bought for $50 from a gymnasium in Trenton that had gone out of business. Primitive though it was, students found it a good place "to loosen the joints and strengthen the limbs stiffened by study" until one night during the summer of 1865 when townspeople burned it to the ground after hearing a rumor that a tramp suffering from smallpox had been sleeping there.

The College's second gymnasium, a gray stone building, was built in 1869, near the site of Campbell Hall, at a cost of $38,000, shared equally by Robert Bonner and Henry G. Marquand. A modest affair by today's standards (inside it was a little smaller than a regulation-size basketball court), it was considered the finest gymnasium in the country when it was built, and its bars, rings, trapezes, ladders, weights, clubs, bells, and ropes were put to constant and effective use by student gymnasts for more than thirty years.

The Bonner-Marquand gym had two celebrated accessories: at its front a bronze statue of a gladiator, in its basement the College's first bathtubs. The gladiator, whose only adornments were a sword, a shield and a fig-leaf, was a favorite butt of student pranks; once when Anthony Comstock, secretary of the Society for the Suppression of Vice, came to give a public lecture, he found the gladiator decorously clothed in red flannel underwear. The dozen enameled iron tubs in "the murky steaming depths" of the basement were difficult to get to and uncomfortable to use. So much so, that it was the custom at that time (when sophomores had to pass a "biennial" examination on the work of the first two years) to observe, on meeting a classmate who had a conspicuously well-scrubbed appearance, "Ah, I see you have taken your biennial."

The Bonner-Marquand Gymnasium was razed in 1907 to make way for Campbell Hall. Meantime, the University Gymnasium had been built in 1903 by general alumni subscriptions. A connecting building contained a swimming pool, which had been built in the early 1890s in memory of Frederick Brokaw 1892, a varsity baseball catcher, who had lost his life trying to save a drowning girl. For four decades the University Gymnasium was used for physical education, athletic contests, student dances, and alumni dinners. It was destroyed by fire in 1944, and replaced in 1947 by Dillon Gymnasium (q.v.).

Jadwin Hall, headquarters of the Department of Physics, was dedicated in 1970 as a memorial to Stanley Palmer Jadwin, whose widow on her death in 1964 left $27 million—virtually the entire family estate—to the University. Portions of this gift were used for the construction of the gymnasium in memory of her son, L. Stockwell Jadwin '28 (q.v.), as well as for the mathematics-physics-statistics center, represented by Jadwin Hall and Fine Hall (q.v.).

Jadwin and Fine Halls stand just west of Palmer Stadium and southwest of Peyton Hall and are connected by a joint library located beneath the plaza between them. Counting the two levels beneath the plaza, Jadwin Hall has altogether six floors, containing ninety laboratories, eighty-four offices, and eight classrooms. On the main floor is a meeting room for the physics faculty named for Princeton's first physicist, Joseph Henry, and adjacent to it a lounge named for its donor, Peter A. Ballentine '35.

Jadwin Hall was designed by Hugh Stubbins & Associates of Cambridge, Massachusetts. Its basic construction, like Fine Hall's, is of reinforced concrete and steel, and the principal exterior materials are Canadian granite and brick. The plaza is paved with a stone known as London Walk.

Jefferson, Thomas, The Papers of, "one of the greatest editorial and publishing ventures in the nation's history," had its genesis at the time of Jefferson's 200th birthday in 1943. The project, President Dodds said, was "truly the child of the creative imagination" of Julian P. Boyd, University Librarian, later Professor of History, who was then serving as historian to the Thomas Jefferson Bicentennial Commission. Encouraged by the commission's warm endorsement and a gift of $200,000 from the New York Times Company, the University assumed editorial responsibility as sponsor of the project, and Princeton University Press agreed to publish the sixty-volume series. Other contributions have come from the Ford Foundation, the National Historical Publications and Records Commission, and individual donors. Invaluable assistance has been given by the Library of Congress, the Library of the University of Virginia, the National Archives, and upwards of 600 archival and historical institutions and private collectors all over the world.

The *Papers*, when completed, will include 18,000 letters written by Jefferson, 25,000 letters written to him, his public papers, and all his writings on the varied topics his wide-ranging mind touched upon—in Professor Gilbert Chinard's words, "the richest treasure house of historical information ever left by a single man."

Julian Boyd has been editor of the *Papers* from the beginning. Serving as associate editors for a time were Mrs. Mina R. Bryan (1944-1956) and Lyman H. Butterfield (1946-1951). Douglas Southall Freeman was chairman of the advisory committee from 1944 to 1953, Fiske Kimball from 1953 to 1955, David K.E. Bruce '19 from 1955 to 1977.

The first of the volumes appeared in 1950; by 1974 nineteen had been published, winning wide critical acclaim for their thorough editing, impeccable scholarship, and beautiful design. They also served as the prototype for such projects as the Hamilton Papers at Columbia, the Franklin Papers at Yale, the Adams Papers (edited by Lyman H. Butterfield) at the Massachusetts Historical Society, the Madison Papers at Chicago and Virginia, and the Wilson Papers at Princeton—the first fruits of what the eminent historian Adrienne Koch called "a bloodless revolution in American historiography." The "revolution" had begun with President Dodds's presentation of the first volume of the Jefferson Papers to President Truman, who issued an Executive order committing the National Historical Publications and Records Commission to a national program of documentary publication which has enabled 200 different projects to undertake publication of the records of Americans in all fields of endeavor.

Jefferson visited Princeton in 1783 as a member of the Continental Congress, which met that year in Nassau Hall. Princeton gave him an honorary LL.D. in 1791; as President Dodds has pointed out, the College showed a fine sense of balance by awarding the same degree at the same time to Alexander Hamilton. Jefferson gave Princeton $100 toward rebuilding Nassau Hall after the fire of 1802.

Jones Hall, designed by Charles Z. Klauder, was built in 1930 as the first home of the mathematics department.

It was originally named in memory of the department's founding chairman, Dean Henry B. Fine (q.v.). When the new Fine Hall was completed in 1969, the old one was renamed in honor of its donors, Thomas D. Jones and his niece Gwethalyn Jones, and made the home of the Departments of East Asian and Near Eastern Studies.

Thomas Jones and his older brother David, sons of a farmer from Wales who settled in Wisconsin in 1850, shared first honors at graduation from Princeton in 1876. Both were lawyers in Chicago and became wealthy in the practice of their profession and in business. Both were trustees of the University and strong supporters of Woodrow Wilson when he was its president.

In 1907, when the cornerstone of Palmer Hall was laid, the Jones brothers gave a $200,000 endowment for the physics and electrical engineering departments. In the late twenties, Thomas Jones and Gwethalyn Jones (daughter of David, who died in 1923) were the University's most generous benefactors when it was seeking $2,000,000 for scientific research to match a conditional $1,000,000 gift from the General Education Board. Thomas gave professorships in mathematics and in physics to express "the debt of gratitude" he owed Henry Burchard Fine and Cyrus Fogg Brackett "as teachers and friends."At the same time, Gwethalyn endowed a chair in chemistry in memory of her father and another in mathematical physics in honor of her uncle. Two years later, they gave an additional $500,000 with which to supplement the income from the four $200,000 chairs in case salaries had to be raised, because, Jones said, his niece and he could not "comfortably contemplate the possibility that the University might have to forego the services of men of the very first rank for these professorships."

In 1928 Jones agreed to be one of ten alumni to subscribe $100,000 each to the $2 million Alumni Fund for Faculty Salaries. He said he felt that it was only fair that the largest part of this fund should come from those "who have what I may loosely call superfluous wealth," rather than from those "who have their hands full supporting their families." Unable to secure the nine other subscribers, the Committee suggested that Jones make his subscription conditional on the completion of the entire fund. Jones declined this honor and, instead, made his subscription unconditional. "I am not a general education board," he wrote "and I do not quite like the pose of insisting that I shall have the privilege of placing the finial on the completed fund." Jones later provided in his will for a $500,000 bequest for faculty salaries.

Shortly after Dean Fine's death, in 1929, Jones and his niece provided for the erection of a mathematics building in his memory (the original Fine Hall, now Jones Hall), and, what was rarer, an endowment for its upkeep. Feeling that "nothing is too good for Harry Fine," Jones said that the building to bear his name should be a place which "any mathematician would be loath to leave." The finished building provided spacious wood-panelled library, common rooms, and faculty studies. It also contained a locker room with shower-bath for faculty wishing to use the then-nearby tennis courts; this amenity inspired these lines about the department chairman in the Faculty Song:

He's built a country-club for Math
Where you can even take a bath.

Loath as the mathematicians were to leave, in 1969 the increased size of the department compelled them to move into the new Fine Hall, leaving their marks in the old one—mathematical formulas and figures in the leaded design of the windows, and Einstein's famous remark over the fireplace in what is now the Lounge: Raffiniert ist der Herr Gott, aber Boshaft ist Er nicht (God is subtle, but He is not malicious).

Kemmerer, Edwin Walter (1875-1945), first Walker Professor of Economics and International Finance, developed an interest in monetary theory during his student days. At Wesleyan University he devoted his senior thesis to a defense of the quantity theory of money, and in his doctoral dissertation at Cornell he devised statistical methods to support his arguments. In 1903, on receiving his Ph.D., he was appointed financial adviser to the United States Philippines Commission. In this capacity he drafted the currency law of the Islands and put them on the gold exchange standard, thus inaugurating a lifetime career as an international "money doctor." Between 1917 and 1934 he served as financial adviser to the governments of Mexico and Guatemala, and headed financial missions to Colombia, South Africa, Chile, Poland, Ecuador, Bolivia, China, Peru, and Turkey. In 1924 he was banking and monetary expert to the Dawes Commission on European reparations.

Kemmerer came to Princeton from Cornell in 1912, joining Frank A. Fetter (q.v.), who had come from Ithaca a year earlier. In 1929 he helped establish the International Finance Section (q.v.), contributed to its endowment, and became its first director as well as first Walker Professor, serving in these positions until his retirement in 1943.

He wrote more than a dozen books. Perhaps the most important for other economists was his *Modern Currency Reforms* (1916). Best known was *The A B C of the Federal Reserve System* (1918), which ran to twelve editions.

Among the honors bestowed on him were the presidency of the American Economic Association; election to the American Philosophical Society and to the American Academy of Arts and Sciences; decorations by the governments of Belgium, Colombia, Ecuador, and Poland; and honorary degrees from universities in Bolivia and Ecuador as well as from Columbia, Occidental, Oglethorpe, Rutgers, and Wesleyan. One distinction that especially delighted him was the honorary membership the Princeton Class of 1916 voted him because he and they "were Freshmen together."

He left bequests to the three universities with which he had been connected—Wesleyan, Cornell, and Princeton.

Kennedy, John Fitzgerald (1917-1963), 35th president of the United States (1961-1963), was admitted to Princeton in 1935, as a member of the Class of 1939. He fell ill with jaundice in London that summer and did not matriculate until October 26, 1935, a month after college opened, and withdrew on December 12, 1935, because of a recurrence of jaundice. He later entered Harvard from which he graduated cum laude in 1940. While at Princeton he roomed in 9 South Reunion with Kirk LeMoyne Billings '39 and Ralph Horton, Jr. '39. Reunion Hall, condemned as a fire hazard, was torn down in 1965. Bricks from the fireplace in their living room, rescued by his classmates, frame a bronze plaque about him in the south entry of the Class of 1939 Dormitory. In his application for admission he

wrote: "To be a Princeton Man is indeed an enviable distinction."

Lacrosse, which originated among North American Indians and was adopted and developed by the French in Canada—they called the stick with which they played "la crosse" because it reminded them of a bishop's crosier—was introduced to the United States by two Canadian teams in a series of exhibition matches in 1877. Columbia, Harvard, and New York University took up the game in 1880; Princeton followed in 1881; and an intercollegiate lacrosse association was organized by the four in 1882. Yale joined later.

Harvard was dominant in the 1880s, winning the championship six years out of nine. Princeton won the title in 1884, 1888, 1889, and then gave up the sport a year later because of the lack of space for practice (in competition with baseball and track), and the feeling that lacrosse's training value for other sports—its chief appeal at the beginning—had been overestimated.

Harland W. Meistrell '25, star lacrosse player from Erasmus Hall High School in Brooklyn, revived lacrosse at Princeton in 1921, as he had previously done at Rutgers before transferring to Princeton. A trophy bearing his name is awarded to the winner of the annual Rutgers-Princeton game.

Princeton won championships in 1924, 1926, and 1929, and enjoyed three successive undefeated seasons in 1933, 1934, and 1935.

The undefeated 1937 team shared the national championship with Maryland; the undefeated 1942 team won it outright. Two players of this period died in World War II: John E. Higginbotham '39, captain his senior year, and

Tyler Campbell '43, All-American defenseman in 1941 and 1942. Higginbotham is memorialized by a lacrosse trophy for sportsmanship, play, and influence; Campbell, by a playing field for lacrosse.

Princeton excelled in the 1950s and 60s. The 1951 team tied with Army for the national championship; the 1953 team won sole possession of the title. After the formal organization of the Ivy League, Princeton was champion seven consecutive years, 1957 through 1963, and then shared the championship with Harvard in 1964 and with Dartmouth in 1965. Cornell toppled Princeton in 1966, but Princeton regained first place the next year with a perfect 6-0 Ivy League record.

Princeton lacrossemen named to All-American teams have been: Kenneth A. Dittmar '23, Conrad J. Sutherland '24, Henry W. Jeffers, Jr. '26, Walter McN. Woodward '37, Lawrence P. Naylor III '41, Joseph D. B. King '41, Tyler Campbell '43, Frederick A. Allner, Jr., '46, Ernest L. Ransome III '47, Henry E. Fish '48, Leonard M. Gaines, Jr. '49, Frank J. Hoen '49, Donald P. Hahn '51, David C. Tait '53, Ralph N. Willis '53, Henry F. Baldwin '54, Douglas G. Levick III '58, John D. Heyd '59, Howard K. Krongard '61, Timothy C. Callard '63, Gray G. Henry '63, John D. Baker '67.

Varsity coaches have been: Albert B. Nies, 1921-1935; William F. Logan, 1935-1945; Richard Colman, 1946-1949; Ernest Ransome III '47, 1950-1951; Ferris Thomsen, 1951-1970; Arthur E. Robinson, 1970-1976; Michael J. Hanna 1976-. Thomsen was named coach of the year by the U.S. Lacrosse Coaches Association in 1967.

Four Princetonians have been elected to the Lacrosse Hall of Fame: Conrad J. Sutherland '24, Harland W. Meistrell '25, and Coaches William F. Logan and Ferris Thomsen.

A women's lacrosse team, coached by Penelope Hinckley, was organized in 1972; high scorer for three seasons was Kienbusch Sportswoman Emily Goodfellow '76.

Lafayette, Marquis de, French soldier, statesman, and liberal leader, who was a general in the American Revolutionary army and a close friend of George Washington, was made an honorary Doctor of Laws by the Trustees of the College in 1790 in recognition of his contribution to the American cause of independence. His full name, as recorded in the official list of honorary graduates, was Marie Jean Paul Joseph Roche Yves Gilbert du Motier, Marquis de Lafayette.

Its honorary degree having been conferred *in absentia*, the College took the occasion of a visit by Lafayette thirty-four years later to award him his diploma. He stopped at Princeton, on the way from New York to Washington, in September 1824, at the beginning of the triumphal American tour he made on the invitation of Congress. Soon after arrival (according to John Maclean, Jr., the Professor of Mathematics), the Marquis, his son George Washington Lafayette, and members of his escort were entertained at a "very bountiful" breakfast in the gaily decorated college refectory, "then the largest room in town." Later, the Marquis was escorted to a circular canopy, which had been erected near the central gate of the front campus. Here, before a throng of students and people from the town and neighboring countryside, President Carnahan presented to Lafayette the doctor of laws diploma, which President Witherspoon had signed in 1790, in ceremonies at which the College's Peale portrait of Washington was conspicuously displayed.

Law School, A, had a brief existence at Princeton in the middle of the nineteenth century. Its faculty included the former chief justice of New Jersey, Joseph C. Hornblower of Newark, and two local attorneys of high standing, James S. Green and Richard S. Field 1821. Its classes were held in a brownstone building on Mercer Street, which Field had built at his own expense for this purpose. The school was formally opened at the College's centennial celebration in 1847, with an extended discourse by Chief Justice (later Chancellor) Henry Woodhull Green 1820 on the need for a well-educated bar.

Despite its auspicious beginnings, the Law School failed to become viable. Lacking any special endowment, the College depended solely upon tuition fees for its expenses, and enrollment was insufficient to provide adequate salaries for the lecturers. Only seven men qualified for the degree of bachelor of laws—four in 1849, two in 1850, one in 1852. The announcement of the school was dropped from the catalogue in 1852 and the names of the three professors in 1854. Later the law school building was given the name, Ivy Hall, and used for other purposes; it was eventually acquired by its neighbor, Trinity Episcopal Church.

The venture of 1847 represented the trustees' third attempt to found a law school. In the 1820s they had begun preparations for courses of lectures in law and in medicine to be given by two of their members, ex-Senator Richard Stockton 1779 and Dr. John Van Cleve 1797, a local physician; but before the plans could be matured, both men died.

In 1835, on being assured by a committee that they had promises of enough financial support to make an experiment "without encroaching on the means of the Board," the trustees had elected ex-Governor Samuel L. Southard 1804 and two other eminent members of the bar as professors of law, but they all declined appointment.

These three unsuccessful attempts notwithstanding, the desirability of having some kind of program of legal studies has been revived several times. President Patton brought the subject up in 1890. "We have Princeton philosophy, Princeton theology, but we have to go to Harvard and Columbia for our law," he told an alumni gathering. "Gentlemen, that is a shame. Just as soon as I find a man with half a million, I am going to found a law school."

Nothing came of this pronouncement, however, much to the disappointment of the professor of jurisprudence—Woodrow Wilson. Shortly after his election as president in 1902, Wilson, in a report to the trustees, proposed a school of jurisprudence in which law would be taught "only to university graduates and by men who could give it full scholarly scope and meaning without rendering it merely theoretical or in any sense unpractical,—men who could, rather, render it more luminously practical by making it a thing built upon principle, not a thing constructed by rote out of miscellaneous precedents." But in his order of priorities, new funds for faculty salaries, preceptorships, the library, a recitation hall, science laboratories, and a graduate school of arts and sciences took precedence, and when Wilson resigned in 1910, the school of jurisprudence had not been realized.

Two developments in the seventies gave new emphasis to Princeton's continuing interest in legal education. The first was the initiation in 1973 of a four-year joint Master of Public Affairs-Doctor of Jurisprudence program by the Woodrow Wilson School in collaboration with Columbia and New York University law schools. The second was President Bowen's appointment in 1974 of a committee to explore the factors which might enter into a University decision on a program in law. Following a year-long study, this committee, which was composed of Woodrow Wilson School Dean Donald E. Stokes '51, chairman, New York lawyer Robert Owen '52, and Politics Professor Dennis F. Thompson, submitted an extensive report to President Bowen. While concluding that a law program with qualities adapted both to Princeton's special characteristics and the special needs of legal education "could bring new strength to Princeton and could make a genuine contribution to the nation," the committee emphasized that very substantial gifts would be needed to endow such a program and to meet its initial plant and library costs. President Bowen and the trustees' executive committee accepted the Stokes committee's recommendation that in view of the "serious financial constraints" facing Princeton, active consideration of a law program be postponed, but they suggested that the committee's "thoughtful and creative" report deserved wider distribution, and a summary was accordingly published in the *Alumni Weekly*.

Lee, Henry (1756-1818) American Revolutionary cavalry officer known as "Light-Horse Harry" Lee and father of Robert E. Lee, graduated from Princeton in 1773. He and his younger brother Charles entered Princeton in the summer of 1770, when they were fourteen and twelve, after a ten-day journey from Virginia, by stage and on horseback, with their friend James Madison 1771.

The Lee brothers roomed together in Nassau Hall. Charles, who graduated two years after Henry, later became attorney general of the United States. Henry was a good student, won prizes in classics, and read widely in English poetry. He spent one vacation making a line-by-line comparison of Pope's translation of the *Iliad* with Homer's original. He joined the Cliosophic Society but later transferred to its rival, Whig, of which Madison was a founder.

Lee came into prominence in 1779 when, as a twenty-three-year-old major, he led a daring capture of the British fort at Paulus Hook (now in Jersey, City), New Jersey. Washington had previously invited him to become his aide but Lee had declined, preferring the more exciting opportunity of adventure in the field. He later served brilliantly as cavalry commander in the southern campaign under General Nathanael Greene.

After the war Lee was elected governor of Virginia and, later, a member of Congress. A close friend of George Washington all his adult life, Lee was the author of the historic tribute, "first in war, first in peace, and first in the hearts of his countrymen." He used these words in the resolutions adopted by Congress on the death of Washington and again in a eulogy he delivered at the state funeral service held for the first president in Philadelphia.

Lee had been at his best as a dashing cavalry officer in the Revolution—"a Rupert in battle," Woodrow Wilson called him, "a boy in counsel, highstrung, audacious, wilful, lovable, a figure for romance." He was less well fitted for civil and domestic life, and his later years were marred by financial reverses and long periods away from home. He lost heavily in land speculations and spent a year in debtor's prison when Robert E. Lee (his fifth child by his second wife) was only two. While in prison he wrote his memoirs of the Revolution. In 1812, in Baltimore, he was seriously injured while in the company of a group opposed to "Mr. Madison's War," who were under attack by an angry mob. Madison denounced the rioters as barbarians and offered Lee a commission as major-general in the army, but he was too weak to accept. Ill and impoverished, he spent his last years in the West Indies in a vain effort to regain his health.

After the Civil War, Robert E. Lee brought out a new edition of his father's memoirs, with a biographical sketch in which he showed a high regard for his military exploits.

Lefschetz, Solomon (1884-1972) came to the United States in 1907 as an engineer, but turned to mathematics when he lost both hands in an accident while working for the Westinghouse Company. He eventually became world renowned for his contributions to the topological study of all algebraic geometry and the algebraic study of topology. At Princeton, as Fine Professor and department chairman, he carried on where Fine, Eisenhart, and Veblen (qq.v.) left off in making Fine Hall world-famous as a center for mathematics.

He was born in Moscow and grew up in Paris, where he graduated from the École Centrale in 1905 with a degree in mechanical engineering. Following the accident, in 1910 he won a fellowship in mathematics at Clark University and gained his Ph.D. there after only one year. He came to Princeton in 1924

from the University of Kansas, was named Fine Professor in 1933 and appointed department chairman in 1945; he continued in both offices until his retirement in 1953.

Lefschetz was brought to Princeton by Dean Fine as part of a continuing effort to develop a first-rate mathematics department. After the newly founded Institute for Advanced Study took James W. Alexander II, Oswald Veblen, and John von Neumann from the University in the early 1930s, Lefschetz supplied the creative drive that maintained the department's research strength and the energy and imagination that led it to new heights. As chairman, the University Orator later said in presenting him for an honorary degree, he ruled "with some pepper, much salt, and an invigorating and impetuous impishness." Under Lefschetz's dynamic guidance the *Annals of Mathematics* which he edited for twenty-five years, became one of the world's foremost mathematical journals.

In his early research in algebraic geometry Lefschetz made innovative use of topological methods, winning the Bordin Prize of the Paris Academy of Sciences in 1919 and the Bôcher Prize of the American Mathematical Society in 1924. In the twenties he began to concentrate on topology itself, proving his famous "fixed point formula" and the "Lefschetz duality theorem." "Topology" is a word he coined in 1930 as the title for a monograph that brought this subject to the forefront of pure mathematics. During the Second World War, he turned his attention to more applied mathematics—nonlinear differential equations, stability theory, and control theory—in which he continued to work the rest of his life. He wrote over 100 papers, as well as a number of books and monographs.

On his retirement from the University in 1953, he embarked on a period of strenuous activity that lasted almost a score of years. He helped organize at Martin Company's Research Institute for Advanced Study in Baltimore a Mathematics Center which, when it moved to Brown University, became known as the Center for Dynamical Systems. His efforts to make known recent Soviet advances in mathematics and his leadership in developing an American school in nonlinear differential equations and kindred subjects were of strategic importance to American space technology. At the same time, he helped build a school of pure mathematics at the National University of Mexico, and in recognition of this achievement received Mexico's Order of the Aztec Eagle. Two international conferences in his honor were held, one on algebraic geometry and topology in Princeton in 1954 on the occasion of his retirement and the other on differential equations and dynamical systems in Puerto Rico in 1965.

His distinction in his field brought him the presidency of the American Mathematical Society, membership in the American Philosophical Society and the National Academy of Sciences, and foreign membership in the Royal Society of London and the Academies of Sciences in Madrid, Milan, and Paris. He received honorary degrees from Mexico, Paris, and Prague, as well as from Brown, Clark, and Princeton. In 1956 he received the Feltrinelli Prize of the Academia dei Lincei. In 1965, when he was eighty-one, he was awarded the National Medal of Science "for indomitable leadership in developing mathematics and training mathematicians." And his colleagues in Fine Hall, on his death in 1972 at age eighty-eight, added to the many honors he had received in his long career a final tribute which only they could make, when they cited as qualities they would always remember, his love of life, his courage, vigor, and humor, his incessant curiosity, and his "towering genius."

Library, The University. Book collections were among the first concerns of the founders and benefactors of Princeton and of other American colonial colleges. Two years after its founding, Harvard received by bequest the library of the man for whom the college was named, while Yale traditionally traces its beginning to a donation of books by ten Connecticut clergymen. Just before it acquired its permanent home in Princeton, the College of New Jersey was presented with 474 volumes from the library of Jonathan Belcher, royal governor of the province.

Gifts of books came in from other friends of the College, and in 1760 a catalogue of the library, compiled and published by President Samuel Davies, listed 1,281 volumes. This catalogue was in part a fund-raising venture; President Davies indicated in the preface that it was published to provide information for those "watching for Opportunities of doing Good," and to afford "particular Benefactors the Pleasure of seeing how many others have concurred with them in their favorite charity." President Davies also described the Library's purpose—in eloquent terms that have continued to have meaning for more than two centuries:

A large and well-sorted Collection of Books on the various Branches of Literature is the most proper and valuable Fund with which [the College] can be endowed. It is one of the best Helps to enrich the Minds both of the Officers and Students with Knowledge; to give them an extensive Acquaintance with Authors; and to lead them beyond the narrow Limits of the Books to which they are confined in their stated Studies and Recitations, that they may expatiate at large thro' the boundless and variegated Fields of Science [i.e., knowledge].

THE LIBRARY'S MANY HOMES

Over the years the Library has occupied a variety of physical accommodations. When the College moved from Newark to Princeton in 1756, two large boxes of books were sent by water from Newark to New Brunswick and conveyed to a room on the second floor of newly constructed Nassau Hall, which became the College's first library. This historic room suffered the depredation of military occupation in the Revolution, served as the meeting place of the Continental Congress in the summer and fall of 1783, and was almost totally destroyed by the disastrous fire of 1802. Soon after this fire, the Library was reestablished in Stanhope Hall (completed in 1803), its collections now considerably enlarged through generous contributions to replace the losses.

The Library remained in Stanhope Hall until 1860, when it was returned to Nassau Hall, this time to larger quarters in the rear wing (now the Faculty Room), created as a part of the building's restoration following another fire in 1855. Under the dynamic leadership of President McCosh, the College acquired in 1873 its first separate library building, the Chancellor Green Library, donated by John C. Green. This octagonal structure, in most respects admirably functional for a small library, was soon outgrown, and Pyne Library was constructed in 1897, the Sesqui-centennial gift of Mrs. Percy Rivington Pyne, mother of M. Taylor Pyne 1877 (q.v.).

When Pyne Library opened, with collections numbering less than 200,000 volumes, the need for more space seemed far away. But, by the 1920s it in turn began to be desperately crowded, and plan after plan was developed to relieve the situation. Decades of planning eventually culminated in the Harvey S. Firestone Memorial Library, financed by gifts from 1,250 groups and individuals, the largest single gift coming at a critical time from the Firestone family. In the final stages of planning in 1944, Julian P. Boyd, the Librarian, called together representatives of a dozen other universities that were also planning to construct large library buildings as soon as materials became available after the war. This meeting led to the creation of the Cooperative Committee on Library Buildings and to a revolution in college and university library architecture with world-wide influence.

The large university library building erected in the first forty years of the century tended to be a magnificent structure, consisting principally of a large warehouse for books, closed to most students and connected to a cavernous, ill-lighted reading room by an ineffective delivery system. The change that took place following World War II is clearly exhibited in Firestone Library, one of the earliest models of the new architectural thinking. What is important about Firestone is not its exterior shell, vaguely Gothic to harmonize with nearby buildings, but rather its functional interior design, which seeks to bring books and readers together, serving as a scholar's workshop, or as a "laboratory of the humanities," to use the language of the planning period. That this aim has been achieved is indicated by the fact that on a typical mid-week day in the academic year 1974-1975 some 5,000 people passed through its doors to take out books or to use the more than 2,000 study seats dispersed among the stacks and in special function rooms. Flexibility, another goal, was provided for by movable partitions and by spaces designed to serve a variety of purposes. The building has with relative ease been adjusted to changing academic requirements; the exterior walls had by 1971 been penetrated four times for new additions.

While Firestone is the largest library building on the campus and houses nearly all of the Library's administrative functions, the collections have expanded into many buildings. With notable exceptions, the humanities and social sciences are housed in Firestone, and science and technology, with mathematics, are located in the buildings where teaching and research in those disciplines are conducted. These special subject collections plus two small residential area libraries and the annex library for seldom-used volumes occupy space in seventeen buildings. It is, however, essentially one library, with one budget and one administration, dispersed for the convenience of users.

THE BOOK COLLECTIONS

From the beginning, the growth of the collections has depended heavily upon gifts. The largest of the early endowed funds, the Elizabeth Foundation for "the purchase of rare and valuable books needed for the purposes of research and study by literary and learned men," was created by a gift of John C. Green in 1868. Starting in 1875 and continuing through recent years, a steady source of support has been endowed funds for the purchase of books established by alumni classes. Of the $1,633,000 spent for acquisitions in 1973-1974, almost half came from the income of 200 Library endowed funds, with a book value of more than $1¼ million, or from gifts and grants of which the principal could be spent. In addition, there were gifts of books and manuscripts with an appraised value of $436,475.

Gifts of rare books and manuscripts have been particularly important in creating those collections of unique and almost irreplaceable materials which are the special distinction of a great research library. The first major collection on a single subject was the Civil War collection of John S. Pierson of the Class of 1840, which grew to more than 5,000 volumes between 1873 and the donor's death in 1908. Other important gifts followed in the next decades, but not until the 1930s did the frequency of the gifts and the cumulative effect begin to produce a rich and varied collection of rare books and manuscripts.

The gifts of Robert Garrett laid the foundation of one of the five best collections of medieval and renaissance manuscripts in the country and the largest collection of Arabic manuscripts. The Gest Oriental Library contains the finest collection of Chinese rare books outside the Orient. English literature is strong, with the latter half of the nineteenth century particularly rich because of the Morris L. Parrish Collection of Victorian Novelists, the Janet Camp Troxell Rossetti Collection, the J. Harlin O'Connell Nineties Collection, the Miers Cruikshank Collection, and the Gallatin Beardsley Collection. Primary sources of history range from the splendid early Americana of Grenville Kane and Cyrus H.

McCormick to the personal papers of public figures such as John Foster Dulles, James Forrestal, Adlai Stevenson, Bernard Baruch, and John Marshall Harlan.

The Friends of the Princeton Library, founded in 1930, and the *Princeton University Library Chronicle*, published by the Friends since 1939, have helped to establish communication with and among collectors and to make known to the scholarly world the resources of the Library.

It is impossible in a brief acticle to do justice to the collections as they exist today, but one should note that they are substantially richer in most fields represented in the teaching and research program of the University than the relative size of the Library would suggest. In perhaps a dozen fields Princeton's is one of the half-dozen best libraries in the country, and in another dozen fields it is very good indeed. This satisfying state is the product of generous donations of books and funds and the patient work of dozens of faculty and staff bibliographers and cataloguers.

THE LIBRARIANS

For more than a hundred years those who served as Librarian, including, from 1812 to 1873, Philip Lindsly, John Maclean, Jr., George Musgrave Giger, and Henry Clay Cameron, almost always had other responsibilities as vice president, clerk of the faculty, or "overseer of college repairs," as well as professor or tutor. However, their duties in the Library were light, since it was generally open only an hour or two a week for the circulation of books until President McCosh arrived in 1868 and extended the period to an hour on each of five days a week. The hours continued to be increased through the ad-

ministration of Frederic Vinton, brought from the Library of Congress in 1873 by President McCosh as the first full-time librarian. When Ernest Cushing Richardson took office in 1890, he opened the building for study and the circulation of books from 8:00 in the morning until dusk. (The closing hour was extended to 10 p.m. in 1898, to midnight in 1928.)

The Library's various manuscript catalogues were simple lists without any subject arrangements until Cameron in the late 1860s rearranged the books on the shelves by subject, and his successor, Vinton, introduced an author and subject card cataloguing system. The collection was completely recatalogued by Richardson, using his own classification, which is still in use at Princeton in those areas that have not been changed to the Library of Congress classification.

As consultant and adviser Richardson was active in developing the concepts and systems that have made the Library of Congress the center of the nation's bibliographic control procedures, as he was in many other innovative aspects of librarianship. His successors have all been actively involved in national library affairs. James Thayer Gerould, Librarian from 1920 to 1940, was one of the three founders of the Association of Research Libraries. Julian P. Boyd, whose Firestone Library was a remarkable achievement, was a leader in a generation of librarians who developed plans and procedures to strengthen the nation's collections by sharing resources. When Boyd resigned to devote full time to the editing of the monumental *Papers of Thomas Jefferson*, William S. Dix became Librarian after a brief period in which Maurice Kelley of the Department of English was Acting Librarian. Dix, who served from 1953 to 1975, was chairman of the Association of Research Libraries and president of the American Library Association.

Richard W. Boss, appointed Librarian in 1975, was succeeded in 1978 by Donald W. Koepp.

THE LIBRARY TODAY

The Princeton University Library has followed and supported the growth of Princeton from a college to a university, and has become the vital center of its intellectual life. The development of the preceptorial method, junior independent work, and the senior thesis have made the Library more and more important to the academic work of undergraduates. At no other university is there so high a ratio of books circulated per student, even though the open stacks and the generous provision of study areas make it possible for students to use more books without borrowing them than in most libraries in the world. At the same time the Library has gradually become a major research library as the number of faculty members and graduate students engaged in an ever-broader variety of studies has grown.

To fulfill this demanding role, it has been essential that the Library's staff, collections, physical facilities, and budget keep pace with the growth of the University's programs and the volume of worldwide publishing. By 1975, the staff, which had numbered eight in 1900, had grown to about 300. The collections totaled some 3.5 million printed books and microform equivalents; expenditures were more than $4.5 million. In 1973-1974 the Library added to its collections more than one and a half times as many volumes and microform equivalents as were in the total collection at the beginning of the century.

Yet the multiplication of recorded knowledge and the needs of users are so great that the Library seems little more adequate for today's University than the Library of 1900 was in its day. As Julian Boyd pointed out in 1940: "The fallacy of an impossible completeness in any one library should be abandoned in theory and in practice; librarians should now think in terms of completeness for the library resources of the whole country."

The exponential rates of growth of all university libraries cannot go on forever. The Princeton University Library continues to search for ways to increase its service to its community of students and scholars at the same time that in collaboration with its peers in this country and abroad it seeks ways of sharing resources more effectively.

William S. Dix

Lincoln, Abraham, accepted the honorary degree of Doctor of Laws from Princeton in 1864 shortly after his reelection to a second term. The degree was conferred at a meeting of the trustees on December 20th of that year, and President Maclean wrote to Lincoln the same day to inform him of their action. The reply, in Lincoln's own handwriting, is one of the University's treasured possessions—"among the title deeds to our Americanism," as Dean Gauss once put it. The letter is as follows:

Executive Mansion
Washington, December 27, 1864.

My Dear Sir:

I have the honour to acknowledge the reception of your note of the 20th of December, conveying the announcement that the Trustees of the

College of New Jersey have conferred upon me the Degree of Doctor of Laws.

The assurance conveyed by this high compliment, that the course of the government which I represent has received the approval of a body of gentlemen of such character and intelligence in this time of public trial, is most grateful to me.

Thoughtful men must feel that the fate of civilization upon this continent is involved in the issue of our contest. Among the most gratifying proofs of this conviction is the hearty devotion everywhere exhibited by our schools and colleges to the national cause.

I am most thankful if my labors have seemed to conduce to the preservation of those institutions under which alone we can expect good government and in its train sound learning and the progress of the liberal arts.

I am, sir, very truly
    Your obedient servant
                                    A. LINCOLN

Dr. John Maclean.

Linguistics. The graduate Program in Linguistics, established in 1962, was built on a tradition that goes back to the first half of this century, when Harold H. Bender (q.v.) taught Indo-European philology, and Robert K. Root (q.v.) taught the Elements of the English Language (better known as "Root's roots"). This tradition was later carried on by Giuliano Bonfante for Italian, Raymond S. Willis for Spanish, and Samuel D. Atkins for Indo-European, among others.

In the years following World War II, Princeton first responded to the growing interest in this field by inviting distinguished linguists to be visiting professors, and by appointing younger scholars with linguistic training to the language and literature departments. Then, in 1960, William G. Moulton was called from Cornell to organize a graduate program in linguistics, sponsored by the Council of the Humanities. An interdepartmental committee was established, and the program which it proposed was approved in 1961 and first offered in 1962.

From the start, the Program in Linguistics was truly interdepartmental. Its students took modest numbers of courses in general linguistics, supplemented by the offerings of the nine cooperating departments: anthropology, classics, East Asian studies, English, Germanic languages, philosophy, psychology, Romance languages, and Slavic languages. Graduates of the program went on to assume positions in language departments or departments of linguistics.

Though the number of faculty members interested in linguistics was modest at the start, it expanded significantly during the 1960s. Special mention should be made of Albert H. Marckwardt, who came from Michigan in 1963 as Professor of English and Linguistics, and who played a leading role in the program until his retirement in 1972.

Thanks in part to Marckwardt's influence, by the 1970s there was a marked increase in both graduate and undergraduate interest in linguistics. The number of undergraduates choosing "independent concentration" in linguistics was often as large as the number of regular "majors" in some small departments. In order to strengthen the offerings in linguistics, two visiting professors were invited to

Princeton in 1973-1974, and plans were made for a Department of Linguistics with a regular undergraduate major. These plans were frustrated by the economic difficulties that beset all American universities during the mid 1970s, though they remain a hope for the future—a "high priority" once finances are available. In the meantime, Princeton has since 1974 had its first faculty appointments strictly in linguistics (rather than in one of the regular departments): two successive junior faculty members with specialization in syntax.

Though most members of the Interdepartmental Committee on Linguistics are known primarily for their work in related fields, two members have received national and international recognition directly within the field of linguistics. Marckwardt was president of the Linguistic Society of America in 1962, and of the American Dialect Society in 1962-1964. He was also president of the mammoth National Council of Teachers of English in 1967. In that same year, Moulton was president of the Linguistic Society of America; and, during 1972-1977, he was president of the international organization of linguists: the Comité International Permanent des Linguistes. Princeton, through its linguists, continues to serve the nation—and the world.

William G. Moulton

Little, Stafford, Hall, which Scott Fitzgerald likened to a snake winding its way from Blair Hall to the Gymnasium, was built half in 1899, half in 1901. It was Princeton's second collegiate Gothic building and was designed, as was the first—Blair Hall—by the Philadelphia firm of Cope and Stewardson. Little had the honor also of being the first dormitory built with bathrooms.

The donor, Stafford Little 1844, (who also endowed the Stafford Little Lectureship) was a founder and first president of the New York and Long Branch Railroad, and for several years president of the New Jersey Senate. He was a trustee of Princeton from 1901 to 1904.

Log College was the name given to a school that William Tennent, an Irish-born, Edinburgh-educated Presbyterian minister, conducted at Neshaminy, Bucks County, Pennsylvania from 1726 until his death in 1745. Here, in a "log house, about twenty feet long and near as many broad," Tennent drilled his pupils in the ancient languages and the Bible and filled them with an evangelical zeal that a number of them, his four sons included, manifested conspicuously during the religious revivals known as The Great Awakening.

The name "Log College" was at first applied derisively by Old Side Presbyterians who disliked some of the excitable and intrusive methods of its New Side graduates and disdained the narrowness of their training. But in time it took on a prouder connotation as its graduates filled vacancies in the growing number of Presbyterian congregations in the Middle Colonies and in the South and founded schools on the frontier modeled on their Alma Mater.

THE PRINCETON CONNECTION

Some writers have assumed that the College of New Jersey grew directly out of the Log College, that indeed it could be regarded as a continuation of it, but, as President Maclean and Professor Wertenbaker have shown, this assumption is not supported by the facts.

The Log College adherents, Professor Wertenbaker pointed out, were not among the seven original incorporators of the College of New Jersey on October 22, 1746. Moreover, it was the educational ideas of these seven men, all graduates of Yale or Harvard, that were embodied in the charter they obtained, establishing a college for the education of youth in the liberal arts and sciences—*not* those of the adherents of the Log College where personal piety and religious experience were emphasized, and as President Maclean said, "the great benefits of mental discipline . . . and of polite learning were not estimated at their full value."

However, soon after the College of New Jersey was founded, a number of Log College men rallied to its support and joined with their New Side brethern from Yale and Harvard in rendering it conspicuous service. Six months after the granting of the charter, three Log College graduates—Samuel Blair, Gilbert Tennent, and William Tennent, Jr.—and Samuel Finley, who was probably also an alumnus, and Richard Treat, who was one of its adherents, accepted election as Princeton trustees. Finley later became fifth president.

Samuel Davies, who preceded Finley as president, studied with Samuel Blair and thus fell heir to the influence of the Log College. It was, moreover, Davies and Gilbert Tennent who, sent to Great Britain by the trustees in 1753, raised there the funds to build Nassau Hall.

Thus, while the facts do not warrant Princeton's pushing its founding date back to 1726, as has sometimes been proposed, they do show that an historical debt of gratitude is due some of William Tennent, Sr.'s pupils and some of

their pupils for the substantial help—both spiritual and practical—they gave the College of New Jersey during its formative years.

Lourie-Love Hall, a south campus dormitory accommodating seventy-eight students, is a monument to the long, close friendship of Donold Bradford Lourie '22 and George Hutchinson Love '22. They were roommates at Exeter and again at Princeton, where Love was manager of the football team and Lourie an All-American quarterback, and both were members of the Senior Council. At the Cannon Exercises of 1922 they were handcuffed together; these handcuffs were put in the corner-stone of Lourie-Love Hall. After graduation they went back home, Lourie to Chicago, where he eventually became chairman of the board of the Quaker Oats Company, Love to Pittsburgh, where he became chairman of the board of the Consolidation Coal Company and then of the Chrysler Corporation. They remained close friends and, on their not infrequent visits to Princeton, almost inseparable companions. Lourie was elected an alumni trustee in 1934, a charter trustee in 1948; Love an alumni trustee in 1954, a charter trustee in 1961. Together they gave the dormitory in 1964.

Lowrie, Walter, House at 83 Stockton Street was given to the University in 1960 by Barbara Armour Lowrie in memory of her husband, Walter Lowrie 1890. It was used as a University guest house until 1968, when it became the residence of the president.

The house was designed by the Philadelphia architect John Notman (architect also of Prospect and of the 1855 restoration of Nassau Hall) and was built in 1845 by Commodore

Robert F. Stockton U.S.N. for his son, John P. Stockton, Princeton 1843, attorney general of New Jersey and United States senator. It was later occupied by Paul Tulane, Princeton-born founder and benefactor of the university that bears his name. In 1895 the house was acquired by George Allison Armour 1877, and became the childhood home of Barbara Armour and her four brothers. Barbara and Walter Lowrie took up residence there in 1930, following their return from Rome, where he had been for many years rector of the Episcopal congregation at St. Paul's-within-the-Walls.

At the age of sixty-two, Lowrie began teaching himself Danish, and for the next twenty-seven years he devoted himself to the translation of all the works of the Danish philosopher, Søren Kierkegaard, and to the writing of a biography one authority called "the greatest one-volume work on Kierkegaard in any language." Lowrie wrote other books too, including one on Karl Barth; in the period of his so-called retirement he published twenty-seven volumes in as many years.

Lowrie was secretary of his class for the last five years of his life and, in *Alumni Weekly* class notes, regaled his dwindling band of octogenarian classmates with reminiscences of their college days and pungent allusions to their declining years. Once he began his column: "I greet each of my classmates with the cheerful salutation: 'Moriturus te saluto! [I who am about to die salute you!].'" Another time he misconstrued a notice of the change of address of a classmate as a notice of his death and so reported it in the *Weekly*. Several weeks later he announced in the class notes that the classmate "was miraculously raised from the dead by reading my obituary of him . . . and promises to send his contribution to the Alumni Fund." "I cannot now be sorry," Lowrie concluded, "that I published an account of his demise, though it was grossly exaggerated, seeing that it had so salutary an effect."

McCabe, David Aloysious (1883-1974), first Joseph D. Green 1895 Professor of Economics, laid the groundwork for the development of Princeton's distinguished tradition in labor economics. One of the last preceptors appointed by Woodrow Wilson, McCabe was discovered by Winthrop M. Daniels, chairman of the Department of History, Politics, and Economics, who lectured at Johns Hopkins in 1909, the year McCabe took his Ph.D. there under George Barnett, the American pioneer in the study of labor relations. For forty-three years thereafter McCabe was one of the University's most popular teachers and a valued counselor in faculty affairs; he was for a time chairman of the economics department.

His four books dealt with labor relations: the first, the standard wage rate in American trade unions; the second (written with his old Hopkins teacher, Barnett), the handling of industrial disputes; the third, collective bargaining in the pottery industry; and the fourth (written with his younger colleague, Richard A. Lester, later a successor as Green Professor), labor and social reorganization.

He was a member of various commissions for the prevention and settlement of labor disputes, serving notably as chairman of the Regional Labor Board for New Jersey in the 1930s and as arbitrator for the National War Labor Board during the Second World War. His warm personality made him a good negotiator, and he enjoyed his relations with workers and employers. Returning once from arbitrating a wage dispute, he quoted with relish a labor representative who had interrupted an analysis McCabe was presenting with the injunction: "Never mind the statistics, professor, just give us the facts."

Witty, blunt, and demanding, he was a provocative teacher. His lectures were models of clarity and his preceptorials so challenging that places in his sections were always eagerly sought. For many years before his marriage he lived in a campus dormitory (Patton Hall) and was interested in all phases of student life; with Dean Hugh S. Taylor, he helped establish the Catholic chaplaincy in 1928. His short stature was a source of good-natured ribbing by undergraduates, who called him "Shorty": "How about this man, McCabe," the seniors sang, "Who ceased to grow while still a babe?"

McCabe's forensic skill—he had been a prize debater at Harvard—and his bubbling Irish wit made him a vigorous and respected elder statesman in faculty meetings. He was said to have spent much time and ingenuity getting off committees to which his admiring colleagues insisted on appointing him. Once at a tea party the president's wife lavished praise on McCabe as one whose counsel her husband counted on in all faculty matters. "Ah, Mrs. Hibben," Shorty rejoined, "I too have kissed the blarney stone."

When he died, at the age of 90, the faculty memorialized him as "a stalwart exponent of its best traditions in teaching, scholarship, and public service."

McCarter Theatre. Of the Princeton Triangle Club's many contributions to the cultural life of Princeton University and its surrounding region, none is more imposing than the McCarter Theatre, which stands massive and towered on its 2.7-acre plot—much of it in sweeping lawn—at what was once a main approach to the campus: across University Place from the old Pennsylvania "Dinky"station.

What the existence of this 1,000-seat theater has meant to both University and region is immeasurable, for it has been host through the years to an incredible number and variety of important dramatic, musical, dance, film, and other events.

Construction of such a theater was probably inevitable when Princeton students formed an organization (named in 1893 "the Triangle Club" [q.v.]) to begin a tradition of undergraduate musical extravaganzas destined to become nationally famous. After a 1924 fire leveled the rickety 1890 campus "Casino," a serious fundraising effort began for a new theater.

In June 1927, between acts of Triangle's *Samarkand*, Professor Donald Clive Stuart, considered by many the father of performed drama at Princeton, came on stage and introduced Thomas N. McCarter '88 and accepted his check for $250,000 toward a new theater for Triangle and other uses.

Under the devoted stewardship of Benjamin Franklin Bunn '07 (q.v.), Triangle had accumulated a substantial hoard of its own, so that, by June 1928, Mr. McCarter's contribution, plus Triangle's box office kitty, and other gifts, totaled $450,000, and construction could begin.

On February 21, 1930, the McCarter Theatre—designed by architect D. K. Este Fisher, Jr. '13, and built of native shale relieved by red brick on lines described as Georgian with Gothic accents—opened its doors to its first audience, for Triangle's *The Golden Dog*. The next night it was formally dedicated.

Now the Club had a rock-solid house made to order for its annual large-cast shows and the makings of an equally impressive financial headache; for the McCarter, conceived in boom, was born in depression, and into a world in which talking pictures and radio were beginning to give painful competition to "live" performances of all kinds, even before the coming of television.

For some years the McCarter was a popular house for pre-Broadway try-outs of new plays and post-Broadway tours of new plays and post-Broadway tours of established hits. Among its world premieres were *Our Town* by Thornton Wilder, A.M. '26; *Bus Stop* by William Inge; *The Wisteria Trees*, adapted from Chekhov's *The Cherry Orchard* by a Triangle stalwart Joshua Logan '31; *Separate Tables* by Terence Rattigan.

It is hard to name an American stage star of the 1930s and 1940s who did not play McCarter: John Barrymore, Ethel Barrymore, George M. Cohan, Helen Hayes, Katharine Hepburn, Paul Robeson, Cornelia Otis Skinner—the list goes on and on.

But after World War II, not only did the number of touring Broadway hits decline but New York producers began to cut costs by substituting in-town previews for out-of-town tryouts of new works. McCarter's income from these sources shrank, and Triangle's earnings from its own shows had already shrunk, with the result that the Club was going steadily into debt to the University for the high costs of theatrical landlordism: insurance, utilities, repairs, and the like.

In 1950, with the debt at $47,000 and obviously increasing, Triangle and the University made a deal: the University would cancel the debt—"in recognition of Triangle's services to the University and significant contributions to McCarter Theatre"—and would take over the theater, giving Triangle use of it for rehearsals and productions, and maintaining the club's office and workroom.

The loss of booked-in plays left a vacuum at McCarter that Princeton's president Robert F. Goheen sought to fill in the late 1950s with a program of plays produced under University auspices. The aim was to give an undergraduate, in four years, a taste of world drama "from Greek to modern, Oriental plays to musicals" with obvious entertainment and cultural benefits to the region.

That program has continued to this writing, with changes in emphasis and in management: artistic directors have included Milton Lyon, Ellis Raab (for 1960 when his APA Company was in residence), Arthur Lithgow, Louis Criss, and Michael Kahn.

Costs for the theater program, and for theater maintenance in general, have risen sharply, and the University, while continuing to subsidize it, has increasingly taken the line that the community that shares McCarter's benefits should assume more financial responsibility for its operation. The community has shown an impressive willingness to do this, but the surrounding region is relatively sparsely populated for the maintenance of so large a theater.

Meanwhile, McCarter during the cooler months—lacking air-conditioning, it is "dark" in the summer—is one of the busiest theaters in America, offering, in addition to its own drama program, a feast of other experiences for students and the general public. With an illustrious past and present, it has, like most cultural institutions, a promising and precarious future.

William McCleery

Maclean, John, Sr. (1771-1814) was Princeton's first professor of chemistry. Benjamin Rush (q.v.) and others had previously taught chemistry in medical schools, but Maclean's lectures at Princeton constituted the first American undergraduate course in chemistry.

A precocious Scot, Maclean entered the University of Glasgow in his native city at the age of thirteen, determined to become a surgeon like his father. Under the influence of his friend Charles Macintosh (who later invented waterproof cloth) he joined the Chemical Society, before which he read several papers. After completing his preliminary studies in arts and medicine, he did further work in Edinburgh, London, and Paris; and in 1791, when he was only twenty, Maclean was licensed to practice and was admitted to the faculty of physicans and surgeons of the University of Glasgow.

Attracted by American political ideals, he came to this country in the spring of 1795 and, on the advice of Benjamin Rush, established himself in Princeton in the practice of "physic" and surgery. That summer, on President Stanhope Smith's invitation, he delivered a short course of chemistry lectures, which made so favorable an impression that the trustees in October appointed him Professor of Chemistry with the understanding that he would be at liberty to continue the practice of his profession. Two years later, on the death of Walter Minto (q.v.), Maclean assumed responsibility for instruction in mathematics and natural philosophy as well as in chemistry; he gave up his medical practice, and from that time on devoted himself wholly to the College.

In 1797 he published *Two Lectures on Combustion*, which helped to overthrow Priestley's phlogiston theory and to clear the way for acceptance of Lavoisier's "new chemistry," to which he had been won over during his studies in Paris.

Maclean helped Benjamin Silliman, later regarded as one of the fathers of science in America, to prepare for his duties as Yale's first chemistry professor, following his appointment in 1802. In his diary Silliman said he considered Maclean his "earliest master of Chemistry" and Princeton his "starting point in that pursuit."

Maclean died at the age of forty-three in 1814—two years after his resignation (which had been requested by a board of trustees more concerned with training ministers than scientists) and two years before the graduation of his eldest son, John Maclean, Jr., who became the tenth president of the College.

Maclean, John, Jr. 1816 (1800-1886) was a member of the faculty for fifty years, serving successively as tutor, professor, vice-president, and tenth president. It was one of the longest associations in Princeton's history.

Son of the first professor of chemistry, John Maclean, Sr. (q.v.), he was born in Princeton and lived there almost all his life, either on or near the Campus.

At his graduation from the College Maclean was the youngest member of his class. Two years later, after earning a divinity degree at the Princeton Theological Seminary, he began his career in the College as a tutor in Greek. He was then eighteen. He became a full professor at twenty-three, vice-president at twenty-nine, and president at fifty-four.

AS VICE-PRESIDENT

Maclean was the mainstay of the thirty-one-year administration of his predecessor, President James Carnahan (q.v.). When Carnahan, dismayed by the state of affairs he found on his arrival in 1823, thought of resigning, Maclean persuaded him to remain. And when, a few years later, Carnahan thought of closing the College because a further drop in enrollment necessitated cuts in faculty salaries and led to a lowering of morale, Maclean came forward with a bold plan to stop the decline by enlarging and improving the faculty. The trustees accepted his plan and made him vice-president. Maclean secured a few gifts, discovered some funds due the College that had not previously been collected, shifted his own field from mathematics back to classics in order to make way for an able young mathematician, and secured the half-time services of several older men as an inexpensive means of broadening the curriculum. Making the most of the College's limited means, he was able to add to the faculty such outstanding men as Joseph Henry, John Torrey, Stephen Alexander, Albert B. Dod (qq.v.), and James Alexander. These appointments reversed the trend, raising enrollment from 87 in 1829 to 228 ten years later.

IN LOCO PARENTIS

Maclean never married; the time and energy ordinarily expended by a father on his children he gave instead to the students of the College, for whom he quite literally stood *in loco parentis*. In this he was helped by his two maiden sisters, who lived with him.

He was vigilant in detecting wrongdoing, but sympathetic to the culprit once he was caught. Frequently, he would intercede with the faculty to allow the offender to escape with rustication at a nearby farm. This was a mild enough penalty: returning from rustication, one student reported that he had spent the weeks fishing and "thinking what a good man Doctor Maclean was." Sometimes, if the infraction of the rules was minor, Maclean would merely administer a rebuke; and he seldom rebuked, his students said, without making a friend.

His students also recalled often seeing him in his long cloak, armed with a lamp, a teakettle and food, on his way to visit a sick student. In case of serious illness the student was brought to his house, and many a parent also found a home with him until the emergency was over. One student, who broke his leg in a fall from a second floor window of West College after the Senior Ball of 1847, was cared for at Maclean's house by Miss Mary Maclean for six weeks.

Maclean was not without a sense of humor. One night two donkeys from a nearby farm were found on the top floor of Nassau Hall. A student on hand at the discovery asked Maclean, with an innocent air, how he thought they had got there. "Through their great anxiety," Maclean replied, "to visit some of their brethren."

He was generous with students in financial straits: over the years he accumulated a drawerful of watches and other articles, unredeemed pledges for loans he had made from his personal funds.

WORK IN THE COMMUNITY

Maclean showed the same concern for his fellow townsmen. He took a particular interest in the welfare of Negroes in the community, serving as their personal counselor and benefactor and as one of the organizers and supporters of the Witherspoon Street Presbyterian Church, a Negro congregation. Maclean was also the chief support of the Second Presbyterian Church (now united with the First Church), known for many years as "Doctor Maclean's church." A member of the Prison Association, he sometimes walked the ten miles to Trenton on Sundays to conduct services in the State Prison.

He was one of the earliest advocates of public education in New Jersey. An address he delivered in 1829 inspired the state legislature to initiate a system closely following his ideas. Staunch Presbyterian though he was in the affairs of the College, he insisted that the public schools should be completely non-sectarian: "There should be in no case the least interference with the rights of conscience, and no scholar should be required to attend to any lesson relating to morals or religion, to which his parents may be opposed."

PRESIDENCY

Maclean's election in 1854 as President Carnahan's successor was as much a reward for previous service as it was an expectation of future achievement. Indeed, there was a strong feeling among the trustees that the College needed a leader of greater distinction, and many favored calling Joseph Henry to the post. But Henry declined to be a candidate and urged the election of Maclean, stressing particularly his "untiring devotion to the interest of the college."

As it turned out, Maclean's "untiring devotion" was just what the College needed for the two extraordinary challenges it had to face during the years he was president: the loss of Nassau Hall by fire in 1855 and the drop of enrollment during the Civil War. Maclean rallied alumni and friends to contribute funds toward the rebuilding of Nassau Hall, augmented these funds by operating the College on an austerity budget for five years, and then helped liquidate the debt that remained by giving up part of his own salary. More than a third of Princeton's students came from the South, and the College suffered a corresponding drop in enrollment during the Civil War. But Maclean managed to keep his faculty together and to maintain a full program for the students who remained. He and the faculty came out strongly for the Union cause—more strongly than some of his old student friends from the South thought necessary, but less quickly than some from the North thought appropriate—and Maclean conveyed to President Lincoln (q.v.) an honorary degree voted by the trustees.

During his presidency, Maclean added a number of good men to the faculty, including the Swiss geographer Arnold Guyot, but as a whole the appointments during this period lacked the luster of those he had contrived earlier. Professor Wertenbaker concluded from his study of the Maclean papers that while Maclean sought good scholars he also looked for good Presbyterians, and that the second desideratum sometimes interfered with the first.

LAST YEARS

On his retirement in 1868, friends bought a house for Maclean at 25 Alexander Street, where he lived out his years with one of his brothers.

In 1877 he completed a two-volume history of the College, an indispensable source of information about Princeton's early years, assigning the royalties to a fund "for the aid of indigent and worthy students engaged in seeking a liberal education."

Although he stayed away from the Campus during term time—except when he was asked to preach in Chapel—he made brief appearances there at commencement, and whenever a knot of alumni caught sight of him, a cheer went up for "Johnny." His last appearance—six weeks before he died—was at the commencement meeting of the alumni in 1886, the 70th anniversary of his own graduation. As honorary president of the Alumni Association (of which he had been a principal founder and the first secretary), he was given an ovation which, by contemporary accounts, was loud, long and tearful.

"Some of us old fellows . . . who cheered first and cried afterward," one of them said later, "put a meaning into our action which nobody but Doctor Maclean and ourselves knew. There were secrets between us which he was too good ever to tell, and which, perhaps, we were ashamed to. His full biography will never be written. Its materials would have to be gathered from too many hearts."

Maclean, John, House, originally the President's House, shares with Nassau Hall the honor of seniority among University buildings; both are accorded the same date of construction (1756) in official records, although it is probable that the President's House was not ready for occupancy until several months after Nassau Hall. Designed and built by Robert Smith, co-architect and builder of Nassau Hall, it was occupied by ten presidents of the College—Burr, Edwards, Davies, Finley, Witherspoon, Smith, Green, Carnahan, Maclean and McCosh—until Prospect was acquired as the President's residence in 1878. After President McCosh moved into Prospect, James Ormsbee Murray, Professor of English, occupied the old President's House and continued to live there after his appointment to the new office of dean of the faculty in 1883. Thereafter until 1967 it was the residence of the first seven deans of the faculty—Murray, Winans, Fine, Magie, Eisenhart, Root, and Brown—and was called the Dean's House. In 1868, when it became the home of the Alumni Council, it was renamed in honor of John Maclean, Jr., founder of the Alumni Association and the last president to occupy the house throughout his administration; "when he was president," John F. Hageman, historian of the Princeton community wrote in 1878, "he kept his mansion filled with guests as if it were a public house."

McClenahan, Howard (1872-1935), second dean of the College, was brought up in a family of thirteen children—an apt training-ground for the strict disciplinarian his students remember him to be. He completed the electrical engineering course at Princeton in 1895, earned a master's degree in science and became instructor in physics in 1897, and was made a professor in 1906.

He was a good teacher and an able administrator. In his younger days he was principal assistant to Cyrus Fogg Brackett, Professor of Physics and founder of the Department of Electrical Engineering. Later he was largely responsible for the design and construction of Palmer Physical Laboratory and for the choice and organization of its equipment. He had strong convictions and a dry sense of humor. Once while conducting demonstrations in a physics lecture, his foot upset a pail near the end of the demonstration table with a clatter. A voice from the rear of the lecture hall called out "O sir, you've kicked the bucket." "No," said McClenahan coolly, "I merely turned a little pale."

As dean of the College from 1912 to

1925, McClenahan proved a stern disciplinarian whose summons to appear in his office "without fail" aroused appropriate apprehension in the heart of the recipient. His image as the rock of rectitude was regarded as fair game by the seniors in their annual Faculty Song. They poked fun at his baldness ("His polish well becomes a Dean,/As does the polish of his bean."), derided his efforts to enforce Prohibition, called him hard-hearted for enforcing compulsory chapel attendance and, in 1922, when it fell to his lot to have to declare three star athletes ineligible, outrageously suggested that Dean "Mac" had been invited by the authorities at New Haven to have his picture taken on the Yale fence.

In the spring of 1925, when McClenahan resigned to accept appointment as secretary of the Franklin Institute in Philadelphia, the ragging in the Faculty Song was noticeably absent, as the Class of 1925 showed the respect that lay beneath the jibes and protests of other years:

Here's to Dean McClenahan;
He's fair and square with every man.
Our class gives him a friendly grip,
And honorary membership.

During the decade that he directed the affairs of the Institute, McClenahan's most significant contribution was the planning, development, and equipping of an industrial and technical museum, which, at his suggestion, the Institute erected as a memorial to Benjamin Franklin. Both as director of the Museum and secretary of the Institute, he advanced the cause of scientific progress by encouraging and broadening popular interest in the mechanical and electrical arts.

Besides receiving a number of honorary degrees and appointments as an honorary member of the Royal Institution of Great Britain and of the Board of Directors of the Deutsches Museum of Munich, McClenahan was also a trustee of Lincoln University, an associate trustee for graduate study of the University of Pennsylvania, and a member of the American Philosophical Society. In a memorial written for the Society, McClenahan's Princeton colleague Dean William F. Magie paid tribute to his "genial and winning manners" and to his ability "to plan on a large scale" and, at the same time, "to attend to the many details of a complex organization." The *Philadelphia Evening Bulletin* observed that, although he had devoted over a quarter of a century of his life to Princeton, McClenahan had left his chief monument in Philadelphia: "In building to the memory of Benjamin Franklin he wrote his own epitaph."

McCormick Hall was built in 1922 with funds given to the University by Cyrus H. McCormick 1879 and his family; they also gave an addition in 1927. The building was designed by Ralph Adams Cram in a medieval Italian style to harmonize with the varied architecture of its neighbors (Whig, Murray-Dodge, Dod, and Brown). It was used by the School of Architecture as well as by the Department of Art and Archaeology until 1963, when the School was given its own separate building.

In 1965, with funds provided by the $53 million campaign, McCormick was enlarged and its interior completely modernized at the same time that the adjoining Art Museum (q.v.) was erected. More adequate provision was thus made for the offices, classrooms, and lecture halls of the Department of Art and Archaeology, the Marquand Library, and the Index of Christian Art.

Designed by Steinmann and Cain, the extensive additions were built of brownstone to conform with the older structure and done in a contemporary style to harmonize with the new museum.

McCosh, James (1811-1894), eleventh president of Princeton, took office in 1868, precisely a century after his fellow-Scot, John Witherspoon (q.v.), whom he resembled in character, religious ardor, statesmanship, devotion to the task of educating young men, and in the rolling rhythms of his native accent. He had been born on a farm near the banks of the River Doon in Ayrshire, the country of Bobby Burns, matriculated at the University of Glasgow in 1825, and moved on to Divinity Hall, University of Edinburgh, in 1829, for the study of religion, philosophy, and psychology. In the spring of 1834 he was licensed to preach by the presbytery of Ayr. "I preached all around," he later wrote, "both in town and country, but chiefly in the country. I had a good horse, and set out on the Saturday with my sermons in a saddlebag behind me, preached twice on the Sabbath, and returned home on the Monday." His first ministerial charge was the Abbey Chapel in Arbroath, and his second at Brechin, Forfarshire, where the earnest young parson was soon involved, heart and soul, tooth and nail, in the reformation movement within the Church of Scotland. This movement, known as "The Disruption," resulted in the organization of the Free Church, which McCosh himself called "a great event in the history of Scotland," and to which he devoted his considerable powers as thinker, propagandist, and orator.

During his pastorate at Brechin he met Isabella (daughter of the eminent physician Alexander Guthrie), who became his wife in September 1845. "She had a good deal of the Guthrie character," he wrote. "She was characteristically firm, and did not always yield to me. She advised and assisted in all my work as minister and professor."

Having fought valiantly for the establishment of the Free Church, McCosh went on to make his mark as professor of philosophy. He had been trained in the subject at Edinburgh, where his essay on Stoic Philosophy had made a stir in 1833. When John Stuart Mill's *System of Logic* appeared in 1843, McCosh took issue with Mill's apparent refusal to give due weight to supernatural powers, and counterattacked in 1850 with his own lively volume, *The Method of Divine Government, Physical and Moral*, which was instrumental in leading to his appointment to the chair of Logic and Metaphysics at Queen's College, Belfast, founded that year by the British government "for the promotion of nonsectarian education." During his sixteen-year tenure in Ireland, he continued to develop and fortify his philosophical position ("a theory of the universe conditioned by Christian revelation") in a series of brilliant books: *Typical Forms and Special Ends in Creation* (with George Dickie, 1855); *The Intuitions of the Mind Inductively Investigated* (1860); *The Supernatural in Relation to the Natural* (1862); and *An Examination of Mr. J. S. Mill's Philosophy* (1866), in which he returned to the demolition of his British compeer so well begun in 1850. John Grier Hibben (q.v.) called this book "one of the most convincing statements concerning the principles of the Intuitional philosophy in opposition to pure empiricism."

McCosh's fame was now widespread in the English-speaking world, and on his first visit to the United States (1866) as a representative of the Evangelical Alliance, he was treated like a visiting potentate. When President John Maclean (q.v.) resigned his post in 1868, the Board of Trustees invited McCosh to serve as his successor.

Just as the Revolutionary War had attenuated the student body and impoverished the exchequer in Witherspoon's time, so the Civil War had severely inhibited the further development of the College during the conflict and the early years of Reconstruction. McCosh's twenty-year presidency changed all that. Andrew Fleming West (q.v.), who entered as a freshman in 1870, compared the new president's influence to "an electric shock, instantaneous, paralyzing to the opposition, and stimulating to all who were not paralyzed." McCosh raised up a distinguished faculty, revised and greatly modernized the plan of study, developed elective course-options, instituted graduate work, found money for fellowships, brought in an expensive array of scientific equipment, dedicated the new Bonner-Marquand gymnasium to the greater glory of intercollegiate sport, founded schools of science, philosophy, and art, and entered upon an ambitious program of building and plantation that greatly enhanced and beautified the hitherto austere campus.

He was also a teaching president, with regular classes in the history of philosophy and in psychology, as well as *ad hoc* meetings in his personal library at Prospect where guest lecturers presented papers and led discussion over a wide range of philosophical and ethical topics. When Darwin's *Origin of Species* threatened to overturn age-old beliefs in God's creation and government of the world, McCosh "stood out almost alone" among American clergymen in defending evolutionary doctrine, insisting that the Darwinian hypothesis, far from denying the existence of God, only served "to increase the wonder and mystery of the process of creation."

A staunch believer in books as tools for the solution of these and other difficult problems, McCosh strongly supported the building-up of Princeton's collections. Under his aegis the octagonal 70,000-volume Chancellor Green Library was dedicated in 1873 with a stirring address by the poet William Cullen Bryant. "I remember," wrote McCosh, "that some critics found fault with me for laying out too much money on stone and lime; but I proceeded on system, and knew what I was doing. I viewed the edifices as means to an end, at best as outward expressions and symbols of an internal life."

His position on the college curriculum was much the same. He wanted to reject "all that was factitious and pretentious," and to continue "the good old solid" course of study "handed down from our fathers." No one, he said, "should be a graduate of a college who does not know mathematics and classics, the one to solidify the reasoning powers, and the other to refine the taste." At the same time he recognized the enormous advances that were being made in the physical sciences, as well as in philology, history, and psychology. From these branches of knowledge, Princeton students were encouraged to choose a wide range of electives to be taken "side by side with obligatory and disciplinary courses."

In the winter of 1885 President Charles W. Eliot of Harvard came to New York—a sufficiently neutral territory—to conduct a debate with McCosh on the ideal college curriculum. Princeton's president was highly critical of Eliot's scheme which allowed students to choose, virtually *ad libitum*, among some two hundred courses. This, said McCosh, obviously encouraged dilettantism, everything being "scattered like the star dust out of which worlds are said to have been made." Even worse, Harvardians were not obliged to attend classes, with the result that a typical professor often found himself lecturing to a roomful of empty seats. Matters were more sensibly ordered at Princeton, where regular attendance was required, and where the whole curriculum had been carefully weighed and logically worked out for all four years, including obligatory core courses and a reasonable variety of solid electives, so that one subject led to another, and the student could develop his powers in an orderly fashion. Most Princetonians believed that McCosh had won the debate handily despite, or perhaps because of, his seventy-three years.

He was seventy-seven when he retired from the presidency in 1888, moving out of "Prospect" to the new house, planned and built under his supervision approximately on the site later occupied by Quadrangle Club. His parting words to the College reflected the noble simplicity of his nature:

It is not without feeling that I take the step which I now take. It recalls that other eventful step in my life when I gave up my living, one of the most enviable in the Church of Scotland, when the liberties of Christ's people were interfered with. . . . I may feel a momentary pang in leaving the fine mansion, which a friend gave to the college and to me—it is as when Adam was driven out of Eden. I am reminded keenly that my days of active work are over. But I take the step firmly and decidedly. The shadows are lengthening, the day is declining. My age, seven years above the threescore and ten, compels it, Providence points to it, conscience enjoins it, the good of the college demands it. . . . I leave the college in a healthy state, intellectually, morally, and religiously, thanks be to God and man. I leave it with the prayer, that the blessing of Heaven and the good-will of men may rest upon it, and with the prospect of its having greater usefulness in the future than even that which it has had in the past.

His successor, Francis L. Patton (q.v.), observed admiringly that McCosh was "more than a model President: he was a model ex-President." This meant that, having once laid down his staff of office, he made no subsequent attempt to use it as a cudgel. He was, however, deeply touched when the Class of 1889 unanimously requested that their diplomas should carry his signature along with Patton's. He met their delegation in the front hall of his house, listened to their words, dabbed quickly at his eyes with a handkerchief drawn from the inside pocket of his clerical frock-coat, and called to his wife. She felt "no scruples" about her own tears, seizing her husband's handkerchief, vigorously wiping her eyes, and saying tenderly, "James, your lads are nae for forgettin' you."

While McCosh lived, his tall, massive, and somewhat stooped figure was often seen strolling along the walk that bore his name, admiring the shrubs and trees he had planted and the way the sunlight struck the stone of the buildings he had caused to be erected. When passing students bowed to him, his response was often the same: "I

know ye, whooo air ye, whatsyour-
name?" And the students, having identified themselves and listened to a few
"wurruds" of greeting, commonly went
away exalted. For most of them knew
and believed the old man's hearty
boast, "It's me collidge. I made it."
Sixty of them gathered on his eightieth
birthday in 1891 to present him with a
golden pitcher inscribed with a legend
in Greek from *The Clouds* of Aris-
tophanes: "May prosperity attend him
who, while passing into the vale of
man's decline, still cultivates wisdom
and imbues his mind with learning ever
new."

As if the shade of Witherspoon,
which had symbolically presided at his
induction to the presidency, were still
in friendly control, McCosh died
quietly on November 16, 1894—
precisely a hundred years and a day
after the date of Witherspoon's death.
These stalwart Scots, in their respective centuries, had each contributed
mightily to the growth of Princeton,
and the modern university is indebted
to them both.

Carlos Baker

McCosh Faculty Fellowships, named
in honor of James McCosh, the College's eleventh president, are awarded
by the Faculty Committee on Appointments and Advancements for individual scholarship in the humanities
and social sciences. Established in
1962, the McCosh Fellowships are
supported by an annual appropriation
of $50,000 from the Jadwin Foundation.

McCosh Hall (built in 1906) was, as
Woodrow Wilson announced, "the gift
of a small group of friends of the University" who were also "devoted to the

memory of James McCosh." When
constructed it was the largest building
on the Campus, extending four
hundred feet along McCosh Walk and
one hundred feet on Washington Road.
It contained four large lecture rooms,
fourteen recitation rooms, and twenty-
six smaller rooms especially planned for
the preceptorial conferences which had
been introduced the year before.

McCosh Hall was designed by
Raleigh C. Gildersleeve in the Tudor
Gothic style of architecture then dominant at Princeton, with exterior walls of
gray Indiana limestone. Situated at the
crossroads of University life, the locus
during term-time of daily faculty and
student dialogue, the scene over the
years of public lectures, open forums,
class meetings, concerts, celebrations,
demonstrations, and protests, it is like
the man it was built to keep in memory:
substantial, familiar, appealing, handsome, purposeful. It fulfills President
Wilson's expectation that "this noble
memorial to our beloved one-time
leader" would be one of the finest
ornaments and at the same time one
of the most useful buildings on the
Campus.

McCosh Infirmary was erected in
1925, replacing an infirmary built on
the same site in 1892. Both were
named for Isabella McCosh, "whose
kindly sympathy and substantial comforts" in days when students were
fewer and younger, and living conditions rugged, endeared her to her husband's "boys" during the twenty years
of his presidency, 1868-1888. One of
them, Alexander J. Kerr 1879, has left
us this picture of Mrs. McCosh on one
of her missions:

She had given strict orders to the
Scottish college proctor, Matt Gold-

ie, that any student who was ill should be immediately reported to her. Her orders were faithfully obeyed and when any boy was sick . . . she would take her large basket, place in it one of her own bed sheets, a pillow case, a towel, a wash cloth, some of her own jams and jellies, homemade cookies and tempting cakes and a jug of tea, over which she would place a tea caddy to keep it hot. She would then carry the basket to the sickroom, no matter though she had to climb four flights of iron stairs to do so. . . .

She would tap on the door and say, "May I come in?" But without waiting for a reply she would enter and, after expressing a mother's sympathy, immediately proceed to wash the face, chest and hands of the young man, put the clean sheet on his bed, the pillow case on his pillow, brush his hair and make him as comfortable as possible and encourage him to eat the good things she had brought and to drink a cup of her good tea. Then, sitting down at his desk, she would write a note to his mother, telling her she need not worry about her boy, as "we are looking after him here."

Urged on by Mrs. McCosh, who was the daughter of the eminent Scottish physician Dr. Alexander Guthrie, President McCosh repeatedly pressed on the trustees the need for an infirmary, but not until after he had retired was a campaign begun for funds to build one and the decision made to name it for Mrs. McCosh at a trustees meeting in 1891. George B. Stewart 1876, an old student of McCosh's and by then a trustee, was a guest at the McCosh home at the time and broke the news at dinner, to the delight of Dr. McCosh and the dismay of Mrs. McCosh. "Oh, they must not do that," she protested, "I don't want them to call it after me." "You have nothing to do about it, Isabella," said McCosh firmly "they will do as they please."

The necessary funds having been raised in response to an appeal by the Sanitary Committee of the faculty, of which Dean James O. Murray was chairman, the cornerstone of the first infirmary was laid at commencement in 1892 and the building was ready for use the following April. Two years later Mrs. McCosh sent Murray a $1000 bond and asked that the income be used for the support and care of students confined in the infirmary.

Mrs. McCosh's gift was the first of many which Princeton women were to make to the Infirmary. In 1903, on the strong recommendation of Mrs. Woodrow Wilson, a group of women known as the "Ladies Auxiliary," organized the year before to furnish women's lounges for social occasions in the new University Gymnasium, resolved to attach itself to the Isabella McCosh Infirmary in both name and deed.

Annual dues were used for the purchase of supplies and equipment, and gifts were obtained for the initial salary of the first University Physician (appointed by the trustees in 1908 on the recommendation of the auxiliary), for a fund to help needy students pay for extra nursing and special physicians, and for an endowment fund that eventually reached $200,000.

Wives of Princeton presidents, following Mrs. McCosh's example, have shown special concern for sick students and have been frequent visitors to the Infirmary.

With steadily increasing enrollment, the original Infirmary soon became inadequate, and the auxiliary began a fund for a new building. In the capital gifts campaign at the end of the First World War, a committee of women raised an additional sum of $345,000 from 1500 donors, most of whom were women, which made possible the construction of the present Infirmary. Its cornerstone was laid at commencement in 1924, and it was dedicated at a commencement meeting of the auxiliary a year later.

This building was designed by Charles Z. Klauder, who used rough-textured red brick and limestone trim to tie it in with its neighbors, Palmer and Guyot Halls. A portrait of Mrs. McCosh, painted by John W. Alexander a few years before she died in her ninety-third year, hangs in the oak-paneled waiting room. Mrs. John Grier Hibben, who as a young faculty wife in the 1890s took Mrs. McCosh as her model, was president of the Ladies Auxiliary for many years and presided at the building's dedication. After her death a tribute to "her unfailing devotion in guarding and guiding the spirit of this Infirmary" was carved on an oak panel in the entrance hall.

The first doctor attached to the Infirmary was John McD. Carnochan 1896, who was appointed University Physician in 1908 and served in that capacity part-time while carrying on his private practice in town until his death in 1929. Employment of full-time University physicians began after the organization in 1911 of the forerunner of today's University Health Services (q.v.).

The Infirmary has long had a reputation for good food and a cheerful atmosphere. One reason for both was the long-time presence on the housekeeping staff of three members of the Hillian family, the first of whom came north from Cheraw, South Carolina, in 1917.

For half a century they contributed to the Infirmary's healing ways: Mabel and Bessie as cooks, Tom as head orderly. Mabel retired after forty-seven years of service. At the golden anniversary party the Infirmary gave Bessie on her retirement, she spoke of meeting sons of students she had known in earlier years and, recently, their grandchildren, and that this made her proud. When Tom died, the Ladies Auxiliary hung a framed tribute to him in the entrance hall of the Infirmary, which said that for forty-five years he had always been cheerful, dedicated, and thoughtful, fulfilling abundantly the Infirmary motto: "Non ministrari, sed ministrare."

McCosh Walk was named for President James McCosh, who enjoyed strolling there in days when it extended only from Prospect Gate to Washington Road. It grew longer as the Campus expanded, eventually describing an east-west axis from Lockhart Hall on University Place through the gateway north of Little Hall to the steps at Washington Road opposite the Woodrow Wilson School Plaza. A latter-day extension of the walk continues along the south side of Frick and the rear of the University Press, past the Mudd Manuscript Library, to the Engineering Quadrangle.

McMaster, John Bach (1852-1932) began his monumental eight-volume *History of the People of the United States* while he was an instructor in civil engineering at Princeton. His interest in American history had been stimulated by contact with the still expanding frontier on a fossil-collecting trip he led to Wyoming in 1878. His Princeton colleagues were apparently unaware of this interest, and the publication of the first volume of his history in 1883 led President McCosh to remark that "the sun had risen without a dawn." According to William Berryman Scott, who as a graduate student had accompanied McMaster to Wyoming, William Milligan Sloane, Professor of History and Political Science, tried to induce the trustees to establish a chair of American history for McMaster. But, said Scott, Sloane "encountered that density and obtuseness which sometimes afflicts governing bodies. McMaster had been teaching engineering; why shouldn't he stick to that? *Ne sutor ultra crepidam* [Shoemaker, stick to your last]; they remembered that much Latin."

The University of Pennsylvania thereupon called McMaster, who was only thirty-one, to a professorship in American history, which he held for thirty-seven years. His innovative books led the way in the development of social and economic history, which previously had been largely neglected for war and politics.

In 1925 Princeton invited him back to receive an honorary doctorate of letters. "His aim," Dean West said in presenting him for the degree, "was . . . to portray intimately the real life of the American people . . . to live in the times which he described and to see things as they were and thus to see the truth of history."

McMillan, Charles (1841-1927) was the College of New Jersey's first engineering professor. A graduate of Rensselaer Polytechnic Institute, he had been a draftsman and engineer for various New York water works, and a professor at Rensselaer and Lehigh before being called to Princeton in 1875 to organize a Department of Civil Engineering.

He was said to be particularly proficient in applied mathematics, a skillful topographical draftsman, a lucid lecturer, and a man of high professional ideals. His students found him a strict and, at times, severe teacher, but many discovered the kindness behind his somewhat dour exterior, particularly when they returned to him after graduation for help and advice.

As Borough Engineer, McMillan designed Princeton's first sewerage system and planned the town's modern streets. He was often consulted by the College, the Princeton Water Company, and the state of New Jersey about sanitation and water problems.

He retired in 1914, having served thirty-nine years as Professor of Civil Engineering and Applied Mathematics, and lived to see his pioneering efforts culminate in the formation of the School of Engineering in 1922.

MacMillan Building was named in honor of Edward A. MacMillan '14, Superintendent of Grounds and Buildings from 1921 to 1957. Designed by John P. Moran '51 and built in 1962 south of Baker Rink, it brought together under one roof the office of Physical Planning and the offices and shops of the Department of Physical Plant.

Madison, James, Jr., 1771 (1751-1836), statesman and political philosopher, should, by tradition, have attended the College of William and Mary in Williamsburg. Most aspiring young Virginia men of his family's station did so. Three influences, however, diverted him. One was his tutor, Thomas Martin, Princeton 1762, who persuaded him of the merits of the young institution in New Jersey. Another was President John Witherspoon's fame, which had begun to spread through the colonies. The third was Madison's family, which had differences with the administration of the Virginia college. So in the summer of 1769 Madison, the eldest of ten children, set out for the College of New Jersey.

Entering as a sophomore, Madison joined a group of students who remained his close and lifelong friends: William Bradford, Jr., 1772, later U.S. attorney general; Hugh Henry Brackenridge, 1771, jurist and novelist; and Philip Freneau, 1771, the "poet of the Revolution." Other future leaders whom he came to know at the college—which, more than any other, drew its students from throughout the colonies—included Gunning Bedford, Jr., 1771, signer of the Constitution from Delaware; Samuel Spring, 1771, Massachusetts cleric and founder in 1808 of Andover Theological Seminary; and Aaron Burr, Jr., 1772, senator from New York and vice president of the United States, who was later responsible for introducing Madison to the widow, Dolly Payne Todd. Samuel Stanhope Smith, 1769, Witherspoon's successor as president of the College, became Madison's college tutor and lasting friend. And Witherspoon himself served as Madison's moral preceptor and faithful champion. These were, as Madison called them in 1774, his "old Nassovian friends."

The College had begun to feel the winds of revolutionary politics by 1770, but Madison's two years of study were spent in reasonable tranquillity. He worked hard to master the classics and the great works of the Scottish Enlightenment, often sleeping, despite his somewhat sickly disposition, less than five hours a night. Like many later undergraduates, he came to college with a smattering of French, but, unlike them, he spoke it with a Scottish accent. "Jemmy," as he was affectionately called, also revealed a side of himself that others, usually meeting this soft-voiced man on serious public occasions, later mistook for a dour and stiff personality. He was one of the earliest members of the Whig Society, and spent much of his time debating with its members the affairs of government and society. He also wrote lusty, ribald doggerel and must have kept his eye on the alert for female companions, for he later wrote wistfully to his friend Bradford that he knew "no place so overstocked with Old-Maids as Princeton." Witherspoon, however, is said later to have told Thomas Jefferson "that in the whole career of Mr. Madison at Princeton, he had never known him to do or say an indiscreet thing."

After completing his junior and senior work in one year, Madison took his degree in the fall of 1771. However, he remained at the college until the spring of the next year to read some law and learn some Hebrew under Witherspoon's tutelage. Returning in 1772 to the pre-revolutionary calm of the Virginia piedmont, he buckled down to a regimen of reading and tutoring his younger siblings. He had warned Bradford to avoid "those impertinent fops that abound in every city"; yet he himself felt isolated in the Old Dominion. Depression and doubt beset him at the very time that his brilliant mind and celebrated convictions were taking mature shape. Given Witherspoon's influence, Madison might have entered the pulpit, but he did not do so, his thin voice possibly deterring him. The practice of law, it seems, also did not appeal to him. What might otherwise have become of this promising but unsure young man is impossible to say. But, as with so many of his generation, the Revolution helped resolve the dilemma. It gave his life a focus, at last released his energies, and dispelled his gloom. Not hardy enough to join the army, he instead helped govern Orange County, Virginia, as a member of its Committee of Safety and then helped draft the state's first constitution as a member of the Virginia general convention in 1776. These opportunities marked the beginning of one of the most distinguished public careers in the nation's history.

During these early years of national service, Madison continued to harbor doubts about his own capacities. Even after he had served in the Continental Congress as its youngest member and won election to the Virginia House of Delegates, where with Jefferson he played a major role in the passage of the historic Virginia Bill for Establishing Religious Freedom, his continued self-doubting elicited from Samuel Stanhope Smith the exasperated wish that "you had the same high opinion of yourself that others have." Yet Madison steadily accumulated the respect of others with whom he served in Virginia and the Continental Congress. (He returned to Princeton at least once during this period when the Congress fled Philadelphia in 1783 to escape the mutiny of American troops.) Bending all his efforts to serve the union, he attended the Annapolis Convention of 1786 and, at the Philadelphia Convention of 1787, was the guiding spirit behind the far-sighted Virginia Plan, which brought a working federalism into being. Without his careful note-taking during the Convention debates, we should know little of the proceedings of that historic meeting. His presence and intelligence during the Convention, acknowledged by almost everyone, won him enduring renown as "Father of the Constitution."

His work in Philadelphia done, Madison turned to securing the Constitution's acceptance. His efforts toward ratification were essential. His arguments in behalf of the Constitution at the Virginia ratifying convention carried that state for the Constitution, without which the ratification of New York might have been lost and hence the federal union with it. Moreover, his co-authorship, with Hamilton and Jay, of the *Federalist Papers*, written in 1787 and 1788 to win over doubters and opponents to the new Constitution and embodying the ideas and learning that Madison had started to accumulate at Nassau Hall some twenty years before, produced the nation's greatest contribution to Western political science. Madison's *10th Federalist*, which overturned conventional arguments about the dangers of an extended republic and provided an analysis of the social bases of political factions and a plan to check their worst effects, alone worked a revolution in political theory and is rightly considered a classic expression of American thought. For his service during this period, Princeton awarded Madison a Doctor of Laws *honoris causa* in 1787. Witherspoon wrote Madison at the time to say that Princetonians were proud to recognize in this way "one of their own sons who had done them so much honor by his public service."

In the 1790s, Madison served in the U.S. House of Representatives, where he sponsored the Bill of Rights and, with Jefferson's encouragement, created a legislative opposition to Treasury Secretary Alexander Hamilton that helped lay the basis for the Democratic-Republican party, the first modern political party in the world. In 1798, in protest against the infamous Alien and Sedition Acts, he wrote the controversial Virginia Resolution, which put forward for the first time the doctrine of state interposition, a doctrine that would deeply influence the later theories of Nullification and Secession. Upon the inauguration of his close friend Jefferson to the presidency in 1801, Madison became secretary of state. After eight years of demanding State Department service during the era of the Napoleonic Wars, he became in 1809 fourth president of the United States. His two terms in the White House were fraught with the difficulties born of war and bitter partisan struggles. Yet Madison and his administration were able to see the nation through its - Second War for Independence, which finally ended Britain's threat to the growing republic. He retired in 1817 after over forty years of public service, but continued to work for the public good by helping Jefferson found the University of Virginia, by serving as its rector after Jefferson's death, and by participating in the Virginia Constitutional Convention of 1829.

Madison always maintained a lively interest in the College of New Jersey. In 1796, he made a contribution toward the purchase of materials for instruction in chemistry. And in 1826 he accepted election as first president of the newly formed Alumni Association of Nassau Hall, a post he held until his death. He contributed regularly to the Alumni Fund in his last years and, upon his death at 85 as the last surviving signer of the Constitution, he bequeathed $1,000 to the College library from the proceeds of his posthumously published "Notes" on the debates at Philadelphia, the largest gift to the library until after the Civil War. Princeton's sense of Madison's place is perhaps best revealed by the order of honors listed on the plaque beneath his portrait in Maclean House:

James Madison—Class of 1771
First President of the
Alumni Association
Fourth President of the United States

Madison's greatest contribution to the nation's history was his ability to translate theory into institutions and norms. No more apt characterization of him can be found than Jefferson's in 1812: "I do not know in the world a man of purer integrity, more dispassionate, disinterested, and devoted to genuine Republicanism; nor could I in the whole scope of America and Europe point out an abler head."

James M. Banner, Jr.

Madison Hall is the collective designation for the freshmen and sophomore dining halls erected in 1916 at the corner of Nassau Street and University Place and named for James Madison 1771. Five great Gothic dining halls are grouped around a central kitchen— Upper and Lower Cloister (next to the cloister that forms the west side of Holder Court), Upper and Sub Eagle (named for the carvings at the ends of the ceiling beams) on University Place, and Madison Hall on Nassau Street. Designed by Day and Klauder, this imposing group of buildings was the gift of Mrs. Russell Sage, the Classes of 1916, 1917, and 1918, and others. They occupy the site of a hotel called University Hall, which, after eight unprofitable years, was given over to the College in 1883 for use as a dormitory and later as the University dining halls.

Madison, James, Medal is awarded annually to a Graduate School alumnus who has attained distinction in his professional career, in the advancement of higher education, or in public service. It is named for the fourth president of the United States who, after receiving his bachelor's degree from the College in 1771, remained here another year to continue his studies under President Witherspoon. Madison Medalists have included John Bardeen Ph.D. '36, twice a Nobel laureate in physics; Thornton Wilder, A.M. '26, Pulitzer Prize-winning novelist and playwright; William O. Baker Ph.D. '39, president, Bell Telephone Laboratories; General Andrew J. Goodpaster Ph.D. '50, Supreme Commander of NATO 1969-1974; John Willard Milnor '51, Ph.D. '54, mathematics professor in the University and later at the Institute for Advanced Study.

Magie, William Francis 1879 (1858-1943), a founder of the American Physical Society and its president from 1910 to 1912, taught physics at Princeton for almost half a century and was chairman of the department during twenty of its formative years. He was one of the able group of alumni of the McCosh era (e.g., Wilson, Fine, West, Hibben) who nurtured Princeton's development from a college to a university.

Magie's early interests were humanistic. In his sophomore year he tried reading his way through the masterpieces of English literature on his own. As an upperclassman he came under the influence of Cyrus Fogg Brackett, Charles A. Young, and Arnold Guyot (qq.v.), excellent scientists and extraordinary teachers—and President McCosh (q.v.), whose "dogmatic methods aroused our antagonism but made us think."

Magie was an editor of the *Princetonian* as were his classmate Woodrow Wilson and Henry B. Fine 1880. He stood near the top of his class all four years and at graduation was class valedictorian. He had thought of following his father into the practice of law, but, stirred by news of the first

Princeton expedition to the West in 1877 and the subsequent paleontological researches of William Berryman Scott and Henry Fairfield Osborn, Magie "could not help wishing" that he too "might have a chance to work in some scientific field."

His chance came toward the end of his senior year, when Professor Brackett, who was carrying all of the work of physics instruction single-handed, suffered a breakdown, and his friends insisted that he should have an assistant. Brackett offered Magie the job on Commencement Day, and he accepted. "I did not then know it," Magie told his classmates fifty years later, "but I now know that the subject of physics, into which I was inducted in this somewhat casual way, was the one subject which was best suited to my habits of thought. I never had enough originality or mathematical skill to do great original work, but I always loved the fundamental and philosophical aspects of the subject, and loved to teach it."

Magie did not neglect the scholarly side of his career. After collaborating on a small piece of research on the electrical discharge, he and Henry B. Fine were given leave in 1884 and went to Germany, where Magie studied at the University of Berlin under the great Helmholtz, and earned his Ph.D. with a thesis on the measurement of surface tensions. A decade later he collaborated with two physicians in publishing the first paper in this country on the possible use of Roentgen's newly discovered X-rays in surgery. He later published occasional papers on the properties of solutions, and was the author of a highly regarded account of the rise and content of physical theories, *Principles of Physics*.

His greatest contribution, however, was in teaching and administration. After 1889, when Brackett began his graduate program in electrical engineering, Magie took over the undergraduate courses in physics, and shared increasingly in the administration of the department. On Brackett's retirement in 1908, Magie succeeded him as chairman and, a little later, as Joseph Henry Professor of Physics. Magie and Brackett worked closely with Dean Fine in building up a strong physics department as part of Fine's efforts, as President Wilson's dean of the faculty, to strengthen all the science departments. In the controversy between President Wilson and Dean West, Fine supported Wilson, but Magie sided with West.

When Hibben became president in 1912, Magie accepted appointment as Henry B. Fine's successor as dean of the faculty; he held this office until 1925. He continued to serve as chairman of the physics department until his retirement in 1929. At Commencement that year President Hibben conferred on him an honorary Sc. D.

As departmental chairman and dean, Magie was noted for his calmness, patience, and fairness. Allen Shenstone '14, his student, later his colleague, and then his successor as chairman of the department, said that the cordial relationship that had always been maintained in the physics department "through agreements and disagreements" was due to the enduring influence of the personality of Magie, "a man of firm character but gentle manners."

The Magie Apartments for junior faculty on the north side of Lake Carnegie, next to the Hibben Apartments, were named for Dean Magie in 1965.

Mann, Thomas (1875-1955), self-exiled German novelist and winner of the 1929 Nobel Prize in Literature, lived in Princeton for two and a half years 1938-1941, and was formally associated with the University during the academic years 1938-1940.

Mann had left Germany in 1933 when Hitler rose to power. After five years in Switzerland he was encouraged by friends to settle in this country, and President Dodds and Dean Gauss persuaded him to accept appointment as a lecturer in the University. While here Mann gave public lectures on Goethe, Wagner, and Freud and guest lectures in upperclass courses on the German romantic movement and the European novel.

The University made him a Doctor of Letters *honoris causa* at a special convocation in Nassau Hall in May 1939. In a moving response Mann expressed gratitude for his new home in America and spoke of gratitude in general: "To be grateful for all life's blessings, . . . is the best condition for a happy life. A joke, a good meal, a fine spring day, a work of art, a human personality, a voice, a glance—but this is not all. For there is another kind of gratitude . . . the feeling that makes us thankful for suffering, for the hard and heavy things of life, for the deepening of our natures which perhaps only suffering can bring. . . ."

During their stay in Princeton Mr. and Mrs. Mann lived in the red brick Georgian house at the corner of Stockton Street and Library Place. Here, working three or four hours every morning, seven days a week, he completed *Lotte in Weimar* and started the fourth volume of the *Joseph* tales. Here, also, he wrote his essays against Nazism.

Mann found Princeton pleasant. "This town is like a park," he wrote a friend in Europe, "with wonderful opportunities for walks and with astonishing trees that now, during Indian summer, glow in the most magnificent colors." He and Albert Einstein, who had been friends in Germany, met frequently in each other's homes. Eventually a warmer climate lured Mann to California, where he remained until 1953 when he returned to Switzerland to spend his last years.

In 1964 a stone tablet with the words "THOMAS MANN LIVED HERE 1938-1941" was placed in the brick wall at the front of the house at 65 Stockton Street (now occupied by the Aquinas Institute). At its dedication Professor Victor Lange, then chairman of the department of German, expressed the hope that as "a lasting reminder of Thomas Mann's presence in Princeton" it might "strengthen the spirit of courageous humanism among us and reaffirm the vision of a community of free men to which his life and work bore such eloquent testimony."

Maritain, Jacques (1882-1973), French philosopher and man of letters, was a professor of philosophy in the University from 1948 to 1952 and continued to make his home in Princeton until 1960. The author of more than fifty books, he was a preeminent interpreter of the thought of Thomas Aquinas and a creative thinker in his own right in metaphysics, moral philosophy, social and political philosophy, the philosophy of art, and the theory of knowledge.

Maritain, brought up in liberal Protestantism, and his wife, Raissa, a Russian Jew whom he met when they were students at the Sorbonne, were converted to the Roman Catholic faith two years after their marriage in 1904. For many years Maritain was professor of philosophy at the Institut Catholique de Paris. He was in the United States

on a lecture tour in 1940 when the Germans overran France, and he remained here in exile throughout the war. He became a visiting professor at Columbia University; during 1941-1942 he came to Princeton three days a week to give a graduate course in medieval philosophy.

After the war Maritain was French Ambassador to the Vatican from 1945 to 1948. He came back to Princeton in 1946 to take part in a conference on "The Humanistic Tradition in the Century Ahead" and to accept an honorary degree at the University's Bicentennial Celebration. The following year he was tendered an invitation to join the Princeton faculty, under unusual circumstances that he later recalled in his book *Reflections on America* (1958). "In December, 1947, returning to Rome from Mexico City," he wrote, "I stopped in New York for a few hours to change planes. President Dodds was there; he had been so kind as to come to New York to offer me—if I should resign my diplomatic post at the Vatican—a professorship at Princeton University, precisely in my capacity as a philosopher dedicated to the spirit and principles of Thomas Aquinas. The fact that Princeton is a secular university of Presbyterian origin made him only more interested in such a teaching appointment." Maritain accepted and came to Princeton as professor of philosophy in 1948. His years at Princeton were felicitous ones. "In no European university," he wrote, "would I have found the spirit of liberty and congeniality I found at Princeton in teaching moral philosophy in the light of Thomas Aquinas."

In addition to a graduate course in moral philosophy he also contributed to the undergraduate Special Program in the Humanities. He retired in 1952 at age seventy and began to enjoy, in his words, "the Elysian status of an Emeritus." He continued to live in Princeton and to contribute to its intellectual life until the death of his wife in 1960, when he retired to a monastery in Toulouse. There he died on April 28, 1973, at the age of ninety.

Maritain was a warm, gentle man. He was admired, one of his colleagues said, even by those of different philosophical convictions, "for his lifelong zeal for truth and impassioned commitment to freedom . . . his humility, his charity, his fraternal attitude toward all that is."

Marquand, Allan (1853-1924), founded the Department of Art and Archaeology and for more than forty years devoted his talents and his means to making it one of the best in the country. He shared with Charles Eliot Norton of Harvard the distinction of being the first to introduce the serious study of art into the curriculum of the American college.

The son of Henry Gurdon Marquand, a New York banker and one of the founders and a chief benefactor of the Metropolitan Museum of Art, he was educated at St. Paul's School and at Princeton. In college he was an excellent student, an accomplished gymnast, first-place winner in three track events, and president of the Boating Club, which sponsored the crew. He graduated second in his class (1874) and was Latin salutatorian and class president. His classmates rejoiced in his success because, they said, "jealousy and envy of others were not in him."

After graduation he studied theology for three years at Princeton Seminary and at Union Seminary in New York, and then, after a year of study at the University of Berlin, went to Johns Hopkins, where he received his Ph.D. in philosophy. At Johns Hopkins, he invented an ingenious "logic machine" —a forerunner of the computer— which is preserved in Firestone Library. He was called back to Princeton as lecturer in logic and tutor in Latin in 1881. President McCosh, detecting an unorthodox, unCalvinistic bent in Marquand's teaching of philosophy, encouraged him to undertake instead the teaching of the history of art. He became an instructor in this subject in 1882 and, a year later, first incumbent of a professorship of art and archaeology, endowed by his uncle, Frederick Marquand.

He held this chair until 1910 when he relinquished it in order to provide funds for an additional professor in the department; thereafter he served the University without salary. He made important gifts to the Art Museum, of which he was the first director, and supplied the department's library with books and photographs from his own collection and paid for other departmental purchases out of his own pocket. He also founded and financed the *Princeton Monographs in Art and Archaeology*.

His generosity was matched by the personal interest he took in his colleagues and his students and by the influence he exerted on them. "There was in his character," Professor C. Rufus Morey said, "a refinement that had nothing about it of the fastidious, but rejected nonetheless the false and unworthy with unerring discernment. Without conscious effort on his part, his life and work evoked in his pupils and associates a standard of precision and candor in scholarship."

Marquand's devoted effort brought forth a good harvest. In 1882 he was the lone instructor of a few students. Forty years later he presided over an art faculty of thirteen members who gave sixteen courses elected by eight hundred undergraduates. In all the colleges east of the Mississippi, half of the teachers of art had been trained in the graduate curriculum he had developed.

WORK ON THE DELLA ROBBIAS

A chief ornament of the *Princeton Monographs in Art and Archaeology* was Marquand's own life-work—his eight-volume *catalogue raisonné* of the works of the ateliers of members of the Della Robbia family, fifteenth- and sixteenty-century Florentine sculptors and ceramists. His interest in these artists began with an altarpiece by Andrea Della Robbia that his father bought for the Metropolitan Museum in 1882. After publishing a study of this altarpiece in the *American Journal of Archaeology* in 1891, he made a tour of Italy (the first of many) in search of unstudied Della Robbia works, and his preliminary observations appeared in the *Journal* and in *Scribner's Magazine* in 1893.

A lapse of almost twenty years between his initial quest for material and the appearance of the first published results of his investigations, was due in part to the demands of other publications, including his work on *Greek Architecture*, and in part to the thoroughness of his scholarship. The first Della Robbia volume, which inaugurated the *Princeton Monographs*, appeared in 1912; the second, in 1914. Then, after five more years of research, five more volumes appeared in rapid succession between 1919 and 1922. Failing health interrupted completion of the eighth and last volume, but the manuscript he left was so far advanced that it was readily completed by his colleagues after his death. All eight volumes were republished in 1972.

Shy and somewhat hesitant in manner, Marquand was most effective as a teacher in small groups. There his own example generated standards of accuracy and thoroughness, and his kindliness encouraged his students to develop their own views. His famous course in Italian sculpture, through which all the graduate students of the department passed at some time in their careers, was noted for the completeness with which it explored all of the important monuments and the published works about them, and the opportunity Marquand gave to all his students to express their own theories. "Even in his own field of the Della Robbias," one of his former students recalled, "he took the attitude that *we* knew as much about it as he, and in that way gave us a sort of professional courage."

Outside of Princeton he was equally active and generous in promoting his chosen subject. He was one of the founders of the Archaeological Institute of America and of the *American Journal of Archaeology*. For some thirty years he anonymously financed traveling fellowships of the Institute and as chairman of the Committee on Medieval and Renaissance Studies—his own creation —helped initiate the careers of a long line of students and teachers of the fine arts. He also supported the American School of Classical Studies in Rome at which he served a year as professor of archaeology.

According to Professor Morey, his successor as chairman of the department,

> Marquand's work was achieved with no sacrifice of the quiet kindliness which constantly marked his relations with others.

Lacking completely the aggressive force with which other creative spirits have gained their ends, Allan Marquand built unconsciously on the loyalty and devotion which he inspired in all who worked in close contact with him. Like his favorite artist, Luca [della Robbia], he saw life simply and directly, and as something which was ultimately sound and beautiful. This viewpoint, his work, and his influence, derive their common admirable character, in the last analysis, from the outstanding quality which is basic in every estimate of the man, and in every memory his deeds and human contacts have left behind them: his utter and unconscious unselfishness.

THE MARQUAND LIBRARY

Professor Marquand began to build an outstanding art library for his own use early in his career. He transferred it from his house to the Campus in 1900, formally deeded it to the University in 1908, and continued to add to it during his lifetime. It provides the nucleus of the library that has been developed as a memorial to him and that is now considered one of the finest art libraries in the world.

MARQUAND PARK

In 1887 Professor Marquand acquired an estate in the western section of town, which he renamed Guernsey Hall after the island home of his Huguenot ancestors. Here he and Mrs. Marquand, who was a recognized authority on flowers and trees in old paintings and manuscripts and an honorary Master of Arts of the University, frequently entertained faculty and students.

In 1953 their children gave seventeen acres of the estate to Princeton Borough for use as a park. It provides open playing fields and walks among handsome, old, and often rare, trees for the enjoyment of the people of Princeton.

Mathematics has been prominent in the Princeton curriculum since the founding of the College. In 1760, entering students were required to have an understanding of the rules of arithmetic, and underclassmen learned algebra, trigonometry, geometry, and conic sections. In 1853 a Boston newspaper reported that at Princeton the study of mathematics was carried on "to an extent not excelled by any other college in the country." In the early years, instruction in mathematics was given by faculty members who generally taught other subjects as well. The first trained mathematician on the faculty was Walter Minto, who had studied in Pisa and had taught in Edinburgh before being called to Princeton in 1787. Not until a century later did the College again have on its faculty teachers who had studied in the European mathematical centers; the first was Henry Burchard Fine (A.B. Princeton 1880), who received his Ph.D. degree at Leipzig in 1885.

The state of mathematics in Princeton changed dramatically after 1905; the beginning of the development of Princeton as one of the world's great centers of mathematical teaching and research took place that year, and was primarily due to Henry Burchard Fine. Fine had been appointed dean of the faculty by President Woodrow Wilson in 1903; and when the University was organized into academic departments in 1904 he was also appointed the first chairman of the Department of Mathematics. In 1905 Fine persuaded Wilson to extend the new preceptorial system to include mathematics and to appoint as preceptors a very promising group of young mathematicians, including Luther P. Eisenhart, who had come to Princeton as an instructor in 1900 and became a distinguished differential geometer, and Oswald Veblen, a geometer and later a mathematical statesman. Dean Fine's ability to detect mathematical talent is evidenced by even a partial list of other appointments he made to the Princeton faculty: James Jeans, Professor of Applied Mathematics, who shortly returned to Cambridge University; George David Birkhoff, who later became the leading mathematical figure at Harvard; J.H.M. Wedderburn, an algebraist whose name is familiar to all mathematicians; James W. Alexander II (B.S. Princeton 1910, Ph.D. 1915), the topologist; and Solomon Lefschetz, the algebraic geometer and topologist. These appointments produced a mathematics faculty of the first rank during the 1920s, and an atmosphere of freshness and enthusiasm that lured a great many of the ablest young mathematicians to postgraduate study at Princeton as National Research Fellows. The publication of the Annals of Mathematics was taken over from Harvard in 1911; and under the direction of Wedderburn and Lefschetz (successively chief editors of that journal for over forty years) the Annals became one of the principal journals of research mathematics in the world.

During this period, mathematics in Princeton, and indeed throughout the United States, was still under a severe handicap in comparison with mathematics in the great European centers. All of the mathematicians in this country were primarily teachers; faculties were small, and the teaching loads, consisting mainly of rather routine courses, were heavy. In Europe by contrast there were forty or fifty posts that were essentially research professorships of mathematics, with limited teaching duties and considerable prestige. The situation changed in 1928, when Princeton instituted the scientific research fund, which made possible a stream of distinguished visiting mathematicians such as G. H. Hardy and P.A.M. Dirac of Cambridge and P. A. Alexandroff of Moscow. At that time too Princeton established the first research professorship in mathematics in the United States, the Henry Burchard Fine Professorship, a gift of Thomas D. Jones 1876. In addition, Jones and his niece Gwethalyn Jones endowed a memorial building to honor Dean Fine, who died in 1928. This building, dedicated in 1931, was commodious and elegant, with handsome wood-panelled library, common rooms, and faculty studies; it housed the department in comfort and style for almost forty years, and Fine Hall became synonymous with the Princeton Department of Mathematics.

Mathematical research in the United States was further advanced when the Institute for Advanced Study was founded in Princeton in 1930. Although the Institute and the University are separate institutions, they have had close and productive relations from the beginning. The School of Mathematics was the first branch of the Institute to be staffed in 1932, and had temporary quarters in Fine Hall until 1939. Two of the Institute's first five professors, Alexander and Veblen, had been at the University for many years, John von Neumann had been professor of mathematical physics since 1930, and Hermann Weyl had been the Thomas D. Jones Professor of Mathematical Physics at Princeton in 1928-1929.

Only Einstein had never held a position at the University, although he had delivered a series of lectures there on the theory of relativity in 1921. The Institute joined the University in the publication of the Annals of Mathematics, and in the founding of the Princeton Mathematics Series (1939) and the Annals of Mathematics Studies (1940), both of which were originated and edited for many years by Albert W. Tucker and continue to be published by Princeton University Press.

Under the chairmanship, from 1929 to 1945, of Fine's successor, Luther P. Eisenhart, the department continued to make outstanding appointments of promising young mathematicians, such as Alonzo Church, a noted logician; Eugene P. Wigner, Thomas D. Jones Professor of Mathematical Physics and later a Nobel laureate; Salomon Bochner, known for the breadth of his contributions to many different areas of analysis; and Samuel S. Wilks, a distinguished mathematical statistician. With the permanent mathematical faculties and visiting members of the University and the Institute, Princeton became an intensely active center for mathematical research in the 1930s. Reporting on an International Congress of Mathematicians held in Oslo in 1936, a Norwegian newspaper ran this headline: "Princeton is the mathematical center of the world but at the moment it is in Oslo."

During the 1920s and 1930s Princeton's uniquely successful graduate program in mathematics also developed. For two decades after 1935, Princeton produced more Ph.D. degrees in mathematics than any other American university; and an American Mathematical Society study in 1974 showed that the Princeton graduate program is by far the largest producer of the tenured faculty members in the country's leading mathematics departments. The characteristic aspects of the Princeton Ph.D. program in mathematics are freedom from formal course requirements, an emphasis on original research at an early stage of the student's education, and a spirit of cooperative study and research in which the students and faculty participate jointly.

Political developments in Europe in the 1930s increased the flow of talented refugees to the United States, and the University and the Institute helped to channel many mathematicians to positions in this country. This vast influx of talent altered the mathematical balance of the world, and finally raised American mathematics to the level of that of the older centers of research in Europe. The first postwar international gathering of mathematicians—over a hundred leaders from nine nations—took place in Fine Hall in 1946, as part of Princeton's bicentennial celebration. The greater amount of mathematical teaching and research required in the more technologically oriented postwar world led to an increase in the size of the faculty. Among those added to the faculty during Solomon Lefschetz's chairmanship, from 1945 to 1953, were Ralph Fox and Norman Steenrod in topology; Emil Artin in algebra; John Tukey in mathematical statistics; Valentine Bargmann and Arthur Wightman in mathematical physics; William Feller in probability; and Donald C. Spencer in analysis.

Lefschetz was succeeded as chairman by Albert W. Tucker, who served from 1953 to 1963. Thereafter the character of the departmental administration changed to a more cooperative undertaking, with duties shared by almost the entire senior faculty; John W. Milnor, Gilbert A. Hunt, Elias M. Stein, William Browder, Joseph J. Kohn, and Robert C. Gunning served successive short terms as chairmen after 1963. Milnor (Princeton A.B. 1951, Ph.D. 1954, winner of the Madison medal, 1977), who had written his first published paper as a freshman, was promoted to full professor in 1960, the youngest in 50 years. He became a professor at the Institute for Advanced Study in 1969. His age record for professorial precocity was broken by Charles L. Fefferman (Princeton Ph.D. 1969), who became full professor of mathematics at the University of Chicago in 1971, and a year later, at the age of 23, was elected by the trustees to a professorship at Princeton, thus equaling a record set a century and a half earlier by another professor of mathematics, John Maclean, later president of the College. These and other appointments during this period gave Princeton a strong faculty in topology (traditionally an area of excellence at Princeton), in algebraic number theory and algebraic geometry, in various branches of analysis (Fourier analysis, partial differential equations, complex analysis, probability), and in mathematical physics (a unique interdepartmental program).

During the 1950s and 1960s the heightened national interest in science and mathematics following Sputnik and the space program led to a further expansion of the department. The number of graduate students increased considerably, with generous support through the National Science Foundation and Woodrow Wilson Foundation Fellowships; undergraduate majors increased from a handful to over two dozen each year; and by the mid-sixties the faculty had more than doubled

since the war. Altogether, the department was nearly five times larger than when it had moved into Fine Hall in 1931, so that that elegant building was no longer large enough. A new building, adjacent to the new physics building, was erected in 1969 to house the Department of Mathematics and the new Department of Statistics, which had separated from the Mathematics Department in 1965 under the chairmanship of John W. Tukey. The new building, with a tower containing faculty studies, a large underground library, and extensive study areas, was a sharp contrast to the old building; but to mark fittingly the continuity of what had by now become the distinguished tradition of Princeton mathematics, the name Fine Hall was transferred to the new building, and the old one renamed Jones Hall in honor of the original donors. The Department has continued to flourish in its new quarters, and to uphold its reputation as a world center for teaching and research in mathematics.

Robert C. Gunning

Mather Sun Dial, The, in the court of McCosh Hall, is a replica of the historic Turnbull Sun Dial constructed in 1551 at Corpus Christi College, Oxford. It was given by Sir William Mather, governor of Victoria University, Manchester, England, to "symbolize the connection between Oxford and Princeton [and] . . . Great Britain and America," and was unveiled on his behalf by Viscount James Bryce, then British ambassador to the United States, in 1907. The monumental shaft, rising from a broad base to a height of more than twenty feet, is topped by a pelican, religious symbol of Corpus Christi. Inscribed around the base are these words from Samuel Butler's *Hudibras*:

Loyalty is e'er the same
Whether it win or lose the game
True as the dial to the sun
Although it be not shined upon.

Mathey, Dean '12 (1890-1972), who served as a trustee under Presidents Hibben, Dodds, and Goheen, was one of the most devoted, energetic, and generous supporters of the University in modern times. His association with Princeton covered a period of sixty-five years and included a wide acquaintance among trustees, faculty, and alumni.

He first came to Princeton in 1907 to play in the University's annual interscholastic tennis tournament, which he won. In his book of Princeton reminiscences, *Men and Gothic Towers*, he recalled the "lovely starlit early May evening" when, as an overnight guest of an upperclassman in Blair Hall, he heard the seniors singing on the steps of Nassau Hall, and was stirred by the program, "a medley of sentiment, humor, loyalty to Alma Mater and the nation." He was also inspired by the beauty of the Gothic buildings, by "Blair Arch with its spectacular steps, the clock in the tower."

The next summer, in 1908, he won the national interscholastic tennis championship at Newport, Rhode Island, and that fall he entered Princeton. He twice won the national intercollegiate doubles championship—in 1910 with a classmate, Burnham N. Dell; in 1911 with another classmate, Charles T. Butler—and was captain of the University tennis team in his senior year. He was elected to Phi Beta Kappa and graduated with honors. He also "had the good fortune" to hear Woodrow Wilson lecture in his popular course in

jurisprudence a short time before Wilson left Princeton to run for governor of New Jersey in the fall of 1910, and was Wilson's great admirer, "as was the entire student body." In 1912, he cast his first presidential vote for Wilson and for many years thereafter liked to identify himself as a "Woodrow Wilson Democrat," which, to his amusement, perplexed some of his Republican associates on Wall Street. Later, as a trustee, he headed the campaign that raised funds for an increased endowment for the School of Public and International Affairs as a memorial to Wilson.

On graduation, Mathey started to work as a bond salesman, at $15 a week, for William A. Read & Co. and eventually became a partner of its successor, Dillon, Read & Co. He found Wall Street a satisfying outlet for his competitive spirit and gradually built up a sizable fortune.

He came to live in Princeton in 1927 in an old farmhouse that he had remodeled with the help of his architect classmate Arthur Holden, on property he had bought from the estate of Moses Taylor Pyne (q.v.). Here he gave luncheons for classmates on Reunion Saturdays and for University trustees and officers on Baccalaureate Sundays and entertained University guests when need arose.

He was alumni trustee of the University from 1927 to 1931, charter trustee from 1931 to 1960, trustee emeritus from 1960 until his death; he served at various times on every one of the board's nine standing committees.

His twelve years as chairman of the finance committee, 1949 to 1960, and of its subcommittee on investments, were marked by a sixfold increase in the University's budget and a doubling in value of its investment pool. He was fond of saying, if asked about some attractive investment his committee may have overlooked, "Well, you can't kiss all the pretty girls," but, as one of his associates said, "Mathey didn't miss many of them."

His greatest love was the committee on grounds and buildings, on which he served for thirty-four years and of which he was chairman from 1942 to 1949. "He gave countless hours to every phase of the committee's work," President Goheen said, "from the smallest details to the largest matters of policy, with unfailing concern for the preservation of the beauty and, in his words, 'the human feel' of the Princeton campus."

Mathey's love of architectural niceties, his affection for his family and friends, and his regard for the traditions of the place can be seen here and there across the campus. He conceived of the Henry B. Thompson Memorial Court within the East Pyne Building. With Mrs. Harold W. Dodds, he planned the garden in memory of President Hibben and the bench in memory of Beatrix Farrand (q.v.) on the north side of the chapel. He gave the Dean Samuel Winans wall enclosing the rear garden of the John Maclean House, in memory of his father-in-law, and the Gertrude Winans Mathey faculty housing near the Graduate College, in memory of his first wife. He proposed, and with another Princeton tennis captain, Joseph L. Werner '21, was co-donor of the pavilion between the rows of tennis courts on Brokaw Field. When his classmate Sanford B. White, a legendary athlete of their college days, died in 1964, Mathey led the Class of 1912 in providing in White's memory another pavilion which stands in the midst of the Bedford, Gulick, and Pardee playing fields.

In 1933 he served on the committee appointed to wait on Harold W. Dodds to notify him of his election as president, and in 1957 on the committee that recommended Robert F. Goheen's election as president.

Mathey held that the trustees of a university cannot delegate their responsibilities but that they can and should delegate to the president the authority vested in them by charter. "They should choose . . . the best educator . . . they can find," he wrote, "and [then], though there may be differences between members of the board and even the whole board of trustees about minor policies from time to time, they should back up their president in his over-all educational policies and [defend him] from the heckling of chronic alumni gripers who think the old place is going to the dogs."

As a trustee Mathey practiced what he preached, supporting the University with an open-minded concern and a large generosity.

Perhaps his most consistently felt—and generously shown—interest [President Goheen wrote] was the development of faculty housing. . . . How much he did by generous gift, as well as by wise judgment, in this area of the University's needs, is little known, for he preferred not to take the credit; but I can tell you it was very large.

And this is a clue to the personality of Dean Mathey—so cheerful and outspoken in everything—and all the while modestly concealing his own role. The full extent of his many gracious and generous thoughts and acts on behalf of Princeton and Princetonians was probably not fully understood by anyone—perhaps not even by himself.

. . . Financier he was, overseer of buildings and grounds he was, but he always placed the human concern ahead of all others. Liveliness and warmth went with keen intelligence and shrewd judgment. Dean liked people.

Mathey never revealed to anyone the extent of his benefactions to the University, but he did disclose the philosophy behind them in an essay he wrote for the Class of 1912's *Fifty Year Record*: "Why do we, along with the alumni . . . of our sister colleges, return to our campuses with a certain solemnity—even though it be on joyous occasions such as a reunion or a traditional football game?" he asked his classmates. "And why do so many of us so often lay so much of our treasure at our Alma Mater's feet?"

I believe the causes of this loyalty to our private colleges [he wrote] . . . go back to the first law of nature, namely survival. For, it seems to me, we sense how fleeting all things are, not only the things we build with our hands, but life itself and even our posterity. And along with this we also sense, subconsciously perhaps, that the great seats of learning . . . some established as far back as the eleventh century—have withstood the ravages of time better than any other thing to which we ourselves may contribute.

Minto, Walter (1753-1796), one of Princeton's earliest teachers of mathematics, was perhaps the first deserving the designation "mathematician." Born in Scotland, in a family of Spanish origin, he read in theology at Edinburgh, and after studying mathematics and astronomy in Pisa, became a professor of mathematics at the University of Edinburgh. In 1783 he published a treatise on the recently discovered planet Uranus, which contained mathematical formulas for determining astronomical magnitudes; and in 1787 he collaborated on a biography of John Napier, the Scottish inventor of logarithms.

A warm supporter of the cause of American independence, Minto came to America in 1786. He spent a year as principal of Erasmus Hall, a newly founded boy's school at Flatbush, Long Island, and in 1787 accepted a call to Princeton as professor of mathematics and natural philosophy at a salary of £200 a year plus room and board.

Minto was successful as a teacher and well regarded by the College authorities. When he died at the age of forty-two, he had been treasurer of the College and clerk of the Board of Trustees for a year, and had almost completed the manuscript for a book on mathematics.

Minto's inaugural oration, delivered on Commencement eve in 1788, and printed by Isaac Collins of Trenton, contains an account of the progress of mathematical science up to that time and a persuasive statement of its importance as an intellectual discipline ("there is no occupation so well adapted . . . to brighten and enlarge that reasoning power which forms the most distinguishing feature of man . . ."). The oration also reveals, in its concluding prayer, Minto's love of liberty as well as of reason, and his faith in their place in his adopted land:

Father of truth and reason and of every thing that lives! Be pleased to prosper the interests of science and literature in the United States of America: to make those interests ever subservient to the promotion of liberty, happiness, and virtue . . . to protect this country as a secure and happy asylum to the oppressed in all quarters of the globe . . . to cause truth and reason at length to obtain a glorious and everlasting victory over error and violence. . . .

Moffett Laboratory, which adjoins the eastern wing of Guyot Hall, was built in 1960 to provide additional space for the Department of Biology. Its cost was defrayed jointly by the Whitehall Foundation and the National Institutes of Health, and it was named for George M. Moffett '04, founder of the Whitehall Foundation and donor in 1952 of the Moffett Professorship of Biology.

In addition to teaching laboratories and offices, Moffett Laboratory contains radioisotope laboratories and many types of specialized equipment for the study of physiological and biochemical processes, greenhouse space and plant growth chambers for the study of plant development, and a variety of different temperature-controlled rooms for studies on a wide range of biological phenomena.

Morey, Charles Rufus (1877-1955), chairman of the Department of Art and Archaeology from 1924 to 1945, was a scholar who reminded some people of a prosperous banker, others (as one colleague put it) of a good bishop "respected by the mighty and loved by the poor."

With his A.B. and A.M. from the University of Michigan and three years' experience as Fellow of the American School of Classical Studies in Rome, Morey came to Princeton in 1903 as a fellow in classics. Three years later, he accepted the invitation of Allan Marquand (q.v.) to become a Wilson-appointed preceptor in art history.

In his thirty-nine years in the department, Morey not only helped establish the budding discipline as a respected field of learning but, as Professor Erwin Panofsky has pointed out, was one of those responsible for the fact "that the contribution of American scholarship has left its imprint on the history of art all over the world." His books, *Early Christian Art* and *Medieval Art*, both published in 1942, rank at the top of his voluminous bibliography. One critic thought that in *Early Christian Art* "Morey alone provided a theory comprehensive enough to guide research," and found his "union of theoretical breadth and minute observation of particulars . . . extremely rare in English writing on art."

Morey taught renaissance and modern art as well as his specialities, practicing his own precept that his faculty should be knowledgeable in all fields. Demanding much of co-workers, he gave much. When called to another university, his price to Princeton for refusing was a sabbatical every seventh semester for his faculty to study abroad. He increased endowment for his department by "soaking the rich," apparently with their cordial approval. In his publications grateful acknowledgement of his graduate students' research built their self-confidence and pleasure in their work (exuberantly expressed by them in a hymnal parody: "He cited me . . . His faithful slave I'll ever be. For in his book he cited me.") His faith in his younger faculty led to long lists of recommended promotions which, it is said, once caused the dean of the faculty, Robert K. Root, to exclaim: "ALL Rufus's ducklings are swans!"

Ambition for his department never limited his concern for the University, for art history, or for humanism in general. He was an active, at times formidable, participant in faculty meetings. In 1932 he distributed at one meeting a booklet printed at his expense, *A Laboratory-Library*, describing "a workplace for students as well as teachers rather than a storehouse for books." Thus he planted the seed for some unique and widely copied features of Firestone Library, built fifteen years later to serve the University generally in ways that the Marquand Library had so well served art historians. Similarly he helped develop New York University's Institute of Fine Arts and the Institute for Advanced Study's School of Humanities, endeavors cited by Panofsky as evidence that Morey "could not prevent the force of his personality from acting upon his surroundings much as the force of gravity operates in the physical world."

There were numerous other manifestations of this force. Morey originated the Index of Christian Art (q.v.) in 1917 and later initiated and directed the Vatican's catalogue of Christian art. For seven years he guided a consortium of five institutions (including Princeton) in a joint excavation of Antioch, and he supervised the ensuing publications. He helped found and nurture the College Art Association and its publication, *The Art Bulletin*. Finally there were the five years (1945-1950) he spent as Cultural Affairs Officer at the United States Embassy in Rome.

During his tour of duty in Rome, he was credited with healing more war wounds than would have been possible for a professional diplomat. Using army trucks and naval vessels, he reopened the flow of journals, books, and photographs between Italy and America before the usual postal channels were operating. Aided by former students, some still in uniform, he located and

restored to Italy paintings, sculptures, even whole libraries, which the Nazis had removed. He drew Roman archaeological and historical institutions into a union that helped their depleted staffs become effective once again. In spite of great difficulties, he even met the Metropolitan Museum's request for a loan of two statues (one a Michelangelo) for its Diamond Jubilee. Finding Lloyd's premiums exorbitant, Morey resolutely shipped the precious packages uninsured, commandeering a fleet of MP's on motorcycles and the battleship *Missouri* for their transportation.

This was the same man who, lecturing one night at the Morgan Library, became so absorbed in a hitherto unnoticed detail of one of his slides that he ceased talking until the director sent up a note inviting him "to share his thoughts with his audience." His style—in thought, action, and personal relations—was total involvement. As a teacher, one of his strongest motivating influences was his obvious distress when students failed, his real delight when they succeeded. In soliciting contributions to his projects he responded genuinely to the interests of others (even to the point of admiring one prospect's dog, which had just bitten him) before drawing them toward his own concerns.

Panofsky spoke for many when, in commenting on Professor Morey's fundamental goodness and strength of character, he wrote:

No one can number those who . . . owed to him their place in the world, their scale of values, their sense of direction in life. No one who knew him can forget the brief, warm smile that could suddenly illumine his strong, often stern-looking face and give confidence to the timid and courage to the troubled.

Martha Lou Stohlman

Mudd, Seeley G., Manuscript Library is named for the dean of the University of Southern California School of Medicine whose will established a $44 million fund for American university and college buildings. The trustees of this fund made a grant of $1,125,000 to Princeton toward the $2,500,000 needed for a manuscript library; the balance was contributed by other donors.

The Mudd Library houses the personal papers of Bernard Baruch, James Forrestal '15, John M. Harlan '20, David E. Lilienthal, Adlai E. Stevenson '22, and other twentieth-century public figures. Located here also are the University Archives. Situated on Olden Street opposite the Engineering Quadrangle, the three-story library contains two levels of stacks for the storage of both bound and boxed papers, office space for visiting scholars, a reading room, conference room, and visitors' lounge, in addition to the usual office and work space for library staff. The building, which was completed in 1976, was designed by Hugh Stubbins and Associates of Cambridge, Massachusetts.

Munro, Dana Carleton (1866-1933), first Dodge Professor of History, graduated from Brown University in 1887 and, soon after, studied in Germany, where he acquired what became a life-long interest in the Crusades. He died before completing his *magnum opus*—a history of the Crusades based on exhaustive and critical use of con-

temporary sources, and on field work in the Near East; but he published five other books that testify to his learning and industry. One of these, *The Middle Ages*, first published in 1902, went through several revised editions and was known to generations of college students.

Munro's students admired him for his profound knowledge and for the generous way he shared his learning. Many leading medieval historians were trained in his graduate seminars; a group of them wrote *The Crusades and Other Essays*, published in his honor in 1928.

As chairman of the history department from 1916 to 1928, he built up the faculty, raised teaching standards, and stimulated research by his own example and counsel.

Munro's geniality and capacity for making friends, coupled with his wide intellectual interests, made him a leader in many scholarly organizations. He was president of the American Historical Association, managing editor of the American Historical Review, and active in the affairs of the American Philosophical Society. He was chosen as chairman of the advisory board of the American Council of Learned Societies when that organization was formed in 1928, and was elected president of the Medieval Academy in 1930. He served in both capacities until his death in 1933.

Murray, James Ormsbee (1827-1899), a graduate of Brown University and Andover Theological Seminary, was Holmes Professor of Belles Lettres from 1875 to 1899 and dean of the faculty from 1883 to 1899. He was Princeton's first dean.

"The office was at first a difficult

one," Professor George McLean Harper later noted in a biographical sketch, "for it included discipline and the enforcement of standards of scholarship, but Dean Murray soon obtained general good will without sacrificing just severity. He had an enthusiastic, impulsive, and affectionate disposition."

This judgment of a junior colleague corroborated the opinion of a senior one. "For sixteen years," President McCosh reflected at the time of his retirement in 1888, "I had the somewhat invidious task of looking after the morals and discipline of the College. Since that time this important work has been committed to Dean Murray, who has shown more patience than I did in the discharge of his duties. Parents may be satisfied when they know that he is looking after the best welfare of their sons."

On Dean Murray's death in 1899, alumni gave funds for a professorship of English in his memory.

Dean Murray's son, George R. Murray, who graduated from the College in 1893, was general athletic treasurer from 1900 to 1932.

Murray-Dodge Hall consists of two buildings, joined by a cloister, each a memorial to a Princetonian who died young. Murray Hall was built in 1879 with a bequest left by Hamilton Murray 1872, who went down with the S.S. *Ville de Havre* when it sank in mid-ocean on November 22, 1873; he had written his will the night before he sailed. Dodge Hall was built in 1900 in memory of Earl Dodge 1879 (a former president of the student religious organization, the Philadelphian Society) who died five years after graduation, in 1884. The funds were given by his

father William Earl Dodge, Jr., and his brother Cleveland H. Dodge 1879. Both buildings were originally used by the Philadelphian Society. Dodge Hall continues to be a center for religious activities, housing the offices of the dean and assistant dean of the chapel, the denominational chaplains, and various student religious and social service organizations. Murray Hall, once used for weekday chapel services, has since the 1920s been the home of Theatre Intime.

Music, Department of. Although music is a late-comer to the University's curriculum (Yale Congregationalists have attributed this to the severities of Presbyterianism) it has nevertheless held an important place in Princeton life since the early days of the College. President Davies wrote odes to "Peace" and "Science," which were sung by students at Commencement in 1760; and when President Witherspoon was married in 1791, a student orchestra celebrated the event with music from the belfry of Nassau Hall. Student singing has long been a prominent feature of campus life, whether in the Glee Club, founded in 1874, or in step-singing, in vogue since the 1880s.

An approach to a more formal program came in 1917 when Henry C. Frick donated the great organ in the Graduate College's Procter Hall, and Alexander Russell, appointed part-time organist and director of music, began weekly organ recitals and public lectures on music. Ralph Downes, first organist and choirmaster in the University Chapel, dedicated in 1928, also taught several music courses for undergraduates. The work of Russell and Downes was supplemented by a committee, made up principally of faculty wives, which organized the University's public concert series.

In 1934, on recommendation of a faculty committee, Roy Dickinson Welch, Professor of Music at Smith College, was invited to Princeton to give two undergraduate courses in music and to design a future plan of study. Student response to Welch's offerings was so enthusiastic that he was prevailed upon to stay and to build the music program himself, thus becoming the father of the Music Department at Princeton.

Welch's embryonic program was incorporated within the Department of Art and Archaeology as a Section of Music. Growth was rapid. By 1937 the two experimental courses had increased to seven and the original thirty-five students had grown so that one tenth of the student body was taking at least one music course sometime in their college career. The enlarged curriculum allowed undergraduates to begin concentrating in the theory and history of music. Welch made several distinguished appointments for the future—Roger Sessions in theory and composition, Oliver Strunk in history and literature, and in 1940 a one-year M.F.A. program was begun. Several new instructors were appointed, including: Milton Babbitt and Edward Cone, two of the department's earliest M.F.A.'s, and Merrill Knapp. The latter was Glee Club director as well as teacher, as, later, Elliot Forbes was for eleven years before he left to return in 1958 to his alma mater, Harvard.

The phenomenal progress of the early years occurred despite the fact that there was very little money and no building. Instruction was given in the basement of Alexander Hall, the Peking Room of Murray-Dodge (shared with Theatre Intime), and the crypt of the Chapel. Books and scores were stored in McCormick Hall, and practice facilities were virtually non-existent.

In 1946 the music section attained departmental status and shortly thereafter was given Clio Hall for a home. Although Clio was not ideal (Stravinsky in the basement often collided with Bach on the second floor via the heating pipes—a wondrous conduit for sound), music was finally under one roof and began to flourish. The graduate program was extended to include the award of Ph.D.s; the first one was conferred in 1950. The Record Lending Library (soon to possess some 8000 recordings) became popular among undergraduates and faculty, and concert activities expanded greatly. The necessary support was provided by Paul Bedford 1897 (the department's perennial godfather), David H. McAlpin '20, William R. McAlpin '26, and many other of the Friends of Music.

In 1951 the department suffered a grievous loss in the early death of its founder, Roy Dickinson Welch. In a moving tribute the faculty praised him as a brilliant teacher and able administrator and as one whose life illustrated the truth of his own belief that "music offers infinite capacity for infinite self-renewal."

Arthur Mendel, an authority on the music of Bach who was called to Princeton in 1952, brought the department professional recognition and eminence during his fifteen years as chairman. Mendel's own scholarship and teaching led in the development of excellence particularly in the graduate program. He was strongly supported by the eminent American composer Roger Sessions, who returned in 1953, after an eight-year absence in Berkeley, as first incumbent of the Conant chair in music, and by Oliver Strunk, one of the nation's leading musicologists.

Almost as important was the influence these men exerted on younger colleagues who were to take their places. In theory and composition, Milton Babbitt became widely known as a contemporary theorist and composer; Edward Cone, as composer, pianist, and writer on musical structure and form; Earl Kim, as composer and performer; James K. Randall, as composer of electronic music; Peter Westergaard, as composer and teacher of theory. This group helped found *Perspectives of New Music*, a leading periodical in the field.

In musicology, Merrill Knapp (Handel and the English eighteenth century), Kenneth Levy (Byzantine and medieval music), Lewis Lockwood (Renaissance studies and Beethoven), have all published widely in their respective fields.

Carl Weinrich, organist and choirmaster in the University Chapel for thirty years, brought renown to Princeton by his organ recitals and recordings of Bach. He was also Glee Club director from 1952 to 1958, when Walter Nollner took over. Nollner proved markedly successful in this position, and in 1973 succeeded Weinrich as choirmaster as well.

After years of careful planning, Arthur Mendel brought the department into the Woolworth Center of Musical Studies—more soundproof than Clio!— in the fall of 1963. During the late 1960s and 1970s, when Kenneth Levy, Lewis Lockwood, and Peter Westergaard were chairmen, the department continued to progress and expand, particularly after the advent of coeducation. Practical music-making, student concerts, and demand for practice

space filled Woolworth to overflowing only ten years after its completion, and the abundance and frequency of musical notices in the *Weekly Bulletin* showed how pervasive music had become in the life of the campus.

Appointments of Claudio Spies (composer and authority on Stravinsky) and Harold Powers (ethno-musicologist and opera scholar) in the early 1970s further strengthened the department. As of 1972, Princeton's graduate program in music was rated as one of the best in the country.

J. Merrill Knapp

Nassau Club, The, was organized in 1889 to advance the social life of its members, who were drawn from both town and gown. It acquired its present clubhouse at 6 Mercer Street in 1903 when Woodrow Wilson was its president. The house had been built about 1814 for Professor Samuel Miller of the Theological Seminary. Two of the Club's most famous parties were those it gave for ex-President Cleveland when he came here to live and for Professor Bliss Perry when he left Princeton to become editor of the *Atlantic Monthly*. The Club's best known activity in modern times has been its weekly Wednesday luncheon talks, which have been drawing on the community's rich resources for the edification of its members since 1914. Originally, the Club had thirty-two members; by 1977 the number was approaching 1900—nearly 800 resident and 1100 nonresident members, most of the latter alumni of the University.

Nassau Hall was, at the time of its completion in 1756, the largest stone building in the colonies. It was much admired and provided the inspiration for other college buildings, notably Hollis Hall at Harvard, University Hall at Brown, Dartmouth Hall at Dartmouth, and Queens Hall at Rutgers.

"We do everything in the plainest and cheapest manner, as far as is consistent with Decency and Convenience, having no superfluous Ornaments," President Aaron Burr, Sr., wrote a benefactor in Scotland, and this was the guiding principle in the design of Nassau Hall. The trustee minutes mention a plan by William Worth, a local stonemason, and another plan by Dr. William Shippen of Philadelphia and Robert Smith, a carpenter-architect who later designed Carpenter's Hall in Philadelphia. No doubt Dr. Shippen contributed to the design of the building, as William Worth may have done in addition to the considerable contribution he made to its execution, but the major responsibility must have been Smith's, since an account of the College published by the trustees in 1765 declared that Nassau Hall was "designed and executed by that approved architect, Mr. Robert Smith, of Philadelphia."

The trustees originally voted that "the College be built of Brick if good Brick can be made at Princeton and if sand can be got reasonably cheap," but they later changed their plans and "the College" was built of a light brown sandstone from a nearby quarry. That it was good stone and that it was well and truly laid by William Worth, the mason, is substantiated by the fact that the exterior walls, which were twenty-six inches thick, withstood the extraordinary shocks and strains the building had to endure: the depredations it suffered during two years of military occupation in the Revolution, devastating fires in 1802 and 1855, and disturbances of rebellious students, who on one occasion exploded a hollow log charged with two pounds of gunpowder inside the main entrance, cracking the adjacent interior walls from top to bottom.

It took two years to erect this building and even before it was completed the trustees voted to name it for the governor of the Province, Jonathan Belcher (q.v.), who staunchly befriended the College in many ways. "Let BELCHER HALL proclaim your beneficent acts . . . to the latest ages," they wrote the governor, but, "with a rare modesty," as President Maclean later noted, the governor declined the honor, and at his suggestion the building was named Nassau Hall in memory of "the Glorious King William the Third who was a Branch of the Illustrious House of Nassau."

SMITH'S NASSAU HALL

Smith's Nassau Hall had three stories and a basement. It was about 176 feet long and 54 feet wide at the ends, with a central element projecting about four feet in front and about twelve feet in back. Over the center of the hip roof was a modest cupola. There were three entrances at the front of the building and two at the back.

On each of the three floors, a central corridor ran the whole length of the building east to west and all the rooms opened on these corridors. There was a two-story prayer hall, 32 by 40 feet, at the rear of the central projection, and a library on the second floor above the main entrance hall. On the three main floors were 42 chambers, some used for classes and for tutors, most of them for student lodging. In the basement were the kitchen, dining room, steward's quarters, and, after 1762, additional rooms for students.

Nassau Hall suffered severely in the Revolution. British and American troops quartered there at different times plundered the library, ruined the organ in the prayer hall, used furniture and woodwork for fuel. In the Battle of Princeton, Nassau Hall changed hands three times and once when the British were in possession, felt the effects of Washington's artillery. One American cannonball came through a window of the prayer hall, destroying a portrait of George II, and another hit the south wall of the west wing and left a scar that is visible today.

Funds being in short supply, recovery was slow; yet by 1783 Nassau Hall was ready to serve as the national capital. For four months that year, July through October, the Continental Congress met in the library on the second floor, using the prayer hall for state occasions. Here Congress congratulated George Washington on his successful termination of the war, received the news of the signing of the definitive treaty of peace with Great Britain, and welcomed the first foreign minister—from the Netherlands—accredited to the United States.

At this time, Washington complied with a request of the trustees to sit for a portrait by Charles Willson Peale, which, at their direction, was placed in the prayer hall in the frame that had been occupied by the portrait of King George II.

LATROBE'S RECONSTRUCTION

The fire of 1802 left only the outside walls of Nassau Hall standing. To restore the building the trustees called on Joseph Henry Latrobe, the first professional architect in America, who later worked on the restoration of the na-

tional capital after it was burned in 1814.

The changes Latrobe made in Smith's original design were chiefly practical ones to lessen the hazards of fire. Instead of wood, the floors were laid with brick and the stairs rebuilt of stone with iron railings. The building was given a sheet-iron roof—a new idea in this country and an experiment on the part of Latrobe.

The roof was raised about two feet from its former position to allow space for transom lights over the doors; this improved the whole exterior appearance of the building. The horizontal lintels over the three entrances at the front of the building were replaced by triangular pediments, and the circular window in the central pediment rising from the eaves line was replaced by a fan-light. The belfry was raised on a large square base to accommodate a clock and to give the cupola added height. Latrobe's changes gave Nassau Hall a Federal rather than a Colonial style, adding grace without marring the original simplicity.

NOTMAN'S REMODELING

The fire of 1855 was just as disastrous as the fire of 1802, and once more only the walls of Nassau Hall were left standing. Again the trustees called on a Philadelphia architect, this time John Notman, who had designed three residences in the village ("Prospect" and those later named Lowrie House and Guernsey Hall). Notman's modifications were far more extensive than Latrobe's and reflected his predeliction for the Italian Rennaissance style, then much in vogue.

Interior changes again were chiefly concerned with fireproofing. Iron beams and brick arches were used to support the floors. The roof was made of slate, laid upon and fastened to iron-laths. Most important of all, since the 1855 fire was believed to have been caused by a spark from a stove in a student's room, nine furnaces were installed to provide central heating. The old prayer hall, no longer needed for that purpose since the erection of a separate chapel, was extended further southward to more than twice its previous size for use as the College library.

Notman made even greater changes in the exterior appearance. Two of the three entrances at the front of the building were removed and towers built on either end to house the stairways which were removed from interior halls. The doorway at the center of the building was replaced by a larger, arched doorway of Florentine style with more massive steps below and a similarly arched window, with a balcony, above. The vertical emphasis thus achieved culminated in a cupola even loftier than Latrobe's.

The tops of the Italianate towers housing the staircases on either end of the building, which rose high above the roof line, were removed in 1905.

LATER CHANGES

The use of Nassau Hall as a dormitory declined steadily toward the end of the nineteenth century with the erection of new dormitories, and as students moved out, museums, laboratories, and classrooms moved in. In the east wing, part of the third floor was removed to create a two-story well for a natural history museum and a skylight cut in the roof to provide light. With construction of Palmer Laboratory and Guyot Hall these facilities were no longer needed, and in 1911, Nassau Hall began to be used for administrative offices; President Hibben (1912-1932) was the first president to have his office there. By 1924, when Eno Hall was completed and the Department of Psychology had departed, Nassau Hall was devoted entirely to offices of the central administration.

In 1967 additional space was obtained by flooring over the two-story well in the east wing, and the exterior appearance improved by the removal of the skylight above it.

THE BELL

A bell rang from the cupola of Nassau Hall soon after its completion. Made in England, it had to be recast after the fire of 1802 and was completely melted in the fire of 1855. A second bell cast in West Troy, New York, was hung in the cupola in 1858. It struck the hour and called students to classes and chapel for ninety-seven years. In time it developed a slight crack and by 11:30 a.m. on February 18, 1955, its peal was reduced to what the *Alumni Weekly* called "a plaintive croak." Thanks to the generosity and foresight of Charles D. Hart 1892, a new bell, which had been cast in France under the direction of the University Bellmaster, Arthur Bigelow, was waiting in the wings. It was hoisted into place on February 22 and the following day at 9:00 p.m. rang out the hour in a D tone, a half note lower than that sounded by the earlier bell.

For many years, the Nassau Hall bell was rung with a rope pulled by a campus policeman or, in the hour-long ringing after a football victory in New Haven or Cambridge, by freshmen and, at least on one occasion, by a dean, whose signature, Christian Gauss, appeared on the wall among the other bell ringers'. With the electrification of bell ringing in 1962, visits to the third floor bell rope by policemen, freshmen, and deans came to an end.

Another custom, which persisted for almost a century, began in the 1860s when an undergraduate disrupted the College's schedule by removing the clapper from the bell one dark winter's night. In later years the stealing of the clapper lost some of its excitement as the College authorities became resigned to the custom, and the Grounds and Buildings Department kept a barrel of clappers on hand to assure rapid replacement. Clinton Meneely '30, president of the family company which made the 1857 bell, said his firm received more orders for clappers for the Princeton bell than for any other bell in the firm's history.

THE CLOCK

A tower clock was first installed sometime after Latrobe's restoration of 1802 when the cupola was raised; it was probably destroyed in the fire of 1855. The clock with the four faces one sees today was donated by the Class of 1866 at the tenth anniversary of their graduation. The works of this clock were modernized in 1919 and again in 1955; its faces are periodically regilded to offset weathering.

THE FACULTY ROOM

In Notman's rebuilding after the fire of 1855, the former prayer hall was more than doubled in size for use as the College library and portrait gallery. After the completion of Chancellor Green Library in 1873, this room was used for the College museum until 1906 when it was remodeled by Messrs. Day and Klauder as the present Faculty Room. The cost was defrayed by a bequest from Augustus S. Van Wickle, a descendant of Nathaniel FitzRandolph, who gave the land on which Nassau Hall was built; Van Wickle's bequest also provided the FitzRan-

dolph Gateway. When the Faculty Room was formally opened on November 2, 1906, President Wilson, in accepting the bequest on behalf of the trustees, said "there could be no more appropriate gift from a descendant of Nathaniel FitzRandolph than one which touched with added beauty his original gift."

Peale's portrait of Washington still hangs in the place of honor in this room along with replacements of the portrait of King George II, damaged in the Battle of Princeton, and of Governor Belcher, lost probably in one of the fires. Now they are accompanied by a portrait of William III, Prince of Nassau, as well as portraits of all of Princeton's presidents and some of its illustrious early graduates.

THE TIGERS

The bronze tigers on either side of the front steps were presented in 1911 by Woodrow Wilson's classmates to replace the lions that they had given on their graduation in 1879. The lions were beginning to show the effects of weather and the tiger had become established as the symbol of Princeton. The tigers were modeled by A. P. Proctor, noted for his animal sculptures. Recumbent, with a "placidity suiting their decorative purpose" (as one critic put it), they have invited generations of small boys and girls to climb up on their backs.

MEMORIAL HALL

The entrance hall, remodeled in 1919 by Day and Klauder as a war memorial, bears on its marble walls the names of Princetonians who have died in this country's wars: ten in the American Revolution, one in the War of 1812, seventy in the Civil War, five in the Spanish-American War, 152 in World

War I, 353 in World War II, twenty-nine in Korea, and twenty-four in Southeast Asia.

Nassau Herald, The, published annually by the graduating senior class, first appeared in 1864. Beginning as a four-page newspaper, it took the form of a paperback book in 1869 and added a hard cover in 1892. At first the contents were limited to the text of senior orations and lists of participants in student activities. Gradually the editors added vital statistics and facts about the habits and opinions of the seniors, as gathered in an annual class poll. The Class of 1892 revealed that 84 of its 155 members smoked and 13 chewed, 41 had read the Bible through entirely, 36 had had to pawn some of their possessions to meet their bills, and 35 had written poetry. It also showed that 43 had supported themselves partly, 7 entirely, and that, among those who cared to express an opinion, 46 preferred brunettes, 35 blondes.

In 1891 the seniors chose their favorite professor and thus started a practice which revealed such recurring favorites as Woodrow Wilson, Stockton Axson, George B. McClellan, Edwin Grant Conklin, Walter P. Hall, David A. McCabe, E. Baldwin Smith, and Roy Dickinson Welch. In 1909 they began also to pick their favorite preceptors, singling out repeatedly Frank Mac-Donald, Albert M. Friend, Jr., George Modlin, Alpheus T. Mason, and Willard Thorp.

"Most likely to succeed" was added to the class poll in 1904. John D. Rockefeller, 3rd, got the most votes in 1929 as did his brother Laurance in 1932 and his nephew Steven in 1958.

The Class of 1915 was the first to publish a photograph and biography of each of its members, thus introducing the modern form of the *Herald*. The biography enumerated the senior's successes at school and college and indicated what he intended to do next. The future Secretary of Defense James V. Forrestal '15 said he was undecided. Edmund Wilson '16 said he would "enter the field of literature." F. Scott Fitzgerald '17 said he would do graduate study in English at Harvard and then go into newspaper work; instead he joined the army and wrote *This Side of Paradise*. George F. Kennan '25, who became ambassador to the Soviet Union, was another senior who "didn't know" what he was going to do.

One of the oldest *Nassau Herald* customs has been the inclusion of senior nicknames. In earlier years, when classes were smaller and campus life more leisurely, the nicknames could be pungent, as may be evident from the following garland of familiarities: Punk, Paddlefoot, Cupid, Toad, Bum, Phoebe, Sleepy, Wrinkle, Grouch, Biffy, Itchy, Rummy, Spider, Sourball, Fats, Runt, Tank, Welsh Rabbit, Wobbles, Noisy, Tubby, Booze, Giddle-Guy, Purity, Beowulf, Satan.

Nassau Lit, The, the country's second oldest college literary magazine, first appeared in 1842 as the *Nassau Monthly*.* In 1847 it changed its name to the *Nassau Literary Magazine* and in 1930 adopted its briefer title.

Its primary object, the first editor said, was "to afford a medium through which young writers might publish incognito their first lucubrations to the world." Since manuscripts were submitted under assumed names or initials, they were not returned, and rejections were often publicly announced in "Notices to Correspondents"— sometimes scornfully: "The 'Parting,' by D.L.D.," the editors asserted about one poem, "is between the writer and common sense." Dissecting another "effusion," they thought "Philo's" request of his "Dulcinea" toward the end of the poem—"O, deem me not a fool"—absolutely indispensable, "for the natural inference from the preceding verses," they said, "would be that their maker was rather leaning that way."

THE FOUNDERS

During the first few years, a large part of the *Lit's* contents was the work of three writers—Theodore L. Cuyler 1841, George H. Boker 1842, and Charles G. Leland 1845.

Cuyler, who contributed frequent essays on European and American culture, also wrote "A Chapter on College Writing" that would have evoked an affirmative nod from many latter-day *Lit* editors:

> . . . A college student should write often [he counseled]. . . . In order to produce the highest effect, he must use short, simple, pointed words. . . . Nor let him be content to write a composition once, but rewrite, and rewrite it again, until he is well assured that there is not a word in it which is not *the very word*, in *the very place*.

Cuyler became a minister in Brooklyn, and wrote eleven books and many articles for the religious press. The *Westminster*, a Presbyterian periodical, called him "the greatest writer of spiritual English since John Bunyan."

George H. Boker (q.v.), the first editor, contributed numerous poems and essays to its early issues, and in later life published two volumes of poetry and wrote eleven plays, besides serving as United States Minister to Turkey and to Russia.

Charles G. Leland was the *Lit's* most prolific contributor during the first four years. One piece of his that did not appear was his *Educatio Diaboli*, a ballad about Satan's admission to Princeton, his involvement in student escapades, and his suspension by the faculty. In this work the poet's allusions to members of the faculty are less complimentary than his references to the Devil, which may explain why the *Lit* denied itself the pleasure of its publication. All his life Leland published widely in a variety of fields, including gypsy lore and language, German literature, industrial arts, and sexual psychology, but he became best known for the many editions of his German-dialect *Hans Breitmann's Ballads*.

THE 1890s

The *Lit* carried brief reports of campus happenings until the *Princetonian* was founded in 1876. About this time some authors began signing their names to their contributions, and by the 1890s the use of pseudonyms and initials had disappeared.

In the early 1890s an informal literary club called the Coffee House provided a focal point for writers such as Jesse Lynch Williams 1892, Booth Tarkington 1893 (qq.v.), and McCready Sykes 1894, during what was one of the *Lit's* strongest periods. Williams was their leader, and Robert Bridges, who had been managing editor of the *Lit* in 1879, was a valuable older friend; as editor of *Scribner's Magazine* he helped them and later generations of young Princeton writers break into print. Tarkington and Williams became Pulitzer Prize winners; Sykes won the affection of his Princeton contemporaries with his accounts—in which he mimicked Chaucerian style—of Princeton football exploits in *Poe's Run and Other Poems* (1904).

THE "GOLDEN AGE"

A remarkable group of writers made the years 1912 to 1917 one of the most fruitful periods in the *Lit*'s history. Its leader was Edmund Wilson '16 (q.v.), around whom campus writers gathered "by a law [Dean Christian Gauss said] of literary gravitation." Other talented members included John Peale Bishop '17, Scott Fitzgerald '17 (qq.v.), and John Biggs '18.

The members of this inner circle exhibited qualities reminiscent of those of the original founders. Bishop was the same patrician poet in his day that Boker had been in his, both drawing much of their inspiration from European culture. Like Leland, Fitzgerald was an *enfant terrible*, although he was less well-read than Leland as an undergraduate and more successful as a writer in later life. Although their views and ultimate vocations were very different, Wilson shared Cuyler's interest in having the right word in the right place, and went even further, desiring that "every word, every cadence, every detail should perform a definite function in producing an intense effect."

QUESTIONS OF PROPRIETY

Usually an unobtrusive member of the campus community, the *Lit* has on occasion been made conspicuous by alleged lapses in taste. Early in the 1930s the Undergraduate Council suspended the editor of the *Lit* for publishing a poem which the Council deemed "obscene and un-Princeton." This unprecedented action brought a flood of student protests to the *Daily Princetonian*. One undergraduate, who had read the poem more carefully than most, reported that its meaning was rather obscure and that the poem was not therefore completely successful, but that far from being obscene, its object was highly moral and indeed didactic. Another student expressed the hope that the Undergraduate Council would not rest on its laurels, but would now seek out other "un-Princeton" matters with which the University abounded, citing certain authors taught to freshmen by the classics and English departments and referring darkly to many "un-Princeton" books in the Library, including one by a writer, named Shakespeare, "which is full of bastards." The Undergraduate Council relented and changed its suspension to a reprimand. The unhappiness that prevailed during this episode was shared by almost everyone except the circulation manager of the *Lit*.

On another occasion in the 1950s, the dean of the college felt obliged to place the editor and the author of a story on probation because of the author's use of pithy Saxonisms in the dialogue. The *Prince* condemned this action, too, but this time there was no flood of letters, and the author reacted tolerantly: "I'm not completely unsympathetic with the Dean," he said, "but, on the other hand, I'm also sympathetic with myself."

RETROSPECTIVES

In February 1942, the *Lit* brought out a 196-page centennial issue, reprinting specimens of poetry and prose from the previous century together with new articles by President Dodds, Jacques Maritain, Booth Tarkington '93, Norman Thomas '05, and others. For that issue Frederick Morgan '43 and Richard M. Morse '43 were co-chairmen, Joseph D. Bennett '43, managing editor. A few years later, Morgan, Bennett, and William Arrowsmith

'45 founded *The Hudson Review*, which became one of the best known and most respected American literary reviews.

In 1976 the *Nassau Lit* published another retrospective issue, featuring contributions from past *Lit* notables like Tarkington and Fitzgerald, as well as from more recent contributors, among them, poets William Meredith '40, Galway M. Kinnell '48, and W. S. Merwin '48, authors George Garrett '52 and John McPhee '53, and artist Frank Stella '58.

* The Yale Literary Magazine was started in 1836.

National Academy of Engineering, The, was established in 1964 "to honor distinguished engineers of the nation and to bring to bear an unusual depth and breadth of engineering knowledge on matters of national concern." Engineering had been a separate section of the National Academy of Sciences since 1919, and although the new Academy was founded under the larger group's charter and made responsible to its Council, it is largely autonomous.

Princeton faculty members have been elected to the Academy in the following years:

1968	Richard H. Wilhelm
1969	Courtland D. Perkins
1973	Mac E. Van Valkenburg
1975	Wallace D. Hayes
1976	Leon Lapidus
1977	Seymour M. Bogdonoff

Professor Perkins became President of the Academy in 1975.

National Academy of Sciences, The, is a society of scholars "dedicated to the furtherance of science and its use for the general welfare." It was established in 1863 by an Act of Congress, which empowered it to create its own organization and by-laws and called upon it to serve as an official adviser to the federal government on any question of science or technology.

Among the Academy's fifty founding members were four scientists associated with Princeton: Stephen Alexander, Arnold Guyot, Joseph Henry, and John Torrey. Henry was the Academy's second president, 1866 to 1878; and Frederick Seitz Ph.D. '34 its seventeenth, 1962 to 1969.

Two associated organizations, the National Academy of Engineering and the Institute of Medicine, were founded by the Academy in 1964 and 1970. The National Research Council, established in 1916, serves as the operating arm of the science and engineering academies.

New members are elected annually by the current membership in recognition of distinguished achievements in scientific research. Princeton professors who have been members of the Academy, and the years of their election, follow:*

1863	Stephen Alexander (astronomy)
	Arnold Guyot (physical geography)
	Joseph Henry (physics)
	John Torrey (botany)
1872	Charles A. Young (astronomy)
1900	Henry Fairfield Osborn (biology)
1906	William Berryman Scott (geology)
1908	Edwin Grant Conklin (biology)
1918	Henry Norris Russell (astronomy)
1919	Augustus Trowbridge (physics)
	Oswald Veblen (mathematics)

1922	Luther P. Eisenhart (mathematics)	
	George A. Hulett (chemistry)	
1924	Karl T. Compton (physics)	
1925	Solomon Lefschetz (mathematics)	
1930	James W. Alexander (mathematics)	
1934	E. Newton Harvey (biology)	
1937	John von Neumann (mathematical physics)	
1940	Ernest G. Wever (psychology)	
	Hermann Weyl (mathematical physics)	
1943	Arthur F. Buddington Ph.D. (geology)	
1945	Henry Eyring (chemistry)	
	Eugene P. Wigner (mathematical physics)	
1950	Salomon Bochner (mathematics)	
	Edward C. Kendall (biochemistry)	
1951	Howard P. Robertson (mathematical physics)	
1952	Harry H. Hess (geology)	
	Lyman Spitzer Jr. (astronomy)	
	John A. Wheeler (physics)	
1955	Charles P. Smyth (chemistry)	
1956	Martin Schwarzschild (astronomy)	
	Norman E. Steenrod (mathematics)	
1957	Walter M. Elsasser (geophysics)	
	Donald F. Hornig (chemistry)	
1959	Walker Bleakney (physics)	
1960	William Feller (mathematics)	
	Hollis D. Hedberg (geology)	
1961	John W. Tukey (statistics)	
	Donald C. Spencer (mathematics)	
1963	Marvin L. Goldberger (physics)	
	John W. Milnor (mathematics)	

	Colin S. Pittendrigh (biology)
1964	Walter J. Kauzmann (chemistry)
1965	Vincent G. Dethier (biology)
1966	Val L. Fitch (physics)
1967	Philip W. Anderson (physics)
	Robert H. Dicke (physics)
1968	Arthur B. Pardee (biochemistry)
1969	Robert H. MacArthur (biology)
	Marshall N. Rosenbluth (astrophysics)
1970	James W. Cronin (physics)
	Arthur S. Wightman (mathematical physics)
1972	Kurt M. Mislow (chemistry)
	Sam B. Treiman (physics)
1973	John T. Bonner (biology)
	Ansley J. Coale (demography)
	John J. Hopfield (physics)
1974	Jeremiah P. Ostriker (astrophysics)
	Elias M. Stein (mathematics)
1975	Stephen L. Adler (physics)
1976	John N. Bahcall (astrophysics)
	Harold P. Furth (astrophysics)
1977	Julian Wolpert (geography and urban planning)

* Some fifty non-faculty alumni have also been elected, among them Arthur H. Compton, Clinton J. Davisson, Philip Bard, John R. Paul, Edwin M. McMillan, Frederick Seitz, Donald H. Menzel, John Bardeen, Richard Feynman, Robert Hofstadter, William O. Baker.

National Institute of Arts and Letters, The, was founded in 1898 and incorporated by Act of Congress in 1913 for the purpose of furthering literature and the fine arts in the United States. Limited to a membership of 250, the Institute presents medals and other awards for distinguished achievement, makes grants to further creative work of outstanding merit, and maintains a revolving loan fund to aid artists, musicians, and writers who are unable to continue their work without financial help.

The American Academy of Arts and Letters was founded by the Institute in 1904, and incorporated by Act of Congress in 1916. Its membership is limited to fifty persons chosen for special honor from those who at any time have been members of the Institute. The Academy participates with the Institute in the award of grants and loans and also administers additional awards.

Alumni and members of the faculty have been elected to the Institute, in one of its three departments—art, literature, music—in the following years:

1898	Parke Godwin 1834
	*Henry Van Dyke 1873
	*Woodrow Wilson 1879
1906	Robert Bridges 1879
	Samuel McC. Crothers 1874
	*Basil L. Gildersleeve 1849
1908	*Booth Tarkington 1893
	Ridgley Torrence 1897
	Jesse Lynch Williams 1892
1911	George McL. Harper 1884
	Andrew Fleming West 1874
1912	John Grier Hibben 1882
1913	*Frank Jewett Mather Jr.
1914	*William J. Henderson 1876
1916	Howard Russell Butler 1876
	Ernest Poole '02
1923	*Gifford Reynolds Beal '00
	*Eugene O'Neill '10
1926	Struthers Burt '04
1927	Paul Van Dyke 1881
1928	Burton E. Stevenson 1894
	*Thornton Wilder A.M. '26
1930	Abram Poole Jr. '04
1932	*John Taylor Arms '09
1938	James Boyd '10
	*Roger Sessions
1942	Ralph Barton Perry 1896
1946	David Adler '04
	Robert P. Tristram Coffin A.M. 1916

	Aymar Embury II '00
1949	*Allen Tate
1956	Richard P. Blackmur
1962	*George F. Kennan '25
1965	Milton Babbitt
1968	William Meredith '40
1969	Andrew W. Imbrie '42
1975	Austin Warren Ph.D. '26

Henry Van Dyke was president of the Institute from 1909 to 1911. George F. Kennan was president of the Institute from 1965 to 1968 and of the Academy from 1967 to 1971. Allen Tate was president of the Institute in 1968-1969.

Five Princetonians have been awarded the Institute's annual gold medal:

1922	Eugene O'Neill (drama)
1933	Booth Tarkington (fiction)
1952	Thornton Wilder (fiction)
1955	Edmund Wilson (essays and criticism)
1961	Roger Sessions (music)

* Subsequently elected also to the Academy.

Near Eastern Studies at Princeton go back to the turn of the century when, as elsewhere, interest in this field, Biblically oriented, centered on the ancient history of the "cradle of civilization." The roots were diffuse, albeit vigorous; there were pioneer scholars of distinction and beginnings of a superlative library for teaching and research.

The most dynamic pioneer was Howard Crosby Butler (q.v.), a specialist in ancient Near Eastern archaeology and architecture who mounted expeditions to Syria and Anatolia in 1899, 1904, and 1909 and headed the notable excavations at Antioch and Sardis; he was Princeton's charter trustee of the Jerusalem School for Oriental Research. In 1901 he brought to Princeton the noted German epigrapher, Enno Littmann, who had accompanied him in Syria; Littmann served as librarian of the Oriental collections and as lecturer in Semitic philology until 1906 when he returned to Tübingen. Four years later he was succeeded by another German scholar, Rudolph Brünnow, who was Professor of Semitic Philology. After Brünnow's death in 1917, the teaching of Semitics declined, and the development of Sanskrit and Indo-European philology began auspiciously under Harold H. Bender (q.v.), who was appointed Professor of Indo-Germanic Philology in 1918. In 1927 Bender organized the precursor of the Departments of Near Eastern and East Asian Studies—the Department of Oriental Languages and Literatures (later Oriental Studies); he served as its first chairman until 1944.

Meanwhile ancient history and Semitics had been well served by David Paton 1874, a self-made Egyptologist who toiled in the western tower of Pyne Library translating important works in this field. In 1919 his mother founded the Paton chair in Ancient and Modern Literature, first occupied by William Robert Rogers of Drew Theological Seminary, a popular lecturer during his ten years as visiting professor, and then by Philip Khuri Hitti, who worked with Bender on comparative Indo-European and Semitic studies, and later gave his attention to Islamic and modern Near Eastern studies.

Princeton's superlative Near Eastern library collections were begun with Arabic manuscripts collected by Robert Garrett 1897 (q.v.) and deposited in the University Library in 1900. He continued to acquire and lend to the University valuable Near Eastern collections, and in 1941 gave them all to Princeton. The collections were further enriched by Littmann's acquisitions and by bequests of the personal libraries of Brünnow and Paton. In 1943 Garrett climaxed his contributions with the gift of the Cairene Yahuda Collection of over 5,000 medieval Arabic items. Thus Princeton has come to possess one of the two greatest collections of books on the Near East in the United States and by far the greatest collection of manuscripts in the Western Hemisphere.

In 1944 Hitti succeeded Bender as chairman, serving until 1954. The department's founding of the country's pioneer Program in Near Eastern Studies after World War II was largely due to Hitti's vision and fund-raising abilities. This program concentrated on the modern Near East. Initially, the three major Islamic languages—Arabic, Turkish, and Persian—constituted the core of the program around which were grouped integrated courses in history, politics, sociology, economics, and related subjects. Three appointments were made to the department to implement the new program: Walter L. Wright in Turkish studies, T. Cuyler Young in modern Persian, and Lewis V. Thomas in Arabic. On Wright's death in 1949, Thomas took over the work in Turkish.

In 1951 the Program in Near Eastern Studies was reorganized as a separate interdisciplinary program emphasizing the social sciences, administered by a committee of representatives from the departments of economics, history, and politics, as well as of the department of oriental languages and literatures. The Program undertook to meet the lack of teacher-scholars in the sociology and politics of the Near East by providing language study and research opportunities in the area for two social scientists. One of them, the sociologist Morroe Berger, later served twice as Director of the Program for a number of years. The other, the political scientist Denkwart Rustow, eventually became Distinguished Professor of Political Science at City University of New York; his place was taken by Manfred Halpern in 1959.

The department expanded during Young's chairmanship (1954-1969), with major emphasis on Arabic and Islam, including modern history and contemporary affairs. The teaching was enriched by foreign scholars who came frequently as visiting professors. Two regular appointments in the mid-1950s, Norman Itzkowitz and Martin Dickson, strengthened the Turkish and Persian fields respectively. John H. Marks, who came in 1954, has specialized in ancient Near Eastern history and West Semitic languages. A year later Rudolph Mach became Curator of Near Eastern Collections; within a decade he had made the Islamic collection, especially for the medieval period, the best in North America; he has continued to add hundreds of important items to the manuscript collection.

In 1956 the department added to its staff the Sinologist Frederick W. Mote—its first appointment in the East Asian field. Under him and Japanologist Marius Jansen, this field of studies developed rapidly, and in 1969 the Department of Oriental Studies divided into the two departments of Near Eastern Studies and East Asian Studies (q.v.).

In the mid-1960s Near Eastern Studies suffered grievous losses with the deaths of Ottoman historian Thomas and Arabic linguist Majid Sa'id, and were further depleted by the departure, to head up new programs elsewhere, of Bayly Winder and Farhat Ziadeh, teachers in the Arabic-Islamic field. Reconstruction involved some change in emphasis. Medieval Islam and modern Arab and North African studies were strengthened by L. Carl Brown's arrival from Harvard; he served as chairman from 1969 to 1973. New depth in Islamic history was provided by Abraham Udovitch, from Cornell. He is a Semitist and medieval Islamist with a special interest in neglected economic history; he became departmental chairman in 1973. These Arabists were joined in 1968 by Andras Hamori, a specialist in classical Arabic literature, and subsequently by similar specialists in Persian and Turkish. In 1970 modern Hebrew language and literature were added to the department's curriculum. In 1972 John Willis was appointed for Islamic civilization in Africa.

In the early 1970s the family of Cleveland and Bayard Dodge (both Class of 1909) endowed twin chairs in Near Eastern Studies to honor these two eminent alumni whose careers, in various and distinguished ways, were connected to that area of the world over the past half century. These two chairs made it possible to add faculty of unusual distinction to the department. Bernard Lewis, the leading historian of the Near East in the English-speaking world, came to Princeton from the University of London in September 1974. He accepted the joint appointment of the University as first Cleveland Dodge Professor of Near Eastern Studies, and of the Institute for Advanced Study as a long-term member of its School of Historical Studies. In September 1975, Charles P. Issawi, the most renowned economist and economic historian of the Middle East, came to Princeton from Columbia University as the first incumbent of the Bayard Dodge Professorship in Near Eastern Studies.

On July 1, 1977, the department was further enriched when the eminent historian Nina G. Garsoian came from Columbia as dean of the Graduate School and professor of Byzantine and Armenian Studies. The same year, John H. Marks succeeded Abraham Udovitch as departmental chairman.

Over the years Princeton's pioneering has contributed much to the national development of Near Eastern Studies. The department has provided leadership in cooperative ventures such as Princeton's National Critical Languages Program, the Inter-University Summer Language Program, the Center for Arabic Study Abroad in Cairo, and the founding of the Middle East Studies Association; and also by its consultation with the Department of Health, Education, and Welfare in the administration of the National Defense Foreign Language Act. Cooperative scholarship in the field has been furthered by the department's annual conference, begun in 1949; in 1974 it brought together in Princeton the first large international group of scholars in Islamic economic history. Not the least important contribution has been the number of well-trained Ph.D.'s the Department has sent out to universities in the United States and Canada, and in the Near East itself, as well as the personnel contributed by the Program to business, government, and public affairs.

T. Cuyler Young
A. L. Udovitch

New South, unlike its semantic opposite, Old North—as Nassau Hall was once called—is a building with little history, having been erected in 1965. However, its name was in the newspapers four years later when fifty members of the Association of Black Collegians occupied it for eleven hours to protest University policy on investments in companies doing business in South Africa. But this "sit-in" was a temperate exercise compared with the frequent and sometime riotous "barring out" of the faculty by students living in "Old North" early in the last century, not to mention the even livelier events that Nassau Hall survived in the century before.

New South was built to provide more ample space for some of the business departments of the University and to release for faculty use the offices which these departments had occupied near the library. One of the first of the University's high-rise buildings, it has two stories below ground and seven above. Designed by Edward Larrabee Barnes of New York, and built of glass and concrete, it stands in the southern section of the Campus. The windows of the cafeteria on the seventh floor afford superb views of the campus and countryside.

Nobel Prizes have been awarded to seven Princeton graduates and two faculty members.

Woodrow Wilson, of the Class of 1879, 28th president of the United States won the Nobel peace prize for 1919.

Arthur H. Compton, B.S. College of Wooster, 1913, Ph.D. (physics) Princeton, 1916, shared the physics award in 1927, while professor of physics at the University of Chicago, for his discovery of the change in wave length of scattered X-rays—the "Compton effect."

Clinton J. Davisson, B.S. University of Chicago 1908, Ph.D. (physics) Princeton 1911, shared the physics award in 1937, while a research physicist at the Bell Telephone Laboratories, for his part in the diffraction of electrons by crystals which furnished the first experimental proof that the electron, previously conceived of as a material particle, could also manifest itself as a wave. At Princeton he prepared his dissertation under the direction of Professor O. W. Richardson.

Edwin M. McMillan, B.S. California Institute of Technology 1928, Ph.D. (physics), Princeton 1932, shared the 1951 prize in chemistry, while professor of physics at the University of California, Berkeley, for his part in the discovery of transuranium elements.

John Bardeen, B.S. University of Wisconsin 1928, Ph.D. (mathematical physics) Princeton 1936, shared the physics award in 1956 for his part in the invention and development of the transistor at the Bell Telephone Laboratories, where he was a research physicist, and in 1972 shared his second Nobel physics prize for his work in superconductivity while professor of physics and electrical engineering at the University of Illinois. At Princeton he wrote his dissertation under the guidance of Professor Eugene P. Wigner.

Robert Hofstadter, B.S. City College of New York 1935, Ph.D. (physics) Princeton 1938, shared the physics prize in 1961, while professor of physics at Stanford University, for his determination of the size and shape of atomic nucleons. At Princeton he did his dissertation under the direction of Professor Walker Bleakney.

Eugene Paul Wigner, Dr. Ing. Technische Hochschule, Berlin 1925, who joined the Princeton faculty in 1930 and became Thomas D. Jones professor of mathematical physics in 1938, shared the physics prize in 1963 for his contributions to the theory of the atomic nucleus and elementary particles.

Richard P. Feynman, B.S. Massachusetts Institute of Technology 1939, Ph.D. (physics) Princeton, 1942, shared the physics award in 1965, while professor of physics at California Institute of Technology, for helping to solve the difficulties in carrying out quantitative calculations of the interplay between charged particles—a contribution that opened up the field of quantum electrodynamics. At Princeton Feynmann worked on his dissertation under the guidance of Professor John A. Wheeler.

Philip W. Anderson, A.B. Harvard University 1943, Ph.D. 1949, previously professor of theoretical physics at Cambridge University, England, and currently Joseph Henry Professor of Physics at the University and consulting director of the physical research division of Bell Laboratories, shared with two other physicists the physics prize in 1977 for their "fundamental theoretical investigations of the electronic structure of magnetic and disordered systems."

Princeton takes pride, if no credit, in three other Nobel awards.

Owen W. Richardson, a professor of physics at Princeton from 1906 to 1913 who left a strong mark on the department before his return to England, won the Nobel Prize in 1928.

Eugene O'Neill, who spent a year at Princeton as a member of the Class of 1910, received the Nobel Prize in Literature in 1936.

Edward C. Kendall, B.S. Columbia 1908, Ph.D. 1910, who shared the Nobel Prize in physiology and medicine in 1950 for his part in the discovery of cortisone at the Mayo Clinic, joined Princeton in 1951 as Visiting Professor of Chemistry at the Forrestal

Research Campus, where he served until his death in 1972.

Oates, Whitney Jennings (1904-1973), successively Ewing Professor of Greek, West Professor of Classics, and Avalon Professor of the Humanities, was a prime mover in the founding and development of a number of important University programs. Mike, as he was known to his colleagues and students, first came to Princeton from the Evanston Township High School in Illinois as a member of the Class of 1925. He graduated *summa cum laude* in classics, earning his A.M. in 1927 and his Ph.D. in 1931. As student and teacher, he was associated with Princeton for forty-nine years.

Chairman of the classics department for sixteen years, Oates published extensively in his special fields of interest, Greek drama and philosophy, and played a leading role in the teaching of the classics in translation. He was frequently voted a favorite preceptor and lecturer in annual senior class polls.

In the 1930s he was a principal organizer, and from 1945 to 1959 was chairman, of the Special Program in the Humanities, an interdisciplinary plan of study that exerted lasting influence on the form and spirit of education at Princeton. According to the seniors' Faculty Song, the Program was concocted over coffee mugs in the old Baltimore Dairy Lunch:

Here's to Princeton's esthete band,
Making culture's final stand.
In the Balt they all convene,
Hinds, Godolphin, Oates, and Greene.

During World War II, Oates served with the Marines in the Southwest Pacific. Soon after he came back to Princeton in 1945, he conceived and found the money for a plan to attract returning servicemen into college teaching; under his dynamic guidance this project eventually became the National Woodrow Wilson Fellowship Program (q.v.).

Carrying further the essential ideas of the Special Program in the Humanities, he was largely responsible for the establishment in 1953 of the Council of the Humanities (q.v.)—as a means of fostering significant teaching and research throughout this field—and was its chairman until his retirement from the faculty in 1970.

Outside of Princeton, he showed similar leadership as a founding member of the National Commission on the Humanities, whose 1963 report did much to secure the establishment by Congress of the National Foundation for the Arts and the Humanities. He was also president of the United Chapters of Phi Beta Kappa, a senior fellow of the Center of Hellenic Studies in Washington, and a director of the American Council of Learned Societies.

Oates's ardent advocacy of humanistic learning nationally was matched at Princeton by the stimulating example he provided generations of Princetonians through his own humanity—his good humor, kindheartedness, and unfailing cheerfulness. Robert F. Goheen, in turn Oates's student, colleague, and president, said that "In his person and in his work he stood in the long, strong line of Christian humanists who have helped give spiritual as well as intellectual quality to this university down through the years. . . . He was imbued, in Professor Osgood's phrase, with 'an affectionate concern, incorrigible and dominant, for his fellow men.' "

Old Nassau has been Princeton's anthem since 1859. Its words were written that year by a freshman, Harlan Page Peck 1862, and published in the March issue of the *Nassau Literary Magazine*. When an effort to sing it to the tune of "Auld Lang Syne" proved unsuccessful, Karl A. Langlotz, who taught German in the college and directed a choral group, was persuaded to write music for it. Langlotz had studied music in Weimar under Liszt and had once played the violin in an orchestra conducted by Wagner. He wrote the music for *Old Nassau* on the porch of his house at 160 Mercer Street one fine spring afternoon.

The words and music appeared together for the first time in *Songs of Old Nassau*, published in April 1859. A few days after this collection appeared, a group of students gathered near the Bulletin Elm at the northeast corner of Nassau Hall, after evening prayers, to try some of the songs. Most of the college had assembled to hear the singing;

when the group had finished their singing of *Old Nassau*, the listeners responded with an enthusiastic skyrocket cheer, which forecast the devotion with which succeeding generations of Princetonians would sing "in praise of old Nassau."

There has been some change in the words over the years. The opening line, originally "Tune every *harp* and every voice," became "Tune every *heart* and every voice" early in the 1890s. Peck wrote seven verses, but three—those about "virtue's amaranthine wreath," "a zeal beyond compare," "a flowery chaplet"—had dropped out of use by 1914.

The words and music of the first verse and chorus are displayed below. The words of the other three verses are as follows:

Let music rule the fleeting hour,
Her mantle round us draw;
And thrill each heart with all her
*   power,*
In praise of Old Nassau.

H. P. Peck, '62   Karl A. Langlotz

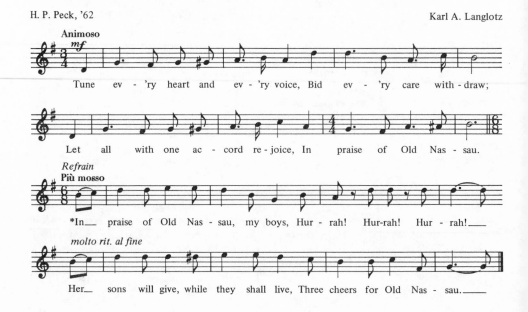

*And when these walls in dust are
    laid,
With reverence and awe,
Another throng shall breathe our
    song,
In praise of Old Nassau.*

*Till then with joy our songs we'll
    bring,
And while a breath we draw,
We'll all unite to shout and sing,
Long life to Old Nassau.*

Olympians from Princeton have placed among the top three in twenty-four events since the ancient games were revived in their modern form in 1896: fifteen in track and field, three in swimming, two in fencing and rowing, and one in basketball and pistol-shooting. In the first Olympic Games, Robert Garrett 1897 set a Princeton record that has yet to be equalled when he won a third place, a second, and two firsts—one in the discus throw, an event in which he had never competed before. Princeton's most recent Olympic winner was oarswoman Carol Brown '75, who earned a bronze medal as a member of the United States eight-oared crew that finished third at Montreal in 1976. Princetonians who have placed among the top three in their events have been:*

1896-ATHENS
Robert Garrett 1897, first place, discus throw (95 feet, 7½ inches); first place, shot put (36 feet, 2 inches); second place, long jump (20 feet, 3¼ inches); third place, high jump (5 feet, 7³/₈ inches).
Herbert B. Jamison 1897, second place, 400-meter run (55.2 seconds).
Albert C. Tyler 1897, second place, pole vault (10 feet, 8 inches).

1900-PARIS
Frank W. Jarvis '00, first place, 100-meter dash (10⁴/₅ seconds).
John F. Cregan 1899, second place, 800-meter run (2 minutes, 1.2 seconds).
Robert Garrett 1897, third place, shot-put (40 feet, 7 inches).

1904-ST LOUIS
William W. Coe '03, second place, shot-put (47 feet, 3 inches).
John R. DeWitt '04, second place, hammer throw (164 feet, 11 inches).
G. P. Serviss '03, second place, high jump (5 feet, 9 inches).

1920-ANTWERP
Karl T. Frederick '03, gold medal, free pistol shooting at range of 50 meters (496 points).
Henry Breckinridge '07, bronze medal, as member of the U.S. foil team which placed third.

1924-PARIS
William E. Stevenson '22, gold medal as member of winning team in 1600-meter relay (3 minutes, 16 seconds—a new Olympic record).
Ralph G. Hills '25, bronze medal, shotput (48 feet, ½ inch).

1928-AMSTERDAM
Benjamin van D. Hedges, Jr., '30, silver medal, high jump (6 feet, 3¼ inches).

1932-LOS ANGELES
Tracy Jaeckel '28, bronze medal, as member of U.S. epee team, which placed third.

1936-BERLIN
Albert Vande Veghe '40, silver medal, 100-meter backstroke (1 minute, 7.7 seconds).

1964-TOKYO
William W. Bradley, Jr. '65, gold medal as member (and captain) of winning

U.S. basketball team which beat the U.S.S.R. team in the final game, 73-59.

Jed R. Graef '64, gold medal in 200-meter backstroke (2 minutes, 10.3 seconds—a world and Olympic record).

Seymour L. Cromwell II '56, silver medal in double sculls (7 minutes, 13.16 seconds).

1968-MEXICO CITY

Ross Wales '69, bronze medal, 100-meter butterfly (57.2 seconds).

1976-MONTREAL

Carol Brown '75, bronze medal, as member of women's eight-oared crew that placed third.

In addition to the foregoing medalists, a score of other Princetonians have represented the United States on various Olympic teams, and members of the faculty and administration have played key roles in the organization and development of the Games. Professor William M. Sloane was a member of the international committee that organized the first Olympics in 1896, and Professor Charles W. Kennedy '03 and Dr. Joseph W. Raycroft both served as vice-chairman of the United States Olympic Committee, with which Asa S. Bushnell '21 was identified in various capacities for almost forty years. University Physician Harry R. McPhee was head physician for the United States teams in 1952, 1960, and 1964, and Princeton's head trainer Edward G. Zanfrini was trainer for the United States teams in 1952, 1956, 1960, 1964, and 1968.

* The practice of awarding gold, silver, and bronze medals to winners of first, second, and third places was not begun until 1908.

O'Neill, Eugene [Gladstone] (1888-1953), dramatist, entered Princeton in the fall of 1906 as a member of the Class of 1910 but, after encountering disciplinary as well as scholastic difficulties, left at the end of freshman year without taking final examinations. He worked for a mail-order house and then went to sea. Later he was a newspaper reporter and studied for a time in George Pierce Baker's celebrated '47 Workshop at Harvard before embarking on the career that brought him the Nobel Prize in Literature in 1936.

Orange Key Society was organized in 1935 on the model of Dartmouth's Green Key Society which had won President Dodds's admiration when he visited Hanover to speak at a conference there. Due at midnight, he missed a train connection and, arriving at two in the morning, was surprised and pleased to find a Green Key undergraduate waiting for him with a car, a thermos of hot coffee, and a friendly greeting.

Originally the Orange Key's primary mission was to welcome visitors to the University and to shepherd athletic teams from other colleges around Princeton. Gradually it assumed other functions: the campus guide service, the Red Cross blood drive, the sponsorship of student-faculty get-togethers, the organization of dances and other social events, and—its most distinctive activity—the Freshman Keycept Program. The Keycept Program, whose name and methods were derived from the preceptorial system, helped to introduce freshmen to life at Princeton through periodic meetings in small groups with a Keyceptor from the Junior Class.

In recent years, in order to meet an expanding demand by visiting groups, the Orange Key has made the campus guide service its principal function.

Orchestra, University, can lay claim to rudimentary antecedents as far back as June, 1791, when a number of student musicians, seated in the belfry of Nassau Hall above the glow of six hundred candles illuminating its facade, entertained the crowd that had gathered to celebrate President Witherspoon's second marriage—with, the *United States Gazette* reported, "a most agreeable and delightful concert from different kinds of instruments."

Almost a century later, a small "Instrumental Club" occasionally appeared in concerts with the newly formed Glee Club. Among its early members was flutist Henry B. Fine 1882, later dean of the faculty and of the departments of science.

During their freshman year, the Class of 1890 formed a college orchestra, which flourished until they graduated. Cellist William Shubael Conant 1890 eventually pursued a successful career as a consulting engineer, and on his death in 1952 left the University $250,000 to endow the music professorship which bears his name.

Early in this century, student musicians formed the Orphic Order, which carried on until the outbreak of the First World War. The University Orchestra came into being after the war, under the direction of Richard L. Weaver. Since 1935, directors have been arranged for by the music department, among them Harold Berkeley, Moritz von Bomhard, Russell Ames Cook, Nicholas Harsanyi, Robert S. Freeman, Peter T. Westergaard, Mordechai Sheinkman, Bruce Ferden, and Michael Pratt, who became director in 1977.

One of Princeton's most memorable concerts took place in May 1973, when the University Orchestra, conducted by Peter Westergaard, and accompanied by a chorus prepared by Walter Nollner, performed Beethoven's Ninth Symphony before an enthusiastic audience that filled Alexander Hall to overflowing.

In recent years, as the opportunities for music study at Princeton have become more widely known, a steady increase in the number of highly qualified undergraduate instrumentalists has brought new strength to the University Orchestra and the programs it can offer.

Osborn Clubhouse, The, is located at the northeast corner of Olden and Prospect Avenues, adjacent to the site of the former University Field (now occupied by the Engineering Quadrangle). For almost three quarters of a century, it provided training table facilities for Princeton and visiting athletic teams. Built in 1892, it was the gift of Henry Fairfield Osborn 1877, a member of the Faculty Committee on Outdoor Sports, then Professor of Comparative Anatomy in the College and later director of the American Museum of Natural History in New York City. In 1971, the clubhouse became the headquarters of the Third World Center (q.v.).

Osgood, Charles Grosvenor (1871-1964), Holmes Professor of Belles Lettres, was distinguished for the breadth of his learning and the influence of his teaching. Well before his long life ended, he had become, in President Dodds's words, "the dean of Princeton humanists."

His alma mater was Yale, where he earned an A.B. in 1894 and a Ph.D. in 1899, and where he was teaching in 1905 when Woodrow Wilson called him to Princeton as one of the original preceptors. He found the life of a preceptor in Princeton congenial.

The town is small, the college large [he told his Yale classmates in their Twenty Year Record]. It is properly secluded, but not remote; and it gives a chance for the rearing of ideals upon equal support of the active and contemplative life. Friendliness between colleagues and, by the help of preceptorial teaching in small groups, between student and teacher . . . does much to effect in students just what a university ought—to teach them the art of living a good life.

He excelled as a preceptor. To him teaching was "the intimate engaging of personality with personality through the medium of some liberal subject," and he gave weekly demonstrations of this concept in preceptorial conferences in his house at 92 Stockton Street—in the winter, around the fireplace in his study.

Osgood early acquired a taste for music, painting, and the classics, which he cultivated all his life. While still at Yale he taught classics for two years (Charles Seymour, later president of that university, was one of his students), but then concluded that he would find greater freedom in the teaching of English. "Yet," he remarked in later years, "my first love never died, and I have lived a life of happy and unashamed bigamy." His course in "English Literature and the Classics," was long a favorite among undergraduates, and the breadth of his interests is revealed by the subjects of some of his early works: *The Classical Mythology of Milton's English Poems;* the Middle English poem, *The Pearl; Selections from the Works of Samuel Johnson; Vergil and the English Mind; Boccaccio on Poetry.*

His favorite English poet was Ed-

mund Spenser. With the help of his wife, he prepared a concordance to Spenser's poems and was later general editor of a ten-volume variorum edition of his works, a monumental task extending through a quarter of a century. Knowing that undergraduates were often careless spellers, he always began his lectures on Spenser by printing on the blackboard: EDMUND SPENSER. He could discourse for hours on Spenser's love of English rivers, the poetic skill of his sonnet sequence the *Amoretti*, and the social, political, and esthetic backgrounds of *The Faerie Queene.*

In 1935 he was persuaded to write a history of English literature for classroom use. It was called *The Voice of England.* "I have small excuse, I know," he wrote in the preface, "for rehearsing the old tale herein set down, except that it *is* an old story, and a good one, and many are the ways of telling it." Osgood's way, reviewers agreed, was one of the best, and one colleague doubted that any textbook was ever written with such grace and lucidity.

Osgood's broad learning was matched by a wide acquaintance with all kinds of people. Outside the University he made many friends as an elder in the First Presbyterian Church and as a trustee of the Princeton Public Library, and he joined the Masonic Order to enlarge his acquaintanceship.

On the train to New York one day a younger colleague heard Osgood, then in his sixties, quote Samuel Johnson to the effect that as a man grows older, he is willing to accept life on easier terms. Later he learned that Osgood was on his way to Artie McGovern's gymnasium, where he went twice a week to sweat it out with, among other people, Babe Ruth.

Osgood voluntarily retired in 1937 to concentrate on his writing. In 1941 he brought out his greatly admired *Poetry as a Means of Grace*, and in 1956 he put the capstone on the variorum edition of Spenser. The same year saw his *Boccaccio on Poetry*, first printed in 1930, reissued in a paperback edition. His preface for this was typically Osgoodian:

At eighty-five a man has no more right to tamper with the work of his fifties than with the work of another man. Indeed this book was the work of another man, younger by a generation than I, and, among all my issue of lesser years, my favorite. I am content that it should survive without correction or change.

Many honors came to Osgood during his later years. His old student, President Seymour, conferred on him a Yale Litt. D. on the fiftieth anniversary of his graduation; Princeton awarded him the same degree a few years later. A former student anonymously endowed the Osgood Book Fund, and the trustees established four advanced graduate fellowships in his name. But, as Willard Thorp, his successor as Holmes Professor, observed, his greatest "honor" was the devotion of hundreds of his former students who visited him and wrote to him until virtually the day of his death.

Outing Club. Except for a year during World War II, the Princeton Outing Club has been in continuous existence since 1941. With a donated cabin in Vermont and a vehicle purchased with annual dues, the club's original raison d'être was to promote skiing. In fact it began as a ski club and was a member of the Eastern Ski Association. More recently its program has broadened "to facilitate and promote the participation in and enjoyment of outdoor activities." Since its inception, the Outing Club

(and for a brief period of time a spin-off Mountaineering Club) has specialized in outdoor activities: climbing, deep sea fishing, skiing, canoeing, hiking and cruising. For a fifteen-year period (until the early sixties) it was the second largest organization on campus with 125 members. In the mid-1970s it experienced a revival, partly due to the influence of a more recent development, the Outdoor Action program.

Under the aegis of the dean of student affairs office, Outdoor Action began in 1973. So far, over 1000 students, staff, and faculty have participated in its programs. Essentially, it is a student staffed and operated program designed to enable diverse members of the university community to share experiences in the outdoors. As in the case of Outward Bound, its groups became involved in canoeing, hiking, backpacking, climbing, caving, and orienteering. Most of the trips are taken in the Delaware Water Gap or in the New Jersey Pine Barrens. It is increasingly being used as a teaching resource by academic departments.

John Andrew Brown

Oznot, Joseph David, was probably the best known character admitted to the University in his time. His qualifications were eminently meritorious. The Admission Office's file on him showed that at high school in East Lansing, Michigan, he was a top student, a classicist, a concert pianist, and class treasurer, with College Examination Board scores in the 700s.

Notice of his admission to the Class of 1968 was accordingly sent him on April 16, 1964, and on the same day his name duly appeared on the official admission list posted in West College. Two days later newspapers from coast to coast carried an Associated Press report that Joseph David Oznot "was not," that the University had been tricked into admitting a fictitious character by a clever, well-executed hoax, perpetrated by six sophomores, four at Princeton, one at Columbia, one at Michigan State University.

The Michigan State sophmore had submitted Oznot's preliminary application for admission in October, giving his fraternity house as Oznot's address. During the Christmas recess the Columbia sophomore came to Princeton for Oznot's interview at the Admission Office and made a favorable impression. In January two of the Princeton sophomores took Oznot's College Board exams, with highly creditable results. The final application papers, with space for marks and comment by the high school, were received by the Michigan State sophomore, and carefully filled out by the six conspirators. They settled on April 1 for Oznot's birthday and private detective as the occupation of his father, William H. Oznot (W.H.O.).

E. Alden Dunham, who was then Director of Admission, found the hoax "ingenious," and took a professional view about Joseph David Oznot. "We would have loved," he said, "to have had him."

EPHRIAM DI KAHBLE '39

A somewhat similar personage, Ephriam Di Kahble, was much talked about in earlier days by the Class of 1939. Ephriam did not, however, surmount the hurdle of the Admission Office. He appeared out of nowhere sometime in his sophomore year and similarly disappeared in his senior year. His name kept cropping up on chapel attendance cards in the Dean's office and the Registrar received examination

grades for him in several courses. His classmates recall last seeing him at an intercollegiate cross-country race in Van Cortlandt Park one hazy Indian summer afternoon. Ephriam started out with the other runners but never returned.

BERT HORMONE '17

Another Princetonian of some renown, Bert Hormone '17, was completely unknown in student days. As sometimes happens he did not blossom out until after graduation. In his case he was first mentioned in 1917's class notes in the *Alumni Weekly* in the spring of 1937, shortly before their twentieth reunion. He sounded like an intriguing person but, although several in the class had vague stirrings of their memories, no one could place him with certainty. Under questioning, the class secretary, Harvey Smith, admitted that Adelbert l'Homme-dieu X. Hormone —Bert's full name—was his brain child, created to stimulate interest in the reunion.

The class made Bert welcome and in later years from time to time different members reported chance encounters with him all over the world. Hormone became a Colonel in the Foreign Legion of France, and Smith faithfully chronicled his global exploits, marital as well as martial. Shortly before the class's fiftieth reunion he reported that Bert had died and been buried in his beloved Tahiti, his grave covered with flowers kept fresh by the tears of his several grieving widows.

Palmer Hall was given by and named for Stephen S. Palmer, trustee of the University from 1908 to 1913. At its dedication in 1909 he said he had made this gift in recognition of the "absolute necessity of extending Princeton's usefulness in the field of science and of placing her in a position where she can respond to the demands that will be made upon her."

The facilities thus provided for instruction and research (three floors with a total area of about two acres) enabled the Department of Physics to respond to the demands made upon it for its first thirty years. But the accelerating demands in the next three decades were such that facilities three times the size of Palmer were needed, and when Jadwin Hall (q.v.) was completed in 1969, the eastern portion of Palmer was given over to underclass instruction in physics, and other subjects, the western portion to East Asian Studies and the Program in the History and Philosophy of Science.

Statues of Benjamin Franklin and Joseph Henry, by Daniel Chester French, flank the front entrance of Palmer Laboratory, and high up on the rear wall of the west wing—to remind posterity that Palmer was built during the tenure of the twenty-sixth president of the United States—an energetic figure shakes a big stick.

Palmer House, named for charter trustee and benefactor Edgar Palmer, was bequeathed to the University by his widow in 1968 on condition that it be used exclusively for "college purposes" for at least twenty-five years. Mrs. Palmer also left $250,000 for the development of the house and grounds and a $200,000 trust fund to provide for maintenance. Since its acquisition Palmer House has been used to provide accommodations and meeting rooms for trustees and guests of the University.

Situated at the northeast corner of Bayard Lane and Nassau Street, it was designed and built by Charles Steadman in 1825 for the daughter of John Potter, wealthy merchant of Charleston, South Carolina, who had married the naval hero, Robert F. Stockton 1813. In 1923 it became the home of Edgar Palmer '03, a charter trustee from 1936 to 1949, who gave Palmer Stadium in memory of his father, Stephen S. Palmer, also a trustee and the donor of Palmer Hall.

Palmer Stadium was given by Edgar Palmer '03 as a memorial to his father, Stephen S. Palmer, a trustee of the University from 1908 to 1913 and the donor of Palmer Hall.

Designed by Henry S. Hardenburgh, the stadium was completed in 1914, the same year as the Yale Bowl. Yale diminished Princeton's enjoyment of the Palmer Stadium dedication on November 14 by winning the annual football game, 19 to 14; but Harvard took even more away from Yale's pleasure at the dedication of the Bowl a week later with a 36 to 0 triumph that led one sportswriter to observe: "Yale had the bowl, but Harvard supplied the punch."

Like Harvard's stadium, which was built in 1903, Princeton's followed the U-shape of the ancient Greek stadium, while the Yale Bowl was modeled on the elliptical design characteristic of the Roman colosseum and the amphitheater at Pompeii. The completely enclosed Yale Bowl had no facilities for track meets. The open end in the Harvard and Princeton stadiums, which reduced the number of seats available for football games, made possible the 220-yard straightaway essential for track meets.

Palmer Stadium is slightly longer and a good deal wider than the standard ancient Greek stadium, which was used only for track and got its name from the Greek word for the distance of its most common race, the *stade*, which was approximately an eighth of a Roman mile, or a little shorter than our 220-yard dash.

Palmer Stadium's capacity is 42,000, which has sometimes been stretched to 52,000 by the erection of wooden stands at the open end.

A new all-weather-surface track was constructed in Palmer Stadium in 1978. It was named the Erdman-McGraw Track in honor of Charles R. Erdman '19, track captain in 1919 and 1920, and Curtis W. McGraw '19, football captain in 1919.

Pate, Maurice '15 (1894-1965), a founder (with Herbert Hoover) and first executive director of UNICEF, was born in Pender, Nebraska, of Welsh ancestry and came to Princeton from East Denver High School in Colorado. His college classmates later remembered him as "a tall, dark, wavy-haired figure of boundless geniality and seemingly infinite energy, whose view of the world was much more advanced than that of most of us." He majored in mathematics and physics, managed the business affairs of the *Lit*, worked on the undergraduate Red Cross Committee, ran the launch on Lake Carnegie for rowing coach J. Duncan Spaeth, took his meals with a nonclub group who called themselves the Gargoyles, won election to Phi Beta Kappa, and graduated with high honors.

The following spring he left his job as bank clerk in Iowa and won a place, after much persistence, on Herbert Hoover's Commission for Relief in Belgium, thus beginning a lifelong friendship with Hoover. After spending 1917 and 1918 overseas with the A.E.F., he was again associated with Hoover, this time for three years as a member of the

American Relief Administration in Poland, with special responsibility for feeding Polish children. In the Second World War, after seventeen years as salesman, importer, and investment banker, he returned to relief work, first as president of the Commission for Polish Relief, then with the American Red Cross as director of Relief to Prisoners of War.

At the end of the war Pate was once more called on by Hoover, in this case to assist him in filling a request by President Truman to help in "the organization of measures to alleviate the postwar famine." Pate accompanied Hoover on a tour of stricken areas. On their return, Hoover's recommendations led to the establishment of the United Nations International Children's Emergency Fund (UNICEF) with Pate as Executive Director. (Later, when this organization was given permanent status, it was renamed the United Nations Children's Fund, but it retained its original acronym.)

Under Pate's leadership, UNICEF grew to be the United Nations's most famous and respected agency, a world-wide operation providing, during his administration, food and medical aid for upwards of a hundred million children. Many people helped: political leaders whose nations contributed funds, artists who designed UNICEF greeting cards, school-children who collected money at Halloween. But it was Pate's personal integrity and selflessness that inspired all the others. Speaking of the United Nations, Dag Hammarskjöld said, "The work of UNICEF is at the heart of the matter—and at the heart of UNICEF is Maurice Pate." During the Hungarian uprising of 1956, when the government would admit no other U.N. official, Pate went to Budapest and, after walking the streets in a three-day survey, dispatched orders for the UNICEF aid he saw was needed. In 1960 he arrived in Leopoldville soon after the outbreak of the Congo crisis to provide badly needed food, having been summoned for this mission by Dag Hammarskjöld, from a movie house, only three nights before. Introducing Pate at a UNICEF dinner, Herbert Hoover called him "the most efficient human angel I have ever known."

He was decorated by Belgium, Ecuador, France, The Netherlands, and Poland, and was honored—closer to home—by the award of the Class of 1915's Merit Cup in 1950 and Princeton's honorary degree of Doctor of Philanthropy in 1958. In 1960 the Norwegian Committee for UNICEF proposed his nomination for the Nobel Peace Prize. Declining this honor for himself, Pate suggested that UNICEF be nominated instead. This was done, and UNICEF received the prize in 1965, the year that Pate died.

At his funeral, the organist played "He Shall Feed His Flock," from Handel's *Messiah*; U Thant said that "the United Nations and the world's children" were "infinitely the richer for his long and devoted service"; the minister read the Parable of the Loaves and Fishes; and a children's choir sang the anthem "Let All Things Now Living," to a traditional Welsh melody. The service closed with these words from the *Bhagavad Gita*, chosen by Mrs. Pate:

One who does one's duties for the love of God, who considers God to be the Supreme Goal of life, who has no attachment, no personal ambition or self-interest, who has no inimical or bitter feelings against anyone in the whole world, will surely reach God.

Paterson, William (1745-1806), one of the principal founders of the governments of New Jersey and the United States, was brought up in the village of Princeton, where his father, a Scotch-Irish immigrant tinsmith and shopkeeper, settled when William was five years old. As a boy of ten he watched the local mason, William Worth, erect Nassau Hall and when he was fourteen he went there to live as a student in the College.

For four years he followed the classical curriculum of that day, excelling in the monthly orations then required of every student, and graduated near the top of his class in 1763. While reading law with Richard Stockton 1748, the leading attorney in Princeton, he kept in touch with the College and helped found the Well Meaning Club, forerunner of the Cliosophic Society. At Commencement in 1766 he received the degree of Master of Arts and delivered an eloquent and widely admired oration on "Patriotism."

In 1769, shortly after he had begun the practice of law (supplementing his meagre income by keeping a general store), he wrote a college friend that "to live at ease and pass through life without much noise and bustle" was all he wished for. Six years later, however, when he was thirty, he embarked on one of the most active public careers of his generation, serving successively as secretary of the New Jersey Provincial Congress, member of the convention that drafted the state constitution, first attorney general of New Jersey, head of the New Jersey delegation to the federal Constitutional Convention, one of the first two United States senators from New Jersey, governor of New Jersey, and finally, for the last thirteen years of his life, associate justice of the United States Supreme Court. From

1787 to 1802 he was also a trustee of the College.

At the federal Constitutional Convention (q.v.) Paterson offered the New Jersey "small states" plan in opposition to the Virginia "large states" plan drafted by James Madison 1771, but then accepted the Connecticut compromise supported by Oliver Ellsworth 1766, which was adopted. Paterson was short, modest, and unassuming in appearance, but he was one of those men, William Pierce, a delegate from Georgia, noted in his journal, "whose powers break in upon you, and create wonder and astonishment."

While senator, he helped Oliver Ellsworth draft the Judiciary Act of 1789. While governor he undertook the codification of all existing New Jersey laws—the English statutes which by the state constitution remained in force, as well as acts adopted by the legislature since the Revolution. He continued this monumental task after his elevation to the Supreme Court, and the results of his labors, the first published Laws of the State of New Jersey, appeared in 1800.

Patton, Francis Landey (1843-1932), twelfth president of Princeton, was born in Warwick, Bermuda, on January 22, 1843. His early schooling was at Warwick Academy; later he attended Knox College of the University of Toronto and studied for two years at Princeton Theological Seminary. After ordination in June 1865, he held pastorates in New York City, Nyack, Brooklyn, and Chicago. His teaching career began in 1872 with his appointment as Cyrus Hall McCormick Professor of Didactic and Polemical Theology at the Presbyterian Theological Seminary of the Northwest (now McCormick Seminary).

In conjunction with his faculty duties, Patton was expected to defend conservative Presbyterianism against the new liberal currents of thought that had all but taken over the Chicago Presbytery. Thin, bespectacled, wearing side whiskers, a white lawn tie and a black frock coat, Patton looked every bit the part he was called to play. He plunged into the task with zeal, as editor of the *Interior*, a Presbyterian weekly, and as professor and public speaker. The culmination of his crusade came in April 1874, with a much-publicized heresy trial of the Rev. David Swing, the most popular representative of Chicago liberalism, whom Patton charged with serious departures from the faith. Patton lost his case before the Presbytery, but gained a great reputation as the eloquent champion of orthodoxy, leading to his election as Moderator of the General Assembly in 1878. Three years later, Princeton Theological Seminary appointed him to a new chair in the Relations of Philosophy and Science to the Christian Religion, endowed especially for Patton by Robert L. Stewart.

When Patton arrived in Princeton in the spring of 1881, he retained the stiff, formal appearance that seemed to reflect his conservative views, but his manner mellowed during the years that followed. The side whiskers disappeared, the high collar came down, the white lawn tie gave way to a simple black business tie. His reputation as a teacher and theologian grew rapidly, and his services as an after-dinner speaker were soon much in demand. Even those who disagreed with his orthodox beliefs admired his platform brilliance embellished as it was with literary allusions and laced with incisive wit. In 1884, he added to his Seminary schedule the teaching of a course at

Princeton College in Ethics and the Philosophy of Religion. But the severest test of his career came in 1888, when he was elected by the trustees of the College to the office of the presidency held so ably for many years by the much-revered McCosh.

Patton's election did not enthuse all Princetonians. Alumni had hoped not only for an educator, but also for an experienced administrator who would bring efficiency and system to the expanding business needs of the College. Some noted that he was not even an American citizen. Undergraduates feared that they were to be "admonished, sermonized, disciplined after the John Knox fashion." But Patton managed to allay many doubts in his first speaking engagement. Before the New York alumni in March 1888, he alluded to his predecessors, particularly Witherspoon and McCosh, saying, "It is manifest that there is more joy among the Alumni over the one President who has been naturalized than over the ninety-and-nine that have needed no naturalization." Amid frequent laughter and applause, he referred to the criticism that he lacked business acumen by saying that he believed that a "college president ought to know an interest-coupon from a railway-ticket, and that he ought to be able to understand a balance-sheet as well as to grade an examination-paper." Continuing, Patton referred to the value of diversity among a student body and explained, "I am not prepared to say that it is better to have gone and loafed than never to have gone at all, but I do believe in the *genius loci*; and I sympathize with Sir Joshua Reynolds when he says, that there is around every seminary of learning, an atmosphere of floating knowledge where every one can imbibe something pecul-

iar to his own original conceptions." Perceptive though this observation was, unfortunately the subordinate clause, "it is better to have gone and loafed than never to have gone at all," was to be most remembered and later often quoted out of context as evidence of Patton's casual attitude toward scholarship.

The classes of the nineties—the "golden nineties" to their members—were unanimous in their respect and affection for Patton. His course in ethics was popular, and when he preached at Chapel, one of his students recalled, "the most indifferent of loafers slouched over to hear him." His kindly wisdom and ready wit soon became legendary, and students frequently sought him out for guidance and counsel.

During Patton's administration, Princeton underwent great change. The student body increased from slightly over 600 to more than 1300, while the faculty, too, more than doubled. Patton appointed a number of both promising and accomplished scholars and teachers who soon brought new lustre to the community. Among them were Woodrow Wilson, Bliss Perry, John Grier Hibben, Winthrop More Daniels, George McLean Harper, Paul and Henry van Dyke, and Howard Crosby Warren. During the same time, more than a dozen major buildings were completed, The social life of the students was also changing as eating clubs proliferated. The clubs, together with the surging interest in athletics, particularly football, created a new atmostphere on campus and an emphasis on "college life" rather than college studies. The climax of the "golden nineties" came in 1896 during the Sesquicentennial Celebration when Patton proclaimed that the College would "in all future time be known as Princeton University."

The change in title, hailed as signaling the beginning of a new era in the history of Princeton, also marked the beginning of the end for the Patton administration, for it brought sharply into focus the president's failures as an administrator. Even by standards of that day, the administrative structure of Princeton was spare to the extreme. Patton conducted college affairs from his study in Prospect. He had no personal secretary until 1895 when he assigned that position to his son, George Stevenson Patton '91, and there was no college or university secretary until the election of Charles Williston McAlpin in December 1900. Patton was assisted by only one dean for most of his term, during which he turned aside the faculty's urgent appeals to inaugurate a system of deans to accommodate the expanding institution. Faculty accounts indicate that Patton lacked initiative in important policy matters, resisted meaningful curriculum reform, was lax in matters of discipline and in scholarly standards—in short, as one faculty member put it, was "a wonderfully poor administrator."

To many of the faculty, enthused by the high promise of the Sesquicentennial, the time seemed at hand to take concrete measures toward making Princeton in fact what she now claimed to be in name. With little help from the president, the faculty did manage an important step forward with the establishment, by the trustees, of the Graduate School in 1900. In its administrative structure, Patton was effectively circumvented, since the dean, Andrew Fleming West, appointed directly by the trustees, was given nearly autonomous powers. On the other hand, faculty committees labored for

nearly two years to reform the curriculum, but Patton remained unconvinced that a student's performance could thus be improved and succeeded in shunting aside the proposals.

Significantly, the efforts of the faculty reformers gained the sympathetic attention of many influential trustees who, although they continued to admire Patton as a teacher, preacher, and public speaker, were becoming deeply concerned about his administrative inadequacies. The Board of Trustees itself had changed its profile during the 1890s as the traditional clerical majority was slowly reduced by the election of more business and professional men. Most of the sixteen new trustees elected in the last five years of the century were successful businessmen and lawyers, products of a burgeoning industrial America, who valued efficiency and who were not inclined to be patient for long with Patton's methods.

The climax came during the spring of 1902 when several trustees and faculty proposed to Patton that an executive committee of two trustees and three faculty members be formed to assume many of the president's administrative powers. Patton protested this reduction in his control of university affairs, but even his friends on the board gave him little encouragement. Finally, after some negotiation, he decided that resignation was the better part of wisdom, and he resigned at the trustees' meeting on June 9, 1902. The board, with Patton's strong endorsement, immediately chose Woodrow Wilson to be his successor.

Patton did not leave his office empty-handed. To compensate him for retiring six years earlier than he had intended, a group of trustees, alumni, and friends agreed to give him a sum in cash that, together with his yearly salary of $4000 as Professor of Ethics for one term a year, would equal for six years his salary as president of the University. His career was by no means ended, for not only did he continue to teach at both University and Seminary, but in the fall of 1902 he accepted election to the new office of president of Princeton Theological Seminary.

Whatever his deficiencies as an administrator, Patton continued high in the affection of students, faculty, and alumni. He also retained his sense of humor. At one time, when asked by a Seminary visitor if he had any connection with the University, he wryly replied, "Yes, indeed, I am President of Princeton University—once removed."

Patton retired from the Seminary in 1913 and returned to his beloved Bermuda, there to write and preach, coming to the States occasionally to lecture. He went on speaking out on behalf of scriptural and doctrinal integrity in numerous controversies that arose in the Presbyterian church, and he presented his case for orthodoxy most fully in his book, *Fundamental Christianity*, published when he was 83. "We cannot change Christianity," he wrote, "We may reject it if we please, but its meaning is plain." He died in Bermuda on November 25, 1932.

David W. Hirst

Penfield, Wilder [Graves] '13 (1891-1976), world-famous brain surgeon, reflected toward the end of his long, productive life that "the only certain virtue" that came into the world with him at his birth in Spokane, Washington on January 26, 1891 was "tenacity of purpose."

When his father's medical practice failed and he was unable to support the family, his mother took his elder brother and sister and eight-year-old Wilder to live with her parents in Hudson, Wisconsin. Following his graduation from the Galahad School in Hudson, which his mother had helped found, Penfield entered Princeton, where he was determined to make himself an all-round scholar, athlete, and leader so that he might qualify for a Rhodes Scholarship—an ambition his mother had encouraged in him from the time he was thirteen. The best he could do in football his first year, in competition with many heavier and speedier players from large eastern schools, was to qualify as a substitute on the freshman team. That winter, on the advice of Heff Herring '07, Princeton football player, wrestler, and Rhodes Scholar, he went out for wrestling, and thereby developed large neck muscles, outgrew his shirts, won the interclass freshman-sophomore wrestling match, and eventually found a place on the varsity football team as a first-string tackle (at 170 pounds, a weight he maintained all his life).

He had previously thought he would never want to enter the profession in which his father had failed, but at the end of his sophomore year, an enthusiasm engendered by Professor Conklin's biology lectures—and a long-standing desire to help his fellow man inculcated in him by his mother—led him to decide on a career in medicine.

Penfield looked forward to beginning his medical education at Oxford, but—despite his having been football tackle, baseball manager, class president and, according to his classmates, "the most respected" and "best all-round man"—he lost out for the Rhodes Scholarship from New Jersey to an "excellent fellow" from Rutgers. Instead, he devoted the year after graduation to earning money for his medical education by coaching the Princeton freshman football team and then teaching at the Galahad School. In the middle of the year, he received word that a Rhodes Scholarship for the following year had been awarded him, and he was accepted for admission to Merton College, which granted him special permission to defer his entrance until the end of the autumn of 1914 so that he might fulfill an agreement to coach the Princeton varsity football team.

At Oxford, he was deeply influenced by Charles Sherrington, "in his heyday, the world's foremost neurophysiologist," who made him realize that in the nervous system was "the unexplored field—the undiscovered country in which the mystery of the mind of man might some day be explained." He was also strongly affected by Sir William Osler, Canadian-born Regius Professor of Medicine ("a hero to the rising generation of medical men") at whose home he convalesced in 1916 after a German torpedo blew up the ship on which he was crossing the English channel to serve in a Red Cross hospital in France.

After two years at Oxford, he entered the Johns Hopkins Medical School where he received his M.D. in 1918. The following year he was surgical intern at the Peter Bent Brigham Hospital in Boston, serving an apprenticeship under brain surgeon Harvey Cushing. But the memory of the "undiscovered country" he had glimpsed through Sherrington's lectures continued to intrigue him. He accordingly returned to Oxford for the third and final year of his Rhodes Scholarship as a graduate student in neurophysiology under Sherrington and followed that with a year as a research fellow in neurology at the National Hospital in London.

Returning to the United States in 1921, he rejected a lucrative position as a surgeon at the Henry Ford Hospital in Detroit—because it would have afforded him no opportunity for research—and accepted a post as associate in surgery at Columbia University and Presbyterian Hospital. There he developed his surgical techniques under Allen O. Whipple, Princeton '04, and organized and pursued research in a laboratory of neurocytology.

During his postgraduate years in Oxford and London, Penfield had turned from experimental neurophysiology toward neurosurgery because he believed that, since the neurosurgeon could lay bare the living human brain, he should be able to study and influence the brain's physiological activity and thus become "a neurologist-in-action." As he came to realize that he could not carry out an effective approach to knowledge of the human brain and make use of that knowledge all by himself, he began to dream of organizing an institute where neurologists, neurosurgeons, and neuropathologists would work together with the kind of team work he had learned as football player and coach. Thinking he might be better able to realize this dream in Montreal, Canada, he joined the medical faculty of McGill University in 1928 and became at the same time neurosurgeon at the Royal Victoria and Montreal General Hospitals.

A few months after his arrival in Montreal, Penfield was called upon to remove a tumor from the brain of his sister Ruth. After finding that the tumor was malignant and far advanced, he performed a more radical operation than most neurosurgeons would have dared to attempt, but could not safely remove all of the malignant cells. Although the operation made it possible for his sister to enjoy a normal life again, the symptoms eventually returned and she died three years later.

The difficulties of his sister's case spurred him to make his first effort to realize his dream of an endowed neurological institute for "investigation of the brain and mind as a way to human betterment." His application to the Rockefeller Foundation resulted in a grant of $1,232,000 and the opening in 1934 of the Montreal Institute of Neurology, whose fame in neurological research and treatment attracted observers and graduate students, as well as patients, from all over the world.

In treating 1,132 patients during Penfield's directorship, the Institute greatly improved the techniques of brain surgery and added materially to neurological knowledge. Penfield himself perfected the surgical operation for severe epilepsy and—by observing directly the living brain and mapping out its responses to electrical stimulation in the course of bringing therapeutic relief to conscious patients under local anesthesia—catalogued a great body of information about the physiology of the brain and recorded observations "of classical importance" on the speech-cortex and the interpretative-cortex. His "distinguished contributions," his successor, William Feindel, said, were "recognized as unique by his neurosurgical and scientific colleagues." The eminent British neurologist Nobel Laureate Edgar Douglas Adrian described Penfield as "a skilled neurosurgeon, a distinguished scientist, and a clear and engaging writer" with qualities of leadership which attracted "devoted colleagues," but that "his first concern" was always the patient who needed "his surgical skill."

Honors were bestowed on Penfield by societies, universities, and governments in North America, Europe, and Asia. President of the Royal College of Physicians and Surgeons of Canada and of the American Neurological Association, he was a fellow of the prestigious Royal Society of London and twenty-five other scientific and professional organizations and a recipient of honorary degrees from as many universities, among them Princeton, Oxford, McGill, and Montreal. He was also awarded half a dozen prizes here and abroad and was the first recipient of the $50,000 Royal Bank Centennial Award. Twice decorated by Canada, he was also awarded the United States Medal of Freedom, crosses of the French Legion of Honor and the Greek Legion of George I—and the British Order of Merit, which is conferred on only twenty-four living persons.

HIS SECOND CAREER

Penfield retired from the McGill medical faculty in 1954, but he continued to serve as director of the Neurological Institute and to lecture frequently. He visited Princeton in 1956 to deliver the Vanuxem lectures, later published by Princeton University Press as *Speech and Brain Mechanisms*. He also traveled to Russia, India, and China in successive years as an invited lecturer before scientific groups. At the same time, he began a second career, as he completely rewrote his late mother's novel, *Story of Sari* (based on a Biblical tale), which was published under the title *No Other Gods*.

On his retirement as director of the Neurological Institute in 1960, he intensified work on his second career in line with his belief that "rest, with nothing else, results in rust." That same year he published *The Torch*, a biographical novel about Hippocrates. Three years later, at age 72, he brought out *The Second Career*, a collection of essays and addresses reflecting his myriad interests and encouraging others to use retirement for the development of a new career.

In 1967, Penfield produced two more books: *The Difficult Art of Giving*, a biography of Alan Gregg, director of the medical sciences division of the Rockefeller Foundation, who had engineered the grant that had made the Montreal Neurological Institute possible, and *Man and His Family*, which grew out of another facet of his second career—his presidency of the Vanier Institute of the Family, which he helped found "to promote and guide education in the home—man's first classroom."

In 1974, when he was eighty-three, he completed and dedicated to Sir Charles Sherrington, *The Mystery of the Mind*, an account for laymen of his investigation of the brain for almost forty years, published by Princeton University Press in 1975.

Three weeks before his death at the age of eighty-five on April 5, 1976, Penfield completed the draft of his autobiography, *No Man Alone*, a phrase repeated frequently in the book to underline his emphasis on the team approach to neurological research and treatment. Published in 1977, his final work was dedicated "with affection and gratitude" to the memory of his mother who had helped make it possible for him "to see things as they were" by preserving, editing, and typing the letters he had written her almost every week from 1909, when he entered Princeton, until her death in 1935.

Perry, Ralph Barton (1876-1957), author of a Pulitzer Prize-winning biography of William James, one-time president of the American Philosophical Association, and philosophy professor at Harvard for forty years, graduated from Princeton in 1896. He was later made an honorary member of the Class of 1896 at Harvard (as well as an honorary doctor of letters at both Princeton and Harvard). In 1941 he attended the forty-fifth reunion of both classes and gave the same talk at the two class dinners. This talk, printed in the *Princeton Alumni Weekly* and the *Harvard Alumni Bulletin* and later published in a little book by the Vanguard Press of New York, decried the tendency of youth to shelve those past forty, and made a *Plea for an Age Movement*.

Let us make virtue of our necessities [Perry counselled his Princeton and Harvard classmates]. Age should not have its face lifted, but rather teach the world to admire wrinkles, as the etchings of experience and the firm lines of character. Let us not *suffer* from insomnia, or regret the fact that we cannot sleep; but rather rejoice that we need not. . . . And when we are told that you cannot teach an old dog new tricks, our answer should be that old dogs have already learned their bagful, and may now practice the tricks they know.

. . . There is a pride of youth, and I would not have it one whit abated. But there is also a pride of age, which is ours if we will only affirm it. . . .

Peyton Hall, home of the Department of Astrophysical Sciences, was built in 1966 with grants from the National Science and Ford Foundations and other gifts and named for William Charles Peyton, father of Bernard Peyton '17 (chairman of the department's Advisory Council), who made the largest individual gift. With its neighbors, Fine Hall of Mathematics and Jadwin Physical Laboratory, it stands just west of Palmer Stadium. Peyton Hall was designed by Minoru Yamasaki, who was also the architect of Woodrow Wilson Hall. The building contains a library, laboratories, faculty offices, lecture and seminar rooms, and two telescopes, one 9½-inch and the other 4-inch, for student instruction. The smaller telescope belonged to William Charles Peyton, a life-long amateur student of astronomy.

The department's facilities also include a 36-inch reflecting telescope in the FitzRandolph Observatory east of Palmer Stadium.

Phi Beta Kappa Society, founded at the College of William and Mary in 1776, has had a Princeton chapter since 1898. Membership is based on general academic performance throughout the college course; normally about a tenth of a class is elected. The society takes its name from the intitials of its Greek motto: *Philosophia Biou Kubernetes—* "Love of wisdom the Helmsman of Life."

Two Princeton faculty members have served as president of the national organization of Phi Beta Kappa: Dean Christian Gauss and Professor Whitney J. Oates.

Philosophy, The Department of. The history of Princeton philosophy goes back to the College's earliest years, long before the present departmental structure was instituted in 1904. To be a philosopher in those days was compatible with being a theologian. It virtually always involved lecturing on ethics and political theory. And it often involved being president of the College. President John Witherspoon, for example, listed as Professor of Theology, was fa-

mous for his lectures on moral philosophy.

A decade prior to Witherspoon, Princeton had as her president, for only a few weeks, one of the greatest philosophers America ever produced: Jonathan Edwards. Never mind the brevity of the period. It is a feather in Princeton's cap that she was able to lure such a giant, and a matter of great regret that his contribution was cut short by his premature death from smallpox.

Witherspoon too was a giant, but in a different way. Edwards's philosophical ideas were stunningly original, though he used them in defense of Calvinistic doctrines that were rapidly losing favor. While not particularly original, Witherspoon was a man of unusual intellectual power. A disciple of Thomas Reid at Glasgow, he brought to Princeton Reid's "Common Sense Realism," when he became president in 1768. James McCosh, who became president exactly one hundred years after Witherspoon, represented the same philosophy. Intellectual histories of the United States use the phrase "The Princeton School" to refer to the powerful point of view espoused by these two Scots.

In the late nineteenth century and the early twentieth, philosophical academia was dominated by the Kantian-Hegelian point of view. Princeton philosophy finally joined in the Germanic chorus, contributing some important voices. Best known internationally was Norman Kemp-Smith, who came to Princeton in 1906. His commentary on Kant's *Critique of Pure Reason*, written while he was at Princeton, was studied wherever philosophy was taught. Archibald Bowman, who joined the department in 1912, lectured on Hegel, as well as Plato. Like Kemp-Smith, he was a Scot;

neither could resist the call homeward, Kemp-Smith to Edinburgh in 1919, Bowman to Glasgow in 1926. A third member of this group was Alexander T. Ormond, one of the first Stuart Professors under McCosh, and the department's first chairman from 1904 to 1913. Still another was John Grier Hibben, a popular teacher and the last philosopher to be president of Princeton.

Early in the twentieth century there were numerous signs of revolt from the predominant Kantian-Hegelian point of view. One movement, peculiarly American, was undertaken by six men who jointly published *The New Realism* in 1912. In various ways, four of the six were associated with Princeton. Two were among the five original "preceptor guys" in philosophy, appointed by Woodrow Wilson in 1905: Edward G. Spaulding, who continued his service to Princeton for thirty-five years, and Walter T. Marvin, later dean at Rutgers. The third was Ralph Barton Perry, professor at Harvard, who was a product of Princeton's Class of 1896. The fourth, Edwin B. Holt, a Harvard graduate and professor, was later, for a decade, visiting professor of psychology at Princeton. (Another original "preceptor guy" in philosophy, Roger B.C. Johnson, served as departmental chairman from 1926 to 1934.)

The new realism was but one straw in the wind. In America, the pragmatism of James and Dewey; in England, the realism of Moore and Russell; on the Continent, the so-called "positivism" of the Vienna Circle; all these were bombarding the Hegelian citadel. The years preceding and immediately following the Second World War were crucial to the future of philosophy departments throughout the country. The bright young men were attracted to the various strands in the revolt. Some departments, where Hegelianism was so entrenched as to resist revolt, tended not to hire these younger men. Other departments, by emphasizing a single strand in the revolt, ran the risk of eventual narrowness in point of view. Fortunately, Princeton followed a middle course in this difficult period of transition, under its chairman from 1934 to 1952, Robert M. Scoon. As a classical scholar he was committed to tradition; his sensitivity to new trends was evident in his admiration of Dewey's pragmatism. The department did not flourish during his chairmanship, but it followed a sensible and even course that paved the way for the future. The key to this period was Scoon's favorite word: "balance."

The towering figure through these years was Walter T. Stace (q.v.), who taught theory of knowledge and metaphysics; many of the best known philosophers in the United States in the 1970s were products of his teaching. Scoon taught Plato and Aristotle, and also Aquinas until the appointment in 1948 of the eminent French philosopher, Jacques Maritain (q.v.). For forty-three years Ledger Wood upheld the tradition of scholarly competence in the history of modern philosophy. Spaulding kept alive philosophy's contact with the natural sciences. Theodore M. Greene vigorously represented philosophy's contact with the arts and humanities.

Throughout the forties, the appointment of younger men was always made with an eye on balance. One of them, Walter Kaufmann, appointed in 1947 to teach modern European philosophy, achieved world-wide recognition in his field. But the forties brought losses with Spaulding's death in 1940 and Greene's resignation in 1945; and so did the fifties with Maritain's retirement in 1952 and both Scoon's and Stace's in 1955. It was clear that the future of the department depended on a series of major appointments.

In 1955, Carl G. Hempel, one of the most eminent men in philosophy of science and theory of knowledge, was lured from Yale. In the same year, Gregory Vlastos, possibly the leading scholar of classical philosophy in this country, was called from Cornell. In 1963, Stuart Hampshire, one of England's foremost philosophers, came from the University of London. In 1967, Donald Davidson, whose work in ethics and the philosophy of language was becoming proverbial, came from Stanford. And, finally, Dana Scott was brought in 1969 to contribute distinction in the area of logic.

It is little wonder that, by 1969, in a survey conducted by the American Council on Education, Princeton's Philosophy Department was ranked first in the nation in both quality of faculty and effectiveness of doctoral program. The department's continuing distinction has not rested solely on the eminent philosophers just mentioned. For one thing, not all remained. Hampshire left after seven years to become Warden of Wadham College, Oxford. Davidson left after three years to accept a post at Rockefeller University. Scott left after only two years to become a University Professor at Oxford. Much of the strength of any department lies in its younger members, and much of Princeton's strength in philosophy lies not only in the ability of these younger scholars but also in the breadth of their interests.

As of 1977, tenured members of the department, by order of date of first appointment, were as follows: James Ward Smith, Political Philosophy; Walter Kaufmann, History of Philosophy;

Arthur Szathmary, Philosophy of Art; George Pitcher, Theory of Knowledge; Paul Benacerraf, Philosophy of Mathematics; Richard Rorty, Metaphysics; Gilbert Harman, Philosophy of Language; Thomas Nagel, Ethics; Thomas Scanlon, Political Philosophy; Margaret Wilson, History of Philosophy; David Lewis, Metaphysics; Richard C. Jeffrey, Philosophy of Science; Michael Frede, Classical Philosophy; Saul Kripke, Logic and Metaphysics.

James Ward Smith

Physics, The Department of. Was it good advice or inspiration that prompted the trustees of the College of New Jersey to appoint Joseph Henry (q.v.) to the Professorship of Natural Philosophy in 1832? Whichever it was, they appointed the greatest, perhaps the only, American research physicist of his time. Henry was the only American whose name was adopted for one of the principal international electrical units. Moreover, he was a great teacher, first exemplifying in physics the Princeton ideal of the teacher-scholar.

After Henry's departure in 1848 to become the first head of the Smithsonian Institution, physics at Princeton had an arid period until the appointment of Cyrus Fogg Brackett (q.v.) in 1873 and of William Francis Magie (q.v.) in 1882. Both men brought distinction to the teaching of physics and prepared the way for the transition into a great department. In the 1890s they, with Henry B. Fine (q.v.), concluded that both mathematics and physics had to be strengthened if Princeton was to become a real university. Consequently, they began, under Woodrow Wilson, to build up both departments by appointing promising young men.

In 1905 and 1906, the trustees brought to Princeton two brilliant young Englishmen, James H. Jeans in applied mathematics and Owen W. Richardson in physics. At that time there was no Palmer Laboratory and physics lectures were given in the old John C. Green School of Science. Richardson described the research facilities he found there in a letter written nearly fifty years later:

I remember getting quite a shock when I was first introduced to the part where I was expected to set up a research laboratory. This was a kind of dark basement, ventilated by a hole in the wall, apparently accidental in origin, and inhabited by an impressive colony of hoptoads which enjoyed the use of a swimming pool in one corner. However, with the help of the Clerk of Works these visitors and their amenities were got rid of and a lot of good work was done in it. Looking back on those days, I think they were in many ways the most satisfactory of my life.

Professor Richardson lived up to his high reputation, and when he went back to England in 1914, he left an enthusiasm for research which has never faltered to this day. The quality of the training under him and his successors is evidenced by the Nobel laureates (q.v.) who have been members of the faculty or graduate students. In the chronological order of their awards they are: Arthur H. Compton, Owen W. Richardson, Clinton J. Davisson, Edwin M. McMillan, John Bardeen, Robert Hofstadter, Eugene P. Wigner, Richard P. Feynman, Philip W. Anderson. Bardeen is the only person who has ever received the physics prize twice. Wigner is also a recipient of the

Fermi Prize and the Atoms for Peace Award.

William F. Magie was chairman of the department from 1908 to 1929. He was a man of firm character but gentle manners, and the influence of his personality on the department still endures. He was blessed with a wife of equally strong personality and a quick wit. She was the source of the often quoted aphorism "A physicist is a man who knows what is wrong with the electric bell but can't fix it," and also of the answer to Professor Cooke's hope that his son would become a scientist: "Oh no, Lester, think of the scientists you know."

The expansion of the department under Dean Magie included the appointment in 1925 of four new assistant professors, Henry D. Smyth, Allen G. Shenstone, Louis A. Turner, and Charles Zahn. Smyth became well known as the author of *Atomic Energy for Military Purposes* (the "Smyth Report"). For his service as the United States representative, with rank of ambassador, on the International Atomic Energy Agency he was given the Atoms for Peace Award. Smyth and Shenstone, between them, served for 25 years as chairmen of the department.

Following those appointments came several in the field of theoretical physics, notably Eugene P. Wigner and John von Neumann, the first of the remarkable group of Hungarians whose effect on physics in the United States has been so very great. With that start, the field of theory became more and more important in the University. The combination of the Institute for Advanced Study and the University made the town of Princeton, at one time, the greatest center for theoretical physics in the world.

In the thirties, Princeton became

part of the nuclear age when Milton G. White was brought to the department and the decision was made to build a cyclotron. Such a decision was much more difficult to make then than now. No government grants were then available, and the University and the department had to find the necessary support from the University Scientific Research Fund. To save money, the machine had to be built in Palmer Laboratory, and the only room large enough was the ventilating room in the basement, which had not been in more than partial use for some time. The cyclotron, until the acquisition of the 3 Bev accelerator in the late fifties, was the most important single piece of apparatus in the department's history.

The years of World War II found most of the physics faculty engaged in war research either in Princeton or at some national laboratory. A considerable number went to the new Radiation Laboratory at M.I.T., which was founded to exploit the magnetron, the short wave transmitter tube invented in England. Professors White and Turner headed large sections of that very important laboratory. Other faculty members were involved in the highly secret atomic bomb development, especially Professor Wigner, whose theoretical and practical abilities were of the greatest importance. Despite a decreased physics faculty, teaching of physics had to be expanded to include all the servicemen being trained at Princeton. This was accomplished by bringing in from other sources every available teacher who could master enough elementary physics to keep one step ahead of the students. A teaching force of over seventy was assembled in that way.

The period between 1945, when the department started to renew itself, and the 1970s was one of continuous expansion in many directions. That was the era of enormous support of fundamental research by various government agencies. Princeton received grants in many fields, involving many millions of dollars. The largest acquisition was the 3 Bev accelerator.

That kind of affluence for departments of physics is now much reduced, so that many physicists are turning towards other fields of research, such as biophysics or astrophysics. Theoretical work is much less affected than is experimental, and Princeton, with its extremely powerful theoretical group, is in an excellent position.

The transformation of Princeton from a college to a university required an increasing emphasis on research and therefore on the assessment of every new faculty member as a research scholar as well as a qualified teacher. It might seem that the emphasis on research could militate against the teaching of undergraduates. That is not in general true in Princeton and particularly in an advancing science such as physics, where an understanding of the philosophy of modern research is necessary even in the teaching of elementary physics; and the upperclass courses would lack all vitality if they were not under the influence of a research faculty. Even the most research-minded faculty members teach not only advanced courses but the highly important elementary courses as well. John A. Wheeler, one of the department's most eminent professors of theoretical physics, lectured in the largest freshman course for five years and found it so exhilarating that he was loath to give it up.

The teacher-scholar tradition, initiated by Joseph Henry and later developed by Brackett, Magie, and their successors, is now carried on by a department of physics that has grown to about sixty faculty members with twenty teaching assistants and over a hundred graduate students. Nor has size diminished the quality of the faculty. In fact it has frequently been said that it is one of the best departments, if not even the best, in the country.

The contrast between the faculties of 1905 and the present day is equalled by the improvement of physical facilities. Instead of the "dark basement," the department enjoyed sixty years of that magnificent building, Palmer Laboratory. In 1970 the faculty's size and the increased room needed for research compelled the two departments, mathematics and physics (which have always had a close relationship and had to remain together), to move into the new complex of buildings comprising the new Fine Hall and Jadwin Hall (qq.v.). Here the two departments live in amity separated only by their joint library.

Allen G. Shenstone

Plasma Physics Laboratory (PPL), The, was founded in 1951 by Lyman Spitzer, Jr., chairman of the Astronomy Department. As an astrophysicist, Spitzer had studied the behavior of ionized gases, or plasmas, in interstellar space. Inspired by the hope of finding a new source of power for peaceful applications, he conceived the idea of confining a plasma in a figure-8 shaped tube using magnetic forces generated by coils wrapped around the outside. Spitzer reasoned that, at sufficiently high temperature, the nuclear particles in a plasma so contained would undergo fusion and release energy. Because only very low density plasma could be contained in this way, there would be no possibility of explosion.

Spitzer called his concept "the stellarator," and took it to the United States Atomic Energy Commission on May 11, 1951. A contract was soon written, and work was begun at the University's newly acquired Forrestal Research Center. The code name Project Matterhorn was used to designate the stellarator program and, for a short time at the beginning, other classified work. Theoretical work was supplemented by experiments, and over a period of twenty years, a series of research devices of progressively larger size bore such names as Model A, B-3, Model C, Spherator, and FM-1. Meanwhile, in 1958, fusion work had been declassified. Graduate instruction in plasma physics was immediately introduced, graduate students made their appearance at Project Matterhorn, and in 1961, the name Plasma Physics Laboratory was adopted. The same year, Melvin B. Gottlieb succeeded Spitzer as Director of the laboratory.

Magnetic confinement proved to be subject to a bewildering variety of instabilities which theoreticians, experimentalists, and engineers attacked one by one. Late in the 1950s the figure-8 geometry was abandoned in favor of the "racetrack," and this in turn gave way in 1970 to the "tokamak," a Russian design closely related to the stellarator concept. Princeton's Symmetric Tokamak (1970-1974) achieved the same greatly improved plasma confinement previously reported by the Russians. It was followed by the Adiabatic Thoroidal Compressor (1972-1976), which investigated new heating methods and reached an electron temperature of 22,000,000°C, and the $14,000,000 Princeton Large Torus (1975-   ) designed for the scaling of results to larger size. Other facilities projected are the $18,000,000 Poloidal Divertor Experiment (1978), dedicated to controlling the level of plasma impurities and the $228,000,000 Tokamak Fusion Test Reactor (1981), which should actually produce short bursts of fusion energy for test purposes.

By 1976 the number of employees had increased to 800 and the annual operating budget was approximately $28,000,000.

Earl C. Tanner

Playing fields within easy reach of dormitories have long been a special feature of Princeton undergraduate life. They have increased in number with the growth of student enrollment and moved southward and eastward as new dormitories were erected. Among the first were Brokaw Field (1893) in memory of Frederick Brokaw 1892; Goldie Field (1912) in honor of George Goldie, first coach of gymnastics and track; and Poe Field (1916) named for John Prentiss Poe 1895, a football hero who was killed in France in 1915 while serving with the Black Watch. Other fields have been named for Paul Bedford 1897, charter trustee; Tyler Campbell '43, lacrosse star who died in World War II; William J. Clarke, who coached thirty-four varsity baseball teams; the Class of 1895; John M.T. Finney 1884, charter trustee; Peter H.B. Frelinghuysen '04; Archibald A. Gulick 1897, charter trustee; Ario Pardee 1897, Herbert Bradley Sexton 1865; and John Kelley Strubing '20, a baseball star.

Poe Brothers, The, contributed to many Princeton football victories in the twenty years beginning in 1882 and were the special nemesis of Harvard and Yale. There were six of them, sons of John Prentiss Poe 1854, attorney general of Maryland (and a cousin of the writer Edgar Allan Poe) who sent them to his Alma Mater, as he put it,

"from a full paternal quiver." They were all short and stocky, strong, and fast:

(1) Samuel Johnson Poe 1884, the eldest, played halfback in 1882 and 1883, and was also a lacrosse All-American.

(2) Edgar Allan Poe 1891 was quarterback and captain in his junior and senior years. In 1889, the year he was named All-American, he played a leading part in the 41 to 15 defeat of Harvard at Cambridge. During the excitement, a Harvard man asked a Princeton alumnus whether Poe was related to the great Edgar Allan Poe; the alumnus looked at him in astonishment and replied, "He *is* the great Edgar Allan Poe." He graduated Phi Beta Kappa and became, like his father, attorney general of Maryland.

(3) John Prentiss Poe, Jr., 1895 had a reckless courage and a generous nature that endeared him to his contemporaries. His freshman year he was a star halfback on the varsity and class president. That spring, when he was required to withdraw from college for scholastic reasons, his whole class turned out at the Junction to see him off. He was readmitted in the fall, and played even more brilliantly. Later that year, again in academic arrears, he was obliged to leave, this time for good. For a time he coached football at other colleges, and then embarked on an adventurous career as cowpuncher, gold prospector, surveyor, and soldier of fortune. When World War I broke out he hastened to England and "took the King's shilling" as a private in the Royal Garrison Artillery. He later applied for transfer to the infantry and was assigned to the 1st Black Watch. He was killed in action in France on September 25, 1915. A portrait, showing his stocky figure with the kilts and bonnet of the

Black Watch, hangs in Madison Hall; it was given by the Princeton Alumni Association of Maryland. Poe Field, provided in his memory by classmates and friends, is used for lacrosse and intramural athletics. The John Prentiss Poe Football Cup, given by his mother, is awarded annually to that member of the varsity football team who has best exemplified courage, modesty, perseverance, and good sportsmanship. It is Princeton's highest football award.

(4) Neilson (Net) Poe 1897 played in the backfield in 1895 and 1896 and returned to coach in later years. He served overseas with the A.E.F. in World War I and was awarded the Distinguished Service Cross for gallantry in action. For twenty years between the World Wars, he was in charge of the scrubs, who were called Poe's "Omelettes" because "they were good eggs who were beaten up." For another twenty years he maintained a close association with coaches and players, watching the daily practices and traveling with the team for its games away. Courteous and light-hearted, he was well liked by everyone who knew him.

(5) Arthur Poe '00, another All-American, made the decisive score that beat Yale in two successive years. In 1898 he ran ninety yards for a touchdown and the only score of the game. Newspapers reported that he had recovered a Yale fumble, but Poe said that he had grabbed the ball from a Yale halfback's arms, that he had a clear field and a ten-yard start for the goal line, and that he had never felt happier in his life. In the 1899 game, with less than a minute to play, and with the score 10 to 6 in Yale's favor, Bill Roper '02 of Princeton recovered a fumble on Yale's 30-yard line. It was getting dark and time was running out. The only feasible strategy was to try for a field goal, then

worth 5 points, but Princeton's two drop-kickers were out with injuries. Arthur Poe volunteered to try a drop-kick even though he had never kicked in a college game before. The others agreed, Poe dropped back to the 35-yard line, and (the newspapers said) made a perfect dropkick. Poe's version was different:

> The pass from center came back perfectly which is more than anyone could truthfully say for the rest of the play. . . . The ball bounded a little too high off the ground as I dropped it and I got under it too much, raising it high into the air almost like a punt. It came down just about a foot over the crossbar and about a yard inside the upright. I wasn't sure it was good until I turned to the referee and saw him raise his arms and heard him say "goal." . . . Then everything broke loose. . . . All I remember after that was being seized by a crowd of undergraduates and alumni who rushed out onto the field, and hearing my brother Net shout: "You damned lucky kid, you have licked them again."

(6) Gresham Poe '02 was first mentioned with his brothers in verses, ascribed to Booth Tarkington 1893, which were read at a victory celebration in 1899. Eli Yale is addressing the Tiger:

> "Sir, I said, "All Poes are gone—
> Johnson, Edgar, Neilson, John;
> Arthur with the toe on which
> Winning goals are kicked galore.
> Tell me, tell me, gentle Tiger,
> Is it possible there are more?"
> "Stop!" the Tiger cried, "there's
>   Gresham,
> Getting ready to refresh 'em—
> Don't forget him, I implore."

As it turned out, Gresham spent most of his time on the bench as a substitute quarterback, but he did get into the Yale game his senior year. He was sent in with other substitutes in the fourth quarter when Yale was leading 12 to 0. The Princeton fans had practically conceded victory to Yale, but when Gresham appeared on the field they rose to their feet with a rousing cheer—such was the magic of the name "Poe." They rose again with a roar when Gresham received a punt and squirmed 23 yards before he was downed. "Poe's presence seemed to rejuvenate the Tigers," *Harper's Weekly* reported, "and for the last ten minutes of the contest they fairly outplayed the weary Elis. The ball was twice carried half the length of the field, but the whistle blew before Princeton could score."

Poler's Recess, a ten-minute break in cramming for exams, was a Princeton custom noisily observed from the turn of the century almost up to the Second World War. The recess occurred every night during the final examination period. As soon as the nine o'clock bell began to ring, all windows on campus were opened and all means employed to produce a din that would divert the most diligent poler from his work. ("Poler" was an old Princeton synonym for "grind.")* Firecrackers were exploded, pistols, revolvers, and shotguns fired with blank cartridges, horns blown, drums and tin pans beaten. As an undergraduate writer observed in 1918, it was "probably the most juvenile" of all campus customs, but it brought "a welcome break for everyone in a long night's hard work."

Poler's Recess was revived after World War II in response to the urging of a young alumnus in a letter to the *Princetonian* of January 20, 1949. He proposed that beginning at 11 p.m. (rather than at 9, so as not to disturb those taking evening exams), with the cry of "Take ten," ten minutes be given over to total pandemonium, and that thereafter absolute silence should prevail.

In the same issue of the *Prince*, "Examinitus" reported that local doctors thought the break would relieve tensions and heighten morale and probably raise each student's marks from one to three grades. He quoted "a prominent psychologist" as saying: "The break will be of incalculable aid to all those suffering from mental blocks, hallucinations, paranoia, schizophrenia, psychosis, neurosis, and blocking of the digestive tract."

That night undergraduates responded enthusiastically, and the next morning the *Princetonian* pronounced the revival an unqualified success, awarding championship honors to Holder Court, where students staged a mock battle with blank cartridges and flaming tennis balls and "let the entire borough know they had discarded their books."

But observance of the "11 p.m. catharsis" was sporadic the next year or two and then faded out. Fairly typical was the reaction of one undergraduate who told the *Prince* that he had enough interruptions already, what with listening to the evening news and then "taking time out for milk, sandwiches, ice cream (and pie)."

---

* B. H. Hall, in *College Words and Customs* (1851), records that at Princeton, and also at Union College, "poler" meant one who studies hard, and he suggests that the meaning was derived by analogy from the laborious poling of a boat.

Politics, The Department of. Although politics did not come into being as a separate department until 1924, the teaching of this subject at Princeton goes back to the early days of the College of New Jersey. We are told that one of the reasons the "Father of the Constitution," James Madison, chose Princeton rather than the College of William and Mary was the fact that Witherspoon, the only clergyman to sign the Declaration of Independence, "extended his course in moral philosophy to include the general principles of public law and politics."

The first course labeled Political Science was introduced in 1871 and taught by Lyman H. Atwater. William M. Sloane, taking over Atwater's work in 1883, offered upperclass courses in the philosophy of history and political science, and graduate work in history. The next year Alexander Johnson gave courses in jurisprudence, political economy, and public and international law. English common law was available as a graduate course.

When Woodrow Wilson joined the faculty in 1890 to fill the vacancy caused by Professor Johnson's death, the curriculum in political studies was extensive. By 1896, the overall Department of Philosophy included history and political science under Sloane, jurisprudence under Wilson, and political economy under Winthrop More Daniels, who had come to assist Wilson in 1892. In 1898, history and political science became simply history, and Daniels entitled his field "political economy and sociology." In 1903-1904, as part of a general reorganization of the curriculum into eleven departments, History, Politics, and Economics were "reassembled" as a single department. On President Wilson's insistence, the name "Politics" replaced Political Science, and so it has since remained.

Beginning in 1905, the influx of President Wilson's "preceptor guys" began. Notable additions in Politics were Edward S. Corwin (q.v.), Charles H. McIlwain, and William Starr Myers, all trained historians. In 1913, when the centrifugal forces of specialization again asserted themselves, History and Politics, and Economics and Social Institutions became two separate departments. Politics broke off in 1924, with Edward S. Corwin, McCormick Professor of Jurisprudence since 1918, as chairman. Having neither taste nor aptitude for administration, Corwin delegated departmental detail to his former student and colleague, William Seal Carpenter, who succeeded him as chairman in 1936.

Corwin stands among the giants of American constitutional commentators—with Kent, Story, and Cooley. More than any other scholar of our time, he justified and illustrated his own incisive observation: "If judges make law, so do commentators." He was one of the few American scholars honored at the Harvard Tercentenary in 1936.

From 1925 until the end of World War II, graduate study in politics at Princeton meant primarily work with Corwin. During this period graduate students, though small in number, were high in quality: Raymond Leslie Buell, Robert J. Harris, Donald Morrison, John Masland, Clinton Rossiter, and Alpheus Thomas Mason. Best known as a judicial biographer and student of American political thought, Mason succeeded Corwin as McCormick Professor of Jurisprudence in 1947. At the undergraduate level, Corwin's course "Con Interp," featuring source material and requiring written "opinions" in cases currently pending in the High Court, enjoyed the reputation of being the toughest one in the University. Then, as now, seniors also voted it "the most valuable."

Until the 1930s the political orientation of the department was predominantly Republican, none more ardent than Professor William Starr Myers. Although a fervent admirer of Woodrow Wilson as a teacher, he voted the straight Republican ticket. Author of a history of the Republican party, his hero was Herbert Hoover. Myers's undergraduate lectures, highlighting personal contacts with political bigwigs, were the subject of a favorite faculty song:

Here's to Myers, William Starr,
Thinks he sees very far.
All the Presidents he knows by sight,
Imagines they're saying, "Myers,
    you're right."

Myers, a southern gentleman of rare charm, took typical undergraduate jest in stride and went right on taking students into his confidence concerning his close ties with "great men" in American politics.

The department's most conspicuous non-conformist was Walter Lincoln Whittlesey. In more recent years H. H. Wilson played, at a higher level, a role not unlike that of Whittlesey. For undergraduates he has created an intellectual ferment, prodding them to think seriously about economic, social, and political inequities. More recently, another dissenter, international law professor Richard Falk, has served as a catalyst, provoking colleagues, students, and the country to question the tragedy of Viet Nam, long before it was popular to do so.

"Princeton in the nation's service" under the auspices of the Politics De-partment took a practical turn in 1930 with the establishment of the School of Public and International Affairs, headed by Harold W. Dodds (later president of the University), and the Princeton Survey in State and Local Government under the direction of John F. Sly. In 1932, Harwood L. Childs came to Princeton to teach and research public opinion, then an uncharted academic field. Childs founded and edited the *Public Opinion Quarterly*, which in a relatively short time became one of the most prestigious journals in the field of politics. With his colleague, international law specialist John B. Whitton, Childs co-authored propaganda abroad by short wave programs during World War II.

During the war members of the department were especially conspicuous in the nation's service. Harold Sprout, who had come to Princeton in 1931, published *The Rise of American Naval Power* (1943). A pioneering work in a burgeoning field, this book, co-authored by Margaret Sprout, quickly established this husband and wife research and writing team as leading authorities. Sprout served as a Washington consultant for various U.S. departments including State, War, and Navy. From 1943 to 1945, he was a member of the staff of OWI, helping to develop propaganda material toward enemy powers.

George A. Graham joined the department as part of the drive that began in the 1930s to expand the curriculum to include public affairs, domestic and international. A specialist in public administration, Graham was in Washington throughout World War II with the U.S. Bureau of the Budget. After the war, he was on call as staff director of the Hoover Commission on Organization of the Executive Branch and consultant in 1951 to the Senate Subcommittee on Ethics in Government.

Meanwhile, members of the department were active in New Jersey state politics and administration. In 1932, a team of twenty-one members of the Princeton faculty (seven drawn from Politics), under the direction of Professor Harold W. Dodds, made a comprehensive survey of the government of New Jersey with a view to recommending economies without impairing essential services. Also serving New Jersey were John F. Sly, chairman of the New Jersey Commission on State Tax Policy, and William S. Carpenter, president of the New Jersey Civil Service Commission. Sly made his mark as a consultant in state and local government throughout the country. His successor, Duane Lockard, a productive scholar no less pragmatic than Sly, brought to his work a liberating humanism.

In 1969, when faculty-student relations reached a crisis stage, it seemed fitting that President Robert Goheen should have asked Professor Stanley Kelley, Jr., to chair a special student-faculty committee to study the administrative structure of the University and recommend alternatives on matters of concern to both faculty and students. For better or for worse, the guiding hand in reorganizing the University as it operates today was that of Kelley, an expert on political parties and campaign techniques.

After 1950, Politics at Princeton moved increasingly toward the scientific approach, toward behaviorism and quantitative analysis, toward comparative study of foreign systems and international relations. Without breaking completely with the Wilson-Corwin-Mason historical tradition, even "Con Interp," under the direction of Walter F. Murphy, fifth McCormick Professor of Jurisprudence, succumbed to the quantitative and comparative approach. Murphy's *Elements of Judicial Strategy* broke fresh ground, not only at Princeton but in the study of constitutional interpretation generally.

By the 1960s personnel and offerings encompassed the whole range of politics, domestic and foreign. Professors Robert Tucker and Stephen Cohen specialize in Soviet affairs, Henry Bienen on sub-Sahara Africa, Manfred Halpern on the Middle East, Edward Taft on the American political system. Robert Gilpin explores the impact of science on international relations. Herman Somers, concentrating on welfare systems, helped draft the medicare program. Political theory, once a neglected area, is now represented by Sheldon Wolin, Dennis Thompson, and Paul Sigmund. At long last the presidency is accorded its due under the leadership of a relative newcomer, Fred Greenstein. Researching a wide range of domestic problems and issues, including ecology, Gerald Garvey brings to each one bold and imaginative dimensions.

Long before co-education at the undergraduate level became an irresistible demand, the Politics Department, following the lead of Oriental Languages, had broken the sex barrier by enrolling women in the Graduate School. Politics was also among the first to admit blacks for graduate study.

In due course, the democratic principle also triumphed in the administration of departmental affairs. The department learned from experience what might have been gleaned from books— "Power tends to corrupt." The first two chairmen, Corwin and Carpenter, carried on 22 years. Finally the affairs of the department, concentrated in the hands of the chairman, became so tyranically administered as to drive Mason, Graham, and Sprout to assert the right of revolution, forcing Carpenter's resignation. The coup d'etat was followed by adoption of a constitution which provided, among other things, for a rotating chairmanship: George A. Graham, 1946-1949; Harold Sprout, 1949-1952; George Graham, 1952-1955; John F. Sly, 1955-1959; William M. Beaney, 1959-1961; Marver H. Bernstein, 1961-1963; Stanley F. Kelley, Jr., 1963-1966; Walter M. Murphy, 1966-1969; Duane F. Lockard, 1969-1972; Dennis W. Thompson, Acting Chairman, 1972-1973; Henry Bienen, 1973-1976.

From the beginning of its history, Princeton has appreciated the educational requirements of a free society. For their day, to some extent in ours, Witherspoon and Madison supplied the model. Reflected in the offerings, under the rubric politics, is recognition of the citizen's need to understand not only the organization, operation, and functions of government but also the problems of industry, commerce, finance, and international relations. The student should learn about people as well as things. "Moral philosophy" is as basic now as in the time of John Witherspoon and James Madison. By the diversity of its instructors and program, as well as its ecumenical approach, the Politics Department continues to maintain Woodrow Wilson's ideal of Princeton in the nation's service.

Alpheus Thomas Mason

Population Research, The Office of, was founded in 1936 when Frederick H. Osborn '10, a charter trustee of Princeton, formerly a trustee at the Milbank Memorial Fund, used his good offices with both of these institutions to persuade the University to found a program in teaching and research in population, and the Milbank Fund to provide much of the initial financing. Osborn, later a major general during World War II, appointed to study and foster improvement in the morale of the armed services, had a deep interest in population matters, as well as in his alma mater. As part of the arrangement between the Milbank Fund and Princeton, Frank Notestein, a demographer then on the staff of the Fund, was appointed to the Princeton faculty, and became the first director of the Office of Population Research. He served until 1959 when he resigned to become president of the Population Council of New York; he was succeeded as director by Ansley J. Coale, and on Coale's resignation as director in 1976, by Charles F. Westoff.

Princeton's venture in demography was a pioneering one. Its program in population studies was the first university-centered combination of research and teaching in the field in the United States. The Office was also an innovator in what was then an all-male institution in the appointment, shortly after the Office was founded, of Dr. Irene Barnes Taeuber as a member of its research staff. Dr. Taeuber, who died in 1974, published nineteen volumes of books and research papers preeminently on the population of Japan, and also on population in the United States, Europe, Africa, and South Asia.

Before World War II, decades before the population explosion became a matter of general concern, Notestein and Taeuber called attention to the prospective acceleration in population growth in the poorer, densely settled areas of the world. Alumni of the Graduate School with degrees in economics, sociology, and statistics who have learned population at Princeton now teach at Princeton, Harvard, Michigan, Johns Hopkins, and Wisconsin, among many others. Nearly 100 foreign students from more than thirty countries have had special training in population at the Office of Population Research. They are employed in the Population Division of the United Nations, at the World Bank, and in many universities and ministries in developing countries.

Ansley J. Coale

Preceptorial method, introduced in 1905 under Woodrow Wilson's leadership, is a method of study whereby a small group of students meets in regular conferences with a faculty member. Wilson first described his proposal as a modified form of the Oxford tutorial that would "import into the great university the methods and personal contact between teacher and pupil which are characteristic of the small college, and so gain the advantages of both." Disclaiming novelty in the concept, Wilson stated that the preceptorial would not only supersede the old-fashioned recitation but also "give the undergraduates their proper release from being school boys." The subject matter was not to be "the lectures of their professors or the handful of text books . . . but the reading which they should do for themselves."

The use of the term "preceptor" seems to have been proposed by Wilson himself; and the title was established by the trustees in June of 1905, when forty-five men were appointed preceptors with the rank of assistant professors.* Twelve were already members of the faculty; the thirty-three others

came from many other campuses across the country. Two more were added in October, and others were appointed in subsequent years, but Wilson's initial goal of fifty is recorded in the students' Faculty Song:

> *Here's to those preceptor guys,*
> *Fifty stiffs to make us wise.*

The new appointments were made in the humanities and social sciences, and also in mathematics; none was made in the "laboratory departments" where, Wilson noted, "direct personal contact between teacher and pupil has long been a matter-of-course method of instruction."

Wilson interviewed each candidate he did not know, and the extraordinary group of teachers he enlisted in a three-month period is one of the remarkable feats in American higher education. His instinct was to place teaching ability ahead of scholarly qualifications, yet many of the preceptors gained distinction as scholars, some as administrators, among them Edward S. Corwin, Luther P. Eisenhart, Christian Gauss, Charles H. McIlwain, Charles G. Osgood, Robert K. Root, and Oswald Veblen.

The original concept was that of a group tutorial. In his junior year each undergraduate was assigned a preceptor to "be his guide in all the reading and work of the Department." As far as possible students continued with the same preceptors for all courses. Lectures were to be complementary to the reading. Students were to be grouped by "aptitudes, training, tastes, and acquirements," abler students being "excused from the ordinary weekly conferences" and encouraged to read independently. Thus Wilson had already envisioned something like the "four-course plan" of independent study established twenty years later.

The new plan brought immediate and far-reaching results. Reporting to the Trustees in December 1905, Wilson asserted that the method "has affected the habits of the University almost as much as if it were an ancient institution." *The Nassau Literary Magazine* declared that it was "generally, even universally, popular." Comments in the press were favorable, and the American educational world watched with interest.

Despite its success the new method brought problems. Wilson had proceeded without the funds required for a greatly enlarged faculty, and the resulting deficit soon came to about $100,000 a year. Preceptors were burdened with reading for too many courses; they lacked tenure, and some resigned. Independent study did not develop as had been expected. Nevertheless the new preceptors quickened the intellectual life of the University, and the preceptorial idea took root. In 1914 a faculty report established procedures for the conduct of preceptorials, but in the years following modifications were gradually made. Preceptors were assigned to fewer courses and allowed to concentrate their interests; the title itself was ultimately abandoned, although later adopted honorifically for Bicentennial Preceptorships (q.v.). A major change came with the "four-course" plan in 1925, when departmental supervisors took over the preceptors' tutorial function—guiding the student through independent study to a senior thesis and comprehensive examination—thus realizing Wilson's original plan of a coherent program of study systematically pursued. Preceptorial instruction came to be more closely attached to courses, including some at the freshman and sophomore levels, and to engage all ranks of the faculty.

Over the years the preceptorial system has continued to be subject to re-examination, with surveys and articles, both critical and supportive, appearing from time to time. A 1933 faculty report found shortcomings, but noted "unanimous and generally enthusiastic approval"; and a student survey and forum in 1938 reflected favorable undergraduate opinion. In 1949, however, a special committee noted scepticism by new faculty members. The faculty were given, in 1953, copies of *Points for Preceptors*, a booklet prepared by the present writer containing helpful suggestions by experienced preceptors. In 1956 the Alumni Day program was devoted to preceptorials on liberal education.

Mounting costs have subsequently led to larger preceptorial groups and, in subjects where knowledge has become increasingly specialized, to more structured seminars and classes. Patterns of education are always changing, but the preceptorial ideal of a close relation between teacher and student continues to be honored at Princeton, in keeping with Wilson's belief that "it is not the whip that makes men but the lure of things worthy to be loved."

Jeremiah S. Finch

* The term "preceptor" appears in *An Account of the College of New Jersey* (1764): "In the instruction of the youth, care is taken to . . . encourage their right of private judgment, without . . . demanding an implicit assent to the decisions of the preceptor."

President of the University is its chief executive officer. He presides at all meetings of the Board of Trustees and of the Faculty and at all academic functions at which he is present and represents the University before the public. The Trustee by-laws charge him with the general supervision of the interests of the University and with special oversight of the departments of instruction. Princeton presidents have been:

1. Jonathan Dickinson   1747
2. Aaron Burr, Sr.   1748-1757*
3. Jonathan Edwards   1758
4. Samuel Davies   1759-1761
5. Samuel Finley   1761-1766
6. John Witherspoon   1768-1794
7. Samuel Stanhope Smith 1795-1812
8. Ashbel Green   1812-1822
9. James Carnahan   1823-1854
10. John Maclean, Jr.   1854-1868
11. James McCosh   1868-1888
12. Francis Landey Patton 1888-1902
13. Woodrow Wilson   1902-1910
14. John Grier Hibben   1912-1932
15. Harold Willis Dodds   1933-1957
16. Robert Francis Goheen 1957-1972
17. William Gordon Bowen   1972-

Acting presidents during the interregnums were: Jacob Green, 1758-1759; John Blair, 1767-1768; Philip Lindsly, 1822-1823; John Aikman Stewart, 1910-1912; and Edward Dickinson Duffield, 1932-1933.

The first five presidents together served less than twenty years. Their tenures were cut short by untimely deaths owing in part to overwork and in part to the backward state of the art of medicine at that time: Edwards died at 55 of a fever after an innoculation for smallpox; Davies who was tubercular, died at 38, after being bled for a bad cold.

In the early years there were two instances of succession by in-laws: Aaron Burr, second president, was succeeded by his father-in-law, Jonathan Edwards. John Witherspoon, sixth president, was succeeded by his son-in-law, Samuel Stanhope Smith.

Two presidents were imported from Scotland, John Witherspoon in 1768 and James McCosh, a hundred years later, in 1868, and both left their marks on Princeton and on the nation. They died in Princeton, Witherspoon on November 15, 1794, McCosh on November 16, 1894—a century and a day apart.

Aaron Burr, Sr., at thirty-two, was the youngest man ever elected president; Jonathan Dickinson, at fifty-nine, the oldest. James Carnahan's administration has been the longest (thirty-one years), Jonathan Edwards' the shortest (five weeks).

The royal charter of 1746, which gave the trustees power to "elect . . . such qualified persons as they . . . shall think fitt to be the President" also empowered them "at any time [to] Displace and discharge such President." Three presidents were induced to resign: Smith in 1812, Green in 1822, Patton in 1902.

The first three presidents—Dickinson, Burr, and Edwards—were graduates of Yale. The next two lacked college degrees; they were trained in classics and divinity, both in Pennsylvania—Davies in Samuel Blair's school at Faggs Manor, Finley in William Tennent's "log college" at Neshaminy. Witherspoon was a graduate of Edinburgh, McCosh of Glasgow and Edingurgh, Patton of Knox College in Toronto. Nine earned degrees at Princeton—Smith, Green, Carnahan, Maclean, Wilson, Hibben, Dodds, Goheen, Bowen.

The President's Lot in the Princeton Cemetery on Witherspoon Street contains the graves of all the deceased presidents of Princeton, except four: Dickinson, who died and was buried in

Elizabethtown, before the college was moved to Princeton; Finley, who died and was buried in Philadelphia (there is a cenotaph for him in the President's Lot, however); Patton, who died and was buried in Bermuda; and Wilson, who died in Washington, D.C. and was interred in the Washington Cathedral.

* Although Burr was formally elected President in November 1748, he had been in charge of the College since Dickinson's death in October 1747.

Presidents of the United States who attended Princeton are:

James Madison A.B. 1771 (Va.)
   1809-1817
Woodrow Wilson A.B. 1879 (N.J.)
   1913-1921

John F. Kennedy also attended Princeton as a member of the Class of 1939 but withdrew after several months because of illness and later graduated from Harvard in the Class of 1940.

Two Princeton graduates have been unsuccessful candidates for the Presidency: Norman M. Thomas '05, the Socialist party's candidate in six successive campaigns 1928 through 1948; and Adlai E. Stevenson '22, the Democratic party's candidate against Dwight D. Eisenhower in 1952 and 1956.

Press Club, The, whose undergraduate members serve as Princeton correspondents for metropolitan newspapers and national wire services, was first organized in 1900, although it seems probable that campus correspondents were functioning long before that. President McCosh may have had them in mind some twenty years earlier when, in an effort to ward off threatened misbehavior, he warned students that "tomorrow it will be in all the New York

papers and the next day in the Philadelphia papers."

Ex-President Grover Cleveland, who lived in Princeton after completing his second term in Washington, was a good source of copy in the early days of the Press Club. He disliked being interviewed but he granted exceptions for students. "It may mean five or ten dollars for the boy," he told a faculty friend, "and that would pay his board for a week." Once, however, he felt obliged to rebuff an undergraduate reporter who pressed him for his opinion on President McKinley's Philippine policy. "That, sir," Cleveland said, "is a matter of too great importance to discuss in so brief an interview, now rapidly drawing to a close."

In the early years, Press Club members usually worked free lance and came together only for social occasions. Seniors approaching graduation sold their rights as correspondents for particular newspapers to the highest bidders—a process that gave more weight to the new reporter's credit at the bank than to his nose for news or his ear for a good sentence.

All of this was changed in 1915 when, following a study he made at the request of the Graduate Council, Professor Christian Gauss reorganized the club along the lines it has followed ever since. He persuaded the Graduate Council to purchase all of the correspondents' rights from club members (the Council was later repaid) and replaced the old auction system with freshman and sophomore competitions for membership. He also introduced the practice of having club members pool their efforts. Most significant of all, he accepted appointment as faculty adviser, a position he held until 1924, when he left Princeton for a year's leave of absence before becoming dean of the

College. Press Club advisers after him included Alexander Leitch '24, Frederick S. Osborne '24, Edmund S. De Long '22, Dan D. Coyle '38, and George B. Eager.

Sometimes when University news was scarce, Press Club stringers created stories. In the twenties, at the suggestion of Dean Gauss, they asked a number of professors what ten books they would want to have with them if they had to spend the rest of their lives on a desert island. The composite results were unsensational (Shakespeare and Homer led, followed by the Bible, Plato, Dante, and Vergil), but the story got a good play, nevertheless. During a slack period several years later, the club asked another group of professors to list the six most important words ("loyalty" was mentioned most frequently), and once more the story ran widely.

There were other occasions when Press Club members had more than enough real news to keep them busy— the Wilson-West row and Wilson's entrance into politics in the early 1900s; the kidnapping of Charles A. Lindbergh's infant son in nearby Hopewell in 1932; the panic caused by Orson Welles's 1938 radio broadcast of "an invasion from Mars" which "landed" four miles from Princeton; and the University's year-long Bicentennial Celebration in 1946-1947.

Among Press Club members who made a career of journalism were David Lawrence '10, founder of the *U.S. News and World Report*; Alfred S. Dashiell '23, managing editor of *Reader's Digest*; Franklyn S. Adams '25, city editor of *The New York Times*, Mark Anthony Beltaire III '37, daily columnist for *The Detroit Free Press*.

Princeton Club of New York, The, has had four homes since its incorporation

on December 7, 1899. It occupied the old Vanderbilt house at the corner of 34th Street and Park Avenue for eight years before moving into its second home, the former residence of the architect Stanford White, on Gramercy Park North at Lexington Avenue, where it remained until the outbreak of the First World War. During the war, when younger members were absent in war service, older members enjoyed the hospitality of the Yale Club on Vanderbilt Avenue at 44th Street; in gratitude they endowed the Princeton Club of New York scholarship at Yale. Beginning in 1922, the Princeton Club made its third home at 39th Street and Park Avenue in an old Murray Hill mansion with a ten-story annex. At different times Princeton shared these facilities with the Brown and Dartmouth Clubs. It occupied this home for almost forty years until the early 1960s, when it built its present nine-story limestone clubhouse at 15 West 43rd Street under the leadership of its president, Frank H. Connor '25. Ground was broken on June 15, 1961; while awaiting completion of the building, rooms were leased in the Columbia University Club across the street. The new clubhouse, which was opened in February 1963, provided a family club, with facilities open to wives of alumni (and, after coeducation, husbands of alumnae), and certain other family members. In the mid-seventies, when many university clubs were consolidating, the membership of the Columbia Club moved across the street to join forces with Princeton. In the spring of 1978, the Club's membership totaled more than 6,000.

An outstanding feature of the Club is the Princeton Library in New York, an eductional corporation chartered by the New York Board of Regents, which in cooperation with the University Library maintains a 9,000-volume library on the fifth floor of the Club for the use of all Princeton alumni and faculty, and other accredited scholars. The Library also sponsors informal lecture evenings with faculty, students, and alumni as guest speakers.

Princeton Education Center at Blairstown is an outgrowth of the Princeton Summer Camp, which was founded in 1909 near Bay Head on the New Jersey shore and was moved in 1930 to its present 170-acre site on Bass Lake near Blairstown in the northwestern part of the state. Originally overseen by the trustees of the Philadelphian Society and later of the Student Christian Association, the facility has been governed since 1974 by a board of trustees under its present name.

The original camp program involved special two-week summer sessions for boys from New York and Philadelphia and from the black and Italian communities of Princeton. In 1970, it became coeducational and since then has included young people mainly from the Princeton-Trenton area as well as from northern New Jersey and Philadelphia.

Over the years the camp has provided an enjoyable and educational experience for more than 10,000 young people as well as for 750 undergraduate counselors, who according to former Student Director Everard Pinneo '48, "will always remember the youngsters who came from the hot city streets for a few weeks of fun and adventure. It was a positive experience for them and an equally important one for us. The special satisfaction of working with the campers has significantly affected many of our careers and voluntary activities since graduation."

The Blairstown facilities have also served for many years as a retreat and as workshop quarters for student, faculty, and staff groups as well as for community organizations.

The camp has been supported by many devoted alumni including Dean Mathey '12, Bernard Peyton '17, Laurance Rockefeller '32, and the McAlpin and McCormick families. Some buildings bear names of individual benefactors, while cabins memorialize the alumni classes that supported their construction. Another major source of financial aid has been the annual Campus Fund Drive conducted by undergraduates.

In 1971, recognizing that program development and major renovation of the physical plant were necessary, the board began a long-range rebuilding program. Architecture Professor Harrison Fraker '64 directed a team of Princeton students and outside consultants in designing the new facilities. Their plans involve using natural power —sun, wind and flowing water—both to conserve energy and to give campers and other program participants a first-hand lesson in ecology. The reconstruction program began in 1977.

The Reverend T. Guthrie Speers, Jr. '50, chairman of the Blairstown Board of Trustees during the 1960s and 1970s, has described the Princeton Summer Camp/Princeton Education Center at Blairstown as "a kind of neutral ground for learning, a non-threatening environment, a place where human interaction is greatly facilitated. . . . Simply put, something extra and significant happens, both individually and to the group, in the setting of Blairstown."

Since 1930, directors of this project have been: Reverend Laurence Fenninger '09 (assistant dean of the Chapel) 1930-1945; Howard Stepp hc '39 (swimming coach and registrar) 1946-1966; David Rahr '60 (director, Alumni

Council) 1966-1970; and John Danielson '58 (assistant dean of students) since
1971.

John G. Danielson

Princeton Engineer, The, began publication in January 1941. Its founding
editors, Theodore Rockwell III '43 and
William P. Stadig '43, announced that
its threefold purpose was to unite the
undergraduate engineers in a new kind
of cooperative project, to keep alumni
and students informed about the
school's activities and facilities, and to
help procure for the engineering school
"the recognition it deserved" in the
outside world. The magazine appeared
to be well on its way to achieving the
third aim in 1956, when Dean Elgin
disclosed that ten paid subscriptions
were going regularly to Moscow.

Princetonian, The, came into existence
on June 14, 1876, to provide, in the
words of one of its early editors, Woodrow Wilson 1879, "an impartial record
of College incident and a medium for a
bold, frank, and manly expression of
College opinion."

From the beginning, the *Princetonian* caused occasional unhappiness
in Nassau Hall. President McCosh had
been at one time uncomfortably aware
that it was "in the way of attacking the
faculty," although by 1888, when he retired, he thought the paper was being
conducted "in the most admirable spirit." His only complaint then was that it
gave "more space to gymnastics than to
literature," an imbalance that led an
Oxford don to say to him, after reading
several issues of the paper, "Pray, are
you the president of a gymnastic institution?"

In its formative years, the *Princetonian* was closer in form and style to an
eighteenth-century coffeehouse journal
than to a modern newspaper. Brief essays considered topics such as American Education, Conceit, The Utility of
Women, Life on the Nile, and the College Loafer. Editorials condemned the
faculty's disciplinary action following a
classroom disorder, curtly dismissed
the "visionary schemes" of "puerile
graduates" for the improvement of college discipline, opposed coeducation
("Our belief and hope is that it is destined . . . to die and go the way of all
isms."), and declared, on the subject of
faculty preaching in chapel, "In plain
English the College sermon cannot
keep the congregation awake."

One of the first issues contained a
plea for unproctored examinations, a
cause the *Princetonian* continued to
advocate until the honor system was
adopted by the faculty in 1893. The
editors also showed enterprise in reporting what news there was, publishing an extra with a telegraphic report of
a Yale-Princeton baseball game at New
Haven in 1895—one of the first, if not
the first, uses of the telegraph by a college newspaper.

As the college grew and its activities
multiplied, the original "fortnightly"
became a weekly in 1883, a tri-weekly
in 1885, and began appearing as the
Daily Princetonian five afternoons a
week in 1892 and six mornings a week
in 1895. This last change created a
problem because students began reading the paper during morning chapel, a
practice that was eventually moderated
in response to editorial warnings that
the displeasure it caused the faculty
was endangering the continuance of the
morning edition.

Two events around this time inspired
special coverage: on President Mc-
Cosh's death in 1894, a whole issue was
devoted to a tribute that must have dis-

pelled any suspicion that he had been the "president of a gymnastic institution," and after the College's celebrated Sesquicentennial Exercises in 1896, extensive coverage of these ceremonies included the full text of all the addresses, among them Woodrow Wilson's famous "Princeton in the Nation's Service."

After Wilson became president in 1902, he was a frequent subject of editorials and news. When he made known his intention to build a fence around Prospect, the *Prince* objected on aesthetic grounds, but when the fence was built, and a group of students tore part of it down, an editorial castigated them for their "vandalism." The editors were enthusiastic about Wilson's preceptorial system, skeptical of his quad plan, and regretful when he resigned to enter political life. On his election as president of the United States in 1912, front-page stories caught the spirit of jubilation that swept the campus and culminated in a midnight student procession to Wilson's house on Cleveland Lane.

The pre-World War I years saw further advances in news coverage and editorial policy. In 1910 the paper enlarged its page size and began publishing Associated Press dispatches. The following year a letter to the editor touched off an extended argument about compulsory chapel attendance—a perennial source of comment in the *Prince* until 1964 when the last vestige of the requirement was removed by the trustees. In 1915, when women suffrage was being voted on in New Jersey, the *Prince* carried on a strong and well-articulated campaign on its behalf, calling it "the greatest social question of the day—the enfranchisement of the other half of the people." Two years later, the paper

came out in favor of the Cleveland revolt against the eating clubs, an early response to an issue destined to achieve editorial popularity exceeding even that of compulsory chapel.

In the twenties, the *Prince*, true to the times, was enterprising, prosperous, lighthearted, and—on occasion—careless of official dignity. Its editors added a weekly photographic supplement and a monthly "Literary Observer" (both of which succumbed to the Depression), introduced a number of popular humorous columns such as "Diogene's Lamp," "The Ivory Tower," and "The Crow's Nest," and initiated two antic diversions that were carried on for many years, the *Gaily Printsanything* and the April Fool's story.

The *Gaily Printsanything* was the title retiring boards gave their last issue, in which they celebrated release from their sober duties. Advertised as "a scurrilous sheet dedicated to yellow journalism," it usually contained lurid tales (accompanied by doctored photographs) of public misbehaviour of the president, deans, and faculty, invariably depicted as dissolute rogues and scoundrels.

The April Fool's story that caused the greatest stir was the announcement on April 1, 1927, that the trustees had accepted a gift of $20 million from the executors of the estate of "Nettie Green" to establish coeducation at Princeton. At the end of the article, pointed attention was called to the date, but not everybody read that far, and Nassau Hall was besieged with protesting telephone calls, telegrams, and letters.

It came as no surprise to President Hibben's associates when he once confided that he made it a rule never to read the *Princetonian* until *after* breakfast.

In the eventful decade before World War II, the *Princetonian* played a more serious role. It collaborated with the Harvard *Crimson* in marshaling student opposition to Prohibition. It issued emergency scrip for student use during the 1933 bank holiday. It gave increased attention in news and editorials to the developing world crisis, and as time for decision drew nearer, it opened its columns to opposing views on American intervention. With President Roosevelt's declaration of an unlimited national emergency in May 1941, the paper headlined a front-page editorial "The Debate is Over," and the day after Pearl Harbor, proclaimed in a banner headline: PRINCETON PRESENTS UNITED FRONT AS UNITED STATES FACES TOTAL WAR. In February 1943, the *Princetonian* suspended publication for the duration of the war.

The decades following the war saw the paper through one of its busiest periods. The *Prince* brought out an extra the morning of Albert Einstein's death in 1955 and devoted most of the next day's regular issue to tributes from friends and colleagues. Another extra in 1956 reported President Goheen's election a little more than three hours after it had been announced at a faculty meeting. The following year there were special editions on the retirement of President Dodds and the death of Football Coach Charlie Caldwell. Eating club elections continued to be an important source of news and editorials through the fifties and sixties, with emphasis first on the ideal of 100 percent sophomore elections and later on the need for social alternatives to the club system itself.

In 1963 an extra covered President Kennedy's assassination and the cancellation of University events that weekend, and for a week following Martin Luther King's assassination in 1968, the paper featured editorials, letters, and accounts of various meetings on how best to advance the cause he embodied as "the responsible leader of a race striving to obtain peacefully the rights which belong to all Americans."

Editorials of this period were sharply critical of the war in Vietnam and called for early disengagement, while pressing on the University front for a larger student role in campus affairs, for the adoption of coeducation, and for support of the administration's efforts to increase the enrollment of minority groups. In 1968 a feature on "A New Era for the Negro at Princeton" won an award as the best college newspaper story of the year.

In the next two years the *Princetonian* published some of the most significant news in its history. In the spring of 1969 banner headlines announced trustee approval of coeducation beginning that fall; the same issue reported trustee acceptance of the proposal that a member of each graduating class be elected to a four-year term on the board, and added a word of congratulation to the trustees for their "courage" and "foresight" in an editorial captioned "Victory for the Student Voice." At Commencement, the paper distributed a two-page reunion extra headlining the fact that the newly constituted electorate—juniors, seniors, and members of the two youngest alumni classes—had chosen Princeton's first black alumni trustee. These and other innovations, and the new responsibilities and opportunities they presented, were summed up in the annual June issue for incoming freshmen in a lead editorial headed "The times, they are a changin'."

In 1970, the *Prince* took an active part in the growing campus protest against the war in Vietnam, which culminated in an unprecedented student strike following the extension of the war into Cambodia. Besides providing up-to-the-minute schedules of strike activities, the *Prince* staff hand-set and distributed a special Sunday 2 a.m. strike extra, gave detailed coverage of student rallies, faculty meetings, and a community-wide Jadwin Gym assembly, and in the place traditionally used for University condolences, extended its sympathy to the families and friends of the four Kent State University students killed while protesting the war. The editors also helped promote adoption of a two-week recess for student political campaigning before the November congressional elections, made possible, they later wrote, by "the remarkable unity of community opinion," which allowed the University "to channel the energy of the strike into constructive action."

The paper celebrated its hundredth anniversary in 1976 with a June seminar on "The Ethics of Leaks" and a two-day symposium on "The Press and Social Change." In its day-to-day activities, it was still committed to the objective it had set for itself at its founding, but now the operation was considerably larger and faster. The fortnightly that a staff of eight or nine produced in the beginning took five days to print by hand press in Trenton. A hundred years later, the five-times-a-week daily tabloid required the efforts of more than a hundred editors, reporters, photographers, and business people, and took only hours to print by the photo-offset process it converted to in 1972. Thanks to the revenues produced by energetic advertising and circulation departments, it was one of the country's few financially independent college newspapers.

Over the years the *Princetonian* has maintained a respected position in campus life. In senior polls it was usually voted the most highly regarded extracurricular activity outside athletics. Places on the board were eagerly sought, and competition for them could be strenuous, as Hamilton Fish Armstrong '16, suggests in this picture of half a dozen surviving "heelers" his freshman year:

> We were exhausted, suspicious, eating little, sleeping little, barely hanging on to passing grades in our academic work, bleary-eyed, pimply, scavenging for bits of news to supplement the stories assigned to us, fighting in every way possible, fair or foul, to add to our lineage in the paper.

For their part, most editors would probably agree with the 1879 board's valedictory statement that "the duties of editing" had given them "a closer and more perfect view of college life and affairs." Nassau Hall, for its part, apparently has come to accept the fact that as long as there is a Princeton, there will be a *Princetonian* carrying on the time-honored mission of college journalism, which is, President Dodds once ruefully observed, "to comfort the afflicted and to afflict the comfortable."

Former *Princetonian* editors have achieved prominence, particularly in government and journalism. Government leaders have included, in addition to Woodrow Wilson, Adlai E. Stevenson '22; Secretary of Defense James Forrestal '15; Supreme Court Justice John M. Harlan '20; Secretary of the Air Force James Douglas '20; Under Secretary of the Treasury H. Chapman Rose '28; General Counsel of the Treasury Nelson P. Rose '31; and Ambassadors Livingston T. Merchant '26, Jacob D. Beam '29, Shelby C. Davis '30, Robert H. McBride '40, and William H. Attwood '41.

Among those conspicuous in journalism and letters have been: Robert McLean '13, publisher, *Philadelphia Evening Bulletin*; Henry A. Laughlin '14, president, Houghton Mifflin Company; Hamilton Fish Armstrong '16, editor, *Foreign Affairs*; Richard Halliburton '21, world traveler, explorer, and writer; John S. Martin '23, managing editor, *Time*; Edward W. Barrett '32, Dean, Columbia School of Journalism; John B. Oakes '34, editorial page editor, *New York Times*; William H. Attwood '41, publisher, *Newsday*; John N. Brooks, Jr. '42, author and staff member, *The New Yorker*; Peter D. Bunzel '49, op-ed page editor, *Los Angeles Times*; Donald Oberdorfer, Jr. '52, national affairs correspondent, *Washington Post*; R. W. Apple '57, chief of the London bureau, *New York Times*; Robert A. Caro '57, Pulitzer prize-winning biographer; Donald Kirk '59, national correspondent, *Chicago Tribune*; James Ridgeway '59, editor and writer, *New Republic* and *Village Voice*; B. Frank Deford '61, writer, *Sports Illustrated*; and José M. Ferrer III '61, associate editor, *Time*.

Princeton-in-Asia is the outgrowth of a relationship that began in 1898 when the Philadelphian Society sent Robert R. Gailey A.M. 1896 (a football All-American) to north China to pioneer Y.M.C.A. work there. He was subsequently joined by Dwight Edwards '04 (honorary Doctor of Philanthropy 1949), Louis D. Froelick '06 (later editor of *Asia* magazine), and others. With student and alumni support, they evolved a program, called Princeton-in-Peking, which for twenty years sent Princetonians to China to help staff the Peking Y.M.C.A. Under the leadership of John S. Burgess '05 and Sidney D.

Gamble '12, whose social survey of Peking (published in 1921) was the first ever made of an Oriental city, the program in 1930 became the Princeton-Yenching Foundation, which helped to organize a sociology department in Yenching University and to develop it into a college of public affairs.

In the 1950s the organization's name was changed to Princeton-in-Asia, and support was shifted to colleges in Taiwan, South Korea, and Hong Kong. With the expansion of the University's efforts in East Asian Studies, the program further broadened its scope, sending recent graduates as teaching fellows to colleges in Japan, China, Hong Kong, and Indonesia, helping alumni and undergraduates to obtain summer jobs in teaching or in business in these countries, and providing scholarships for Asian students in Asian universities.

Princeton Inn College was founded in 1970 in response to a need and an idea. The need, resulting from the admission of women to the university, was housing; the idea was to create a special kind of undergraduate community, a residential college.

The old Princeton Inn, built in 1924-25, was a gracious, rambling hotel.* On the rear terrace, overlooking the pond of Springdale golf course, where the British had made a temporary stand during the Battle of Princeton, guests could sip a cocktail and listen to the music of the carillon float down from the Cleveland Tower. Now the college occupies the main building of the Inn, as well as the former employees' quarters, called the Annex, and a new building opened in 1971, the Addition. Four hundred and forty undergraduates live in these facilities. On the terrace, where waiters in formal dress once served mint juleps, coeds now sun themselves or play frisbee in the spring.

The new Inn was planned as a residential college, a community to join what Princeton has traditionally put asunder: academic and social life; different classes; undergraduates, graduate students, townspeople, and faculty; men and women. (Even Princeton Borough and Township come together at the Inn, since the boundary line runs through the center of the lobby.) This purpose has given the college an informal, egalitarian way of life. Even in relation to its fellow colleges, Wilson and Stevenson, Princeton Inn tends to be regarded as the edge of campus. Spiritually as well as geographically, it can seem either a promising frontier or too far to walk (ten minutes from Firestone Library). In its early days the college became known for its raffish, bohemian air. The first Master announced his goal as "perpetual Woodstock"; the mural in the coffee house sprouted an enormous shaggy *Love*. Eventually, as the counterculture faded, the look and style of the Inn became respectable: solid furniture, chamber music, and Shakespeare. But the spirit of democracy remains strong. Appropriately, the only name officially honored by the Inn belongs to a respectable socialist. In May 1975, the 10,000-volume college library was dedicated to Norman Thomas '05.

More social and cultural activities take place at Princeton Inn, probably, than anywhere else on campus. Almost every evening something will be happening: a dance, party, or poetry reading; Black Thoughts or French conversation; a festival of Latin-American movies or a conference on Virginia Woolf. Most of these events are run by students, supported by student funds, and responsible to a student council.

Assistant and Associate Masters (graduate students and faculty residents) help look after the college as a whole, as do the Masters (scholars as well as administrators). The Masters of the Inn have been Albert Sonnenfeld (1970-1973), Lawrence and Joanna Lipking (1973-1976), and Gerald and Lou Ann Garvey (1976-   ).

Lawrence Lipking

* A still older Princeton Inn, located on the site of the current Borough Hall, had been in use for twenty-five years (1893-1918).

"Princeton in the Nation's Service" is the title of an oration Woodrow Wilson delivered at the Sesquicentennial celebration (q.v.), when Princeton looked back to its founding in 1746. For his inaugural address as president of the University in 1902, when he outlined a program for Princeton's future, he used almost the same title: "Princeton *for* the Nation's Service" (italics ours). But the 1896 oration is more memorable and its title the one so frequently quoted.

Wilson began with a brief sketch of Princeton's first twenty years, under its five earliest presidents, and then devoted the major part of his address to the administration of Princeton's sixth president, John Witherspoon (q.v.), divine, scholar, and statesman, whose "vitality entered like a tonic into the college, kept it alive in . . . time of peril—made it as individual and inextinguishable a force as he himself was, alike in scholarship and in public affairs."

He then told how Witherspoon, who came from Scotland in 1768 and was president of the College until he died in 1794, helped make a new constitution for New Jersey, became her spokesman in the Continental Congress, and voted for and signed the Declaration of Independence. He "stood forth in the sight of all the people a great advocate and orator, deeming himself forward in the service of God when most engaged in the service of men and of liberty."

Wilson went on to describe dramatically the events that took place in Princeton during the Revolution, how Nassau Hall became a military hospital, then a barracks, and finally on January 3, 1777, a stronghold that changed hands three times. On that memorable day, there was fighting in the streets and cannon fire against Nassau Hall, as Washington, who only a few days before had been beaten and in full retreat, after crossing the Delaware, defeated the British and changed "the whole face of the war."

Princeton, Wilson pointed out, became as much a center of politics as it was of fighting: the state legislature and its revolutionary Council of Safety sat in Nassau Hall on occasion, and the Continental Congress (to which news of peace came in October) met there in 1783. The Commencement audience that year saw Washington and Witherspoon on the platform together, "the two men, it was said, who could not be matched for striking presence in all the country."

Under Witherspoon, Princeton "became herself for a time . . . the academic center of the Revolution" and sent into public life an extraordinary number of notable statesmen: twenty-one senators, thirty-nine representatives, twelve governors, three Supreme Court justices, one vice-president, and a president, all within a period of about twenty-five years, and from a college which seldom had more than a hundred students. Nine Princeton men were delegates at the Constitutional Convention, and five of these were Witherspoon's students.*

It would be absurd, Wilson said, to pretend that one could single out a distinctive Princeton mark in the Revolution or the Constitution:

We can show nothing more of historical fact than that her own president took a great place of leadership in that time of change, and became one of the first figures of the age; that the college which he led, and to which he gave his spirit, contributed more than her share of public men to the making of the nation, outranked her elder rivals in the roll call of the constitutional convention, and seemed for a little a seminary of statesmen rather than a quiet seat of academic learning. What takes our admiration and engages our fancy in looking back to that time is the generous union then established in the college between the life of philosophy and the life of the State.

Coming down to the present, Wilson declared it the duty of institutions of learning in a democracy not merely to inculcate a sense of duty, "but to illuminate duty by every lesson that can be drawn out of the past." He then spoke of the contributions various disciplines could make to this purpose. Toward the end of his address, he urged that the College identify itself with the needs of the nation—in a passage often quoted, which was an essential idea in the founding, in 1930, of the School of Public and International Affairs, later named for Wilson:

. . . It is indispensable, it seems to me, if [a college] is to do its right service, that the air of affairs should be admitted to all its classrooms. I do not mean the air of party politics, but the air of the world's transactions, the consciousness of the solidarity of the race, the sense of the duty of man toward man, of the presence of men in every problem, of the significance of truth for guidance as well as for knowledge. . . . We dare not keep aloof and closet ourselves while a nation comes to its maturity. The days of glad expansion are gone; our life grows tense and difficult; our resource for the future lies in careful thought, providence, and a wise economy; and the school must be of the nation.

Additional information on Princeton's record "in the nation's service" will be found in the following articles:

Ambassadors and Ministers
Cabinet Officers
College and University Founders
College and University Presidents
Constitutional Convention of 1787
Continental Congress
Governors
House of Representatives
Presidents of the United States
Senate
Supreme Court Justices
Vice-Presidents of the United States

* In this paragraph, the numbers President Wilson used have been amended in light of later research.

Princeton Theological Seminary. An offspring of the College, the Theological Seminary draws upon the common heritage of the vigorous reawakening of "New Light" Presbyterianism in the mid-1700s. In 1811, the Presbyterian General Assembly decided that the College was becoming too secular in its curriculum and general climate and that ministers required a quality of professional training beyond the scope of a liberal arts college. The College, on its part, had come to feel that the influ-

ence of the church was too restrictive. The founding of the Seminary deprived the College of the financial support of the Presbyterian establishment and only after the lay graduates of the College, many years later, began to acquire both wealth and concern for the welfare of their alma mater did the College regain its momentum in evolving into a leading liberal university.

From its opening in 1812, the Seminary has been blessed with able leadership, including its first professor, Archibald Alexander, and soon thereafter, Samuel Miller and Charles Hodge. It became the dominant influence in Presbyterianism in the United States for more than a century. Administered by its faculty with a rotation of leadership until 1902, its first president was Francis Landey Patton, previously president of the University, who was followed by J. Ross Stevenson in 1914, John A. Mackay in 1936, and James I. McCord in 1959.

Today, the Princeton Theological Seminary not only is the outstanding Presbyterian Seminary in the country but is one of the leading seminaries in the world. Its distinguished faculty of thirty-eight is supplemented by fourteen adjunct and visiting professors and more than fifty pastors and chaplains cooperating in field training. Its 740 students come from throughout the world and from many confessions. It awards advanced degrees and provides mid-career instruction to large numbers of ministers through institutes and special seminars. Its Speer Library is one of the best research libraries in its field. While remaining separate institutions, the Seminary and the University have cooperated in many ways in enriching the intellectual life of an academic community.

J. Douglas Brown

Princeton Tiger, The, first appeared in March 1882 but ceased publication that December after only nine issues. The evidence is not clear whether this was for lack of funds or, as has been suggested, because the editors had incurred faculty displeasure for having pressed too far their discovery (in Somerset Maugham's phrase) that "impropriety is the soul of wit."

In 1890 the *Tiger* was born again. This time it survived, despite the fact that its early efforts were made difficult by an unsympathetic faculty and by advertisers "far from warm-hearted." McCready Sykes 1894 recalled involving President Patton in a discussion of Greek syntax in order to avoid the difficult task of having to demonstrate why the *Tiger* should not be required to discontinue publication. Booth Tarkington 1893 (q.v.) remembered two editors spending a Saturday in New York in search of ads, and returning with an expense account for two round-trip tickets, eight hours hansom cab service, and an "enviable lunch at the Hoffman House," and, to offset these items, "a single, almost-promised ad that would bring—it was hoped—five dollars."

Tarkington, a frequent contributor of jokes and pen-line drawings, also recalled that it was easy to get students to accept membership on the *Tiger* board, but harder to get them to write, draw, or edit. This proved a continuing problem. In their day F. Scott Fitzgerald '17 (q.v.) and John Biggs, Jr. '18, produced whole issues of the *Tiger*, unassisted, by working through the night together.

In the 1920s the *Tiger* prospered greatly. Circulation reached 10,000; average issues numbered sixty pages, many of them heavy with ads. A sinking fund was started to finance a building like the *Harvard Lampoon's* (a hope never realized), and the 1924 board contributed $1,000 to the new chapel, thus showing that the oft-offending *Tiger* was, after all, on the side of the angels.

In 1932 the *Tiger*, tracing its date of birth back to 1882, celebrated its golden jubilee by issuing in book form "A Compendium of Half a Century of Princeton Wit and Humor, if any, in Prose, Picture, and Poesy."

Two board members of the thirties used the talents they demonstrated in college to make their marks in later life. Whitney Darrow Jr. '31's *Tiger* cartoons showed the beginnings of the distinctive style he later developed as a regular cartoonist for *The New Yorker*. Lewis Thomas '33, who wrote for the *Tiger* while majoring in biology, later became well known as a leader in medical education and cancer research and as the author of a widely praised volume of essays, *The Lives of a Cell*.

In May 1942 the *Tiger* announced that it was suspending operations for the duration of the war, although many thought the suspension had been hastened by Nassau Hall's disapproval of the improprieties of their wit. In 1947 the editors secured reluctant permission to resume publication. In these years Henry R. Martin '48 drew cartoons for the *Tiger* while majoring in art history; later he joined Whitney Darrow as a frequent contributor to *The New Yorker*.

In 1952 the *Tiger*, again experiencing difficulties, sought to appeal to a wider campus audience by becoming "concerned with all things relevant to Princeton," while continuing to run cartoons and a few other bits of its old fare. The managing editor, John A. McPhee '53's pungent columns in the *Tiger* gave a hint of the style that later distinguished his widely known writing for *The New Yorker*.

Though the *Tiger* was still strong

enough in 1957 to produce a "Roar of Laughter" (the title of its 75th anniversary number), there were hard times ahead, and when the fortunes of college humor magazines declined in the late sixties and early seventies, the plight of the *Tiger* was highlighted in a feature story in the *New York Times*, and in an editorial headlined "Tiger, tiger burning low" lamenting the implications of this trend "in a world badly in need of laughter and satire." If the *Tiger*'s more frequent appearances in the mid-seventies are any indication, there is still a chance that it will be burning bright again one day.

Princeton University Press was founded in 1905 by a gift from Charles Scribner 1875, and incorporated in 1910 as a non-profit corporation "to establish, maintain, and operate a printing and publishing plant, for the promotion of education and scholarship, and to serve the University by manufacturing and distributing its publications."

The first director was Whitney Darrow '03, who brought the Press into being. He was succeeded by Paul Tomlinson '09, who built up the printing plant and published many notable books during his long term, 1917-1938. The brief tenure, 1938-1941, of Joseph Brandt was a turning point in the development of the Press; from then on there was increasing emphasis on publishing rather than printing. This emphasis was further developed by Datus C. Smith, Jr. '29, with whom began the Press's greatest period of growth and achievement, continued since 1954 under the directorship of Herbert S. Bailey, Jr. '42.

Like many other good things in life the Press had a humble beginning. It started by buying out a small local printer and setting up shop in rented quarters over a drugstore on Nassau Street. In 1911 Charles Scribner gave the Press its handsome and unique building on William Street. At first the Scribner Building was mainly a printing plant, but in 1967 it was completely renovated and became the offices of the publishing division. An additional building was erected in nearby Lawrenceville to house the modern printing plant, warehouse, and accounting department. It was named the Laughlin Building, after Henry A. Laughlin '14, a former trustee and president of the Press's Board of Trustees.

Although closely connected with the University, the Press is a separate, financially independent corporation which has its own fifteen trustees, nine of whom must be members of the faculty, administration, or alumni of Princeton. The president of the University is an ex officio trustee, and he appoints four faculty members to the Editorial Board, which controls the imprint of the Press.

True to the purpose for which it was founded, the Press publishes scholarly books and continues to print most of them in its own plant. It prints for the University and some other non-profit organizations.

The Press has published nearly 3,000 titles since its first book, John Witherspoon's *Lectures in Moral Philosophy*, appeared in 1912. These have included such seminal volumes as Einstein's *The Meaning of Relativity*, von Neumann and Morgenstern's *The Theory of Games and Economic Behavior*, and Edward S. Corwin's *The Constitution and What It Means Today*. Currently it publishes about 100 new books each year, selected from about 1,000 manuscripts submitted. The Press is responsible for a number of long-term projects intended to serve scholarship for many decades and perhaps centuries. One of these is *The Papers of Thomas Jefferson*, edited by Julian P. Boyd; the first volume was published in 1950, and over 60 are expected. Another is *The Papers of Woodrow Wilson*, edited by Arthur S. Link, for which about 45 volumes are planned.

Princeton University Press is cooperating with the National Endowment for the Humanities' program to produce authoritative editions of classic American authors by issuing *The Writings of Henry D. Thoreau*, which is expected to encompass some 20 volumes. Another major project is the *Princeton Encyclopedia of Classical Archaeological Sites* (1976), which contains descriptions of about 2,800 sites by some 400 authors and is a unique reference work in its field. In 1972 it was announced that the Press will publish *The Writings of Albert Einstein* with the cooperation of Princeton University and the Institute for Advanced Study, where Einstein's archives are housed.

The Bollingen Series, begun in the 1940s by the Bollingen Foundation, was given to the Press in 1969 with the responsibility for carrying on its work in the fields of aesthetics, archaeology, cultural history, ethnology, literary criticism, mythology, philosophy, psychology, religion, and symbolism. It includes such great projects as *The Collected Works of C. G. Jung, The Collected Works of Samuel Taylor Coleridge*, and *The Collected Works of Paul Valéry*, which the *New York Times Book Review* called "undoubtedly one of the most distinguished and ambitious series of books ever issued by an American publisher."

Over the years Princeton University Press books have won numerous honors, including at different times Pulitzer Prizes, National Book Awards, Bancroft Prizes, and various awards from the professional scholarly associations. The Press has also received many awards for excellence in printing and design.

The Press publishes three scholarly journals: *World Politics*, issued for the University's Center of International Studies; *The Annals of Mathematics*, sponsored by the University and the Institute for Advanced Study; and *Philosophy & Public Affairs*, with no outside sponsorship, which is written for those concerned with the philosophical exploration of public issues in law, sociology, political science, and economics.

Since its inception, the Press has printed and published the *Princeton Alumni Weekly* (q.v.), one of the nation's oldest alumni magazines. It is editorially directed by an alumni board, but managed by the Press, and has its offices in the Scribner Building. Some 40,000 copies of each issue are distributed.

In 1976, 98 new clothbound titles and 42 new paperbacks were published; 725,000 books were sold—320,000 hardcover, 405,000 paperback. Approximately 75 percent of total sales are from the backlist. The Press's paperback program, with over 300 titles in print, has been in operation since 1965, and is one of the largest among university presses.

Princeton University Press achieves a worldwide distribution of its books, and about 25 percent of them are sold abroad. The Press's largest foreign customers, in order, are: the United Kingdom, Japan, Canada, Germany, Holland, Italy, Australia, and India. Princeton's bestselling hardback book is the Wilhelm/Baynes translation of the *I Ching, or Book of Changes* in the Bollingen Series, with over 400,000 copies sold. The bestselling paperback is R. R. Palmer's translation of Lefebvre's *Coming of the French Revolution*, sales of which exceeded 160,000.

The authors come from many different institutions and countries. About 25 percent are affiliated with the University. Others have come from a wide variety of colleges and universities in America and, in recent years, in Australia, Canada, Germany, Greece, Israel, Switzerland, Thailand, and the United Kingdom.

Thus Princeton University Press, in fulfillment of its Charter, serves the University and the world of scholarship through printing and publishing. Its motto is: "Putting Knowledge to Work."

Herbert S. Bailey, Jr.

Princeton University Store, The, colloquially known orignally as the Univee Store, later as the U-Store, has been doing business since 1905. It was an outgrowth of a student-managed bookstore that began modest operations in a corner room of West College in 1896. Robert C. McNamara '03, first manager 1905-1908, added athletic supplies and extended the Store's quarters into two more rooms. (He eventually became chairman of the board of Scott, Foresman & Co.) B. Franklin Bunn '07, manager 1908-1947, added most of the Store's present departments and extended its quarters to include the entire first floor of West College, with a separate shop for music in town. Under the direction of Frederick John Worthington (B.A., University of Colorado, 1937, M.S., New York University 1938) who became manager in 1947, the Store in 1958 combined all of its activities under one roof in a new building of its own at 36 University Place, designed by Eldredge Snyder '22.

When McNamara left in 1908, annual sales were $60,000, and when Bunn retired in 1947 they were $1,100,000. For the fiscal year ending June 30, 1976, they were $5,500,000.

The Store is a cooperative society whose membership is open to University members and alumni and also members of the Theological Seminary and the Institute for Advanced Study. It pays its members an annual rebate, which reached a peak of 12½ percent the first year after World War II and leveled off at 7.64 in the mid-seventies.

The Store is governed by a board of trustees, composed of undergraduates, graduate students, faculty, administration, alumni, and the manager. Dean of the Faculty Henry B. Fine '80 and University Secretary Charles W. McAlpin '88, who were prime movers in the founding of the Store, were trustees for many years. Dean of the Faculty J. Douglas Brown '19, Chandler Cudlipp '19, one-time vice-president of McCutcheon's and later head of his own interior designing firm in New York City, and John H. Leh '21, senior partner of the H. Leh and Co. department store, Allentown, Pennsylvania, made notable contributions as trustees to the Store's later development.

The Store's membership as of June 30, 1976, numbered some 46,000.

Proctor, The Office of, was instituted in 1870 by President McCosh to help him discharge the heavy disciplinary burden that his predecessor, John Maclean, had carried almost single-handed. The first incumbent, Matthew Goldie (brother of George Goldie, director of the gymnasium), had good rapport with the undergraduates. "He was square and honest," one of them said, "and played no favorites. He hated cant and hypocrisy, and was a watchdog without being a spy." Matt's assistant, known to the students only as "Dennis," was less popular. As McCosh's messenger to undergraduates suspected of wrong-doing, his stock phrase was: "You are to see the Doctor in his study tonight"; he was regarded as "a bird of ill omen whose very presence contaminated the atmosphere."

When Goldie retired in 1892 his place was taken by Johnny Topley. Apparently Topley had to discharge the baleful mission once performed by Dennis, for the seniors had this song about him:

Johnny, Johnny Topley,
Johnny, Johnny Topley,
Do you want me?
No-O, Sir-ee.
Not this afternoon-ter-noon-
ter-noon-ter-noon.

In 1907 Topley resigned his proctorship and, to the delight of the students and the discomfort of the Dean, opened a saloon across the street from FitzRandolph Gateway. The seniors continued to sing about him; but now they gave the question "Do you want me?" an enthusiastically affirmative answer:

Yes, Sir-ee,
Every afternoon-ter-noon-
ter-noon-ter-noon.

After Topley sold his saloon in 1913, he was soon lost sight of, but seniors continued to sing about his legendary services on into the twenties.

Bill Coan, who followed Topley, was born and reared in Princeton, and it was said that his expertise about student escapades had been acquired through his own participation in similar happenings in earlier days. A chastened sophomore, on leaving a meeting of the Discipline Committee, was once heard to complain, "Bill knew what I did before I did it." A faculty member of the committee, learned in Greek mythology, likened Coan to Argus of the hundred eyes.

Hank Bovie, who took over from Coan in 1919, was tall and handsome and cut a magisterial figure, but the seniors thought him slow in crime detection. One year they sang:

Although it seems beyond belief,
They say that once he caught a thief.

Another year:

We lose fur coats in winter's chills,
And get them back with the daffodils.

Thus recommended, Hank became chief of detectives of the Borough in 1926.

Francis X. Hogarty, who assumed Bovie's mantle, was an earnest somewhat stolid guardian of campus morals. Once, when the Discipline Committee was examining a charge of intoxication, Dean Gauss, leaning over backward to be fair, said, "Frank, how can you be sure this student was intoxicated?" "Well, Dean," the ever solemn Frank replied, "I saw him fall flat on his face. I think he was drunk."

Frank was ably assisted by Michael Kopliner and by Harry Cawley. Frank, Mike, and Harry inspired the Proctor's Song of the thirties and forties:

There are three men in Princeton
*   town,*
They look us up, they look us down;
Like the plague, they're all around,
Heigh-ho, the proctors!
Heigh-ho, the proctors, the proctors,
*   the proctors!*
Heigh-ho, the proctors, the
*   Pinkertons of Princeton.*

There were other verses with other intimations: "They try on us to place the blame," . . . "Under our beds they look for drinks," . . . "Who the Hell will furnish bail?" . . . "Hist the sound of stealthy feet!" . . . all concluding: ". . . the Pinkertons of Princeton."

Mike Kopliner, who joined the staff in 1924, had one of the longest tours of duty on record—36 years—and became one of the best remembered proctors. Once, in 1931, toward the end of the Prohibition Era, he was grilling a visiting bootlegger in his room at the Princeton Inn when a sophomore telephoned to place an order and gave his name and address before he realized it was Kopliner he was talking to:

So just take care in buying wine
To see that Mike's not on the line.

Mike became head proctor in 1945. One May in the 1950s he got word that some undergraduates were planning to disrupt the customary R.O.T.C. review near Palmer Stadium. He took a strategic position on the lower Campus, and, a few minutes before the review was to start, heard an approaching cadence: "Hip-two-three-four . . ." Presently, around 1915 Hall came five undergraduates in Confederate uniforms, with a Confederate flag, a snare drum, a sword, and two rifles. Mike hurried ahead on the road to the Stadium and at the Vivarium below Guyot drew a chalk line. When the invading Confederates arrived, he said, "Look, boys. Up to this point you've had a lot of fun. You go beyond this line and you're in trouble. What do you intend to do?" Then, according to Mike's tape-recorded memoirs, the student with the sword turned to the others and said, "Well, boys, we have met the enemy and we are theirs."

Mike died of cancer, at age 63, in the summer of 1960. The previous fall, between the halves of a football game, the band had demonstrated the respect and affection in which he was held by forming a giant K as they played the Proctor's Song.

In 1960 the proctors and the campus police were placed under the supervision of a new officer, the director of security. Incumbents of this post have been Walter Dodwell, former member of the New Jersey State Police, 1960-1969; Allan N. Kornblum, former special agent of the Federal Bureau of Investigation, 1969-1975; Jerrold L. Witsil, former director of public safety at the University of Maryland, 1975-
Mike Kopliner's son, James M. Kopliner '51, a former borough policeman, has been Assistant Director of Security since 1965.

By 1977 the University security department numbered ninety-nine persons, including the director, two assistant directors, the chief of the uniformed division, the captain of Forrestal security, eight security sergeants, sixty security officers, four proctor supervisors, eighteen proctors, and four secretaries.

Prospect, once the home of the president and now a social center for University faculty, administration, and staff, was acquired by the College in 1878. At that time it occupied a thirty-acre estate that extended as far east as the present site of Woodrow Wilson School.

The land on which Prospect stands was originally part of a large tract owned by Richard Stockton, one of the first settlers of Princeton and grandfather of Richard Stockton 1748 (q.v.). It was later acquired by Benjamin Fitz-Randolph, who conveyed it to his son, Nathaniel FitzRandolph (q.v.). Still later the property was deeded to Colonel George Morgan, western explorer, United States Agent for Indian Affairs, and gentleman farmer. Morgan built a stone farmhouse on the crest of the hill and, observing the superb view of the landscape to the east, called it "Prospect."

Colonel Morgan's estate became famous in Revolutionary times as "Prospect near Princeton." A delegation of ten Delaware Indian chieftains spent a few days in wigwams on its lawns as guests of Colonel Morgan in 1779, preparatory to going to Philadelphia to confer with Continental Congress. Some two thousand mutinous soldiers of the Pennsylvania Line pitched camp there in 1781, also en route to Philadelphia to demand a redress of their grievances. Continental Congress held a number of its sessions at Prospect in 1783 before establishing itself in Nassau Hall.

John Potter, a wealthy merchant from Charleston, South Carolina, acquired Prospect in 1824. In 1849, his son, Thomas F. Potter replaced Colonel Morgan's stone farmhouse with the present mansion, which was designed by John Notman in the Florentine style, much used at that time for country residences. The grounds were laid by an Englishman named Petrey who, according to Mrs. Allan Marquand, undoubtedly planned the flower garden and brought over the beautiful Cedar of Lebanon, the large hawthorn, and the fine English yew, on the west of the house.

In 1878 Alexander and Robert L. Stuart, wealthy Scottish-American merchants and Presbyterian-minded philanthropists, bought Prospect and presented it to the College for use as the residence of President McCosh and his successors. McCosh thought it the finest college president's house in the world and on leaving it said he felt like Adam leaving Eden. In the 1890s President Patton kept a cow and pastured it where Palmer Hall now stands. Prospect's Eden-like qualities diminished with the passing years. Undergraduates going to their eating clubs took short cuts across the Prospect grounds and one year football crowds trampled on the garden. The following summer (1904) President Wilson had an iron fence built around the Prospect grounds, enclosing five acres of the Campus, to the annoyance of undergraduates who tore part of it down. Mrs. Wilson made over the garden approximately in its present form and planted the background of evergreens.

One spring night in 1925, a caravan of student cars drove through the Prospect grounds to protest an edict of the trustees banning automobiles from the Campus, and during a spring riot in the early sixties undergraduates tore down a section of the fence at the back of the garden.

After the official residence of the president was changed to the Walter Lowrie House (q.v.) in 1968, Prospect was converted for the social use of the faculty and administration, and later of all full-time University employees. The president continued to use its grounds for official receptions at the opening of the University in September and at Commencement.

Provost, The, serves as general deputy to the president, giving particular attention to the overall academic development of the University, and, in the president's absence or disability, exercises the presidential power and duties relating to the general supervision of the University, if no acting president has been appointed. The position was created by the trustees in 1966 to permit the president to share more of his administrative load so that he might have time for the essential task of shaping educational policies. Provosts have been:

J. Douglas Brown 1966-1967
William G. Bowen 1967-1972
F. Sheldon Hackney 1972-1975
Albert Rees 1975-1977
Neil L. Rudenstine 1977-

Psychology, The Department of. For such a relatively young discipline, Psychology's history at Princeton is surprisingly long. In the 1868 catalog, Psychology was listed as a required course for the Junior class and for the next two decades was taught by President James McCosh, assisted by Professors Henry Fairfield Osborn and William Berryman Scott. In 1893 a laboratory for experimental psychology was established under J. Mark Baldwin. Housed in Nassau Hall, it thrived as a center for research and scholarship in the then-fledgling science. The *Psychological Review*, founded jointly by Baldwin and by Cattell of Columbia University in 1894, soon became the leading publication in American psychology.

Following a pattern that developed throughout the western world, psychology was initially treated as a subfield of philosophy. When the departmental system was instituted by President Wilson in 1904, psychology was taught as part of the philosophy department. In 1915, it received recognition in the title, the Department of Philosophy and Psychology. Finally, in 1920, a Department of Psychology was established, largely through the efforts of Howard C. Warren (q.v.), who was its first chairman.

The next step was to find a home for the burgeoning science, and in 1924 Eno Hall became the first university building in America to be devoted entirely to experimental psychology. There Psychology remained and grew until 1963, when Green Hall, the former engineering building, was renovated to house the Departments of Psychology and Sociology, and Psychology began occupying every nook and cranny of its part of this large building.

But important as space and facilities are, the department's real history lies in the contributions of its faculty and students. From the beginning Psychology at Princeton has been among the foremost programs in the country. McCosh was one of the first to bring the "new" experimental psychology of the German psychologists Wundt and Fechner to the attention of scholars in this country. Baldwin continued this tradition, studying both with Wundt and with McCosh, and then went on to become one of this country's most distinguished psychologists, serving as president of the American Psychological Association in 1898. Warren was no less eminent, serving also as president in 1913.

Warren was succeeded as chairman of the department by Herbert Langfeld, whose textbook, written with Boring and Weld, was considered the first modern survey-introduction to psychology. Under Langfeld, the department's progrm was further strengthened by the appointment of such men as Ernest Wever, pioneer in the study of hearing; Hadley Cantril, noted for his work in public opinion and his study of people's reactions to Orson

Welles's Martian invasion broadcast; and Harold Gulliksen, one of the country's foremost authorities on mental testing.

This blend of theoretical and practical interests continued under the chairmanships of Carroll Pratt, Hadley Cantril, and John L. Kennedy in the two decades following the Second World War. During this period Sylvan Tomkins, a leading figure in personality theory and assessment, brought Freud, Jung, and Adler alive for hundreds of enthralled undergraduates. Frank Geldard came from the University of Virginia, expanding the department's scope by his work on cutaneous perception and communication.

The department began to take on a new character and form after it moved to Green Hall in 1963. For the first time laboratories could be built and equipped to house the various new branches of rapidly developing experimental psychology. Professors John L. Kennedy and Joseph M. Notterman, who were instrumental in planning and supervising the building's reconstruction, also brought in young scientists to expand the department's coverage of modern psychology. In 1968, Leon J. Kamin assumed the chairmanship with a clear mandate to build on the solid foundation that already existed. Since then, the department has concentrated on four major areas: physiological psychology and the neurosciences, social psychology, cognitive processes and perception, and the psychology of learning and motivation. In addition, the study of behavioral development has been emphasized within each of these areas.

The decision to build depth as well as breadth resulted in a vigorous and popular department. Interdisciplinary research and scholarship has flour-ished, with faculty and students working across traditional lines: biology and biochemistry have become part and parcel of the work in neuroscience; linguistics and anthropology an integral part of work in cognition; mathematics and computer sciences a necessary and useful tool in the study of memory, perception and learning.

Student interest has grown correspondingly. In the early 1970s, Leon J. Kamin's introductory psychology lectures averaged over 300 students. John M. Darley and Joel Cooper attracted as many to each of their courses in Social Psychology and Personality, respectively, and the faculty were trying to keep pace with 150 undergraduate concentrators. Despite the constriction of the academic job market, the department attracted many more graduate students than could be accommodated, and it had an enviable record in placing its Ph.D.'s in suitable positions throughout the country. President McCosh would have been pleased with the growth and development of experimental psychology at Princeton. Even though psychology was no longer thought of as Mental Philosophy, McCosh's spirit of vigorous inquiry and teaching and his commitment to excellence and service continued to prevail.

Sam Glucksberg

Public lectures on topics of general interest are provided by five special endowments given by the following alumni and friends of the University: in 1891 by Spencer Trask 1866; in 1899 by Henry Stafford Little 1844, donor also of the Stafford Little dormitory; in 1912 by Louis Clark Vanuxem 1879; in 1939 by George L. Farnum 1894; and in 1957 by the family of Governor Walter E. Edge. Among those who have occupied these lectureships are Grover

Cleveland, Theodore Roosevelt, Albert Einstein, Bertrand Russell, Robert Frost, Felix Frankfurter, Martin Buber, William O. Douglas, Edmund Wilson, Ralph Bunche, C. P. Snow, and Linus Pauling.

Some 500 other lectures, seminars, and colloquia, given mainly under departmental auspices, are also open to the University community and the general public without charge each year.

Pulitzer Prizes, established in 1917, have been awarded to the following Princeton alumni and faculty:

FICTION

1918 Ernest Poole '02, *His Family*
1919 Booth Tarkington 1893, *The Magnificent Ambersons*
1922 Booth Tarkington 1893, *Alice Adams*
1928 Thornton Wilder A.M. '26, *The Bridge of San Luis Rey*

DRAMA

1918 Jesse Lynch Williams 1892, *Why Marry?*
1922 Eugene O'Neill '10, *Anna Christie*
1928 Eugene O'Neill '10, *Strange Interlude*
1938 Thornton Wilder A.M. '26, *Our Town*
1943 Thornton Wilder A.M. '26, *The Skin of Our Teeth*
1950 Joshua L. Logan '31 (with Richard Rodgers and Oscar Hammerstein II), *South Pacific*
1957 Eugene O'Neill '10, *Long Day's Journey Into Night*

HISTORY

1924 Charles H. McIlwain 1894, *The American Revolution, A Constitutional Interpretation*

1934 Herbert Sebastian Agar '19 Ph.D. '22, *The People's Choice*
1957 George F. Kennan '25, *Russia Leaves the War*

BIOGRAPHY

1934 Tyler Dennett (Professor of Politics), *John Hay*
1936 Ralph Barton Perry 1896, *The Thought and Character of William James*
1961 David Donald (Professor of History), *Charles Sumner and the Coming of the Civil War*
1968 George F. Kennan '25, *Memoirs (1925-1950)*
1971 Lawrance R. Thompson (Holmes Professor of Belles Lettres), *Robert Frost: The Years of Triumph*

POETRY

1971 William S. Merwin '48, *The Carrier of Ladders*

COMMENTARY

1977 George F. Will Ph.D. '68 (Columnist for the Washington Post Writers Group)

GENERAL NONFICTION

1977 William W. Warner '43 *Beautiful Swimmers: Watermen, Crabs, and the Chesapeake Bay*

The Putnam Collection of Sculpture is a memorial to John B. Putnam, Jr. '45, Lieutenant U.S.A., who was killed in action in World War II. It consists of the works of twenty major twentieth-century sculptors purchased in 1969 and 1970 through a fund given by an anonymous donor.

The sculptors represented in the Collection, their works, and the location of these works follow:

Reg Butler, *The Bride*, in Hamilton Court.

Alexander Calder, *Five Disks: One Empty*, on the plaza between Fine and Jadwin Halls.

Jacob Epstein, *Albert Einstein*, in the Fine Hall Library.

Naum Gabo, *Spheric Theme*, between 1879 Hall and Architecture Building.

Michael Hall, *Mastodon VI*, in front of MacMillan Building.

Gaston Lachaise, *Floating Figure*, in the Compton Quadrangle, Graduate College.

Jacques Lipchitz, *Song of the Vowels*, between Firestone Library and the University Chapel.

Clement Meadmore, *Upstart II*, at entrance to Engineering Quadrangle.

Henry Moore, *Oval with Points*, between West College and Stanhope Hall.

Masayuki Nagare, *Stone Riddle*, in the courtyard of Engineering Quadrangle.

Louise Nevelson, *Atmosphere and Environment X*, at the Nassau Street entrance to the Campus near Firestone Library.

Isamu Noguchi, *White Sun*, in the lobby of Firestone Library.

Eduardo Paolozzi, *Marok-Marok-Miosa*, in the lobby of the Architecture Building.

Antoine Pevsner, *Construction in the 3rd and 4th Dimension*, in the courtyard of Jadwin Hall.

Pablo Picasso, *Head of a Woman*, in front of The Art Museum.

Arnaldo Pomodoro, *Sfero*, in the Lourie-Love dormitory quadrangle.

George Rickey, *Two Planes Vertical Horizontal II*, between East Pyne and Murray-Dodge.

David Smith, *Cubi XIII*, near Spelman Hall.

Tony Smith, *Moses*, on the front lawn of Prospect.

Kenneth Snelson, *Northwood II*, in Compton Quadrangle, Graduate College.

A recapitulation, arranged alphabetically by locations, follows:

Architecture Building lobby: Paolozzi
Architecture Building-Seventy-Nine Hall: Gabo
Art Museum front lawn: Picasso
Engineering Quadrangle: Meadmore, Nagare, Snelson
Fine Hall, library: Epstein
Fine-Jadwin plaza: Calder
Firestone plaza: Lipchitz
Firestone Library lobby: Noguchi
Firstone Library near Nassau Street: Nevelson
Graduate College, Compton Court: Lachaise
Hamilton Court: Butler
Jadwin Hall courtyard: Pevsner
Lourie-Love dormitory quadrangle: Pomodoro
MacMillan Building: Hall
Murray-Dodge: Rickey
Prospect lawn: Tony Smith
Spelman Hall: David Smith
West College-Stanhope Hall: Moore

These sculptures were selected by a committee of alumni who were directors or former directors of art museums: Alfred H. Barr, Jr. '21 (Museum of Modern Art), Thomas P.F. Hoving '53 (Metropolitan Museum of Art), P. Joseph Kelleher Ph.D. '47 (The Art Museum, Princeton University), William M. Milliken '11 (Cleveland Museum of Art).

John B. Putnam, Jr. '45, who came to Princeton from Cleveland, Ohio, left college at the end of his sophomore year to enlist in the Army Air Corps. He made a brilliant record as a squadron flight leader with the Eighth Fighter Command in England, winning the Distinguished Flying Cross and the

Air Medal with six Oak Leaf Clusters. He was killed in a crash in England shortly after D Day in 1944.

Pyne, Moses Taylor (1855-1921), gave to his Alma Mater so generously of himself and his means that it was once said of him (by Cambridge Vice-Chancellor Sir Arthur Shipley) that he did more for Princeton than any other man had done for any college.

A man of great inherited wealth, accumulated originally by his maternal grandfather, Moses Taylor (first president of the National City Bank of New York and the principal stockholder in the Delaware, Lackawanna and Western Railroad Company), Pyne devoted most of his adult life, and much of his fortune, to helping Princeton grow from a college into a university. During his thirty-six years on the Board of Trustees he did not miss a single meeting.

A member of the famous Class of 1877, Pyne acquired at Princeton a lasting taste for Latin and Greek. A year after receiving his LL.B. at Columbia Law School in 1879, he married Margaretta Stockton, a great-great-granddaughter of Richard Stockton 1748 (q.v.), and became general counsel for the Delaware, Lackawanna & Western Railroad Company. In 1891 he resigned from this office in order to give more time to his other interests, especially Princeton.

Pyne was elected to the Princeton Board of Trustees in 1884, when he was twenty-eight. His election was engineered by President McCosh, who told Pyne's classmate, Henry Fairfield Osborn, that the Board was "full of old dotards" and that it badly needed "a fine young man" like Pyne.

His first concern was to organize the alumni in support of the College. He collected, and stimulated others to collect, information about alumni, which resulted in rich archival material and comprehensive address lists—a formative contribution to the present-day University Archives and Bureau of Alumni Records. With his classmate, Professor William Libbey, Jr., he prepared and published in 1888 the first edition of the modern Alumni Directory. He was one of the founders and first presidents of the Princeton Club of New York and helped establish other alumni associations throughout the country. In 1900 he took a leading part in the adoption of the plan for electing alumni trustees, and in the founding of the *Alumni Weekly*, serving as first chairman of its executive committee. In 1905 he was one of the organizers of the Committee of Fifty, the original forerunner of the Alumni Council. His classmate, Henry Fairfield Osborn, said Pyne "virtually created the modern alumni spirit" at Princeton.

As chairman of the trustees' committee on grounds and buildings, Pyne exerted a strong influence in favor of the use, originally suggested by Dean West, of collegiate Gothic for the buildings which were erected at the time of the Sesquicentennial in 1896. Two of these he himself built and gave to the University; they were named Upper and Lower Pyne in his honor (q.v.). Another was the Pyne Library, which he persuaded his mother to give.

Later, as chairman of the trustees' committee on finance, Pyne sought the necessary funds to finance President Wilson's preceptorial system and dipped into his own pocket yearly to meet whatever deficit remained. To provide housing for the influx of the original preceptors and other new faculty members, he acquired the necessary land and built twenty-three houses in the Broadmead section of town.

These he rented at modest charges during his lifetime and bequeathed to the University on his death.

At the same time Pyne took a deep interest in furthering Dean West's plans for the development of a residential graduate college. In 1905 he acquired Merwick, a mansion on Bayard Lane, which he made available to the University rent-free as a residence hall for graduate students, pending the erection of the Graduate College. When President Wilson proposed the Quad Plan for undergraduates in 1907, Pyne favored an experimental approach, but opposed its total adoption at that time because of the trustees' prior commitment to provide a residential graduate college.

After ex-president Grover Cleveland's death in 1908, Pyne gave up the finance committee chairmanship to take Cleveland's place as chairman of the committee on the graduate school. In this capacity he sided with Dean West's proposal to locate the graduate college at a distance from the main campus—in opposition to Wilson's wish to have it integrated with the undergraduate college.

On reunion day in 1910, in recognition of Pyne's twenty-five years of extraordinary service as trustee, the alumni presented him with a hand-wrought gold cup, eighteen inches high, its body ornamented with tiger lilies, its cover surmounted by a tiger resting on a base of four University shields. President Wilson, who made the presentation, told Pyne: "It has been in no small part through the stimulation of your example that hundreds of Princeton men have learned how to translate their affection into action." Pyne replied that when he thought of men like James McCosh and Grover Cleveland, he could only say,

"What have I done that you should thus honor me? Non sum dignus, amici."

After Wilson's resignation in the fall of 1910, Pyne was urged by his friends to accept the presidency of the University, but he refused because he felt he could be more useful as a trustee. He continued his efforts on behalf of the Graduate School, contributing funds for the construction of the Pyne Tower at the Graduate College and for the endowment of a professorship. After World War I he took a leading part as contributor and canvasser in the 1919 endowment campaign. Pyne's generosity to the University was matched by many acts of kindness, frequently anonymous, on behalf of faculty, students, alumni, and townspeople. A *New York Evening Post* editor, reflecting on Pyne's benefactions, wrote: "He went around doing good as Pater said of Leonardo, like a man on a secret errand."

Pyne's estate, "Drumthwacket," was for many years the focus for much of the social life of the University and the town. The grounds were always open to visitors, and many a Princetonian spent pleasant hours strolling along the path that led from a rustic gate on Lover's Lane past a deer park and through the woods to a series of small lakes amid flower gardens.

During Pyne's last illness, the trustees voted to name the first of the new post-World War I dormitories, then under construction, in his honor, and President Hibben was able to tell him of their intention and to secure his consent before he died.

The day he was buried, the whole community joined in tribute. University activities were suspended and all business stopped on Nassau Street. After the services at Drumthwacket the funeral cortege drove slowly through the grounds of the Graduate College, past the site of the Pyne Dormitory, by Upper and Lower Pyne, to the Fitz-Randolph Gateway where it entered the Campus. To the tolling of the Nassau Hall bell the procession passed through a student guard of honor to the steps of Nassau Hall, then westward around the rear of the building, and through the arches of Pyne Library, and then back to Nassau Street. After the procession left the Campus, the students walked down Witherspoon street in a body to the cemetary where they encircled the grave and awaited the arrival of the cortege.

In addition to the buildings and the professorship that bear his name, Pyne is remembered by the Pyne Honor Prize (q.v.), founded in 1921. His portrait hangs in Procter Hall of the Graduate College.

Pyne Hall, one of the largest undergraduate dormitories, enjoys the further distinction of having been in 1969 the first to house female candidates for bachelor degrees. It was designed by Day and Klauder and built in 1922 with funds given by the alumni. Entries are designated as gifts of the Classes of 1902, 1906, 1908, 1912, 1920, 1921, 1922, and 1923. It was named in memory of Moses Taylor Pyne 1877, a trustee of the University and one of its most generous benefactors (q.v.).

Pyne Honor Prize, The, established in 1921 by Mrs. May Taylor Moulton Hanrahan and named for her cousin M. Taylor Pyne, is awarded annually by the president on Alumni Day to that member of the senior class who has most clearly manifested excellent scholarship and effective support of the best interests of the University. It is the highest general distinction conferred upon an undergraduate.

Among those awarded the prize in earlier years were Charter Trustee H. Chapman Rose '28, President Robert F. Goheen '40, and United States Senator Paul S. Sarbanes '54. Reflecting the larger undergraduate body and the greater diversity of its interests, the prize in recent years has sometimes been shared by two or three seniors. Howard W. Bell, Jr. '70 was the first black to receive the prize, and Marsha H. Levy '73, the first woman.

Ramsay, David 1765 (1749-1815), physician, patriot, and historian, delivered what was probably the first Fourth of July oration ever given in America.

The son of a Scotch-Irish Pennsylvania farmer, Ramsay graduated from Princeton at the age of sixteen, and taught school for five years before undertaking the study of medicine at the College of Philadelphia. After receiving his bachelor of physic degree, he went to Charlestown, South Carolina, bearing a letter from his friend and medical teacher, Benjamin Rush 1760 (q.v.), who said he was "far superior to any person we ever graduated at our college." His practice in Charlestown was successful and his permanent contributions to medicine were recognized in 1789 when Yale granted him an honorary M.D. He was also active in politics, serving in the assembly and senate of South Carolina and the Continental Congress.

It was as an historian, however, that Ramsay made his most notable contribution. His works included *The History of the Revolution of South Carolina* (1785), *History of the American Revolution* (1789), *The History of South Carolina* (1809), and *History of the United States*, which remained unfinished at his death and was completed by his brother-in-law, S. Stanhope Smith (q.v.). (The second of Ramsay's three wives, all of whom predeceased him, was—like Mrs. Smith—a daughter of John Witherspoon.)

Modern historical scholarship has tended to dismiss the histories of the Revolution written by Ramsay, William Gordon, and others, but some historians have insisted on the importance of these early histories nevertheless. "What matters," Professor Frank Craven has said, "is that they were written and read, and that they present the first attempts by Americans to deal comprehensively with an important segment of our common history."

In 1965 Professor Page Smith of the University of California at Los Angeles published an extensive study of Ramsay's *History of the American Revolution* in which he stressed the advantage that accrued to Ramsay through his involvement in the events of which he wrote and the wisdom he exercised in availing himself of this opportunity. "The generosity of mind and spirit which marks his pages, his critical sense, his balanced judgment and compassion," Professor Smith concluded, "are gifts that were uniquely his own and that clearly entitle him to an honorable position in the front rank of American historians."

The Independence Day oration believed to be the first delivered in the United States was given by Ramsay on July 4, 1778. A century later it was asserted by some that William Gordon had delivered the first such oration in Boston in 1777. But the Reverend Mr. Gordon's discourse was a sermon, on a text from the third book of Kings in the Old Testament, preached before the General Court of Massachusetts, whereas Dr. Ramsay's was an oration on "the Advantages of American Independence" delivered to "a Publick Assembly of the Inhabitants of Charlestown in South Carolina"—a more likely forerunner of the Fourth of July orations that became a part of the American tradition.

Reeve, Tapping 1763 (1744-1823) was the founder of one of America's earliest and most important law schools. A classmate of the eminent jurist, William Paterson, Reeve taught for a number of years after graduation before going to Connecticut to read law in the office of Judge Root in Hartford. In 1773, he married Sally Burr, the daughter of Princeton's second president, and moved to Litchfield. He began giving law instruction in his office—his brother-in-law, Aaron Burr, Jr. 1772, was one of his first students —and in 1784, to accommodate a growing number of students, built a cottage next to his house, which became known as the Litchfield Law School.

Although not the first institution for instruction in the law—the first American chair of law was established at the College of William and Mary in 1779—Reeve's school represented a major advance in the development of legal education in this country.

Reeve operated the school single-handedly until 1798, when he was appointed to the Connecticut Supreme Court (of which he was later Chief Justice). He then invited James Gould, Yale 1791, who had just graduated from the school, to join him in its management. Reeve and Gould attracted students from almost every state in the Union, who came by horseback, steamboat, and stage to study law in their unheated, one-room school. Students received systematic instruction, with carefully prepared lectures and moot courts for practical instruction.

The school trained some of the most eminent men in public life in the early nineteenth century, including in addition to Aaron Burr, John C. Calhoun, Horace Mann, Noah Webster. It numbered among its some 1,000 graduates sixteen United States senators, fifty congressmen, forty justices of higher state courts, two justices of the United States Supreme Court, ten governors, and five cabinet officers.

Tapping Reeve retired from active connection with the school in 1820 when he was 76. Gould continued to lecture until 1833 when growing physical infirmity obliged him to close the school. Other law schools meantime had been founded at Harvard (1817), and Yale (1824).

Tapping Reeve's house and the law school are still standing in Litchfield.

Registrar, The, has been an officer of the College and the University since 1840. Originally he was a recent graduate who held the office briefly while also serving as tutor. Henry Nevius van Dyke 1872 (no relation to Henry van Dyke, the author) was the first long-term registrar; he served from 1873 to 1910. He was followed by Charles J. Jones '00, 1910-1918, who was succeeded by Fred LeRoy Hutson, 1918-1925. Hutson was known for his compassion. "He never stoops to rulings mean," the seniors sang in their Faculty Song, "We wish to God they'd make him Dean." Another spring they took a different turn: "If he had his dope down straight,/Half the class would get the gate." Hutson's successors have been Wilbur F. Kerr, 1925-1947, Howard W. Stepp, 1947-1969, and Bruce Finnie, 1969-

During van Dyke's tenure the registrar was first given an office of his own, located in Stanhope Hall. The registrar's office was moved to Nassau Hall in 1911 and to West College in 1959.

Originally the registrar kept the academic records of undergraduates only. Since 1970 the registrar has also kept the records of graduate students, previously the responsibility of the office of the dean of the graduate school.

Religion, The Department of. Speaking at the 1957 Alumni Day Luncheon in honor of Harold W. Dodds who was soon to retire as president, President Pusey of Harvard said:

> Because of a blindness which has infected much of modern education, Princeton appeared almost alone to be blazing a new trail when she set out to build a strong Department of Religion. This may well prove in time to have been not the least memorable achievement of an administration filled by constructive advance.

President Pusey was referring to a development in American higher education little noted outside Princeton in 1940, but by the early 1950s frequently emulated by many private colleges and universities and, more recently, by state universities and colleges.

By the appointment of George F. Thomas in 1940 as the University's first Professor of Religious Thought, Princeton was recognizing the lack of specific instruction in religion since the nineteenth century, when it had been taught as part of other academic disciplines, such as philosophy, literature, and history. More importantly, the University was affirming, in the words of the faculty committee created in 1935 to study the matter, that "the study of religion . . . is an intellectual discipline, and as such has a proper place in the curriculum of instruction of a university which pretends to devote itself to liberal studies."

Since the appointment of Thomas in 1940, the creation of a department in 1945, and the establishment of a graduate program in 1955, a strong group of teacher-scholars have together established the department's international reputation for excellent instruction and scholarship in religion. George Thomas in the Philosophy of Religion and R.B.Y. Scott in the Old Testament were honored authorities in their disciplines when they retired in 1968. Others, Horton M. Davies and John F. Wilson in the History of Christianity; Paul Ramsey in Religious Ethics; Malcolm L. Diamond and Victor Preller in the Philosophy of Religion; and Philip H. Ashby in the History of Religion, have striven to maintain the standards of excellence of Scott and Thomas. They, and their junior colleagues, know that they are engaged in a still pioneering and exciting endeavor. They receive frequent inquiries from other universities seeking to learn from Princeton's past experience, present methods, and future plans. Other members of the faculty have gone on to Brown, Duke, Harvard, Pennsylvania, Syracuse, the University of California at Los Angeles, Yale, and other universities from which they report that their Princeton experience was invaluable in developing their conception of religion as an academic discipline in the humanities.

But what of the undergraduate program, the primary reason for the department's existence? During Thomas's first year at Princeton, 21 students elected courses in religion. Fifteen years later, in 1955, over 700 students took at least one course in the department and 28 upperclassmen concentrated in religion. In the 1960s and 70s yearly enrollments were as high as 1300, with as many as 69 concentrators. The majority of students concentrating in religion head toward careers in medicine, law, teaching, and business; they study religion because they recognize, in the words of the faculty committee of 1935, that it "is an independent power, the study of which is worthy of an independent place . . . as an element of liberal culture and as one of the humanities."

Nor has Princeton been content to pioneer only in the undergraduate study of religion. Since the establishment of the graduate program in 1955, Princeton, along with a few other universities not associated with divinity schools or seminaries, has been a leader in establishing high standards for the scholarly study of religion. Its Ph.D.'s now teach in colleges and universities in the United States, Canada, Australia, Japan, and the Union of South Africa. A comparative study of graduate education in religion sponsored by the American Council of Learned Societies in 1971 reported: "Princeton is clearly established in the front rank according to all the objective indices and has been the most rigorously disciplined."

The 1935 faculty committee's careful study of the place of religion in the study of the humanities, the appointment of George F. Thomas with his dedication to teaching and concern for scholarly rigour, the vigorous support of Presidents Dodds, Goheen, and Bowen—all of these have combined to establish Princeton as the leader in an area of study that before 1940 was almost totally ignored by the leading universities of America.

Philip H. Ashby

Research Board, University, a university-wide committee formed in 1959, is composed of members of the faculty and administration. The Board, advisory to the president, recommends policy in the acceptance and administration of research grants and contracts throughout the University and gives general supervision to the implementation of policy. Its administrative arm is the Office of Research and Project Administration, formed at the same time as the Board.

During its existence the Board has supervised sponsored research on a remarkable variety of subjects. Computerized music and an orbiting astronomical observatory; the editing of the Thoreau papers and the engineering application of laser beams; continental drift and Fifth Century BC excavations in Sicily; moon rocks and the luminescence of fireflies—these represent but a few of the more than 700 research projects that have fallen within its oversight annually.

The Board's immediate predecessor was the Committee on Project Research and Invention, which had been established in 1946 under a directive from George A. Brakeley, vice president and treasurer of the University. Initial membership included Brakeley, Kenneth H. Condit (Dean of Engineering), Henry DeW. Smyth (Chairman of the Department of Physics), Hugh S. Taylor (Dean of the Graduate School), who served as first chairman, and Raymond J. Woodrow, who was executive officer and secretary.

When the Research Board succeeded the Project Research Committee in 1959, Professor Smyth, who had served as chairman of the committee for several years, became the Board's first chairman, serving, as have his successors, with the rank of dean. The new Board was drawn from the faculty (some appointed by the president and some elected by the faculty) as well as from the senior administration. The other original members were Ricardo A. Mestres (University Treasurer), Raymond Woodrow, Carlos H. Baker (English), Joseph R. Strayer (History), Donald F. Hornig (Chemistry), Lester V. Chandler (Economics), Arthur K. Parpart (Biology), and Joseph C. Elgin (Dean of Engineering).

Smyth served as Chairman through June 1966. His successors have been Lyman Spitzer, Jr. (Astrophysical Sciences), 1966-1972, Sheldon Judson (Geological and Geophysical Sciences), 1972-1977, and Robert M. May (Biology) since September 1, 1977.

By 1976 about $50 million was being spent annually on sponsored research. Of this amount, $30 million went to the Plasma Physics Laboratory on the Forrestal Campus for its attempts to control fusion as a peaceful energy source, and some $20 million of sponsored research was conducted by the several departments and programs on the main campus. About 95 percent of the funds represented federal grants and contracts. Exclusive of Plasma Physics, 54 percent of the research funds were for Natural Sciences, 29 percent, Engineering and Applied Science, 12 percent, Humanities and Social Science, and 5 percent, Interdepartmental Programs.

Through various subcommittees, the University Research Board has oversight of expenditures from the Higgins Trust (shared equally with Columbia, Harvard and Yale), the Scientific Research Fund of the University, as well as institutional grants from the National Science Foundation and the National Institutes of Health. In addition, the Board ensures the conformance of University practice with certain governmental regulations such as, for example, those governing research involving experimentation with animals, the use of human subjects, and the use of biohazardous materials. The Board originally had supervision of the senior professional and technical staffs that are organized into ladders parallel with those of the faculty. In 1975 this function was transferred to a committee (with the University Research Board Chairman as presiding officer), which reported to the dean of the faculty. This group, informally known as the "committee-of-seven," is a counterpart of the so-called "committee-of-three," which advises the president on appointments, promotions, and salaries of faculty members.

Over the years, general policies for the conduct of sponsored research have developed, and the University Research Board reviews each piece of proposed research in the light of these policies, e.g., that research at Princeton should promote the education of students, both undergraduate and graduate, and that it should provide for the advancement of knowledge and for its preservation and dissemination. The University does not administer funds whose purpose and character cannot be publicly disclosed nor does it accept contracts or grants for the support of classified research except under the most extraordinary conditions.

Sheldon Judson

Reserve Officers Training Corps (R.O.T.C.) at Princeton began quietly in the fall of 1919 with the establishment of an army field artillery unit. Princeton was "an ideal location" for such a unit, according to Major John McMahon, Jr., the first Professor of Military Science and Tactics. "It is out in the country where there is plenty of available land for riding," he wrote. "The soft country roads are only a few minutes ride from the stables, thus affording the students a wonderful opportunity to ride in the midst of the pleasantest surroundings." The military training unit under his command soon included a half dozen Regular Army officers, two dozen enlisted men, a battery of French '75s, and ninety horses.

The field artillery unit remained horse-drawn long after Nassau Street was clogged by automobiles; indeed, the first trucks did not make a caisson roll till 1937, and "seventy horses" were still listed in the 1940 catalogue. A course on Hippology and Military Law was offered in the 1922 catalogue ("The conformation of the horse, lameness and disease, age by the teeth, bitting, stable hygiene, shoeing, gaits . . .") and, about the same time, polo was established as an intercollegiate sport at Princeton (indoor champions in 1921) with polo ponies furnished the ROTC by the War Department.

The start of the program in 1919, coming so soon after the Armistice that ended the "war to end all wars," had not been a propitious time to start military training on the campus. Early enrollments lagged, but an unlikely combination—the *Daily Princetonian* and President John Grier Hibben ("We all pray . . . we may never have to undertake another war, but the fallacy of unpreparedness would be . . . a great national sin.")—urged students to participate. By late fall, 127 had enrolled, and in 1925 the number had grown to 600. By the time of Pearl Harbor, more than 2,000 Princetonians had been comissioned in the field artillery. Many of them served in World War II, and some gave their lives. One ROTC graduate, Lt. Colonel John U.D. Page '26, later won the Medal of Honor and lost his life at the Pusan Reservoir in Korea.

Suspended during World War II, the Army unit was reactivated in 1946— this time with 2½ ton trucks and 105-mm. howitzers. With the establishment of a Naval ROTC unit in 1946 and an Air Force unit in 1951, ROTC became a significant presence on campus, with annual reviews, military balls, and commissioning by the president as part of Class Day ceremonies. The Cold War and the draft exemption for ROTC students, along with the scholarships offered by the three services, and a chance for a commission, pushed enrollments to an all-time high of 1107 undergraduates in 1951. But even with the support given ROTC by Presidents Hibben and Dodds, there were always some who questioned the presence of a military training unit on a liberal arts campus. As early as 1927, an article in the *Alumni Weekly* had foreshadowed the principal arguments later put forth against ROTC when it declared that "the course is not . . . properly . . . a part of a University curriculum, . . . and . . . is detrimental to the furtherance of permanent peace, toward which the University . . . should constantly strive."

In the 1950s these problems multiplied. Faculty grew restive about granting academic credit for ROTC courses; students were increasingly reluctant to give up one course a semester for ROTC; and a number of professional associations, most notably in engineering, threatened not to accredit programs that gave course credit for ROTC. The University, under the leadership of Dean J. Douglas Brown, made an effort to add academic substance to ROTC by creating a series of special, alternative University-taught courses—in psychology, politics, economics, and military history. Army and Air Force responded; but the Navy, which valued the "readily employable ensign," did not. The "Princeton Plan" for reforming ROTC found little support outside the University and, even locally, proved at best a short-run solution to a mounting problem.

In the 1960s, as Vietnam emerged as the great issue on campus, enrollments dwindled and tensions mounted. By 1964 there had been a 70 percent decline to only 334 in all three units. Student groups, the Undergraduate Assembly, and members of the faculty began to insist upon an end to course credit for ROTC, as well as to departmental standing for ROTC programs and faculty status for on-campus military officers. President Goheen appointed a special faculty committee, which recommended such changes, and in the spring of 1969, the faculty overwhelmingly approved proposals that, in effect, converted ROTC into non-credit programs with the status of extra-curricular activities.

The invasion of Cambodia in May 1970 (when there were a mere 113 students in ROTC) brought the high point of campus anti-militarism—a firebombing of the Armory. A month later, the trustees approved a proposal by faculty and students to terminate all three ROTC programs no later than June of 1972.

Yet within a year—paralleling the unanticipated pendulum swing of student opinion that came with the end of the draft and the winding down of the war—students in a 1971 Undergraduate Assembly referendum voted in favor of retaining ROTC under the conditions set by the faculty in 1969. Although the Air Force and the Navy were unwilling to accept the University's requirements and closed down their programs, the Army agreed to the contract the trustees offered in June 1972. That fall ROTC quietly returned to Princeton—not as field artillery and not for course credit, but as a non-credit elective program of officer education. Thereafter, growth was modest but sustained. By 1976, seventy-four students (thirteen of them women) were enrolled, with the prospect of the first co-ed being commissioned in 1978.

Richard D. Challener

Residential, dining, and social facilities for undergraduates, which now occupy some fifty University buildings, were once concentrated in Nassau Hall, after the College of New Jersey moved to Princeton from Newark in 1756.

All undergraduates lived in Nassau Hall (or had lodgings in town) until 1833, when the first dormitory, East College, was built. As other dormitories were erected, Nassau Hall in time was taken over exclusively for administrative and faculty use, but one or two students continued to live there as late as 1903.

By 1973, when Spelman Halls, the first to offer apartment living, were completed, Princeton had built forty dormitories, all but six of which were still being used for their original purpose. Three had been razed: East College in 1896, Upper Pyne in 1963, and Reunion Hall in 1965. Three had been converted to other uses: Lower Pyne in 1950 for business offices, Seventy-Nine Hall and West College in the early 1960s for departments of instruction, and administrative offices, respectively.

Nassau Hall also contained the College's dining room and kitchen (originally in the basement, later in a connecting wing) until 1804, when they were moved to the first floor of Philosophical Hall, built that year where Chancellor Green now stands. For a dozen years, starting in 1834, a second refectory, situated on William Street, supplied board at a cheaper rate for those desiring it (one dollar and fifty cents a week rather than the regular two dollars). Students called it the "poor house."

Meals in those early days were Spartan. Breakfast often consisted of bread and butter with coffee, supper of bread and butter with milk and occasionally chocolate. Students sometimes filled out their meagre evening fare by stealing chickens or turkeys in town and roasting them over their chamber fires—a common college custom at that time. Mid-day dinner was more adequate, usually offering meat, fish, or poultry, potatoes, fresh vegtables in season, "small beer and cyder," and sometimes for desert "pye" or cake. Not surprisingly, one of the rules for refectory conduct issued in 1759 directed that "none shall eagerly catch at a share, but wait till he is served in turn."

In diaries and in letters home, students complained about the poor quality and sameness of their meals. In the 1840s their protest began taking a forceful turn: at a given signal, up would go the windows and out would fly the tablecloths and all that was on them.

Beginning in 1843 students were permitted to take their meals with families in town, where the cost was somewhat higher than in the college refectory, although in some cases, the college catalog announced, "select associations of students have been formed, whose expenses do not exceed $1.25 a week."

The college refectory gradually lost out in competition with the local boardinghouses and was finally closed in 1856 (as Harvard's had been, for similar reasons, seven years earlier). The "select associations of students" in boarding-houses grew in number and gradually evolved into a system of eating clubs (q.v.). Attempts to revive the college commons in 1877 and 1891 failed, and it was not until 1906 and 1908 that first freshman, and then sophomore, commons were instituted in the old University Hall. Their place in campus life was made more secure in 1916 by the erection of Madison Hall (q.v.).

WILSON'S QUAD PLAN

Two years after introducing the preceptorial system, President Wilson tried to translate its principles into a plan for the social reorganization of the University which he also hoped would check the domination of the eating clubs and thus rectify what he feared was "the almost imperceptible and yet increasingly certain decline of the old democratic spirit of the place." The Quad Plan called for the establishment of residential quadrangles or colleges, each with its own dining hall, common room, resident master, and resident preceptors. Every undergraduate would be required to live in a college, the particular one to be determined by lot or assignment. Although the trustees approved the Quad Plan in principle, they later withdrew their support in response to the opposition of club alumni and undergraduates, and their own concern about the cost.

After the defeat of Wilson's Quad Plan, a campus center, strongly favored by President Hibben, was frequently urged as a means of improving the fabric of student life. Plans for a million dollar complex containing a University club, theater, and quarters for undergraduate activities were announced in the mid-twenties, but suspended during the depression. A campus center for servicemen established in Murray-Dodge during World War II continued in use for undergraduates until 1954 when the University created Chancellor Green Student Center (q.v.), renovating the north wing of Pyne Library for the cafeteria, and the large reading room in Chancellor Green Library for the main lounge. The Center's accessibility made it an instant success. To meet the heavy patronage of students, faculty, and staff, a second cafeteria was set up in the main lounge. When the legal age for drinking was lowered to eighteen in 1973, a pub was installed there also, and student bartenders began serving draught beer, wine, and soft drinks, and student cooks started to bake "the best pizza in town."

In the late 1960s a special committee of the trustees working with the faculty committee on undergraduate life concluded that more diverse social opportunities were needed—not only to reduce the disproportionate emphasis on membership in the upperclass eating clubs but also to create an improved social environment for all undergraduates. These objectives soon began to take shape, and by the time the University entered the seventies, it could offer students a variety of alternatives ranging from a modified version of the club life of earlier years to an approach to Wilson's ideal of residential colleges. Though some eating clubs became non-selective and two were converted in 1969 to a University-operated social facility, named Stevenson Hall (q.v.), others continued to maintain their former autonomy.

Modern Princeton's first approach to the Quad Plan had come in 1968 with the creation of Wilson College (q.v.). Two years later when additional space was needed following the advent of coeducation, the Princeton Inn College (q.v.) was founded. Another option first offered in this period was the student-organized Madison Society, a low-cost alternative to the eating clubs that provided up to two hundred members varied dining opportunities— breakfast at Wilcox Hall, lunch at Commons or the Student Center, and "candlelight and beer" dinners in the restaurant atop the New South Building. Some hardy "independents" preferred to choose their own bill of fare, sometimes by shopping around in restaurants, more often by cooking their meals in dormitory kitchens.

All things considered, Princetonians of the 1970s were faring better than their hungry forebears in the lean days of the college refectory.

Reunion Hall, a five-story dormitory, was built in 1870 to commemorate the reunion of the Old and New Schools of the Presbyterian Church. It was razed in 1965 after it had been condemned as a fire hazard. The space it occupied between Stanhope Hall and West College has been left open. During his short stay at Princeton, John F. Kennedy (q.v.) lived in this dormitory.

Reunions of alumni classes began soon after the Civil War, and with them class gifts. At its tenth reunion the Class of 1859 endowed a senior prize in English, and at *its* tenth, the Class of 1860 founded a graduate fellowship in experimental science. When the Class of 1866 observed its decennial, it gave the College the clock in the cupola of Nassau Hall.

By the 1890s class reunions at Commencement time had become fairly numerous. They were modest affairs at first: meetings held in classrooms in old

Dickinson Hall or Nassau Hall, followed by a dinner in University Hall or the old Princeton Inn. Stimulated by an alumni torchlight procession at the Sesquicentennial (q.v.) which brought 2,000 alumni back to Princeton in 1896, attendance at reunions grew and programs became more elaborate, sometimes lasting two or three days. Houses were rented to accommodate class members, bands engaged for their entertainment (and to welcome classmates arriving by train), and various means of identification gradually adopted—class banners, hatbands, blazers, costumes. Later, beginning in the early 1950s, headquarters and sleeping quarters were provided on the Campus for most major reunions.

Very early it became the custom for each class to have a major reunion at five-year intervals following graduation. For these occasions alumni have made a determined effort to return to Princeton even from distant places. In between, at the "off year" reunions, a smaller number keep the pilot light burning.

The twenty-fifth reunion, when most alumni have reached the peak of their careers, has come to be regarded as the most important of all, and the twenty-fifth year class has accordingly been given the place of honor at the head of the Alumni Parade (q.v.). The Class of 1942 dramatically demonstrated the importance of a twenty-fifth reunion when, in 1967, it gave more than $300,000 to Annual Giving (q.v.), the first class to do so. It brought back to its reunion that year another gift, the Nassau Hall bell clapper it had stolen in what was a traditional freshman year prank, and, having had the clapper split in two, gave half to the golden anniversary Class of 1917 and half to the graduating Class of 1967.

The fiftieth has come to be another big reunion. There is usually a large turnout of septuagenarians who step out briskly when the Alumni Parade leaves the front of Nassau Hall. One alumnus, Dr. William H. Vail 1865, walked fifty miles to attend his fiftieth, reaching the campus just in time to join his classmates in the Parade to and around University Field—"the last mile."

The Class of 1887's sixty-fifth reunion dinner at Merwick, Bishop Matthews' home on Bayard Lane, was attended by five of the seven living members of the class and several relatives. It started out rather sadly, when one man noted that classmates had begun to drop off soon after the fiftieth reunion and that by the time the sixtieth came two-thirds had gone. Bishop Matthews served some excellent Burgundy (the class historian recorded) and spirits gradually lifted. Banter and jokes followed, and one of the sons present was moved to compliment himself on having picked '87 for his father's class. Toward the end of the evening, following more stories and reminiscences, one man exclaimed that if President McCosh were present he would say that 1887 was the greatest class that ever graduated. Then after a few seconds' reflection, he wryly added, "as he said of every class."

The sixty-fifth is usually the last major reunion, although there is on record at least one later one. In 1967, two members of the Class of 1897, Paul Bedford and Leander H. Shearer, sat down together in the lobby of the Princeton Inn and there received a formal visit from President Goheen on the occasion of their seventieth reunion.

While a member of the faculty and during his presidency of the University, Woodrow Wilson 1879 attended all of his class's reunions. In 1914 he came up from Washington for his thirty-fifth, but in 1919, because he was in Paris for the Peace Conference, he was obliged to send his regrets to his classmates when they gathered for their fortieth. "I shall miss what would be the greatest possible refreshment to me in meeting the boys then," he cabled his friend and classmate Robert Bridges a few days before the reunion, "and so I beg that you will give them the most affectionate messages from me and tell them how cheering it is to me always to think of their friendship and of the old days we spent together."

Norman Thomas '05, clergyman and perennial Socialist candidate for president, rarely—if ever—missed a reunion of his class. "Some things in life justify themselves emotionally, without necessity for analytic reasoning," he once said. "On the whole, Princeton reunions fall in that category. In my moralizing moments, I may regret that reunions are too greatly inspired by the prayer: 'Make me a sophomore again just for tonight,' which prayer, with the aid of a sometimes excessive consumption of the spirituous, rather than the spiritual, often seems to be granted."

Sometimes reunion days are extended. In 1969 thirty classmates topped off the Class of 1939's thirtieth reunion by flying to Russia. There, according to the *New York Times*, they gave the first rendition of "Old Nassau" ever heard in Moscow University.

Even more distant duties than Wilson's in Paris have kept a class notable away. In 1973 astronaut Charles Conrad, Jr., sent word to his reunion chairman that he could not be present at 1953's twentieth because "he was out of town on business." He sent his message from the country's first space station, Skylab I, to the Johnson Space

Center at Houston, which relayed it to Princeton.

CLASS ATTENDANCE AWARDS

In 1912 the Class of 1901 gave a silver cup to be awarded annually to the class having the largest proportion of its living members present at a reunion. Attendance of winners has ranged from 52 percent (the Class of 1919 at its fiftieth) to 77.3 percent (the Class of 1898 at its twenty-fifth). The winner in 1916, the Class of 1866, had 18 of 27 classmates present at its fiftieth reunion; their attendance percentage was especially appropriate and pleasing to them: 66.66.

Other awards were begun in the 1930s: the 1921 plaque for the greatest number at a major reunion, the Class of 1894 bowl for the largest percentage at an off-year reunion, the Class of 1915 cup for the greatest number at an off-year reunion. Another one was begun in 1967: the Class of 1912 trophy for the largest percentage present at the reunion of a class graduated more than fifty years.

Rhodes Scholarships, for study at Oxford University in England, have been awarded to some 140 Princeton undergraduates since their founding early in this century. Each year, thirty-two American scholars are chosen from more than 600 applicants for their "intellectual attainment, character, leadership, and physical vigor." In many years there have been at least two Princeton recipients, and frequently three or four, and in 1960 and 1976 there were five. In the twenty years between 1950 and 1970, Princeton was represented every year. The Class of 1925 was represented by six Rhodes Scholars—more than any other Princeton class.

Princeton Rhodes Scholars have for the most part followed professional careers—law, medicine, the ministry, and education. Those in public service have included Supreme Court Justice John M. Harlan '20, Career Ambassador William W. Butterworth, Jr. '25, Attorney General Nicholas DeB. Katzenbach '43, and Senator Paul S. Sarbanes '54. There have been a number of college presidents: William E. Stevenson '22 (Oberlin), Paul S. Havens '25 (Wilson), Caleb F. Gates, Jr. '26 (University of Denver), James Harlan Cleveland '38 (University of Hawaii), and James McN. Hester '46 (New York University and United Nations University). Princeton called back seven Scholars to teach classics, English, or history: Paul R. Coleman-Norton '19, Donald A. Stauffer '23, E.D.H. Johnson '34, Gordon A. Craig '36, James H. Billington '50, Arthur W. Litz, Jr. '51, and Neil L. Rudenstine '56 (later Provost). Among those in medicine have been two classmates in 1913: Wilder Penfield, the brain surgeon, and Wilburt C. Davison, Dean of the Duke University Medical School, and among those in music, Frank E. Taplin '37, President of the Metropolitan Opera. Journalists include John B. Oakes '34, editor of the *New York Times* editorial page.

Henry Allison Page III, Rhodes Scholar in 1935, was killed in action in World War II and awarded a Congressional Medal of Honor. Dan Sachs, Rhodes Scholar in 1960, who was an outstanding football player, died in 1967 after a three-year struggle with cancer. In his memory, friends, classmates, and fellow football players established a scholarship enabling a graduating senior who desires, like him, to go into public service, to study abroad, as he did.

The best known Princeton Rhodes

Scholar in recent years has been basketball All-American and Olympic gold medalist Bill Bradley '65.

Rittenhouse Orrery, The, one of Princeton's oldest instruments for the teaching of science, is on display in the lobby of Peyton Hall. Devised to represent the motions of the planets about the sun, orreries were regarded as essential teaching equipment of eighteenth-century lecturers on "natural philosophy." They derived their name from the Earl of Orrery, for whom one of the most famous was built in England about 1713.

Princeton's Rittenhouse Orrery is the first of two remarkably accurate orreries made by the Pennsylvania clockmaker and self-educated astronomer, David Rittenhouse. He made the second one for the College of Philadelphia, now the University of Pennsylvania. Princeton's orrery was purchased by President Witherspoon and installed in Nassau Hall in 1771. It was damaged during the Revolution and later repaired. It was in active use for about a half-century; thereafter it became merely a curiosity and did not come to attention again until it was exhibited at the World's Fair in Chicago in 1893. Then it disappeared and was thought permanently lost until it was discovered, in 1948, still crated, in the basement of McCosh Hall. Through the generosity of Bernard Peyton '17, it was once more restored and given a place of honor in Firestone Library until Peyton Hall was built. In the restoration one concession was made to the twentieth century: electric motors were added to provide smooth motive power, thus eliminating the damage to the intricate wheelwork which in earlier days resulted from hasty and irregular turning of the crank that set the orrery in motion.

Romance Languages and Literatures, The Department of. The first romance language ever taught at Princeton was smuggled in by none other than President John Witherspoon. As early as 1769, when only Hebrew, Greek, and Latin were respectable enough to warrant inclusion in the curriculum, Witherspoon himself offered, free-of-charge, extracurricular instruction in French, as did also outside teachers who were engaged by the students for a fee. Not until 1830 did the College appoint a regular instructor of French and Spanish, Louis Hargous, who taught these languages until 1836. Hargous was followed by Benedict Jaeger, who became a one-man language department, offering German, Italian, French, and Spanish, all as Professor of Modern Languages, a rubric that lasted till 1958, when by amoeba-like fission the Department of Modern Languages divided into the two Departments of Germanic and Romance Languages and Literatures.

Although Hargous, Jaeger, and their followers had faculty standing, no academic credit was given for their offerings. A century after Witherspoon's early efforts, President McCosh made instruction in modern languages a regular part of the curriculum for which credit was given. Finally, in 1904, Woodrow Wilson raised the living languages to a par with the dead ones, when he created the present organization of departments, among them Modern Languages.

During the administration of the first chairman, Williamson U. Vreeland, 1904 to 1913, Wilson summoned a generation of fine teacher-scholars to the department: Christian Gauss (q.v.),

Douglas L. Buffum, Donald Clive Stuart, and Percy A. Chapman. From here on, the stars in the department's *Pléiade* become too numerous to be accorded the space they deserve; but not to be forgotten is their predecessor, the inimitable Frank L. Critchlow (remembered in the Faculty Song as "hatless, coatless, kids in hand") who contributed rare humor, coupled with solid scholarship in the little-known Catalan language.

Of the "preceptor guys" Wilson appointed in 1905, Gauss was beyond question the most spectacular. He is remembered by alumni not only as a brilliant lecturer and preceptor but also as twice chairman of the department (1913-1936, 1943-1946), as dean of the college for almost twenty years, and as a wise expositor of American college life.

A dozen years after the first preceptors, two outstanding scholars were called from Johns Hopkins: Charles C. Marden, first Emory L. Ford Professor of Spanish, and Edward C. Armstrong. Marden became internationally known as editor, and twice as discoverer, of medieval Spanish texts. Armstrong was the founder of the famed Elliott monographs in romance studies, and head of a research project on the medieval Alexander romances. Under Armstrong's guidance as director, graduate studies prospered greatly. Among the first to earn Princeton Ph.D.'s in the early twenties were F. Courtney Tarr, later second Ford Professor, and Ira O. Wade, chairman from 1946 to 1958.

For the first two decades, the department was staffed primarily by native Americans, but in 1923 it imported Augusto Centeno from Spain and Maurice Coindreau from France. Centeno became a popular lecturer and preceptor; Coindreau, through his sensitive translations, acquainted France with American authors such as Faulkner, Hemingway, and Dos Passos.

About this time Kenneth McKenzie accepted a professorship in Italian, and Alfred L. Foulet was called to assist Armstrong, whose Alexander studies he continued splendidly. A little later the department took in two young Princeton graduates who became fixtures in their specialties: E.B.O. Borgerhoff in French classicism, and Raymond S. Willis in Spanish middle ages and renaissance.

After 1930 the department's reputation attracted an imposing array of scholars who served as visiting professors, such as André Maurois, P. Laumonier, Salvador de Madariaga, and R. Lapesa.

Under a different policy, Princeton called to tenure appointments three foreign scholars: a Frenchman, Gilbert Chinard; an Italian, Giuliano Bonfante; and a Spaniard, Américo Castro. Bonfante's stay was relatively brief; Chinard and Castro left indelible impressions on Princeton. Chinard's specialty was eighteenth-century America and its relations with France, and it created deep and lasting interest among students and faculty. Castro revolutionized Spanish historiography with his thesis that Spain was born of the symbiotic relationship of three medieval "castes": Christians, Muslims, and Jews.

In the wake of World War II, far-reaching changes to the department took place. Language learning by listening and speaking, as developed by the army, was instituted under the guidance of Archibald T. MacAllister, Jr. Russian, a wartime innovation, was expanded into a field of literary study, chiefly by two women, Ludmilla Turkevich and Valentine Bill; and it remained with Romance Languages until it was converted into an independent department in 1961.

Another important postwar change was introduced by soft-spoken Ira Wade, who turned out to be a radical innovator, devising unprecedented schemes to convert young Americans into world citizens. With the cooperation of foreign business, students were placed in summer jobs in Europe and Latin America, and they also did research there on anything from labor problems to contemporary poetry. Wade's Special Program in European Civilization (including Latin America at first) eventually enlisted the collaboration of four social science and six humanistic departments, from whose offerings students tailored their own programs on the civilization of a foreign land.

Even after the separation of German and Russian, the department steadily increased its offerings. By 1974 it presented seventy undergraduate, one-term courses for which there were 2,000 student elections. The program included French, Italian, Portuguese, and Spanish; also offered were linguistics, European literature in English translations, and, at the graduate level, medieval Provençal and Catalan literature.

Faculty recruitments, beginning in the late 1940s, strengthened the department in medieval and modern languages, literature, civilization, and linguistics. They included Blanchard W. Bates, Edward D. Sullivan, later chairman and then dean of the college; Edmund L. King, another chairman; Vicente Llorens; Armand Hoog; Leon-Francois Hoffman; Albert Sonnenfeld; Karl D. Uitti, also chairman; Antonio Alatorre; Victor H. Brombert; J. Lionel Gossman and Sylvia Molloy,

the first woman in the University ever to be promoted "from the ranks" to tenure (in 1973). Together with their associates, they have formed a team of romance scholars whose distinction has been recognized the world over.

Raymond S. Willis

Root, Robert Kilburn (1877-1950), Chaucer scholar and fourth dean of the faculty, first came to Princeton in the spring of 1905. President Wilson had written him about the University's plan to institute the preceptorial system and had asked whether it would be convenient for Root to come down from New Haven for an interview.

As he journeyed to Princeton on a bright day in April, Root later recalled, he had misgivings "as to this new-fangled method of teaching and more personally as to whether a Yale man could be happy in Princeton." His interview lasted some forty minutes. Wilson asked Root no questions about himself but spoke "with winning eloquence" about his plans for Princeton.

"Before five minutes had passed," Root remembered, "I knew that I was in the presence of a very great man . . . that I never before talked face to face with so compelling a person. Before the talk was over my loyalties were entirely committed to him. Had Woodrow Wilson asked me to go with him and work under him while he inaugurated a new university in Kamchatka or Senegambia I would have said 'yes' without further question."

This loyalty and devotion, Root said, were shared by the other teacher-scholars who made up the original group of preceptors; they felt that "they were embarked upon a great educational adventure under the immediate guidance of a great and wise innovator."

Root committed his loyalty and devotion to President Hibben after Wilson left to enter political life, and to President Dodds after Hibben retired, and when Root's turn came (in his own phrase) "to go on the retirement shelf" some forty years after his first interview with Wilson, the trustees declared that his life and labor here had been "informed by a union of critical judgment and unabashed partisanship in all things Princetonian."

Root proved adept in the use of the "new-fangled method of teaching," and eventually earned the distinction of having led the longest-lived preceptorial group in Princeton's history. A group of men in the Classes of 1917, 1918, and 1919 who had enjoyed their preceptorials with him as undergraduates asked him to lead an alumni preceptorial group after graduation. Starting in the 1920s and continuing until his death in 1950 they met with him two or three times a year for dinner at one of the eating clubs, followed by a preceptorial discussion of some literary work.

Root was also a popular lecturer. Whether the subject was Chaucer, Eighteenth Century Literature, or The Elements of the English Language ("Root's Roots" the students called it), his lectures were models of organization and lucidity. Every year in Root's Roots he analyzed the probable origin of the surname of each student in the course.

His graduate seminars were infused with rigorous intellectual discipline, and many students who were trained by him were forever grateful, as one of them put it, "because he first sharpened" their "instruments of precise thought."

Root wrote many articles and books on Chaucer, Shakespeare, and Pope. His most important work was a definitive edition of Chaucer's *Troilus and Criseyde* (1928). In the course of his study of this poem Root performed a notable piece of literary detective work. Scholars had long been puzzled over the date of the writing of *Troilus*, which they variously placed some time between 1373 and 1386. Root thought perhaps he had found a clue in the lines of the poem beginning "The bent moone with hire hornes pale, / Saturne and Jove, in Cancro joyned were." He wondered if the astronomical phenomenon thus described—the conjunction of Saturn, Jupiter and the crescent Moon (her horns pale from the lingering twilight) in the sign of Cancer—was possible; and he speculated that if it were, Chaucer might have used it because it occurred when he was writing the poem. Root consulted his colleague, Professor Henry Norris Russell, the astrophysicist, who said that the conjunction of the three heavenly bodies within a single segment of the heavens was possible, but extremely infrequent. After complicated calculations Russell informed Root that the configuration described by Chaucer would have occurred in the month of May or early June of 1385, for the first time in six hundred years.

Root then carried the study a step further. In the poem the unusual heavenly configuration was followed by a violent thunderstorm, which prevented Criseyde from leaving her uncle's home after having supper with him and thus resulted in her first encounter with Troilus. From his studies of medieval astrology Root knew that the conjunction of the two planets and the Moon in the sign of Cancer would be followed by a deluge and wondered if he could find evidence of such a storm. On consulting the chronicles of the medieval historian, Thomas Walsingham, he discovered that a terrific thunderstorm had in fact flooded England in July 1385.

From these findings Root and Russell concluded, in a joint paper in the *Publications of the Modern Language Association of America* (1924), that *Troilus and Criseyde* was not finished earlier than the spring or summer of 1385, thus establishing the fact that *Troilus* was a product of Chaucer's mature years, written shortly before he began the *Canterbury Tales*.

Among his publications, Root took pride, according to his colleagues, "in slyly including" a volume on *Machine Gun Sights for Aircraft Use*, which he wrote while serving as a major of ordnance in World War I.

Root became dean of the faculty when Harold W. Dodds assumed the presidency in 1933 and was able to help achieve economies which permitted the University to avoid salary cuts during the depression of the 1930s.

In World War II Root showed a capacity to deal with complexities as he guided the faculty and adjusted the curriculum to the sudden shifts and strains brought on by the war. At the end of the war, the trustees asked him to continue in office a year after he reached the age for retirement so that he might contribute his wisdom and experience to the initiation of the University's program for returning servicemen.

"To all of his many activities," his faculty colleagues said, "he brought unfailing qualities of integrity and self-sacrifice. . . . His opinions were sharp and clear; if at times they seemed impersonal or cold, their austerity stemmed from the high value he set upon institutions and order—whether of the law, or of the University, or of the Church."

Dean Root was an Episcopalian and a faithful communicant of Trinity Church. One November Sunday, Father Williams, who was then rector, thanked God, in his opening prayer, for Princeton's football victory over Yale the day before. At that point Dean Root got up and walked out. Undergraduates thought it was because he was a Yale graduate but older friends knew that in Bob Root's theology, not even a *Yale* football victory would be worthy of notice in a service of worship.

In his seventy-fourth year, he went to St. Louis to deliver a public lecture at Washington University on "The Fierce Indignation of Dean Swift." In the midst of an animated discussion about Alexander Pope while at lunch the day before his lecture, Dean Root suddenly died of a heart attack.

Dean Root had never married. He bequeathed to the trustees his house at 25 Mercer Street and the rights to all his published books and writings, and directed that the income be used for the purchase of books in English literature for the University Library. He also left the trustees some antique furniture he had used in the Dean's House and several pieces of presentation silver. One of them was a loving cup that had been presented to him by his alumni preceptorial group.

Roper Lane, which extends between Cap and Gown Club and Cottage Club from Prospect Avenue to the main entrance of Palmer Stadium, is named for William W. Roper '02, varsity football coach during the years 1906-1908, 1910-1911, and 1919-1930. This short passage way is a modest memorial, but on autumn Saturdays, when it is crowded with Princetonians inching their way to or from football games, it is a lively and appropriate one.

Bill Roper was, in President Dodds's phrase, "a vibrant personality." He was one of the last of the inspirational coaches; his staccato talks to the teams between halves and his oratorical periods at rallies before big games were histrionic masterpieces.

Roper's style was eclectic, opportunistic. He tended to borrow plays from teams that did well against Princeton. For example, in the fifth game of the 1919 season, West Virginia overwhelmed Princeton with its spread formation, 25 to 0. On the next two weekends, Princeton employed the same formation to good advantage, tying Harvard 10 to 10 and beating Yale 13 to 6.

Roper applied his gift for improvisation to language as well as to football. "The trouble with you," he once told a recalcitrant star, "is that you're too indegoddamnpendent."

Newspapermen called Roper an evangelist; his fiery talks at rallies before the big games did indeed have a smell of brimstone about them. In 1920, before the Harvard game in Cambridge, Roper, looking in profile like General Sherman, strode up and down the front of the platform in Alexander Hall where the Princeton team was seated, and going down the list of players on both teams, position by position, declared in each case that the Princeton player was plainly superior to his opposite number at Harvard. He then announced that he had purchased one-way railroad tickets for the team and that if they didn't win, they would have to make their own arrangements for getting home. Harvard and Princeton played a 14-14 tie game, so hard-fought and so exciting that no one

remembered to inquire whether any of the Princeton team had to walk home.

Roper was not a methodical type, and sometimes his associates had to improvise for him. In that same fall of 1920 Roper forgot about a Yale game invitation he had extended to some of his colleagues on the Philadelphia city council until a few days before the game, when all the seats had been sold. The best that George R. (Joe) Murray 1893, graduate manager of athletics, could do was to put a bench between the wooden stands and the goal-posts at the open end of the Stadium and to give Roper hand-written notes, instructing the ushers to seat the visiting councilmen there. As it turned out, these proved to be the best seats in the Stadium.

The game's first score came in the second quarter, when Frank Murrey drop-kicked a 34-yard field goal that sailed over the heads of the Philadelphia councilmen. Later Don Lourie, aided by Stan Keck's stalwart blocking, sprinted forty-seven yards across the goal-line and touched the ball down a few yards from their feet, and Keck placed-kicked the ball over their heads for the extra point.

In the third quarter, Captain Mike Callahan recovered a Yale fumble on the Yale fifteen-yard line and crossed the goal line right in front of the councilmen for a touchdown, and Keck sent the ball over their heads for the extra point. Later, with Lourie holding, Keck place-kicked a 36-yard field goal, and once again the ball went spinning over the heads of the councilmen.

After the game, as the Princeton fans snake-danced around the field, tossing their hats over the goal-posts in celebration of Princeton's 20 to 0 victory, the Philadelphia councilmen hurried to the Princeton dressing rooms to thank

Roper for the marvelous arrangements he had made for them.

For many years Roper was the principal speaker at the annual meeting to acquaint freshmen with the history and principles of the honor system in examinations. "No one," Dean Gauss said, "ever had a more withering scorn for the dishonest, the hypocritical, and the unsportsmanlike. No one ever had a higher faith in the human spirit and in its possibilities."

In addition to Roper Lane, Roper is remembered by a trophy, established in 1939 by his widow and the Class of 1902, which is awarded annually to that senior who best combines high scholastic rank and sportsmanship with general proficiency in athletics.

Rothschild Arch, The, connecting Dickinson Hall with the University Chapel, was given in 1930 by Simon F. Rothschild and his son, Walter N. Rothschild '13, in memory of Walter's mother and his brother, Howard F. Rothschild '21; inscribed at the top of the arch are these words: MATRI FILOQUE IN AMORE DEDICATUS.

Rowing, begun as an undergraduate sport at Yale and Harvard in the 1840s, developed more slowly at Princeton, which was less well endowed by nature for aquatic sports. Lamenting the absence of this strong deterrent to dissipation ("boating and spreeing are, physically at least, incompatible"), the senior editors of the *Nassau Literary Magazine* in their last issue in 1860 suggested the possibility of rowing on the Delaware and Raritan Canal; they thought the canal no less serviceable than the "diminutive Cam" of Cambridge University, whose rowers were then the champions of England, and

urged "the men of '61" to pursue this matter the following year "with class spirit and enterprise."

The outbreak of the Civil War prevented the Class of 1861 from acting on this suggestion, and it was not until 1870 that half a dozen undergraduates began a "navy" at Princeton. "Uniting their purses as well as their purposes," an undergraduate observer recorded, they bought from Yale two old six-oared gigs, which proved to be "respectable imitations of Noah's Ark." One gig sank to the bottom of the canal the first time it was taken out, but the other proved buoyant, and in it the crew "learned to feather an oar, sit in a boat fairly, and judiciously expend their strength on the stroke."

Later, the Princeton Boating Club was organized, and gradually more equipment was secured: a six-oared shell, a four-oared shell, a barge for practice, and, in 1874, a boathouse on the canal. The same year Princeton and Wesleyan were admitted to membership in the Rowing Association of American Colleges, despite the objection of Amherst "that a line must be drawn somewhere." That summer Princeton entered freshman and varsity crews in the association's annual intercollegiate regatta at Saratoga. In the first event, the Class of 1877 crew got off to a very bad start, but by determined effort made up the lost distance and, with a magnificent spurt toward the end of the three-mile course, finished ahead of the Yale and Brown freshmen, the only other entrants, thus giving Princeton a victory in its first intercollegiate race. Elated members of the Class of 1877 held a victory celebration in the College gymnasium, where the crew's oars stood crossed and beribboned on the platform and their shell hung from the rafters. Each of the six oarsmen was given a ten-inch silver loving cup, lined with gold.

Princeton's first intercollegiate victory proved to be its last in the nineteenth century. During the dozen years, 1872 to 1884, that the Boating Club survived, the varsity came in last in most of its races—in six-oared boats at Saratoga, in four-oared shells on the Schuylkill River at Philadelphia in competition for the Childs Cup, begun in 1879. The chief reason for Princeton's lack of success was the inadequacy of the Delaware and Raritan Canal as a place for practice. In comparing the canal with the Cam, the 1860 *Nassau Lit* had overlooked one important difference: the steady stream of commercial traffic on the canal. In those days the canal was crowded with boats, some propelled by steam, others drawn by mules on the towpath. Passing them on half-oar was difficult and dangerous, and an arduous job for the bow oar who served as coxswain, steering with his right foot as he rowed.

Several alumni who rowed on the canal in the 1870s dreamed of securing a lake for Princeton rowing. One of them, Howard Russell Butler 1876, persuaded Andrew Carnegie to build such a lake, and Lake Carnegie (q.v.) was dedicated in 1906.

For the first few years after the lake was completed, competitive rowing was limited to interclass races under the supervision of Constance J. Titus, a former United States single sculls champion.

In 1909 a group of oarsmen, led by Norman Armour '09, then crew captain and later a career ambassador, asked J. Duncan Spaeth, Professor of English, who had been captain of the University of Pennsylvania crew in 1888, to help develop a varsity boat for intercollegiate competition. Professor Spaeth agreed.

"I thought it was to be a temporary affair," Spaeth later recalled, "but found myself in the position of a spectator at a fire who catches a baby thrown out of a window and can discover no one who will claim it. 'It's yours,' the crowd says."

Spaeth served as amateur rowing coach through 1925. Under his guidance Princeton committed itself to the idea of short races, ranging from the Henley distance of a mile and five-sixteenths to two miles, rowed exclusively on college water in contrast to the four-mile races at Poughkeepsie and New London.

In 1911 Princeton celebrated its return to intercollegiate rowing with a triangular regatta on Lake Carnegie in which it finished two lengths behind Cornell (the Poughkeepsie champions) and nine lengths ahead of Yale. This creditable performance helped stimulate the Class of 1887 to give a boathouse the following year. The 1913 varsity scored the University's first major victory by winning from Harvard and Penn on the Charles River. The 1916 varsity defeated Yale, Harvard, Columbia, Navy, and Pennsylvania, losing only to Cornell by the length of the forward deck.

HEINIE LEH'S CREW

Spaeth's greatest crew was the 1921 eight, stroked by Phi Beta Kappa oarsman Heinie Leh. It emerged from obscurity—most of its members had been junior varsity oarsmen the year before—to defeat every crew it met: Navy, Harvard, Cornell, Yale, and California. It rowed its fastest race against California, that year's Pacific Coast champion, setting a record (8:53.8) for the Lake Carnegie upstream course of 1⅞ miles. But its most spectacular victory was in the triangular regatta with Navy and Harvard in which Leh stroked the Princeton crew to a four-length victory over Harvard, and a half-length victory over Navy, the previous year's Olympic champions and afterwards winner of the regatta at Poughkeepsie. Some of the excitement of this event was conveyed in the *Alumni Weekly*'s eyewitness account by Dr. Spaeth, who watched from the car of Trustee Henry B. Thompson 1877 as it followed the course of the race, moving along the towpath between the lake and the canal. Harvard got off first, Navy second, Princeton last. But before the half-mile mark was reached, Princeton had pulled ahead and was still leading by ten feet as the crews passed the mile flag.

But about 200 yards beyond the mile mark [Spaeth recounted], Leh lost his oar-handle just as he was getting ready to answer Navy's last desperate challenge for the lead. For two . . . [beats] the Princeton crew was without a stroke, and the Navy shell in a flash shot into a lead of half a length. Brigham at 7 heroically stroked the crew until Leh recovered his oar, and then . . . the plucky Princeton stroke dug in again at a raised beat. In a long, hard mile and a quarter by desperate meeting of every Navy spurt he had managed to pull out a lead of ten feet. And now in less than five seconds Navy had gained half a length. But instead of discouraging Leh, it seemed to rouse him and his crew. Before the mile-and-a-half mark was reached the lost half-length was regained, and the blue flag of the Navy and the white flag of Princeton dropped simultaneously.

Into the last stretch the two leaders shot, prow and prow alternating by inches. "Will they last?" called out Mr. Thompson. "They'll last," I

said, "but I wish they had stored up for the last twenty strokes the power that went into regaining the lost lead a minute ago."

Twenty more strokes to go and still even! Then the emergency signal came and was answered; up went the stroke for the final dash and on the second stroke of that final spurt I whispered to Mr. Thompson, "We've got 'em!" Stroke by stroke we went ahead; the time interval at the finish between Princeton and Navy was 2⅘ seconds. Four seconds make a length on Lake Carnegie. And that decisive lead was gained in the last twenty strokes!

Charles P. Logg, former University of Washington oarsman, was varsity coach from 1925 to 1931. His 1927 crew, five of whom were sophomores, was the first Princeton crew to win both the Childs Cup (from Penn and Columbia) and the Carnegie Cup (from Cornell and Yale), which was given by Andrew Carnegie's widow in 1920.

LIGHTWEIGHT ROWING

Meantime Gordon G. Sikes '16, a member of the University administration who had been coxswain of Spaeth's 1916 varsity crew, introduced 150-pound rowing at Princeton in 1920, serving, like his mentor, as an amateur coach. Two of his crews, the 1926 eight and the 1930 eight won the Joseph Wright Challenge Cup (named for the Pennsylvania coach who initiated lightweight rowing in the United States) in the annual regatta of the American Rowing Association, thus earning the lightweight championship of the East. The 1930 crew competed for the Thames Challenge Cup in the English Henley, winning two races before it was eliminated.

In 1931, when Sikes succeeded Logg

as varsity heavyweight coach, the University's Presbyterian chaplain, Wilhemus B. Bryan '20, began his eight years as amateur coach of the fifties. Both his 1933 and 1935 crews won the Goldthwait Cup from Harvard and Yale, and the Joseph Wright Cup in the American Henley on the Schuylkill. The 1933 crew made an unsuccessful bid for the Thames Challenge Cup in the English Henley.

Delos C. ("Dutch") Shoch, former University of Washington oarsman, coached the lightweight crew in 1939 and 1940, James A. Rathschmidt in 1941 and 1942. After losing to Pennsylvania and Harvard early in the season, the 1942 eight outrowed them and all the other competitors for the Wright Cup over the Henley distance on Lake Carnegie, lowering the course lightweight record by almost six seconds.

After the Second World War, Gordon Sikes returned to his first love, coaching the fifties in 1946 and 1947. Later, some of the oarsmen who had rowed under him in the 1920s, in tribute to his "courage, enthusiasm, and devotion to Princeton," founded the Gordon Sikes Medal, awarded annually to the outstanding senior lightweight oarsman.

The decade 1948 through 1957 was a golden age for lightweight rowing at Princeton. The 1948 crew, coached by Davis Spencer '45, won the Joseph Wright Cup in the American Henley and the Thames Challenge Cup at the Henley Royal Regatta—the first Princeton crew to win in this ancient British tournament. The 1949 eight, coached by Charles von Wrangell, won the Goldthwait Cup from Harvard and Yale and, although twice defeated in other races in this country, performed superbly in the British Henley Regatta,

twice equaling the record for the course, to retain the Thames Challenge Cup for Princeton.

In five successive years from 1953 through 1957, Princeton won the Goldthwait Cup from Harvard and Yale and in 1953, 1956, and 1957, also won the Joseph Wright Cup for the eastern sprint championship. The 1953 crew, coached by Arthur Sueltz, pared three-tenths of a second off the record for the Wright Cup race, and lost the final for the Thames Challenge Cup after breaking the English Henley course record by six seconds in one of its preliminary races. Coach Donald Rose's undefeated 1956 eight, which twice broke the Lake Carnegie course record for the Henley distance, and his undefeated 1957 eight, which lowered a sixteen-year-old Charles River course record by nearly nine seconds, became the third and fourth Princeton winners of the Thames Challenge Cup.

OUTSTANDING HEAVYWEIGHT CREWS

Gordon Sikes's 1933 and 1934 varsity heavyweight crews, both stroked by Aikman Armstrong '34 (another Phi Beta Kappa oarsman), defeated Harvard and M.I.T. for the newly instituted Karl Taylor Compton Cup, presented by the former Princeton physicist who had become president of M.I.T., and they also outrowed Navy, Columbia, Pennsylvania, and Cornell —losing both seasons only to Yale, unofficial Eastern sprint champion. The 1934 eight competed for the Grand Challenge Cup in the Royal Henley Regatta in England and, in its second round, forced Leander, premier rowing club of England, to set a new course record to win.

Fred Spuhn succeeded Sikes as varsity heavyweight coach, serving from

1938 to 1942. His 1939 and 1941 crews won the historic Childs Cup, and although the 1942 crew lost it to Penn by four feet, they went on to score an upset victory over Yale and Cornell for the Carnegie Cup.

Dutch Schoch was heavyweight coach from 1946 to 1965. After achieving only moderate success in the regular season, his 1948 crew rowed its way into the finals of the Olympic tryouts and placed second to California. Winners of both the Carnegie and the Childs Cups, the 1949 eight set a new record for the Lake Carnegie downstream course of 1¾ miles. The 1952 crew finished second to Navy in both the Intercollegiates and the Olympic trials. The 1956 crew not only won the Childs Cup, but took the Compton Cup with the best time recorded since it was first placed in competition in 1933.

Peter W. Sparhawk, stroke of Cornell crews in the early 1950s, became Varsity heavyweight coach in 1966. His 1968 crew was the first since 1952 to win the Carnegie Cup from Yale and Cornell, setting an example for the 1969 and 1970 crews, who made it three in a row.

THE SEVENTIES

The seventies brought new vitality to Princeton's century-old rowing tradition. Thanks to gifts from some 300 crew alumni and other friends, a long-awaited year-round training facility became available in 1972 with the dedication of an enclosed rowing tank, built next to the boathouse. A year later, the men's lightweight crew, coached by Gary Kilpatrick, capped an undefeated season by winning the Thames Challenge Cup; at Syracuse the previous summer, five of its members had won the national championship for freshmen four-oared crew with coxswain. In 1976, the men's heavyweight crew, coached by Peter Sparhawk, edged out Wisconsin for second place in the Intercollegiate Rowing Association's annual regatta for the national championship, won by California.

These years also brought exciting achievements, both here and abroad, by the newest arrivals at the Class of 1887 Boathouse. In 1972, the first women's crew ever to represent Princeton won the Eastern Intercollegiate Regatta, shaving nine seconds off the national women's record, and their captain, Amy Richlin '73, became one of the first women to wear the white sweater with black "P," traditionally awarded captains of championship teams. Undefeated in dual meets, the 1973 women's varsity placed third in the national women's rowing championships.

In 1974, Carol Brown '75 and Janet Youngholm '75 won the national collegiate title for women's pairs without coxswain, and at the world championships in Lucerne, Switzerland, finished a length ahead of a strong Soviet pair on their way to the finals, where they ranked as fifth best in the world. Carol Brown also won a silver medal at Nottingham, England, in 1975 and a bronze medal at the Montreal Olympics a year later.

Rugby at Princeton began with the founding of the Princeton Rugby Club in the spring of 1931 by a pair of British graduate students, H. Cooper and Monti Barak. Coaching was provided by Professor John Whitton, who actively supported the club throughout its first forty-five years. The initial season was highly successful, as both Harvard and Yale were defeated twice. In 1934 the team, captained by Ed Lee '34, lost only to a touring Cambridge University side.

Suspended during World War II, rugby was propitiously revived in the spring of 1948, when the club won the Bermuda Cup, and the Missouri Cup, and was featured in an article in *Life* magazine. In the fall of 1959 and the spring of 1960, the club put together successive undefeated seasons. The team of 1962, led by Bill Swain, won the first Commonwealth Cup tournament. In 1969, captain Terry Larrimer's team won the first Ivy League Rugby tournament, the Easterns Championship, and the prestigious Washington 7's tournament.

In 1970, the Princeton Rugby Alumni Association was formed to support the undergraduate teams and to play an occasional "Old Boys" match. This created a new tradition at Reunions when the alumni take on the students for the Doc Whitton Cup—a match remarkable for the quality of rugby played and for the fierce yet friendly rivalry that exists between students and alumni.

Thomas Pirelli

Rush, Benjamin 1760 (1746-1813) was a physician, teacher, and man of affairs who played a dramatic role in the early history of his country, his college, and his profession. A man of contradictions, he practiced and taught the backward medical art of bloodletting, yet was far ahead of his time in the care of the mentally ill. He was a vigorous foe of slavery and capital punishment, an advocate of better education for women

and of free public schools. More than any other person he was responsible for bringing John Witherspoon to America as Princeton's sixth president.

He lost his father when he was six, and was brought up by his mother who kept a grocery shop in Philadelphia to help support and educate her seven children. When he was eight, he entered an academy conducted by his uncle, Samuel Finley (later president of Princeton) at Nottingham, Maryland, where he made such progress that on entering Princeton five years later he was admitted to the junior class; he graduated in 1760 when he was not quite fifteen.

Although of a pious nature, he did not think he would make a good minister. President Davies was inclined to think he should take up the law, but his uncle, Dr. Finley, persuaded him to study medicine with Dr. John Redmond in Philadelphia. He served an apprenticeship with Dr. Redmond for almost six years and attended the first lectures of Dr. John Morgan and Dr. William Shippen, Jr. 1754 in the newly formed medical department of the College of Philadelphia (later the University of Pennsylvania).

In the summer of 1766, when he was twenty, he sat up every night for several weeks with Dr. Finley, then president of the College, during his last illness, and "finally performed the distressing office of closing his eyes." That fall he went to Edinburgh, Scotland, then the medical center of the world, where after two years of study, and some heroic experiments with emetics on his own person for his doctoral thesis on the digestion of food in the stomach, received his M.D. degree.

While in Scotland he rendered his alma mater an incalculable service, when in cooperation with Richard

Stockton, a trustee, he persuaded John Witherspoon to come to America as Princeton's president. Stockton's authority and dignity were indispensable to the mission, but it was Rush's confident, audacious, and engaging youth that won the day. From Edinburgh, twenty-one-year-old Rush wrote forty-four-year-old Witherspoon "your talents have been in some measure buried, but at Princeton they will be called into action, and the evening of your life will be much more effulgent than your brightest meridian days have been." When Witherspoon felt obliged to decline because of his wife's fear of leaving home—the very mention of going to America made her physically ill—Rush asked Witherspoon "And must poor Nassau Hall be ruined?" and "Will you then suffer your sun to set so soon?" A little later he urged Witherspoon to reconsider the Princeton invitation and offered to help him make another appeal to his wife. Soon, on Witherspoon's invitation, Rush spent several days with the Witherspoons at their home in Paisley. Shortly afterward a friend of Witherspoon wrote to Richard Stockton in Princeton that "to Mr. Witherspoon's great satisfaction, his wife has at last given a calm hearing to Mr. Rush, argued the Matter with him, and received a satisfying Answer to all her objections; so that now she is willing if the Doctor is rechosen . . . to go with him without Grudge." Witherspoon was re-elected in due course and he and Mrs. Witherspoon came to America in August 1768.

Rush spent the following year in London, where he attended medical lectures, and in Paris. In London he was on friendly terms with Benjamin Franklin, and at Benjamin West's dined with Sir Joshua Reynolds, who in turn had him to dinner with Samuel Johnson and Oliver Goldsmith. In Paris he met Diderot, who gave him a letter of introduction to David Hume.

Soon after his return home Rush was appointed to a chair of chemistry in the College of Philadelphia's medical department, thus becoming at the age of twenty-three the first professor of chemistry in America. He built up a large private practice, at first among the poor, but he found time to further other interests. He published a pamphlet on the iniquity of the slave trade, and helped organize the Pennsylvania Society for Promoting the Abolition of Slavery and the Relief of Free Negroes Unlawfully Held in Bondage, the first antislavery society in America; he later became its president. In the growing quarrel between the colonies and the mother country, he associated with such leaders as Thomas Paine, John Adams, and Thomas Jefferson. It was on his urging that Thomas Paine wrote a strong tract on behalf of complete American independence to which he gave the title, suggested by Rush, *Common Sense*.

In the summer of 1775 while visiting President Witherspoon and Richard Stockton in Princeton, he met Stockton's sixteen-year-old daughter, Julia. The following January, a few days after his thirtieth birthday, he and Julia were married by the Reverend President Witherspoon. Less than seven months later, the bridegroom, who had been elected a delegate to the Continental Congress from Pennsylvania, joined his father-in-law and Dr. Witherspoon, both delegates from New Jersey, in signing the Declaration of Independence.

While Surgeon-General of the Middle Department of the Army during the Revolution, Rush became outraged by the conditions he found in army hospitals and, failing to get the remedial action he sought from the director general, Dr. Shippen (his former teacher), he sent a protest to General Washington, accusing Dr. Shippen of maladministration. Washington referred the protest to Congress, which ruled in favor of Shippen, and Rush resigned his commission. Rush lost confidence in Washington's ability and became associated indirectly with the Conway cabal to replace him; later he deeply regretted this action, and supported Washington politically.

Returning to Philadelphia, Rush resumed his practice, his teaching, and his humanitarian endeavors. At the medical school of the College of Philadelphia, he added courses on the theory and practice of medicine to his lectures in chemistry, and became the most admired teacher of medicine in Philadelphia, then the medical center of America. All told, he taught more than three thousand medical students, who carried his influence to every corner of the growing nation.

Rush founded the Philadelphia Dispensary for the relief of the poor, the first of its kind in the United States, and for many years gave it hours of service without pay. He also founded Dickinson College, was one of the charter trustees of Franklin College (later Franklin and Marshall), and—being persuaded of the importance of removing "the present disparity which subsists between the sexes in the degrees of their education and knowledge"— became an ardent incorporator of the Young Ladies Academy in Philadelphia.

He worked heroically during the yellow fever epidemic of 1793; although he was severely censured for his stubborn reliance on bloodletting, his account of the epidemic published the fol-

lowing year won him recognition by several European learned societies.

His greatest contributions to medical science were the reforms he instituted in the care of the mentally ill during his thirty years of service as a senior physician at the Pennsylvania Hospital. In the words of one of his biographers, Dr. Carl Binger, a psychiatrist, "he took on heroic stature," substituting kindness and compassion for cruelty, and replacing routine reliance on archaic procedures by careful clinical observation and study. The year before he died, he published *Medical Inquiries and Observations upon the Diseases of the Mind*, the first textbook on psychiatry in America, which Dr. Binger called "the crowning achievement of his professional life."

Benjamin and Julia Rush had thirteen children; one of them, Richard Rush 1797, served as cabinet officer or ambassador under four presidents.

In 1837 some of Rush's former students founded a medical college in Chicago; which they named for him. The American Psychiatric Association, whose official seal bears Rush's portrait, placed a bronze plaque at his grave in Philadelphia in 1965, designating him the "Father of American Psychiatry."

Russell, Henry Norris (1877-1957), for many years the leading theoretical astronomer in America, was graduated from Princeton in 1897 at the age of nineteen *insigni cum laude* (with extraordinary honor)—a designation by the Faculty never used before or since. His father was a Presbyterian minister; his mother and maternal grandmother had both won prizes in mathematics. He recalled his parents' showing him the transit of Venus in 1882 when he was five years old. His favorite study in college was mathematics (his favorite sport, mountain-climbing); an interest in astronomy was stimulated by Professor Charles A. Young (q.v.), with whom he continued to study after graduation, earning his Ph.D. *summa cum laude* in 1900. Following study as an advanced research student at Cambridge University, England, he was appointed instructor in astronomy by Woodrow Wilson in 1905; became a full professor in 1911, and director of the Observatory in 1912. He took an active part in the affairs of the Class of 1897 and attended reunions frequently. His classmates were very proud of him; at their thirtieth reunion in 1927, they honored him and their old astronomy teacher by endowing the Charles A. Young Research Professorship of Astronomy with Russell as the first incumbent.

Russell pioneered in the use of atomic physics for the analysis of the stars and thus played a principal part in laying the foundations of present-day astrophysics. He analyzed the physical conditions and chemical compositions of stellar atmospheres and evaluated the relative abundance of the elements. His assertion of the overwhelming abundance of hydrogen, was accepted, after prolonged controversy, as one of the basic facts of cosmology.

His name is perpetuated by the Hertzsprung-Russell color magnitude diagram (stellar evolution), the "Russell mixture" (composition of solar and stellar atmospheres), Russell-Saunders coupling (spectrum analysis), and the Henry Norris Russell Lectureship of the American Astronomical Society, endowed at his retirement by gifts from fellow astronomers and Princeton classmates.

Russell's position as America's leading astronomer was recognized by his presidency of the American Astronomical Society, the American Association for the Advancement of Science, and the American Philosophical Society. He was awarded the gold medal of the Royal Astronomical Society of England, two medals of the French Academy, five other medals of American scientific societies, and numerous honorary degrees. Mexico conferred on him its Order of the Aztec Eagle, and issued a postage stamp in his honor—done in orange and black.

Russell attracted to Princeton an outstanding group of graduate students who went on to occupy positions of leadership in observatories throughout the country. Notable among his students were Harlow Shapley, Ph.D. 1913, who became director of the Harvard Observatory in 1921; Donald H. Menzel, Ph.D. 1924, who succeeded Shapley at Harvard in 1952; and Lyman Spitzer, Jr., Ph.D. 1938, who succeeded Russell as director of the Princeton Observatory in 1947.

Harlow Shapley said that it was generally agreed that the word "genius" more rightly applied to Russell than to any other American astronomer of his or earlier times. F.J.M. Stratton, leading British astrophysicist, thought Russell "the most eminent and versatile theoretical astrophysicist in the United States if not in the world," and described him as "a man of overflowing energy, never sparing himself in his own work or in assisting in the researches of others."

Among Russell's 241 published papers were articles written jointly with Princeton colleagues in both astronomy and physics and a joint paper with Robert K. Root, Professor of English, on "A Planetary Date for Chaucer's *Troilus*"; they also included a paper "On the Navigation of Airplanes," for which Russell made observations in airplanes flying at 105 miles per hour, at heights up to 16,000 feet, as a consultant to the federal government in World War I.

Lyman Spitzer, Jr. has given us this vivid picture of Russell:

> Those who knew him in his later years remember him for his unbounded energy and his enthusiasm for ideas. It is characteristic of the man that he would frequently be so carried away in his graduate lectures that he would talk enthusiastically for an additional hour or two, carrying his fascinated audience into exciting new realms of research. He brought this same keenness and enthusiasm to all the many experiences in his full and active life—to his extensive travels, his wide reading of both prose and poetry, and his happy hours with his grandchildren. He would keep small children engrossed for hours with the paper boats, balls, birds, and animals that he constructed with facility, his long, dextrous fingers folding and creasing the paper with unerring speed. His knowledge was encyclopedic; it included facts and theories not only in all branches of science but also in such varied subjects as the Bible and the wild flowers of New Jersey.

Russell spoke frequently on the so-called "conflict" between science and religion, seeking to assure those who feared science as "a dangerous foe" to religion that their feeling was "altogether ill-advised." In his 1925 Terry Lectures at Yale, he fully accepted the mechanistic theory of nature, "not as a demonstrated natural law, but as a working hypothesis" and held that this hypothesis "far from being hostile to religion . . . is capable of rendering religion important services." He concluded his Terry Lectures with this statement of his personal belief:

> The need for some venture of faith still remains; one must stake one's life upon something. For myself, if I am to stake all I have and hope to be upon anything, I will venture it upon the abounding fullness of God—upon the assurance that, as the heavens are higher than the earth, so are His ways higher than our ways, and His thoughts than our thoughts. Just what future the Designer of the universe has provided for the souls of men I do not know, I cannot prove. But I find that the whole order of Nature confirms my confidence that, if it is not like our noblest hopes and dreams, it will transcend them. . . .

> And, when immortality becomes for us no longer a matter of academic discussion, but the most vital of all questions; . . . we shall find our comfort where so many before us have found it, in the ancient words, *"In manus tuas, Domine."*

Sailing. The Princeton University Yacht Club, which maintains facilities for sailing and racing on Lake Carnegie, was founded in 1928. In that same year, a "Big-Three Regatta" in eight-meter yachts initiated intercollegiate racing and also provided an auspicious beginning for the Princeton Sailing Team, which was skippered to victory by Arthur Knapp, Jr. '28.

Intercollegiate competition was firmly established in 1930 with the McMillan Cup (donated by William McMillan '28), which endures as the premier regatta. Princeton has won this event seven times, more than any other competitor.

With the passage of time, the yachts have become boats and the regattas more numerous. Princeton has continued to field successful teams, winning the National Intercollegiate Dinghy Championship three times.

With the advent of coeducation, the sailing team expanded its membership to include women. The women's team has been notably successful, winning the National Women's Intercollegiate Championship three out of the first four years of its existence.

In 1976, the facilities of the Yacht Club were enhanced by construction of the Lockwood Pirie '27 Boathouse on Lake Carnegie, made possible by the generosity of alumni and other Friends of Princeton Sailing.

H. C. Curtiss, Jr.

Salutatory Oration, The, which dates back to the first commencement in 1748, is Princeton's oldest student honor. Contrary to the usual practice elsewhere, the salutatory, rather than the valedictory (q.v.), which came later, was traditionally delivered by the highest ranking member of the senior class. In recent years, the faculty has chosen both speakers for their special qualifications for the parts as well as for their high scholastic standing.

The first salutatorian, Daniel Thane, delivered his address "in a modest and decent manner," according to an account of commencement in *Parker's Gazette and Post Boy* of New York. He apologized "for his Insufficiency" (customary in those days), enumerated "the Numberless Benefits the liberal Arts and Sciences yield to Mankind in private and social life," and addressed "becoming Salutations to his Excellency [the governor] and the Trustees, the President and whole Assembly." All of this was "performed in good Latin from his Memory in a handsome oratorical Manner in the Space of about half an Hour." Thane later employed his oratorical talents as a preacher.

Two salutatorians became Princeton presidents: Samuel Stanhope Smith 1769 and Robert F. Goheen '40. Others have become eminent professors in the University: Allan Marquand 1874 (art and archaeology), Samuel R. Winans 1874 (classics), William Berryman Scott 1877 (paleontology), Henry Burchard Fine 1880 (mathematics), Henry Norris Russell 1897 (astrophysics), Edward T. Cone '39 (music). When Marquand and Winans tied for first place in 1874, Marquand gave a salutatory in Latin, Winans in Greek.

Two brothers, David B. Jones and Thomas D. Jones, later trustees, tied for first place in 1876 and gave Latin and English salutatories, respectively. Two other brothers were salutatorians in the thirties: Lewis H. Van Dusen, Jr. '32, later a lawyer in Philadelphia, and Francis L. Van Dusen '34, who became a circuit court judge in the same city.

The memorized half-hour oration, as delivered by the first salutatorian, eventually gave way to a ten-minute address, usually read from manuscript, and its tone, once in keeping with the formal proceedings of commencement, came to provide a kind of comic relief from them. In modern salutatories the humor of the text itself is heightened by the reaction of the other degree candidates, most of whom know no Latin but have at their places printed copies of the salutatory, with footnotes indicating the responses the salutatorian expects of them (*hic plaudite, hic vociferate, hic deplorate,* etc.); and they always do respond, though sometimes hesitatingly at first, with exuberance—to the delight and surprise of the audience.

In 1938 Wolfgang K. H. Panofsky, later professor of physics at Stanford University, carried this joke one step further by quoting in English a "memorable saying" of a "foreign" poet (Shakespeare), "a knavish speech sleeps in a foolish ear," and then for the benefit of his "Roman" classmates, translating it into Latin, "Dormit sermo astutus in aure insipientis."

In 1971, following a year in which no salutatory was given, Donald J. Mathison, a classics major, revived the tradition with verve and wit, calling this restoration a "classical renaissance" and likening it to the one in Europe that "prevailed over the ignorance and barbarity of the Dark Ages." With tongue in cheek, he departed from the conventional expressions of gratitude, assuring the trustees, "We are willing to listen to your advice on how to run our university," and lamenting to the faculty, "I can not say, as is customary, that you have in large part made our minds and souls what they are not because this is more than true, but because it is perhaps less than complimentary."

A wise salutatorian knows that his address will get more attention if it contains here and there a well-known Latin phrase which will be recognized by non-Latinists. Mathison played this principle to the hilt by piling one Latin aphorism on another in mock words of advice to his classmates, e.g., "ut aliquando sit in vino veritas, non credendum est post hoc ergo propter hoc." Having talked at some length, he suddenly stopped, looked at his watch, sadly announced "Heu, eheu! Tempus fugit," quickly came to a climax with "Dei sub numine viget," and concluded, "Itaque, amici, avete atque valete," as his classmates stood and cheered his bravura performance.

The first woman salutatorian, Lisa Siegman '75, introduced a variation on the usual footnotes, calling for shouts from the boys ("Pueri, hic vociferate") when she observed that for 229 years the greeting of commencement audiences in Latin had been the duty of a male student ("*discipuli*") and for shouts from the girls ("Puellae, hic voc-

iferate") when she added with spirit that at last it was the duty of a female student ("*discipulae*").

Sayre, Daniel Clemens (1903-1956), first chairman of the Department of Aeronautical Engineering and first director of the James Forrestal Research Center, was born in Columbus, Ohio, the same year that two other Ohioans, Orville and Wilbur Wright, made the first controlled and sustained flights in a power-driven airplane. Sixteen years later Sayre began the study of civil engineering at Massachusetts Institute of Technology but, after taking a year off to work on dams in Ohio and Alabama to earn money for his expenses, changed his course to aeronautical engineering, earning his B.S. in 1924 and his M.S. in 1929.

While still a student he earned his pilot's license and then organized the Boston Airport Corporation, which played a leading part in establishing this country's first commercial airline run, between New York and Boston. He served as instructor and assistant professor at M.I.T. from 1927 to 1933. During the last two years, he conducted an extensive investigation of American air masses. The data he and his associates gathered during almost daily flights, at altitudes from 16,000 to 18,000 feet in an instrument-laden plane, proved of great value in the development of commercial and military aviation. They frequently encountered difficult atmospheric conditions. On one flight visibility was so poor that, coming down through a cloud layer for a landing, Sayre found he had drifted some 150 miles out to sea. With a rapidly dwindling fuel supply, he barely managed to get back, landing on a golf course near the coast. The newspapers played up the mishap, and, as

Sayre liked to recall, more than one New England editor was unable to resist headlining the story: "Professor Lost in Fog."

Sayre was later on the editorial staff of the magazine *Aviation*, then, aviation editor of *Newsweek*, director of Statistics and Information for the Civil Aeronautics Authority, chief of the Safety Division of the Civil Aeronautics Board. In 1941 he was called to Princeton to organize an aeronautical engineering department to help meet the nation's critical needs in this field. He recruited some of the ablest aeronautical scientists in the country and secured the necessary support for their work from outside sources as well as from the University. As a result, the department rose in a very few years to a position of national leadership, evidenced in 1949 when the Guggenheim Foundation selected Princeton and the California Institute of Technology as the places for the two Guggenheim Jet Propulsion Centers.

In 1951, when the University was given the opportunity to acquire new laboratory facilities for the natural and engineering sciences from the Rockefeller Institute for Medical Research, Sayre played a leading role—"indeed," President Goheen later said, "he was the catalyst for the efforts of all others"—in the establishment of the James Forrestal Research Center, later renamed the Forrestal Campus. A man of wide interests, Sayre also contributed his judgment and enthusiasm to the development of the Firestone Library and the Council of the Humanities. He died at the age of fifty-three after a five-year struggle with cancer, "gratefully remembered," President Dodds said, "for his many constructive contributions to the growth of the modern Princeton and by his colleagues for

his cheerfulness, his contagious wit, and his very great courage throughout his long illness."

A short time after his death, one of the original buildings of the Forrestal Campus was named Sayre Hall in his memory.

Scholarships. James Leslie, Class of 1759, attended Princeton with the help of a gift of thirteen British pounds from a "Fund for Pious Youth." After graduation, he became a school teacher in New York City. When he died, he left his frugally guarded savings to the College as a perpetual fund "for the education of poor and pious youth."

In grateful recognition, President John Witherspoon designated this fund "The Leslie Fund" and, over the years—as part of the University's endowment—it has helped hundreds of young Princetonians prepare themselves for lives of usefulness and honor.

From the beginning, Princeton has welcomed students from differing economic backgrounds, and by now it has seven hundred endowed scholarship funds to help meet their needs. These funds have come from many sources: from graduates and their families; from members of the faculty, various classes, alumni associations, and friends of the University. Their total "book value" is nearly $30 million; their "market value" more than twice as much.

The number and the needs of students have also risen over the years. Today, about half of the undergraduate body qualifies for some kind of financial help. To provide this, there are some outside sources of funds—from corporations and foundations, state and federal governments—but the "Tiger's share" (75%) comes from the University. And when necessary, Princeton augments the income from scholarship endowment with her own unrestricted funds.

Scholarship assistance generally requires a complementary expenditure of time, energy, and future resources from the student recipients. Those who receive outright scholarship grants work a certain number of hours in campus jobs: in the Library, Dining Halls, University Store, Laboratories and other places—earning well over a million dollars annually. They also assume interest-bearing loans to repay after graduation.

By good fortune, DEI SUB NUMINE VIGET, the University has so far been able to assist any student who can meet the requirements for admission.

Frederic E. Fox

Scott, William Berryman 1877 (1858-1947), the eminent vertebrate paleontologist who was Blair Professor of Geology from 1886 to 1930, spent almost all of his long, happy, productive, and rather secluded life in Princeton. He was born a few months before the Lincoln-Douglas debates and about two years before the publication of Darwin's *On the Origin of Species*, the son of a Presbyterian minister (who died before William's fourth birthday) and the grandson of the theologian, Charles Hodge 1815, who was often called "The Presbyterian Pope."

Throughout his life Scott demonstrated an apparent but unintended aloofness and formalness that, he later realized, resulted in part from his lack as a child of comradeship outside of his close-knit family, which was strongly dedicated to God, hard work, educational eminence, and an unwavering conviction of its own quality. A frail and sickly child, Scott became precociously devoted to books. He expected to fol-low the family tradition of life as a cleric, but instead became a noted and much-honored scientist.

As a Princeton student, researcher, and teacher, he discovered and studied many fossil vertebrates, and thereby helped initiate and develop important theories that tested and expanded some of Darwin's ideas about organic evolution. Scott's life interests in geology and in religion are reflected in a verse about him in the Faculty Song:

Here's to Bill Geology Scott,
He has a carboniferous knot,
He tells us how the earth was made,
And how the Lord his sidewalks laid.

He was "Professor Princeton" to the many students who enjoyed his famous lectures in which he combined scientific discourse with salty tales of his graduate study abroad and his expeditions to the American West. At his retirement in 1930, after half a century of teaching, many alumni voiced regret that students would no longer learn science from his stories of "The Johnstown Flood" and "Chief Red Cloud's Arrest."

As a boy of nine, Scott read proof on Charles Hodge's book "What is Darwinism?" and agreed with his grandfather's conclusion that "Darwinism is Atheism"; but he changed his mind during his early professional years when the ideological tussle between Darwin and Genesis was at its height, compelling commitment or compromise. Scott chose compromise. President McCosh, whom Scott regarded as one of the greatest of teachers, conferred with Scott in writing *The Religious Aspects of Evolution* (1888), in which he declared that he was "in favor of evolution properly limited," because it is "the method by which God works."

For his descendants Scott wrote his memoirs, parts of which were published in *Some Memories of a Palaeontologist* (Princeton University Press, 1939). These charming accounts are a valuable source of information about his family and ancestors, his education, travels, friends, publications, University politics, and philosophies.

In his *Memories* Scott said that no account of his life would be complete that omitted the tale of how he, Henry Fairfield Osborn, and Francis Speir (called "the triumvirate" by their awed classmates of 1877), after a swim in the canal on a hot June day in 1876, decided to make a fossil-collecting trip to the Far West. The expedition that resulted from this historic decision (encouraged by Professor Guyot and financed by the trustees) marked the beginning of the scientific careers of Scott and Osborn and of the acquisition for Princeton of what has become one of the finest collections of vertebrate fossils. Later, Osborn was largely responsible for the development of paleontology at the American Museum of Natural History in New York and the growth of its fossil collection into the largest in the world.

The famous Princeton Patagonian Expeditions (1896-1899) were originated and financed by one of Scott's assistants, John B. Hatcher, who developed many new ways of collecting fossils in the field and, in the Princeton Museum of Natural History, devised new methods of exhibiting them. Scott spent most of his time on his own research and had little interest in developing the Museum or in training graduate students. These tasks were assumed by William J. Sinclair, who joined the Princeton faculty in 1904, and later by Glenn L. Jepsen, who joined it in 1930. Sinclair instituted the William Berryman Scott Fund for research in vertebrate paleontology and secured contributions to it. A principal donor was Childs Frick '05. Sinclair willed his own estate to Princeton for the Sinclair Professorship of Vertebrate Paleontology as a means of continuing the tradition of research and teaching in that subject begun by Scott in the 1880s.

A measure of Scott's influence on students of paleontology is found in more than a dozen species of fossil mammals in different genera named "scotti" in his honor. Later these evidences of respect by younger men gave him as much pleasure as his many medals and honorary degrees.

Although Scott was proud of having Benjamin Franklin, Charles Hodge, and other personages in his ancestral line, he maintained that his favorite family tree was that of the fossil camels. From the study of such fossil phylogenies, he concluded that they are not satisfactorily accounted for by the Darwinian factor of natural selection; and many scientists now agree.

Scott's splendid long career exemplifies the dedicated life of a gifted teacher in a privileged University environment, the way a man and an organization make reciprocal contributions to each other's welfare, and the ways they change. On Scott's eightieth birthday at a big party his colleagues had for him in Procter Hall, he made an observation about a fossil that was strongly contrary to a statement he had made on the previous day. When reminded of this, he said, "Yes, but that was yesterday."

Glenn E. Jepson

Scribner, The publishing house of, was founded in 1846 and ever since has been presided over by successive generations of Princeton graduates: by the founder, Charles Scribner 1840 (1846-1871); by his three sons, John Blair Scribner 1870 (1871-1879), Charles Scribner 1875 (1879-1930), Arthur H. Scribner 1881 (1930-1932); by his grandson, Charles Scribner '13 (1932-1952); and by his greatgrandson, Charles Scribner '43 (1952-   ). Longest leadership by far has been given by those—all in a direct line—whom Ellery Sedgewick, editor of the *Atlantic Monthly*, once designated "Charles the First, Charles the Second, Charles the Third . . . Charles the Fourth." The Scribners descended from Benjamin Scrivener, who was in Norwalk, Connecticut, in 1680; the family changed its name to Scribner after 1742. Charles Scribner 1840 married a daughter of John Insley Blair, donor of Blair Hall.

The Scribners have been consistently devoted Princeton workers and benefactors. Charles Scribner 1875 was a trustee of the University 1912-1930 and chairman of its library committee 1915-1930. Founder of Princeton University Press, the donor of its first building, and its first president, he was also one of the organizers of the *Alumni Weekly*, first president of the Princetonian Publishing Company, and president of the Princeton Club of New York. He was awarded an honorary Litt.D. in 1925. On his death in 1930, he left Princeton University Press $50,000 toward its endowment fund; when his portrait by Wilford Seymour Conrow '01 was unveiled at the Press in 1935, Dean Christian Gauss said the richest legacy the Press had received was the spirit of Charles Scribner himself.

Charles Scribner '13 followed in his father's footsteps as president of Princeton University Press 1940-1948. He also carried on his father's interest in the University library—he was a frequent donor of rare books and manuscripts. In 1946, under his presidency, Charles Scribner's Sons, in celebration of its centenary and Princeton's bicentenary, gave the University $50,000 for a conference room in the Firestone Library in memory of his four predecessors.

Charles Scribner '43, who was class salutatorian at his graduation, has carried on the family tradition of service to Princeton as president of Princeton University Press, as chairman of the advisory councils of the department of classics and the department of English, and, like his grandfather, as a trustee of the University and chairman of its library committee. He was given an honorary degree in 1966. In 1967, under his presidency, the Scribner firm turned over to the University its archives of more than a quarter-million documents, including correspondence with Winston Churchill, William Faulkner, F. Scott Fitzgerald, and Ernest Hemingway.

Seal of Princeton University, The, which is in the custody of the Secretary of the University, is in effect the corporate signature of the trustees. It is embossed on diplomas and printed on other official documents authorized by them and affixed by the secretary to legal instruments requiring its use.

The seal of the College of New Jersey, used for almost a century and a half, comprised the following details: In the upper part of a circle, an open Bible with Latin characters VET NOV TESTAMENTUM signifying the Old and New Testaments. Over the Bible, the motto VITAM MORTUIS REDDO (*I restore life to the dead.*) Underneath, on the right, a table with books signifying scholarship. On the left, a diploma, signifying the goal of the student. On the outside of the circle, SIGILLUM COLLEGII NEO-CAESARIENSIS IN AMERICA (seal of the College of New Jersey in America).

Since 1896, when at the Sesquicentennial of its founding the College of New Jersey became Princeton University, the corporate seal has been simpler—as described in the trustees' minutes of February 13, 1896: ". . . a shield resting upon a circle. In the upper part of the shield an open Bible with Latin characters VET NOV TESTAMENTUM signifying the Old and New Testaments . . . In the lower part a chevron, denoting the rafters of a building. In the spaces between the sides of the shield and the circle the motto DEI SUB NUMINE VIGET [*Under God's power she flourishes*]. On the outside of the circle SIGILLUM UNIVER-

SITATIS PRINCETONIENSIS [seal of Princeton University]."

The shield from the official seal, minus the circle and with the motto in a ribbon beneath the shield, serves as the

University's insignia and may be employed for decorative purposes by any organization or individual connected with the University where the use of Princeton's symbol is appropriate.

The full seal is strictly reserved for the purpose described in the college's original charter namely as "a Common Seal under which they [the trustees] may pass all Diplomas, or Certificates of Degrees, and all Other the Affairs & Business of and Concerning the said Corporation. . . ."

Secretary of the University, The, assists the clerk of the Board of Trustees and in this capacity makes arrangements for meetings of the board and of its executive committee, and prepares the minutes; he is secretary of the committee on honorary degrees. He notifies by letter all persons in the faculty or administration elected or appointed to office by the board or appointed by action of the president. As secretary of the corporation known as "The Trustees of Princeton University," he has custody of the University seal and affixes it to all documents that require its use, including diplomas. In the words of the Charter he is "the agent . . . upon whom process against the corporation may be served." He also has oversight of Commencement and other University convocations.

The office of the secretary serves as an arm of the president's office, and at one time or another has been headquarters for a variety of University activities including alumni affairs, student aid, public information, and departmental advisory councils. For many years the office housed archives of the University, and during his incumbency V. Lansing Collins wrote extensively about the history of the University and of the town of Princeton. Until 1974 the secretary was responsible for the preparation and distribution of the several catalogues and other publications issued under the heading, "The Official Register," as well as *The Weekly Bulletin*.

The By-Laws charge the secretary with "responsibility, under the President, for such other areas of the University's affairs, not specifically assigned to another officer, as the Board or the President may designate." One incumbent characterized the office as "the department of everything else." Those who have endeavored with the help of their loyal associates to cope with these manifold obligations have been: Charles W. McAlpin 1888, 1901-1917; V. Lansing Collins 1892, 1917-1936; Alexander Leitch '24, 1936-1966; Jeremiah S. Finch hc '31 and '42, 1966-1974; Thomas H. Wright '62, 1974-

Senate of the United States has numbered among its members seventy-nine Princeton alumni from twenty-four states. Since its establishment in 1789 it has been without a Princetonian only twenty years.

Following is a list of Princeton senators, compiled from biographical material in the 1972 edition of *The Biographical Directory of the American Congress* and supplemented by additional information from subsequent Congressional directories. Where known, the party affiliation is given in parentheses, viz., Democratic (D), Federalist (F), Republican (R), Whig (W).

ALABAMA
John W. Walker 1806 (D) 1819-1822

CALIFORNIA
John S. Hager 1836 (D) 1873-1875

CONNECTICUT
Oliver Ellsworth 1766 (F) 1789-1790
Henry W. Edwards 1797 (D)
    1823-1837

DELAWARE
James A. Bayard 1784 (F) 1804-1813
Nicholas Van Dyke, Jr. 1788 (F)
    1817-1826
Arnold Naudain 1806 (R) 1830-1836
Richard H. Bayard 1814 (W)
    1836-1839, 1841-1845
George Gray 1859 (D) 1885-1899

GEORGIA
George M. Troup 1797 (D) 1816-1818,
    1829-1833
John Forsyth 1799 (D) 1818-1819,
    1823-1827, 1829-1833
John M. Berrien 1796 (D) 1825-1829,
    (W) 1841-1852
Alfred Cuthbert 1803 (D) 1835-1843
Walter T. Colquitt (D) 1843-1848
Alfred Iverson 1820 (D) 1855-1861
Alfred H. Colquitt 1844 (D) 1883-1894

KENTUCKY
John Brown 1778, 1792-1805
George M. Bibb 1792 (W) 1811-1814,
    1829-1835

LOUISIANA

Edward Livingston 1781 (D)
1829-1831
Edward J. Gay '01 (D) 1918-1921

MARYLAND

John Henry 1769 (D) 1789-1797
Samuel Smith (D) 1803-1815,
1822-1823
Robert G. Harper 1785 (F) 1816
James A. Pearce 1822 (W) 1843-1862
Blair Lee 1880 (D) 1914-1917
Daniel B. Brewster '46 (D) 1963-1969
Paul S. Sarbanes '54 (D) 1976-

MASSACHUSETTS

Jonathan Mason, Jr. 1774 (F)
1800-1803

MISSISSIPPI

*Thomas B. Reed (D) 1826-1827, 1829
John Henderson 1812 (W) 1839-1845

MISSOURI

Francis P. Blair, Jr. 1841 (D)
1871-1873
George H. Williams 1894 (R)
1925-1926
John C. Danforth '58 (R) 1976-

NEW HAMPSHIRE

Samuel Livermore 1752, 1793-1801

NEW JERSEY

William Paterson 1763 (F) 1789-1790
John Rutherford 1776 (F) 1791-1798
Frederick Frelinghuysen 1770 (F)
1793-1796
Richard Stockton 1779 (F) 1796-1799
Jonathan Dayton 1776 (F) 1799-1805
Aaron Odgen 1773 (F) 1801-1803
Mahlon Dickerson 1789 (D) 1817-1833
Samuel Southard 1804 (D) 1821-1823,
(W) 1833-1842
Jacob R.T. Frelinghuysen 1804 (D)
1829-1835
William L. Dayton 1825 (W)
1842-1851
Robert F. Stockton (D) 1851-1853
John R. Thomson (D) 1853-1862
Richard S. Field 1821 (R) 1862-1863

James W. Wall 1838 (D) 1863
John P. Stockton 1843 (D) 1865-1866,
1869-1875
David Baird, Jr. '03 (R) 1929-1930
H. Alexander Smith '01 (R) 1944-1959

NEW YORK

Aaron Burr 1772 (D) 1791-1797
John Armstrong 1800-1802, 1803-1804
John Foster Dulles '08 (R) 1949

NORTH CAROLINA

Benjamin Hawkins (F) 1789-1795
Alexander Martin 1756, 1793-1799
David Stone 1788 (D) 1801-1807,
1813-1814
Nathaniel Macon (D) 1815-1828
James Iredell 1806 (D) 1828-1831

OHIO

Jacob Burnet 1791 (F) 1828-1831
Atlee Pomerene 1884 (D) 1911-1923

OKLAHOMA

Dewey F. Bartlett '42 (R) 1972-

OREGON

James K.Kelly 1839 (D) 1871-1877

PENNSYLVANIA

George M. Dallas 1810 (D) 1831-1833
James D. Cameron 1852 (R)
1877-1897
David A. Reed '00 (R) 1922-1935
Joseph F. Guffey 1894 (D) 1935-1937
James H. Duff '04 (R) 1951-1957

RHODE ISLAND

Claiborne D. Pell '40 (D) 1960-

SOUTH CAROLINA

John E. Colhoun 1774 (D) 1801-1802
John Taylor 1790 (D) 1810-1816
Daniel E. Huger 1798 (D) 1843-1845
James Chesnut, Jr. 1835 (D)
1858-1860
John L.M. Irby (D) 1891-1897

TENNESSEE

George W. Campbell 1794 (D)
1811-1814, 1815-1818

VERMONT
Isaac Tichenor 1775 (F) 1796-1797,
1815-1821

VIRGINIA
Abraham B. Venable 1780, 1803-1804
William B. Giles 1781 (D) 1804-1815
John Randolph (D) 1825-1827

* Although attendance of Princeton was indicated in the *Biographical Directory of the American Congress*, precise confirmation of the fact was not possible when this list was compiled.

Service of Remembrance, conducted annually by the Alumni Association, had its origins in a memorial service for Princeton war dead first held in Nassau Hall on Baccalaureate Sunday of 1919. The service was broadened in 1943 to include remembrance of all alumni who had died during the preceding year and was held thereafter in the University Chapel. In 1970 the time was changed to the mid-winter Alumni Day.

The service is conducted by three or four alumni ministers and concludes with a procession of class representatives, bearing floral tributes in memory of their classmates who have died in the preceding year.

Sesquicentennial Celebration, The, took place on October 20, 21, and 22 in 1896, reaching a climax when the College of New Jersey, on the 150th anniversary of its founding, formally announced its change of title to Princeton University. More than two years were spent in the celebration's preparation, and it was, according to contemporary accounts, the largest and best organized academic festival ever held in America. The previous winter and spring, President Patton and classicist Andrew Fleming West, the organizing genius of the celebration, had toured the country, arousing alumni interest, while mathematician Henry B. Fine

and art historian Allan Marquand had gone about Europe, inviting eminent scholars to attend. That summer a trustee-faculty committee had assured the Sesquicentennial's national significance by securing President Cleveland's agreement to give the principal address. The entire affair was a brilliant success, thanks to careful planning—and to Princeton's good fortune in having for the occasion three days of beautifully crisp and sunny weather in an otherwise wet and foggy October.

Visitors to the celebration found the town and campus bright with color—the red, white, and blue and the orange and black of flags, banners, and ribbons, set off against the brilliant fall colors of the trees and of autumn flowers coming into bloom. Princeton banners hung from dormitory windows, American flags were raised on every flagpole, and in the streets carriage and draft horses wore orange ribbons in their manes. Triumphal arches set up on Nassau Street for the occasion—one given by the town, the other provided by the College—added a touch of classical dignity to the scene. The town's arch bore a Latin inscription for "God Save the Republic," and the College's bore mottoes bidding farewell to the old (AVE VALE COLLEGIVM NEOCAESARIENSE) and welcoming the new (AVE SALVE VNIVERSITAS PRINCETONIENSIS).

During the week preceding the celebration, a fitting prelude to Princeton's assumption of university status was provided by a series of eighteen learned lectures given by six outstanding foreign scholars: Leipzig's Karl Brugmann on "Noun Genders in the Indo-Germanic Languages"; Dublin's Edward Dowden on "The French Revolution and English Literature"; Utrecht's A.A.W. Hubrecht on "The Descent of Primates"; Göttingen's

Felix Klein on "The Mathematical Theory of the Top"; Edinburgh's Andrew Seth on "Theism"; and Cambridge's J. J. Thomson on "The Discharge of Electricity in Gases." The American Mathematical Society held a special meeting in Princeton in honor of Professors Klein and Thomson, and less formal gatherings were held to honor the other lecturers.

The first day of the celebration included a sermon by President Patton in the morning, a reception of delegates in the afternoon, and an orchestral concert that evening. At the convocation for the reception of delegates, Harvard's president, Charles W. Eliot, speaking on behalf of American universities, congratulated Princeton on the contributions it had made to public service, medicine, history, and science, through such men as John Witherspoon, Oliver Ellsworth, James Madison, Benjamin Rush, David Ramsay, and Joseph Henry (qq.v.). The speaker for European universities, Professor J. J. Thomson of Cambridge, extolled the achievements of three Princeton scientists, physicist Joseph Henry, geologist Arnold Guyot, and astronomer Charles A. Young (qq.v.)

The main events of the second day were a convocation in the morning, a football game in the afternoon, and a torchlight procession at night.

At the convocation, Henry van Dyke 1873, representing the Cliosophic Society, recited an ode, "The Builders," which he had composed for the occasion, and Woodrow Wilson, speaking for the American Whig Society, delivered an oration, "Princeton in the Nation's Service" (q.v.). Wilson's eloquent address—a British delegate said there had been "nothing to equal it since Burke"—brought a long continued ovation.

In the football game, watched by many of the delegates as well as by students and alumni, Princeton defeated the University of Virginia, 48-0.

The torchlight procession, more than a mile long, began behind Nassau Hall, and was led through the town by a picked group of a hundred students, wearing reproductions of the blue and buff uniforms of the Mercer Blues, a Princeton company that had fought in the Revolution. They were followed by a delegation of twenty-five Yale seniors, eight hundred Princeton undergraduates, and two thousand alumni, representing classes back to 1839. Everyone carried an orange torch or lantern of some kind, and most of the alumni classes wore costumes and carried transparencies. "It was an unforgettable sight," William Berryman Scott recalled in his memoirs forty years later; the lights against the red and yellow autumn foliage, he wrote, "made a fairy scene." In front of Nassau Hall, where the procession ended, each class paused, as it passed in review, to cheer President and Mrs. Cleveland.

The main features of Nassau Hall, from the ground to the top of the cupola, were outlined in orange electric lights, the front campus was strung with Chinese lanterns, and overhead a full moon shone. Further color was added to the spectacle by fireworks, set off along the front fence on Nassau Street—large dynamite rockets, fiery wheels, bursting bombs, fountains, showers, and set figures, ending with the final "Good-night, Princeton 1746-1896."

On the third morning, the historic City Troop of Philadelphia, whose forebears had served under Washington in the Battle of Princeton, led a splendidly costumed academic procession from Marquand Chapel to Alexander Hall for the concluding Sesquicentennial anniversary exercises. President Patton thanked the delegates for their participation in the celebration and for their continuing interest in Princeton; announced that, despite the business depression, a special committee on endowment had raised more than $1,350,000 for professorships, fellowships, a new library, and a new dormitory; and, finally, proclaimed that "from this moment on, what heretofore for one hundred fifty years has been known as the College of New Jersey shall in all future time be known as Princeton University." With this announcement, Professor George McLean Harper recorded, "the audience broke into immense applause . . . [and] cheering, each cheer ending with the triple, 'Princeton University.' "

Following the conferring of fifty-eight honorary degrees, President Cleveland delivered the principal address, in which he made a plea for more earnest participation by educated men in the political affairs of the nation; he received a tumultuous ovation.

The Sesquicentennial was a turning point in Princeton's history. It marked the occasion when the old college gave way to the new university, and its effects influenced the University's growth years after the celebration was over. Andrew Fleming West demonstrated organizing talents that he later used as dean of the graduate school, and developed friendships with alumni, which proved invaluable in raising funds for the Graduate College. President Cleveland, warmed by the reception he had received, came to live in Princeton the following spring; he was elected a university trustee and served as first chairman of its graduate school committee. Henry B. Fine's contacts with foreign scholars, especially with his Sesquicentennial house guest J. J. Thomson, helped him further his ideas

for making Princeton a great center for mathematics and science; some of his earliest appointments were students of Thomson. And Woodrow Wilson's celebrated address, formulating a continuing ideal of Princeton service to the nation, brought him to the fore as a potential leader of the university—and of the nation.

Seventy-Nine Hall was presented to Princeton by Woodrow Wilson's classmates in 1904. They said it was a small gift that came from great love or, in the more elegant Latin inscribed above the fireplace in the oak-paneled tower room, EX AMORE MAGNO DONUM PARVUM. This was a modest appraisal of a handsome 25th reunion gift made long before the age of affluence by a class of only 170 members. All their names are recorded in bronze in the vaulted passageway beneath the tower.

Seventy-Nine's architect, Benjamin Wistar Morris, Jr., followed the Tudor Gothic style previously employed in Blair and Little but instead of stone used red brick with limestone trim, materials later chosen for neighboring buildings. Gutzon Borglum carved the monkey and tiger grotesques that peer out from the mouldings on the tower arches. The vaulted passageway beneath the tower provides a favorite spot for impromptu concerts by undergraduate singing groups. The tower room, which is large and high, with fine mullioned windows at either end, was used as an office by Woodrow Wilson when he was president of the University.

Seventy-Nine was originally a dormitory much coveted by upperclassmen because of its proximity to the eating clubs. In 1960 when new dormitories were being erected elsewhere on the campus, and increased academic office space was needed in this area, Seventy-Nine was converted for use by the philosophy and sociology departments. When sociology moved to Green Hall in 1964, the religion department took its place.

For sixty years two lions guarded the Washington Road steps to the passageway beneath the tower. Designed by Frederic Auguste Bartholdi, the French sculptor who designed the Statue of Liberty, they were given to the University by the Class of 1879 at their graduation and flanked the front door of Nassau Hall until 1911, when the Class presented the bronze tigers that took their place and moved the lions to Seventy-Nine Hall. Made of soft and malleable "white metal," the lions deteriorated with the passage of time and eventually had to be removed to a University storeroom for preservation.

Sigma Xi, The Society of, founded in 1887 by a group of undergraduate students at Cornell University, has had a Princeton chapter since 1932. There are two classes of membership: full members—faculty and graduate students who have published results of scientific research; and associate members—graduate and undergraduate students who have shown promise of marked achievement in scientific research.

Sir Hugh Taylor was national president of Sigma Xi from 1951 until 1953, and editor-in-chief of its publication *American Scientist* from 1954 to 1969, when its editorial offices were at Princeton.

Slavic Languages and Literatures. Russian language instruction at Princeton began during World War II, when a group of interested students asked to have John Turkevich of the Chemistry Department give them a course, and President Dodds granted their petition. Professor Turkevich's efforts were continued by Pierre Eristoff, Professor Turkevich's wife Ludmilla, and eventually, by Valentine Bill, who continued until her retirement in 1974.

Russian offerings were later incorporated into the Department of Modern Languages, and, after it was divided, Russian became a part of Romance Languages, where it remained until an independent Program in Slavic Languages and Literatures was finally organized in 1961. Shortly thereafter a graduate program was initiated, and the faculty was expanded considerably, with additions primarily from Yale and Harvard. This period also saw the establishment of a Program in Russian Studies, in which students could work jointly, while taking courses in Slavic. In 1967 the Program in Slavic became a full-fledged Department of Slavic Languages and Literatures. In 1971, because of a budgetary crisis and the cessation of support from the government, the Graduate Program in Slavic was, unfortunately, suspended, but not until it had trained fifteen excellent people who now teach at Harvard, Yale, Columbia, and Pennsylvania, among other institutions. The Slavic Department now focuses on an excellent undergraduate program, but continues its efforts to have its Graduate Program restored.

The department concentrates much of its activity on a rigorous four-year language program in which all professors are involved. In addition, a wide variety of Russian and Soviet literature courses are offered, including such individual authors as Dostoevsky, Tolstoy, and Solzhenicyn. Advanced courses are often taught primarily or solely in Russian. Undergraduate majors in Slavic may emphasize literature, but they may also involve themselves more directly with the language and study the structure and history of Russian and Slavic. Though Russian itself is certainly the main language in the Princeton Slavic Department, a course in Czech is now offered, and Polish and Serbo-Croatian have also been available in the past.

The Slavic department maintains close cooperation not only with Russian Studies but also with the Departments of Comparative Literature and Linguistics, and its students frequently take courses in these departments.

Charles E. Townsend

Smith, Samuel Stanhope 1769 (1751-1819), was the seventh president of the College and the first alumnus to hold the office. He was born March 15, 1751 (not 1750, as often has been said, even on his tombstone), the year in which his father, Robert Smith, was installed as pastor of the Presbyterian church in Pequea, Pennsylvania. The father was a trustee of the College from 1772 to 1793. Elizabeth, his mother, was a daughter of Samuel Blair, one of its founding trustees. Two younger brothers, John Blair and William Richmond Smith, graduated with the Class of 1773. His own ties to Princeton were strengthened when on June 28, 1775, he married Ann, the oldest daughter of President Witherspoon, whom he would succeed in 1795.

Samuel was prepared for college by his father, who conducted a famous school at Pequea, from which Samuel was admitted to the College in 1767 as a member of the junior class. Having excelled in mathematics and having become one of the earlier members of the

Whig Society, he graduated two years later with the highest honor of delivering the Latin salutary address at commencement. He returned to Pequea to assist his father in the school and to begin with him the study of theology. In 1770 he was brought back as a tutor to Princeton, where he continued his preparation for the ministry with Witherspoon. Licensed to preach in 1773, he went then as a missionary to Virginia.

There Smith had a leading part in the founding of two academies. One of them, located first in Augusta County, later became Washington College and still later Washington and Lee University. Prince Edward Academy, of which Smith was appointed first rector in 1775, became in 1783 Hampden-Sydney College. He also assumed a lead in bringing the support of Virginia's Presbyterians to the hope of Jefferson and Madison for the separation of church and state. In 1779 he was called back to Princeton as Professor of Moral Philosophy.

Smith and his family reached Princeton in December, taking up residence in the President's House, as Witherspoon moved to Tusculum, the house and farm he owned outside the village. Smith would occupy the President's House (now Maclean House) for almost 33 years, one of the longest tenures in the some 220 years of its history. Witherspoon, who remained active in the affairs of state and church, promptly turned over a large part of his administrative responsibilities to his son-in-law, who was named vice president in 1786. As the venerable president advanced in years, becoming totally blind during the last three years of his life, Smith's responsibilities grew. On Witherspoon's death in 1794 there was no question as to who should succeed him, and no problems of transition into the new administration.

Tall and well proportioned, with finely formed features and noticeably blue eyes, Smith by all accounts was an unusually handsome man who paid close attention to his dress and manners. Archibald Alexander recalled that when he first saw him at a meeting of the Presbyterian General Assembly he thought him the most elegant person he ever had seen. Elegance seems also to have contributed to his fame as a pulpit orator. There is an oft-repeated story, probably apocryphal, that his brother John once said to him: "You don't preach Jesus Christ and Him crucified, but Sam Smith and him dignified." Any one who turns to the collection of his sermons published in 1799, or to the two volume edition of them brought out after his death, will be impressed by their quality and their readability even today.

President Smith was fortunate in the reputation he enjoyed as a scholar. Elected to the American Philosophical Society in 1785, he delivered before that body *An Essay on the Causes of the Variety of Complexion and Figure in the Human Species*. It argued that all mankind belonged to the same family, and attributed diversity within the species to environmental influences. Although the paper brought nothing original to discussion of an old question, it displayed a respectable command of the existing literature, and was important enough, after its initial publication at Philadelphia, to be reprinted at Edinburgh and London, and to bring attacks from other scholars which caused Smith to respond with an enlarged edition in 1810. Above all, the *Essay* expressed Smith's abiding faith that there could be no conflict between science and revealed religion.

That faith provides the key to his educational policies at Princeton. Without challenging the fundamental place of classical languages and literature in education, he sought more time for the study of science and modern languages. One device was to strengthen requirements for admission so that further classical instruction might be limited to the first year. Another proposal, with agreement of the trustees in 1799 that was withdrawn in 1809, was to allow students to pursue a special program leading to a certificate of achievement, a significant step toward the later Bachelor of Science degree.

Smith did not achieve all that he hoped for in the way of curricular reform, but his achievements in other areas were impressive. The College in 1795 was still struggling to recover from the disastrous effects of the war years. Especially critical was the financial problem. Smith's success in getting from the state legislature in 1796 a grant of £600 per year for three years provided only partial relief. The grant was not renewed, and the College remained primarily dependent upon tuition fees for its income. An enrollment of just above 75 students in 1794 had grown to a total of 182 in 1805, and the 54 A.B. degrees awarded in 1806 was the largest number since the founding of the College. A faculty of two professors, including the president, had grown to one of four professors in addition to the president, the usual two or three tutors, and an instructor in French. Among the professors was John Maclean, a graduate of Edinburgh whose special interest was chemistry. Faculty minutes, which had their beginning in 1787 and for a time dealt almost exclusively with a nagging problem of student discipline, reveal that the faculty increasingly was consulted on academic questions.

Smith himself continued to carry a teaching schedule that any modern teacher will regard as unbelievably heavy. The two volumes of his *Lectures . . . on . . . Moral and Political Philosophy* published in 1812 testify to the high quality of the instruction he gave. He acutely estimated the special opportunity the College faced in the light of its history and the growing competition from other colleges. He was fond of describing Princeton as a mecca for students drawn from the region reaching southward from the Hudson to Georgia. How accurate was the estimate is suggested by the origins of students attending the College in January 1805. From New Jersey there were 32, Pennsylvania 31, Maryland 28, Virginia 22, South Carolina 13, and Georgia 9. Of the other states, only New York had as many as Georgia.

The high point in Smith's presidency came just after the fire that in 1802 destroyed Nassau Hall. The constituency of the College rallied to its support so well that funds were raised not only for the reconstruction of Nassau Hall but for the addition of two new buildings to flank it on the front campus, Stanhope Hall and Philosophical Hall, which no longer stands. Except for the unhappy sequel that followed, this would have to be described as an unqualified tribute to the man who headed the institution.

The sequel is not easily explained. A student riot in 1807, resulting from Smith's mishandling of a problem of discipline, brought the suspension of 125 students and a growing distrust by the trustees of the president. For some of them his educational reforms had gone too far, and there was discontent over the declining number of students preparing for the ministry. Enroll-

ments declined, four professors resigned, Maclean the last in 1812. In that year, too, Smith was given no choice but to resign. He was provided a pension and a house. He died on August 21, 1819.

W. Frank Craven

Soccer became an organized sport at Princeton on the evening of November 2, 1905, when several dozen undergraduates crowded into 2 Middle Dod in response to a call in that morning's *Prince* for a meeting of "all men interested in forming an association football team." Less than a month later, Princeton played its first game, defeating a Merion Cricket Club team, 3 to 0.

In the early years, the teams received only such coaching as they could procure themselves. For a while they were fortunate in having the services of Jack Taylor, a former All-England soccer player, who gave them what time he could spare from his major occupation—bartender at the old Princeton Inn.

The Intercollegiate Association Football League was formed in 1905 by Columbia, Cornell, Harvard, Haverford, and Penn, and joined by Yale in 1908 and by Princeton in 1911. Princeton competed in this league until 1926, in the larger Intercollegiate Soccer Football Association until 1932, in the Middle Atlantic League until 1955, and after 1955 in the Ivy League.

Princeton's best season in the early years came in 1916 when it tied for first place but lost the postseason play-off to Penn, 3 to 2, on a snow-covered field a week before Christmas. Center forward Arthur Preyer '19, who had learned to play soccer in Holland, scored both of Princeton's goals. Two of Penn's three goals were scored by its inside right, an

All-American whose name was William Nassau. "Just how we let this man get away from us," the *Alumni Weekly* commented, "is a matter worthy of consideration."

Al Nies, the first full-time coach, who served from 1919 to 1934, saw Princeton soccer through one of its most successful eras. Five of Nies's sixteen teams were league champions: 1921, 1922, 1925, 1926 (tied), and 1927; and five finished second: 1919, 1920, 1923, 1924, and 1932 (tied).

Two brothers played leading roles on the 1922 team. Defending Princeton's goal, Captain Crossan Cooper '23 held league rivals to three goals, while, up front at center forward, Joe Cooper '25 scored a third of Princeton's twenty-three points. The 1925 team was undefeated but suffered one tie. The 1927 team's record was unmarred by either defeat or tie. Center forward Jack Packard '28 accounted for more than half the goals scored by Princeton in the championship seasons of 1925, 1926, and 1927.

Bill Logan was coach from 1935 through 1937 and in his last two years guided Princeton to league championships.

Jimmie Reed was coach for almost three decades, from 1938 through 1966. His teams won 188 games, lost 103, and tied 33. Six were league champions: 1939, 1940, 1942, 1946 (tied), 1957, and 1960, and three finished second: 1938, 1941, and 1959.

A spirited member of the forward line in the late 1930s was Bob Goheen '40, later freshman soccer coach, and still later sixteenth president of the University.

The 1940 team, which won eight games and tied Yale 3 to 3 in the ninth, shared with Penn State the title of Eastern Collegiate champion.

The 1942 team, whose record was marred only by a scoreless tie with Yale, was one of Princeton's strongest. In nine games it scored 42 points and allowed only 2, holding all of its opponents scoreless, except Penn. Leading a well-balanced team were Captain Ward Chamberlain '43 at outside left, Bud Palmer '44 at center halfback, and Chan Brewer '45 at goal.

Princeton won the Ivy championship in 1957 and again in 1960. The captain of the 1964 team, Dave Hackett '65, was killed in action in Vietnam; in his memory, his teammates provided a soccer trophy which is awarded annually. Jack Volz was coach from 1967 through 1972. Bill Muse, an All-American soccer player at Springfield College in Massachusetts in 1968, became coach in 1973. His 1976 team finished 10-4 overall and 5-2 in the Ivy League, tying with Cornell for second place.

Sociology became an independent department in Princeton only in the 1960s, but in 1895 a course was given with this description: "Sociology. A historical review of the evolution of modern industrialism. . . . The genesis and development of a science of sociology." The instructor was Walter A. Wyckoff 1888 (q.v.), Lecturer in Sociology and later Assistant Professor of Political Economy, who was called "Weary Willie" because from 1891 to 1893 he made his way, mostly on foot, from Connecticut to California, supporting himself as a laborer in order to learn by experience about America's emerging "labor problem" and poverty.

Beginning in 1912, the economist Frank A. Fetter (q.v.) continued this ameliorative approach to the new "industrialism" with a course in "Social Economics." After 1913, this course was offered in the Department of Economics and Social Institutions, which split off from the Department of History, Politics, and Economics, set up in 1904 by Woodrow Wilson.

The establishment of the Office of Population Research in 1936 provided a further impetus to Sociology through the work of its first director, Frank W. Notestein, and later of demographer-sociologists Dudley Kirk, Kingsley Davis, and Wilbert E. Moore. Under Moore's guidance, Sociology took a more scientific direction, complementing the earlier and continuing interest in social problems and reform. Soon after the Second World War, Frederick F. Stephan joined the department as professor of social statistics along with three younger scholars, Marion J. Levy, Jr., specializing in general theory and East Asia; Melvin M. Tumin, in social class and race relations; and Gerald W. Breese, in urban studies. In 1948, on the recommendation of an inter-departmental committee, a doctoral program was established; the first Ph.D. was granted in 1951.

Sociology grew slowly in the 1950s. Morroe Berger joined the sociology faculty and also the recently expanded Program in Near Eastern Studies in 1952, adding to Sociology's specialization in foreign "area" studies and comparative social structure. In 1954, the Department of Economics and Social Institutions became Economics and Sociology.

Growth was rapid in the next decade, beginning in 1960, when the junior partner of Economics and Sociology became the senior partner of the Department of Sociology and Anthropology. Charles H. Page came from Smith College to be the first chairman, and he was joined a few years later by Charles F. Westoff, a demographer, and Marvin

Bressler, a specialist in the sociology of education.

In 1963, the department moved to Green Hall (vacated by the School of Engineering), which it shared with the Psychology Department. Sociologists continued to be active as teacher-scholars and administrators in the Woodrow Wilson School, the Office of Population Research, the "area" programs on East Asia, the Near East and Russia, and the newer Program in Afro-American studies; Bressler headed the Commission on the Future of the College, which conducted a three-year review of undergraduate education at Princeton.

In 1965, Anthropology assumed separate status, and the department's title became simply the Department of Sociology. Under the new chairman Westoff and his successor, Bressler, Sociology attracted new faculty members and large numbers of students. Suzanne Keller joined as visiting professor in 1965 and three years later became the first woman full professor in Princeton's history.

During the national crises of the later 1960s, students took a heightened interest in sociology, seeking "relevance" to problems of the war in Viet Nam, race and sex relations, and the environment. Several young instructors made the subject even more attractive, among them Robert A. Scott and Stephen L. Klineberg, whose course attracted hundreds of undergraduates. The number of undergraduate concentrators rose from 20 in 1965 to about 150 in 1969 and 1970, the largest in the University.

This great influx ended as student unrest declined. Sociology, under Berger's chairmanship, faced the problem of orderly contraction. Modest, regular growth seemed to have returned by

1974. Meanwhile the department acquired several new professors: in 1970, Norman Ryder, a demographer who was one of the first Princeton Ph.D.'s in sociology, and Gilbert F. Rozman, specializing in East Asian and Russian Studies; in 1972, Walter L. Wallace, a specialist in general theory and in Afro-American studies; and in 1973, Howard F. Taylor, a social psychologist, who was also appointed director of the Program in Afro-American Studies.

By the mid-1970s, Sociology at Princeton was on a more even course. In the face of rapid change, it had maintained a combination of specialization and breadth that saved it from the fluctuations of fashion. The department continued its commitment to effective teaching, and its scholarly work gave it a place, despite its small size, among those ranked highest in the country.

Morroe Berger

Spelman Halls, completed in 1973, provided the first on-campus apartment living for undergraduates. They were named for Laura Spelman Rockefeller, who, with her husband, John D. Rockefeller, Sr., founded Spelman College in Atlanta, Georgia, the first American college for black women. A former public schoolteacher, Mrs. Rockefeller maintained a life-long interest in education, particularly for women. Her grandson, Laurance S. Rockefeller '32, a charter trustee, gave the University $4 million in 1969 to help institute coeducation. Most of the gift was used for Spelman Halls, which helped meet the increased housing needs of an expanded student body.

The eight-building complex, which was designed by I. M. Pei and Partners, contains fifty-eight apartments for 220 students. Each unit includes a living and dining area, outside balcony, kitchen, bath, and, typically, four study-bedrooms. Six of the apartments, with single large bedrooms, are for student married couples.

Set in a naturally wooded landscape on the western edge of the main campus, the interdependent halls are arranged along a diagonal axis extending south from Pyne Hall and Dillon Gymnasium in such a way as to preserve vistas and to provide pleasant spaces between Spelman and its neighbors. An innovative use of pre-cast concrete slabs, glass, and light enabled the architects to integrate the eight buildings into an architecturally varied campus, according to one observer, "in an elegant, respectful, and restrained manner."

In 1977, Spelman Halls was given an honor award by the American Institute of Architects as a "distinguished accomplishment in architecture."

Squash became an intercollegiate sport at Princeton in 1929, and within the first five years of competition the University had produced undefeated teams in 1931 and 1932 as well as the 1933 intercollegiate individual champion and the runner-up, William G. Foulke II '34 and his classmate Sheldon Stephens. Six years later Princeton had another champion—Stanley W. Pearson, Jr. '41.

John Conroy, who became coach in 1940, said his major problem was making undergraduates understand that squash was something else besides "a vegetable they don't like." Judging by his thirty-year won-lost record (184-69 for a winning percentage of .727), the problem was not insoluble. His teams won national championships in dual meet competition in 1942, 1943, and 1955 (finishing second in 1960, 1964, and 1965), and in post-season tournaments in 1959 and 1960 (finishing second in 1961).

Seven national collegiate individual championships were won by Princeton players during Conroy's years: in 1941 and 1942 by Charles M. Brinton '42, in 1954 and 1955 by Roger Campbell '55, and in 1959, 1960, and 1961 by Stephen T. Vehslage '61—first three-time winner in the history of the championship. Princeton's first national intercollegiate doubles championship was won in 1953 by Charles Warner '53 and Benjamin F. Edwards III '53.

Conroy retired at the end of the 1969 season. He was succeeded by his assistant coach, William M. Summers, who in turn was succeeded, in the fall of 1974, by David A. Benjamin, a former squash star and tennis captain at Harvard.

Varsity squash continued to flourish in the seventies after the move from the old courts at Dillon to the new ones in Jadwin, which the *New York Times* called "the nation's finest squash facilities." From 1975 through 1978, Princeton squash teams led by Coach Dave Benjamin achieved one of the most impressive four-year records in Princeton athletic history. In dual meet competition they won the nine-man national championship with undefeated seasons in 1975, 1977, and 1978, and placed second in 1976 to Harvard, which gave Princeton its only defeat in four years. In the post-season intercollegiate championship tournaments, Princeton won the six-man team title in 1976 and again in 1978—the first time Princeton won both championships in the same year.

In addition to their success in intercollegiate competition, Princetonians have won the men's national championship eight times: Donald Strachan '31 in 1935 and 1939; Charles M. Brinton '42 in 1941, 1942, 1946, and 1947; Stanley W. Pearson, Jr. '41 in 1948; Stephen T. Vehslage '61 in 1965. Princeton alumni were also men's national doubles champions three years running: Strachan and Brinton in 1946, Pearson and David McMullin '30 in 1947, Brinton and Pearson in 1948.

WOMEN'S SQUASH

Women's teams, coached by six-time national champion Betty Constable, earned an A+ in their early years. Undefeated in 1972, their first season, they captured four successive national collegiate championships from 1973 through 1976, won a fifth in 1978, and produced five national collegiate champions—Wendy Zaharko '74 in 1972, 1974, and 1975; Sally Fields '73 in 1973; and Nancy Gengler '78 in 1976.

Stace, Walter Terence (1886-1967), Stuart Professor of Philosophy for twenty years, grew up in an English military family (his great-grandfather, General William Stace, served in the Battle of Waterloo), and it was expected that, like his father and brother, he would follow a military career. In his teens, however, he experienced a religious conversion and entered Trinity College, Dublin, with a view to a career in the Anglican Church. At Trinity, he became interested in systematic philosophy, but on graduation, yielding to family pressure, he entered the British Civil Service. From 1910 to 1932, he served in various posts in the government of Ceylon; there is still a Stace Street in Colombo, where he was mayor for many years. At the same time, he continued to study philosophy; every morning he was awakened with early tea at six to read and write for two hours before breakfast. In this way he produced three books: *A Critical History of Greek Philosophy, The Philosophy of Hegel,* and *The Meaning of Beauty.*

He was called to Princeton in 1932 and appointed Stuart Professor of Philosophy in 1935. After coming to the University he published a book-length poem, many scholarly articles, and books of major importance in the theory of knowledge, metaphysics, ethics, social and political thought, and the philosophy of religion. One book won an American Council of Learned Societies award, another the Reynal and Hitchcock prize. His publications, according to the *New York Times,* established him as "one of the preeminent philosophers of the English-speaking world."

Stace was an empiricist in the British tradition. Professor James Ward Smith, a colleague and former student, has said that his basic position was that empiricism does not require the confinement of belief to propositions that are in any strict sense demonstrable.

The boy who had experienced religious conversion [Professor Smith wrote] was never smothered by the mature clearly-reasoning empiricist. . . . "Either God is a mystery or He is nothing at all," Stace wrote. "To ask for a proof of the existence of God is on a par with asking for a proof of the existence of beauty. If God does not lie at the end of any telescope, neither does he lie at the end of any syllogism. . . ."

Stanhope Hall, the University's third oldest building, was erected in 1803. It originally housed the college library, study halls, and the two literary societies, Whig and Clio, and was called the Library. Later it contained the "geological cabinet" and lecture rooms and was known as Geological Hall. Still later it contained the offices of the treasurer and the superintendent of Grounds and Buildings and, for a time, the meeting room of the Faculty and was called the College Offices and then the University Offices. In 1915 the trustees gave it its present name in honor of Samuel Stanhope Smith, who was president when it was built. In recent years Stanhope has housed the University's communications and security offices.

Another building, an exact duplicate of the present Stanhope, was also built in 1803 on the other side of Nassau Hall facing the "Library." In its basement were the college kitchen and refectory, on its upper floors rooms for the college's "philosophical apparatus" and for the classes in mathematics and natural philosophy. Known at first as the Refectory it was later called Philosophical Hall. It was here that Joseph Henry conducted his experiments in electromagnetism and in telegraphy. Philosophical Hall was razed in 1873 to make room for Chancellor Green library.

Statistics at Princeton was the creation of Luther P. Eisenhart and Samuel S. Wilks. Its history falls naturally into four periods: Wilks alone, World War II, postwar under Wilks, the early years as a department.

Dean Eisenhart's vision brought Wilks to Princeton's Department of Mathematics in 1933. For the next eight or ten years, Wilks was the lone statistician in that department, building a sequence of courses, stimulating undergraduates, and starting to turn out Ph.D.'s. Much of his important research was carried out and published during this era. His influence on a variety of areas of application grew rapidly, and his editorship of the *Annals of Mathematical Statistics* carried that journal through its crucial and formative decades. His pattern of "write mathematics, and do applications" became well established and was thoroughly conveyed to his students.

During World War II Wilks became deeply involved in the activities of the National Defense Research Committee, both in the Applied Mathematics Panel and at Princeton, where SRG-P (Statistical Research Group-Princeton) and its branch at Columbia ("SRG-P Jr") involved graduate students T. W. Anderson, P. J. McCarthy, F. Mosteller and D. F. Votaw, and brought in R. L. Anderson, W. G. Cochran, A. M. Mood, L. S. Savage, J. W. Tukey, J. D. Williams, and C. P. Winsor for varying periods. (Many of these names were to become familiar to statisticians in the decades that followed.)

Merrill Flood became responsible for the Fire Control Research Group, involving in addition to mathematicians, physiologists, and engineers, C. P. Winsor, an engineer-turned-physiologist-turned-statistician, J. W. Tukey, a chemist-turned-topologist-turned-statistician, and G. W. Brown, a mathematician-turned-statistician.

During these years the flavor was, of course: "do crucial applications, and any mathematics that can help."

This increase in the number of statisticians made statistics much more visible in Princeton (and vice versa) and must have played a part in the administration's approval of a Section of Mathematical Statistics in the Department of Mathematics. This section, which initially consisted of Wilks, Tukey (part-time Princeton, part-time Bell Telephone Labs), and usually a visitor, grew in 1956 by the addition of Francis J. Anscombe (a former visitor). The old

flavor of "write mathematics and do applications" continued, although some were now much more willing not to look to mathematicians as the source of approval. Undergraduate courses and interest grew somewhat, and there were steady streams of Ph.D.'s and faculty research.

The Korean War stimulated the establishment of the Analytical Research Group, of which Forman S. Acton was director from 1952 to 1956, and about half of whose work was statistical. George E. P. Box was then brought to Princeton as director of the Statistical Techniques Research Group (1956-1959), whose participants included E.M.L. Beale, J. Stuart Hunter, Colin Mallows, Mervin E. Muller, and Henry Scheffé. Again there was a larger critical mass and mutual stimulation, with a further broadening of interests and a further recognition of mathematics as important but not all embracing.

After Wilks's death in 1964, with encouragement from some mathematicians and the administration, an independent Department of Statistics was formed in 1966. Tukey was its (part-time) chairman from 1966 to 1969 and after an administrative review and approval of expansion, he was succeeded by Geoffrey S. Watson in 1970. A new stream—undergraduate majors —joined the streams of Ph.D.'s, faculty research, and involvement in statistical applications; emphasis on undergraduate study became comparable with the emphasis on graduate study.

Frederick F. Stephan, who had come to Princeton in 1947 in Sociology, transferred to the new department, broadening its interests significantly. J. Stuart Hunter, who had returned to teach in the School of Engineering in 1968, also took an active role for a time.

John Hartigan returned in 1964 to help hold the fort and, after Watson's arrival, the department was strengthened by Donald McNeil (1971-1976) and Peter Bloomfield (1971, acting chairman 1976-1977) among others.

Tukey's interest in data analysis (regarded as encompassing statistics), now that the pressure of needing to teach "mathematics" was removed, led first to a Freshman course in Exploratory Data Analysis and then to a book (preliminary edition 1970-71, first edition 1977) emphasizing simple arithmetic and careful thinking. In December 1974 a PDP 11-40 computer was installed. Both these steps illustrate the continued broadening in the Department's attitude, where very mathematical questions remain important but other Ph.D. theses focus on specific applications or even on the analysis of important sets of data.

Robustness (in the technical sense of that word) and time series continue to be strong interests in the department, as they have been for decades. More recently, collaboration with the Office of Population Research and the Center for Environmental Studies has been prominent. The department is proud that the first two chairmen of the Department of Statistics, both at Harvard and at Yale, came from Princeton and that, in the early seventies, those of its undergraduate majors who wished to do their graduate study in statistics were able to do so at Harvard, Stanford, or Yale.

John W. Tukey

Stevenson, Adlai Ewing (1900-1965), governor of Illinois, twice Democratic candidate for president, and ambassador to the United Nations, was born to politics. His maternal great-grandfather, Jesse Fell, a founder of the Republican party, was a close friend of Abraham Lincoln and the first to propose him for the presidency. His paternal grandfather, Adlai E. Stevenson, was vice-president during Grover Cleveland's second term. His father, Lewis Stevenson, also a Democrat, was once secretary of state for Illinois.

As a boy of twelve, Adlai accompanied his father when he called on Governor Woodrow Wilson at his summer home in Sea Girt to discuss the presidential campaign of 1912. Wilson, Stevenson later recalled, was extremely courteous to him, asking whether he was interested in politics and referring casually to the fact that he had been president of Princeton before becoming governor of New Jersey. "That's what decided me on going to Princeton, right then, and there," Stevenson said. "I came away with the feeling: I'm his deathless friend. His supporter. His admirer. That's my man."

At Princeton he studied principally history and literature and although, as he himself said, he "was never threatened by Phi Beta Kappa," it became obvious in later life that he absorbed a great deal from his reading, lectures, and preceptorials. He joined Whig Hall, took a course in public speaking which he thought "could prove very worthwhile," became managing editor of the *Princetonian*, and was elected one of the fifteen members of the Senior Council, the original agency of student government. He lived in 42 Patton Hall and took his meals at Quadrangle Club in upperclass years. In the senior class vote at his graduation in 1922, as he informed another senior class thirty-two years later (with characteristic humor at his own expense), he received only eight votes for "biggest politician" but twenty-eight for *"thinks* he is. . . ." He also received two votes for "most likely to succeed." ("I still don't know who the other fellow was," he said.)

As a young lawyer in Chicago, following legal studies at Harvard and Northwestern, he developed his skill as a public speaker and his knowledge of world problems while serving as president of the Chicago Council on Foreign Affairs. In the early 1930s he spent a year in Washington with the New Deal and during World War II was special assistant first to the secretary of the navy and later to the secretary of state. He was an active participant in the formulation of the charter of the United Nations in San Francisco in 1945, chief of the United States delegation at the meeting of the U.N. Preparatory Commission in London, and a member of the United States delegation at the first three sessions of the General Assembly.

GOVERNOR OF ILLINOIS

Stevenson won the governorship of Illinois from the Republican incumbent in 1948 by 572,067 votes—the largest majority ever received in Illinois up to that time. His achievements during his four-year term as governor were impressive. He recruited first-class men—some of them Republicans—for top positions on his staff, eliminated many useless jobs, and instilled a sense of public responsibility in the surviving state employees. He took the state police out of politics, knocked out commercial gambling, started a highway improvement program, and overhauled the state's welfare system. He almost doubled the state's appropriations for local schools and made its mental health program, which had been one of the worst, very close to the best.

His veto messages were remarkable both for substance and for style. He courageously vetoed a bill, overwhelmingly passed by both houses, which would have set up elaborate procedures for detecting subversives and require loyalty oaths of teachers and state officials: "Basically, the effect of this legislation . . . will be less the detection of subversives and more the intimidation of honest citizens." In a lighter vein, he explained his refusal to approve a bill that sought to protect birds by restricting the movement of cats: "If we attempt to resolve [this problem] by legislation, who knows but what we may be called upon to take sides as well in the age-old problems of dog versus cat, bird versus bird, even bird versus worm. In my opinion, the state of Illinois and its local governing bodies already have enough to do without trying to control feline deliquency."

THE PRESIDENTIAL CAMPAIGNS

Stevenson was the unsuccessful Democratic candidate for president in 1952 and again in 1956, losing both elections to General Eisenhower. Asked on a television program some time later if he had any advice to give to young politicians, he said, "Yes, never run against a war hero."

As a presidential candidate Stevenson elevated American political discussion, beginning with his speech of acceptance in 1952: "Let's talk sense to the American people. Let's tell them the truth, that there are no gains without pains, that we are now on the eve of great decisions, not easy decisions . . . but a long patient, costly struggle which alone can assure triumph over the great enemies of man—war, poverty and tyranny—and the assaults upon human dignity which are the most grievous consequences of each."

In 1952 when it was not considered politically prudent to tangle with Senator Joseph R. McCarthy, Republican of Wisconsin, Stevenson publicly denounced McCarthyism in the senator's own state. "Because we believe in the free mind," he said, "we are also fighting those who, in the name of anti-Communism, would assail the community of freedom itself."

In 1956 he urged a treaty to ban nuclear testing even though public opinion polls supported the view of some of his associates that he would lose votes thereby. "There are worse things than losing an election," he said, "the worst thing is to lose one's convictions and not tell the people the truth."

Although he failed to win two presidential elections, Stevenson exercised extraordinary influence on American politics in his time. He attracted a large group of young college people into the active ranks of the Democratic party. As one of them (Richard Goodwin, Harvard '52) said, "He told an entire generation there was room for intelligence and idealism in public life, that politics was not just a way to live but a way to live greatly."

Stevenson lost his party's nomination in 1960 to John F. Kennedy but, as Arthur Schlesinger, Jr., pointed out, the transformation of the Democratic party in the 1950s was largely Stevenson's work and "by 1960 the candidates . . . were talking in the Stevenson idiom."

HIS WIT AND HUMOR

Stevenson also brought to the hurly-burly of politics a lively imagination and a ready wit. During the 1952 campaign, a news photographer caught a picture of him with a large hole in the sole of his shoe. "Better a hole in the shoe than a hole in the head," said Stevenson, and the hole in the shoe became a campaign symbol.

Partly because of his appeal to the intellect, partly because of his balding head, his opponents called him and his supporters "eggheads." In his Godkin Lectures at Harvard (published as *Call to Greatness*) he admitted that "*Via ovicipitum dura est*, or . . . the way of the egghead is hard."

On election day in 1952 he gave a talk to schoolchildren in front of a polling place near his home on "this business of voting" and to break the ice at the beginning said: "I would like to ask all of you children to indicate, by holding up your hands, how many of you would like to be Governor of Illinois, the way I am?" After a show of hands, he said, "Well, that's almost unanimous. Now, I would like to ask all of the governors if they would like to be one of you kids," and then raised *his* hand, exclaiming "yeh, yeh, yeh."

Sometime later, he asked a Radcliffe commencement audience, "Do you know the difference between a beautiful woman and a charming one?" and then responded, "A beauty is a woman you notice; a charmer is one who notices you."

AMBASSADOR TO THE UNITED NATIONS

On his inauguration in 1961, President Kennedy appointed Stevenson ambassador to the United Nations, and Stevenson served in that post until his death. During his four and a half years as ambassador he was probably the best known and most popular representative at the United Nations. Of the 116 governments then represented there were only six whose capitals he had not visited and whose leaders he had not talked with. Soon after he took office he visited the respresentatives of all 116 governments.

He was especially appreciated by representatives of the developing nations. "He had that quality," said Barbara Ward, the British economist, "for which the Africans . . . have found a special term . . . 'Nommo,' . . . the Bantu word for the gift of making life rather larger and more vivid for everyone else."

He was admired for his eloquence and for the moderation and reason he brought to discussions. "Even when policies and interests diverged violently," Miss Ward wrote, he remained "a symbol of America's readiness to live within the limits of civilized and responsible power."

Speaking to the United Nations Economic and Social Council in Geneva [on July 9, 1965,] Stevenson declared:

We travel together, passengers on a little space ship, dependent on its vulnerable reserves of air and soil; all committed for our safety to its security and peace; preserved from annihilation only by the care, the work, and I will say, the love we give our fragile craft. We cannot maintain it half fortunate, half miserable, half confident, half despairing, half slave—to the ancient enemies of man—half free in a liberation of resources undreamed of until this day. No craft, no crew can travel with such vast contradictions. On their resolution depends the survival of us all.

Five days later, while visiting in England on his return from Geneva, Stevenson fell dead of a heart attack on a London sidewalk. "To the public dialogue of his time he brought intelligence, civility and grace," the *New York Times* said in tribute, "We who have been his contemporaries have been companions of greatness."

Stevenson was awarded an honorary LL.D. by the University in 1954 and was the 1963 recipient of the Woodrow Wilson Award for his exemplification of Wilson's phrase, "Princeton in the Nation's Service." He is memorialized at Princeton by Stevenson Hall, an open membership social and dining facility, and also by a bronze bust (sculptured by Elizabeth Gordon) in the Woodrow Wilson School of Public and International Affairs and a stained glass window (designed by Ellen Simon) in the University Chapel, both of which were given by his Class of 1922. On a marble pedestal supporting the bust are carved these words of Stevenson:

And now we shall have to address ourselves to the unending tasks of greatness. For the quest for peace and security is not a day's or a decade's work. For us it may be everlasting.

Stevenson Hall was formed as a non-bicker University-managed dining facility at the initiative of undergraduate students in the Classes of 1968 and '69 when it became apparent that the original Court Club and Key and Seal Club would not long remain economically successful institutions. Stevenson was formed with approximately 130 members to occupy these buildings, at 83 and 91 Prospect Avenue, in response to growing student calls for a "viable social alternative," i.e., an alternative to membership in one of the traditional Prospect Avenue clubs.

Malcolm Diamond (Religion) served as first Master, 1969-1971. He was succeeded by Gerald Garvey (Politics), 1971-1974, followed by Maitland Jones (Chemistry), whose wife, Susan Hockaday, served as full Co-Master, 1974-1977.

In the early years, Stevenson Hall membership gained a reputation for strong commitment to political activism—but activism "within the system." During the Cambodia controversy in the spring of 1970, for example, the suggestion for a regular midterm University recess to permit active student participation in political campaigns originated at a Stevenson Hall protest meeting. During the same period, Stevenson Hall became a focal point of the Movement for a New Congress. It also served as the headquarters for various campaign efforts on behalf of insurgent (i.e., anti-Vietnam War) candidates for the U.S. Congress.

Through the early 1970s, the Stevenson Hall membership broadened. Sophomores were permitted to become full members in 1972. The same year, a Kosher dining facility was opened in the building at 83 Prospect; freshmen desiring to keep the dietary laws were admitted to membership in this section. The Kosher section represents the first of its type in any Ivy League university. Membership in the Kosher section grew in the first four years from 35 to 145.

The membership has also become increasingly diversified as liberal arts and engineering members have joined Stevenson Hall, along with the Woodrow Wilson School majors, historians and political scientists who have traditionally favored the Hall.

Gerald Garvey

Stockton, Richard 1748 (1730-1781), a member of the first graduating class, and the first alumnus elected a trustee, was born in Princeton of a Quaker family that was among the community's earliest settlers. His grandfather came to the colonies in 1696 and a few years later acquired from William Penn a large tract of land that embraced the present borough of Princeton. His father inherited the portion of the property that included the dwelling later named "Morven" where Richard was born, and was, for many years, presiding judge of the court of common pleas; a liberal patron of the College, the elder Stockton's influence contributed to its being located in Princeton.

Richard received his preparatory education at Samuel Finley's (q.v.) academy in Nottingham, Maryland, and graduated from the College in 1748 when it was still located in Newark. All of his five classmates went into the ministry. Stockton read law in the Newark office of David Ogden, a leading member of the New Jersey bar, and was admitted to the bar in 1754. He opened an office in Princeton and acquired a reputation for being the most eloquent and persuasive advocate in New Jersey. Among the able young men who read law with him were Joseph Reed 1757 and Jonathan Dickinson Sergeant 1762, both of whom later served as attorney general of Pennsylvania, and William Paterson 1763 (q.v.), later attorney general and governor of New Jersey.

In 1757, when he was twenty-seven, Stockton was elected a trustee of the College. Ten years later, while on an extended visit in Great Britain, he was asked to go to Scotland to extend to John Witherspoon the trustees' invitation to succeed the recently deceased Samuel Finley as president of the College. Stockton was "successful in removing all the objections which originated in Witherspoon's mind," but not those in Mrs. Witherspoon's, and he wrote his wife, "I have engaged all the eminent clergymen in Edinburgh and Glasgow to attack her in her intrenchments, and they are determined to take her by storm, if nothing else will do." Finally, with the help of Benjamin Rush 1760 (q.v.), then a medical student at the University of Edinburgh, Mrs. Witherspoon was persuaded to consent, and her husband accepted the call.

After his return, Stockton took an increasingly active part in the political life of the Province of New Jersey. In 1768 he was made a member of its council and in 1774 a judge of its supreme court. Elected a delegate to the Continental Congress on June 22, 1776, he took his seat in Philadelphia in time to hear the closing debate on the Declaration of Independence and to sign it along with Witherspoon and Rush. Two months later, in a vote by the state legislature, he was narrowly defeated for the governorship of New Jersey by William Livingston, and was then chosen first chief justice of the state, but declined this office, preferring to continue in the Continental Congress.

The following November, when British troops were rapidly approaching Princeton, Stockton took his family to the home of a friend in Monmouth County for safekeeping. While there, he was betrayed to the British by Loyalists and was dragged in bitterly cold weather to Perth Amboy. He was later taken to New York and put in the notorious Provost Jail, where he suffered brutal treatment until January 3, 1777, when a formal remonstrance from Congress led to his release.

Upon Stockton's return to Princeton, it became known (according to a letter from President Witherspoon to his son, David) that during his imprisonment the British had persuaded him to sign General Howe's Declaration, which required an oath of allegiance to the King—an act Stockton revoked later

that year by signing oaths of adjuration and allegiance prescribed by the New Jersey legislature. His health shattered, his estate pillaged, his fortune depleted, he continued to live in Princeton, an invalid, until his death from cancer on February 28, 1781, in his fifty-first year. "It was one of his earliest honors to have been a son of this college," said Vice President Samuel Stanhope Smith at Stockton's funeral in Nassau Hall, "and it was one of the first honors of his college to have given birth to such a son." He was buried in the Quaker burial ground at Stony Brook Meeting House.

Stockton's wife was Annis Boudinot, daughter of a merchant and silversmith who was for a time postmaster of Princeton. Their eldest daughter Julia married Benjamin Rush. Stockton's descendants occupied prominent places in the College and town, the state, and the nation. Among them were a United States secretary of the treasury, Richard Rush 1797; two judges of superior courts; three state attorneys general; and four United States senators.

A portrait of Stockton hangs in the Art Museum, one of his wife, in the John Maclean House. The Stockton family home, Morven, became the official residence of the governor of New Jersey in 1951. New Jersey's Richard Stockton State College was dedicated in his honor in 1971.

Street Library, The, which is a wing of Wilcox Hall, was given in 1961 by Graham D. Mattison '26 in memory of the writer Julian Street (1879-1947), who lived in Princeton in the 1920s and befriended many undergraduates, of whom Mattison was one. The Street Library provides residents of Woodrow Wilson College with a selection of some ten thousand books in greatest demand by undergraduates.

Mattison's gift built the library and purchased the original selection of books; it also provided an endowment for the addition of new books each year.

Street, whose son, Julian Street, Jr., graduated from Princeton in 1925, wrote that "as an outsider" he was fascinated by college life in Princeton as a "vision of . . . life in miniature." Before coming here to live he had collaborated with Booth Tarkington 1893 in writing a comedy, *The Country Cousin*, which had a successful run on Broadway. During the decade that he lived in Princeton, Street wrote a novel and three volumes of short stories, one of which ("Mr. Bisbee's Princess") won the O'Henry Prize for 1925. He was best known as a gourmet and author of books on wine, food, and travel.

Student government did not begin at Princeton until the turn of the century, but its essential spirit was evident years earlier. In James Madison 1771's time, the debating and literary societies, Whig and Clio, were governed entirely by undergraduates, and their strict parliamentary rules were sometimes applied with severity to erring faculty graduate members. During Woodrow Wilson 1879's undergraduate years, athletic, literary, and musical activities were all student-governed, and in the 1890s a later generation saw the beginning of another form of undergraduate self-government—the student-controlled honor system in examinations (q.v.).

Princeton's first formal agency of student government, the Senior Council, was founded in June 1905 on the initiative of undergraduates in the Class of 1906 and welcomed by President Wilson as a means of calling lead-

ers of undergraduate opinion into consultation with trustees and faculty "upon matters of moment in which it was not only proper but desirable that authority should wait upon opinion."

Although the Senior Council profited from the experience and influence of its members, its weakness was its lack of continuity; each year its membership was entirely new—a disadvantage that became particularly apparent in the 1920s when, after the Council had failed to produce an acceptable system of regulations for the safe use of automobiles by undergraduates, the trustees issued an edict forbidding student car use after July 1, 1927. The 1927 Senior Council thereupon resigned, and although the reason given was that they had not been properly consulted, the underlying difficulty in President Hibben's view was one of continuity and the Council's understandable reluctance to make decisions "which would not affect their own liberty but would affect only their successors."

The following fall, an Undergraduate Council representing all four classes was formed to replace the Senior Council. Among the products of its forty-year existence were a marriage course for seniors, chartered flights to Europe, an extension of Firestone Library hours, an increase in carrel space for upperclassmen, and the end of required chapel attendance. The Council also agitated successfully for the repeal of the edict prohibiting student use of automobiles, the improvement of club elections, the development of alternative social facilities, and the extension of curfew hours for women visitors in dormitories.

The late sixties and mid-seventies found Princeton student government in a state of flux. In 1967 the Undergraduate Council gave way to a larger

Undergraduate Assembly designed to provide wider student participation through the campus-wide election of representatives from dormitory areas and the scheduling of frequent meetings open to any undergraduate who wanted to attend. According to one student observer, the Assembly was "more constructively vocal" than the old Council. But the operation of the larger organization proved unwieldy, attendance fell off, and in time, the Assembly, like its predecessor, was being criticized for its failure to effectively represent student opinion, and was accordingly superseded in 1975 by a body known as the Undergraduate Student Government.

The new organization gave more power to existing committees on academic matters and undergraduate life and to the projects board, and replaced the old Assembly with the Undergraduate Caucus, a smaller deliberative body made up of student government officers, committee chairmen, class presidents, class delegates, and the undergraduate members of the Council of the Princeton University Community (q.v.).

Supreme Court of the United States, since its establishment in 1789, has numbered among its justices eight Princeton graduates. With the presidents who appointed them, they are:

WASHINGTON
William Paterson 1763 (N.J.)
  1793-1806
*Oliver Ellsworth 1766 (Conn.)
  1796-1800

JEFFERSON
William Johnson, Jr. 1790 (S.C.)
  1804-1834
(Henry) Brockholst Livingston 1774
  (N.Y.) 1806-1823

MONROE
Smith Thompson 1788 (N.Y.)
  1823-1843

JACKSON
James Moore Wayne 1808 (Ga.)
  1835-1867

TAFT
Mahlon Pitney 1879 (N.J.) 1912-1922

EISENHOWER
John Marshall Harlan '20 (N.Y.)
  1955-1971

* Chief Justice

Swimming at Princeton got off to a good start in the spring of 1906 with a victory over Yale in that season's only meet. The following year, the 1907 team won every meet in Princeton's first full season, taking the championship of the newly founded Intercollegiate Swimming Association; and a year later the 1908 team won the association's postseason meet to determine individual championships.

Frank Sullivan was coach from 1911 to 1928. His 1912 team defeated Yale but lost to Penn, finishing second in the league. His 1924 team won the league championship, beating Yale twice in close contests, while going undefeated in dual meet competition. The first of the two defeats of the Elis broke their seven-year string of 44 straight intercollegiate victories. Both meets were decided in the final event by Princeton's victorious 200-yard relay team, whose anchorman, John H. Hawkins '26, won the national collegiate championship in the 440-yard free-style the following year.

When Sullivan suddenly resigned in 1928, the University accepted Yale's offer to lend its assistant coach, Howard W. Stepp, for the rest of the season—and then kept him at

Princeton as swimming coach for twenty-five years and as Registrar from 1947 until his retirement in 1969. Stepp's teams won 162 of their 228 meets for an overall percentage of .711. His 1938 team was the first to beat perennial champion Yale since 1924.

Stepp swimmers included seven national collegiate champions: Edwin J. Moles, Jr. '31, Richard R. Hough '39, and Robert L. Brawner '52 in the 200-yard breast stroke; Albert Vande Weghe '40 and James Shand '48 in the 100-yard backstroke; Edward P. Sherer '32 in the 50-yard free style; Robert L. Brawner '52 in the 100-yard butterfly; Albert Vande Weghe '40, Richard R. Hough '39, and Hendrik Van Oss '39 in the 300-yard medley relay. In 1939 Hough was awarded the N.C.A.A. Trophy as the "outstanding swimmer of the year." Another Stepp swimmer, Howard L. Canoune '37 followed his mentor as varsity coach for five years from 1953 to 1958.

Robert L. Clotworthy (Ohio State '53), 1956 Olympic gold medalist in the three-meter dive, was coach from 1958 to 1970. "A bubbly little man who treats swimming with . . . an enthusiastic reverence" (in the words of Frank Deford '61), Clotworthy guided his 1962 swimmers to Princeton's first Eastern Seaboard team championship, and his twelve teams scored 104 victories in 148 dual meets for a winning percentage of .703. He trained three national collegiate champions: G. Gardiner Green, Jr. '63 (100-yard breast stroke), Jed R. Graef '64 (200-yard backstroke), and Ross E. Wales '69 (100-yard butterfly). Graef won an Olympic gold medal, in world-record time, in the 200-meter backstroke in 1964, and Wales was bronze medalist in the 100-meter butterfly at the 1968 Olympics.

Clotworthy's successor in 1970 was William W. Farley (Michigan '66), 1964 Olympic bronze medalist in the 1500-meter freestyle. His 1972 team, which completed Princeton's first undefeated season since 1924, captured the Eastern League championship and further distinguished itself by beating Yale by the widest Princeton margin achieved up to then—83 to 31.

In 1973 Princeton won its first Eastern Seaboard title since 1962, outscoring North Carolina by 120 points, as Captain Charles Campbell '73 earned four gold medals and Curtis Hayden '75, three, in individual and relay events.

Farley's 1974 team, which crushed Yale 91 to 22 during the regular season, won Princeton's second straight Eastern Seaboard championship with a breathtaking 419 to 411 victory over Harvard, accomplished in the last event of the meet when Princeton's 400-yard freestyle relay anchorman, Mal Howard '75, outstretched his Crimson opponent by half a stroke and touched home 47-100ths of a second sooner.

Entering the last day of the Eastern Seaboard championships in 1975, Princeton trailed North Carolina by 13 points, but a one-two-three sweep by Joe Loughran '77, Curtis Hayden '75, and Rob Maass '78 in the 1650-yard freestyle, and winning scores for diver Bill Heinz '75 on the three-meter board, helped Princeton pull ahead by nine points to win its third successive Eastern Seaboard title.

Runner-up in both the 1-meter and 3-meter dives at the 1974 N.C.A.A. Championships, Heinz was a student of two-time Olympic gold medalist Bob Webster (diving coach from 1966 to 1975), who also trained Eastern champions Holt Maness '69, John Huffstutler '71, Collins Landstreet '72, and Cece Herron '74, Princeton's first woman diving champion. Webster was succeeded by John Andrews '63 in 1975 and by another Olympic gold medalist, Leslie Bush Hickcox, in 1976.

The 1976 Princeton swimmers shared the Eastern title with Harvard and then outpointed them 344 to 252 in the Eastern Seaboard meet to win that championship for the fourth successive year.

In 1977, Princeton completed an undefeated season, won the league championship outright, and came from behind to beat Harvard 344 to 309 for an unprecedented fifth straight Eastern Seaboard title. That year's team, which Bill Farley said was the "best we've ever had," was the first to win both league and the Eastern Seaboard championship titles.

In 1978, after losing out to Harvard for the dual-meet championship by a bare .69 second in the closing 400-yard freestyle relay, Princeton came back a month later to beat Harvard in the same event, with an Eastern Seaboard record time that gave Princeton its sixth straight Eastern Seaboard championship.

WOMEN'S SWIMMING TEAMS

Intercollegiate swimming by Princeton women began informally, and auspiciously, in 1971 when a freshman and a sophomore entered the Eastern Intercollegiate Women's championships and together scored enough points to win fifth place for Princeton—Jane Fremon '75 by setting new Eastern records in the 100-yard butterfly and the 100- and 200-yard freestyle, Cece Herron '74 by finishing second in a field of seventeen divers.

A women's team was formally organized the following year, and from 1972 through 1975, Princeton women placed third, second, and then first twice in succession in the Eastern Intercollegiates.

At the 1973 Women's Nationals, Princeton finished third behind Arizona State and Florida as Cathy Corcione '74 set national records in the 100-yard freestyle and 100-yard butterfly, while joining Captain Carol Brown '75, Barbara Franks '76, and Jane Fremon '75 to set a national record in the 200-yard freestyle relay. That same year, the other pioneer, Cece Herron '74, was both the 1-meter and 3-meter diving champion at the 1973 Easterns. The following year at the 1974 Easterns, Cathy Corcione set another national record—in the 100-yard individual medley—and Eastern records in four other events.

Led by Captain Liz Osborne '76, who took first in the 50-, 100-, and 200-yard breaststroke, Princeton placed second in the 1976 Eastern Intercollegiates. The following year, paced by Mary Sykes '79 and Beth Mauer '80, the Princeton team decisively outpointed Yale, 657 to 520, to win the first official women's Ivy championship.

Coached initially by the men's varsity coach, Bill Farley, the women's team has had its own full-time coach, since the fall of 1975. Dave Garretson '72 was coach until the fall of 1977, when he was succeeded by Jane Barkman Tyler, former American record holder and Olympic medalist. Her 1978 team took second place in both the Ivy and Eastern championships. Beth Mauer '80 set four Princeton records in the backstroke, butterfly, and the 200- and 400-yard individual medley.

Tarkington, [Newton] Booth (1869-1946), novelist and playwright, spent his first two years of college at Purdue, his last two at Princeton. He was a founder of the Triangle Club, and editor of the *Nassau Literary Magazine*, a contributor of humorous drawings and literary wit to *The Tiger*, and the most popular man in his class. Bliss Perry said he was "the only Princeton man who had ever been known to play poker (with his left hand), write a story for the *Nassau Lit* (with his right hand), and lead the singing in a crowded room, performing these three acts simultaneously." These pleasurable activities Tarkington carried on at some expense to his studies, and when his class graduated in 1893 he lacked sufficient credits for a degree. His later achievements, however, won him an honorary A.M. in 1899 and an honorary Litt.D. in 1918.

Tarkington's singing of Kipling's ballad, "The Hanging of Danny Deever" was a highlight of student life in his time. Sooner or later, when the seniors gathered on the steps of Nassau Hall for their singing, the call would go up "Tark! Tark! Danny Deever!" and although he would always protest and suggest another song—and sometimes even try to slink away—his classmates would call for him until he had performed. In later years at class reunions the cry continued, and as one of his classmates related in the *Alumni Weekly*, Tarkington continued to respond reluctantly:

The same old Tark—just watch him shy
Like hunted thing, and hide, if let,
Away behind his cigarette
When "Danny Deever!" is the cry.
Keep up the call and, by and by
We'll make him sing, and find he's yet
The same old Tark.

Tarkington wrote a series of cheerful, realistic novels about life in the Middle West, beginning with *The Gentleman from Indiana* (1899) and including two Pulitzer Prize winners, *The Magnificent Ambersons* (1918) and *Alice Adams* (1921). He also, as Dean West said in presenting him for his second honorary degree, "rediscovered the American boy and wrote the idyll of his life" in *Penrod* (1914) and its sequels. He dramatized several of his novels, wrote other plays, short stories, essays, and *The World Does Move* (1928), a book of reminiscences.

In a commemorative tribute to Tarkington written for the American Academy of Arts and Letters Professor Chauncey B. Tinker of Yale quoted this remark of the critic, Hamilton Basso:

In his books as nowhere else, we get an understanding of how that earlier, more stable world of clipped lawns, gabled houses, and long summer holidays seemed from the inside of those who, like Tarkington himself, looked upon it as the best of all possible environments in a none too perfect world.

"In that happy environment," Tinker added, "he had many blessings. Experience of a sadly different kind in later life he bore with fortitude, and remained undefeated to the end. He was a gallant gentleman."

Taylor, Hugh Stott (1890-1974), who was born in Lancashire, England, and educated at the University of Liverpool, came to Princeton in 1914 expecting to remain only a few years. He stayed the rest of his long and productive life. Starting as a chemistry instructor, he rose quickly to full professor at age thirty-two and became first David B. Jones Professor in 1927. He served as chairman of the Department of Chemistry for twenty-five years and was dean of the graduate school from 1945 until his retirement in 1958.

Before receiving his doctorate at Liverpool, Taylor had done research in physical chemistry at the Nobel Institute in Stockholm and at the Technische Hochshule in Hanover. He soon became known for his work in this field and in 1919 gained international recognition when he wrote with Sir Eric Rideal the first significant book on catalysis. He was frequently consulted by both government and industry. During the First World War he returned to England to work in the Munitions Inventions Department. In the Second World War he played a prominent role in American scientific effort, directing a number of research projects, and contributing to the development of the atomic bomb with his discovery of the most effective catalyst for producing heavy water.

As an authority on catalysis, Taylor attracted to the University able young scientists from all over the world, among them future leaders in America, England, Japan, Belgium, and Sweden. While chairman of the department from 1926 to 1951, he was influential in securing Frick Chemical Laboratory and vigorously led the way in the development of chemistry at Princeton. His enthusiasm kept the department alive with excitement, which affected the work not only of postdoctoral fellows but of undergraduate students.

While he was dean, the Graduate School trebled its enrollment, added nine Ph.D. programs (in five engineering departments and in architecture, music, religion, and sociology), and strengthened its ties with former students through the creation of the Association of Princeton Graduate Alumni.

As devoted a churchman as he was a scientist and educator, Taylor was largely responsible for the establishment of a Catholic chaplaincy at Princeton in 1928, and he spoke frequently on the Campus about the relation of science and religion. He held to Thomas Aquinas's thesis that "Science is a revelation of the mind of God," and insisted, as in a *Princetonian* article in 1939, that true education could not be "divorced from the spiritual values of life." He was president of Pax Romana, the international Roman Catholic movement for intellectual and cultural affairs, and a member of the Pontifical Academy of Sciences.

His achievements brought him many honors. He was awarded the Nichols Medal of the American Chemical Society in 1928, elected a Fellow of the Royal Society of London in 1932, and made a Commander of the Belgian Order of Leopold II in 1937. The ensuing years brought him other medals, numerous honorary degrees, and membership in many American and foreign academies and societies. He was notably honored in 1953, when in April he presided over the Faraday Society's golden jubilee celebration in London, and when the following month he was twice knighted, first by Pope Pius XII in the Order of St. Gregory the Great, and, five days later, by Queen Elizabeth in the Order of the British Empire.

After his retirement, he served as president of the Woodrow Wilson National Fellowship Foundation and as editor-in-chief of *American Scientist*, the periodical publication of the Society of Sigma Xi, of which he had been president.

In 1962 an anonymous donor provided an enduring memorial of Sir Hugh's lifelong contribution to Princeton with a $500,000 gift establishing the Hugh Stott Taylor Chair of Chemistry.

Teacher preparation, as part of the undergraduate curriculum, was initiated in 1965, when President Goheen appointed a faculty committee to develop a program appropriate to a liberal arts college. The members were Professors William M. Beaney, chairman, Jeremiah S. Finch, Heinrich D. Holland, Sheldon Judson, André Maman, Albert H. Marckwardt, James W. Smith, and Albert W. Tucker. The committee's recommendations were based on the belief that a broad undergraduate program with concentration in one subject, combined with adequate experience as a student teacher under competent supervision, would prepare a person to teach that subject at the secondary school level.

The Teacher Preparation Program was approved by the faculty in 1967 and begun in that year under the direction of Henry Callard, former headmaster of the Gilman School, who had guided the proposal through its presentation to the faculty. He was joined in 1968 by Henry Drewry, former chairman of social studies at the Princeton High School, who became director following Callard's retirement. In 1969 the program was approved by the New Jersey Department of Education, and the first graduating senior received a permanent certificate for secondary school teaching.

For many years students had gone out from Princeton to enter the teaching profession, most of them in independent schools; lack of certification was an impediment for those who wished to become public school teachers. The advent of the program made certification possible on graduation, thus extending the possibilities for service to public as well as to private schools. As the program has evolved, it has adhered to the basic ideas of the original proposal: completion of full departmental requirements, selection of elective courses important to prospec-

tive teachers, and extended classroom experience of directed observation and teaching with competent counsel and instruction. Certification is possible in English, foreign languages, mathematics, science, and social studies. By 1976 nearly 300 had completed the program and received certification, more than half of whom had gone directly into teaching.

Besides achieving the purpose for which it was founded, the program has provided an added benefit for its participants. Orderly consideration of the teaching process and of the organization of ideas and materials to assist others to learn can enhance one's ability to view and evaluate one's own education. Thus the Teacher Preparation Program is not only consonant with a liberal education but supports and strengthens it for a significant part of each undergraduate class.

Henry S. Drewry
Jeremiah S. Finch

Tennis, long the most popular game played at Princeton, began as an organized sport in 1882 when undergraduates formed the Princeton Lawn Tennis Association. Two years later, Princeton joined the newly founded Intercollegiate Lawn Tennis Association and by the turn of the century had produced three intercollegiate champions: Samuel G. Thomson 1898, Raymond D. Little '01, and Frederick B. Alexander '02. Little and Alexander also shared Princeton's first doubles championship in 1900.

Led by Dean Mathey '12 and George M. Church '15, Princeton teams excelled in the years 1910 through 1915. Mathey twice shared intercollegiate doubles championships—in 1910, with his classmate Burnham N. Dell; and in

1911, with another classmate Charles T. Butler. Singles champion in both 1912 and 1914, Church also won the doubles in 1912 with his classmate Winfred H. Mace. Church later gave the University ten tennis courts, while Mathey, for many years a charter trustee, and Joseph L. Werner '21, a former tennis captain, gave the pavilion in the center of the tennis courts on Brokaw Field.

Princeton had one undefeated team in the first decade of the century (1906), two in the second (1913 and 1915), and five in the third (1921, 1922, 1926, 1928, 1929). Princeton's most renowned player John Van Ryn, Jr. '28 and his roommate Kenneth B. Appel '29 were intercollegiate doubles champions in 1927. Van Ryn, who was noted for his superb low volleying, later teamed with Wilmer L. Allison (University of Texas) to win the Wimbledon doubles championship in 1929 and 1930 and the United States doubles in 1931 and 1935—a partnership honored in 1963 by their joint election to the National Lawn Tennis Hall of Fame.

Under Mercer Beasley, who became coach in 1933, Princeton completed three undefeated seasons in 1933, 1934, and 1938, won Eastern intercollegiate championships in 1933, 1938, and 1941, and produced the 1935 Eastern intercollegiate singles champion —Norcross S. Tilney '35.

Assistant Coach John Conroy took over as head coach in 1942. During his thirty-year tenure, he directed eight undefeated teams, one in 1942, three from 1950 through 1952, and four from 1961 through 1964. Princeton won the Eastern intercollegiate championship in each of these years, as well as in 1953, 1957, and 1971, and shared it in 1954, 1965, 1968, and 1969. Two of Conroy's teams gained national recog-

nition: the 1942 team was ranked Number 1, the 1951 team Number 2. In the five years from 1949 to 1953, his teams won 42 consecutive victories—an all-time, all-sport Princeton record which stood only until six more Conroy teams accumulated 54 consecutive victories from 1960 to 1965.

Princeton players of this period won the Eastern intercollegiate doubles championship four times: Edgar M. Buttenheim '44 and Richard J. Bender '44 in 1942, Chadwick Johnson '46 and Frederick C. Prior '47 in 1944, John C. Taylor '48 and Joseph D. Scheerer '48 in 1945, and James S. Farrin '58 and David O. Brechner '59 in 1957. Two of them were singles champions: Chadwick Johnson in 1944, James Farrin in 1956 and 1957. Another outstanding player in the Conroy years was Herbert Fitzgibbon II '64, who played number one on all three undefeated teams in 1962, 1963, and 1964.

Conroy retired as tennis coach at the end of the 1971 season with a Princeton career winning average of .877.

Freshman coach William M. Summers took over the varsity coaching duties in 1971 and was succeeded in the fall of 1974 by David Benjamin, who had been captain of Harvard's 1966 Ivy League championship tennis team. Princeton teams continued in the Conroy tradition, finishing first for four consecutive years: they took the Eastern intercollegiate championship outright in 1974 and 1975, shared it with Harvard in 1976, and won it outright again in 1977.

WOMEN'S TENNIS

First organized in 1970, women's tennis teams proved to be equally formidable, taking the Eastern intercollegiate women's championship the first five years and sustaining a 35-match winning streak from 1971 through 1975. Marjory Gengler '73, the first Princeton woman to be awarded the white sweater with black P traditionally given captains of championship teams, was also Princeton's first winner of the Eastern intercollegiate women's singles championship, in the fall of 1970. Her classmate Jane Kincaid took the same title in both succeeding years, and in 1975, Linda Rice '78 became Princeton's fourth Eastern women's singles champion in six years. In doubles, Susan Epstein '76 and Julie Kirkham '76 won the Eastern championship in 1972. Eve Kraft coached the women until 1973 when she resigned to devote full time to the Princeton Community Tennis Program, in which she was co-director with John Conroy. Her successors have been Anne Marie Hicks, Carla Geiser, and Marie McCallum.

Theatre Intime, born for the self-amusement of three juniors on the third floor of Witherspoon Hall in 1919-20, has produced over 500 plays and involved some 10,000 people. It has always been run entirely by students, independent of University supervision. The experience gained in being responsible for every aspect of running a theatre is often cited as the reason for the unusual number of Intime graduates who have had outstanding careers in the professional theatre.

In 1921, Theatre Intime moved into Murray-Dodge under the leadership of Louis Laflin '24 and became a "legitimate" campus organization. The emphasis at first was on serious and/or original plays. (Some 150 student-written plays have been put on. Of "classical" authors, Shakespeare leads with 18 different plays produced, followed by Shaw with 16 and O'Neill with 8.)

A fire in June 1933 gutted the interior of Murray Theatre. It was remodeled that summer into roughly its present shape. World War II posed a more serious crisis. After three years in which Murray was given over to Navy lectures, a group of former Triangle and Intime members re-established the organization, reaching heights in 1948 with a memorable production of "Richard II." Their momentum carried over into the formation of the summer University Players. This was nothing new, for some of Intime's leading spirits had helped found the original University Players at Falmouth, Massachusetts, in 1928. A third outcropping of talent in 1968 brought to life "Summer Intime," which at this writing is still going strong.

Some Intime "stars" who have sparkled in professional theatre are Bretaigne Windust and Erik Barnouw '29; Joshua Logan, Norris Houghton, and Myron McCormick '31; Robert Chapman '41; Philip Minor '50; Charles Schultz, Hugh Hardy and Daniel Seltzer '54; Clark Gesner '60. Among Intime's "memorable" productions were Tolstoy's "Tsar Fyodor Ivanovitch" (1929); Toller's "Man and the Masses" (played in the new McCarter Theatre in 1931); "Time of Their Lives" (a play about Princeton by Robert Nail '33); "The Great God Brown" (1936), which earned a telegram of congratulation from Eugene O'Neill; and Giraudoux' "The Trojan War Will Not Take Place" in the early 1950s. For over half a century Intime has steered a generally successful course between the demands of the box office and the desire to do seldom-produced plays.

Herbert McAneny

Third World Center, The, was created in 1971 when the trustees approved the designation of the old Osborn Field House as a University facility to be used primarily, but not exclusively, by minority students.

Because the University's cultural and social organizations have largely been shaped by students from families nurtured in the Anglo-American and European traditions, it has not always been easy for students from different backgrounds to enter the mainstream of campus life. As trustee John M. Doar pointed out to the Board of Trustees, students from minority groups may miss something in their educational experience—not owing to a failure on the part of the University, but rather because the situation in which they find themselves is often different from the circumstances to which they have been accustomed. Minority students thus felt uneasiness and in many instances a sense of insecurity.

In 1971 the University began to recruit actively students who, while qualified, had not been a substantial part of the community. It was then believed and has since been established that increased participation of students from various backgrounds would stimulate and enrich the intellectual and cultural life of the University. With the increased enrollment of minority students in the early 1970s, Princeton had to give particular attention to ways in which these students could come together on an intellectual and cultural basis, to help them appreciate better their own backgrounds and to enhance their self-confidence. The University also recognized the need to have a means whereby the rest of the University community could better understand and appreciate the backgrounds and views of minority students.

During the academic year 1970-71, leaders of various minority groups expressed a strong interest in a facility for activities of their own that would include seminars, colloquia, exhibits, cultural shows, and social events. After a proposal had been carefully worked out and subjected to the most searching review, such a center was opened in the fall of 1971. As with other University-sponsored collegiate facilities, the Third World Center is open to all students. Its academic and cultural program is shaped by the students, the Master, and a Program Director. The Center is not residential and does not normally serve meals. Its aim is to provide through intellectual and social activities a setting and a program that will help students to reinforce each other and also to create a forum for greater awareness and understanding among people of differing cultural backgrounds. In doing so, the Third World Center has become a vital part of the University's cultural life and a resource for the whole University community.

Conrad D. Snowden

Thomas, Norman [Mattoon] 1884-1968), six times Socialist candidate for president of the United States, 1928 through 1948, began what he called a lifelong "love affair with Old Nassau" when, as a "gangling lad" in Marion, Ohio, a family friend gave him a copy of Jesse Lynch Williams's *Princeton Stories*.

After a year at Bucknell, Thomas was admitted to Princeton in the fall of 1902 as a "heavily conditioned" sophomore, thus becoming "a member of the glorious Class of 1905." He passed off his conditions, qualified for the "first general group" all three years, and was chosen class valedictorian at graduation. He did not think the education he received first-rate; "the curriculum . . . should have set higher, more demanding goals," and there were not enough good teachers—Wilson's preceptorial system was not to begin until the year after his graduation. He thought his lecturers good, particularly Professors Daniels and Wyckoff in economics. To Mr. Daniels he owed "a sound grounding in a laissez faire economy" so that later in life he "knew what he was rejecting." He also thought "Weary Willie Walter Wyckoff did a pretty good if by no means lasting job" in teaching him "why socialism would never work." He was enthusiastic about the honor system in examinations ("a major contribution to any man's education").

He excelled in Whig Hall activities, especially in competitive debate. He remembered a formal debate in Alexander Hall at which President Wilson presided, when all the participants wore academic gowns. "Just as we were about to go in," he recalled, "Mr. Wilson looked at my legs and where the gown stopped observed my gray trousers—they were pressed—and said, 'Mr. Thomas, it is proper to wear dark trousers.' In spite of that I won the debate."

At graduation, the 1905 *Nassau Herald* revealed, he regarded himself as a Presbyterian and a Republican, was called "Tommy" by his classmates, and intended to become a minister (like his father and his grandfather). The first two years after graduation he worked at Spring Street Church and Neighborhood House in New York City; he told his class secretary that he had come to see that "as a nation we face a social problem of tremendous gravity, whose solution will take the best that we have in us of thought and service."

For 1905's Five-Year Record, Tommy began his report: "Bliss has no history. This letter will be brief." He had just been married to Frances Violet Stewart (granddaughter of John Aikman Stewart, financial adviser to President Lincoln and to President Cleveland, and a trustee of Princeton for many years), whom he had met at a tuberculosis clinic where she was a social worker. They were living in an apartment in a crowded tenement district where he was doing social work for Christ Church while attending Union Theological Seminary, and where all 1905 men would be welcome. He ended his letter: "With sincere sympathy for all the unmarried."

In the Twenty-Year Record in 1925 Thomas reported that he was now executive director of the League for Industrial Democracy. He had been a parish minister in East Harlem, an editor of three publications, and an "advocate of unpopular causes." "My path has led me away from the road travelled by many old friends," he wrote. "That I regret, but nothing else."

Thomas later recalled that he had been barred as a speaker from the Princeton campus from 1917 to 1924 but that to his "pleased surprise" he was given an honorary degree in 1932. It was President Hibben (an ardent interventionist in World War I) who barred him from the campus, and it was Hibben also who persuaded the trustees to give Thomas the degree at Hibben's last Commencement.

The conferring of his degree, which was to have occupied an unobtrusive position third from the end, involved a minor mishap. The University Orator, Dean Augustus Trowbridge, completed the presentation of honorary graduands without any mention of Thomas, concluding in a resonant voice: "And finally, Mr. President, for the degree of Doctor of Laws, *honoris causa*, Benjamin Nathan Cardoza. . . ." Justice Cardoza's degree conferred, the University Orator started to return to his seat. The Chief Marshal, Secretary V. Lansing Collins, caught him by the sleeve and whispered in his ear. The orator wheeled back into position, riffled through his papers, and announced, "And *finally*, Mr. President, I have the honor to present for the degree of Doctor of Letters, *honoris causa*, Norman Thomas."

After the exercises Trowbridge explained to Thomas that the sheet containing his citation had got attached to the preceding sheet by a paper clip. "I know," said Thomas, "a capitalistic clip."

Trowbridge's citation called Thomas "a brilliant and successful clergyman . . . who for conscience's sake gave up a conventional form of ministry . . . to become the fearless and upright advocate of change in the social order." "Irrespective of party preferences," Trowbridge concluded, "we join to honor this valiant and distinguished son of Princeton."

Thomas gave "critical support" to American participation in World War II because he feared an Axis victory would condemn the world to the "lowest circle of hell." But when the United States used the atomic bomb against Japan, he cried out in protest.

In 1955 the editors of 1905's half-century record said Tommy was beloved by all his classmates and no 1905 gathering was complete without his presence and some utterance from his "silver tongue." All of them, the editors said—"even those in violent dissent" —agreed that he was "a man of the highest integrity, of utter, self-effacement [and] concern for the welfare of his fellow men, and of kindliness rarely seen in . . . iconoclasts." Thomas, for his part, wrote his classmates:

I've failed—doubtless to your general satisfaction!—in the chief purpose of my career. That was to bring about, or help bring about, in our country a more realistic political alignment which might give us two major responsible parties, one of them democratic socialist in principle whatever its name.

None of us at Princeton in 1905 could possibly have dreamed what this half-century has brought forth. But I suspect that in years of war and turmoil, among our comforts has been satisfaction that Princeton and the things it stands for has endured. Often we have warmed our hearts at the flame of our Princeton loyalties.

And Princeton's beauty, present before our eyes or in memory, has been like Princeton's friendships, an abiding joy, a part of life's wealth that cannot be taken away.

In his later years Thomas was almost sightless, hard of hearing, and crippled by arthritis, but he maintained his keen interest in people and affairs until the every end. Interviewed by long distance telephone on his eighty-first birthday, while listening by radio to the Princeton-Dartmouth football game, he told a reporter: "I like human beings. I'm very glad I'm one of them. But I think we're crazy."

In a speech to students from thirty countries just before his eighty-third birthday, delivered according to one reporter "at 200 words a minute," he castigated the United States for its policies in Vietnam and its inadequate antipoverty efforts, but he insisted nevertheless that he had affection for his country as well as criticism. He didn't like the sight of young people burning the American flag. "A symbol?" he asked, "if they want an appropriate symbol they should be washing the flag, not burning it." He thought loyalties necessary in life. "Most of us live by our group loyalties . . . but we have to rise above them to the values of humanity so that we can co-exist lest we don't exist at all."

He died in his sleep soon after his eighty-fourth birthday. In the *Alumni Weekly* the secretary of 1905 reminded his forty-five surviving classmates that in senior year they had voted Tommy the brightest man in the class. "If we could have foreseen the future," the secretary added, "we must also have acclaimed him the most courageous."

Thompson, Henry Burling 1877 (1857-1935) probably had more to do with the physical appearance of Princeton during the period of unprecedented expansion in the Wilson and Hibben administrations than any other man. A textile manufacturer in Wilmington and president of the board of trustees of the University of Delaware, he was a Princeton trustee for almost thirty years.

Thompson was chairman of the trustees' committee on grounds and buildings from 1909 to 1928. He early saw the need for the formulation of a master plan for the development of the Campus; he proposed the creation of the offices of supervising architect and consulting landscape gardener, and was influential in bringing Ralph Adams Cram and Beatrix Farrand to Princeton to fill these positions. During his chairmanship, twenty-five campus buildings were erected, beginning with Holder Hall and ending with the University Chapel.

A friend of Woodrow Wilson since their college days, Thompson supported Wilson's quad plan and graduate college proposals, but when these were defeated and Wilson left to enter politics, he gave the same loyal support to John Grier Hibben. "He never hesitates, he never draws back," President Hibben told Thompson's classmates, "and when he once puts his mind and spirit to any enterprise for the sake of Princeton, its successful accomplishment is assured."

Thompson headed the 1919 drive that raised $10 million in new endowment and helped found the School of Engineering in 1921. He was chairman of a trustees' committee that drew up the University's basic plan of physical education and encouraged the development of a greatly expanded number of tennis courts and playing fields near the dormitories. He spoke out against undue emphasis on gate receipts in intercollegiate athletics and pushed the idea of "athletics for all." He had a special (and partisan) interest in rowing—he was chairman of the alumni rowing committee for ten years—and every spring the editor of the *Alumni Weekly* confidently awaited Thompson's annual letter asking why crew was not given more space.

Thompson is commemorated by a memorial court, created in 1956 with a gift from his family, at the center of the walk that passes through the arches of East Pyne Building, on the site of East College, where he roomed as an undergraduate.

Thompson Gateway and the adjacent brick wall on Prospect Avenue near Olden Avenue were given in 1911 by Ferris S. Thompson 1888. Until the early 1960s when the Engineering Quadrangle was built, the wall marked the southern boundary of the athletic grounds known as University Field, and the gate was opened annually to admit the alumni parade to the baseball game with Yale on Reunion Saturday. The gateway and wall were designed by McKim, Mead, and White, who also designed the FitzRandolph Gateway (q.v.) in front of Nassau Hall.

Ferris Thompson was the grandson of the founder of the Chase National Bank in New York. As an undergraduate he held the Princeton record for the mile walk and was president of the Princeton Athletic Association in his senior year.

On his death in 1913, he left the University $3 million, a third by immediate bequest, the balance in his residuary estate which came to the University in 1948. His gifts were used for general endowment, for Bicentennial Preceptorships, and for the Ferris S. Thompson faculty houses on College Road.

Tiger, The, emerged as a symbol of Princeton, ironically, not very long after Woodrow Wilson's class, at its graduation in 1879, gave the College a pair of lions to guard the main entrance to Nassau Hall. The growing use of the tiger—rather than the lion—as Princeton's totem has been ascribed by Princetonians of that period to two things: the college cheer, which, like other cheers of that time, contained a "tiger" as a rallying word; and the growing use of orange and black as the college colors.

In 1882 the senior class issued a humor magazine called *The Princeton Tiger*, depicting on its title page a lively tiger cub being born beneath the legend Volume I, Number 1. This tiger's influence was short-lived, however, since after only nine issues no other issue appeared until 1890 when another generation brought forth a second Volume I, Number 1. Meanwhile, football players of the early 1880s were wearing broad orange and black stripes on their stockings and on their jerseys, and sometimes on stocking caps. Watching their movements in the wan-

ing light of late autumn afternoons, sports writers began to call them tigers.

The tiger soon began to appear in Princeton songs, begining with "The Orange and the Black," written in the late 1880s by Clarence Mitchell 1889:

Although Yale has always favored
The violet's dark hue,
And the many sons of Harvard
To the crimson rose are true,
We will own the lilies slender,
Nor honor shall they lack,
While the tiger stands defender
Of the Orange and the Black.

A few years later, Ernest Carter 1888's lovely "Steps Song" began, despite the awkward presence of Seventy-Nine's lions:

Our lofty elms so gently break
The twilight crescent moon's soft
*   light;*
Old Nassau's tigers slow awake;
The Seniors hold the steps tonight.

In 1905 Kenneth S. Clark '05 composed a song about a Princeton tiger "who will eat right off your hand." "But," he warned, "when he gets in battle with the other beasts of prey, he frightens them almost to death in this peculiar way":

Wow, wow, wow-wow-wow
Hear the Tiger roar;
Wow, wow, wow-wow-wow,
Rolling up a score.
Wow, wow, wow-wow-wow,
Better move along
When you hear the Tiger sing his
*   jungle song.*

In 1893, a three-year old eating club called The Inn changed its name to Tiger Inn.

In 1902, a pair of marble tigers, holding shields, appeared on the posts of the gateway north of Little Hall;

another pair appeared on the north wall of McCosh Hall when it was built in 1907.

In 1911, with the tiger firmly established as the Princeton symbol, the Class of 1879 substituted A. P. Proctor's bronze tigers for the lions flanking the front steps of Nassau Hall.

That same year, carved marble tigers looked down from the tops of the pillars flanking the newly constructed Ferris Thompson Gateway at University Field, as many small tigers worked their way into the wrought iron gates below.

Thanks to the infinite variety possible in Gothic decoration, the tiger continued to put in an appearance in different places and in various ways: as brass weathervanes on top of Holder and Henry towers; on mouldings of 1879 Hall and Dillon Gym; above a fireplace at the west end of Procter Hall at the Graduate College, where, if one looks carefully, he can discern a tiger peering out from the foliage carved in the stone.

All these tigers were undoubtedly conceived of as male. In 1969, the year coeducation was introduced, Bruce Moore's bronze tigers for the Adams Mall between Whig and Clio were created male and female.

In 1923, a live tiger who had been captured in India by the father of a football player, Albert F. Howard '25, was brought to Princeton as a mascot; but after several weeks of mounting community anxiety he was given to a zoo.

Since World War II a less ferocious and more convivial tiger—an undergraduate clad in a tiger skin—has appeared regularly at football games, cavorting with the cheerleaders and the band, and delighting young and old alike. At the 1973 Yale game this friendly tiger was accompanied, for the first time, by a comely tigress, a large orange bow on her mane and a smaller one on her tail.

Torrey, John (1796-1873), pioneer American botanist, was professor of chemistry at the College of Physicians and Surgeons in New York from 1827 to 1855 and concurrently professor of chemistry and natural history at Princeton from 1830 to 1854.

Although obliged to devote much of his time to his duties as a teacher, mainly of chemistry, and after 1854 as United States Assayer of the Mint at New York, Torrey was able to carry on his interest in botany and to establish himself as a foremost American botanist. His pioneering work in the identification and classification of American plants greatly influenced all subsequent taxonomic work. He wrote *Flora of the State of New York* and, with the collaboration of his pupil and friend, Asa Gray, compiled their great work, *Flora of North America*.

Torrey tried to secure an appointment for Gray at Princeton. "Asa Gray has no superior in botany," he wrote to Joseph Henry, ". . . It is good policy for the College to secure the services & affections of young men of talent, & let them *grow up* with the Institution." But the requisite funds were not available. Torrey's own appointment had been part of an ingenious series of faculty recruitments Vice President Maclean had earlier contrived with meagre resources. Later, Gray was called to Harvard as the first Fisher Professor of Natural History and developed there a distinguished department of botany.

Torrey had a genial and unselfish character, and was the friend and helper of every young American botanist of his time. "As an investigator," Gray wrote in a memoir for the National Academy of Sciences, which he and Torrey helped found, "he was characterized by a scrupulous accuracy, a remarkable fertility of mind, especially shown in devising ways and means of research, and perhaps by some excess of caution."

A mountain peak in Colorado was named for Torrey by a former student. Torrey climbed this peak for the first time when he was seventy-six, and there gathered alpine plants which he had himself named fifty years before when botanical study of the Colorado Rocky Mountains was first begun.

Also named for him was a genus of evergreen trees, *Torreya*, somewhat like the yew. All over the world, Gray concluded in his memoir, Torreya trees, as well as his own important contributions to botany, keep John Torrey's memory green.

Track and field athletics had their beginning at Princeton in an intramural meet on June 21, 1873—the first collegiate track contest held in the United States. The meet was organized by George Goldie, Scottish-born director of the gymnasium from 1869 to 1911, and called the Caledonian Games because of his success as an all-round champion in games staged by American and Canadian Caledonian Clubs. The names of some of the events reflected their Caledonian origin—standing long jump, running high leap, hitch and kick, vaulting with the pole. The Caledonian Games survived until 1947; thereafter they gave way to the fuller intercollegiate schedule of modern times.

In the first Caledonian Games Allan Marquand 1874, later the founder of the college's art department, won three

first places and one second. In the fourth Caledonian Games Andrew J. McCosh 1877 won four first places, one second. Introducing him to a friend about this time, President McCosh remarked, "This is my son, Andrew, whose brains are in his heels." This was fatherly hyperbole: Andrew graduated with honors and became an eminent surgeon.

In 1876, at the first meet held by the newly formed Intercollegiate Association of Amateur Athletes of America (the IC4A), Princeton won the team championship with four first places and four seconds.

Francis Larkin, Jr. 1879 won intercollegiate championships in the shot-put, hammer throw, standing high junp, and standing broad jump in both 1878 and 1879. He was the first four-event winner in the country and the only one in Princeton history.

Walter C. Dohm 1890, double winner in 1890 of the half-mile and the broad jump, was the first intercollegiate champion to do the half-mile under 2 minutes. A double winner in 1891, Luther H. Cary 1893 was the first American sprinter to use the crouching start, and the first intercollegiate champion to do the 100 in 10 seconds flat and the 220 under 22 seconds.

Robert Garrett 1897, twice team captain, earned an unequalled place of honor on the roll of Princeton Olympians (q.v.) as the winner of two first places, a second, and a third at the first of the modern Olympic games in 1896.

Princeton's outstanding track athlete of the nineteenth century was John F. Cregan 1899. Twice team captain and three times intercollegiate champion in the mile, he won both the half-mile and the mile in the 1898 intercollegiates, the first runner in the country to accomplish this feat. A year later, he won the first intercollegiate cross-country championship, and at the 1900 Penn Relays, he was anchor man on the Princeton team which won the two-mile relay championship and set a new intercollegiate record (8:05). In a meet with California, he won the quarter-mile as well as the mile; and against Cornell he took first place in the half-mile, the mile, and the two-mile runs. (In later life a metallurgist, he lived to be 88.)

John R. DeWitt '04 was intercollegiate hammer-throw champion four straight years from 1901 through 1904—Princeton's only four-time winner in the intercollegiates. In the words of a Harvard contemporary, he was "a giant in strength and a master of the art of the double turn."

Princeton's first dual meet was with Columbia in 1877, but regular annual meets did not begin until the 1890s, first with Columbia, later with Cornell, Yale, Harvard.

Following Goldie, other trainers who worked with the varsity track squad were James Robinson, Jack McMasters, Walter Christie, Alfred F. Copland, Charles H. Wilson.

THE FITZPATRICK ERA

Keene Fitzpatrick, the leading track coach in the country, was called to Princeton from the University of Michigan in 1910. His 1911 team was the first Princeton team to beat Yale in a dual meet. The victory was not assured until the last event, the high jump, in which a sophomore, John F. Simmons '13, later chief of protocol of the State Department, "rose to the occasion," as the *Alumni Weekly* put it, and tied for first place, giving Princeton a 60-56 edge over Yale. In 1915, a Princeton team won the two-mile relay championship at the Penn Relays,

setting a new intercollegiate record (7:55.4), and the anchor man, Captain Ian Douglas Mackenzie '15, set a new Princeton record for the mile (4:20) in the Yale-Princeton meet that year.

Fitzpatrick's most brilliant years were those after World War I when five teams beat both Yale and Harvard in 1918, 1920, 1922, 1925, and 1932, and four placed second in the Intercollegiates in 1920, 1922, 1923, and 1925. In 1932, his last team, captained by Hunter P. Dawson '32, won its three dual meets with Cornell, Harvard, and Yale, and was, he said, the best-balanced team he had ever coached.

Fifteen Princetonians trained by Keene Fitzpatrick won individual intercollegiate championships. Two of them were double winners: Charles R. Erdman '19 in the 120-yard high hurdles and 220-yard low hurdles in 1918; Randolph E. Brown '20 in the 100- and 220-yard dashes in 1920. Two were two-time winners, J. Coard Taylor '23 in the 220-yard low hurdles in 1922 and 1923; Ralph G. Hills '25 in the shot-put in 1923 and 1925. Each also won a national championship, Taylor in 1922, Hills in 1925.

The most versatile trackman of this era was S. Harrison Thomson '23, national all-round champion in 1919 and 1921, national decathlon champion in 1922. In the Harvard meet in 1922 he took first place in the 120-yard high hurdles, shot-put, and discus throw; second in the high jump and broad jump. Theodore W. Drews '25 was national pentathlon champion in 1926. Another versatile performer was Benjamin van D. Hedges '30. In the Cornell meet in 1929 he took first place in the 120-yard high hurdles and broad jump and tied for first in the high jump and pole vault. Hedges was amphibious; 1929 intercollegiate champion in the high jump, that same year he was adjudged the second best diver in the swimming intercollegiates.

On Fitzpatrick's retirement in 1932, Princeton's appreciation of the contribution he had made was summed up by Dean Gauss in these words: "Born one of Nature's gentlemen, in his disappointments as in his triumphs he was and remains for all of us the perfect sportsman."

THE OXFORD-CAMBRIDGE MEETS

In 1920 a friendship struck up at the Penn Relays between Charles R. Erdman '19, Princeton track captain, and Bevil Rudd, Oxford track captain, led to an Oxford-Princeton meet in 1920 which in turn led to a series of ten meets between Oxford-Cambridge teams and Princeton-Cornell teams held between 1921 and 1949. Princeton won from Oxford in 1920. Of the other ten meets, the first, in 1921, resulted in a tie, Oxford-Cambridge won four (1925, 1926, 1934, 1937), and Princeton-Cornell won five (1929, 1930, 1933, 1938, 1949). These meets were held alternately in England and the United States. Athletes from both teams lived and trained together, and at one post-meet dinner, a speaker from the British Embassy said he couldn't tell them apart until on that warm July evening, all present took off their coats. Then, he said, he recognized the Oxford and Cambridge men by their "braces." Champion quarter-miler William E. Stevenson '22 was the most equitable contributor to international amity. After losing to England's Olympic champion Bevil Rudd, in 1920, he beat him in 1921; and then in 1925, as a Rhodes Scholar, won the event for Oxford-Cambridge against both Princeton-Cornell and Harvard-Yale.

THE GEIS YEARS

Keene Fitzpatrick was succeeded in 1932 by Matthew T. Geis, an energetic, warm-hearted coach who had made a distinguished record at the Lawrenceville School. An old middle-distance runner himself, Geis had among his earliest protégés another middle-distance runner, William R. Bonthron '34, who attained pre-eminence among Princeton track athletes similar to that of Johnny Cregan in the late nineties. Indeed their careers followed parallel courses. Bonthron's double victory in the 800 and 1500 meters in the 1933 and 1934 intercollegiates duplicated Cregan's in the 1898 intercollegiates, and his triple victory in the 800, 1500, and 3000 meter runs in the 1933 and 1934 Yale meets matched Cregan's feat against Cornell in 1900. His 4:08.7 mile in 1933 set a Princeton record which survived until 1968. In 1934 the Amateur Athletic Union's James E. Sullivan medal was awarded to Bonthron as the outstanding amateur athlete of the year and a track trophy was established in his honor at Princeton.

In Bonthron's senior year Asa S. Bushnell '21, then graduate manager of athletics, organized, with Matty Geis, an invitation track meet at reunion time which was continued as an annual event through 1940. These meets brought into competition some of the outstanding track athletes of the day, and produced a number of new world's records.

Two other protégés of Geis were double winners in the intercollegiates: Harvey M. Kelsey Jr. '45 and Paul F. Cowie '46, champions in the 100 and 220-yard dashes in 1943 and 1948 respectively. Three others were two-time intercollegiate winners: Standish F. Medina '37 in the pole vault in 1936 and 1937, Anson Perina '40 in the broad jump in 1938 and 1939, F. Morgan Taylor, Jr. '53 in the broad jump in 1952 and 1953.

The greatest team of the Geis era was Captain Peter B. Bradley's in 1938. It beat all six opponents in dual meets and placed first in the Heptagonal Games (established in 1935 by Columbia, Cornell, Dartmouth, Harvard, Penn, Princeton, and Yale).

When Geis retired in 1956, only one past Princeton record remained intact: Ben Hedges' 6'4½" high jump of 1929.

RECENT YEARS

Under Peter J. Morgan, Jr., successor to Geis, Princeton track athletes continued the inexorable process of running faster, leaping higher or longer, or throwing farther than their predecessors. Hedges' 32-year-old high-jump record was finally broken by a freshman, John Hartnett '64, who cleared the cross-bar at 6'6 in 1961; he later did 6'9½. That same year, Charles Mitchell '63, a poetry-writing sophomore, bettered Stan Medina's twenty-four-year-old pole-vault record with a leap of 14 feet; a year later he made it 15 feet. Mitchell found pole-vaulting not unlike poetry ("You can put emotion and feeling into it; there's real beauty and timing in pole-vaulting. When I'm vaulting I feel alone, apart from everyone. That's how it is with my poetry.")

In 1968, the two-mile relay team set a new Princeton record for that event (7:25). In the same year, one of its members, Alan J. Andreini '68, shaved seven-tenths of a second off Bonthron's thirty-five-year-old record for the mile, and another member, Werner E. Endrikat '68, set a new Princeton record in the half-mile (1:48) and became

Princeton's only three-time winner in the Heptagonals.

Lawrence Ellis succeeded Morgan as track and cross-country coach in 1970. A graduate of New York University, where he was a top-flight middle-distance runner and an intercollegiate champion in cross-country, Ellis was the first black to be appointed a head coach in the Ivy League.

Under Ellis, Princeton's participation in indoor track has expanded, helped by the new facilities made available with the completion of the Jadwin Gymnasium in 1969. Princeton teams have become noted for their success in dual meet competition, indoors as well as outdoors.

True to the tradition begun in Johnny Cregan's day, and carried on in Ian Mackenzie's, Bill Bonthron's, and Alan Andreini's, Ellis's two-mile relay teams captured both the IC4A and NCAA championships in 1975, and the Heptagonal championship in 1976 and again in 1977. The relay's anchor man, Craig Masback '77, added further luster to the Cregan-Mackenzie-Bonthron-Andreini tradition in the mile run by winning that event in the 1977 indoor IC4A championships with the best time ever recorded by a Princeton miler—4:01.8.

Treasurer, The, occupies one of Princeton's oldest offices, the first incumbent having been appointed in 1748, a year after the election of the first president. In the eighteenth century and during most of the nineteenth, it was a part-time office, usually held by a trustee, occasionally by a member of the faculty. Beginning in 1885, the following served as treasurers full-time: Edwin C. Osborn, 1885-1901; Henry G. Duffield 1881, 1901-1930; George C. Wintringer 1894, 1930-1941.

George A. Brakeley '07, who came to Princeton in 1939 as financial vice-president, assumed the office of treasurer also in 1941. Ricardo A. Mestres '31 succeeded Brakeley as treasurer in 1953, and was financial vice-president and treasurer from 1959 to 1972. Carl W. Schafer was treasurer from 1972 to 1976 (while Paul B. Firstenberg '55 was financial vice-president) and became financial vice-president and treasurer in 1976.

The financial vice-president and treasurer has oversight, under the president, of the business operations of the University. He has charge, under the trustees' committee on finance, of all the Corporation's assets—funds, stocks, securities, real estate—and is responsible for preparing the annual budget for approval by the trustees.

Triangle Club, The, evolved from the Princeton College Dramatic Association, which changed its name to Triangle Club in 1893, ten years after its founding. Two years before, the association had given up formal drama for musical comedy, and, according to Booth Tarkington 1893, the new name, which fittingly referred to a musical instrument, was inspired by a favorite walk* on which students would sing Henry Van Dyke 1874's Triangle Song: "Well the Old Triangle knew the music of our tread / How the peaceful Seminole [Seminary student] would tremble in his bed / How the gates were left unhinged, the lamps without a head / While we were marching through Princeton."

In his senior year, as president of the Dramatic Association, Tarkington wrote "The Honorable Julius Caesar," a musical parody of Shakespeare's play that was performed again the following year as the Triangle Club's first production. Tarkington played the part of Cas-

sius, for whose "lean and hungry look" he was well cast, being, as Jesse Lynch Williams 1892 wrote, "woefully gaunt, almost cadaverous."

To provide a home for the Triangle Club—its early performances were staged in University Hall's dining room—Tarkington initiated a campaign that raised funds for a small building erected in 1895 on what was then the lower campus. For more than a quarter of a century this modest structure, which was called the Casino, served as a home for club rehearsals and local performances, as a place for dances, tennis, and bowling, and as an armory for a local company of the National Guard.

Outstanding among early Triangle shows was "Tobasco Land" (1905-06), which was enthusiastically received. "What these players lack in technique," Professor Stockton Axson said in a *Prince* review, "they make up for by their superior intelligence and manifest glee in acting"—an observation that could apply to a long line of shows that followed. "Tobasco Land" was distinguished by the music and lyrics of Kenneth S. Clark '05 (composer of "Going Back to Nassau Hall"). One of Clark's hits was "Floating on a Marcel Wave":

And it's oh, my lads, yo-ho,
How the ladies all pursue me!
And it's ev'ry where I go,
They are always clinging to me.
As a breaker-up of homes
I'm a reckless sort of knave,
Whene'er I go a-floating on a Marcel
*   wave.*

In the years just before the First World War, Triangle shows were enlivened by the lyrics of F. Scott Fitzgerald '17, who also appeared on stage as a very attractive chorus girl. One show entitled "Fie, Fie, Fi-Fi!" (1914-15) became "Ha-Ha Hortense!"

in *This Side of Paradise*, where Fitzgerald, describing a classically hectic rehearsal, says: "How a Triangle show ever got off was a mystery, but it was a riotous mystery anyway, whether or not one did enough service to wear a little gold triangle on his watch-chain." Another show, "The Evil Eye" (1915-16), for which he wrote the lyrics, employed the talents of two other students who became well-known writers, Edmund Wilson '16, who wrote the book, and John Peale Bishop '17, who was a member of the cast.

In the postwar years the club attained a high point in its history under Donald Clive Stuart, Professor of Dramatic Literature, who directed performances from 1919 to 1934. An updated version of "The Honorable Julius Caesar," (1918-19) and "The Isle of Surprise" (1919-20) introduced a Gilbert and Sullivan kind of show, remarkable for the clever dialogue and lyrics of Hope Coffey '20 and the tuneful melodies of Erdman Harris '20, whose evocation of Triangle music at alumni reunions in later years made him one of the best known of Triangle men.

A memorable song of this period, "One Hour More" ("Just one hour more is all I crave / For one hour more I'll be your slave"), from the 1921-22 show "Espanola," was still being hummed at reunions fifty years later. It was composed by Louis E. Tilden '22 and played by him on his accordion, as it was sung by his classmate J. Russell Forgan '22. The song's opening notes are inscribed on a piano at Prospect as well as outside Woolworth Music Center's Room 108, which was given by Forgan and Tilden to commemorate their Triangle collaboration and lifelong friendship.

Another star of the twenties was Wallace H. Smith '24, one of the finest comedians in the club's history. In his senior year he wrote "Drake's Drum," based on a poem about Sir Francis Drake by the English poet Alfred Noyes, a visiting professor at Princeton. Critics called this the best Triangle production ever; its book, dialogue, music, lyrics, costumes, scenery, acting, and dancing were all effectively combined to make it a standard by which succeeding shows were judged. Best known and longest remembered among several outstanding hits was "Ships That Pass In The Night," whose lyrics and music, by Smith, appear on the following page. Four other numbers in the show were written by Robert M. Crawford '25, who also did the orchestration and played the part of Sir Francis Drake.

"Drake's Drum" was the first of seven shows that were put on without a local theater, the old Casino having burned down in January 1924. By 1930 the club had secured a permanent home, whose cost was met by a $250,000 gift from Thomas N. McCarter 1888, for whom the theater was named; by Triangle Club earnings of over $100,000; and by other gifts, including the proceeds of a benefit performance by the Hasty Pudding Club of Harvard.

The last years of Dr. Stuart's directorship were enlivened by a very talented group of undergraduates who produced a number of notable shows and who later made their marks in the performing arts. Best known among them in college and afterward were Joshua Logan '31, James Stewart '32 and José Ferrer '33. Logan helped write the book and played leading roles in "Zuider Zee" (1928-29), "The Golden Dog" (1929-30), and "The Tiger Smiles" (1930-31). Stewart had parts in the last two of these and also played the lead in "Spanish Blades" (1931-32). Ferrer, who joined the Triangle Club

SHIPS THAT PASS IN THE NIGHT

From the Triangle Club show "Drake's Drum"

Words and Music by
W. H. Smith, '24

Slowly and dreamily

All the ships that pass in the night For ha - vens far and landsout of sight, Like maid-ens — we have known of yore, Soon van-ish, — to be seen no more. They bow and smile, then fade in the dark - ness, har - bin-gers so bright. — Sail on! We will meet a-gain all the state-ly ships that pass us in the night. night.

46511 *Copyright, 1923, by The John Church Company*

his senior year, was the bright spot in "It's the Valet" (1932-33).

Other talented members of this group were actor Charles Arnt '29, who went on to a career in Hollywood; writer Eric Barnouw '29, who became dramatic arts professor at Columbia; writer and actor A. Munroe Wade '30, later a leader in theater productions and a drama teacher in the Princeton community; set designer Norris Houghton '31, later a founder of the Phoenix Theater and a drama professor; and Myron McCormick '31, who was a comic hit in "The Tiger Smiles" as he was later in Logan's "South Pacific." "The Tiger Smiles," a satire on student life put together by Logan when he was club president, was highly praised by the *Prince* as "a grand show, brilliant and original."

Following Dr. Stuart's retirement, the club had a succession of directors including Logan and several other Triangle alumni. The first of several shows that Logan was associated with, "Stags at Bay" (1934-35), earned enthusiastic reviews on its tour, sold out two nights running in New York, and had three memorable songs: "Will Love Find a Way?" by Brooks Bowman '36 and Kirkland B. Alexander, Jr. '37, and "Love and a Dime" and "East of the Sun (and West of the Moon)" by Bowman. "East of the Sun" was probably the most popular and longest-lasting hit nationally ever to come out of the Triangle Club.

The 1940s brought several good shows. "Ask Me Another" (1941-42), a swift-paced review based on the Gallup Poll and organized by club president Mark Lawrence, prompted *Variety* to say "the Princeton lads really have something this year." The first postwar show, "Clear the Track" (1946-47), satirized the University's Bicentennial

Year to the delight of the *Prince*, which pronounced it an undoubted hit because of its spontaneous gaiety and its excellent music.

In 1955-56 Milton Lyon began a long and successful directorship with the production of "Spree de Corps," which one veteran reviewer thought "the best of them all." This show was put together in its initial stages by Triangle president D. Brooks Jones '56, who later became head of Cincinnati's Playhouse in the Park.

The 1960s produced a number of creditable performances, some of them displaying the talents of exceptional writers. "Breakfast in Bedlam" (1959-60) and "Tour de Farce" (1961-62) made summer tours of United States army bases in Europe. All of the music and some of the lyrics of the tuneful "Breakfast in Bedlam" were written by Clark Gesner '60, in later years author of the popular off-Broadway musical "You're a Good Man, Charlie Brown." Jeffrey Moss '63, who collaborated with John Simon '63 in writing the book, music, and lyrics for "Ahead of the Game" (1962-63) was head writer for TV's "Sesame Street" during its formative years. "Funny Side Up" (1963-64) found much favor with alumni for its pleasing revival of songs and skits from past productions. "Grape Expectations" (1964-65) and "A Different Kick" (1968-69) won prizes as the best college shows in the country.

In 1971 alumni representing fifty years of the club's history came back to Princeton to honor Benjamin Franklin Bunn '07, graduate treasurer from 1908 to 1965, who had died at the age of ninety-six. At their memorial gathering in McCarter, called "One Hour More for Uncle Ben," they sang hits from the past and listened to affectionate reminiscences by Josh Logan and others about the man who had "chaperoned" their Christmas tours for half a century. At the conclusion, Jimmie Stewart read the text for a plaque in memory of Bunn, and as the lights dimmed, undergraduate men and women from the current show, holding lighted candles, lined the aisles of the theatre, and sang "All the Ships That Pass in the Night."

With the advent of coeducation in 1969, the Triangle Club was able to assign to women the female roles formerly taken by men. In the chorus lines, however, the club on occasion managed to enjoy the best of the old and new worlds by having men portray women, as was done in the successful 1974-75 production, "American Zucchini." This entertaining examination of a day in the life of a Princeton undergraduate, was directed, as were most of its twenty predecessors, by Milton Lyon.

What Triangle has meant to generations of undergraduates was summed up by Joshua Logan in the foreword to its history, *The Long Kickline* by Donald Marsden '64, which the club's Board of Trustees brought out in 1968:

> . . . The Triangle Club, smiling like a basketful of cats, lives on as though it had nine-times-nine lives. It is the Great Vitrine for youth, the Bulletin Board for young ideas, the proving ground for talent that still is permitted to fumble; it is a place to sing, to do pratfalls, to thumb one's nose at authority, to test the last liberties of adolescence, to taste the true wine of being an American. . . .

George S. Stephenson

* The sides of the Triangle Walk were Stockton and Mercer Streets, the apex their junction at University Place, the base of the "Little Triangle," Lover's Lane, and of the "Big Triangle," Quaker Road.

"**Trustees of Princeton University**" is the legal title of the corporation that is empowered to "conduct a university not for profit."

There are a maximum of forty trustees, of whom two (the governor of the state and the president of the University) serve ex-officio; thirteen are elected by alumni and students, and the remainder are chosen by the board itself. Four of those chosen by the Board are called term trustees and serve four years, as do all of the thirteen trustees elected by alumni and students. The rest of those chosen by the board are called charter trustees; those elected prior to 1969 serve until their seventieth birthday, those elected in 1969 and thereafter, for terms of ten years.

Of the original twelve trustees named in the College's first charter in 1746, nine were clergymen, one was a merchant, one—the person who drafted the charter—a lawyer, and the twelfth was that indispensable adjunct of a privately endowed college—"a man of leisure and wealth and given to good works."

The youngest of the twelve was twenty-three. The oldest, Jonathan Dickinson, the first president of the college, was fifty-eight.

The twenty-three trustees named in a second charter, granted in 1748, represented a broader spectrum of society and reflected the founders' avowed purpose of raising up men who would be "ornaments of the State as well as the Church." Added were the governor of the Province, Jonathan Belcher, and four members of the provincial council of New Jersey as well as two judges and a merchant in Philadelphia. Now there were twelve clergymen—a clerical majority of one.

The clergymen maintained this majority of one for more than a century. As the number of trustees was increased after the Civil War, more laymen were appointed, and although there were still twelve clergymen they were now outnumbered. As late as 1905 the by-laws stipulated that at least twelve trustees should be clergymen, but the following year the number was reduced to eight, and in 1913 this requirement was removed completely. The present by-laws make no occupational stipulation whatever.

Most of the original trustees were graduates of Yale, Harvard, or William Tennent's "Log College" in Neshaminy, Pennsylvania, but a decade later graduates of the College began infiltrating its Board of Trustees. Richard Stockton (q.v.), a member of the first graduating class of 1748, who practiced law in Princeton, became the first in 1757 and was joined four years later by his classmate, Israel Read, minister at Bound Brook. By 1768, when John Witherspoon became president, there were five graduates of the College on the board; a century later, under McCosh, there were seventeen. In recent years, with few exceptions, every trustee has been a Princeton alumnus.

One non-Princetonian, John A. Stewart, was an active member of the board longer than any other trustee in Princeton's history. A graduate of Columbia College in 1840, and a trusted financial adviser to President Lincoln and later to President Cleveland, Stewart was elected a Princeton trustee in 1868 and continued to serve until his death in 1926 at the age of 104. He was acting president of the University in the interregnum between the Wilson and Hibben administrations.

ALUMNI TRUSTEES

In 1900, in recognition of the increasing part that alumni were playing in Princeton's growth, the board amended the charter and by-laws to permit adding to its membership five trustees to be elected annually by the alumni. This number became eight in 1917, and the method of election was subsequently modified several times, resulting in a plan adopted in 1934 which provided that two alumni trustees be elected annually, one from a region by vote of alumni living in that region, the other chosen at large by vote of the entire alumni body, in both instances from among candidates nominated by a nine-man committee of the Alumni Council.

The range of alumni trusteeships was further extended by two developments in the 1960s. The first came in 1963 with the addition of a ninth alumni trustee representing the graduate school, elected for a four-year term once every four years from among candidates nominated by the Princeton Graduate Alumni Association and voted upon by the entire alumni body.

Further additions were made in 1969 when increasing student interest in the governance of the University led the board to provide for four more alumni trustees, one elected each year from the graduating class by vote of the members of the junior and senior classes and of the two most recently graduated classes, to serve a term of four years.

The latter provision was made retroactive by the election of two trustees in May 1969. Richard W. Cass '68, aged twenty-two, was elected for a three-year term and Brent L. Henry '69, aged twenty-one, was elected for a four-year term. Henry had the double distinction of being the youngest man and the first black to be elected a Princeton trustee.

At the same time the board revoked the rule that alumni trustees elected by regions and at large must have been members of classes out of college at least ten years.

CHARTER AND TERM TRUSTEES

Meanwhile changes had been made affecting trustees elected by the board itself. In 1942, in an act of self-restraint led by Albert G. Milbank 1896, the board renounced the right to life tenure that trustees had enjoyed for almost two centuries. "Life trustees" became "charter trustees," committed to retirement at age seventy with the title "trustee emeritus." This change opened up vacancies for oncoming generations at earlier dates and compelled a more rapid change-over of committee chairmanships traditionally retained by the same persons over long periods of time.

In 1956 the board reduced the number of charter trustees by four, replacing them with term trustees, elected by the board for four-year terms. This new classification permitted the board to use the services of a greater number of persons whose special knowledge and judgment might be needed at various times in the University's development.

As a further means of achieving greater diversity in the age, interests and background of trustees, the board in 1969 set a ten-year limit for terms of service of charter trustees elected on or after July 1 of that year.

The Board added women to its membership for the first time in 1971 when it elected as charter trustees, Mary St. John Douglas and Susan Savage Speers (daughters of alumni in the classes of 1905 and 1920 and wives of alumni in the classes of 1943 and 1950).

TRUSTEE COMMITTEES

Until 1939, the governor of New Jersey was the presiding officer of the Board. Since then, the president of the University has presided and, in his absence, the chairman of the Executive Committee of the trustees, who serves as spokesman for the board.

Starting with the McCosh administration, most of the work of the trustees has been done by standing committees, of which there are now nine: executive, finance, curriculum, grounds and buildings, plans and resources, library, student life, health and athletics, and honorary degrees. Between board meetings, the executive committee has all the powers and duties of the board except that of removing or electing a trustee or the president.

The Executive Committee (originally called the Administrative Committee, and headed by the president) was first instituted in 1919. Its chairmen have included Edward D. Duffield 1892, Walter E. Hope '01, Fordyce B. St. John '05, Harold H. Helm '20, James F. Oates, Jr. '21, John N. Irwin II '37, and R. Manning Brown '36.

TRUSTEES' ROLE AND FUNCTION

Relations between the trustees and the administration and faculty have sometimes been strained. Early in the nineteenth century the trustees made frequent visitations to Princeton and interfered with the faculty in matters of discipline. "Unhappily," President Maclean later observed, "there were no railroads to take the trustees to their homes in those days." President McCosh complained that the board was "full of old dotards and sometimes they go to sleep," and Moses Taylor Pyne recalled that "the Trustees spent most of their time fighting Doctor McCosh."

In recent times, the situation has changed markedly. In a speech to the alumni at the close of his administration, President Dodds commended the trustees for their understanding of the function of a university, and "for the respect they pay to the professional province of the faculty and to the responsibilities which pertain to the administration." "I have known college presidents," President Dodds said, "who always took to their beds for the weekend following a meeting of their trustees. My sworn testimony is that I have never attended a meeting of our board which did not give a lift to my heart."

In his annual report of 1968, President Goheen said that he had often been struck by how little is known about the role and function of university trustees in general and about Princeton's board in particular, and that "this is the more regrettable because, in my close observation, Princeton's Trustees merit so much trust."

Their sense of their role [he continued] is almost always one of service and the best interests of the University, not a matter of vested rights or of power.

They hold a public trust to carry out specified educational purposes . . . They . . . have a general responsibility for the kind of education and kind of research conducted by the University, and for their bearing on the public interest . . . [leaving] the specific determination of academic programs and the conduct of instruction to professionals—that is, the faculty and academic administration.

With this basic public trust . . . go also binding legal and fiscal obligations. It is the Trustees alone who can hold title to the material assets and property of Princeton University, and responsibility for the management of its funds rests directly on them. With respect to the latter, Princeton's twentieth-century record is superb. Even during the Great Depression, when salary slashes were the order of the day on American campuses, Princeton managed to avoid them through the Trustees' good management of the funds in their charge. More recently, the simultaneous growth of the University's endowment and of the annual return on this endowment has been impressive. . . .

More than any one in the University, the Trustees have to carry the sense of a trust held in perpetuity. On them rests the responsibility to a university whose future is no less important than its present or its past . . . On many fronts—provision for the Library, for health and athletics, for student affairs, for faculty and staff housing and benefits, for curricular developments and the enlistment of financial support; in interpreting the University to those outside and defending its best interests; in trying to assess the varied opportunities and obligations which confront the University at any and all times—the Princeton Trustees are, indeed, working trustees.

Twain, Mark, who visited Princeton in the early 1900s, considered coming here to live. "Princeton would suit *me* as well as Heaven," he wrote his friend, Laurence Hutton, a former editor of *Harper's* who was a lecturer in the University, "better in fact, for I shouldn't care for that society up there."

University League, The. On April 13, 1920, at the suggestion of Mrs. Dana Munro, 171 "women of the Faculty, Library and Administration" were invited by the faculty tea committee to meet at Prospect. At this meeting, with Mrs. Hibben presiding, the University League was founded "to promote a friendly spirit among wives and families of men connected with the University." Membership in the League has been broadened in recent years to include all "women who are, or whose husbands are, members of the University faculty, administration or staff."

The four presidents' wives during the life of the League, Mrs. Hibben, Mrs. Dodds, Mrs. Goheen, and Mrs. Bowen, have been very close to it, serving as president or chairmen as well as giving support and entertainment.

In the early days teas were a larger part of the League's social activities than they are today, with weekly teas often honoring different departments in the University. League-sponsored parties at Prospect on Christmas night, when all the faculty could fit comfortably into the president's home, were especially gala occasions with dancing, mah-jong, bridge, music, and refreshments.

As late as 1941, a leaflet on "Advice to Newcomers in the University League" advised women what to wear, when to return calls, and how many calling cards to leave. Hats, white gloves, and calling cards are gone, but League-sponsored dances, teas, buffet suppers, theatre parties, and trips are still part of the program. The varied social activities have helped newcomers to feel a part of the University family and have encouraged friendships across age limits, departmental lines, and national barriers. Special interest groups have covered foreign languages, travel, child care, literature, the performing arts, sports, and a wide variety of other subjects ranging from Shakespeare to international cooking.

The service activities of the League have continued to increase in importance. A Business Registry was started in 1927, so that members' skills might be matched with faculty needs. In 1967 the League began a Job Roster for professional women seeking employment, which in 1972 was merged with the Professional Roster, a volunteer community organization.

One of the League's concerns has been to make foreign visitors feel welcome. For many years host families have been matched with foreign families. A very active English Conversation Group has held weekly sessions with foreign visitors. The League was instrumental in creating the International Center, an office and lounge to serve students and faculty from foreign countries.

Two other important League services have been the University Nursery School, where parents assist the four teachers and repair equipment to keep tuition costs low, and the Furniture Exchange, where furniture is acquired, reconditioned, and made available, at minimal fees, for members of the University community.

The service objectives of the League have been helped by memorial gifts for medical emergencies and for scholarships for the University League Nursery School. Among those honored by funds for these purposes are Jenny Davidson Hibben, Mary Blanchard Magie, Ethel Palmer Morgan, Sir Hugh and Lady Taylor, Esther Bentley, and Elise Fitch.

In 1967 the University League and the Art Museum began two programs, a Docent or Lecture Guide Program and an Art Interest Group featuring Gallery talks and lectures. Both programs were incorporated into the Museum Volunteers, who conduct guided tours, present slide shows to community school children, and serve at the Art Museum desk answering questions and selling books, catalogues, and cards.

In recent years the League offices were moved to 171 Broadmead where the Dorothy Brown Room, the Grace Marckwardt Room, a workroom, and a kitchen provide much-needed space.

Jane G. Dix

Upper and Lower Pyne, gifts of Moses Taylor Pyne 1877, were built in 1896. Lower Pyne still stands at the northeast corner of Nassau and Witherspoon streets. Upper Pyne was razed in 1963 to make way for the Princeton Bank and Trust Company building at 76 Nassau Street. Upper and Lower Pyne were designed by Raleigh C. Gildersleeve on the model of sixteenth-century houses in Chester, England. They were planned to provide space for shops at the street level, dormitory rooms for undergraduates in the stories above. In 1950 the dormitory rooms were converted to offices.

A sundial on the front of Upper Pyne bore on its face a Latin epigram about the passing hours which proved to be prophetic: VULNERANT OMNES: ULTIMA NECAT (They all wound, the last one kills).

Valedictory Oration, The, was first given by a graduating senior in 1760. Originally, a high-ranking student with particular talents for the part delivered the valedictory, and the highest ranking senior gave the salutatory (q.v.). In recent years the faculty has chosen both speakers for their special qualifications for the parts, as well as for their high scholastic standing.

One of the earliest valedictorians was James Roosevelt 1780, great-grandfather of Franklin D. Roosevelt. George Mifflin Dallas, valedictorian in 1810, became the eleventh vice-president of the United States. William Jay Magie, valedictorian in 1852, became chancellor of New Jersey; his son, William Francis Magie was valedictorian in 1879 and later dean of the faculty.

John Grier Hibben, fourteenth president of the University, was valedictorian in 1882; Norman Thomas in 1905; John Foster Dulles in 1908; Henry P. Van Dusen, later a trustee, in 1919. Several valedictorians became members of the faculty: Donald A. Stauffer '23, E. Harris Harbison '28, Gordon A. Craig '36, James H. Billington '50.

Over the years valedictory orations have, by and large, tried to sum up the Princeton experience in relation to the world the seniors were entering. Woodrow Wilson's Sesquicentennial oration, "Princeton in the Nation's Service" (q.v.), has provided the background for a number of valedictories. "We owe this University a debt we cannot pay," Donald A. Stauffer told his classmates in 1923. "The least we can do is to remember and honor the tradition of national service, the obligation Princeton imposes upon us to use our minds, never to let them yield on the rack of this tough world."

Using the Wilson motto in his valedictory oration at the 1936 commencement, Gordon A. Craig, later professor of history at Princeton, and Stanford, said it was of the utmost importance that this tradition be preserved, "for, at no time in the life of the state, has there been a greater need for men with trained minds."

In 1964, Wilfried Schmid, who, at twenty-six, became professor of mathematics at Columbia, said that world developments in recent years suggested a broader interpretation of Wilson's ideals—already implicit in his Sesquicentennial speech—"that the University has not only national, but also international responsibilities"; and, speaking for students from abroad, of whom he was one, he commended Princeton for the way it was meeting these responsibilities.

In recent years, many valedictorians have been reluctant to exhort their classmates on political and social questions. The 1972 valedictorian, Halbert L. White, while expressing a similar reluctance, nevertheless voiced his own "fervent hope for . . . the emergence of an awareness on the part of our country that we no longer can act as an isolated national entity fighting for world dominance, but must instead act as an integral member of the human and natural community of this planet."

Van Dusen, Henry Pitney '19 (1897-1975), world churchman, Christian statesman, and a long-time University trustee, came from a family with strong Princeton associations. His father, George R. Van Dusen 1877, was a lawyer, as were his maternal grandfather, New Jersey Vice-Chancellor Henry C. Pitney 1848, and three uncles, Henry C. Pitney, Jr. 1877, Supreme Court Justice Mahlon Pitney 1879, and Princeton trustee John O.H. Pitney 1881.

Pit Van Dusen was one of the leaders of his college generation, serving as chairman of the Undergraduate Council, president of the Philadelphian Society (the student Christian association), and captain of the University debating team. As a sophomore, he took part in the revolt against the eating clubs led by his classmate, Richard F. Cleveland. The winner of Phi Beta Kappa honors, he gave the Ivy oration on Class Day and the Valedictory at Commencement, and was voted by his class "the best all-round man outside athletics" and the "most likely to succeed."

After college, Van Dusen served as graduate secretary of the Philadelphian Society for two years and then took up theological study, the first year at New College, Edinburgh, the next two at Union Theological Seminary in New York, obtaining his bachelor of divinity degree there, *summa cum laude*, in 1924. Later, in the early 1930s, he returned to Scotland, where he completed graduate work for his Ph.D. at Edinburgh and was married in Inverness to Elizabeth Coghill Bartholomew, daughter of the late cartographer to the king.

The year he graduated from Union, his ordination was challenged by a conservative-minded judicial commission of the Presbyterian General Assembly because he declined to affirm the literal Biblical account of the virgin birth. He overcame the challenge with the help of a notable brief in his support by John Foster Dulles '08.

Following his ordination, Van Dusen spent two years visiting American colleges from coast to coast seeking to interpret religion to undergraduates, and then began his long career at Union Theological Seminary as an instructor in 1926. He became dean of students in 1932, Roosevelt professor of systematic theology in 1936, and tenth president in 1945, occupying that office for eighteen years. Under his vigorous leadership, the seminary attained world-wide significance as a center for theological study.

Van Dusen left his mark on world Christianity as a leader in the ecumenical movement, playing a prominent part in the founding of the World Council of Churches and paving the way for its union with the International Missionary Council as chairman of the joint commission representing both bodies. He traveled around the world twice, touching down at some sixty countries on six continents.

A tireless worker, he was a trustee of a dozen institutions, among them the Rockefeller Foundation, Vassar, and Smith—as well as Princeton, where he held one of the University's longest trustee tenures: thirty-four years, twenty-one of them as chairman of the curriculum committee. Also included among some fifty "extracurricular" responsibilities were his services as chairman of numerous committees of various religious organizations, and as president or board chairman of the Association of American Theological Schools, the United Board for Christian Higher Education in Asia, and the Union Settlement Association.

Van Dusen was the author or editor of some twenty-five books, among them *For the Healing of the Nations: Impressions of Christianity Around the World* (1940), *The Vindication of Liberal Theology* (1963), and *Dag Hammarskjöld: The Statesman and His Faith* (1967), written in tribute to the United Nations' second Secretary-General, who, in Van Dusen's words, "affirmed 'The Communion of Saints' and—within it—an eternal life."

Van Dusen's achievements were acclaimed by the Union Faculty and Board of Directors in their final tributes. "In the long history of the Seminary," the Faculty declared, "Van Dusen's presidency stands out as the high-water mark of its achievement. He

... enlarged not only the personal and physical resources of the Seminary, but above all, its spirit and its outreach." The Board of Directors saluted him as "one of the first World Churchmen of our era, a scholar, a statesman, a leader, and—not least—a friend."

After his retirement as president of Union Seminary in 1963, Van Dusen and his wife made their home in Princeton. Besides continuing to write, he served on various boards, and visited churches around the world to keep in touch with seminary alumni and to promote world Christianity—until 1970, when he suffered a severe stroke that limited his physical activity and made normal speech impossible. At the same time, Mrs. Van Dusen was the victim of a steadily worsening and increasingly painful arthritic condition. In January 1975, the Van Dusens—both members of the Euthanasia Society—took overdoses of sleeping pills to end their lives. Mrs. Van Dusen died immediately, Van Dusen fifteen days later. A letter they left for their three sons and other relatives and friends said that they had led happy lives, but that increasingly poor health no longer permitted them to do what they wanted to do, and that they were not afraid to die. They acknowledged that some would be disappointed, and asked for their understanding.

One of Van Dusen's successors as president of Union Theological Seminary, Roger L. Shinn, said he had never seen anybody physically or mentally less cut out to be an invalid: "He had a very strong belief in immortality. His attitude was that, when your time is up, when you have lived out the possibilities, it is all right to stop, and to go on to the next life."

Van Dusen's letter concluded with this prayer: "O Lamb of God, that takest away the sins of the world, have mercy upon us. O Lamb of God, that takest away the sins of the world, grant us Thy peace."

van Dyke, Henry 1873 (1852-1933) was called to Princeton in 1899 from the pastorate of New York's Brick Presbyterian Church to occupy a chair especially endowed for him by alumni and named for Dean Murray (q.v.), who had preceded him as pastor of the Brick Church and as professor of English at Princeton.

His younger brother, the historian Paul van Dyke 1881, had joined the faculty several years earlier, and the seniors welcomed Henry in the Faculty Song of 1900:

Here's to Henry the brother of Paul.
He has a large head, but he's not
very tall.

Although "not very tall," his carriage was erect, and his "large head" well-formed and handsome. Whether driving his Adirondack horses and smart trap to lecture hall in his early years or walking in academic procession in the scarlet gown of an honorary Oxford doctor of letters in later years, van Dyke was always a striking figure.

Although he strongly opposed Woodrow Wilson's Quad Plan, Wilson never held this against him, and later appointed him Minister to the Netherlands and Luxembourg. He was one of the most popular lecturers in his time, and when he retired in 1923 the trustees congratulated him on having developed in his students "an appreciation of the best in literature and a genuine love of reading."

He was a prolific writer, producing more than fifty books of stories, essays, and verse. His Christmas story *The Other Wise Man* was a best seller,

translated into many languages, and two books about the outdoors, *Little Rivers* and *Fisherman's Luck*, also sold well. He himself considered *The Book of Common Worship of the Presbyterian Church*, produced in 1906 by a committee which he headed, and revised in 1932 under his direction, his most important contribution.

Veblen, Oswald (1880-1960), who played a major role in the development of Princeton and American mathematics, was the grandson of a Norwegian cabinet maker who came to Wisconsin in 1847 and took up farming. He was the son of Andrew Anderson Veblen, a professor of mathematics and physics at the University of Iowa, and the nephew of the economist and social theorist Thorstein Veblen.

Oswald Veblen took an A.B. at the University of Iowa in 1898, a second A.B. at Harvard in 1900, and a Ph.D. at the University of Chicago in 1903. Dean Fine, who was then building up the mathematics department, heard of Veblen's work at Chicago and, at his suggestion, President Wilson called Veblen to Princeton as one of the original preceptors in 1905.

Dean Fine had a remarkable knack for picking promising young mathematicians, and none of his excellent choices was more successful than Veblen. He soon established himself as a leading geometer whose articles and books were noted for their completeness, precision, and clarity. He attracted many able graduate students, some of whom were added to the faculty, and he helped Dean Fine recruit other distinguished men for the growing department. His research and that of his students covered many fields, including the foundations of geometry, differential geometry and its connection with relativity theory, symbolic logic, and analysis situs (later known as topology). Under his leadership Princeton became one of the world's great centers in topology.

His influence in his profession extended beyond Princeton, earning him his reputation as a "statesman of mathematics." As president of the American Mathematical Society in 1923-24, when its funds were low, he led a successful effort to make better known the importance of mathematics generally and to obtain gifts from foundations, business corporations, and individuals for mathematical research and publication. It was on his urging that the National Research Council began granting postdoctoral fellowships in mathematics in 1924.

When the Henry Burchard Fine Professorship, the first American research chair in mathematics, was founded in 1926, Veblen was named its first incumbent. On Dean Fine's death in 1928, Veblen paid him an impressive tribute in a memoir for the *Bulletin* of the American Mathematical Society, written in the lucid style that Fine had so admired. And when the Jones family provided funds for the original Fine Hall in 1929, Veblen supplied most of the ideas that went into its design.

He conceived of Fine Hall as a center about which mathematicians could (in his words) "group themselves for mutual encouragement and support," and where "the young recruit and the old campaigner" could have "those informal and easy contacts that are so important to each of them." The Common Room, which he hoped would increase the solidarity of the mathematics faculty and students and encourage their closer relation to the physics group from nearby Palmer, was placed so that everyone had to pass it to get to the li-

brary on the top floor. There was another room of this sort reserved for professors on the principle, "not always understood by those who try to bring about closer relations between faculty and students," Veblen said, "that in all forms of social intercourse the provisions for privacy are as important as those for proximity."

In 1932 Veblen resigned the Fine Professorship to accept appointment as the first professor in the Institute for Advanced Study (q.v.), which had just been established. He was largely responsible for selecting the other members of its original mathematics faculty (James W. Alexander II, Albert Einstein, John von Neumann, and Herman Weyl) and also for determining the Institute's policy of concentrating on postdoctoral research. He helped relocate many distinguished foreign mathematicians after Hitler's rise to power, and in his later years (as the Institute's director J. Robert Oppenheimer observed) "provided a real clearing house at the Institute for mathematicians from all over the world." The year he retired as professor at the Institute, 1950, his life-long devotion to the advancement of mathematics was recognized by his selection as president of the International Congress of Mathematicians, held at Harvard.

All his life Veblen loved the outdoors. He was influential in the purchase of a large tract of land for the site of the Institute, whose woods provide attractive walks for its members and for the Princeton community. In 1957, he and his wife deeded eighty-one acres of an extent of wooded land where they lived in later years, called by them Herrontown Wood, to Mercer County to provide a place where, in their words, "you can get away from cars and just walk and sit."

Veblen was a member of the American Philosophical Society and the National Academy of Sciences and a foreign member of the academies of science in Denmark, England, France, Ireland, Italy, Peru, Poland, and Scotland. He was awarded honorary degrees by Chicago and Princeton, and also by Edinburgh, Glasgow, Hamburg, Oslo, and Oxford. And, like his father before him, he was made a Knight of Norway's Royal Order of St. Olaf.

Veterans of Future Wars, so goes the legend, sprang full-blown from a tea party at Terrace Club in March 1936. The Founding Father was Lewis Jefferson Gorin, Jr. '36, of Louisville, a politics major then writing a senior thesis, appropriately enough, on Niccolo Machiavelli.

Gorin and the other tea drinkers—Urban J.P. Rushton '36, Thomas Riggs, Jr. '37, Archibald Lewis '36, Robert G. Barnes '37, John C. Turner '36, Alexander Black, Jr. '36, and a young member of the history faculty, Lynn White, Jr.—were disturbed by an act of Congress that had advanced by ten years—from 1946 to 1936—the date at which the veterans of World War I would receive their long-sought and controversial soldiers' bonuses. This legislation, the consequence of intensive lobbying by the American Legion and the Veterans of Foreign Wars, struck the Princetonians as an intolerable raid upon the United States Treasury for the benefit of an organized minority.

The Veterans of Future Wars was created to satirize the bonus hunters. Their first manifesto in the *Princetonian* argued that sooner or later there would be another war and that it would only be an act of justice for Congress to grant a $1000 cash bonus to all men between the ages of 18 and 36. Legally the bonus would be payable in 1965, but since Congress seemed bent on paying bonuses before they were due, the actual payment date should be June 1936, with, of course, an additional 3 percent annual interest compounded back from 1965 to 1936. In this way the future veterans would receive their benefits while all were still alive to enjoy them. A national salute was adopted, a modified version of the then famous Fascist greeting: an arm held straight out in the direction of Washington, the palm turned up receptively.

The Press Club sent out stories, the wire services got interested, and all across the country newspapers ran articles on the Future Veterans. Overnight, local chapters mushroomed on college campuses; by June 1936 there were more than 500 chapters and a paid-up membership of over 50,000 students.

The Future Veterans were discussed —and denounced—in Congress, and they were vigorously criticized and condemned by the organized veterans movement. The Commander of the Veterans of Foreign Wars, James Van Zandt, called them "insolent puppies" who ought to be spanked. "They'll never be veterans of a future war," he predicted, "for they are too yellow to go to war." The Princetonians replied that since the Veterans of Future Wars was a genuinely patriotic organization, Van Zandt clearly must be a "Red."

Activity at other colleges took various forms, but most of what happened at Princeton headquarters was intended simply to laugh the bonus movement to death. This spirit was well summed up by the student who happily noted, as the memberships rolled in, "Manifest Destiny has laid another golden egg."

What made the Future Veterans an instant success was their rare appeal both to conservatives and to liberals. Conservatives saw the Princetonians as heaven-sent allies who would help them keep FDR from spending the country into bankruptcy. College liberals who were pacifist, anti-war, and anti-military saw in the movement an opportunity to satirize war itself. Still, more than a few liberals did suspect that the Princetonians were at heart merely conservatives who really didn't care about anything except the bonus issue. This, to a considerable extent, was right. At Princeton the emphasis was upon the joke, the satire, the bonus. But not always, and not exclusively. Dean Christian Gauss, who had originally lent only grudging support, sensed this when he wrote a critic of the Future Veterans that the movement "was founded partly in a spirit of high jinks and partly in a spirit of protest against the glorification of war." Later on, Gauss mused that the Future Veterans "might have consequences that no one can yet see and that it demonstrates the determination of youth to rebuild the disordered world of their fathers a little closer to sanity."

The liberal, anti-war note was most evident at Princeton toward the end. In June 1936 the national headquarters adopted a resolution calling upon Congress to declare that the United States would not enter a foreign war except by majority vote of the residents of three-fourths of the States of the Union. In spirit and language this resolution paralleled the then pending Ludlow Amendment, which in 1937 barely failed of passage in the House of Representatives.

Future Veteran activity had peaked by the close of the academic year. After the summer vacation the treasury was bare, the joke was stale, and national attention was focused on the Roosevelt-Landon campaign. The Princetonians gamely issued a few proclamations and sent questionnaires to the presidential candidates about the bonus—and also about conscription and wartime controls over capital. But it was clear that the last golden egg had been laid. Operations were suspended in the fall, and in April 1937, with the treasury showing a deficit of forty-four cents, the Veterans of Future Wars closed their books forever.

One last note. Except for one student who was hurt in an automobile accident, every one of the Princetonians who founded the Veterans of Future Wars served in the armed forces of the United States in World War II.

Richard D. Challener

Vice-President was the title accorded several persons serving as acting president during brief interregnums in the early years of the college, but the first vice-president in the usual sense was Samuel Stanhope Smith, son-in-law of President John Witherspoon, who was appointed in 1786 to act for the president when he was away from Princeton, as he frequently was, on affairs of state. This office was filled sporadically as a means of granting the president much-needed aid by:

Samuel Stanhope Smith 1786-1795
Elijah Slack 1812-1817
Philip Lindsly 1817-1824
John Maclean 1829-1854

Two of these vice-presidents became presidents: Smith and Maclean.

In modern times the duties discharged by the four vice-presidents listed above have been performed by deans (beginning in 1883), and more recently by provosts (beginning in

1966). Since 1939 the title vice-president has been associated with business rather than academic matters:

Financial Vice-President
George Brakeley '07 (1939-1953)
Ricardo A. Mestres '31 (1959-1972)
Paul B. Firstenberg '55 (1972-1976)
Carl W. Schafer (1976-   )

(These financial vice-presidents have also served as treasurer: Brakeley, 1941-1953; Mestres, 1953-1972; Schafer, 1972-   ).

Administrative Vice-President
Edgar M. Gemmell '34 (1959-1965)

Vice-President for Development
Henry E. Bessire '57 (1969-   )
Vice-President for Public Affairs
William H. Weathersby (1970-1978)
Robert K. Durkee '69 (1978-   )

Vice-President for Administrative Affairs
Anthony J. Maruca '54 (1972-   )

Vice-President for Facilities
John P. Moran '51 (1973-   )

Vice-Presidents of the United States who attended Princeton are:

Aaron Burr A.B. 1772 (N.Y.) 1801-1805
George Mifflin Dallas A.B. 1810 (Pa.) 1845-1849

Viner, Jacob (1892-1970), third Walker Professor of Economics and International Finance, was one of the ablest economists of his generation, and "in the range and depth of insight and erudition," according to the British economist Lionel C. Robbins, "the outstanding all-rounder of his time in our profession." His primary interests were in international economics, economic theory, and the history of economic thought, but his influence pervaded all areas of economics and spread to the fields of history, philosophy, literature, and religion. President Bowen, who was one of his students, called him "one of the great Renaissance scholars of the world."

Born in Montreal, Canada, of Rumanian immigrant parents (he later became a naturalized citizen of the United States), he graduated in 1914 from McGill, where Stephen Leacock was one of his teachers, and received his Ph.D. in 1922 from Harvard, where he was a pupil and became a close friend of Professor Frank Taussig.

He became an instructor at the University of Chicago in 1916 and was promoted to full professor in 1925, at the age of thirty-two. Chicago had a remarkably brilliant group of economists in those years; according to Simeon E. Leland, his first graduate student and later his colleague, "the brightest star in this galaxy was Viner . . . the most industrious and the toughest teacher of the lot."

Viner's first book was *Dumping* (1923); when a dowager asked him why anyone would write a book on *that* subject, his reply was the subtitle: "*A Problem in International Trade.*" His second book, *Canada's Balance of International Indebtedness* (1924), was his doctoral dissertation; a pioneering work, it set the style for a highly productive series of studies in the working of international financial mechanisms. His *Studies in the Theory of International Trade* (1937), was, Robbins said, "at once the main source of historical knowledge regarding the evolution of thought in this sphere and a work in which some of his main theoretical developments play a pivotal part." During his eighteen years as editor of the *Journal of Political Economy*, he brought that journal to the peak of its distinction.

Viner frequently interrupted his academic work to serve as an adviser to the government and as a delegate to many international conferences. During the First World War, he was associated with the United States Tariff Commission and the Shipping Board. In the thirties he was an adviser to the Treasury Department, participating in the original planning of the Social Security Program. He was later a consultant to the State Department and to the Board of Governors of the Federal Reserve System.

Viner made several close friends in other countries, among them, Lionel Robbins, who has described their first encounter at Oxford in 1927 and "the impression he at once made—the short alert figure with his candid and penetrating eyes, now brimming over with fun, now sober with deep reflection, his quick wit, his delight in argument and the general sense of intellectual vitality that informed even his casual remarks."

Later Robbins discovered other qualities: Viner's scrupulousness, his candor, his catholic outlook, his "zest for the exchange of ideas and the pursuit of the thought wherever it led him which made any session with him an exciting and strenuous adventure." Robbins said of Viner what Dr. Johnson said of Edmund Burke: "That man calls forth all my powers."

THE PRINCETON YEARS

In 1946, after serving for thirty years as a member of the faculty of the University of Chicago, Viner accepted President Dodds's invitation to come to Princeton, where he made a remarkable contribution to the intellectual life of the University for almost twenty-five years.

His insight and erudition delighted his Princeton colleagues. Time and again, Professor William Baumol recalled, Viner would pose propositions to him "involving complex interrelations arrived at by some inexplicable intuitive process." Occasionally, Baumol would argue with him that his propositions were obviously incorrect, but always it turned out that Viner had been right. "Sometimes it took me days of painstaking calculation to arrive at his result," said Baumol, "but I can remember no case in which the mathematics failed to support his assertion."

His reputation as a tough teacher continued. Graduate students knew that in doctoral examinations his would be the most difficult questions, Baumol recalled, but what they did not know was that afterward his would be the most generous marks proposed—and usually adopted. Once a colleague asked Viner how he could possibly propose such a good grade for a student who had failed completely to answer what Viner had asked him. With a playful gleam in his eyes, Viner replied "Surely no one could reasonably have been expected to answer *that* question."

A familiar figure in Firestone Library, Viner exercised a lively influence on its other users. "No one," the University Librarian, William S. Dix, said, "could measure the value of his informal teaching as he stood near the catalogue or in the stacks talking with a graduate student or a colleague . . . teaching by example the pleasure and the integrity of sound scholarship." An expert bibliographer and an inveterate reader of booksellers' catalogues, he delighted in discovering obscure but useful books and pamphlets which he acquired and gave to the University library, with meticulous notes on their bibliographical significance.

He also contributed his tough-mindedness and his infectious humor to the affairs of the University Press as a member of its editorial board and as a trustee. Under his influence standards and procedures were established for the publication of scholarly books that have helped set the Press's guidelines ever since. Remarking on Viner's influence, Herbert S. Bailey, Jr., Director of the Press, spoke of the "witty seriousness" that was characteristic of everything he did. "He rarely told a joke," Bailey recalled, "but conversations with him were filled with laughter. . . . Even on the most serious occasions when he was righteously aroused by some scholar's carelessness or infidelity, a flash of wit could suddenly turn everything to smiles—though the carelessness or infidelity was not excused."

HIS "MODEST PROPOSAL"

Viner's wit as well as his humanistic approach to learning are illustrated in an address delivered at Brown University in 1950, entitled "A Modest Proposal for Some Stress on Scholarship in Graduate Training." His "modest proposal" was that graduate schools should assume more responsibility than they ordinarily do for scholarship as distinct from research.

Although he admitted that graduate students could not become "finished scholars as well as finished economists" in the short time available to them, he pointed out that graduate study is followed by another stage in education "lasting to the end of one's life." He suggested, therefore, that doctoral degrees should be granted, and accepted, somewhat in the spirit in which the University of Avignon handled the case of a capable but negligent candidate in 1650; "after some hesitation it conferred the doctoral degree . . . *sub spe futuri studii* . . . 'in the hope of future study.' "

He did not plead on behalf of scholarship that it would save the world ("although this had conceivably happened in the past and might happen again") or that it would bring material rewards to the scholar or that it was an invariably exciting activity. All that he would plead, at least on this occasion, he said, was that once the taste for it has been aroused,

it gives a sense of largeness even to one's small quests, and a sense of fullness even to the small answers to problems large or small which it yields, a sense which can never in any other way be attained, for which no other source of human gratification can, to the addict, be a satisfying substitute, which gains instead of loses in quality and quantity and in pleasure-yielding capacity by being shared with others—and which, unlike golf, improves with age.

Viner's ground-breaking study of *The Customs Union Issue* appeared in 1950, his essays on *International Economics* in 1951, and his lectures at the National University of Brazil, *International Trade and Economic Development*, in 1952. In 1957, on his sixty-fifth birthday, his students and friends brought out a selection of his writings, entitled *The Long View and the Short*.

In 1960 Viner nominally retired, but despite his reply to an old friend who asked what he was doing now— "basking amid the laurels of my students"—he continued to spend most of his time in Firestone Library, "pursuing with concentrated intensity at once the detail of how the subject of his study actually happened and what its significance was in the broad evolution of thought and affairs."

In 1962 he was awarded the Francis A. Walker Medal, presented by the

American Economic Association once every five years to an economist who has made a contribution of the highest distinction to economics. In presenting this award, Fritz Machlup, Viner's successor as Walker Professor, said that in all the fields to which Viner had contributed, he would be remembered as "a deflator of pretentious nonsense as well as an original creator." What all of his colleagues might learn from him, Machlup added, was "intellectual honesty and fearlessness," with "a willingness to stand firm on the unpopular side of any issue, theoretical or practical, whether that side be 'radical' or 'conservative,' 'newfangled' or 'old-fashioned.' "

During his retirement he spent a year at Harvard as Taussig Research Professor, wrote a monograph on monetary control and another on Adam Smith, and gave the Jayne Memorial Lectures of the American Philosophical Society on "The Role of Providence in the Social Order."

Viner was a permanent member of the Institute for Advanced Study in Princeton and an honorary fellow of the London School of Economics. President of the American Economic Association in 1939, he was also a fellow or member of a number of honorary academies in the United States as well as in Great Britain, Sweden, and Italy. He received honorary degrees from thirteen American and foreign universities including Princeton.

"A deep love of justice and liberty and a profound sense of compassion" were for Viner "the underlying justifications for thought and public action," Lionel Robbins wrote in his final tribute:

Jack was not a believer in any orthodox creed. But he believed passionately in the liberal values: equality before the law, the maximum freedom for the individual compatible with similar privileges for his fellows, sympathy and help for the unfortunate. Nothing stirred him to anger more than an infringement of these norms, nothing more aroused his contempt than bogus substitutes for them. . . . He did not believe that life on this planet was likely to become perfect. But he believed that, with forethought, it could be made less imperfect than it is.

von Neumann, John (1903-1957), world-famous mathematician who was professor of mathematical physics in the University and later a professor at the Institute for Advanced Study, was born on December 28, 1903, the son of a well-to-do banker in Budapest, Hungary. From the age of thirteen he showed a pronounced interest in mathematics, which was fostered by his teachers at the Lutheran High School of Budapest where Princeton's Nobel laureate physicist Eugene Wigner was also a student.

After graduation from high school, von Neumann studied chemistry for two years in Berlin and for two years in Zurich but spent much of his time with mathematicians, taking a Ph.D. in mathematics at the University of Budapest not long after receiving his chemistry diploma at Zurich. Thereafter, he concentrated on mathematics and theoretical physics in further study at Göttingen and Hamburg and after 1927 as a privatdozent in Berlin.

In 1929 von Neumann accepted an invitation to come to Princeton as a visiting professor for one term. Given a continuing half-time appointment the following year, he spent one term each year in Princeton and one in Germany until 1933 when, at the age of 30, he accepted appointment as the youngest and one of the first professors in the newly founded Institute for Advanced Study. In 1937 he became a United States citizen.

Von Neumann's brilliant work in mathematics also carried him into theoretical economics and technology as well as theoretical physics—areas where he was able to make vital contributions not only to science but also to the welfare of his adopted country. His work in quantum mechanics gave him a profound knowledge concerning the application of nuclear energy to military and peacetime uses, enabling him to occupy an important place in the scientific councils of the nation. During the Second World War, he played a major role among the Los Alamos group of scientists who developed the atomic bomb. After the war he served on the advisory committee of the Atomic Energy Commission and on the commission itself from 1954 until his death.

In collaboration with the University's Class of 1913 Professor of Political Economy, Oskar Morgenstern, he developed further the interest in game theory he had first evidenced in a treatise published in 1928. Their joint endeavors resulted in *Theory of Games and Economic Behavior* (published by Princeton University Press in 1944), which aimed to demonstrate that "the typical problems of economic behavior become strictly identical with the mathematical notions of suitable games of strategy." The theory was also considered of value for the study of government and sociology and for its application to problems of military strategy by the United States.

Probably the best known and most dramatic of von Neumann's accomplishments was his development of one of the speediest, most accurate, and most useful computers, which made the essential calculations that enabled the United States to build and test its first full model of the hydrogen bomb. Another computer he later developed enabled the Navy to do twenty-four-hour weather predictions in a few minutes and helped the armed forces plan the movement of men and material by mathematically simulating logistic problems

Von Neumann received many honors for his contributions to science and to the nation. In 1937, when he was 34, he won the American Mathematical Society's highest award, the Bocher Prize, and soon thereafter, at a comparatively early age, was elected a member of the National Academy of Sciences, the American Philosophical Society, and the American Academy of Arts and Sciences, and a foreign member of scientific academies in Amsterdam, Lima, Milan, and Rome. In 1947 he was awarded the Presidential Medal for Merit and the Navy Distinguished Civilian Service Award for his work during the Second World War. That same year he was one of a select group of scholars awarded Princeton honorary degrees at the concluding convocation of its Bicentennial Year; he was later honored by a number of other institutions, including Harvard and Pennsylvania. From 1951 to 1953 he was president of the American Mathematical Society, and in 1956 he received three top honors: the Albert Einstein Commemorative Award, the $50,000 Enrico Fermi Award for his contributions to the design and construction of computing machines used in nuclear research and development, and the Medal of Freedom "for exceptional meritorious service in promoting the scientific progress of this country's armament program."

Analyzing the qualities of mind that made possible von Neumann's extraordinary contributions, Eugene Wigner emphasized the accuracy of his logic, his brilliance, and his exceptional memory. Observing that von Neumann was ever-ready to help and was genuinely interested in every problem that presented a challenge, Professor Wigner said that he himself had learned more mathematics from von Neumann than anyone else and much more about the "essence of creative thinking in mathematics" than a lifetime's study without von Neumann could have taught him. Professor Wigner also quoted Atomic Energy Commission Chairman Lewis L. Strauss's comment on von Neumann: "If he analyzed a problem, it was not necessary to discuss it any further. It was clear what had to be done."

In the summer of 1955, only a few months after his appointment to the Atomic Energy Commission, von Neumann became ill with what was soon diagnosed as cancer. His last public appearance came early in 1956 when, in a wheel-chair at the White House, he received the Medal of Freedom from President Eisenhower. That April he was taken to Walter Reed Hospital where he died on February 8, 1957.

In a memoir written for the American Philosophical Society, Professor Eugene Wigner, von Neumann's close friend since their high school days in Budapest, declared: "His accomplishments were manifold, his was a great mind—perhaps one of the greatest of the first half of this century." A tribute from President Eisenhower cited the "rare and great gifts of mind" von Neumann had given "for the defense of his adopted land and the cause of freedom."

Warren, Howard Crosby (1867-1934), first chairman of the Psychology Department, was badly burned by a lamp when eighteen months old, and suffered great pain from a succession of operations during the first five years of his childhood. As a result of this ordeal, he developed powers of endurance and emotional restraint that remained dominant traits of his personality. Although he carried through life deep facial scars and a useless hand and eye, there were apparently no emotional scars—in his autobiography he said his early life was "the story of a happy childhood, a pleasant home life, and congenial playmates."

His family was financially able to give him every assistance in coping with his early handicap (and later to leave him a substantial inheritance, which he used with characteristically self-effacing generosity to advance the science of psychology). Although brought up in a puritanically religious household, he developed at an early age a skepticism toward conventional beliefs and explanations, which in college ripened into a revolt against religious mysticism and a belief in a deterministic interpretation of mental processes.

He prepared for college under a private tutor, graduated from Princeton in 1889, and received an A.M. two years later. In 1893, after advanced study in Leipzig, Berlin, and Munich, he became a demonstrator in Princeton's new psychological laboratory in Nassau Hall. His advance was rapid: he became professor in 1902, director of the laboratory in 1904, and Stuart Professor of Psychology in 1914. He worked with persistence toward the formal separation of psychology and philosophy, and in 1920 became the first chairman of a separate department of psychology. Through his efforts and with his financial help, Eno Hall, a building devoted entirely to psychology, was erected in 1924.

Warren was profoundly honest and deeply scornful of insincerity and vanity; he also had a fine sense of humor. These qualities were in evidence when in 1916, two years after his appointment to the Stuart Professorship, he became a candidate for the degree of Doctor of Philosophy at Johns Hopkins University. He had not bothered to take a degree at the normal time in his career and now concluded that it was not proper for him to examine Ph.D. candidates without having the degree himself. He spent the entire academic year 1916-17 in residence at Hopkins, where he gave lectures instead of attending them, presented a thesis, and successfully completed the final oral examinations in which, one observer said, "one could not tell who was the examiner and who was the candidate." He thus earned his Ph.D. three years after the completion of his term as president of the American Psychological Association.

Toward the end of his life Warren was threatened with total blindness; "it will be an interesting psychological experiment," he told a colleague, "to find out what personal adjustments I shall have to make." He patiently carried on the work of compiling a dictionary of psychology, with which he had been occupied for a decade, and pushed it almost to completion, even though he could see the print only with the greatest difficulty. He left the manuscript, and $5,000 for editorial expenses, to the trustees of Princeton, and the dictionary was published posthumously, "a memorial," his faculty colleagues said, "to his careful scholarship and . . . supreme courage."

He also left to Princeton his extensive psychological library; it is housed in Green Hall, which replaced Eno Hall as the home of psychology in 1963.

In his honor the Society of Experimental Psychologists, which he helped found, annually awards to one of its members the Howard Crosby Warren Medal.

Washington, George, made two memorable visits to Princeton. The first took place in 1777 when, ten days after crossing the Delaware on Christmas night and defeating the British at Trenton, he made the early morning surprise attack that drove the British from Nassau Hall and sent them in retreat from Princeton. The second visit occurred in 1783, in the closing days of the war, when he came here at the request of the Continental Congress, which had fled from Philadelphia to avoid mutinous troops and was meeting in Nassau Hall.

Since no suitable house could be found for Washington in the village of Princeton, "Rockingham" was rented for him at Rocky Hill, four miles distant. Here he arrived late in August and stayed until November. He became a familiar figure in Princeton and was a frequent visitor to Nassau Hall where he conferred with the committee of Congress on peace establishment.

In August, at a formal audience of Congress in Nassau Hall, he received the thanks of his countrymen for his conduct of the war. That September he attended the College's Commencement in the First Presbyterian Church in company with the members of Congress who, as a compliment to the College, had adjourned their meetings so that they might attend. Ashbel Green (later president of the College), delivered the valedictory oration, observing that "there had never been such an audience at a Commencement before, and perhaps, there never will be again." He concluded with this tribute to Washington:

Some future bard . . . shall tell in all the majesty of epic song, of the man whose prudent conduct, and whose gallant sword, taught the tyrants of the earth to fear oppression, and opened an asylum for the virtuous and free to all the world.

The trustees met immediately after the Commencement exercises. Their only business was the adoption of the following resolution:

The Board being desirous to give some testimony of their high respect for the character of his Excellency General Washington, who has so auspiciously conducted the armies of America,

Resolved, That the Rev. Drs. Witherspoon, Rodgers, and Johnes be a committee to wait upon his Excellency to request him to sit for a picture, to be taken by Mr. Charles Wilson Peale, of Philadelphia. And that this portrait be placed in the Hall of the College, in the room of the picture of the late King of Great Britain [George the Second], which was torn away by a ball from the American artillery in the battle of Princeton.

At a meeting on the following day President Witherspoon reported to the board that "his Excellency General Washington had delivered to him fifty guineas . . . as a testimony of his respect for the College." The board thereupon resolved to direct the committee it had appointed to solicit his portrait, to present to him at the same time "the thanks of the Board for . . . his politeness and generosity."

Washington consented to the portrait, which was completed in time for presentation at Commencement the following year. It depicts Washington with uplifted sword at the battle of Princeton, at his side the mortally wounded General Hugh Mercer, a surgeon, and another officer bearing an American flag, with Nassau Hall in the distance. The portrait has escaped two fires and today hangs in the Faculty Room on the right side of the president's chair. It is one of the University's finest paintings and one of its proudest possessions.

Washington continued to maintain his respect for Princeton, sending his ward, George Washington Parke Custis, to study here in 1796 under President S. Stanhope Smith. In a letter to Custis in 1797, Washington cautioned him against letting his former tutor, Zechariah Lewis, divert him from the course recommended by President Smith:

Mr. Lewis [Washington wrote] was educated at Yale College, and, as is natural, may be prejudiced in favor of the mode pursued at that seminary; but no college has turned out better scholars or more estimable characters than Nassau.

Water Polo was played at Princeton before packed galleries from 1907 to 1930. It was a rugged game, with no holds barred (no one, except those involved, ever knew what went on under water), but there were those who loved it. Archibald MacLeish, the poet, played right forward on the Yale team that suffered its only loss to Princeton in 1914.

Ably coached by Frank Sullivan, Princeton teams won championships in the water polo league of the Intercollegiate Swimming Association in ten of the twenty-three seasons in which they participated: 1912 through 1917; 1919; 1921 through 1923. Princeton did not lose a single game in any of these years. The 1912 and 1913 teams added to their laurels by post-season victories over the University of Illinois, intercollegiate champions of the West. The 1916 team was exceptionally strong defensively: it permitted its opponents only 12 points—against its own 335—during the entire season. The 1917 team was outstanding on offense, scoring a total of 370 points, a league record. Herbert W. Warden, Jr. '18 led in scoring with 230 points in 1916, and 210 in 1917. Some other outstanding players were Goulding K. Wight '13, Robert L. Nourse, Jr. '17, Robert C. Tait '22, Fred M. Phillips '23, Henry M. Matalene, Jr. '26.

In February 1930, the Faculty Committee on Athletics announced that 19 of the 23 members of the varsity squad and 14 of the 17 members of the freshman squad were suffering from ear injuries or nose and throat infections and that water polo would be discontinued for the rest of the season. Later, on recommendation of the medical staff, the committee announced the abolition of the sport at Princeton. Since then, water polo has been revived informally several times under revised rules that have sought to make the game less hazardous.

Wertenbaker, Thomas Jefferson (1879-1966), second Edwards Professor of American History, was born in Char-

lottesville and took his bachelor's and his doctor's degrees at the University of Virginia, where his grandfather, appointed librarian by Thomas Jefferson, had served for half a century.

He made his reputation with his doctoral thesis, *Patrician and Plebeian in Virginia*, which he followed with his *Virginia under the Stuarts*, and his master work *The Planters of Colonial Virginia*. In all of these, his student and colleague Joseph R. Strayer has written, "he showed the same complete honesty, historical insight, and appreciation of the role of the common man in our early history."

Brought to Princeton as a preceptor by Woodrow Wilson in 1910, Wertenbaker was a member of the History Department for thirty-seven years and its chairman from 1928 to 1936. He encouraged good undergraduate teaching; his own course on Colonial American history, familiarly known as "House and Garden," was a student favorite. He was a popular preceptor among undergraduates and in great demand for "alumni preceptorials." For many years he carried, with Dana C. Munro, the major burden of graduate instruction in history and strove to advance the scholarly reputation of the department.

His three volumes on *The Founding of American Civilization* "added new dimensions of social and cultural history to what had been the standard economic-political treatment of the colonial period." His other works include a general history of the American people, and a history of Princeton's first one hundred and fifty years, written for the University's Bicentennial in 1946.

Wertenbaker was president of the American Historical Association and a member of the American Philosophical Society. He was twice appointed Harmsworth Professor of American

History at Oxford and was a visiting professor at the University of Göttingen. Even in retirement he continued to receive important appointments, e.g., as visiting professor at the University of Munich, Thomas Jefferson Research Fellow at the University of Virginia, and John Hay Whitney Professor at Hampden-Sydney College.

Besides being one of the leading historians of his time, Wertenbaker was also a newspaper editor and an amateur architect; he designed his own home in Princeton, enclosing the garden with a serpentine wall modeled after Jefferson's at the University of Virginia. A courtly gentleman and scholar, he endeared himself to generations of students and colleagues. He was even-tempered in argument with his associates and went out of his way to be helpful to younger men. "In character and versatility," his faculty colleagues declared in their memorial minute, "he was a worthy representative of his beloved Golden Age of Virginia."

When he died, his friends established the Thomas Jefferson Wertenbaker Memorial Fund for the purchase of University Library books in American colonial history.

West, Andrew Fleming (1853-1943), first dean of the Graduate School, was born in Allegheny, Pennsylvania on May 17, 1853. He entered Princeton in 1870, but soon withdrew because of poor health and for two years attended Centre College in Danville, Kentucky, where his father was a professor in the Danville Theological Seminary. He returned to Princeton in 1872, graduating in the Class of 1874. After college, he taught high school Latin in Cincinnati for six years and, following a period of study in Europe, served for two years

as principal of the Morris Academy in Morristown, New Jersey.

In 1883 he was called to Princeton by President McCosh to fill the newly founded Giger chair in Latin. Early in his career he published a book about the teacher of Charlemagne, *Alcuin and the Rise of Christian Schools*, and a Latin grammar he hoped would lead secondary school students "without too many scratches" through what Alcuin had called "the thorny thickets of grammatical density." He was president of the American Philological Association, a trustee of the American Academy in Rome, one of the founders of the American School of Classical Studies in Rome, and the principal founder of the American Classical League, which he organized in an effort to stem the decline of interest in the classics—in his view, "the gold standard of education."

The organizing and fund-raising talents West used in his efforts on behalf of the classics, also found dramatic expression in the University's highly successful sesquicentennial celebration in 1896. As secretary of the committee in charge of the celebration, he organized a splendid three-day affair, including a distinguished program of public lectures by visiting scholars from abroad that set a pattern for other, later university celebrations, and a spectacular torchlight procession of 2,000 gaily costumed alumni that stimulated the development of the most colorful event of the annual Commencement season— the alumni parade.

West also helped to obtain President Cleveland's participation in the celebration, and after his second term as president, Cleveland moved to Princeton, naming the house and grounds that West found for him "Westland." On his election as a University trustee, Cleveland became chairman of the trustees' committee on the graduate school and West's strong supporter.

As secretary of the committee that sought gifts in connection with the sesquicentennial celebration, West played a significant role in the raising of funds for endowment and for a library and three dormitories ("Here's to Andy three million West," the seniors sang, "At gathering money he is the best"); he was also largely responsible for introducing collegiate gothic architecture at Princeton, communicating his enthusiasm for the gothic of Oxford and Cambridge to M. Taylor Pyne and other donors and—through Pyne's influence as chairman of the grounds and buildings committee—to other members of the board of trustees.

With his appointment in December 1900 as first dean of the graduate school, West devoted his energy and talents to the development of the school and particularly to the creation of a residential graduate college. He wanted Princeton to lead the way in providing adequate residences for American graduate students. In the spring of 1903, after visiting Oxford, Cambridge, and other universities in Britain and on the continent, he outlined his proposal for a residential college in a handsomely illustrated book, which he proceeded to use, with great effectiveness, in raising funds for this project. One of the first results of his effort was a $275,000 bequest left in the spring of 1906 by Mrs. Josephine Thomson Swann, of Princeton, for a graduate college in memory of her first husband, United States Senator Robert S. Thomson, of the Class of 1817.

The Swann bequest brought to light a disagreement between West and President Wilson regarding the location of the graduate college that marked the onset of the great controversy between these two strong and stubborn sons of Presbyterian ministers. From the beginning, Wilson had wanted the graduate college "at the heart" of the University as "a means of vitalizing the whole intellectual life" of the place. West appeared to be in agreement at first: in his book, he spoke of the influence the proposed graduate college would have on "every undergraduate who passes it in his daily walks." However, as his plans developed, he settled on a location geographically separate from the main campus, where, as he put it, the graduate college would be free from the distractions of undergraduate life, and thus able to develop "its own true life."

West's position was greatly strengthened in the fall of 1906 when he received an invitation to the presidency of Massachusetts Institute of Technology. What his loss would mean to Princeton was widely discussed in the nation's press as well as in the *Princetonian* and the *Alumni Weekly*. After the adoption of a trustees' resolution (drafted by Wilson) declaring that the board would consider his loss "quite irreparable" because it had "particularly counted upon him to put into operation the Graduate College which he conceived and for which it has planned," West finally declined the invitation, and the *New York Sun* headlined its announcemnt "WEST WON'T GO."

West suffered a setback in the spring of 1908, when the trustees voted to locate the Thomson graduate college between Prospect and Seventy-nine Hall. A year later, however, West's continuing efforts were rewarded by a letter he received from Procter and Gamble Company President William Cooper Procter 1883, whose wife had been a student of West's at the Hughes high school in Cincinnati. Procter offered the University $500,000 for the graduate college, provided the trustees raised an equal amount from other sources and selected some site other than the Prospect one.

The stalemate that followed the Procter offer ended abruptly in May of 1910 with the death in Salem, Massachusetts, of Isaac C. Wyman 1848, a wealthy bachelor West had visited a number of years before, and sought to persuade to leave his money to Princeton for a graduate college to be built near where his father had fought in the Revolutionary battle of Princeton. From Salem, where he had gone for the funeral and probate of the will, West telegraphed President Wilson and Trustee M. Taylor Pyne (by then chairman of the graduate school committee) that Wyman had left his residuary estate (estimated originally at upwards of $2 million but eventually realized at a little less than $800,000) for the purposes of the Graduate College and had named West as one of two executors and trustees. "I laid a spray of ivy from Nassau Hall on Mr. Wyman's casket," West reported in a letter to Pyne describing the funeral, "and I planted an ivy root from Nassau Hall at his grave."

President Wilson having acknowledged defeat in the matter of location, the Board, on his recommendation, unanimously authorized acceptance of the Procter gift; it also voted to extend its thanks to West for his "great services to the University" in obtaining the Wyman bequest.

Built on the north edge of the University's golf links, half a mile from the main campus, its chief supporters remembered by Thomson College, Procter Hall, Wyman House, Pyne Tower,

and Cleveland Tower, the graduate college was dedicated on October 22, 1913, with speeches by, among others, Dean West and ex-President Taft.

Although his main ambition was now fulfilled, West continued to exercise his money-raising talent. When Henry Clay Frick, on being shown Procter Hall, observed that it "looked too damn much like a church—all it needs is an organ," West quickly persuaded him to give one. Nor was he discomfited by Edward W. Bok's comment that Princeton needed a memorial to Woodrow Wilson; he promptly exacted from Bok endowment for a Woodrow Wilson professorship.

A large man (the undergraduate Faculty Song described him as "63 inches around the vest") with an impressive voice, West was an unforgettable personage. A wit and a satirist, he delighted in epigrams and limericks. He also took special pleasure in writing the honorary degree citations, and was always ready to respond to a request for an elegant inscription for a new building. He enjoyed dining out, fine food, good conversation, a good cigar, a good detective story, and a good joke.

West retired in 1928 after forty-five years as Giger professor of Latin and twenty-seven as dean of the graduate school. Classicist Edward Capps, who had been called from the University of Chicago by Wilson and had been one of his strongest partisans, wrote to West: "You are entitled to reflect, as few of us are, that you have seen most of your dreams come true. The Graduate School and the Graduate College are your sole creations, and they are splendid." At the same time, the university conferred on West an honorary doctor of letters, and the *Daily Princetonian* issued a 32-page special edition to recount his achievements. A few months earlier, R. Tait McKenzie's bronze statue of him, given by William Cooper Procter, had been erected in the main quadrangle of the Graduate College and a small house was completed next to Wyman House for his use the rest of his life.

In his retirement years, he recommended Princeton as "a good place to grow old in" to members of the Nassau Club, when they gave him a dinner on his eighty-first birthday, learned with satisfaction of the endowment by the Carnegie Corporation and anonymous donors of The Andrew Fleming West chair in classics, and, with the help of President Dodds, who went to see him at his request, planned his funeral. After "some bantering back and forth and a considerable amount of laughter," they outlined a full service and left copies at the office and home of the president and the dean of the graduate school—West "had never been prone to leave things at loose ends," Mr. Dodds later recalled, "and his funeral was to be no exception."

He died on December 27, 1943, and the funeral service—as planned—was held in the University Chapel three days later.

A faculty memorial minute lauded West's "vision, wisdom, and tenacity of purpose," his "keen understanding of human nature," his "powers of persuasion," and his "genius for strong and enduring friendships."

John D. Davies

West College, built in 1836, probably from the plans of John Notman, was Princeton's second dormitory. The first was East College (q.v.). West College was remodeled in 1925-1926 by Aymar Embury 1900, who removed a mansard roof that had been added about 1870, restoring the original Colonial roof line.

He also added the second-floor balcony along the front, redesigned the two main entrances, and built a new addition in the rear. Except for the ground floor, which was once occupied by the University Store, West continued to serve as a dormitory until 1964 when its interior was converted for use by deans and other officers concerned with the academic administration of the undergraduate college.

Whig-Cliosophic Society, The American, is the oldest college literary and debating club in the United States. Originally two separate groups, Whig and Clio (as they have been known commonly for most of their history) grew out of two earlier student societies, the Plain Dealing Club (Whig) and the Well Meaning Club (Clio), founded about 1765 to promote literary and debating activities. Similar groups had appeared in other American colleges during the eighteenth century; most of them had been short-lived. Such was the fate of the Plain Dealing and Well Meaning Clubs; conflicts between the two groups led to their suppression in March 1769.

Command of the subtler uses of the written and spoken word was a major instrument of professional and political success in the eighteenth as well as in the nineteenth century. Undergraduate interest in literary and debating activities, therefore, did not end with the dissolution of the clubs. The prime agent in their revival appears to have been William Paterson, later governor of New Jersey. After graduation in 1763, Paterson remained in Princeton to study law. During these years he maintained close contact with students, encouraging their more constructive activities. It seems to have been Paterson, along with a few other alumni, who persuaded the new president, John Witherspoon, to permit the formation of successors to the Plain Dealing and Well Meaning Clubs.

The American Whig Society was born on June 24, 1769, and the Cliosophic Society on June 7, 1770. The name "American Whig" derived from a recent series of essays by a new trustee of the College, William Livingston, shortly to become first governor of the state of New Jersey. It signified adherence to ancient principles of British political and religious dissent, principles that later found concrete form in the Revolution and in the founding of the American Republic. The adjective "Cliosophic" seems to have been invented by Paterson. Signifying "in praise of wisdom," it bears no relation to the muse of history.

The years immediately preceding the Revolution were active ones for the societies. They afforded an arena in which many future leaders of the Republic, such as James Madison (Whig) and Aaron Burr (Clio) developed and sharpened the skills of persuasion, exposition, and cooperation (and conflict) with peers.

The disruptions caused by the Revolutionary War brought a hiatus in the societies' activities. Revived in 1781, they then entered their period of greatest influence and usefulness, one that extended to the 1880s. Housed at first in two small chambers in Nassau Hall, in 1805 Whig and Clio moved into more spacious apartments on the second floor of newly constructed Stanhope Hall. By the 1830s the societies had outgrown these rooms. They then constructed handsome wooden neo-classical halls for their own exclusive use, which were completed in 1838. The present marble halls, opened

in 1893, are greatly enlarged copies of the buldings of the 1830s.

Whig and Clio, like similar literary societies at other American colleges, were the main focus of undergraduate life for much of the nineteenth century. Elaborately organized, self-governing youth groups (though often receiving advice from alumni and faculty), they were, in effect, colleges within colleges. They constructed and taught their own curricula, selected and bought their own books, operated their own libraries (often larger and more accessible than that of the college itself), and developed and enforced elaborate codes of conduct among their members. Intense competition for members and for college honors led to creative emulation between the two societies. Their libraries afforded undergraduates easy access to the world outside; their debates trained generations to consider the great public issues of the day, from slavery to American expansion, from women's rights to the dismemberment of the union. Surviving the challenge of Greek letter fraternities in the 1850s and 1860s, the societies reached their apogee in the 1880s. Then Princeton, like many other old American colleges, underwent a rapid transformation. It became a university college. In the process enrollment increased enormously, while a network of social clubs, expanded library facilities, and a widened curriculum replaced many of the functions once performed by Whig and Clio. By the time of World War I, Whig and Clio were only two among the scores of student groups that appealed to a wide range of undergraduate intellectual, social, and physical interests.

Dormant during World War I, when the societies were revived in the early 1920s they faced a student generation largely indifferent to their traditional concerns. In an effort to attract interest, in 1925 the Polity, Law and Fine Arts Clubs, along with the Speaker's Association, were absorbed into the Halls. However, interest continued to decline; in 1928 the two societies merged and moved into Whig Hall. In 1941 Whig Hall and the assets of the society were transferred to the trustees of the University, with the understanding that the building and funds were to be "used for purposes associated with undergraduate activities in the fields of public speaking, debate, conferences on public affairs, literature and journalism." These were the main pursuits of the society over the succeeding three decades. In following them Whig-Clio sponsored successfully several subsidiary organizations, such as the Princeton Senate, the International Affairs Council, and the National Affairs Council. But from the 1930s on, Whig-Clio's most conspicuous public role was in bringing important public figures to speak on the campus. Sometimes controversial, the speakers linked the undergraduates in a direct and personal manner to the wider world beyond Princeton. And, when Whig Hall was gutted by fire in November 1969, its speedy and strikingly innovative reconstruction testified to widespread and continuing support for one of the older organizations in the United States.

James McLachlan

Whig Hall has been the home of the American Whig-Cliosophic Society, commonly known as Whig-Clio, since the merger of the American Whig and Cliosophic Societies in 1929. Whig Hall was built in 1893 at the same time as its twin, Clio Hall (q.v.). Both buildings were designed in marble by A. Page Brown in the Ionic style of a Greek temple, which had also been used for their stucco and wood predecessors, built in approximately the same locations in 1838. After Whig was gutted by fire in November 1969, extensive renovations, including a modern treatment of the destroyed east wall, were designed by the firm of Gwathmey and Siegel and completed in 1972.

Wilcox Hall is the nucleus of a group of buildings on the south campus that house Woodrow Wilson College (q.v.). It was completed in 1961 and named in honor of its donor, T. Ferdinand Wilcox '00, senior partner in a New York banking and brokerage firm, who was an officer of his class and a member of the Alumni Council. It contains dining facilities, lounges, conference rooms, overnight accommodations for guests, and a 12,000-book working library, named for Julian Street (q.v.).

Wilder, Thornton [Niven] 1897-1975) came to Princeton frequently in the early 1920s to browse in the stacks of the old Pyne Library on evenings when he was off duty at Lawrenceville School, where he taught French and was a master of Davis House. He entered the Princeton Graduate School in the fall of 1925 and received an A.M. in Modern Languages here in June 1926. He had previously attended Oberlin and Yale, where he received his A.B. in 1920. He got the idea for his Pulitzer Prize-winning novel, *The Bridge of San Luis Rey*, "on the winding walk from the golf club to the Graduate College." He began to write *The Bridge* in his rooms on the top floor of the eleventh entry of the Graduate College and finished it in Davis House the following year while teaching again at Lawrenceville. He left this area in 1928. A decade later, in 1938, his first play, *Our*

Town, opened in McCarter Theatre. It won a Pulitzer Prize and became one of the most frequently produced plays in America. He won a third Pulitzer Prize in 1943 for his play *The Skin of Our Teeth*.

Wilhelm, Richard Herman (1909-1968), a teacher of chemical engineering for thirty-four years and chairman of the department for fourteen, was regarded by his colleagues as one of the leading engineer scientists in Princeton's history. His innovative drive made itself felt in teaching, in research, and in administration. Under his leadership the Department of Chemical Engineering rose to be one of the most eminent in the country.

Born and raised in New York City, Wilhelm earned his three degrees (B.S. in Eng., Ch.E., and Ph.D.) at Columbia, and then spent his entire professional career at Princeton. He came here as an instructor in 1934, became a full professor in 1946, and chairman of his department in 1954.

An authority on chemical reaction engineering, he pioneered in fluidization and the development of fluid beds, which revolutionized the petroleum-cracking process. During his last years he discovered and refined the principle of parametric pumping, a process for separating the components of fluid mixtures, which has possible uses for separating salt from ocean water and waste from streams and may explain certain processes in living cells.

Although always an energetic and productive investigator, he gave first priority to teaching. "The primary function of the university is to teach," he once said, "and its most important focus of education should be on the undergraduate." According to the *Princeton Engineer*, "his chief pleasure was working with students in the classroom and the laboratory." He was at the same time a magnet for graduate students—their number increased from ten to seventy during his chairmanship—and his Ph.D.'s are to be found on chemical engineering faculties across the country. His faculty colleagues described him as "a gracious man, always sensitive to the concerns of those around him." In his presence, they said, his students and his associates "felt welcome, at ease, and reassured by his confidence in them."

His research and teaching won him many professional honors, including three awards from the American Institute of Chemical Engineers: the William H. Walker Award and the Professional Progress Award for his contributions to research and publication, the Warren K. Lewis Award for his "distinguished and continuing contributions to chemical engineering education." He was elected a Fellow of the American Academy of Arts and Sciences in 1964 and was given the American Chemical Society's award in industrial and engineering chemistry in 1966.

Wilhelm's creative energies spread to all parts of the University. He directed a conference on "Engineering and Human Affairs" as part of the University's Bicentennial Celebration in 1946. Three years later he organized a program of study combining elements of chemical engineering, biology, chemistry, and mathematics, to prepare students for careers in the biological industry and for postgraduate research in this area. Later he helped devise a program in engineering and public affairs, jointly administered by the engineering school and the Woodrow Wilson School. In 1966 he helped organize a University-wide committee to coordinate and strengthen Princeton's work in the life sciences.

In June 1968, two months after his election to the National Academy of Engineering, he was appointed by the trustees to the Henry Putnam University Professorship, a chair of special distinction used "for recognition of a scholar of extraordinary ability in any discipline." Six weeks later while on vacation he died of heart attack at the age of fifty-nine. Thus, his faculty colleagues wrote, "Princeton University and the science and art of engineering . . . lost far too soon the contributions of a creative teacher-scholar."

The R. H. Wilhelm Award in Chemical Reaction Engineering was established by the American Institute of Chemical Engineers in 1973. The following year, the University, with contributions from colleagues, friends, and students, instituted the Richard H. Wilhelm Lectureships in Chemical Engineering.

Wilks, Samuel Stanley (1906-1964), the father of mathematical statistics at Princeton and a leader in the development of that discipline in the United States, was born on his father's farm near the town of Little Elm in northern Texas. He began his education in a one-room schoolhouse in Little Elm, and later attended high school in nearby Denton. He took his bachelor's degree at North Texas State Teachers College, his master's at the University of Texas, and his Ph.D. at the University of Iowa, then the center for statistical study in the United States. He came to Princeton in 1933, and in 1944 was appointed professor of mathematics and director of the newly founded Section of Mathematical Statistics, positions he held until his death twenty years later.

The twenty-one men who took their Ph.D.'s under Wilks played a leading role in the development of statistics in the United States and Canada. As graduate students, they had been inspired by his high expectations of them. Wilks was delighted when a student produced a fresh solution to a problem. "Kind of a nice result," he would say in his Texas drawl, "kind of pretty." Undergraduates responded equally well to his generous sharing of ideas and his challenging teaching; a number of senior theses written under him were published.

Wilks was concerned with keeping theoretical and applied mathematics in close association and in having them contribute to other disciplines. As one of his students, Frederick Mosteller, first chairman of the Harvard department of mathematical statistics, said, "Boundaries between disciplines, organizations, and people never lasted long in his mind, for he thought in terms of bridges, entrances, and opportunities."

Wilks sought to improve the teaching of mathematics at all levels, from kindergarten through high school as well as in college and graduate school. He organized courses on quality control inspection sampling for industry and made wartime contributions to antisubmarine warfare and the solution of convoy problems. He was chairman of the committee that analyzed the reasons public opinion polls had erroneously predicted the outcome of the 1948 Dewey-Truman presidential election. And it was at his suggestion that Princeton's football coach Charlie Caldwell used game movies, replayed many times, to grade each player on every play, in order to evaluate his effectiveness under varying conditions more accurately.

Although Wilks was responsible for a

considerable body of original research, his major contribution to his profession was as committeeman and adviser. "He was a hard-working, modest committee member," his Princeton colleague John Tukey recalled, "who was always there; who always knew, though he would only admit it indirectly, more about related programs than anyone else." Because of these qualities he was widely sought as a leader in scholarly organizations and as an adviser to the federal government. Professor Mosteller called him the "Statesman of Statistics"—a title borne out by even a partial listing of the offices Wilks held: president of the American Statistical Association as well as of the Institute of Mathematical Statistics, of which he was a founder; chairman of the Conference Board of the Mathematical Sciences, which he helped to create, and also of the Division of Mathematics of the National Research Council; director of the Social Science Research Council; member of the United States Commission for UNESCO; member of the Applied Mathematics Panel of the Office of Scientific Research and Development during World War II; and later adviser and consultant to many agencies in the Executive Office of the President, in the Department of Defense, and in the National Science Foundation. He was editor of the *Annals of Mathematical Statistics* during eleven crucial years in which it became the foremost journal in its field. He was a member, and active committeeman, of the American Philosophical Society and the American Academy of Arts and Sciences.

Wilks impressed his students and his colleagues as a vigorous, wise, and devoted man, sensitive to the feelings of others, and possessing a technical skill adequate to any demand. But, in the words of Professor Tukey, he is remembered by them above all for "his Scottish canny knack for finding a way through their intellectual or organizational brambles."

Williams, Jesse Lynch 1892 (1871-1929), began his literary career early in his junior year when he won a short story contest conducted by the *Nassau Literary Magazine*. He was later an editor of the *Lit* and, with Booth Tarkington, co-founder of the Triangle Club. While a graduate student (he earned his A.M. in 1895) he wrote *Princeton Stories*, in which the American undergraduate, who had usually been presented as a football hero, was portrayed at work and at play in his everyday campus setting. Williams was one of the founders of the *Alumni Weekly* and from 1900 to 1903 its first editor.

In the quarter-century from 1904 to 1929 Williams wrote six novels and four plays. His comedy, *Why Marry?* (1917) won the first Pulitzer Prize for Drama. The University made him an honorary Doctor of Letters in 1919.

Willis, Clodius Harris (1893-1964), first Arthur Le Grand Doty Professor of Electrical Engineering, was a Virginian who did his undergraduate work at the University of Richmond and took his Ph.D. in physics and electrical engineering at Johns Hopkins. He came to Princeton in 1926 during the formative years of the School of Engineering and, as a teacher for thirty-two years and departmental chairman for fourteen, was influential in developing the School's basic concepts of engineering education.

During most of his career, he was consultant to the research laboratories of the General Electric Company, and, for several years, to the Brookhaven

National Laboratory of the Atomic Energy Commission. He held thirty-five patents relating to electronic power converters, and was one of the first to recognize, in the 1930s, the advantages of using direct current for the long-range transmission of electric power.

Professor Willis's introductory course in the principles of electrical engineering, required of all engineering students regardless of department, was frequently voted the most popular course in the School of Engineering. His tests were noted for their toughness but, as one student said, his "cheerful countenance and rosy smile never failed to win back your confidence after an hour's struggle with heavy formulas."

During World War II he supervised four teaching programs that operated concurrently but on different schedules: Army, Navy, and civilian programs at the undergraduate level, and a postgraduate program that graduated 790 Navy radar officers. He also intensified his advisory work and his consultation with the government. After the war he began to suffer from Parkinson's disease, which compelled him to curtail his activities. He gave up the chairmanship of the department in 1950 and retired from teaching at the age of 65 in 1958.

At his death in 1964, his colleagues paid him this tribute:

> Clodius Willis believed that engineering as an applied science should be based upon central principles and concepts rather than upon mere collection of facts, and that it must, therefore, have at its base a sound knowledge of mathematics and the pure sciences, tempered with a true insight into . . . the humanities and the social sciences. When the

scientific and technological explosions of recent years revealed deficiencies in engineering education in the country at large, Princeton required no revolution in its way of doing things. Instead it had only to press more rapidly the evolution of its original principles established years ago by a small group of wise men. Clodius Willis was a leading member of this distinguished group.

Wilson, Edmund '16 (1895-1972), beginning as a brilliant undergraduate ("red-haired, eager, tireless," wrote Dean Christian Gauss, "he bubbled with ideas and threw them out by the handful"), came eventually to be recognized as the dean of American critics. Through nearly half a century, when not engaged with poetry, plays, and novels of his own, he devoted his energies to the reading and judging of work by others. In so doing, he developed a remarkable art of criticism-in-narrative. His honorary degree citation for the Doctor of Letters degree in 1956 called it "a versatile instrument which he . . . employed both for the reassessment of the literary classics and for the encouragement and appreciation of rising new writers."

His devotion to good writing was one of the great constants of his life. It first became apparent at the Hill School, where he prepared for college, continued at Princeton, where he belonged to Charter Club and helped T. K. Whipple '12 in the great revival of the *Nassau Lit*, and shifted afterward to New York, where he served briefly as reporter for the *Evening Sun*. Although some of his classmates had found him cool and aloof—he looked upon the "circus aspects of undergraduate life," as Dean Gauss said, "with amused toleration"—the best writers on campus had coalesced around him like bees round a hive and soon recognized that he was ready and eager to print anything they wrote unless it was pretentious or shoddy.

In 1917-1919 he was too busy with the Army Intelligence Corps to write much except reports. After the war he made up for the lapse by serving for a year as managing editor of *Vogue*, and subsequently as associate editor of *The New Republic*. Later he was literary critic for *The New Yorker*. Apart from these positions, the record of his life from the late 1920s to the early 1970s is very largely the record of the books he conceived, wrote, and saw through to publication. The bright and lively *Axel's Castle* of 1931 established his critical reputation, which was cemented by *The Triple Thinkers* and *The Wound and the Bow*. Before and after these books came travelogues such as *Europe Without Baedeker*; the novels, *I Thought of Daisy* and *Memoirs of Hecate County*; a volume of verse; and several volumes of plays. Despite some dull stretches, *To the Finland Station* remains an absorbing and informative history of socialism and communism, with sketches of the lives of the major revolutionaries from Marx and Engels to Lenin and Trotsky. Another thick volume, *Patriotic Gore*, first broached in the Gauss Seminars of 1952, offered a reprise of the most important American literature related to the Civil War. He regularly collected his fugitive essays and reviews in what he liked to call "literary chronicles," such as *Classics and Commercials* and *The Shores of Light*. The latter begins with an eloquent testimonial to the intellectual and pedagogical powers of Dean Gauss. Glorying in his reputation as a polymath and a multilingual, Wilson added Hebrew to his arsenal of lan-

guages to facilitate his study of the Dead Sea Scrolls, and showed the range of his sociological interests in *Red, Black, Blond, and Olive*, synoptic studies in Zuñi, Haitian, Russian, and Israeli civilizations. Two of his autobiographical books, *A Prelude*, which deals in part with his undergraduate years, and the crusty "reflections at sixty" that he called *A Piece of My Mind*, bracket the time from his young manhood to the beginnings of his old age.

Ten years after his honorary degree at Princeton, he received the National Medal for Literature. He came with some frequency to Princeton in response to invitations to lecture or to conduct seminars, and several generations of faculty and students came to know him by sight as well as reputation. In his salad days, when his coevals all called him "Bunny," he prided himself on his lithe build and his skill in performing distinctive somersaults, but in his later years he developed a solid and beefy figure which gave him something of the look of an ancient Roman senator and seemed to require that he be called Mr. Wilson.

In the last twenty years of his life, he took particular pleasure in the rehabilitation of an old stone house in upstate New York, willed him by his mother, and acquired the nickname of "Squire." Talcottville was a pleasant hamlet and for Wilson a perennial refuge in which he accomplished a good deal of reading and writing, well away from the social whirl of Wellfleet on Cape Cod, where he lived for a number of years. The last publication of his lifetime was *Upstate*, a chronicle of his periodic residences there, with much about the history and character of the Wilson family, as well as sketches of his neighbors and part-time employees. His friend John Dos Passos, who was well acquainted with his penchant for conversations like those recorded in the book, joshed him with a limerick:

> He says he's the Talcottville squire
> But the facts will prove him a liar
> He don't plow, he don't harrow
> He don't push no wheelbarrow
> He juss sits and holds forth by the
>   fire.

Holding forth, whether viva voce or on the printed page, was one of Wilson's strong points, as farming was not. It was one of the qualities, along with his critical integrity, that he shared with another "great cham of literature" of at least equal stature: Dr. Samuel Johnson.

Carlos Baker

Wilson, [Thomas] Woodrow (1856-1924), thirteenth president of Princeton, was born December 29, 1856, in Staunton, Virginia, the son of Joseph Ruggles Wilson, D.D., a Presbyterian minister. Tommy Wilson, as he was called until after his graduation from college, grew up in Augusta, Georgia, and Columbia, South Carolina. After a freshman year at Davidson College, 1873-74, he withdrew to prepare himself for Princeton, where he matriculated in 1875 as a member of the Class of 1879.

The next four years were a time of rapid maturing for the precocious youth. He supplemented a meager course fare with an ambitious program of reading; kept a commonplace book of passages from his reading; and organized a student club for discussion of public affairs. His peers recognized his leadership abilities, electing him speaker of the American Whig Society, secretary of the Football Association, president of the Baseball Association (he remained an avid supporter of col-

lege sports the rest of his life), and managing editor of the *Princetonian*. He made a number of loyal friends who later played crucial roles in advancing his career.

From 1879 to 1883, Wilson studied law at the University of Virginia and practiced in Atlanta. Disillusioned by the tedium and materialism of damage suits, he entered the Johns Hopkins University in 1883 for graduate work in political science and history. His doctoral dissertation, *Congressional Government* (1885), brought immediate fame and academic appointments at Bryn Mawr College (1885-88) and Wesleyan University (1888-90). Meanwhile he had married Ellen Louise Axson of Rome, Georgia, in 1885. They had three daughters: Margaret Wilson; Jessie Woodrow Wilson, who married Francis B. Sayre; and Eleanor Randolph Wilson, who married William Gibbs McAdoo. Ellen Axson Wilson died in 1914; Wilson married Edith Bolling Galt in 1915.

Wilson's fondest dream came true with his election to a professorship at Princeton in 1890. When his efforts to prod President Francis L. Patton (q.v.) to raise the money for a law school failed, Wilson set about preparing what was undoubtedly the best pre-law curriculum in the country. Year in and year out he was voted the most popular teacher on the faculty; he was also a friend and counselor to numberless students who worshipped him for his warmth and highmindedness. At the same time, his fame as a scholar grew. A regular lecturer at the Johns Hopkins and the New York Law School, he also spoke widely, contributed to popular magazines and wrote best-selling biography and history. However, his greatest triumph during this period was his eloquent and influential oration,

"Princeton in the Nation's Service" (q.v.) at the Sesquicentennial celebration in 1896.

When President Patton was persuaded to retire in June 1902, the trustees with one accord elected Wilson to fill the chair of Witherspoon and McCosh. In his first report to the Board of Trustees, the new president presented a program, to cost $12.5 million, to transform Princeton into a major university. Substantial sums were not forthcoming, so Wilson moved slowly. He tightened academic standards so severely that enrollment declined sharply until 1907. Princeton had no administrative structure to speak of in 1902. One of Wilson's first actions was the creation of departments of instruction with heads directly responsible to the president. He later arranged the creation of new deanships of the departments of science and of the college. At the same time, he took the effectual power of faculty nominations out of the control of the Trustees' Curriculum Committee and lodged it in the president and departments.

These innovations were a prelude to more far-reaching changes. In 1904, Wilson led the faculty in instituting the most significant curricular reform in American higher education in the twentieth century. In place of the aimless, free elective system, which had heretofore prevailed at Princeton as at other institutions, Wilson substituted a unified curriculum of general studies during the first two years, capped by concentrated study in one discipline (the first program for a major) and related fields during the junior and senior years. There was the added provision of an honors program for ambitious students.

The following year, 1905, Wilson revolutionized the teaching system.

Supported by the first organized yearly alumni fund-raising campaign in Princeton's history, Wilson overnight doubled the faculty by the appointment of almost fifty assistant professors called preceptors. (See *Preceptorial Method.*) They were to be the companions and guides of undergraduates. Instead of memorizing lecture notes and textbooks, students would master fields of knowledge through guided reading and small-group discussion. With a remarkable eye for quality, Wilson assembled what was probably the finest young faculty anywhere. Out of this group came many of the professors and administrators who later made Princeton renowned among the universities of the world.

Wilson supported Dean Henry B. Fine 1880, in strengthening the science program, insisting all the while that research in science should be pure research. He took biblical instruction out of the hands of a fundamentalist and appointed a scholar in his place. He broke the hold of conservative Presbyterians over the Board of Trustees, and symbolic of this change was a 1906 Board resolution that formally declared Princeton a non-sectarian institution. He appointed the first Jew and Roman Catholic to the faculty. He was instrumental in the addition to the physical plant of three buildings for instruction (McCosh Hall, Palmer Laboratory, Guyot Hall), four dormitories (Seventy-Nine, Patton, Campbell, and Holder Halls), the gymnasium and Lake Carnegie, the faculty room in Nassau Hall, the FitzRandolph gateway, and the Mather sundial. The University also acquired the Springdale golf links, 221 acres of valuable real estate.

Administration, curriculum, and teaching methods had been brought into organic unity by 1906. However, in Wilson's view the social life of the undergraduates remained not only beyond university control but also detrimental to the intellectual life and social democracy of the University. The social life of about two thirds of the upperclassmen centered in the eating clubs on Prospect Avenue. Wilson said that they were the sideshows that were swallowing up the main tent. Worse still, the clubs encouraged snobbishness and elitism, and the one third of excluded upperclassmen lived in isolation and, frequently, ostracism and humiliation.

In the early months of 1906, Wilson resolved to move against the clubs, but he well knew that it might take years to effect any significant change. A severe stroke in May 1906 threatened his life, and he decided to act while time was left to him. He presented a plan to the trustees, tentatively in December 1906 and in mature form six months later. It proposed the creation of quadrangles, or colleges, in which undergradutes of all four classes would live, with their own recreational facilities and resident faculty masters. Membership would be by assignment or lot, and the clubs would either be absorbed into the quads or abolished.

The trustees approved the quad plan in principle and Wilson announced it at commencement in June 1907. Alumni, particularly in New York and Philadelphia, were soon up in arms against a plan that they said would deprive undergraduates of freedom of social choice and destroy class spirit. Wilson responded patiently, but to no avail. Opposition grew, annual giving declined. Bowing in October 1907, the trustees withdrew their approval of the quad plan. One wealthy trustee and donor, M. Taylor Pyne 1877,

threatened to withdraw his support if Wilson resumed his campaign for the plan.

Wilson did not give up the fight. It sensitized him to glaring social injustice for the first time and transformed him into a radical social democrat by 1909. By then, however, he was embroiled in another controversy, over a residential graduate college.

Andrew F. West 1874 (q.v.), dean of the Graduate School since its creation in 1900, had one great obsession—erection of a handsome graduate college where he could preside in Gothic splendor. At first he said that he wanted the college located in the center of the campus. Wilson heartily concurred, for he believed that the graduate establishment should be the energizing force in the intellectual life of the University. Wilson also worked hard, and successfully, to add distinguished professors in order to strengthen the graduate teaching program.

Relations between Wilson and West deteriorated after 1906 as West made it clear that he wanted a luxurious graduate college with gentlemen scholars, far removed from the bustle of the campus. Josephine Ward Thomson Swann, a Princeton resident, died in 1906, leaving $275,000 for a graduate college. Supporting Wilson, the trustees in 1908 voted that it should be built upon the grounds of Prospect. But while the plans were being drawn, in May 1909, William Cooper Procter 1883, of Cincinnati, announced that he would give $500,000 for the graduate college and program, provided that the trustees raised an equal amount and agreed to an off-campus location for the college. In October, Procter selected the Springdale golf course as his site.

Wilson fought desperately against

the Procter offer, charging that money was trying to dictate educational policies. He finally came out into the open, saying that the fundamental issue was Dean West and his exclusive social ideals. The New York and Philadelphia alumni joined the fray, with Pyne taking leadership of the anti-Wilson element. Procter withdrew his offer in February 1910 before a special trustees' committee could recommend against it. However, Isaac C. Wyman 1848, of Salem, Massachusetts, died on May 18, 1910, leaving his entire estate, estimated to be worth at least $3 million, for the graduate college and program and naming West as one of his two executors. Wilson surrendered at once. "We've beaten the living," he said to his wife, "but we can't fight the dead." Ironically, the Wyman estate turned out to be worth only $794,000.

With West and Pyne in control and the latter maneuvering for Wilson's removal, Wilson now began to turn a receptive ear to George Harvey, New York editor and politician, and James Smith, Jr., of Newark, leader of the New Jersey Democratic party. They had been urging the Princetonian to accept the Democratic nomination for governor of New Jersey, as a stepping stone to the White House. West's triumph did not leave Wilson much choice. He accepted the nomination in September and went on to win the governorship in 1910 and the presidency of the United States in 1912. The story of his political career belongs elsewhere. Although he maintained his voting residence in Princeton, he rarely returned to the scene of his great academic achievements and defeats. He died at his home in Washington on February 3, 1924, and was interred in the Washington Cathedral.

Wilson had a larger hand in the development of Princeton into a great university than any other man in the twentieth century. He left a vision of an institution dedicated both to things of the mind and the nation's service, promoted a spirit of religious tolerance, and held up ideals of integrity and achievement that still inspire the Princeton community.

Arthur S. Link

Wilson, Woodrow, Award founded in 1956, the centennial year of Wilson's birth, is presented annually to an alumnus in recognition of distinguished achievement "in the Nation's Service." Recipients, selected from a broad spectrum of service to the nation and to the world, have included: Allen O. Whipple '04, surgeon and teacher; Bayard Dodge '09, president, American University of Beirut; Henry D. Smyth '18, U.S. Representative on the International Atomic Energy Agency; Adlai E. Stevenson '22, Ambassador to the U.N.; Eugene C. Blake '28, secretary-general, World Council of Churches; John D. Rockefeller 3rd '29, philanthropist; Claiborne Pell '40, U.S. senator from Rhode Island; John M. Doar '44, chief counsel for the House Judiciary Committee at the 1974 impeachment hearings; Ralph Nader '55, consumer advocate.

Wilson, Woodrow, College is a residential community of nearly 400 undergraduates. Its nucleus is Wilcox Hall, which contains dining, social, and educational facilities, including the Julian Street Library of more than 10,000 volumes. Around Wilcox are six dormitories for members of the College— 1915, 1922, 1937, 1938, and 1939 dormitories, and Dodge-Osborn Hall. The College was named in honor of Woodrow Wilson (q.v.), who had sought unsuccessfully to establish a plan of residential colleges at Princeton.

The College evolved from Woodrow Wilson Lodge, which was founded in 1957 by a dozen members of the Class of 1959 "to provide a place where individuals . . . could be accepted for what they are and not forced to conform to the narrow specifications of Bicker [eating club elections]. . . ." Membership burgeoned several years later when Darwin R. Labarth '61, a class officer, led a large group of his classmates into its ranks. Madison Hall, one of the University's dining halls, served as the common dining and social facility until 1961, when the organization moved to the newly completed Wilcox Hall. It thereupon changed its name to the Woodrow Wilson Society to reflect the wider objectives and diversity made possible by its new facilities and by the inclusion of sophomores in its membership.

In these early years, social activities —hayrides in horse-drawn wagons, rock bands, dances, and the like—were made possible by fees paid voluntarily by members who wished to participate. The University provided money for educational purposes, spent with the advice and consent of the Master-in-Residence. As part of its effort to integrate the social and intellectual sides of undergraduate life, the Society sponsored foreign-language tables, evening lectures, art exhibits, music recitals, film series, and poetry and informal play readings. These activities were strengthened by the faculty fellow program, which brought faculty members into the life of the Society and enhanced informal contacts between faculty and students.

In 1967, Julian Jaynes, then master-in-residence, proposed to the University that the Society become a truly residential entity. Accordingly, Woodrow Wilson College was created the following spring, with membership open to all four classes. Whereas previously members had lived in scattered dormitories, they were now required not only to eat at Wilcox but also to reside in the six dormitories in the surrounding quadrangle. In addition to the master, an associate master and two assistant masters-in-residence were named. Apartments in the dormitories were set aside for eight resident faculty fellows; the number of associate fellows swelled to nearly a hundred. Resident advisers were appointed among the junior, senior, and graduate student members to advise incoming freshmen, and a faculty member was named academic adviser. The College itself continued to be directed by student officers and committees chosen by the membership.

Wilcox Hall was remodeled to provide study carrels, seminar rooms, an art studio, a coffee shop, a darkroom, and a small theater in the basement. A successful drama program, which produced several plays each year, a weekly film series, and a literary magazine, the *Catalyst*, were among the tangible results of this reorganization.

From 1966 to 1968, student-initiated seminars were offered in an experimental college, founded under the leadership of Daniel Altman '67. In the early 1970s, the Woodrow Wilson "Knight" School provided training in such areas as auto mechanics, bartending, drawing, music theory, baking, foreign languages, bicycle repair and maintenance, and bridge.

Masters-in-residence have greatly contributed to Wilson's success since its inception: James Ward Smith, Professor of Philosophy, 1963-1965; Julian Jaynes, Lecturer in Psychology, 1966-

1969; John V. Fleming, Professor of English, 1969-1972; Henry N. Drewry, Lecturer in History, 1972-1975; and Norman Itzkowitz, Professor of Near Eastern Studies, 1975-   .

Mark I. Davies

Wilson, Woodrow, Fellowship Program, The, a nationwide search for college teaching talent, grew out of a pioneering effort begun at Princeton at the end of the Second World War. The idea, as conceived by Professor Whitney J. Oates, was to help renew the normal flow of graduate students, which had dried up during the war, by inviting ex-servicemen who were thought to have gifts for teaching to try out a year of graduate study. One of the first invited was Robert F. Goheen '40, who later became president of the University. Fellowship funds to complement G.I. benefits were provided initially by Miss Isabelle Kemp of New York City, Randolph Compton '15, Donald Mixsell '15, and William D. Sherrerd, Jr. '25. These were supplemented by appropriations from the University's general funds and in 1947 by a grant from the Carnegie Corporation of America. Professor Oates and Professor George A. Graham were co-administrators of the program.

The University's program was found to have a continuing value that went beyond the immediate needs of the postwar period, and in 1951 it was taken over by the Association of Graduate Schools (a component of the Association of American Universities) and considerably expanded. Among those who served as national director under the guidance of Dean Hugh S. Taylor, then chairman of the Fellowship Committee of the Association of Graduate Schools, were Princeton Pro-

fessors Courtney C. Smith and Robert Goheen. The fellowships awarded under the enlarged program were underwritten by the thirty-seven universities which comprised the Association of American Universities and by grants from the Carnegie Corporation and the General Education Board.

Not all Woodrow Wilson Fellows became teachers. Ralph Nader '55, for example, went on to become a crusader for consumer interests and other aspects of public welfare.

In 1958 a separate organization, the Woodrow Wilson National Fellowship Foundation, was established with Dean Taylor as President and his eventual successor Hans Rosenhaupt, formerly of Columbia University, as national director. For ten years thereafter Ford Foundation grants totaling $52 million permitted the Wilson Fellowship Foundation to disburse $5 million annually: $3 million in stipends for Fellows, $2 million in grants for graduate schools chosen by the Fellows. Before 1958 about 200 fellowships were awarded annually. In the last year of substantial Ford Foundation support almost a thousand were awarded.

Massive Ford Foundation support ceased in 1967. Between 1968 and 1971, the Wilson Fellowship Foundation continued to identify good candidates for graduate schools even though it was able to provide financial support for only about 150 of them each year.

Thereafter, although fellowships for first-year graduate students were no longer offered, the Foundation continued to conduct a variety of programs concerned with the recruitment and placement of graduate students.

Wilson, Woodrow, The Papers of, sponsored jointly by the Woodrow Wilson Foundation and Princeton University, will, when the approximately forty-five volumes have been completed, constitute the first full-scale edition of the papers of any modern American President. The series has won critical acclaim as one of this century's "distinguished historical enterprises" whose "scholarship, format, and scrupulous editing meet the highest standards of the craft."

The Papers were the outgrowth of the Wilson Centennial Year of 1956 when a national effort to recall Wilson's many-faceted contributions brought to light the need of a full-scale edition of his papers. The Woodrow Wilson Foundation of New York, which had been founded in 1922 for the perpetuation of Wilson's ideals, led the way in meeting this need. The Foundation secured contributions with which to start the project and then suspended all its other activities in order to devote its own capital resources as needed to the completion of *The Papers*. Princeton University became cosponsor in 1959, assuming responsibility for housing the papers and for helping to care for its staff.

Arthur S. Link, author of the definitive biography of Woodrow Wilson, was appointed Editor of the *Papers* in 1958 and was called to Princeton as Professor of History in 1959. Associate editors from the early stages of the project have been John Wells Davidson, who served from 1958 until his retirement in 1972, and David W. Hirst, who has occupied that position continuously since the publication of the first volume. John E. Little has been associate editor since 1971.

The first volume appeared in the fall of 1966, and by the spring of 1978, twenty-six volumes had been published.

The Papers include most of the letters Wilson wrote and a substantial proportion of those he received, most of his speeches, samples of his classroom and lecture notes, all of his important articles, two of his books, central in the development of his political thought (*Congressional Government* and *Constitutional Government in the United States*), and his important political and diplomatic correspondence and other state papers. Volume 1 and Volumes 7 through 20, which cover Wilson's years as Princeton student, professor and president, constitute virtually a documentary history of the University, unique in the annals of American higher education.

The Papers also include transcripts of many of the shorthand notes Wilson made throughout his life, using the Graham method, now almost extinct. The editors had the good fortune to find several older Graham experts to make the transcripts and thus secure for posterity much important material that Wilson wrote in shorthand, including a remarkable diary he kept while an undergraduate at Princeton, which opens with the maxim: "To save time is to lengthen life."

Wilson, Woodrow, School of Public and International Affairs is a memorial to the University's thirteenth president and the nation's twenty-eighth. Designed to prepare students for careers in public service in keeping with the tradition described in Woodrow Wilson's oration "Princeton in the Nation's Service" (q.v.), the school was founded in 1930 as a cooperative enterprise of the History, Politics, and Economics Departments at the undergraduate level. In 1948 the trustees named the school for Wilson and established a graduate program, which was considerably expanded after 1961, when the

University received a generous gift for this purpose.

The prime movers in the founding of the school were Charter Trustees William Church Osborn 1883 and Albert G. Milbank 1896, who obtained financing for its early years and who were key members of its original advisory board. Their contributions to the school's origin and development were later recognized by the creation of a memorial professorship in public affairs for Osborn and one in international law for Milbank.

Initially the school was administered by a faculty committee, of which politics professor Harold W. Dodds, later University president, was chairman. A leading authority on municipal government, Dodds guided the school's first faculty research project, a survey of state expenditures in New Jersey, undertaken at the request of the governor.

The school's first director was Dewitt Clinton Poole, previously counselor of the United States Embassy in Berlin. Called to Princeton to help establish the school, he served as director from 1933 until 1939. Poole was chiefly responsible for the early development of a conference course in which undergraduates were trained to apply the analytical methods of their academic studies to the world's practical problems—a contribution which, President Dodds said, made the School at that time "the most significant experiment in the teaching of the social studies . . . in any American university."

The school's early years saw the beginnings of two research programs. The State and Local Government Section, which was created in 1935, continued active under John F. Sly's direction until 1961. In 1936, the Office of Population Research (q.v.) was founded through the influence of Frederick Osborn '10 (son of William Church Osborn), who was a trustee of the Milbank Memorial Fund, which provided much of the original financing; under the direction of Frank Notestein, later of Ansley J. Coale, and more recently of Charles F. Westoff, it has been internationally famous.

Succeeding Poole as director was Dana Gardner Munro, who had come to Princeton as a professor of history in 1932 after serving as chief of the State Department's Division of Latin American Affairs and as minister to Haiti. His nineteen-year tenure, from 1939 to 1958, brought significant advances in the school's development. In 1939, the School became a separate department for purposes of undergraduate concentration, allowing upperclassmen to do their independent work and take their final examination in the fields of public or international affairs rather than in one of the social science departments, as formerly. Under Munro, the conference course continued to be the most distinctive feature of the program, which was further enriched by senior seminars (and in later years by policy task forces, smaller versions of the conference).

Up to 1948 the director of the school was also director of the undergraduate program. Since then, those in charge of the undergradute program have included William W. Lockwood, Harold Chase, William D. Carmichael, Jameson W. Doig, and Robert van de Velde.

THE GRADUATE PROGRAM

The Munro years also saw the beginning of a graduate program, the strengthening of the faculty, and the creation of the school's first real home. These developments followed the trustees' naming of the school for Woodrow Wilson, thus providing what President Dodds called "a natural and fitting memorial." Wilson, he said, "expressed in one sentence . . . the central truth to which instruction in this School is dedicated: 'We are not put into this world to sit still and know; we are put here to act.'"

Donald H. Wallace, who had been a key economic adviser in the Office of Price Administration during World War II, was called to Princeton in 1947 as first director of the graduate program and was later appointed first incumbent of the William Church Osborn professorship. Wallace's pioneering effort to develop a new approach to professional training in public affairs was cut short by his death in 1953. He was succeeded by Stephen K. Bailey and subsequently by Harold Stein, and followed as Osborn Professor by Bailey in 1954 and by Ansley J. Coale, head of the Office of Population Research, in 1964.

The school's work in the international field was strengthened in 1951 when Frederick S. Dunn (Princeton '14) and six of his associates at the Yale Institute of International Studies, of which he had been director, were called to Princeton. Dunn was appointed first Milbank Professor and first director of the School's Center of International Studies (q.v.), founded with the help of the Milbank Memorial Fund. He was later succeeded in this post by economist Klaus Knorr, and subsequently by historian Cyril E. Black.

In the late 1940s, a committee headed by Charter Trustee Dean Mathey '12, began raising funds to endow the school's development as a memorial to Wilson and to provide a building to suit its special needs. Woodrow Wilson Hall, at the corner of Prospect Avenue and Washington Road, was dedicated in 1952, replacing the temporary quarters the School had previously occupied in Dickinson and Whig Halls and in the former Arbor Inn eating club.

That same year, John D. Rockefeller III '29, then a charter trustee, instituted a program of annual awards for outstanding public service, to be administered by the School. Originally restricted to federal career officials, the program was broadened in 1976 to honor individuals from both within and outside government for outstanding contributions to the public welfare at all levels—local, state, and national.

THE ROBERTSON GIFT

A new era began in 1961 with a $35 million gift designed to develop within the School, in President Goheen's words, "professional education for the public service at a level of excellence comparable to the country's outstanding schools of law and medicine." The donors, Charles S. Robertson '26 and his wife Marie, insisted on anonymity, and for a dozen years the origin of the gift—the largest in Princeton's history—was a well kept secret. But the University was embarassed by continuing speculation about the source of the funds, and in 1973, Robertson reluctantly agreed to let the facts be known.

The Robertson benefaction permitted a marked increase in enrollment of graduate students, enlargement of the faculty, and the creation of new facilities. A new building, designed by Minoru Yamasaki, was erected on the site of the old one, which was moved to its present location and renamed Corwin Hall (q.v.). The new building was dedicated in May 1966 with addresses by President Goheen, Governor Richard J. Hughes, and President Lyndon B. Johnson.

At the dedication, President Goheen

described the contributions trustees and faculty members had made to the school's early development and then paid particular tribute to three men, who had "directed the School so ably in this great new phase of its development": Gardner Patterson, director from 1958 to 1963, Lester V. Chandler, acting director for the year 1963-64, and Marver H. Bernstein, the school's first dean from 1964 to 1969. Patterson became deputy director-general of the General Agreement on Tariffs and Trade, Bernstein, president of Brandeis University.

Bernstein had been the first director of the graduate program after the Robertson gift. He was succeeded in that post by William G. Bowen, later president of the University, and Richard A. Lester, later dean of the faculty. Subsequent directors have been Richard H. Ullman, Michael N. Danielson, Jameson W. Doig, David F. Bradford, and Charles H. Berry.

Since 1961 the faculty of the school has been augmented by appointments from outside Princeton as well as from the University's social science departments. Those called to Princeton included Sir W. Arthur Lewis, authority on the economy of developing nations, who was appointed first incumbent of the School's newly created James Madison Professorship of Political Economy; and Richard Falk, an authority on the international legal order and comparative world order systems, who was named second incumbent of the Milbank Professorship of International Law and Practice.

Two of the new faculty members came to Princeton as deans. John P. Lewis, who had previously served as a member of the President's Council on Economic Advisers and as minister-director of the AID mission to India, was dean of the school from 1969 to

1974. He was succeeded by Donald E. Stokes, an authority on American and British voting habits, who had won high honors in the school on his graduation from Princeton in 1951 and, after taking his Ph.D. in politics at Yale, had gone on to become dean of the graduate school at the University of Michigan.

As the faculty expanded, new specialized research resources were added, including a program, founded in 1967, under the direction of W. Arthur Lewis and later of John P. Lewis, on the economic development of less developed nations. A research program on criminal justice, under the direction of Jameson W. Doig, was begun in 1973 with funds from the Daniel and Florence Guggenheim Foundation. To facilitate student and faculty involvement in public affairs within the state, a new Center for New Jersey Affairs, under the direction of Michael N. Danielson, was established with a federal grant in 1975.

The school in 1966 initiated a small Ph.D. program for selected graduates of its master's program, with substantial experience in public affairs, who plan to pursue public service careers in which a Ph.D. is desirable.

The school's work in mid-career education, begun on a small scale in 1948 to help prepare men and women for positions of greater responsibility in their professions, was considerably expanded in the early 1960s by the development of two new, one-year, non-degree programs. One program, begun in 1962, has brought to the school annually a select group of some twenty officials of federal, state, and local governments. Another, started in 1961 with support from the Albert Parvin Foundation, has brought each year six to eight talented men and women from developing countries as distant and diverse as Chile, India, Korea, Malaysia, Nigeria, the

Philippines, and Sudan. In 1975, a third program was established with support from the Alfred P. Sloan Foundation; it has brought to the school annually eight journalists for training in the application of modern economic analysis to questions of public policy.

In the mid seventies, the school's faculty numbered about forty regular members, each of whom, with rare exceptions, held an appointment in another department as well. Thirty other members of social science departments also participated in the graduate program. The school's student body included about 120 undergraduates equally divided among juniors and seniors, approximately 110 graduate students working toward the Master of Public Affairs or the Doctor of Philosophy degree, and about 40 mid-career fellows.

The essential qualities that distinguish the Wilson School from comparable programs at other universities were outlined by Dean Stokes in a 1976 *Alumni Weekly* interview. Princeton's program, he noted, is one of the few that admits both undergraduates and graduate students—an arrangement that works to the advantage of both groups, undergraduates profiting by exposure to more mature graduate students and experienced mid-careerists, and the latter finding stimulation in their exposure "to the freshness of the undergraduates, their drive, their mental sharpness."

Another difference he mentioned was that, while most other schools are devoted mainly to the study of either domestic or of foreign affairs, the Wilson School is equally committed to both, and the career interests of students reflect a similar balance. "Those whose interests are international," Dean Stokes said, "need to know more about the way things work in Washington and, indeed, in Trenton, N.J. . . . And many jobs in the domestic field require knowledge of how foreign countries handle similar problems. Much can be learned, for example, about the problems of our own cities by studying urban problems overseas, and this thrust toward comparative study is far more likely to be real in a school with a strong international dimension."

However, the characteristic that he personally found most appealing was the "remarkably modern interdisciplinary nature of the School, built in at the very beginning." He liked, for example, the way economics and political science, each a major discipline, interact with one another and with more technical fields. "So many combinations are possible," he said. "There is so much openness. Where a student has an interest in a technological field, we try to work out a joint-degree program. We have close ties as well both to the School of Architecture and Urban Planning and to the School of Engineering and Applied Science. We expect to strengthen our ties with a number of other departments and programs."

Former Woodrow Wilson School students who have become prominent in public life include: G. Mennen Williams '33, six times governor of Michigan; John B. Oakes '34, *New York Times* editorial page editor; Francis L. Van Dusen '34, district court judge; J. Harlan Cleveland '38, assistant secretary of state, and later ambassador to NATO; William E. Colby '40, director of the Central Intelligence Agency; Claiborne Pell '40, senator from Rhode Island; George P. Shultz '42, secretary of the treasury; Nicholas de B. Katzenbach '43, under secretary of state, and later attorney-general; John Doar '44, special counsel of the House

Judiciary Committee; Paul Volcker '49, under secretary of the treasury, and later president of the Federal Reserve Bank of New York; Donald B. Easum MPA '50, assistant secretary of state, and later ambassador to Nigeria; Alexander B. Trowbridge '51, secretary of commerce; Ralph A. Dungan, Jr., MPA '52, ambassador to Chile, and later chancellor, Department of Higher Education of the State of New Jersey; W. Michael Blumenthal MPA '53, chairman of the Bendix Corporation, and later secretary of the treasury; Paul S. Sarbanes '54, senator from Maryland; Ralph Nader '55, consumer advocate.

THE WOODROW WILSON SCHOOL BUILDING

The most striking feature of Minoru Yamasaki's design is provided by fifty-eight elegantly tapered pillars that give a feeling of lightness and grace to the building they surround. These white, quartz-surfaced pillars support the top floor of the building, permitting the use on the first floor of non-bearing walls of travertine marble and allowing a freedom of space within.

The main story, which is twenty-eight feet high, contains a well-lit and comfortable lobby-lounge extending the width of the building, a bowl-shaped auditorium seating 200, a library with two mezzanine levels containing student carrels, and a dining room. On the lower floor, which is below ground level, are conference, seminar, and lecture rooms, and on the upper floor, faculty offices and smaller lounges.

The lobby-lounge contains an abstract sculpture, "The World, 1964," by Harry Bertoia and bronze busts of Woodrow Wilson by Jo Davidson and of Adlai E. Stevenson by Ellen Simon. In the plaza to the north is a reflecting pool and a twenty-foot-high bronze "Fountain of Freedom" by James Fitzgerald.

Witherspoon, John (1723-1794), was the sixth president of Princeton, a signer of the Declaration of Independence, and from 1776 to 1782 a leading member of the Continental Congress. He came from Scotland in 1768 to assume the presidency of the college and held office until his death a quarter of a century later.

A graduate of the University of Edinburgh, who received an honorary doctorate from St. Andrews in 1764, Witherspoon had become widely known as a leader of the evangelical or "Popular Party" in the established Church of Scotland, of which he was an ordained minister. The trustees of the College first elected him president in 1766, after Samuel Finley's death; but Mrs. Witherspoon was reluctant to leave Scotland, and he declined. Thanks very largely to the efforts of Benjamin Rush 1760, then a medical student at Edinburgh, she was persuaded to reconsider. Informed that Witherspoon would now accept the call if renewed, the trustees again elected him to the presidency in December of 1767.

With their five surviving children (five others had died in early childhood), and 300 books for the college library, the Witherspoons reached Philadelphia early in August 1768. When a few days later they moved on to Princeton, they were greeted a mile out of town by tutors and students, who escorted them to Morven, home of Richard Stockton. That evening the students celebrated the occasion by "illuminating" Nassau Hall with a lighted tallow dip in each window.

Witherspoon had arrived in time to

provide the highlight for commencement, which in those days was held in September. Early in October, he wrote Rush that on the preceding 28th he had delivered "an inaugural Oration in Latin" before "a vast Concourse of People." He was obviously heartened by the warmth of his reception, but he also reported a number of disturbing conditions in the state of the college. He found far too many of the students inadequately prepared for college work, a complaint frequently heard since, and one that explains the close attention he subsequently gave to the grammar school conducted by the college. Most worrisome of all was the low state of the college's finances.

With characteristic vigor, Witherspoon moved immediately to find the remedy. Taking advantage of the vacation between commencement and the beginning of a new term in November, he went first to New York and then on to Boston for consultation with friends of the College. During the next fall's vacation, he visited Williamsburg, where, the *Virginia Gazette* reported, he "preached to a crowded audience in the Capital yard (there being no house in town capable of holding such a multitude) and gave universal satisfaction." The concrete measure of that satisfaction was a collection taken at the end of the sermon amounting "to upwards of fifty-six pounds." The following February found him again in Virginia, and this was not the last of his southern tours.

By no means the least of the advantages that accrued to the College from his itinerant preaching was an increased enrollment of students, whose tuition continued to be the major source of revenue. Enrollment had reached a peak under President Finley, with graduating classes of 31 each in

1765 and 1766, but had fallen off thereafter. There were 11 graduates at the commencement of 1768, but 29 in 1773, and 27 in 1776. Simultaneously, a change occurred in the constituencies from which the students were drawn. Now, as before, most of them came from the middle provinces, but the representation from New England, which had been substantial, declined markedly, and a significant enrollment from the southern colonies began to develop.

Not all of Witherspoon's preaching was done on the road. Indeed, when in Princeton he normally preached twice each Sunday to a mixed congregation of townspeople and students, which only recently had acquired a place of worship apart from the Prayer Room of Nassau Hall. Their church had been constructed at the front of the present campus, where stands today a Presbyterian church of much later construction. According to Benjamin Rush, Witherspoon's manner in the pulpit was "solemn and graceful," his voice melodious, and his sermons "loaded with good sense and adorned" with "elegance and beauty" of expression. But Rush was impressed above all by the fact that Witherspoon carried no notes into the pulpit, in sharp contrast with the "too common practice of reading sermons in America." Other contemporary descriptions indicate that he depended upon no oratorical flourishes or gestures. The story is told of a visitor who, observing that Witherspoon's enthusiasm for gardening was confined to growing vegtables, remarked, "Doctor, I see no flowers in your garden," to which came the reply, "No, nor in my discourses either."

To the day of his death, his speech revealed his Scottish birth. A man of medium height, tending toward stoutness, with bushy eyebrows, a prominent nose, and large ears, he had a quality contemporaries were inclined to describe as "presence." One of his students, a later president of the College, recalled that Witherspoon had more presence than any other man he had known, except for General Washington. Witherspoon lived at first in the President's House (now called the John Maclean House), but after several years he moved about a mile north of the village to "Tusculum," a handsome residence he built that still stands on Cherry Hill Road. His route to and from the College is well enough indicated by the street that bears his name.

President Witherspoon was obviously a very busy man, for in addition to managing the College's affairs and preaching twice on Sundays, he bore the heaviest responsibility for instruction of the students. His "faculty" normally included two or three tutors (recent graduates who may have been pursuing, in such free time as they could find, advanced studies in divinity before moving on to some vacant pulpit) and one, later two, professors. Considering himself less than an accomplished scholar in mathematics and astronomy, he secured the appointment of a Professor of Mathematics and Natural Philosophy in 1771. This left to the president the main responsibility for instruction in moral philosophy, divinity, rhetoric, history, and chronology, and also in French, for such students as might elect to study the language.

Witherspoon's administration marks an important turning point in the life of the college, but the changes he made were mainly of method and emphasis within the broad objectives which had been originally set. Thus, he brought to Princeton a fresh emphasis upon the need of the church for a well educated clergy, a purpose to which the college had been dedicated at the time of its founding, but by men who at the height of a stirring religious revival may well have given first place to the church's need for a "converted" ministry. There is no indication that Witherspoon discounted the importance of a conversion experience, but on balance he tended to place the primary emphasis on education. His influence in helping to bring about a final reunion of all Presbyterians, who earlier had been sharply divided, in support of the College was one of his major accomplishments.

The founders had hoped too that the College might produce men who would be "ornaments of the State as well as the Church," and Witherspoon realized this hope in full measure. His students included, in addition to a president and vice-president of the United States, nine cabinet officers, twenty-one senators, thirty-nine congressmen, three justices of the Supreme Court, and twelve state governors. Five of the nine Princeton graduates among the fifty-five members of the Constitutional Convention of 1787 were students of Witherspoon.

Witherspoon broadened and enriched the curriculum of the College. He was the first to introduce the new rhetoric of the eighteenth century, accomplishing his purpose by extending and intensifying instruction in English grammar and composition. He added substantially to the instructional equipment of the College, especially books for the library and "philosophical apparatus" for instruction by demonstration in the sciences, including the famous Rittenhouse Orrery acquired in 1771.

He was not an original thinker, but he was a product of Scotland's leading university in an age when the Scottish universities had a vitality possessed by no others in Great Britain. Although certain leniencies encouraged by the Scottish Enlightenment had offended his orthodox Presbyterianism, Witherspoon introduced to Princeton, and through it to other institutions, some of the more advanced ideas of that movement. He subscribed to John Locke's view of the role of sensory perception in the development of the mind, but vigorously rejected all esoteric interpretations of that view. He saw no conflict between faith and reason; instead, he encouraged his students to test their faith by the rule of experience. He was much inclined to apply the test of common sense to any proposition, and to reduce it to its simplest terms. In lecturing on rhetoric he advised his students of the multiple components into which a discourse traditionally had been divided, and then suggested that it was enough to say that every discourse or composition "must have a beginning, a middle, and an end." His name is rightly identified with certain attitudes and assumptions, considered to be of importance in the development of our national life, that are associated with what is known as the Common Sense Philosophy.

Though a man of strong convictions, he showed no inclination to protect his students from exposure to ideas with which he disagreed. The many books he added to the library gave the undergraduate access to a wide range of contemporary literature, including authors with whom he had publicly disputed. In his famous lectures on moral philosophy, not published until after his death and then probably contrary to his wish, his method was to lay out contending points of view and to rely upon persuasive reasoning to guide the student toward a proper conclusion of his own.

Witherspoon had a helpful sense of humor. He suffered from insomnia, and his tendency to drowse, particularly after dinner, led him, during one of the two terms he served in the New Jersey legislature, to move that the daily sessions be concluded before dinner. When his motion lost, he informed his colleagues that "there are two kinds of speaking that are very interesting . . . perfect sense and perfect nonsense. When there is speaking in either of these ways I shall engage to be all attention. But when there is speaking, as there often is, halfway between sense and nonsense, you must bear with me if I fall asleep."

In his support of the American cause there is no occasion for surprise. He subscribed to John Locke's political philosophy as wholeheartedly as to his psychology, and brought from Scotland a strong sense of "British liberty," which he came to see as greatly endangered by the course of British policy. When John Adams stopped over in Princeton on his way to the first meeting of the Continental Congress in 1774, he met Witherspoon and pronounced him "as high a Son of Liberty, as any Man in America."

Through the years he served in Congress, Witherspoon's patriotism and judgment won the respect of his colleagues, as evidenced by his assignment to many committees, some of them among the most important. He struggled through these years—not always successfully—to keep the College in session, and he became a frequent commuter between Princeton and Philadelphia. He resigned from Congress in November 1782, when a war that had cost him the life of his son James (who graduated from the College in 1770 and was killed in Germantown) was ended, and peace, with American independence, seemed assured.

Witherspoon's later years were filled with difficulty. The college had suffered extensive damage to its building and instructional equipment, and its finances were in disarray. Two years before his death he became totally blind. His wife died in 1789, and a second marriage in 1791 to a young widow of twenty-four occasioned more than a little comment. Through these later years his son-in-law, Samuel Stanhope Smith, increasingly carried the responsibility for conduct of the College's affairs.

But through these later years, too, Witherspoon remained remarkably active and influential. He was a member of the ratifying convention that brought to New Jersey the honor of being the third state to ratify the Constitution of the United States. He contributed greatly to the organization of a newly independent and national Presbyterian Church, and in 1789 opened its first General Assembly with a sermon and presided until the election of the first moderator. Above all, the name he had won as a divine, an educator, and a patriot brought returning strength to the College. He is rightly remembered as one of the great presidents of Princeton.

W. Frank Craven

Witherspoon Hall was named in honor of Princeton's sixth president John Witherspoon. At the time of its completion in 1877, it was considered the most beautiful and luxurious college dormitory in the country. One of its first occupants was Woodrow Wilson, who moved into room no. 7 in the west entry at the beginning of the second term of his sophomore year and lived there until his graduation in 1879.

Women have played a varied and significant part in the life of Princeton from the beginning. Esther Burr, whose marriage at twenty-one to the second president when he was thirty-six created a stir among the students, has added feminine insight to what we know of the College's early years through the pages of her diary. Annis Stockton, wife of the first graduate trustee of the College, had the distinction of being the only woman on the rolls of the American Whig Society, which gratefully voted her honorary membership because she safeguarded Johnson's Dictionary, brass andirons and candle sticks, and other Society treasures during the Revolution. She was also celebrated for the verses she wrote to General Washington while he was in Princeton for meetings of the Continental Congress (asking, in one: "Say; can a female voice an audience gain? / And Stop a moment thy triumphal Car . . .").

Two wives of latter-day presidents made contributions to the University's welfare that have been perpetuated through the work of like-minded women of succeeding generations. Isabella McCosh, wife of the eleventh president, ministered to the health of students and is memorialized in the infirmary that bears her name (q.v.); her example has been emulated over the years by members of the infirmary's Ladies Auxiliary. A similar influence has been exerted by the University League (q.v.), founded in 1920 by Jenny Davidson Hibben, wife of the fourteenth president, "to provide a friendly spirit among the wives and families of men connected with the University."

Wives of deans similarly contributed to the quality of life in the University. Long before Princeton had a music department, Philena Fobes Fine, wife of the third dean of the faculty, pioneered in bringing outstanding musical performers to Princeton, and when she died in 1928 her friends endowed a fund in her name to help carry on the program of concerts she had initiated.

Wives of faculty members, though lacking faculty status, often collaborated with their husbands in their scholarly activities. One of them, Margaret Farrand Thorp, who worked with her English-department husband, was the author of a book of special interest in this context: *Female Persuasion: Six Strong-Minded Women.*

Another woman used her handiwork to beautify the campus. Beatrix Farrand's contribution as consulting landscape gardener for thirty years is commemorated by an inscription on a bench near the Chapel: "Her love of beauty and order is everywhere visible in what she planted for our delight."

Daughters of alumni got their educations—and made their contributions—elsewhere. A notable example was Sylvia Beach (daughter of a graduate of 1876), who published the first edition of James Joyce's *Ulysses* from her renowned Paris bookshop Shakespeare and Company in 1922, thus earning the gratitude of students of literature everywhere and the particular pride of Princeton, which has the bulk of her papers in the Firestone Library's Sylvia Beach Collection.

With the coming of shorthand, the typewriter, the telephone, and the growing complexity of administrative procedures, the contribution of women to the management of University affairs took on increasing importance as women assistants and women secretaries became indispensable helpmates of presidents, deans, professors, and others. A conspicuous example in earlier years was Anna B. H. Creasey, a

"strong-minded" woman who ruled the Graduate School office in Nassau Hall with the same magisterial air with which Dean West presided over the Graduate College and was accordingly nicknamed Dean East by graduate students. During the years after World War II, when secretarial help was in short supply, the University was able to meet its needs with the services of graduate student wives who toiled to supplement their husbands' G.I. benefits (leading one observer to declare that many a student earned his Ph.D. by "the sweat of his *frau*").

Women thus filled a variety of useful roles in Princeton life long before they were accorded full faculty or student status. Although the first woman full professor was not appointed until 1968, when sociologist Suzanne Keller was given that rank, women were discharging research and teaching responsibilities as long ago as the 1930s when the distinguished demographer Irene Taeuber began her career as a research associate in the Population Research Section, and the 1940s when a number of departments began adding women to their staffs to help meet increased student demand for foreign-language instruction.

A first step toward the admission of women as students had been taken as far back as 1887 with the founding of the quasi-coordinate Evelyn College for Women (q.v.), which encouraged *Harper's Bazaar* to look forward to the day when "our country shall come to speak with equal pride of the sons and daughters of Princeton." But the new college, falling on hard times after the Panic of 1893, had to close its doors in 1897, and almost another three-quarters of a century would pass before *Harper's* prophecy could be fulfilled.

A modest extension of Princeton's

educational opportunities for women came in World War II when twenty-three were admitted to a government-sponsored defense course in photogrammetry. More significant changes occurred in the 1960s with the admission of women graduate students (the first Ph.D. was awarded in 1964), and the admission each year of several dozen young women for a year of concentrated study in "critical languages."

The day before the 1967 Commencement the Board of Trustees authorized a careful investigation of "the advisability and the feasibility of Princeton's entering significantly into the education of women at the undergraduate level." At the exercises next day the unexpected appearance of a pretty brown-haired girl, who had been smuggled into the academic procession in cap and gown by a graduating senior friend, prompted President Goheen to interrupt his formal announcement of the trustees' decision to note that one young woman had already "worked her way" into Princeton's midst.

A ten-member committee, headed by Economics Professor Gardner Patterson, thereupon conducted a 16-month study and produced an extensive report which, according to President Goheen, offered evidence that "the presence of talented young women at Princeton would enhance the total educational experience and contribute to a better balanced social and intellectual life." It would also help "sustain Princeton's ability to attract outstanding students," while providing a Princeton education for young women who could be expected "to make worthy contributions to the national life, where clearly women are, and will be, taking increasingly active parts."

A special trustees' committee, headed by Harold H. Helm '20, worked with administration and faculty representatives to test the findings and recommendations of the Patterson Report while meetings were being held in twenty-five cities for discussion of the report with alumni. One such meeting, conducted by the Princeton Area Alumni Association in McCosh 50, produced a long and lively discussion. Toward the end of the evening an alumnus clergyman took as his text Genesis II, 18: "And the Lord God said, It is not good that the man should be alone," adding that since the hour was late and there was not time for a sermon, he would simply say that it appeared that God favored the Patterson Report.

In January 1969 the Helm committee recommended to the board that Princeton undertake the education of women at the undergraduate level. It gave two reasons: first, that both Princeton faculty and Princeton alumni engaged in higher education elsewhere now believed that "the educational experience is improved . . . when it is carried out in mixed, rather than single-sex, circumstances," and second, that the general shift toward a favorable view of coeducation among younger alumni and faculty, combined with the clear preference of today's students, seemed to them "to have very important implications for Princeton's future."

The trustees, by a vote of 24 to 8, approved coeducation in principle and instructed the administration to develop plans for its implementation. An *ad hoc* faculty-administration-student committee, appointed and presided over by the president made an intensive study of all aspects of conversion, including the relative merits of coordinate versus coeducational arrangements; all of its members came to be convinced that if properly worked out, coeducational arrangements would be "both better educationally and generally more economical."

The committee's implementation plans were approved by the trustees in April, and President Goheen announced that coeducation would become a reality in September. The *Prince* congratulated the trustees on their "courage, foresight, and ability to change with the times," and WPRB concluded its broadcast of the news with the *Hallelujah Chorus*.

During the first weekend after Labor Day in 1969, a pioneering band of 171 women arrived in Princeton as candidates for bachelor degrees; among them were 101 members of the freshman Class of 1973 looking forward to full Princeton careers along with their 820 male classmates. Four years later, on Commencement eve, the *New York Times* highlighted some of the achievements of the women in Princeton's first coeducational class. One of them, Marsha H. Levy, was the first woman to win the Pyne Prize and the first to be elected an alumni trustee. Princeton's only Marshall scholarship winner was a woman, as was one of its three Fulbright recipients. Princeton women had fielded undefeated teams in tennis, squash, and swimming, and the women's crew, which practiced daily at 6:30 a.m., had won the Eastern championship in 1972. Marjorie Gengler, captain of the undefeated tennis team, never lost a set in her intercollegiate career, and later became Annual Giving's first woman class agent.

In his concluding remarks at the 1973 Commencement President Bowen declared, "The women among us have now added their gifts of fallibility to our own, and I think we are a far better

university—and a far richer community of people—for them."

Women continued to excel in scholarship and athletics: At the 1975 Commencement Lisa Siegman '75 was salutatorian and Cynthia Chase '75 valedictorian—the first time women had won both honors. A year later Emily Goodfellow '76 became the first Princetonian to win twelve varsity letters, four each in field hockey, squash, and lacrosse. That December, Suzanne Perles '75 of Anchorage, Alaska, was one of the first thirteen American women chosen as Rhodes Scholars.

In 1976, Nancy B. Peretsman '76 became the second woman to be elected alumni trustee, bringing the number of women on the Board to four, Mary St. John Douglas and Susan Savage Speers having been elected charter trustees in 1971.

Although the curricular interests of women in the first coeducational class covered a wide range in the liberal arts and sciences, none of them chose an engineering program. By the spring of 1976, however, thanks to the new directions engineering was taking in America and to the Engineering School's strenuous efforts at recruitment, nearly 14 percent of the University's engineering students were women, compared to a national average of less than 5 percent.

The proportion of women in the undergraduate body as a whole also rose substantially and continued to rise after the trustees removed an earlier quota by adopting, in 1974, a policy of equal access. By 1976, the undergraduate body numbered 1,395 women and 2,965 men.

Among graduate students, the proportion of women also rose—by 1976 there were 367 in a total student body of 1,415.

In 1977 Nina G. Garsoian became Dean of the Graduate School and Joan S. Girgus, Dean of the College—the first women to hold Princeton's second and third oldest deanships.

Woolworth Center of Musical Studies was constructed in 1963. It was largely the gift of Frasier McCann '30 and his sister, Mrs. Helena McCann Charlton, and was named in memory of their grandfather, Frank Winfield Woolworth. Other donors gave some of the rooms, which are marked by memorial plaques.

In addition to classrooms and offices, Woolworth contains a record library and listening rooms, individual and ensemble practice rooms, studios for private lessons, and a rehearsal room that is also used for small student concerts.

Moore & Hutchins, of New York, were the architects; Bolt, Beranek & Newman, of Cambridge, Massachusetts, the accoustical consultants.

A bronze plaque in the entranceway pays tribute to the two men whose dreams and work culminated in the Woolworth Center: Roy Dickinson Welch (1885-1951) founding chairman of the Department of Music, and Paul Bedford 1897, trustee and benefactor.

WPRB, undergraduate radio station, first known as WPRU, was founded in 1940, just twenty years after public broadcasting was introduced in the United States by Station KDKA in Pittsburgh. Henry G. Theis '42 organized the Princeton station in his room in 441 Pyne Hall, using the University's electric wiring system to conduct recorded music, news of sports events, and local advertising to campus listeners three hours daily. Another member of the original staff, James G. Robinson '43, an electrical engineer, helped

guide the development of the station as chairman of its governing board for over twenty years.

In 1955, fifteen years after its founding, WPRU obtained a license to build an FM transmitter and became the first student-owned and operated FM station in the country. From an antenna on top of Holder Tower it beamed a 250-watt signal to potential listeners within a radius of twenty miles, while continuing to broadcast simultaneously to the campus on the A.M. dial.

Its new status as a licensed station required a change in name when it was discovered that a ship at sea was using the same call letters. It accordingly changed from its Princeton University-derived WPRU to a Princeton Broadcasting Service-derived WPRB.

In 1960—its twentieth anniversary year—WPRB asked the Federal Communications Commission for authority to increase its power from 250 watts to 1,000 on the frequency it was using. Its application was denied but it was informed that another frequency, carrying 17,000 watts, was available. WPRB applied, and when the application was granted, it borrowed $10,000 for equipment, and became one of the most powerful FM stations in New Jersey.

At first WPRB had trouble controlling its new-found power. Nearby radio users complained that it was blanketing out half the FM dial. A freshman claimed that he was picking up its music on his electric shoe polisher; an older citizen of the borough, that he was hearing it on his false teeth. These difficulties were eventually ameliorated and some relief granted close neighbors; at the same time, the station was making new friends as far distant as Philadelphia and Greenwich, Connecticut.

One profitable consequence of WPRB's new 17,000-watt signal was its interference with the programs of Station WTFM in Lake Success, Long Island. WTFM offered WPRB $5,000 and technical assistance if it would change its frequency from 103.5 to 103.3. WPRB replied that it would make the change, without any technical assistance, for $10,000 and WTFM agreed. In 1962, with the approval of the F.C.C., the change was made and the proceeds used a year later for purchase of equipment that enabled WPRB to become the first college station in the United States to engage in stereo broadcasting.

By the mid-seventies, WPRB was utilizing the energies of about a hundred undergraduates in its program, business, technical, and public relations departments to provide an estimated audience of 45,000, in a five-state area, with the same basic ingredients it had given its campus listeners in 1940—music, sports, advertising—along with more diverse elements added over the years—national news, public affairs programs, university public lectures, chapel services, and live concerts in stereo. Typical of the staff's enthusiasm for their work was a banner in the station manager's office crocheted by one of the women members, reading "God Bless WPRB."

A number of WPRB alumni have gone on to professional careers in broadcasting, including former station manager Paul Friedman '66, who became producer of NBC's *Today Show.*

Wrestling did not begin as an intercollegiate sport at Princeton until early in this century, although freshmen and sophomores had been practicing a Princeton variant, the cane spree, since the close of the Civil War. Originally, this involved a series of rough-and-tumble bouts between freshmen sporting forbidden canes, and sophomores trying to wrest them away. Later, three specially trained representatives of the freshman and sophomore classes—light, middle, and heavyweight—wrestled for possession of a cane. In the early 1900s the cane spree inspired freshmen-sophomore wrestling matches, which in turn led in 1905 to the formation of the first varsity wrestling team.

In the second year of Varsity competition, Donald G. Herring '07 won the intercollegiate heavyweight championship in record time, throwing one opponent in sixteen seconds, another in thirteen. He was a dapper heavyweight, sometimes appearing at professional wrestling matches in Newark in white tie, tails, and topper.

Five years later, in 1911, Princeton won the Eastern intercollegite team championship when George W. Prettyman '11, Franklin C. Wells, Jr. '11, Alexander T. Ormond, Jr. '12, and Jacob H. Frantz '13 took four of the six individual titles. Ormond's brother, Harold H. Ormond '12, won an individual championship in 1912 as did Harold H. Gile '15 in 1913. The 1911 welterweight champion Jacob Frantz (twice a cane-spree winner) successfully defended his intercollegiate title in 1912 and 1913 to become Princeton's first three-time champion. Frantz had but one hold—the front chancery and bar lock—but he was very proficient at it and lost no time in applying it to his opponent after the customary opening handshake. In three years of varsity competition he was never thrown; the only match he did not win was lost by a close decision; all the others he won by falls.

In the twenties four Princetonians won Eastern intercollegiate individual championships: Charles C.J. Carpenter '21, Robert Morrison '23, Theodore V. Buttrey '26, and William A. Graham '29. Heavyweight champion Carpenter, later Protestant Episcopal Bishop of Georgia, further distinguished himself by scoring a technical victory in a handicap match with the professional wrestler "Strangler" Lewis.

Buttrey and Graham won their titles under Clarence F. Foster, who coached from 1924 through 1934. Other Eastern intercollegiate champions coached by Foster were William D. Barfield '30, Russell H. Hooker '34, and Thomas Snelham '35, as well as Julian Gregory Jr. '35 and George B. Treide '36, who both went on to win second championships under Foster's successor, Jimmie Reed.

A former two-time Eastern intercollegiate champion at Lehigh, Reed was varsity coach for thirty years through 1964. His 1936 and 1937 teams were undefeated, and his 1938 team won seven successive meets before losing their final encounter with Lehigh, thus extending Princeton's unbroken string of victories to twenty-one. The 1937 and 1938 teams took second place in the Eastern intercollegiates, and the 1941 team tied Yale for first place. Reed's wrestlers won the Big Three title in the years from 1936 through 1939, from 1941 through 1943, and in 1947, 1949, 1950, 1953, and 1957.

Reed's roster of Eastern intercollegiate champions was impressive. One, Bradley M. Glass '53, also won the 1951 NCAA heavyweight championship, Princeton's first national title. Richard B. Harding '40 and Robert C. Eberle '41 won Eastern championships in each of their three years of varsity competition. Charles A. Powers '38, who won twice, was awarded the coaches' cup as the most accomplished

wrestler in the 1937 Eastern championship meet. W. Eugene Taylor '43 and Bradley Glass were also double winners. Other Eastern champions were Morris S. Emory '38, Charles H. Toll, Jr. '38, and David A. Poor '50.

John Johnston, a former national champion at Penn State, succeeded Jimmie Reed as coach in 1965, and Princeton soon became a formidable power in Ivy competition, winning sole possession of the League crown in 1967, 1970, and 1971, sharing it with Penn in 1972 and with Cornell in 1973, and winning it outright again in 1975, 1977 and, with a phenomenal 19-0 season record, in 1978, when it also won the Eastern intercollegiate tournament. In 1972, Emil A. Deliere '72 won the Eastern intercollegiate championship in the 190-pound class, and reached the finals of the NCAA championship tournament, where the recurrence of a back injury compelled him to default. Captain John Sefter '78 won the Eastern intercollegiate championship in the heavyweight class in 1977 and 1978, and reached the finals of the NCAA championship tournament in 1978. Steve Grubman '78 won the Eastern intercollegiate championship in the 142-lb. class in 1978, and the same year, along with Keith Ely '79 in the 177-lb. class, reached the quarter-finals of the NCAA championship tournament.

One of Princeton's strongest competitors was Donald Rumsfeld '54, who reached the finals of the Eastern intercollegiates in the 157-pound class his junior year and the semi-finals as captain in his undefeated senior year, and who later became congressman from Illinois, ambassador to NATO, and secretary of defense.

Wyckoff, Walter Augustus (1865-1908), who gave Princeton's first course in sociology, was born in India of missionary parents. As a Princeton undergraduate, he was College champion in the mile run and gave the Ivy Oration at the 1888 Commencement: "Today we are young and gay with no thought of care; tomorrow we are borne out into a fuller experience of life's realities." Three years later, Wyckoff set out with a dollar in his pocket to learn firsthand the life of the unskilled worker. In the course of eighteen months he worked his way as a day laborer from Connecticut to California, much of it on foot. Later, while a lecturer in sociology and then an assistant professor of political economy, he published a two-volume account of his experiences, *The Workers: an Experiment in Reality* (1897 and 1898).

Wyckoff was a popular teacher. His students called him "Weary Willie," and attributed to him, perhaps apocryphally, this definition: "A hobo is a migratory worker; a tramp is a migratory nonworker; a bum is a nonmigratory nonworker."

Wyckoff's career was cut short by an aneurism of the aorta at the age of forty-three. A bronze tablet erected in an East Pyne archway by his classmates honors him as "a lover of mankind, an adventurous traveler who wrote out of his own experience, taught with his heart in his message, and died in peace and welldoing."

Wyman House, the residence of the dean of the graduate school, was built in 1913 at the same time as the Graduate College, which it adjoins. It was named for Isaac C. Wyman, Class of 1848, of Salem, Massachusetts, who left the University his residuary estate of some $800,000 for the development of the Graduate College as "a memorial of my lasting affection and interest in my Alma Mater." Over the fireplace in the Dean's library are hung the long-barreled flintlock musket and powder horn that Wyman's grandfather used in the French and Indian Wars and which his father, as a boy of sixteen, carried in the Revolutionary battle of Princeton. Part of the fighting was on ground now occupied by the Graduate College.

Young, Charles Augustus (1834-1908) was born in Hanover, New Hampshire, of a family long connected with Dartmouth College. He graduated from Dartmouth, at eighteen, at the head of his class. When he was thirty-one, he was appointed to a professorship of science at Dartmouth previously held by his father and his maternal grandfather; eleven years later he accepted a call to Princeton to succeed Stephen Alexander (q.v.) as professor of astronomy and to become first director of the Observatory.

Young was an authority on the sun and a pioneer in spectrum analysis. He devised the automatic spectroscope, which later came into general use, and his observations led to an improved list of important features of the spectrum of the sun. He organized expeditions to different parts of the world to observe solar eclipses, on one of them observing for the first time the reversal of the lines of the solar spectrum—the "reversing layer"—for which he received the Janssen Medal of the French Academy of Sciences. He also made the first good quantitative determination of the rate of rotation of the sun. He served a term as president of the American Association for the Advancement of Science.

His book *The Sun* (1881) went into numerous editions and was translated into several languages; his four textbooks, which were widely used, were generally considered to be among the best in astronomy ever written. His teaching was also, according to his most brilliant student, Henry Norris Russell (q.v.), "superb."

Young was admired by undergraduates, who called him "Twinkle" (as much for the bright, kindly flash of his eye as for his subject), and by the faculty, who thought him "in gifts and character . . . the ideal man of science." At Commencement in 1905, the year he retired, the trustees gave him an honorary LL.D., and the students rose and gave him a triple cheer.

The day he died—January 3, 1908— at his family home in Hanover, New Hampshire, there was a total eclipse of the sun.

BIBLIOGRAPHY

A selected list of books the *Companion* has found helpful and which may be of interest to the reader. Within each division references are arranged by date of publication.

GENERAL HISTORY

Blair, Samuel. *An Account of the College of New Jersey*. Woodbridge, New Jersey: Printed for the trustees by James Parker, 1764.

This pamphlet is the best contemporary statement available of the history, curriculum, and life of the College during its early years.

Maclean, John. *History of the College of New Jersey*. 2 vols. Philadelphia: J. B. Lippincott & Co., 1877.

Hageman, John Frelinghuysen. *History of Princeton and Its Institutions*. 2 vols. Philadelphia: J. B. Lippincott & Co., 1879.

Detailed history of the Princeton community from its first settlement in the seventeenth century.

The Princeton Book: A Series of Sketches Pertaining to the History, Organization and Present Condition of the College of New Jersey. By officers and graduates of the College. Boston: Houghton, Osgood & Co., 1879.

Collins, Varnum Lansing. *Princeton*. New York: Oxford University Press, 1914.

Wertenbaker, Thomas Jefferson. *Princeton 1746-1896*. Princeton: Princeton University Press, 1946.

Lane, Wheaton J. *Pictorial History of Princeton*. Princeton: Princeton University Press, 1947.

The Modern Princeton. Princeton: Princeton University Press, 1947.

Essays by seven Princetonians about trustees, faculty, alumni, graduate school, campus life, architecture, and *genius loci*.

HISTORIC EVENTS

Harper, George McLean, ed. *Memorial Book of the Sesquicentennial Celebration of the Founding of the College of New Jersey and the Ceremonies Inaugurating Princeton University*. New York: Published for the Trustees of Princeton University by Charles Scribner's Sons, 1898.

Collins, Varnum Lansing. *The Continental Congress at Princeton*. Princeton: Princeton University Press, 1908.

Bill, Alfred Hoyt. *The Campaign of Princeton 1776-1777*. Princeton: Princeton University Press, 1948.

Osgood, Charles G. *Lights in Nassau Hall: A Book of the Bicentennial*. Princeton: Princeton University Press, 1951.

Savage, Henry Lyttleton, ed. *Nassau Hall 1756-1956*. Princeton: Princeton University Press, 1956.

SPECIAL TOPICS

West, Andrew Fleming. *The Graduate College of Princeton, With Some Reflections on the Humanizing of Learning*. Illustrated by John P.

Cuyler. Princeton: Princeton University Press, 1913.

Egbert, Donald Drew. *Princeton Portraits*. Princeton: Princeton University Press, 1947.

Photographs of some 200 portraits owned by the University and biographical sketches of those portrayed.

Rice, Howard C., Jr. *The Rittenhouse Orrery: Princeton's Eighteenth Century Planetarium, 1767-1954*. Princeton: Princeton University Library, 1954.

Condit, Kenneth H. *A History of the Engineering School of Princeton University, 1875-1955*. Princeton: privately printed, 1962.

Bush, Alfred L. *Literary Landmarks of Princeton*. Princeton: Princeton University Library, 1968.

A record of works written in Princeton by residents and visitors, both town and gown, through more than two centuries.

Stillwell, Richard. *The Chapel of Princeton University*. Princeton: Princeton University Press, 1971.

PRESIDENTS

Eighteenth Century

Collins, Varnum Lansing. *President Witherspoon*. 2 vols. Princeton: Princeton University Press, 1925.

Butterfield, L. H. *John Witherspoon Comes to America*. Princeton: Princeton University Library, 1953.

Davies, Samuel. *The Reverend Samuel Davies Abroad: The Diary of a Journey to England and Scotland, 1753-1755*. Edited, with an introduction, by George William Pilcher. Urbana: University of Illinois Press, 1967.

Green, Ashbel. *The Life of the Rev^d*

John Witherspoon. Edited by Henry Lyttleton Savage. Princeton: Printed for the Council of the Society of Colonial Wars of the State of New Jersey by Princeton University Press, 1973.

Nineteenth Century

Sloane, William Milligan, ed. *The Life of James McCosh: A Record Chiefly Autobiographical*. New York: Charles Scribner's Sons, 1896.

Howe, M.A. DeWolfe. "James McCosh and Princeton," in *Classic Shades: Five Leaders of Learning and Their Colleges*. Boston: Little, Brown & Co., 1928.

Twentieth Century

Myers, William Starr, ed. *Woodrow Wilson: Some Princeton Memories*. Princeton: Princeton University Press, 1946.

Reminiscences by seven of Wilson's colleagues.

Link, Arthur S. *Wilson: The Road to the White House*. Princeton: Princeton University Press, 1947.

The Papers of Woodrow Wilson. Arthur S. Link, editor. Princeton: Princeton University Press, 1966-

Volumes 1 and Volumes 7 through 20 are of particular value for Princeton history.

Dodds, Harold Willis. *Out of This Nettle, Danger*. Princeton: Princeton University Press, 1943.

Essays based on his baccalaureate and commencement addresses during the Depression and the early years of the Second World War.

Goheen, Robert F. *The Human Nature of a University*. Princeton: Princeton University Press, 1969.

A distillation of the best of his public

papers during his first twelve years as president.

TRUSTEES

Nevins, Allan. *Grover Cleveland: A Study in Courage*. New York: Dodd, Mead & Co., 1932.

Finney, John M.T. [1884]. *A Surgeon's Life*. New York: G. P. Putnam's Sons, 1940.

Mathey, Dean ['12]. *Men and Gothic Towers*. Princeton: privately printed, 1967.

FACULTY

Perry, Bliss. "Princeton in the Nineties," in *And Gladly Teach*. Boston: Houghton Mifflin Co., 1935.

van Dyke, Tertius. *Henry van Dyke, A Biography* [1873]. New York: Harper & Brothers, 1935.

Scott, William Berryman. *Some Memories of A Palaeontologist*. Princeton: Princeton University Press, 1939.

Rodgers, Andrew Denny, III. *John Torrey*. Princeton: Princeton University Press, 1942.

Coulson, Thomas. *Joseph Henry: His Life and Work*. Princeton: Princeton University Press, 1950.

Gauss, Christian. *The Papers of Christian Gauss*. Edited by Katherine Gauss Jackson and Hiram Haydn. New York: Random House, 1957.

Maritain, Jacques. *Reflections on America*. New York: Charles Scribner's Sons, 1958.

ALUMNI

General

General Catalogue of Princeton University 1746-1906. Princeton: Published by the University, 1908.

Contains lists of graduates through 1906, with brief reference to the academic, public, and military careers of each. Included also are lists of trustees, administrative officers, and faculty.

Thorp, Willard, [Ph.D. '26], *The Lives of Eighteen from Princeton*. Princeton: Princeton Univerity Press, 1946.

Eighteenth Century

Alexander, Samuel Davies [1838]. *Princeton College During the Eighteenth Century*. New York: Anson D.F. Randolph & Co., 1872.

Brief sketches of alumni in the Classes of 1748 through 1800.

Brown, William Garrott. *The Life of Oliver Ellsworth* [1766]. New York: Macmillan, 1905.

Boyd, Thomas. *Light-Horse Harry Lee* [1773]. New York: Charles Scribner's Sons, 1931.

Rush, Benjamin. *The Autobiography of Benjamin Rush* [1760]. Edited, with introduction and notes, by George W. Corner. Princeton: Published for the American Philosophical Society by Princeton University Press, 1948.

The Papers of James Madison [1771]. Edited by William T. Hutchinson and William M.E. Rachal. Chicago: University of Chicago Press, 1962-   .

Volume I, which covers the years 1751-1779, includes letters to and from his father, jottings in his commonplace book, collegiate doggerel during his three years at Princeton, and correspondence with classmates and friends during college years and later.

Ramsay, David [1765]. *Selections from His Writings*. Edited by Robert L. Brunhouse. Transactions of the American Philosophical Society, Vol. 55, Part 4, 1965.

Binger, Carl. *Revolutionary Doctor: Benjamin Rush* [1760]. New York: W. W. Norton & Co., 1966.

Ketcham, Ralph Louis. *James Madison: A Biography*. New York: Macmillan, 1971.

McLachlan, James S. *Princetonians, 1748-1768: A Biographical Dictionary*. Princeton: Princeton University Press, 1976.

Rush, Benjamin. *Letters of Benjamin Rush* [1760]. Edited by L. H. Butterfield. 2 vols. Princeton: Published for the American Philosophical Society by Princeton University Press, 1951.

Nineteenth Century

Woodress, James. *Booth Tarkington* [1893]: *Gentleman from Indiana*. Philadelphia: J. B. Lippincott Co., 1954.

Myers, Robert Manson. *The Children of Pride: A True Story of Georgia and the Civil War*. Yale University Press, 1972.

Includes letters of Charles C. Jones, Jr. 1852 and Joseph Jones 1853, members of a Georgia family whose correspondance was woven by the author into a National Book Award-winning history.

Myers, Robert Manson. *A Georgian at Princeton*. New York: Harcourt Brace Jovanovich, Inc., 1976.

Includes letters home from Charles C. Jones, Jr. 1852 and Joseph Jones 1853 during their undergraduate years at Princeton.

Twentieth Century

Mizener, Arthur M. ['30]. *The Far Side of Paradise: A Biography of F. Scott Fitzgerald* ['17]. Boston: Houghton, Mifflin & Co., 1951.

Fosdick, Raymond B. ['05, A.M. '06]. *Chronicle of a Generation: An Autobiography*. New York: Harper & Brothers, 1958.

Steiner, Paul, editor. *The Stevenson Wit & Wisdom*. Pyramid Books, New York, 1965.

Doyle, Edward P., editor. *As We Knew Adlai, The Stevenson Story by Twenty-two Friends*. New York: Harper & Row, 1966.

Martin, John Barlow. *Adlai Stevenson* ['22] *of Illinois*. New York: Doubleday & Co., 1976.

STUDENT LIFE

Alexander, James W. [1860]. *Princeton—Old and New*. New York: Charles Scribner's Sons, 1898.

Mills, W. Jay, ed. *Glimpses of Colonial Society and the Life at Princeton College*. Philadelphia: J. B. Lippincott Co., 1903.

Contains twenty-five letters from William Paterson 1763.

Williams, Charles Richard [1875]. *The Cliosophic Society*. Princeton: Princeton University Press, 1916.

Beam, Jacob N. [1896]. *The American Whig Society*. Princeton: Published by the Society, 1933.

Wilson, Edmund ['16]. "Princeton, 1912-1916," in *A Prelude: Landscapes, Characters and Conversations from the Earlier Years of My Life*. New York: Farrar, Straus & Giroux, 1967.

Marsden, Donald ['64]. *The Long Kickline: A History of the Princeton Triangle Club*. Princeton: Sponsored by the Club's Board of Trustees, 1968.

ATHLETICS

Presbrey, Frank [1879] and Moffatt, James Hugh [1900]. *Athletics at*

Princeton: A History. New York: Frank Presbrey Co., 1901.

Team records and photographs in all sports from the beginning through June 1901.

Edwards, William H. [1900]. *Football Days, Memories of the Game and of the Men Behind the Ball*. Introduction by Walter Camp [Yale 1880]. New York: Moffat, Yard & Co., 1916.

Herring, Donald Grant, Sr. ['07]. *Forty Years of Football*. New York: Carlyle House, 1940.

McPhee, John A. ['53]. *A Sense of Where You Are: A Profile of William Warren Bradley* ['65]. New York: Farrar, Straus & Giroux, 1965.

Davies, John D. ['41]. *The Legend of Hobey Baker* ['14]. Introduction by Arthur M. Mizener ['30]. Boston: Little, Brown & Co., 1966.

Kaufman, Louis, Barbara Fitzgerald, and Tom Sewell. *Moe Berg* ['23]: *Athlete, Scholar, Spy*. Boston: Little, Brown & Co., 1974.

FICTION

Williams, Jesse Lynch. *Princeton Stories*. Charles Scribner's Sons, 1895.

Fitzgerald, F. Scott. *This Side of Paradise*. New York: Charles Scribner's Sons, 1920.

Edgar, Day. *In Princeton Town*. New York: Charles Scribner's Sons, 1929.

GUIDEBOOKS

Williams, John Rogers. *The Handbook of Princeton*. Introduction by Woodrow Wilson. New York: The Grafton Press, 1905.

Collins, Varnum Lansing. *Guide to Princeton: The Town, the University*. Princeton: Princeton University Press, 1919, 1920.

Collins, Varnum Lansing. *Princeton, Past and Present*. Princeton: Princeton University Press, 1931, 1945, 1946.

University League. *A Guide to the Princeton Campus and Its Treasures*. Princeton, 1946, 1955.

Chamberlain, Samuel. *Princeton in Spring: Camera Impressions*. Princeton: Princeton University Press, 1950.

Van Zandt, Helen and Jan Lilly. *The Princeton University Campus: A Guide*. Princeton: Princeton University Press, 1964, 1970.

Grieff, Constance, M., Mary W. Gibbons, Elizabeth G.C. Menzies. *Princeton Architecture: A Pictorial History of Town and Campus*. Princeton: Princeton University Press, 1967.

PERIODICALS, NEWSPAPERS, AND YEARBOOKS

Important sources of information on which the *Companion* has relied are *Nassau Literary Magazine* (1842–); *Nassau Herald* (1864–); *Bric-a-Brac* (1876–); *Princetonian* (1876–); *Princeton Alumni Weekly* (1900–).

MANUSCRIPT RESOURCES

Past trustee and faculty minutes are available for restricted use in the Archives in Mudd Manuscript Library.

Papers of presidents, trustees, faculty, and alumni are on deposit in the Archives and in the manuscript division of the Department of Rare Books and Special Collections in Firestone Library.

INDEX

The titles of the 439 articles that constitute *A Princeton Companion* form the basis of this selected index. Their page numbers are given below in bold face.

552 INDEX

McCleery, William, 14, 123, 295
McClellan, George B., 265, 333
McClenahan, Howard, **299-300,** 19, 35, 128, 174, 249
McCormick, Cyrus H., 300, 354
McCormick, Myron, 465, 479
McCormick Hall, **300-301,** 28
McCosh, Andrew J., 472
McCosh, Isabella Guthrie, 82, 244, 301, 303, 304-305, 306, 527
McCosh, James, **301-304;** landscapes campus, 78; develops graduate studies, 132, 225; represents same philosophy as Witherspoon, 361; pioneer in psychology, 395, 396; on work of deans, 128; on Edwards Hall, 152-153; on the gymnasium, 276; on evolution, 302, 432; on John B. McMaster, 307; on Dean Murray, 326; on the *Princetonian*, 380; on Prospect, 394; on Moses Taylor Pyne, 399; on the trustees, 482-483; other references: 17, 19, 55, 82, 109, 166, 211, 228, 311, 314, 376, 472, 538
McCosh Faculty Fellowships, 304
McCosh Hall, **304,** 78
McCosh Infirmary, **304-306,** 183, 244, 245
McCosh Walk, **306**
MacCoy, Bill, 40
MacDonald, Francis C., 167, 333
McGill University, 358, 359, 492
McGraw, Curtis W., 165, 352
McIlvaine, Joshua Hall, 166, 170, 171
McIlwain, Charles H., 256, 370, 374, 397
McKenzie, R. Tait, 224, 504
McKim, Mead and White, 187, 469-470
McKinney, Stewart B., 263
McMaster, John Bach, **306-307,** 118, 255
McMillan, Charles, **307,** 97
McMillan, Ed, 191, 196
McMillan, Edwin M., 337n, 342, 364
MacMillan Building, **307,** 398
McPhee, Frank, 192, 196
McPhee, Harry R., 245, 346
McPhee, John, 44, 122, 336, 388, 541
Machlup, Fritz, 17, 20, 151, 272, 273, 495
Madison, James, Jr., **307-310;** as "father of constitution," 114, 115, 116-117; and Brackenridge, 63; and Burr, 69; and Ellsworth, 160; and Freneau, 200, 201; and Henry Lee, 283, 284; and Paterson, 354; other references: 20n, 70, 75, 105, 146, 224, 266, 370, 377, 539, 540
Madison Hall, **310,** 148, 409
Madison Medal, **310-311**
Madison Society, 410
Magie, William Francis, **311-312,** 19, 64, 112, 129, 259, 299, 300, 363, 364, 365, 485
Maliszewski, Stas, 193, 196
Malkiel, Burton G., 151
Mann, Joseph McElroy, 39

Mann, Thomas, **312-313,** 212
Manning, James, 104, 181
Marckwardt, Albert H., 168, 290, 291, 463
Marden, Charles C., 414
Maritain, Jacques, **313-314,** 51, 335, 362, 539
Marquand, Allan, **314-316,** 17, 24, 27, 28, 29, 30, 31, 69, 70, 109, 170, 234, 429, 438, 472
Marquand, Henry G., 85, 276
Marquand Chapel, 85, 136, 183, 184
Marquand Library, 28, 29, 316
Marquand Park, 316
Marshall, George, 51
Martin, Alexander, 114, 115, 223, 437
Martin, Henry R., 388
Martin, John R., 28, 29
Martin, Luther, 69, 114, 115, 116
Maruca, Anthony J., 492
Masback, Craig, 125, 475
Mason, Alpheus T., 18, 119, 120, 267, 333, 370, 373
Massachusetts Institute of Technology, 91, 107, 112, 178, 225, 342, 430, 502
Mathematics, **316-319,** 133
Mather, Frank Jewett, 17, 19, 27, 29-30, 174, 338
Mather, Sir William, 319
Mather Sun Dial, **319-320,** 513
Mathey, Dean, **320-322,** 79, 379, 463-464, 520, 539
Mathey, Gertrude Winans, Faculty Housing, 321
Maurois, André, 414
Maxwell, John C., 210
May, Robert M., 18, 405
Meaning of Relativity, The, 153, 154, 389
Medieval Studies, 220
Medina, Harold R., 37, 206, 259
Memorial Hall, 332-333
Mendel, Arthur, 18, 327, 328
Menzel, Donald H., 337n, 427
Merchant, Livingston T., 14, 383
Meredith, William M., 122, 336, 338
Meritt, Benjamin D., 101
Merwick, 70, 225, 400
Merwin, W. S., 336, 397
Mestres, Ricardo A., 275, 405, 476, 492
Metropolitan Museum of Art, 142, 314, 315, 324
Michigan, University of, 102, 118, 159, 191, 205, 290, 374, 459, 473, 521
Middlebury College, 101, 145, 194
Milbank, Albert G., 482, 519
Mill, John Stuart, 301
Milnor, John Willard, 17, 20, 311, 319, 337
Minority Students, 4, 170, 227-228, 466
Minto, Walter, **322-323,** 19, 31, 180, 296, 316
Mislow, Kurt, 18, 95, 337
Mizener, Arthur, 185, 186, 540
Modern European Studies, 134
Modern Languages Department, 205, 212, 413

Library of Congress Cataloging in Publication Data

Leitch, Alexander, 1900-
    A Princeton companion.

    Bibliography: p.
    Includes index.
    1.   Princeton University—Addresses, essays, lectures.
I.   Title.
LD4608.L4   378.749′67   78-51178
ISBN 0-691-04654-9